Strategic Human Resource Management

Strategic Human Resource Management

SECOND EDITION

Randall S. Schuler and Susan E. Jackson
Rutgers University and GSBA Zurich

Editorial material and organization © 1999, 2007 by Blackwell Publishing Ltd

BLACKWELL PUBLISHING
350 Main Street, Malden, MA 02148-5020, USA
9600 Garsington Road, Oxford OX4 2DQ, UK
550 Swanston Street, Carlton, Victoria 3053, Australia

The right of Randall S. Schuler and Susan E. Jackson to be identified as the Authors of the Editorial
Material in this Work has been asserted in accordance with the UK Copyright, Designs, and Patents Act
1988.

First published 1999
Second edition published 2007 by Blackwell Publishing Ltd

2   2008

Library of Congress Cataloging-in-Publication Data

Strategic human resource management / [edited by] Randall S. Schuler, Susan E. Jackson.—2nd ed.
    p. cm.
  Includes bibliographical references and index.
  ISBN: 978-1-4051-4959-4 (pbk. : alk. paper)
  1. Personnel management. 2. Strategic planning. I. Schuler, Randall S. II. Jackson, Susan E.
HF5549.S8832 2006
658.3'01—dc22

                                                                      2006008654

A catalogue record for this title is available from the British Library.

Set in 10/12.5 Galliard
by Newgen Imaging Systems (P) Ltd., Chennai, India

For further information on
Blackwell Publishing, visit our website:
www.blackwellpublishing.com

Contents

Part I   Overview of SHRM   5

Part II   Global Dimensions   139

Figures

Tables

Contributors

Jay B. Barney, *Ohio State University*
Richard W. Beatty, *Rutgers University*
J. Stewart Black, *University of Michigan*
Peter Boxall, *University of Auckland*
Werner Braun, *PA Consulting*
Chris Brewster, *Henley Management College*
Pawan S. Budhwar, *University of Aston*
Wayne F. Cascio, *University of Colorado*
Barry A. Colbert, *York University*
Fang Lee Cooke, *Manchester Business School*
Benjamin B. Dunford, *Cornell University*
Vijay Govindarajan, *Dartmouth University*
Lynda Gratton, *London Business School*
Hal B. Gregersen, *Brigham Young University*
Anil K. Gupta, *University of Maryland*
Michael Harvey, *University of Mississippi*
Mark A. Huselid, *Rutgers University*
Susan E. Jackson, *Rutgers University and GSBA Zurich*
Robert J. Jensen, *Brigham Young University*
David J. Ketchen, Jr., *Cornell University*
David P. Lepak, *Rutgers University*
Wolfgang Mayrhofer, *Vienna University*
Mark E. Mendenhall, *University of Tennessee – Chattanooga*
Milorad M. Novicevic, *University of Wisconsin – La Crosse*
Vladimir Pucik, *IMD*
S. Saini, *Management Development Institute Gurgaon*
Craig Eric Schneier, *Biogen*
Randall S. Schuler, *Rutgers University and GSBA Zurich*

Doone Selbie, *HR Information Systems Consultant*
Scott A. Snell, *Cornell University*
Charles C. Snow, *Pennsylvania State University*
Paul R. Sparrow, *Lancaster University*
Catherine Truss, *Kingston Business School*
Shaun Tyson, *Cranfield School of Management*
Dave Ulrich, *University of Michigan*
Patrick M. Wright, *Cornell University*
Suzanne Zivnuska, *Bond University*

Preface

The discipline that concentrates on the management of people in organizations has witnessed a great deal of change over the past twenty-five years! These changes can be discussed as two major transformations. The first is the transformation from being the field of "personnel management" to being the field of "human resource management." The second is the transformation from being the field of "human resource management" to being the field of "strategic human resource management."

The first transformation incorporated the recognition that people are an important asset in organizations that can be managed systematically. Managing them systematically involved coordinating the shape and substance of the several traditional personnel policies and practices. The need for this orchestration was based upon the increasing evidence that all these policies and practices substantially affect human behavior and that their impact would produce positive results only if they were affecting human behavior in the same way. This required insight and knowledge about the several personnel policies and practices and how they impact human behavior. It also required coordination in formulation and implementation of the several personnel policies and practices. Together, these events in personnel management required a growing body of knowledge and professionalism amongst the professionals engaged in the discipline of managing people. To give recognition to this transformation in the discipline, the field acquired the designation "human resource management."

The second transformation, as the first transformation, has built on, rather than replaced, the preceding knowledge base of the discipline. This transformation is based upon the recognition that, in addition to coordinating human resource policies and practices with each other, they need to be coordinated, or linked, with the needs of the organization. Given that these needs are reflected in discussions of the major issues and directions of the organization, i.e., the strategy of the firm, this transformation of "human resource management" came to be known as "strategic human resource management." For some, there may even be a third transformation, or at least a branch of the second transformation and that is reflective of the increased globalization of organizations.

Strategic human resource management, while certainly a discipline that is still taking form, is based upon the recognition that organizations can be more effective if their human resources are managed with human resource policies and practices that deliver the right number of people with the appropriate behaviors, the needed competencies, and the feasible levels of motivation to the organization. What is right, needed, and feasible is set in the context of the organization as the relevant internal environment and context outside the organization as the relevant external environment. These external and internal environmental components, the relevant stakeholders, are thus important to the practice of strategic human resource management. But they also give enhanced meaning and sense of importance to the discipline. Today, based upon the accumulated evidence, the academics and professionals alike can claim that systematic coordination of human resource policies and practices based upon the needs of the firm, can result in such outcomes as improved: employee satisfaction, customer satisfaction, profitability, environmental and societal impact, strategic partner relationships, and organizational survival.

In order to get these outcomes, however, the practice of strategic human resource management needs to be based upon partnership. The formulation and implementation of the policies and practices affecting human behavior need to involve the collective insights, knowledge and perspectives of employees, customers, managers, board members, union representatives, governmental officials, as well as the human resource professionals. It takes all these groups, working in partnership, to design the human resource policies and practices that will produce the appropriate competencies, the right numbers of employees, the needed behaviors, and feasible levels of motivation from the firm's human resources.

Making this partnership a reality is more challenging and complex than ever because strategic human resource management is practiced in firms operating across several countries of the world. These multinational corporations (MNCs) are stretching out all over the world. For these firms, the practice of formulating and implementing strategy is considerably more complex, thus the linking of human resource management policies and practices is as well. The challenge and complexity are increased for MNCs that pursue more knowledge-based strategies and thus need to transfer knowledge and learning across borders rapidly and effectively. Some MNCs may also take advantage of globalization by engaging in various forms of cross-border alliances such as international joint ventures or international mergers or acquisitions. Increasingly, we know that the success of these alliances depends in large measure on how well human resource issues are managed. Some organizations, whether they consider themselves MNCs or not, may also take advantage of globalization through outsourcing or offshoring some of their operations. For them, as with traditional MNCs, it behooves them to know about the various characteristics of the countries in which they are doing business. For companies outsourcing to India or China, it is useful to know about their human resource practices, labor legislation, cultural qualities, the educational system, and the political and regulatory systems.

But with this challenge and the complexity of managing companies in today's global environment, come a great deal of excitement, opportunity, and need for flexibility and adaptation on the part of the human resource professionals and their departments. Today, human resource professionals are being challenged to learn more about the business, its strategy, its environment, its customers, and its competitors. They are also being challenged to manage the process of change that organizations are going through. To further add to their value, human resource professionals are demonstrating to others that they add significant economic value to the organization and that they are producing competitive advantage for the organization. In the process of doing these things, they are substantially transforming their human resource departments. They are doing this through the creation of organizational structures such as centers of excellence and service centers. They are also reducing the size of their operations through outsourcing some of their traditional activities and focusing on their core competencies.

Doubtless to say, the discipline of strategic human resource management is filled with a great deal of excitement and energy, both for the professionals as well as the academics. There are no easy answers, but times certainly require some answers that are better than others. Times certainly require more knowledge, insight, and understanding than ever before. Helping to find those answers and to offer some knowledge, insight and, understanding of the discipline of "strategic human resource management" is what this reader is all about.

Acknowledgments

The editors and publisher gratefully acknowledge the permission granted to reproduce the copyright material in this book:

1. Jay B. Barney, "Looking Inside for Competitive Advantage," pp. 49–61 from *Academy of Management Executive* 9 (4), 1995. Reprinted by permission of the Academy of Management.
2. Susan E. Jackson and Randall S. Schuler, "Understanding Human Resource Management in the Context of Organizations and Their Environments," pp. 237–64 from *Annual Review of Psychology* 46, 1995. Reprinted with permission from the *Annual Review of Psychology* Volume 46 ©1995 by Annual Reviews (www.annualreviews.org).
3. Suzanne Zivnuska, David J. Ketchen, Jr., and Charles C. Snow, "Implications of the Converging Economy for Human Resource Management," pp. 371–405 from *Research in Personnel and Human Resource Management* 20, 2001. Copyright © 2001. Reprinted with permission from Elsevier.
4. Patrick M. Wright, Benjamin B. Dunford, and Scott A. Snell, "Human Resources and the Resource-Based View of the Firm," pp. 701–21 from *Journal of Management* 27, 2001.
5. Barry A. Colbert, "The Complex Resource-Based View: Implications for Theory and Practice in Strategic Human Resource Management," pp. 341–58 from *Academy of Management Review* 29 (3), 2004. Reprinted by permission of the Academy of Management Review.
6. Dave Ulrich, "Alignment of Human Resources and their Impact on Business Performance," pp. 17–31 from *The Executive Handbook on Compensation: Linking Strategic Rewards to Business Performance* edited by Charles Fay. Free Press, 2001. Reprinted with the permission of The Free Press, a division of Simon & Schuster Adult Publishing Group. Copyright © 2001 by Hay Group, Inc. All rights reserved.
7. Anil K. Gupta and Vijay Govindarajan, "Converting Global Presence into Global Competitive Advantage," pp. 45–58 from *Academy of Management Executive* 15 (2), 2001. Reprinted by permission of the Academy of Management Executive.
8. Paul R. Sparrow and Werner Braun, "Human Resource Strategy in International Context," from M. M. Harris, *Handbook of Research in International Human Resource Management*. Lawrence Earlbaum, 2005. Reprinted by permission of Lawrence Erlbaum Associates Inc. and by permission of the author.
9. Vladimir Pucik, "Reframing Global Mindset: From Thinking to Acting," from *Advances in Global Leadership*, vol VI. Oxford: Elsevier, 2005. Copyright © 2005, reprinted with permission from Elsevier.
10. Randall S. Schuler and Susan E. Jackson, "A Quarter-Century Review of Human Resource Management in the US: The Growth in Importance of the International Perspective," pp. 11–35 from *Management Review* 16 (1), 2005. Reprinted by permission of Rainer Hampp Verlag.

11. Wolfgang Mayrhofer and Chris Brewster, "European Human Resource Management: Researching Developments over Time," pp. 36–62 from *Management Review* 16 (1), 2005. Reprinted by permission of Rainer Hampp Verlag.

12. Fang Lee Cooke, "HRM in China," pp. 18–34 from *Managing Human Resources in Asia-Pacific*. London: Routledge, 2004. Copyright © 2004 Routledge. Reproduced by permission of Taylor & Francis Books UK.

13. Debi S. Saini and Pawan S. Budhwar, "HRM in India," pp. 114–37 from *Managing Human Resources in Asia-Pacific*. London: Routledge, 2004. Copyright © 2004 Routledge. Reproduced by permission of Taylor & Francis Books UK.

14. Peter Boxall, "HR Strategy and Competitive Advantage in the Service Sector," pp. 5–20 from *Human Resource Management Journal* 13 (3), 2003. Reprinted by permission of Blackwell Publishing.

15. David P. Lepak and Scott A. Snell, "Managing the Human Resource Architecture for Knowledge-Based Competition," pp. 127–54 from *Managing Knowledge for Sustained Competitive Advantage*. Jossey Bass, 2003. Reprinted with permission of John Wiley & Sons, Inc.

16. Richard W. Beatty, Mark A. Huselid, and Craig Eric Schneier, "New HR Metrics: Scoring on the Business Scorecard," pp. 107–21 from *Organizational Dynamics* 32 (2), 2003. Copyright © 2003, reprinted with permission from Elsevier.

17. Wayne F. Cascio, "Strategies for Responsible Restructuring," pp. 80–91 from *Academy of Management Executive* 16 (3), 2002. Reprinted by permission of the Academy of Management Executive.

18. Lynda Gratton and Catherine Truss, "The Three-Dimensional People Strategy: Putting Human Resources Policies into Action," pp. 74–86 from *Academy of Management Executive* 17 (3), 2003. Reprinted by permission of the Academy of Management Executive.

19. Mark E. Mendenhall, J. Stewart Black, Robert J. Jensen, and Hal B. Gregersen, "Seeing the Elephant: Human Resource Management Challenges in the Age of Globalization," pp. 261–74 from *Organizational Dynamics* 32 (3), 2003. Copyright © 2003, reprinted with permission from Elsevier.

20. Milorad M. Novicevic and Michael Harvey, "The Changing Role of the Corporate HR Function in Global Organizations of the Twenty-First Century," pp. 1251–68 from *International Journal of Human Resource Management* 12 (8), 2001. Reprinted by permission of Taylor & Francis Ltd (www.tandf.co.uk/journals) and by permission of the author.

21. Shaun Tyson and Doone Selbie, "People Processing Systems and Human Resource Strategy," pp. 117–27, from *International Journal of Human Resources Development and Management* 4 (2), 2004.

Every effort has been made to trace copyright holders and to obtain their permission for the use of copyright material. The publisher apologizes for any errors or omissions in the above list and would be grateful if notified of any corrections that should be incorporated in future reprints or editions of this book.

Introduction

The second edition of this book of readings in strategic human resource management is divided into four parts. Each part covers an important aspect of the discipline of strategic human resource management. The readings or articles assembled here represent the work of authors throughout the world, all of whom have been writing in the field of strategic human resource management virtually since its inception. Indeed, the authors represented here have been the prime movers and shapers of strategic human resource management and increasingly, strategic international human resource management.

The articles in Part I, "Overview of SHRM," illustrate various perspectives the authors have taken in describing and defining the field of strategic human resource management and the field from which it has benefited greatly – strategic management. Common to all the articles is the general conceptualization of strategic human resource management as being about systematically linking people with the firm. In these articles, "the firm" includes all the internal aspects of the organization, i.e., its structure, culture, vision, mission, values, strategies, products, and technology, and all its external aspects, i.e., its customers, competitors, regulators, employees, investors, and suppliers. Also common in all the articles is a discussion and use of theoretical frameworks to support their descriptions of the role of human resources in organizations especially the resource-based view and its focus on firms gaining competitive advantage through the strategic management of their human resources.

The articles in Part II of this reader "Global Dimensions," highlight the unique issues in strategic human resource management that arise in firms that are operating in a global environment. These aspects result from the: unique structural characteristics of multinational corporations; unique alliance or joint venture characteristics; and unique country characteristics. Issues resulting from the unique structural characteristics include those associated with deciding upon the nature of its differentiation, from being truly global to being multi-domestic. There are significant implications for strategic human resource management regardless of the choice of differentiation selected. Similarly, there are major implications for strategic human resource management as the firm decides how to integrate itself, how to coordinate the activities of the far-flung units of the international firm.

It is argued by some that the strategic human resource implications resulting from the differentiation and integration of global firms are not only more complex and challenging that those of domestic firms, but more important as well. There are also several implications for strategic human resource management that arise in cross-border alliances, particularly international joint ventures and international mergers and acquisitions. Complexity, challenge, and implications for strategic human resource management also arise from global firms that need to operate in different countries and understand their external environment components, e.g., national culture, laws and regulations, competition, and political conditions. This need is becoming more important as more companies become multinationals (MNCs) and/or engage in more outsourcing to countries such as India and China. As a consequence, it is important to know as much about these countries as possible.

The articles in Part III, "Strategy to Action," describe the viewpoints of several authors on the topic of linking human resource management activities with the firm. More specifically, they describe the perspectives of the authors on a central question in strategic human resource management: "Is there a one best way to link people with the firm?" In addressing this general question, they provide numerous examples illustrating that the answer may be that there are several best ways to link people with the firm. Those ways depend upon several factors, many of which are discussed by the authors in Part I of this reader. These factors include characteristics of the internal environment such as top management values, the vision and mission of the firm, its strategy, manufacturing or service, size, structure, technology, knowledge intensity, products and services, and customers, and such external characteristics as the customers, degree of competition, size of the market, barriers to entry, ease of substitution for the products and services, legal and regulatory conditions, educational system, demographics, political conditions, degree of unionization, and nature of the investment community. Another major question that the authors address in this part of the reader relates to the purpose of managing human resources strategically. In general, they suggest that the reason is for the benefit of multiple stakeholders. More specifically, they indicate that the purpose is to gain competitive advantage, attain higher levels of performance, satisfy the needs of the employees and customers, and to adhere to the rules and regulations of society.

In Part IV, "Role of the HR Department and HR Professionals," the articles cover several issues related to the role of the HR department and HR professionals in strategic human resource management. Because the field of strategic human resource management depends upon detailed understanding of HR policies and practices, it is often useful for the HR department and HR professionals to be closely involved with, actually working in partnership with, line managers who are more directly involved in the firm's strategy formulation and implementation. In some firms, the senior HR professional may be quite knowledgeable about the strategy of the firm, making the resulting HR policies and practices more aligned with the needs of the firm and the people more linked with the firm. Strategy formulation is only one part of the equation however. It is often in the details of implementation that business strategies get into difficulties. Here partnership among the HR professionals, line managers, and the employees themselves can help overcome the hurdles in implementation. The articles in this part talk about these issues in great detail. They also discuss the implications of strategic human resource management for competency development for the HR professionals, not only at the senior levels but throughout the HR department. They also discuss the implications for the structure of the HR department and what the HR department of the future may look like, particularly as it becomes a real strategic partner, practicing strategic human resource management.

In the Conclusion, Dave Lepak offers an excellent overview of where he thinks the field is now and suggests some directions for future work. In doing so, he identifies the theoretical constructs that are likely to play a key role in the future of SHRM.

The discipline of strategic human resource management is a very exciting one, but also a very challenging one, both to the practitioner and to the academic. Together, all of these articles in this reader convey the sense of the development of this discipline as well as the current issues that are confronting academics and practitioners as they seek to manage human resources in the context of the organization and its environment. We hope that you find these articles as an interesting, informative, well-written, and substantive as we have in your thinking and understanding of strategic human resource management. We also hope that they will have a positive impact on the future work in the field.

Randall S. Schuler
Rutgers University and GSBA Zurich

Susan E. Jackson
Rutgers University and GSBA Zurich

Part I

Overview of SHRM

The chapters in this part illustrate various perspectives authors have taken in describing and defining the field of strategic human resource management. Common to all the chapters is the general conceptualization of strategic human resource management as being about systematically linking people with the firm. In these chapters the firm includes all the internal aspects of the organization, i.e., its structure, culture, vision, mission, values, strategy, products, and technology, and all its external aspects, i.e., its customers, competitors, regulators, employees, investors, and suppliers. Also common in all the chapters is a discussion and use of theoretical frameworks to support their descriptions of the role of human resources in organizations.

In the first chapter, Barney develops the theme of gaining competitive advantage through managing resources that are valuable, rare, and costly to imitate. This theme appears frequently in the strategic human resource management literature. In fact, some imply that because firms can gain competitive advantage through human resources, the function of human resource management has become viewed as a component of management's arsenal of "strategic weapons." Thus, the early work and that based upon Michael Porter's original description of competitive advantage and competitive strategy, provide the basis for the field of strategic human resource management. Since this beginning, the field has certainly expanded, but the theme of gaining competitive advantage through human resources still remains a major objective of strategic management and strategic human resource management. This chapter by Barney provides great detail in understanding the concept of competitive advantage and how firms can gain it. The logic is largely based upon the analysis of the firm's internal strengths and weaknesses. This analysis provides insight and further support for how and when human resources can be used to gain competitive advantage. Clearly, this advantage gained by human resources is achieved through their linkage to the firm.

The Jackson and Schuler chapter sets the broad context for the field of strategic human resource management through its development and explanation of its integrative framework shown in Fig. 2.1. This framework depicts the several aspects of the firm's internal and external environments in both a national and international context, and incorporates a multiple stakeholders' perspective. In addition, it illustrates the variety of outcomes associated with strategic human resource management that reflect the objectives of the various stakeholders. Typical of the chapters in this part, including Barney, the authors then offer several theoretical frameworks that can be used in the understanding of strategic human resource management, and in the development of theory-driven research. The frameworks offered include: general systems theory, role theory, human capital theory, transaction costs theory, resource dependency theory, agency theory, and resource-based theory.

In the third chapter, Zivnuska, Ketchen, and Snow discuss in more detail the impact of the external environment on strategic human resource management. The authors describe three major aspects of the external environment (all convergent factors of the world economy), namely, information technology, globalization, and the increasing importance of intangible assets and their impact on human resource management practices. In their descriptions of each of these aspects the authors identify the resulting challenges for human resource management and the possible human resource management practices that could be created to meet these challenges. Because many firms are and will be facing these aspects of the external environment, what Zivnuska and her colleagues provide to strategic human resource management is a generic outline of how firms can prepare themselves, at least from the viewpoint of human resources, to more effectively deal with the external environment through specific human resource management practices.

The Wright, Dunford, and Snell chapter highlights the strategic role that human resource management plays in organizations. They do this through their review and extension of the resource-based view of the firm, perhaps one of more dominant perspectives used in the field of strategic human resource management. This has resulted in large part because of its closely aligned development with business strategy, particularly concepts such as, but not limited to, Porter's and Barney's competitive strategy and competitive advantage. The authors examine how past work has used the resource-based view to develop theoretical and empirical work related to strategic human resource management and to show how it has provided an accessible bridge between business strategy and human resource management. The authors conclude with several interesting suggestions for future research using the resource-based view.

In the fourth chapter, Colbert continues and further elaborates the discussion begun by Wright and his colleagues on the resource-based view applied to human resource management. He elaborates by investigating the implications for research and practice in strategic human resource management of a complex, living-systems extension of the resource-based view. He offers an integrative framework for strategic human resource management that applies complexity principles to the human resource system. Tables 5.1 and 5.2 are excellent summaries of the resource-based view of the firm and complexity and excellent illustrations of how the two concepts can be aligned and hence applied to advance our thinking and practice in the field of strategic human resource management.

Ulrich's chapter concludes Part I with a very useful review of the literature on the relationship between human resource management strategies and organizational performance. This is the literature that has been explicitly focused at discovering and uncovering the possible relationships between human resource management and firm performance, hence shedding light on the conditions under which being strategic with respect to human resource management really matters to the organization. Ulrich then provides insights and explanations as to when and why strategic human resource really matters. He does this through a capability focus that identifies ten critical capabilities that link human resource management and firm performance. His conclusions and observations are very consistent with the resource-based view of the firm and the early literature on strategic human resource management that suggests managing human resources with an understanding of the organization and its environment can really provide a competitive advantage through people.

Chapter 1

Looking Inside for Competitive Advantage

Jay B. Barney

The history of strategic management research can be understood as an attempt to "fill in the blanks" created by the SWOT framework, that is to move beyond suggesting that strengths, weaknesses, opportunities, and threats are important for understanding competitive advantage to suggest models and frameworks that can be used to analyze and evaluate these phenomena.[1] Michael Porter and his associates have developed a number of these models and frameworks for analyzing environmental opportunities and threats. Porter's work on the "five forces model," the relationship between industry structure and strategic opportunities, and strategic groups can all be understood as an effort to unpack the concepts of environmental opportunities and threats in a theoretically rigorous, yet highly applicable, way.

However, the SWOT framework tells us that environmental analysis – no matter how rigorous – is only half the story. A complete understanding of sources of competitive advantage requires the analysis of a firm's internal strengths and weaknesses as well.[2] The importance of integrating internal with environmental analyses can be seen when evaluating the sources of competitive advantage of many firms. Consider, for example,

- Wal-Mart, a firm that has, for the last twenty years, consistently earned a return on sales twice the average of its industry;
- Southwest Airlines, a firm whose profits continued to increase, despite losses at other U.S. airlines that totaled almost $10 billion from 1990 to 1993; and

J. B. Barney, "Looking Inside for Competitive Advantage," *Academy of Management Executive*, Vol. 9, No. 4 (1995): 49–61.

- Nucor Steel, a firm whose stock price continued to soar through the 1980s and 1990s, despite the fact that the market value of most steel companies has remained flat or fallen during the same time period.[3]

These firms, and many others, have all gained competitive advantages – despite the unattractive, high threat, low opportunity environments within which they operate. Even the most careful and complete analysis of these firms' competitive environments cannot, by itself, explain their success. Such explanations must also include these firms' internal attributes – their strengths and weaknesses – as sources of competitive advantage. Following more recent practice, internal attributes will be referred to as "resources" and "capabilities" throughout the following discussion.[4]

A firm's resources and capabilities include all of the financial, physical, human, and organizational assets used by a firm to develop, manufacture, and deliver products or services to its customers. Financial resources include debt, equity, retained earnings, and so forth. Physical resources include the machines, manufacturing facilities, and buildings firms use in their operations. Human resources include all the experience, knowledge, judgment, risk taking propensity, and wisdom of individuals associated with a firm. Organizational resources include the history, relationships, trust, and organizational culture that are attributes of groups of individuals associated with a firm, along with a firm's formal reporting structure, explicit management control systems, and compensation policies.

In the process of filling in the "internal blanks" created by SWOT analysis, managers must address four important questions about their resources and capabilities:

1. The question of value
2. The question of rareness
3. The question of imitability
4. The question of organization.

The Question of Value

To begin evaluating the competitive implications of a firm's resources and capabilities, managers must first answer the question of value. Do a firm's resources and capabilities add value by enabling it to exploit opportunities and/or neutralize threats?

The answer to this question, for some firms, has been "yes." Sony, for example, has a great deal of experience in designing, manufacturing, and selling miniaturized electronic technology. Sony has used these resources to exploit numerous market opportunities, including portable tape players, portable disc players, portable televisions, and easy-to-hold 8 mm video cameras. 3M has used its skills and experience in substrates, coatings, and adhesives, along with an organizational culture that rewards risk taking and creativity, to exploit numerous market opportunities in office products, including invisible tape and Post-It™ notes. Sony's and 3M's resources – including their specific technological skills and their creative organizational cultures – made it possible for these firms to respond to, and even create, new environmental opportunities.

Unfortunately, for other firms, the answer to the question of value has been "no." For example, USX's long experience in traditional steel-making technology and the traditional steel market made it almost impossible for USX to recognize and respond to fundamental changes in the structure of the steel industry. Because it could not recognize new opportunities and threats, USX delayed its investment in, among other opportunities, thin slab continuous casting steel-manufacturing technology. Nucor Steel, on the other hand, was not shackled by its experience, made these investments early, and has become a major player in the international steel industry. In a similar way, Sears was unable to recognize or respond to changes in the retail market that had been created by Wal-Mart and specialty retail stores. In a sense, Sears' historical success, along with a commitment to stick with a traditional way of doing things, led it to miss some significant market opportunities.[5]

Although a firm's resources and capabilities may have added value in the past, changes in customer tastes, industry structure, or technology can render them less valuable in the future. General Electric's capabilities in transistor manufacturing became much less valuable when semiconductors were invented. American Airlines' skills in managing their relationship with the Civil Aeronautics Board (CAB) became much less valuable after airline deregulation. IBM's numerous capabilities in the mainframe computing business became less valuable with the increase in power, and reduction in price, of personal and mini-computers. One of the most important responsibilities of strategic managers is to constantly evaluate whether or not their firm's resources and capabilities continue to add value, despite changes in the competitive environment.

Some environmental changes are so significant that few, if any, of a firm's resources remain valuable in any environmental context.[6] However, this kind of radical environmental change is unusual. More commonly, changes in a firm's environment may reduce the value of a firm's resources in their current use, while leaving the value of those resources in other uses unchanged. Such changes might even *increase* the value of those resources in those other uses. In this situation, the critical issue facing managers is: how can we use our traditional strengths in new ways to exploit opportunities and/or neutralize threats?

Numerous firms have weathered these environmental shifts by finding new ways to apply their traditional strengths. AT&T had developed a reputation for providing high-quality long-distance telephone service. It moved rapidly to exploit this reputation in the newly competitive longdistance market by aggressively marketing its services against MCI, Sprint, and other carriers. Also, AT&T had traditional strengths in research and development with its Bell Labs subsidiary. To exploit these strengths in its new competitive context, AT&T shifted Bell Labs' mission from basic research to applied research, and then leveraged those skills by forming numerous joint ventures, acquiring NCR, and other actions. Through this process, AT&T has been able to use some of its historically important capabilities to try to position itself as a major actor in the global telecommunications and computing industry.

Another firm that has gone through a similar transformation is the Hunter Fan Company. Formed in 1886, Hunter Fan developed the technology it needed to be the market share leader in ceiling fans used to cool large manufacturing facilities.

Unfortunately, the invention of air conditioning significantly reduced demand for industrial fans, and Hunter Fan's performance deteriorated rapidly. However, in the 1970s, rising energy prices made energy conservation more important to home owners. Since ceiling fans can significantly reduce home energy consumption, Hunter Fan was able to move quickly to exploit this new opportunity. Of course, Hunter Fan had to develop some new skills as well, including brass-plating capabilities and new distribution networks. However, by building on its traditional strengths in new ways, Hunter Fan has become a leader in the home ceiling fan market.[7]

By answering the question of value, managers link the analysis of internal resources and capabilities with the analysis of environmental opportunities and threats. Firm resources are not valuable in a vacuum, but rather are valuable only when they exploit opportunities and/or neutralize threats. The models developed by Porter and his associates can be used to isolate potential opportunities and threats that the resources a firm controls can exploit or neutralize.

Of course, the resources and capabilities of different firms can be valuable in different ways. This can be true even if firms are competing in the same industry. For example, while both Rolex and Timex manufacture watches, they exploit very different valuable resources. Rolex emphasizes its quality manufacturing, commitment to excellence, and high-status reputation in marketing its watches. Timex emphasizes its high-volume, low-cost manufacturing skills and abilities. Rolex exploits its capabilities in responding to demand for very expensive watches. Timex exploits its resources in responding to demand for practical, reliable, low-cost timekeeping.

The Question of Rareness

That a firm's resources and capabilities are valuable is an important first consideration in understanding internal sources of competitive advantage. However, if a particular resource and capability is controlled by numerous competing firms, then that resource is unlikely to be a source of competitive advantage for any one of them. Instead, valuable but common (i.e., not rare) resources and capabilities are sources of competitive parity. For managers evaluating the competitive implications of their resources and capabilities, these observations lead to the second critical issue: how many competing firms already possess these valuable resources and capabilities?

Consider, for example, two firms competing in the global communications and computing industries: NEC and AT&T. Both these firms are developing many of the same capabilities that are likely to be needed in these industries over the next decade. These capabilities are clearly valuable, although – since at least these two firms, and maybe others, are developing them – they may not be rare. If they are not rare, they cannot – by themselves – be sources of competitive advantage for either NEC or AT&T. If either of these firms is to gain competitive advantages, they must exploit resources and capabilities that are different from the communication and computing skills they are *both* cited as developing. This may be part of the reason why AT&T recently restructured its telecommunications and computer businesses into separate firms.[8]

While resources and capabilities must be rare among competing firms in order to be a source of competitive advantage, this does not mean that common, but valuable, resources are not important. Indeed, such resources and capabilities may be essential for a firm's survival. On the other hand, if a firm's resources are valuable and rare, those resources may enable a firm to gain at least a temporary competitive advantage. Wal-Mart's skills in developing and using point-of-purchase data collection to control inventory have given it a competitive advantage over K-Mart, a firm that until recently has not had access to this timely information. Thus, for many years, Wal-Mart's valuable point-of-purchase inventory control systems were rare, at least relative to its major US competitor, K-Mart.[9]

The Question of Imitability

A firm that possesses valuable and rare resources and capabilities can gain, at least, a temporary competitive advantage. If, in addition, competing firms face a cost disadvantage in imitating these resources and capabilities, firms with these special abilities can obtain a sustained competitive advantage. These observations lead to the question of imitability: do firms without a resource or capability face a cost disadvantage in obtaining it compared to firms that already possess it?

Obviously, imitation is critical to understanding the ability of resources and capabilities to generate sustained competitive advantages. Imitation can occur in at least two ways: duplication and substitution. Duplication occurs when an imitating firm builds the same kinds of resources as the firm it is imitating. If one firm has a competitive advantage because of its research and development skills, then a duplicating firm will try to imitate that resource by developing its own research and development skills. In addition, firms may be able to substitute some resources for other resources. If these substitute resources have the same strategic implications and are no more costly to develop, then imitation through substitution will lead to competitive parity in the long run.

So, when will firms be at a cost disadvantage in imitating another's resources and capabilities, either through duplication or substitution? While there are numerous reasons why some of these internal attributes of firms may be costly to imitate, most of these reasons can be grouped into three categories:

1. the importance of history in creating firm resources;
2. the importance of numerous "small decisions" in developing, nurturing, and exploiting resources; and
3. the importance of socially complex resources.

The importance of history

As firms evolve, they pick up skills, abilities, and resources that are unique to them, reflecting their particular path through history. These resources and capabilities reflect the unique personalities, experiences, and relationships that exist in only a single firm. Before World War II Caterpillar was one of several medium sized firms in the heavy construction equipment industry struggling to survive intense competition. Just before the outbreak of war, the US Department of War (now the Department of Defense) concluded that, in order to pursue a global war, they would need one worldwide supplier of heavy construction equipment to build roads, air strips, army bases, and so forth. After a brief competition, Caterpillar was awarded this contract and, with the support of the Allies, was able to develop a worldwide service and supply network for heavy construction equipment at very low cost.

After the war, Caterpillar continued to own and operate this worldwide service and supply network. Indeed, Caterpillar management still advertises their ability to deliver any part, for any piece of Caterpillar equipment, to any place in the world, in under two days. By using this valuable capability, Caterpillar was able to become the dominant firm in the heavy construction equipment industry. Even today, despite recessions and labor strife, Caterpillar remains the market share leader in most categories of heavy construction equipment.[10]

Consider the position of a firm trying to duplicate Caterpillar's worldwide service and supply network, at the same cost as Caterpillar. This competing firm would have to receive the same kind of government support that Caterpillar received during World War II. This kind of government support is very unlikely.

It is interesting to note that at least one firm in the heavy construction equipment industry has begun to effectively compete against Caterpillar: Komatsu. However, rather than attempting to duplicate Caterpillar's service and supply network, Komatsu has attempted to exploit its own unique design and manufacturing resources by building machines that do not break down as frequently. Since Komatsu's machines break down less frequently, Komatsu does not require as extensive a worldwide service and supply network as Caterpillar. In this sense, Komatsu's special design and manufacturing skills in building machines that break down less frequently may be a strategic substitute for Caterpillar's worldwide service and supply network.[11]

In general, whenever the acquisition or development of valuable and rare resources depends upon unique historical circumstances, those imitating these resources will be at a cost disadvantage building them. Such resources can be sources of sustained competitive advantage.

The importance of numerous small decisions

Strategic managers and researchers are often enamored with the importance of "Big Decisions" as determinants of competitive advantage. IBM's decision to bring out the 360 series of computers in the 1960s was a Big Decision that had enormous competitive implications until the rise of personal computers. General Electric's decision to invest in the medical imaging business was a Big Decision whose competitive ramifications are still unfolding. Sometimes such Big Decisions are critical in understanding a firm's competitive position. However, more and more frequently, a firm's competitive advantage seems to depend on numerous small decisions through which a firm's resources and capabilities are developed and exploited. Thus, for example, a firm's competitive advantage in quality does not depend just upon its announcing that it is seeking the Malcolm Baldridge Quality Award. It depends upon literally hundreds of thousands of decisions made each day by employees in the firm – small decisions about whether or not to tighten a screw a little more, whether or not to share a small idea for improvement, or whether or not to call attention to a quality problem.[12] From the point of view of sustaining a competitive advantage, small decisions have some advantages over Big Decisions. In particular, small decisions are essentially invisible to firms seeking to imitate a successful firm's resources and capabilities. Big Decisions, on the other hand, are more obvious, easier to describe, and, perhaps, easier to imitate. While competitors may be able to observe the consequences of numerous little decisions, they often have a difficult time understanding the sources of the advantages.[13] A case in point is The Mailbox, Inc., a very successful firm in the bulk mailing business in the Dallas-Ft. Worth market. If there was ever a business where it seems unlikely that a firm would have a sustained competitive advantage, it is bulk mailing. Firms in this industry gather mail from customers, sort it by postal code, and then take it to the post office to be mailed. Where is the competitive advantage here? And yet, The Mailbox has enjoyed an enormous market share advantage in the Dallas-Ft. Worth area for several years. Why?

When asked, managers at The Mailbox have a difficult time describing the sources of their sustained advantages. Indeed, they can point to *no* Big Decisions they have made to generate this advantage. However, as these managers begin to discuss their firm, what becomes clear is that their success does not depend on doing a few big things right, but on doing lots of little things right. The way they manage accounting, finance, human resources, production, or other business functions, separately, is not exceptional. However, to manage all these functions so well, and so consistently over time is truly exceptional. Firms seeking to compete against The Mailbox will not have to imitate just a few internal attributes; they will have to imitate thousands, or even hundreds of thousands, of such attributes – a daunting task indeed.[14]

The importance of socially complex resources

A final reason that firms may be at a cost disadvantage in imitating resources and capabilities is that these resources may be socially complex. Some physical resources (e.g., computers, robots, and other machines) controlled by firms are very complex. However, firms seeking to imitate these physical resources need only purchase them, take them apart, and duplicate the technology in question. With just a couple of exceptions (including the pharmaceutical and specialty chemicals industries), patents provide little protection from the imitation of a firm's physical resources.[15] On the other hand, socially complex resources and capabilities – organizational phenomena like reputation, trust, friendship, teamwork and culture – while not patentable, are much more difficult to imitate. Imagine the difficulty of imitating Hewlett Packard's (HP) powerful and enabling culture. One of the most important components of HP's culture is that it supports and encourages teamwork and cooperation, even across divisional boundaries. HP has used this socially complex capability to enhance the compatibility of its numerous products, including printers, plotters, personal computers, mini-computers, and electronic instruments. By cooperating across these product categories, HP has been able to almost double its market value, all without introducing any radical new products or technologies.[16]

In general, when a firm's resources and capabilities are valuable, rare, and socially complex, those resources are likely to be sources of sustained competitive advantage. One firm that apparently violates this assertion is Sony. Most observers agree that Sony possesses some special management and coordination skills that enable it to conceive, design, and manufacture high-quality, miniaturized consumer electronics. However, it appears that every time Sony brings out a new miniaturized product, several of its competitors quickly duplicate that product, through reverse engineering, thereby reducing Sony's technological advantage. In what way can Sony's socially complex miniaturization skills be a source of sustained competitive advantage, when most of Sony's products are quickly imitated?

The solution to this paradox depends on shifting the unit of analysis from the performance of Sony's products over time to the performance of Sony over time. After it introduces each new product, Sony experiences a rapid increase in sales and profits associated with that product. However, this leads other firms to reverse engineer the Sony product and introduce their own version. Increased competition leads to the sales and profits associated with the new product being reduced. Thus, at the level of individual products introduced by Sony, Sony apparently enjoys only very shortlived competitive advantages.

However, by looking at the total returns earned by Sony across all of its new products over time, the source of Sony's sustained competitive advantage becomes clear. By exploiting its capabilities in miniaturization, Sony is able to constantly introduce new and exciting personal electronics products. No one of these products generates a sustained competitive advantage. However, over time, across several such product introductions, Sony's capability advantages do lead to a sustained competitive advantage.[17]

The Question of Organization

A firm's competitive advantage potential depends on the value, rareness, and imitability of its resources and capabilities. However, to fully realize this potential, a firm must also be organized to exploit its resources and capabilities. These observations lead to the question of organization: is a firm organized to exploit the full competitive potential of its resources and capabilities?

Numerous components of a firm's organization are relevant when answering the question of organization, including its formal reporting structure, its explicit management control systems, and its compensation policies. These components are referred to as "complementary resources" because they have limited ability to generate competitive advantage in isolation. However, in combination with other resources and capabilities, they can enable a firm to realize its full competitive advantage.[18]

Much of Caterpillar's sustained competitive advantage in the heavy construction industry can be traced to its becoming the sole supplier of this equipment to Allied forces in World War II. However, if Caterpillar's management had not taken advantage of this opportunity by implementing a global formal reporting structure, global inventory and other control systems, and compensation policies that created incentives for its employees to work around the world, then Caterpillar's potential for competitive advantage would not have been fully realized. These attributes of Caterpillar's organization, by themselves, could not be a source of competitive advantage, that is, adopting a global organizational form was only relevant for Caterpillar because it was pursuing a global opportunity. However, this organization was essential for Caterpillar to realize its full competitive advantage potential.

In a similar way, much of Wal-Mart's continuing competitive advantage in the discount retailing industry can be attributed to its early entry into rural markets in the southern United States. However, to fully exploit this geographic advantage, Wal-Mart needed to implement appropriate reporting structures, control systems, and compensation policies. We have already seen that one of these components of Wal-Mart's organization – its point-of-purchase inventory control system – is being imitated by K-Mart, and thus, by itself, is not likely to be a source of sustained competitive advantage. However, this inventory control system has enabled Wal-Mart to take full advantage of its rural locations by decreasing the probability of stockouts and by reducing inventory costs.

While a complementary organization enabled Caterpillar and Wal-Mart to realize their full competitive advantage, Xerox was prevented from taking full advantage of some of its most critical valuable, rare, and costly-to-imitate resources and capabilities because it lacked such organizational skills. Through the 1960s and early 1970s, Xerox invested in a series of very innovative technology development research efforts. Xerox managed this research effort by creating a standalone research laboratory (Xerox PARC, in Palo Alto, California), and by assembling a large group of highly creative and innovative scientists and engineers to work there. Left to their own devices, these scientists and engineers developed an amazing array of technological innovations, including the personal computer, the "mouse," windows-type software, the laser printer, the "paperless office," ethernet, and so forth. In retrospect, the market potential of these technologies was enormous. Moreover, since these technologies were developed at Xerox PARC, they were rare. Finally, Xerox may have been able to gain some important first mover advantages if they had been able to translate these technologies into products, thereby increasing the cost to other firms of imitating these technologies.

Unfortunately, Xerox did not have an organization in place to take advantage of these resources. For example, no structure existed whereby Xerox PARC's innovations could become known to managers at Xerox. Indeed, most Xerox managers – even many senior managers – were unaware of these technological developments through the mid-1970s. Once they finally became aware of them, very few of the innovations survived Xerox's highly bureaucratic product development process – a process where product development projects were divided into hundreds of minute tasks, and progress in each task was reviewed by dozens of large committees. Even those innovations that survived the product development process were not exploited by Xerox managers. Management compensation at Xerox depended almost exclusively on maximizing current revenue. Short-term profitability was relatively less important in compensation calculations, and the development of markets for future sales and profitability was essentially irrelevant.

Xerox's formal reporting structure, its explicit management control systems, and its compensation policies were all inconsistent with exploiting the valuable, rare, and costly-to-imitate resources developed at Xerox PARC. Not surprisingly, Xerox failed to exploit any of these potential sources of sustained competitive advantage.[19]

This set of questions can be applied in understanding the competitive implications of phenomena as diverse as the "cola wars" in the soft drink industry and competition among different types of personal computers.

The Competitive Implications of the "Cola Wars"

Almost since they were founded, Coca-Cola, Inc. and PepsiCo, Inc. have battled each other for market share in the soft drink industry. In many ways, the intensity of these "cola wars" increased in the mid-1970s with the introduction of PepsiCo's "Pepsi Challenge" advertising campaign. While significant advertising and other marketing expenditures have been made by both these firms, and while market share has shifted back and forth between them over time, it is not at all clear that these efforts have generated competitive advantages for either Coke or Pepsi.

Obviously, market share is a very valuable commodity in the soft drink industry. Market share translates directly into revenues, which, in turn, have a large impact on profits and profitability. Strategies pursued by either Coke or Pepsi designed to acquire market share will usually be valuable.

But are these market share acquisition strategies rare or does either Coca-Cola or Pepsi have a cost advantage in implementing them? Both Coca-Cola and PepsiCo are marketing powerhouses; both have enormous financial capabilities and strong management teams. Any effort by one to take share away can instantly be matched by the other to protect that share. In this sense, while Coke's and Pepsi's share acquisition strategies may be valuable, they are not rare, nor does either Coke or Pepsi have a cost advantage in implementing them. Assuming that these firms are appropriately organized (a reasonable assumption), then the cola wars should be a source of competitive parity for these firms.

This has, apparently, been the case. For example, Pepsi originally introduced its Pepsi Challenge advertising campaign in the Dallas-Ft. Worth market. After six months of the Pepsi Challenge – including price discounts, coupon campaigns, numerous celebrity endorsements, and so on – Pepsi was able to double its share of the Dallas-Ft. Worth market from 7 per cent to 14 per cent. Unfortunately, the retail price of Pepsi's soft drinks, after six months of the Pepsi Challenge, was approximately one half the pre-challenge level. Thus Pepsi doubled its market share, but cut its prices in half – exactly the result one would expect in a world of competitive parity.[20]

It is interesting to note that both Coca-Cola and Pepsi are beginning to recognize the futility of going head to head against an equally skilled competitor in a battle for market share to gain competitive advantages. Instead, these firms seem to be altering both their market share and other strategies. Coke, through its Diet Coke brand name, is targeting older consumers with advertisements that use personalities from the 1950s, 1960s, and 1970s (e.g., Elton John and Gene Kelly). Pepsi continues its focus on attracting younger drinkers with its "choice of a new generation" advertising campaigns. Coke continues its traditional focus on the soft drink industry, while Pepsi has begun diversifying into fast food restaurants and other related businesses. Coke has extended its marketing efforts internationally, whereas Pepsi focuses mostly on the market in the United States (although it is beginning to alter this strategy). In all these ways, Coke and Pepsi seem to be moving away from head-to-head competition for market share, and moving towards exploiting different resources.

The Competitive Position of the Macintosh Computer

Building on earlier research conducted by Xerox PARC, Apple Computer developed and marketed the first user-friendly alternative to DOS-based personal computers, the Macintosh. Most Macintosh users have a passion for their computers that is usually reserved for personal relationships. Macintosh users shake their heads and wonder why DOS-based computer users do not wake up and experience the "joy of Macintosh."

The first step in analyzing the competitive position of the Macintosh is to evaluate whether or not "user friendliness" in a personal computer is valuable; i.e., does it exploit an environmental opportunity and/or neutralize an environmental threat? While user friendliness is not a requirement of all personal computer users, it is not unreasonable to conclude that many of these computer users, other things being equal, would prefer working on a user-friendly machine compared with a user-unfriendly machine. Thus, the Macintosh computer does seem to respond to a real market opportunity.

When the Macintosh was first introduced, was user friendliness rare? At that time, DOS-based machines were essentially the only alternative to the Macintosh, and DOS-based software, in those early days, was anything but user friendly. Thus, the Macintosh was apparently both valuable and rare, and thus a source of at least a temporary competitive advantage for Apple.

Was the user friendliness of the Macintosh costly to imitate? At first, it seemed likely that user-friendly software would rapidly be developed for DOS-based machines, and thus that the user-friendly Macintosh would only enjoy a temporary competitive advantage. However, history has shown that user friendliness was not easy to imitate.

Imitation of the user-friendly Macintosh by DOS-based machines was slowed by a combination of at least two factors. First, the Macintosh hardware and software system had originally been developed by teams of software, hardware, and production engineers all working in Apple Computer. The teamwork, trust, commitment, and enthusiasm that these Apple employees enjoyed while working on Macintosh technology was difficult for other computer firms to duplicate, since most of those firms specialized either in hardware design and manufacturing (e.g., IBM) or software development (e.g., Microsoft, Lotus). In other words, the socially complex resources that Apple was able to bring to bear in the Macintosh project were difficult to duplicate in vertically nonintegrated computer hardware and software firms.

Second, Apple management had a different conception of the personal computer and its future from managers at IBM and other computer firms. At IBM, for example, computers had traditionally meant mainframe computers, and mainframe computers were expected to be complicated and difficult to operate. User friendliness was never an issue in IBM mainframes (users of IBM's JCL know the truth of that assertion!), and thus was not an important concern when IBM entered the personal computer market. However, at Apple, computers were Jobs' and Wozniak's toys – a hobby, to be used for fun. If management's mindset is that "computers are supposed to be fun," then it suddenly becomes easier to develop and build user-friendly computers.

Obviously, these two mindsets – IBM's "computers are complex tools run by technical specialists" versus Apple's "computers are toys for everyone" – were deeply embedded in the cultures of these two firms, as well as those firms that worked closely with them. Such mindsets are socially complex, slow to change, and difficult to imitate. It took some time before the notion that a computer should be (or even could be) easy to use came to prominence in DOS-based systems.[21] Only recently, after almost ten years (an eternity in the rapidly changing personal computer business), has user-friendly software for DOS-based machines been developed. With the introduction of Windows by Microsoft, the rareness of Macintosh's user friendliness has been reduced, as has been the competitive advantage that Macintosh had generated.

Interestingly, just as Windows software was introduced, Apple began to radically change its pricing and product development strategies. First, Apple cut the price of the Macintosh computer, reflecting the fact that user friendliness was not as rare after Windows as it was before Windows. Second, Apple seems to have recognized the need to develop new resources and capabilities to enhance their traditional user-friendly strengths. Rather than only competing with other hardware and software companies, Apple has begun developing strategic alliances with several other computer firms, including IBM and Microsoft. These alliances may help Apple develop the resources and capabilities they need to remain competitive in the personal computer industry over the next several years.

The Management Challenge

In the end, this discussion reminds us that sustained competitive advantage cannot be created simply by evaluating environmental opportunities and threats, and then conducting business only in high-opportunity, low-threat environments. Rather, creating sustained competitive advantage depends on the unique resources and capabilities that a firm brings to competition in its environment. To discover these resources and capabilities, managers must look inside their firm for valuable, rare and costly-to-imitate resources, and then exploit these resources through their organization.

NOTES

1. Porter's work is described in detail in M. Porter, *Competitive Strategy* (New York, NY: Free Press, 1980), and M. Porter, *Competitive Advantage* (New York, NY: Free Press, 1985).

2. A variety of different authors has begun to explore the competitive implications of a firm's internal strengths and weaknesses. Building on some seminal insights by Edith Penrose (*The Theory of the Growth of the Firm*, New York, NY: Wiley, 1959), this work has come to be known as the Resource-Based View of the Firm. Resource-based scholarly work includes: Birger Wernerfelt, "A Resource-Based View of the Firm," *Strategic Management Journal*, 5, 1984, 171–80; Richard Rumelt, "Toward a Strategic Theory of the Firm," in R. Lamb (ed.), *Competitive Strategic Management* (Englewood Cliffs, NJ: Prentice-Hall, 1984, 556–70); Jay Barney, "Strategic Factor Markets," *Management Science*, 41, 1980, 1231–41; and Jay Barney, "Organizational Culture: Can It Be a Source of Sustained Competitive Advantage?" *Academy of Management Review*, 11, 1986, 791–800. The framework developed in this chapter draws most closely from Jay Barney, "Firm Resources and Sustained Competitive Advantage," op. cit.

3. For more detailed discussions of the internal resources and capabilities of these firms, see Pankaj Ghemewat, "Wal-Mart Stores' Discount Operations," Case No. 9-387-018 (Harvard Business School, 1986); S. Chakravarty, "Hit 'Em Hardest with the Mostest," *Forbes*, 148, September 16, 1991, 48–54; and Pankaj Ghemewat, "Nucor at a Crossroad," Case No. 9-793-039 (Harvest Business School, 1992).

4. Different terms have been used to describe these internal phenomena, including core competencies (C. K. Prahalad and Gary Hamel, "The Core Competence of the Organization," *Harvard Business Review*, 90, 1990, 79–93), firm resources (Birger Wernerfelt, op. cit., and Jay B. Barney, "Firm Resources and Sustained Competitive Advantage") and firm capabilities (George Stalk, Phillip Evans, and Lawrence Shulman, "Competing on Capabilities: The New Rules of Corporate Strategy," *Harvard Business Review*, March–April, 1992, 57–69). While distinctions among these terms can be drawn, for our purposes they can, and will, be used interchangeably.

5. For details, see B. Schlender, "How Sony Keeps the Magic Going," *Fortune*, 125, February 24, 1992, 76–84; L. Krogh, J. Praeger, D. Sorenson, and J. Tomlinson, "How 3M Evaluates Its R&D Programs," *Research Technology Management*, 31, November/December, 1988, 10–14; Richard Rosenbloom, "Continuous Casting Investments at USX Corporation," Case No. 9-392-232 (Harvard Business School, 1990); and Cynthia Montgomery, "Sears, Roebuck and Co. in 1989," Case No. 9-391-147 (Harvard Business School, 1989).

6. This kind of environmental or technological shift is called a Schumpeterian revolution, and firms in this setting have little systematic hope of gaining competitive advantages, unless the competitive environment shifts again, although they can be lucky. See Jay B. Barney, "Types of Competitors and the Theory of Strategy: Toward an Integrative Framework," *Academy of Management Review*, 1986, 791–800.

7. For a discussion of AT&T's attempt to develop new resources and capabilities, see D. Kirkpatrick, "Could AT&T Rule the World?" *Fortune*, 127, May 17, 1993, 54–6. Hunter Fan's experience was described through personal communication with managers there, and in a publication celebrating Hunter Fan's 100th anniversary in 1986.

8. Prahalad and Hamel's 1990 discussion of NEC's attempt to develop the resources needed to compete in the global telecommunications and computer industry is insightful, especially in comparison to Kirkpatrick's discussion of AT&T's efforts in *Fortune*.

9. Wal-Mart's point of purchase inventory control system and the impact of Wal-Mart's rural stores on its performance, are described in Ghemewat, op. cit., 1986. K-Mart's inventory control response to Wal-Mart is described in L. Steven's "Front Line Systems," *Computerworld*, 26, 1992, 61–3.

10. See M. G. Rukstad and J. Horn, "Caterpillar and the Construction Equipment Industry in 1988," Case No. 9-389-097 (Harvard Business School, 1989).

11. Komatsu's response to Caterpillar's competitive advantage is described in C. A. Bartlett and U. S. Rangan, "Komatsu Ltd.," Case No. 9-385-277 (Harvard Business School, 1985).

12. See Richard Blackburn and Benson Rosen, "Total Quality and Human Resources Management: Lessons Learned from Baldridge Award-Winning Companies," *Academy of Management Executive*, 7, 1993, 49–66.

13. These invisible assets have been described by H. Itami, *Mobilizing Invisible Assets* (Cambridge, MA: Harvard University Press, 1987).

14. Personal communication.

15. See E. Mansfield, "How Rapidly Does New Industrial Technology Leak Out?" *Journal of Industrial Economics*, 34, 1985, 217–23; and E. Mansfield, M. Schwartz, and S. Wagner, "Imitation Costs and Patents: An Empirical Study," *Economic Journal*, 91, 1981, 907–18.

16. See S. K. Yoder, "A 1990 Reorganization at Hewlett Packard Already Is Paying Off," *Wall Street Journal*, July 22, 1991, Section Ak, 1+. This is not to suggest that socially complex resources and capabilities do not change and evolve in an organization. They clearly do. Nor does this suggest that managers can never radically alter a firm's socially complex resources and capabilities. Such transformational leaders do seem to exist, and do have an enormous impact on these resources in a firm. Managers such as the late Mike Walsh at Tenneco, Lee Iacocca at Chrysler, and Jack Welch at General Electric apparently have been such leaders. However, this kind of leadership is a socially complex phenomenon, and thus very difficult to imitate. Even if a leader in one firm can transform its socially complex resources and capabilities, it does not necessarily mean that other firms will be able to imitate this feat at the same cost. The concept of transformational leaders is discussed in N. Tichy, *The Transformational Leader* (New York, NY: Wiley, 1986).

17. See Schlender, op. cit.

18. See Raphael Amit and Paul Schoemaker, "Strategic Assets and Organizational Rent," *Strategic Management Journal*, 14, 1993, 33–46; David Teece, "Profiting from Technological Innovation," *Research Policy*, 15, 1986, 285–305; and Ingemar Dierickx and Karel Cool, "Asset Stock Accumulation and Sustainability of Competitive Advantage," *Management Science*, 35, 1989, 1504–11, for a discussion of complementary resources and capabilities. Of course, complementary organizational resources are part of a firm's overall resource and capability base, and thus the competitive implications of these resources could be evaluated using the questions of value, rareness, and imitability. However, the question of organization is included in this discussion to emphasize the particular importance of complementary organizational resources in enabling a firm to fully exploit its competitive advantage potential.

19. Xerox's organizational problems with Xerox PARC are described, in detail, in David T. Kearns and David A. Nadler, *Prophets in the Dark* (New York, NY: Harper Collins, 1992); Douglas K. Smith and Robert C. Alexander, *Fumbling the Future* (New York, NY: William Morrow, 1988); and L. Hooper, "Xerox Tries to Shed Its Has Been Image with a Big New Machine," *Wall Street Journal*, September 20, 1990, Section A, 1+.

20. See A. E. Pearson and C. L. Irwin, "Coca-Cola vs. Pepsi-Cola (A)," Case No. 9-387-108 (Harvard Business School, 1988), for a discussion of the cola wars, and their competitive implications for Coke and Pepsi.

21. See D. B. Yoffie, "Apple Computer – 1992," Case No. 9-792-081 (Harvard Business School, 1992), for a complete discussion of Apple, IBM, and Apple's new strategies for the 1990s.

Chapter 2

Understanding Human Resource Management in the Context of Organizations and Their Environments

Susan E. Jackson and Randall S. Schuler

Introduction

The need for understanding human resource management (HRM) in context

Applied psychologists have developed sophisticated tools and techniques intended to improve the effectiveness of organizations, and substantial evidence attesting to the value of these has accrued (e.g. Denison 1990; Hansen & Wernerfelt 1989; Kaufman 1992; MacDuffie & Krafcik 1992; Macy & Izumi 1993; Terpstra & Rozell 1993; United States Department of Labor 1993; Huselid unpublished; Schnell, Olian, Smith, Sims Jr, Scully, Smith, unpublished). Nevertheless, US employers have been slow to adopt the "best" practices, that is, those widely discussed in organizations as being the most effective (Bretz *et al.*, 1992; Rynes & Boudreau 1986; Saari *et al.*, 1988). Commentators have suggested that the acontextual nature of the scientific evidence is part of the problem (e.g. Johns 1993; Murray & Dimick 1978); consequently, calls for new human resource management (HRM) research that takes context more seriously have become more frequent (e.g. Begin 1991; Dobbins *et al.*, 1991; James *et al.*, 1992;

S.E. Jackson and R.S. Schuler, "Understanding Human Resource Management in the Context of Organizations and Their Environments," *Annual Review of Psychology*, Vol. 46 (1995): 237–64.

Latham 1988). At the same time, a growing body of empirical evidence is beginning to shed light on the relationship between contextual conditions and HRM. Our objective for this review is to increase the momentum associated with this emerging field.

We use HRM as an umbrella term that encompasses (a) specific human resource practices such as recruitment, selection, and appraisal; (b) formal human resource policies, which direct and partially constrain the development of specific practices; and (c) overarching human resource philosophies, which specify the values that inform an organization's policies and practices. Ideally, these comprise a system that attracts, develops, motivates, and retains employees who ensure the effective functioning and survival of the organization and its members. To understand HRM in Context we must consider how these three components of HRM are affected by the internal and external environments of the organization's members. By implication, effective HRM helps employees meet the expectations of role partners within the organization (i.e. supervisors, peers, subordinates), at organizational boundaries (i.e. customers and clients), and beyond (i.e. family and society). Thus the expectations of these role partners must be incorporated into an understanding of HRM in Context.

Institutional theory
A role theory perspective assumes individuals respond to normative pressures as they seek approval for their performance in socially defined roles. Similarly, institutional theory views organizations as social entities that seek approval for their performances in socially constructed environments. Organizations conform to gain legitimacy and acceptance, which facilitate survival (Meyer & Rowan 1977; Zucker 1977). Because multiple constituencies control needed resources, legitimacy and acceptance are sought from many stakeholders.

Research on institutionalization (Scott 1987; Zucker 1987) focuses on pressures emanating from the internal and external environments. Internally, institutionalization arises out of formalized structures and processes, as well as informal or emergent group and organization processes. Forces in the external environment include those related to the state (e.g. laws and regulations), the professions (e.g. licensure and certification), and other organizations – especially those within the same industrial sector. Regardless of the source of institutional pressures, two central assertions of this perspective are (a) institutionalized activities are resistant to change and (b) organizations in institutionalized environments are pressured to become similar (DiMaggio & Powell 1983; Meyer & Rowan 1977). Thus, in this theoretical perspective, context is the major explanation for both resistance to change and the adoption of new HRM approaches. The first assertion suggests that HRM activities have deep historical roots in the organization, so they cannot be understood completely without analyzing the organization's past. From the second assertion it follows that HRM activities may be adopted by an organization simply because other organizations have done so. Thus, "managerial fads and fashions" ebb and flow in part because a few legitimate organizations become fashion leaders that are imitated by other organizations that view imitation as a low-risk way to gain acceptance (Abrahamson 1991). Tolbert & Zucker (1983) showed, for example, that institutionalization resulting from imitation partially explained the rate at which reforms in civil service selection procedures spread throughout the country at the turn of the century.

Resource dependence theory

Like institutional theory, resource dependence theory focuses on the relationship between an organization and its constituencies. However, resource dependence theory emphasizes resource exchanges as the central feature of these relationships, rather than concerns about social acceptability and legitimacy (Pfeffer & Cohen 1984). According to this perspective, groups and organizations gain power over each other by controlling valued resources. Furthermore, HRM activities and processes are assumed to reflect the distribution of power within a system. For example, personnel departments acquire power over other departments to the extent they make others dependent upon them by controlling the flow of human resources into and through the organization (Osterman 1984, 1992; Pfeffer & Cohen 1984). Thus this theoretical perspective is somewhat similar to an interactionist perspective within psychology in that the actor (an organization or unit) and the environment work in conjunction as explanations for the behavior of the actor.

Institutional theory and resource dependence theory were developed in the context of understanding large public bureaucracies, where efficiency may not be among the most important goals (see Ostroff & Schmitt 1993). In contrast, the theories we discuss next – human capital theory, transaction costs theory, agency theory, and resource-based theory – were developed in the context of understanding business enterprises, for which issues of efficiency are presumed to be central.

Human capital theory

In the economics literature, human capital refers to the productive capabilities of people (Becker 1964). Skills, experience, and knowledge have economic value to organizations because they enable it to be productive and adaptable; thus, people constitute the organization's human capital. Like other assets, human capital has value in the market place, but unlike other assets, the potential value of human capital can be fully realized only with the cooperation of the person. Therefore, all costs related to eliciting productive behaviors from employees – including those related to motivating, monitoring, and retaining them – constitute human capital investments made in anticipation of future returns (Flamholtz & Lacey 1981).

Organizations can use HRM in a variety of ways to increase their human capital (Cascio 1991; Flamholtz & Lacey 1981). For example, they can "buy" human capital in the market (e.g. by offering desirable compensation packages) or "make" it internally (e.g. by offering extensive training and development opportunities). Investments of either type have associated costs, which are justifiable only to the extent the organization is able to productively utilize the accumulated capital (Tsang *et al.*, 1991). In human capital theory, contextual factors such as market conditions, unions, business strategies, and technology are important because they can affect the costs associated with alternative approaches to using HRM to increase the value of the organization's human capital and the value of the anticipated returns, such as productivity gains (e.g. see Boudreau & Berger 1985; Russell *et al.*, 1993).

Transaction costs theory

Transaction cost economics assumes that business enterprises choose governance structures that economize transaction costs associated with establishing, monitoring, evaluating, and enforcing agreed upon exchanges (Williamson 1979, 1981). Predictions about the nature of the governance structure an enterprise will use incorporate two behavioral assumptions: bounded rationality and opportunism (i.e. the seeking of self-interest with guile). These assumptions mean that the central problem to be solved by organizations is how to design governance structures that take advantage of bounded rationality while safeguarding against opportunism. To solve this problem, implicit and explicit contracts are established, monitored, enforced, and revised. The theory has direct implications for understanding how HRM practices are used to achieve a governance structure for managing the myriad implicit and explicit contracts between employers and employees (Wright & McMahan 1992). For example, organizations that require firm-specific knowledge and skills are predicted to create internal labor markets that bind self-interested and boundedly rational employees to the organization, while organizations that do not require these skills can gain efficiencies by competing for self-interested and boundedly rational talent in an external labor market (Williamson 1981, 1991). Contextual factors, in turn, partly determine whether the types and amounts of skills and knowledge a firm needs are likely to be available in the external labor market, the costs of acquiring them from the external market, the organization's capability for developing them internally, and the costs of doing so.

Agency theory
Agency theory focuses attention on the contracts between a party (i.e. the principal) who delegates work to another (i.e. the agent) (Jensen & Meckling 1976). Agency relations are problematic to the degree that (a) the principal and agent have conflicting goals and (b) it is difficult or expensive for the principal to monitor the agent's performance (Eisenhardt 1989). Contracts are used to govern such relations. Efficient contracts align the goals of principals and agents at the lowest possible cost. Costs can arise from providing incentives and obtaining information (e.g. about the agent's behavior and/or the agent's performance outcomes). Agency theory appears to be particularly useful for understanding executive and managerial compensation practices, which are viewed as a means for aligning the interests of the owners of a firm (i.e. principals) with the managers in whom they vest control (i.e. agents). For example, agency theory suggests several conditions under which contracts are more likely to monitor behavior (e.g. salary-plus-merit pay systems) and/or outcomes (e.g. commissions) (see Conlon & Parks 1990; Eisenhardt 1988, 1989; Milkovich *et al.*, 1991; Tosi & Gomez-Mejia 1989). Agency theory also has been used to predict occupation-based differences in job pricing methods (i.e. job evaluation vs market pricing) and in pay variability (Newman & Huselid 1992).

   Agency and transaction costs theories share many similar assumptions about human behavior (Eisenhardt 1989) and may be most useful when combined. For example, using these two theories, Jones & Wright (1992) offer an insightful interpretation of the HRM literature focusing on implications of the economic perspective for HRM utility estimates. Their discussion suggests various reasons for predicting that the utility of HRM activities will vary with conditions in both the internal and external environments of organizations. Such conditions include the other human resource practices that are used by the organization, government regulations and their enforcement, technologies, union activities, and labor market conditions. These contextual factors can affect both the costs and potential gains associated with a particular human resource practice (e.g. a recruitment program, a selection test, or a training program).

Resource-based theory

The resource-based theory of the firm blends concepts from organizational economics and strategic management (Barney 1991; Conner 1991). A fundamental assumption of this view is that organizations can be successful if they gain and maintain competitive advantage (see Porter 1985). Competitive advantage is gained by implementing a value-creating strategy that competitors cannot easily copy and sustain (Barney 1991) and for which there are no ready substitutes. For competitive advantage to be gained, two conditions are needed: first, the resources available to competing firms must be variable among competitors, and second, these resources must be immobile (i.e. not easily obtained). Three types of resources associated with organizations are (a) physical (plant; technology and equipment; geographic location), (b) human (employees' experience and knowledge), and (c) organizational (structure; systems for planning, monitoring, and controlling activities; social relations within the organization and between the organization and external constituencies). HRM greatly influences an organization's human and organizational resources and so can be used to gain competitive advantage (Schuler & MacMillan 1984). Presumably, the extent to which HRM can be used to gain competitive advantage, and the means of doing so, are partly determined by the environments in which organizations operate (Wright *et al.*, 1994). For example, in some industries, technologies can substitute for human resources, whereas in others the human element is fundamental to the business. To illustrate, contrast labor-intensive and knowledge-intensive industries. The latter context may be more conducive to the use of HRM as a means to gain competitive advantage.

Conclusion

This brief and selective overview of theoretical perspectives is intended to facilitate the reader's understanding and interpretation of some of the empirical research we review below. In addition, we believe these perspectives can inform new research on HRM in Context. Although many of the internal and external factors considered below are likely to be related, few studies control for all possible interdependencies; similarly, we treat the contextual factors as if they are independent while recognizing that this approach is overtly simplistic.

Review of Empirical Research

HRM and the internal contexts of organizations

Technology

Technology refers to a system's processes for transforming inputs into usable outputs. These processes can vary along many dimensions, including the degree of continuity in the production system (e.g. Woodward 1965), the types and levels of knowledge required by the system (Hulin & Roznowski 1985), the degree to which tasks are routinized and predictable (Perrow 1967), and the linkages and interdependencies among tasks and people (Thompson 1967). The impact of technology on the social dynamics within organizations has long been recognized, but only recently have US researchers begun to address systematically the implications of technology for HRM (Katzell 1994).

Following human capital theory and a systems theory view of the relationship between human and technical subsystems, Snell & Dean (1992) hypothesized that HRM would be directly influenced by the presence of advanced manufacturing technology (AMT), total quality management (TQM), and just-in-time inventory control (JIT). Using data from 512 manufacturing firms, they found that firms using traditional technologies were less likely than firms using AMT to engage in selective hiring, comprehensive training, developmental appraisal, and externally equitable compensation (see Clark 1993 for a similar conclusion). Jackson et al. (1989) used the role behavior perspective to predict and explain why, compared to firms engaged in mass production, firms using technologies for flexible specialization were more likely to use performance appraisals in determining pay and training needs. Kozlowski & Hults (1987) did not directly invoke roles as explanatory constructs in their study of engineers, but the association they found between an organization's technical complexity and HRM indicative of a "climate for technical updating" also are consistent with the role behavior perspective. It appears that research informed by both role theory and human capital theory could improve our understanding of how technology shapes HRM, as well as the role of HRM in implementing new technology (e.g. see Zammuto & O'Connor 1992).

Structure
Organization structure describes the allocation of tasks and responsibilities among individuals and departments; it designates the nature and means of formal reporting relationships as well as the groupings of individuals within the organization (Child 1977). The structural forms generally recognized for domestic firms include functional departmentalization, product-based divisionalization, geographical divisionalization, and matrix organization (with dual reporting relationships). Different forms are presumed to result from and be associated with a variety of internal and external forces, including technological demands, organizational growth, environmental turbulence, and business strategy (e.g. see Randolph & Dess 1984). Furthermore, each structural form probably faces some unique challenges that have implications for HRM. For example, Jackson et al. (1989) argued that divisionalized firms should be more likely than those structured around functional departments to emphasize results over process, reflecting greater integration across units and a more externally oriented focus. Consistent with this expectation, they found that divisionalized firms relied relatively more on stock ownership and bonuses for company-wide performance as components of their HRM systems.

Van Sluijs et al. (1991) argued that HRM has been shaped by its evolution within the context of functionally departmentalized organizations. Congruent with functional departmentalization, the traditional approach to managing people focuses on selection, training, performance appraisal, and compensation for individuals in specific jobs versus, for example, team players employed as members of an organization (cf Bowen *et al.*, 1991). It also presumes hierarchies of control rather than horizontal work-flow sequences (cf Whyte 1991). A realization is emerging, however, that when organizations are (re)structured around teamwork (in place of individual performers), there are major consequences for HRM. For example, Klimoski & Jones (1994) suggest that organizations with team-based designs may need to use new methods of job analysis, assessment, recruitment, and socialization activities. Jackson *et al.* (1994) argued that greater reliance on teams has been an important factor in generating more concern about the HRM implications of workforce diversity.

The impact of structure on HRM is particularly evident in discussions of multinational firms and international joint ventures. Structures for organizations that span across national borders include multinational, global, international, or transnational forms (Phatak 1992; Ghoshal & Bartlett 1990). These forms represent alternative solutions to the problems of differentiation, integration, uncertainty, and risk management in an international environment (SJ Kobrin, unpublished), and each form has unique implications for HRM (Dowling *et al.*, 1994; Kochan *et al.*, 1992). The fundamental challenge is how to use HRM to link globally dispersed units while also adapting to the societal requirements of host societies (Laurent 1986). Similar problems must be solved when firms from different countries collaborate in a joint venture (e.g. Schuler *et al.*, 1991, 1992; Schuler & van Sluijs 1992; Slocum & Lei 1993).

Size
Institutional theory suggests that larger organizations should adopt more sophisticated and socially responsive HRM activities because these more visible organizations are under more pressure to gain legitimacy. Economic theories suggest that, because of the costs associated with many aspects of HRM, acceptable economies of scale must be reached before sophisticated HRM systems can be implemented. Consistent with both perspectives, considerable evidence shows that HRM varies systematically with organization size.[1] Specifically, compared to smaller organizations, larger ones are more likely to (a) adopt due process procedures (Dobbin *et al.*, 1988); (b) adopt employee involvement practices (Lawler *et al.*, 1992); (c) rely less on temporary staff (Davis-Blake & Uzzi 1993); (d) use more sophisticated staffing (Terpstra & Rozell 1993) and training and development (Saari *et al.*, 1988) procedures, and have more highly developed internal labor markets (Baron *et al.*, 1986a, see also Ferris *et al.*, 1992); (e) pay their employees more (Mellow 1982), but also put more pay at risk through the use of bonuses and long-term incentives (Gerhart & Milkovich 1990); and (f) engage in drug testing (Guthrie & Olian 1991a).

Life cycle stages
The literature on organization life cycle stages directs attention to the changing managerial priorities that characterize organizations in various developmental stages such as start-up, growth, maturity, and perhaps decline and revival (Baird & Meshoulam 1988; Smith *et al.*, 1985). These changing priorities, in turn, have implications for HRM. For example, a description of how managerial roles change across phases of the organizational life cycle was used by Gerstein & Reisman (1983) to argue that selection criteria and assessment methods for top-level executives need to be matched to life

cycle stages. Similarly, Datta & Guthrie (1994) suggested that the role requirements of CEOs in rapidly growing firms help explain why outsider CEOs are more likely to be hired during this phase. Ferris *et al.* (1984) also used a role perspective to develop propositions regarding the staffing needs and their implications under conditions of decline. Research and theory relating life cycle stages to changes in managerial requirements presume that managerial roles change across life cycle stages, but the validity of this assumption has not been established empirically, for example, through the use of systematic job analyses (Szilagyi & Schweiger 1984).

In the studies just described, the research questions address the types of employees who best match the needs of organizations in various life cycle stages. Other studies have addressed the issue of how much attention is directed toward staffing issues, and here economic arguments seem more relevant. For example, Buller & Napier (1993) found that CEOs and human resource executives in rapidly growing firms viewed recruitment and selection as by far the most important aspect of HRM, whereas in mature firms there was more concern for a broad array of activities, such as those related to maintaining an internal labor market (see also Kotter & Sathe 1978). Economic explanations also have been used to predict and explain associations between life cycle stages and pay levels (see Gerhart & Milkovich 1992).

To date, empirical research on HRM and organizational life cycles has adopted a deterministic view, predicting that life cycle stage constrains and shapes HRM. But more complex contingency models also have been proposed. In these models, the assumption is that HRM reflects choices made by organizational decision makers; wise choices lead to a good fit between life cycle stage and HRM, which results, in turn, in organizational effectiveness (e.g. Cook & Ferris 1986; Kozlowski *et al.*, 1993; Lengnick-Hall & Lengnick-Hall 1988; Milliman *et al.*, 1991). The validity of such models has not been assessed empirically, however.

Business strategy

Typologies for characterizing the business strategies used by firms abound, but the two most frequently cited in discussions of HRM were proposed by Miles & Snow (1978) and Porter (1980, 1985). Miles & Snow classified organizations as prospectors, analyzers, or defenders (later, reactors were added). Prospectors actively seek new products and markets and, therefore, seek to grow; analyzers also seek to grow, but in a more stable and predictable way through the internal development of new products rather than creation of new markets; defenders seek to maintain the same limited product line with emphasis on high volume and low cost (Miles & Snow 1984). These postures toward the environment should have implications for the quantity and pace of human resource flows. Defenders, for instance, are less concerned about recruiting new applicants externally and more concerned about developing current employees. Therefore, performance appraisal is used more for developmental purposes than for evaluation (Snow & Snell 1993). In contrast, prospectors are growing and so are more concerned about recruiting and using performance appraisal results for evaluation rather than for longer-term development (Olian & Rynes 1984, see also Slocum *et al.*, 1985).

Porter's (1985) competitive strategies distinguish among firms that compete on the basis of cost leadership, product differentiation, and market focus. In a study of airlines, Johnson *et al.* (1989) showed that, in a deregulated environment, wage rates were related significantly to which of these strategies airlines pursued. In an adaptation of Porter's typology, Schuler & Jackson (1987a) used the role behavior perspective to describe the possible HRM implications of cost-reduction, innovation, and quality enhancement strategies. Jackson *et al.* (1989) supported Schuler & Jackson's argument that, because an innovation strategy requires risk-taking and tolerance of inevitable failures, HRM in firms pursuing this strategy should be used to give employees a sense of security and encourage a long-term orientation. Peck (1994) and Milkovich *et al.* (1991) also support a relationship between an innovation strategy and the use of HRM to support a longer-term orientation. Consistent with predictions regarding behaviors needed for a quality strategy is Cowherd & Levine's (1992) finding that egalitarian pay structures are associated with greater product quality.

This brief review of the strategic HRM literature is by no means exhaustive (e.g. see Lengnick-Hall & Lengnick-Hall 1988) and does not fully consider the possible complexity of and alternative models for describing the relationship between strategy and HRM (e.g. see Kerr 1985; Snow & Snell 1993), but the studies clearly support the assertion that strategy is a contextual factor with important implications for HRM. Thus, we are especially optimistic about recent efforts to establish linkages between strategic considerations and psychologically oriented HRM research on selection and utility (see Russell *et al.*, 1993).

HRM and the external contexts of organizations

Legal, social, and political environments

Within the United States, almost all aspects of HRM are affected by the legal and regulatory environment. In the process of attending to the legal environment, the field also responds to the social and political environments that give rise to and shape the promulgation, interpretation, and enforcement of acts of Congress, executive orders, tax codes, and even funding for HRM innovations (see Cascio 1992; Landy *et al.*, 1994; Mahoney 1987; Miller & O'Leary 1989; Noe & Ford 1992; Sharf 1994; Wigdor & Sackett 1993). As US corporations expand their operations abroad, however, they face additional legal concerns. For example, in European countries, organizations are obliged to set aside specific sums of money for formal training and development (Brewster *et al.*, 1993). And for corporations that employ expatriates abroad, immigration and taxation treaties can influence staffing decisions (Dowling *et al.*, 1994). Global corporations also encounter additional social and political realities. For example, in some countries, civil laws and religious laws coexist and jointly define a legal context for HRM (Florkowski & Nath 1993). Looking ahead, institutional theory and resource dependence theory appear to be particularly useful guides for research on how the legal, social, and political environments impact HRM (see Konrad & Linnehan 1992). Potential topics for investigation include the conditions and processes that facilitate or inhibit the adoption and transfer of HRM innovations (e.g. see Johns 1993) and the feedback processes through which the HRM activities of organizations create changes in their social, legal, and political environments.

Unionization

In the United States, unionized employees have received wages estimated to be up to 33% greater than those of nonunion employees, and unions are often credited with improving working conditions and safety (Lawler & Mohrman 1987). Unions give voice to their members; establish policies and procedures for handling wage and working condition grievances; provide for job security; and secure health and retirement benefits (Baron *et al.*, 1986b; Freeman & Medoff 1984; Jackson *et al.*, 1989; Kochan *et al.*, 1992; Youngblood *et al.*, 1992). In addition to helping their own members, unions have probably motivated nonunion employers to provide many of these same benefits (Foulkes 1980). Nevertheless, recent years have witnessed a decline in unionization due to the environmental forces of deregulation, international competition, and the shift to a service economy. Consequently, some unions have moved out of their traditional collective bargaining roles and adversarial relationships with management and are beginning to work cooperatively on issues such as plant designs and locations (Adler 1993; Lewandowski & MacKinnon 1992; Noble 1993; Woodruff 1993); work team design (Lawler & Mohrman 1987); team-oriented pay plans such as gainsharing and employee ownership (Miller & Schuster 1987; Rosen *et al.*, 1986); recruitment and selection procedures including selecting members for representation on the board of directors (Collins *et al.*, 1993); retraining and relocation (Hoerr 1991; Marshall 1992); and quality improvement (Bognanno & Kleiner 1992; Brett *et al.*, 1990; Lawler *et al.*, 1992; Reid 1992). Changing union-management relations mean that researchers can no longer simply compare union to nonunion firms. Now they must also take into consideration whether union-management relations with each firm are adversarial or cooperative (e.g. see Cutcher-Gershenfeld 1991).

As the process of globalizing unfolds, both unions and multinational enterprises (MNEs) are recognizing that they need to understand how the institutions of union–management relations and collective bargaining differ around the world (Dowling *et al.*, 1994). Prahalad & Doz (1987) found that lack of such understanding often results in conflicts between MNE managers and local communities. To facilitate adaptation to local conditions, it helps US MNEs to know, for example, that in Europe the collective bargaining process and class struggle are more intertwined than they are in the United States (Bournois & Chauchat 1990; Marginson 1992; Poole 1986a,b), and labor institutions are often much stronger (Ofori-Dankwa 1994; Western 1993). MNEs must consider these histories and institutions when developing company-wide human resource philosophies, policies, and practices (Hamill 1983). HRM researchers on almost every topic also must recognize, understand, and incorporate these realities into their work (Kochan *et al.*, 1992) if it is to be useful for organizations operating in a global context.

Labor market conditions

Labor market conditions can be characterized along several dimensions including unemployment levels, labor diversity, and labor market structure. Unemployment levels and labor market structures have long been recognized as important macroeconomic variables, whereas the importance of labor diversity has been recognized more recently.

Unemployment levels reflect the demand for labor relative to the supply. Macroeconomic research conducted at the national level indicates that in the capitalist United States, excess demand typically results in low unemployment while excess supply typically results in high unemployment. Furthermore, as unemployment drops, wages and costs increase and profits and investments decline; these conditions, in turn, reduce demand for labor (Levine & Tyson 1990). Conversely, as unemployment rises, absenteeism and turnover rates tend to decrease (Kerr 1954; Markham 1985) and the link between employee dissatisfaction and turnover is weakened (Carsten & Spector 1987).

Perhaps because recruitment activities regulate organizational inputs, recruitment researchers have been more sensitive than others to the potential importance of unemployment levels (Rynes 1991; Rynes & Barber 1990). Consistent with transaction costs theory, recruitment strategies appear to vary with unemployment levels. When the labor supply is tight, organizations use more expensive and intensive recruiting methods (Hanssens & Levien 1983), increase the geographic scope of their recruitment activities (Malm 1955), and appear to forego preemployment drug screening (Bennett et al., 1994). Other responses to a tight labor supply include improving wages, benefits, and working conditions in order to attract and retain employees (Lakhani 1988) and reducing hiring standards as a means to fill vacant positions (Thurow 1975). Such responses to the labor pool may have significant implications for other human resource practices (e.g. lower selection standards may mean that more training is needed). Thus, the consequences of the external environment may ultimately include fundamental changes in the nature of the employment relationship (e.g. see Levine & Tyson 1990).

The US labor market is evolving toward greater diversity in terms of gender, age, and ethnicity (Johnston & Packer 1987, see also Triandis et al., 1994b), although demographic diversity varies markedly among occupations and across status levels. The implications of increasing diversity have been mostly ignored by HRM researchers, as have the implications of differing degrees of homogeneity across segments of the labor market (cf Katzell 1994; Triandis et al., 1994b). This is somewhat surprising, given the field's long history of research on bias and discrimination and substantial evidence showing that feelings, cognitions, and behaviors are all influenced by conditions of group homogeneity vs diversity (see Cox 1993; Jackson et al., 1994). These effects undoubtedly have consequences for recruitment, selection, and attrition (see Jackson et al., 1991; Pfeffer 1983; Schneider 1987); socialization (Jackson et al., 1993); training, development, and mentoring (Morrison 1992; Ohlott et al., 1994; Powell & Butterfield 1994; Thomas 1993); and perhaps assessment and reward systems (Pfeffer & Langton 1988). To date, however, the HRM implications of increasing diversity have received relatively more attention from large businesses than from academic researchers. Large businesses are experimenting with a variety of HRM interventions in order to adjust systems that evolved in the context of relative homogeneity to fit the new conditions of relative diversity (e.g. see Jackson & Associates 1992; Morrison & Crabtree 1992; Morrison et al., 1993; Zedeck 1992).

The above discussion regarding how unemployment levels can impact HRM implicitly assumes a labor market structure that is undifferentiated. But stratification of the external labor market as well as the internal labor market along the somewhat related dimensions of price and status is acknowledged widely; methods of recruitment, forms of compensation, severance arrangements, employee autonomy, and numerous other aspects of HRM are known to differ as one moves up through price and status levels (e.g. Guthrie & Olian 1991a; Osterman 1984; Rynes 1991; Schuler & Jackson 1987b). Substantial evidence suggests that HRM systems differ across occupational groups, reflecting occupational subcultures that vary in their orientations toward work, control, and authority structures, self-identification, and career expectations (Althauser 1989; Bridges & Villemez 1991; Sonnenstuhl & Trice 1991; Van Maanen & Barley 1984). Thus, even if firms have a single HRM philosophy and a single set of HRM policies, these are likely to manifest themselves in different practices across subgroups of employees. By extension, the "same" HRM intervention should be expected to be differentially interpreted and received across these subgroups.

Industry characteristics
The term "industry" refers to a distinct group of productive or profit-making enterprises. A full discussion of how HRM is affected by industry-level factors would consider HRM in the public vs private sectors (Molnar & Rogers 1976; Rosen *et al.*, 1986), in regulated vs unregulated industries (Guthrie & Olian 1991b; Guthrie *et al.*, 1991; Johnson *et al.*, 1989), and in industries characterized by high vs low stability or change (Evans 1992; Ghoshal & Bartlett 1990), among other topics. Due to space limitations, only the simple classification of manufacturing vs service industries is discussed below.

Bowen & Schneider (1988) described three characteristics that distinguish the activities of services from manufacturing organizations: First, a service is generally intangible; second, in services the customer and employee usually collaborate in the service production-and-delivery process; third, in services, production and consumption are usually simultaneous. Because customers play a central role in services, they can be thought of as partial employees who are subject to human resource management (Bowen 1986; Mills & Morris 1986). Consistent with this notion, Jackson & Schuler (1992) found that employers in the service sector were more likely to include customers as sources of input for performance appraisal. Differences in the nature of manufacturing and service also appear to have implications for other aspects of HRM systems, including recruitment and selection, training, compensation, stress management, use of temporary workers, and the development and maintenance of appropriate organizational climates and cultures (see Davis-Blake & Uzzi 1993; Delaney *et al.*, 1989; Guthrie & Olian 1991a; Jackson 1984; Jackson & Schuler 1992; Schneider *et al.*, 1992; Terpstra & Rozell 1993).

In summary, although not yet widely incorporated into research paradigms, industry characteristics may have far-reaching implications for HRM. Industries, like national cultures, are the contexts within which meanings are construed, effectiveness is defined, and behaviors are evaluated (e.g. see Hofstede 1991).

National culture
The globalization of national economies and the evolution of multinational enterprises have resulted in increased awareness and documentation of the differences in how human resources are managed among countries (Brewster & Hegewisch 1994; Towers Perrin 1992). Because countries often have unique cultures (i.e. values, norms, and

customs) it is widely presumed that multinational enterprises must understand the culture(s) of the region(s) in which they operate in order to effectively manage their human resources.

The most widely known framework for comparing national cultures is that developed by Hofstede (1980), who identified four dimensions of culture: individualism, masculinity, uncertainty avoidance, and power distance. A fifth dimension, time orientation, has been added more recently, but most available research considers only the four original dimensions (Hofstede 1993). Other authors have identified additional dimensions of culture, including informality, materialism, and change orientation (Adler 1991; Phatak 1992; Ronen 1994).

There has been considerable speculation about the possible implications for HRM of cultural variations along these dimensions (Erez & Earley 1993; Mendonca & Kanungo 1994; Slocum & Lei 1993), but empirical studies seldom include direct measures of both culture and HRM. Instead, researchers generally have compared HRM across countries and then argued that cultural values and orientations are determinants of the differences found (see Arvey et al., 1991; Bhagat et al., 1990; Begin 1992; Brewster & Tyson 1991; Carroll 1988; Eberwein & Tholen 1993; Erez 1994; Hickson 1993; Maruyama 1992; Yu & Murphy 1993). It must be recognized, however, that culture may not explain all HRM differences found across countries (Lincoln 1993). Country differences may also be the result of differences in economic and political systems (e.g. Carroll et al., 1988), laws and regulations (e.g. Florkowski & Nath 1993), industrial relations systems (Strauss 1982), and labor market conditions (e.g. Lévy-Leboyer 1994). Recently, Hofstede (1991) even suggested that organizational and industry characteristics may be more important than national cultures as determinants of managerial practices and employee behaviors. This argument is consistent with evidence that some types of HRM systems can be used effectively across countries that are culturally quite dissimilar (MacDuffie & Krafcik 1992; Wickens 1987). Our understanding of the role of national culture in HRM could benefit from investigations that focus on the question of how globally expanding companies develop HRM systems that are simultaneously consistent with multiple and distinct local cultures and yet internally consistent in the context of a single organization (cf Heenan & Perlmutter 1979; Phatak 1992; Schwartz 1992; Tung 1993).

An Integrative Perspective for Research on HRM in Context

Figure 2.1 represents a summary view of the many relationships between context and HRM described in this review. The relationships we described are depicted as part of a larger model, which includes several important components that are beyond the focus of our discussion. The component labeled "Sense-making & Decision-making" has been the subject of a growing body of research that investigates how and why organization leaders, acting individually and in concert, characterize and interpret their environments, and the implications of these processes for eventual action (e.g. Hambrick 1994; Jackson 1992; Jackson & Dutton 1988). In our integrative

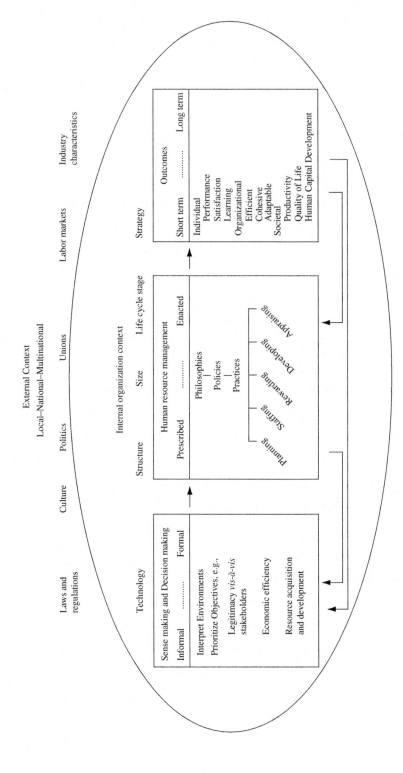

Figure 2.1   Integrative framework for understanding HRM in Context. Copyright by S.E. Jackson & R.S. Schuler. Used with permission.

model of HRM, these processes are assumed to be intimately bound with the implicit and explicit prioritizing of objectives. These, in turn, are translated into HRM philosophies, programs, and practices (Schuler 1992). In other words, our model presumes that the phenomena represented in the left-most box in Fig. 2.1 are key mediators that help explain vertical linkages between context and HRM.

Individual-, organizational-, and societal-level outcomes (right-most boxes in Fig. 2.1) are also major components of an integrative model. A list of specific outcomes could be readily derived by readers familiar with the scientific and practice-oriented HRM literature. We wish to encourage interested researchers to expand their conceptualizations of outcomes to go beyond individual-level behavior in work settings. In addition, outcomes that describe small and large groups (e.g. groups, organizations, society) should be considered and the phenomena studied should reflect the reality that HRM activities may affect outcomes beyond the traditional boundaries of the target organization (e.g. families, schools, communities).

Understanding and advancing HRM in Context requires an integrative perspective that recognizes and incorporates all of the relationships depicted in Fig. 2.1. Within the discipline of psychology, however, linkages involving the macro-level internal and external environments have been largely ignored. Fortunately, a realization is now emerging that this state of affairs should not continue. Much research is needed to understand how internal and external environments shape (a) the nature of human resource philosophies, policies, and practices; (b) the employee behaviors and attitudes that should be valued, and which are likely to be exhibited; (c) the criteria that define employee effectiveness and achieved levels of employee effectiveness; and (d) the criteria that define organizational effectiveness and achieved levels of organizational effectiveness. In addition, future research needs to recognize that contexts may moderate the observed relationships between HRM and various outcomes.

Our review of the literature has revealed to us how seldom research addresses the horizontal linkages among HRM activities, although such linkages are implied by most of the theories we reviewed and, we would argue, by most psychological theories about employee attitudes and behaviors. Employees do not respond to specific human resource policies and practices in isolation. They attend to and interpret the entire array of information available and from this they discern cultural values and behavioral norms. Unfortunately, we know surprisingly little about how various combinations of human resource policies and practices are interpreted by employees, nor do we know how complex HRM systems influence the attitudes and behaviors of current and potential organizational members. Our understanding of vertical linkages between HRM and contexts cannot proceed without attending to the horizontal inter-dependencies that exist among human resource policies and practices.

Theory-driven research

The theories we have identified represent possible explanations for some of the empirical relationships between environmental conditions and HRM, but the available theories are admittedly inadequate. Each deals with pieces of the larger phenomenon and none addresses the whole domain of HRM in Context. Thus, in the near future, the best work will be informed by multiple theoretical perspectives. Furthermore, because the theories we have discussed were generally not formulated specifically for the purpose of understanding HRM in Context, some translation and adaptation of these theories may be required. This translation process is likely to proceed in iterative steps, with consensus emerging slowly. Nevertheless, research driven by incomplete theories is more likely to accumulate to form a meaningful body of knowledge, compared to research driven by no theory at all.

Methodological issues

Although imperfect, potentially useful theories are relatively plentiful. Much less plentiful are psychometrically sound, agreed-upon approaches for measuring relevant constructs and testing key theoretical propositions. Through methodological contributions, industrial–organizational psychology is in an excellent position to contribute to the advance of knowledge about HRM in Context. Contributions will not come through "research as usual," however. Several shifts in approach will be required: from treating organizational settings as sources of error variance to attending as closely to them as we have traditionally attended to individual characteristics; from focusing on individuals to treating social systems as the target for study; from focusing on single practices or policies to adopting a holistic approach to conceptualizing HRM systems; from research conducted in single organizations at one point in time to research comparing multiple organizations and/or studying dynamic changes in organizations across times and places; and from a search for the "one best way" to a search for the fundamental features that characterize the many possible ways to design and maintain effective systems.

These shifts in perspective are fundamental in many respects. In other respects, however, they require little more than a change from defining the essential features of situations as jobs (as industrial–organizational psychology often does) to a recognition that jobs are merely the first level of context in a many-level complex system of contexts. By extension, we would argue that future HRM research should elevate organization analysis (and perhaps extraorganization analysis) to a status equal to that currently enjoyed by job analysis. We already understand and act on the principle that effective selection systems, performance appraisal methods, compensation plans, and training programs cannot be developed without a scientifically valid diagnosis of the job-as-situation. Similarly, the design of effective HRM systems cannot be developed without a valid diagnosis of the organization-as-situation.[2] Current methods for conducting job analysis are not adequate for conducting organizational analysis. However, if motivated to do so, thoughtful researchers undoubtedly could apply the principles of sound job analysis for the purpose of developing sophisticated methods for measuring organizational contexts.

Also needed are measurement tools that capture the essential features of HRM philosophies, policies, and practices, while yielding information that facilitates meaningful comparisons among organizations and across environmental contexts. Research that simply identifies and describes the most common configurations of prescribed HRM systems and the most common forms of received HRM should serve as the foundation for future investigations of HRM in Context. Ideally, such research will reflect the reality of rapid globalization and the international context of most large organizations. Indeed, globalization may be the most potent catalyst for an explosion of research on HRM in Context: for those operating in a global environment, the importance of context is undeniable – it cannot be ignored. Multinational organizations strive for consistency in their ways of managing people on a worldwide basis while also adapting their ways to the specific cultural requirements of different societies (Laurent 1986). To meet this challenge, those responsible for the design of globally effective HRM must shift their focus away from the almost overwhelming variety of specific practices and policies found around the world and look instead at the more abstract, fundamental dimensions of contexts, HRM systems, and dimensions of employees' reactions (e.g. see Fulkerson & Schuler 1992). If they succeed in identifying these dimensions and the relationships between them, they may be able to more easily design HRM systems that can be used effectively in multiple country locations (e.g. see MacDuffie & Krafcik 1992).

NOTES

1. In HRM research, number of employees is the most commonly used size indicator, but financial indicators such as the dollar value of capital assets and/or the dollar value of sales also are reported sometimes.
2. This principle is, of course, widely accepted in the training literature – but it is also widely ignored.

LITERATURE CITED

Abrahamson E. 1991. Managerial fads and fashions: the diffusion and rejection of innovations. *Acad. Manage. Rev.* 16: 586–612

Adler NJ. 1991. *International Dimensions of Organizational Behavior*. Boston: PWS-Kent

Adler PS. 1993. Time-and-motion regained. *Harvard Bus. Rev.* 73: 97

Althauser RP. 1989. Internal labor markets. *Annu. Rev. Sociol.* 15: 143–61

Arvey RD, Bhagat RS, Salas E. 1991. Cross-cultural and cross-national issues in personnel and human resources management: Where do we go from here? *Res. Pers. Hum. Res. Manage.* 9: 367–407

Baird L, Meshoulam I. 1988. Managing the two fits of strategic human resource management. *Acad. Manage. Rev.* 13: 116–28

Barney J. 1991. Firm resources and sustained competitive advantage. *J. Manage.* 17: 99–120

Baron JN, Davis-Blake A, Bielby W. 1986a. The structure of opportunity: how promotion ladders vary within and among organizations. *Admin. Sci. Q.* 31: 248–73

Baron JN, Dobbin FR, Jennings PD. 1986b. War and peace: the evolution of modern personnel administration in US industry. *Am. J. Sociol.* 92: 350–83

Becker GS. 1964. *Human Capital*. New York: Natl. Bur. Econ. Res.

Begin JP. 1991. *Strategic Employment Policy*. Englewood Cliffs, NJ: Prentice-Hall

Begin JP. 1992. Comparative human resource management (HRM): a systems perspective. *Int. J. Hum. Res. Manage.* 3: 379–408

Bennett N, Blum TC, Roman PM. 1994. Presence of drug screening and employee assistance programs: exclusive and inclusive human resource management practices. *J. Organ. Behav.* 15: 549–60

Bhagat RS, Kedia BL, Crawford SE, Kaplan MR. 1990. Cross-cultural issues in organizational psychology: emergent trends and directions for research in the 1990's. *Int. Rev. Ind. Organ. Psychol.* 5: 196–231

Bognanno M, Kleiner M. 1992. Introduction: labor market institutions and the future role of unions. *Ind. Relat.* 31: 1–12

Boudreau JW, Berger CJ. 1985. Decision-theoretic utility analysis applied to employee separations and acquisitions. *J. Appl. Psychol.* 70: 581–612

Bournois F, Chauchat J-H. 1990. Managing managers. *Eur. Manage. J.* 8: 56–71

Bowen DE. 1986. Managing customers as human resources in service organizations. *Hum. Res. Manage.* 25: 371–83

Bowen DE, Ledford GE Jr, Nathan BR. 1991. Hiring for the organization, not the job. *Acad. Manage. Exec.* 5(4): 35–51

Bowen DE, Schneider B. 1988. Services marketing and management: implications for organizational behavior. *Res. Organ. Behav.* 10: 43–80

Brett JM, Goldberg SB, Ury WL. 1990. Designing systems for resolving disputes in organizations. *Am. Psychol.* 45: 162–70

Bretz R Jr, Milkovich G, Read W. 1992. The current state of performance appraisal research and practice: concerns, directions, and implications. *J. Manage.* 18: 111–37

Brewster, C, Hegewisch A, Lockhart T, Holden L, eds. 1993. *The European Human Resource Management Guide.* New York: Academic

Brewster C, Hegewisch A, eds. 1994. *Policy and Practice in European Human Resource Management.* London: Routledge

Brewster C, Tyson S, eds. 1991. *International Comparisons in Human Resource Management.* London: Pitman

Bridges WP, Villemez WJ. 1991. Employment relations and the labor market: integrating institutional and market perspectives. *Am. Sociol. Rev.* 56: 748–64

Buller PF, Napier NK. 1993. Strategy and human resource management integration in fast growth versus other mid-sized firms. *Br. J. Manage.* 4: 273–91

Carroll GR, Delacroix J, Goodstein J. 1988. The political environments of organizations: an ecological view. *Res. Organ. Behav.* 10: 359–92

Carroll SJ. 1988. Asian HRM philosophies and systems: Can they meet our changing HRM needs? In *Personnel and Human Resource Management*, ed. RS Schuler, SA Young-blood, VL Huber, pp. 442–55. St. Paul, MN: West

Carsten JM, Spector PE. 1987. Unemployment, job satisfaction, and employee turnover: a meta-analytic test of the Muchinsky Model. *J. Appl. Psychol.* 72: 374–81

Cascio WF. 1991. *Costing Human Resource: The Financial Impact of Behavior in Organizations.* Boston: PWS-Kent

Cascio WF. 1992. Reconciling economic and social objectives in personnel selection: impact of alternative decision rules. *New Approaches Empl. Manage.: Fairness Empl. Sel.* 1: 61–86

Child J. 1977. *Organization.* New York: Harper & Row

Clark J. 1993. Managing people in a time of technical change: conclusions and implications. In *Human Resource Management and Technical Change*, ed. J Clark, pp. 212–22. Newbury Park, CA: Sage

Collins D, Hatcher L, Ross TL. 1993. The decision to implement gainsharing: the role of work climate, expected outcomes, and union status. *Pers. Psychol.* 46: 77–104

Conlon E, Parks J. 1990. The effects of monitoring and tradition on compensation arrangements: an experiment on principal/agent dyads. *Acad. Manage. J.* 3: 603–22

Conner KR. 1991. A historical perspective of resource-based theory and five schools of thought within industrial organization economics: Do we need a new theory of the firm? *J. Manage.* 17: 121–54

Cook DS, Ferris GR. 1986. Strategic human resource management and firm effectiveness in industries experiencing decline. *Hum. Res. Manage.* 25: 441–58

Cowherd DM, Levine DI. 1992. Product quality and pay equity between lower-level employees and top management: an investigation of distributive justice theory. *Admin. Sci. Q.* 37: 302–20

Cox T Jr. 1993. *Cultural Diversity in Organizations: Theory, Research and Practice.* San Francisco: Berrett-Koehler

Cutcher-Gershenfeld J. 1991. The impact on economic performance of a transformation in workplace relations. *Ind. Labor Relat. Rev.* 44: 241–60

Datta DK, Guthrie JP. 1994. Executive succession: organizational antecedents of CEO characteristics. *Strat. Manage. J.* 15: 569–77

Davis-Blake A, Uzzi B. 1993. Determinants of employment externalization: a study of temporary workers and independent contractors. *Admin. Sci. Q.* 38: 195–223

Delaney JT, Lewin D, Ichniowski C. 1989. *Human Resource Policies and Practices in American Firms.* Washington, DC: US Dept. Labor, US Govt. Print. Off.

Denison D. 1990. *Corporate Culture and Organizational Effectiveness.* New York: Wiley

DiMaggio PJ, Powell WW. 1983. The iron cage revisited: institutional isomorphism and collective rationality in organizational fields. *Am. Sociol. Rev.* 35: 147–60

Dobbin FR, Edelman L, Meyer JW, Scott WR, Swidler A. 1988. The expansion of due process in organizations. In *Institutional Patterns and Organizations: Culture and Environment,* ed. LG Zucker, pp. 71–98. Cambridge, MA: Ballinger

Dobbins GH, Cardy RL, Carson KP. 1991. Examining fundamental assumptions: a contrast of person and system approaches to human resource management. *Res. Pers. Hum. Res. Manage.* 9: 1–38

Dowling PJ, Schuler RS, Welch DE. 1994. *International Dimensions of Human Resource Management.* Belmont, CA: Wadsworth

Eberwein W, Tholen J. 1993. Euro-manager or splendid isolation? *Int. Manage. – An Anglo–German Comparison* 9: 266

Eisenhardt KM. 1988. Agency and institutional explanations of compensation in retail sales. *Acad. Manage. J.* 31: 488–511

Eisenhardt KM. 1989. Agency theory: an assessment and review. *Acad. Manage. Rev.* 14: 57–74

Erez M. 1994. Towards a model of cross-cultural I/O psychology. See Triandis *et al.,* 1994a, pp. 559–608

Erez M, Earley PC. 1993. *Culture, Self-Identity, and Work.* New York: Oxford Univ. Press

Evans P. 1992. Management development as glue technology. *Hum. Res. Plan.* 15: 85–106

Ferris GR, Buckley MR, Allen GM. 1992. Promotion systems in organizations. *Hum. Res. Plan.* 15: 47–68

Ferris GR, Schellenberg DA, Zammuto RF. 1984. Human resource management strategies in declining industries. *Hum. Res. Manage.* 23: 381–94

Flamholtz EG, Lacey JM. 1981. *Personnel Management, Human Capital Theory, and Human Resource Accounting.* Los Angeles: Inst. Ind. Relat., Univ. Calif.

Florkowski GW, Nath R. 1993. MNC responses to the legal environment of international human resource management. *Int. J. Hum. Res. Manage.* 4: 305–24

Foulkes FK. 1980. *Personnel Policies in Large Nonunion Companies.* Englewood Cliffs, NJ: Prentice-Hall

Freeman RB, Medoff JL. 1984. *What Do Unions Do?* New York: Basic

Fulkerson JR, Schuler RS. 1992. Managing worldwide diversity at Pepsi-Cola International. In *Diversity in the Workplace: Human Resources Initiatives*, ed. SE Jackson, pp. 248–76. New York: Guilford

Gerhart B, Milkovich GT. 1990. Organizational differences in managerial compensation and financial performance. *Acad. Manage. J.* 33: 663–91

Gerhart B, Milkovich GT. 1992. Employee compensation: research and practice. In *Handbook of Industrial and Organizational Psychology*, ed. HC Triandis, MD Dunnette, LM Hough, 3: 481–569. Palo Alto, CA: Consult. Psychol.

Gerstein M, Reisman H. 1983. Strategic selection: matching executives to business conditions. *Sloan Manage. Rev.* 24: 33–49

Ghoshal S, Bartlett CA. 1990. The multinational corporation as an interorganizational network. *Acad. Manage. Rev.* 15: 603–25

Guthrie JP, Grimm CM, Smith KG. 1991. Environmental change and management staffing: an empirical study. *J. Manage.* 17: 735–48

Guthrie JP, Olian JD. 1991a. Drug and alcohol testing programs: Do firms consider their operating environment? *Hum. Res. Plan.* 14: 221–32

Guthrie JP, Olian JD. 1991b. Does context affect staffing decisions? The case of general managers. *Pers. Psychol.* 44: 283–96

Hambrick DC. 1994. Top management groups: a conceptual integration and reconsideration of the "team" label. *Res. Org. Behav.* 16: 171–214

Hamill J. 1983. The labor relations practices of foreign-owned and indigenous firms. *Empl. Relat.* 5: 14–16

Hansen GS, Wernerfelt B. 1989. Determinants of firm performance: relative importance of economic and organizational factors. *Strat. J. Manage.* 10: 399–411

Hanssens DM, Levien HA. 1983. An econometric study of recruitment marketing in the US Navy. *Manage. Sci.* 29: 1167–84

Heenan DA, Perlmutter HV. 1979. *Multinational Organization Development.* Reading, MA: Addison-Wesley

Hickson DJ. 1993. Management in Western Europe. *Soc. Cult. Org. Twelve Nations* 14: 290

Hoerr J. 1991. What should unions do? *Harvard Bus. Rev.* May–June: 30–45

Hofstede G. 1980. *Cultures Consequences.* Beverly Hills, CA: Sage

Hofstede G. 1991. *Cultures and Organizations.* London: McGraw-Hill

Hofstede G. 1993. Cultural constraints in management theories. *Acad. Manage. Exec.* 7: 81–94

Hulin CL, Roznowski M. 1985. Organizational technologies: effects on organizations' characteristics and individuals' responses. *Res. Organ. Behav.* 7: 39–85

Jackson SE. 1984. Organizational practices for preventing burnout. In *Handbook of Organizational Stress Coping Strategies*, ed. AS Sethi, RS Schuler, pp. 89–111. Cambridge, MA: Ballinger

Jackson SE. 1992. Consequences of group composition for the interpersonal dynamics of strategic issue processing. *Adv. Strat. Manage.* 8: 345–82

Jackson SE, Associates, eds. 1992. *Diversity in the Workplace: Human Resources Initiatives.* New York: Guilford

Jackson SE, Brett JF, Sessa VI, Cooper DM, Julin JA, Peyronnin K. 1991. Some differences make a difference: individual dissimilarity and group heterogeneity as correlates of recruitment, promotions and turnover. *J. Appl. Psychol.* 76: 675–89

Jackson SE, Dutton JE. 1988. Discerning threats and opportunities. *Admin. Sci. Q.* 33: 370–87

Jackson SE, May KE, Whitney K. 1994. Understanding the dynamics of diversity in decision making teams. In *Team Decision Making Effectiveness in Organizations*, ed. RA Guzzo, E Salas. San Francisco, CA: Jossey-Bass. pp. 204–61

Jackson SE, Schuler RS. 1992. HRM practices in service-based organizations: a role theory perspective. *Adv. Serv. Mark. Manage.* 1: 123–57

Jackson SE, Schuler RS, Rivero JC. 1989. Organizational characteristics as predictors of personnel practices. *Pers. Psychol.* 42: 727–86

Jackson SE, Stone VK, Alvarez EB. 1993. Socialization amidst diversity: the impact of demographics on work team oldtimers and newcomers. *Res. Organ. Behav.* 15: 45–109

James LR, Demaree RG, Mulaik SA, Ladd RT. 1992. Validity generalization in the context of situational models. *J. Appl. Psychol.* 77: 3–14

Jensen M, Meckling W. 1976. Theory of the firm: managerial behavior, agency costs, and ownership structure. *J. Financ. Econ.* 3: 305–60

Johns G. 1993. Constraints on the adoption of psychology-based personnel practices: lessons from organizational innovation. *Pers. Psychol.* 46: 569–91

Johnson NB, Sambharya RB, Bobko P. 1989. Deregulation, business strategy, and wages in the airline industry. *Ind. Relat.* 28: 419–30

Johnston WB, Packer AE. 1987. *Workforce 2000: Work and Workers for the 21st Century.* Washington, DC: US Dept. Labor

Jones GR, Wright PM. 1992. An economic approach to conceptualizing the utility of human resource management practices. *Res. Pers. Hum. Res. Manage.* 10: 271–99

Katz D, Kahn RL. 1978. *The Social Psychology of Organizations.* New York: Wiley

Katzell RA. 1994. Contemporary meta-trends in industrial and organizational psychology. See Triandis *et al.*, 1994a, pp. 1–89

Kaufman R. 1992. The effects of IMPRO-SHARE on productivity. *Ind. Labor Relat. Rev.* 45: 311–22

Kerr C. 1954. The Balkanization of labor markets. In *Labor Mobility and Economic Opportunity*, ed. EW Bakke, PM Hauser, GL Palmer, CA Myers, D Yoder, C Kerr, pp. 93–109. New York: Wiley

Kerr JL. 1985. Diversification strategies and managerial rewards: an empirical study. *Acad. Manage. J.* 28: 155–79

Klimoski RJ, Jones RG. 1995. Suppose we took staffing for effective group decision making seriously? In *Team Decision Making Effectiveness in Organizations*, ed. RA Guzzo, E Salas, pp. 64–92. San Francisco, CA: Pfeiffer

Kochan TA, Batt R, Dyer L. 1992. International human resource studies: a framework for future research in research frontiers. In *Industrial Relations and Human Resources*, ed. D Lewin, OS Mitchell, PD Sherer, pp. 147–67. Madison, WI: Ind. Relat. Res. Assoc.

Konrad AM, Linnehan F. 1992. The implementation and effectiveness of equal opportunity employment. In *Best Papers Proceedings*, ed. F Hoy. pp. 380–84. Anaheim, CA: Acad. Manage.

Kotter J, Sathe V. 1978. Problems of human resource management in rapidly growing companies. *Calif. Manage. Rev.* Winter: 29–36

Kozlowski SWJ, Chao GT, Smith EM, Hedlund J. 1993. Organizational downsizing: strategies, interventions, and research implications. *Int. Rev. Ind. Org. Psychol.* 8: 263–332

Kozlowski SWJ, Hults BM. 1987. An exploration of climates for technical updating and performance. *Pers. Psychol.* 40: 539–63

Kozlowski SWJ, Salas E. 1994. A multilevel organizational systems approach for the implementation and transfer of training. In *Improving Training Effectiveness in Work Organizations*, ed. JK Ford & Associates. Hillsdale, NJ: Erlbaum

Lakhani H. 1988. The effect of pay and retention bonuses on quit rates in the US Army. *Ind. Labor Relat. Rev.* 41: 430–38

Landy FJ, Shankster LJ, Kohler SS. 1994. Personnel selection and placement. *Annu. Rev. Psychol.* 45: 261–96

Latham GP. 1988. Human resource training and development. *Annu. Rev. Psychol.* 39: 545–82

Laurent A. 1986. The cross-cultural puzzle of international human resource management. *Hum. Res. Manage.* 25: 91–102

Lawler EE III, Mohrman SA. 1987. Unions and the new management. *Acad. Manage. Exec.* 1: 293–300

Lawler EE III, Mohrman SA, Ledford GE. 1992. *Employee Involvement and Total Quality Management: Practices and Results in Fortune 1000 Companies.* San Francisco, CA: Jossey-Bass

Lengnick-Hall CA, Lengnick-Hall ML. 1988. Strategic human resources management: a review of the literature and a proposed topology. *Acad. Manage. Rev.* 13: 454–70

Levine DI, Tyson LD. 1990. Participation, productivity, and the firm's environment. In *Paying for Productivity*, ed. A Blinder, pp. 183–235. Washington, DC: Brookings Inst.

Lévy-Leboyer C. 1994. Selection and assessment in Europe. See Triandis *et al.*, 1994a, pp. 173–90

Lewandowski JL, MacKinnon WP. 1992. What we learned at Saturn. *Pers. J.* 37: 31–2

Lincoln JR. 1993. Work organization in Japan and the United States. In *Country Competitiveness: Technology and the Organizing of Work*, ed. B Kogut, pp. 93–124. Oxford: Oxford Univ. Press

MacDuffie JP, Krafcik J. 1992. Integrating technology and human resources for high-performance manufacturing. In *Transforming Organizations*, ed. T Kochan, M Useem, pp. 210–26. New York: Oxford Univ. Press

Macy B, Izumi H. 1993. Organizational change, design, and work innovation: a meta-analysis of 131 North American field studies – 1961–1991. In *Research in Organizational Change and Development*, ed. R Woodman, W Pasmore, 7: 147–70. Greenwich, CT: JAI

Mahoney TA. 1987. Understanding comparable worth: a societal and political perspective. *Res. Organ. Behav.* 9: 209–45

Malm FT. 1955. Hiring procedures and selection standards in the San Francisco Bay area. *Ind. Labor Relat. Rev.* 8: 231–52

Marginson P. 1992. European integration and transnational management-union relations in the enterprise. *Br. J. Ind. Relat.* 30: 529–45

Markham SE. 1985. An investigation of the relationship between unemployment and absenteeism: a multi-level approach. *Acad. Manage. J.* 28: 228–34

Marshall R. 1992. The future role of government in industrial relations. *Ind. Relat.* 31: 31–49

Maruyama M. 1992. Changing dimensions in international business. *Acad. Manage. E.* 6: 88–96

Mellow W. 1982. Employer size and wages. *Rev. Econ. Stat.* 64: 495–501

Mendonca M, Kanungo RN. 1994. Managing human resources: the issue of cultural fit. *J. Manage. Inq.* 13: 751–56

Meyer JW, Rowan B. 1977. Institutionalized organizations: formal structure as myth and ceremony. *Am. J. Sociol.* 83: 340–63

Miles RE, Snow CC. 1978. *Organizational Strategy, Structure, and Process.* New York: McGraw-Hill

Miles RE, Snow CC. 1984. Designing strategic human resources systems. *Org. Dyn.* 16: 36–52

Milkovich GT, Gerhart B, Hannon J. 1991. The effects of research and development intensity on managerial compensation in large organizations. *J. High Technol. Manage. Res.* 2: 133–50

Miller CS, Schuster MH. 1987. Gainsharing plans: a comparative analysis. *Org. Dyn.* Summer: 44–67

Miller P, O'Leary T. 1989. Hierarchies and American ideals, 1900–1940. *Acad. Manage. Rev.* 14: 250–65

Milliman J, von Glinow MA, Nathan M. 1991. Organizational life cycles and strategic international human resource management in multinational companies: implications for congruence theory. *Acad. Manage. Rev.* 16: 318–39

Mills PK, Morris JH. 1986. Clients as "partial" employees of service organizations: role development in client participation. *Acad. Manage. Rev.* 11: 726–35

Molnar JJ, Rogers DL. 1976. Organizational effectiveness: an empirical comparison of the goal and system resource approaches. *Sociol. Q.* 17: 401–13

Morrison AM. 1992. *The New Leaders: Guidelines on Leadership Diversity in America.* San Francisco, CA: Jossey-Bass

Morrison AM, Crabtree KM. 1992. *Developing Diversity in Organizations: A Digest of Selected Literature.* Greensboro, NC: Cent. Creative Leadersh.

Morrison AM, Ruderman MN, Hughes-James M. 1993. *Making Diversity Happen.* Greensboro, NC: Cent. Creative Leadersh.

Murray VV, Dimick DE. 1978. Contextual influences on personnel policies and programs: an explanatory model. *Acad. Manage. Rev.* 12: 750–61

Newman JM, Huselid MA. 1992. The nature of behavioral controls in boundary occupations: agency theory at the edge. *Adv. Global High-Technol. Manage.* 2: 193–212

Noble BP. 1993. More than labor amity at AT&T. *New York Times* March 14: F25

Noe RA, Ford JK. 1992. Emerging issues and new directions for training research. *Res. Pers. Hum. Res. Manage.* 10: 345–84

Ofori-Dankwa J. 1994. Murray and Reshef revisited: towards a typology and theory of paradigms of national trade union movements. *Acad. Manage. Rev.* 18: 269–92

Ohlott PJ, Ruderman MN, McCauley CD. 1994. Gender differences in managers' developmental job experiences. *Acad. Manage. J.* 37: 46–67

Olian JD, Rynes SL. 1984. Organizational staffing: integrating practice with strategy. *Ind. Relat.* 23: 170–83

Osterman PO. 1984. *Internal Labor Markets.* Cambridge, MA: London

Osterman PO. 1992. Internal labor markets in a changing environment: models and evidence. In *Research Frontiers in Industrial Relations and Human Resources,* ed. D. Lewin, OS Mitchell, PD Sherer, pp. 273–308. Madison, WI: Ind. Relat. Res. Assoc.

Ostroff C, Schmitt N. 1993. Configurations of organizational effectiveness and efficiency. *Acad. Manage. J.* 36: 1345–61

Peck SR. 1994. Exploring the link between organizational strategy and the employment relationship: the role of human resources policies. *J. Manage. Stud.* 31: 715–36

Perrow C. 1967. A framework for the comparative analysis of organizations. *Am. Sociol. Rev.* 32: 194–208

Pfeffer J. 1983. Organizational demography. *Res. Organ. Behav.* 5: 299–357

Pfeffer J, Cohen Y. 1984. Determinants of internal labor markets in organizations. *Admin. Sci. Q.* 29: 550–72

Pfeffer J, Langton N. 1988. Wage inequality and the organization of work: the case of academic departments. *Admin. Sci. Q.* 33: 588–606

Phatak AV. 1992. *International Dimensions of Management.* Boston: PWS-Kent

Poole M. 1986a. Managerial strategies and styles in industrial relations: a comparative analysis. *J. Gen. Manage.* 12: 40–53

Poole M. 1986b. *Industrial Relations: Origins and Patterns of National Diversity.* London: Routledge

Porter ME. 1980. *Competitive Strategy: Techniques for Analyzing Industries and Competitors.* New York: Free Press

Porter ME. 1985. *Competitive Advantage: Creating and Sustaining Superior Performance.* New York: Free Press

Powell GN, Butterfield DA. 1994. Investigating the "Glass Ceiling" phenomenon: an empirical study of actual promotions to top management. *Acad. Manage. J.* 37: 68–86

Prahalad CK, Doz YL. 1987. *The Multinational Mission: Balancing Local Demands and Global Vision.* New York: Free Press

Randolph WA, Dess GG. 1984. The congruence perspective of organization design: a conceptual model and multivariate research approach. *Acad. Manage. Rev.* 9: 114–27

Reid J Jr. 1992. Future unions. *Ind. Relat.* 31: 122–36

Ronen S. 1994. An underlying structure of motivational need taxonomies: a cross-cultural confirmation. See Triandis *et al.*, 1994a, pp. 241–70

Rosen CM, Klein KJ, Young KM. 1986. *Employee Ownership in America.* Lexington, MA: Lexington

Russell CJ, Colella A, Bobko P. 1993. Expanding the context of utility: the strategic impact of personnel selection. *Pers. Psychol.* 46: 781–801

Rynes SL. 1991. Recruitment, job choice, and post-hire consequences: a call for new research directions. In *Handbook of Industrial and Organizational Psychology,* ed. MD Dunnette, LM Hough, 2: 399–444. Palo Alto, CA: Consult. Psychol.

Rynes SL, Barber AE. 1990. Applicant attraction strategies: an organizational perspective. *Acad. Manage. Rev.* 15: 286–310

Rynes SL, Boudreau JW. 1986. College recruiting in large organizations: practice, evaluation, and research implications. *Pers. Psychol.* 39: 729–57

Saari LM, Johnson TR, McLaughlin SD, Zimmerle DM. 1988. A survey of management training and education practices in US companies. *Pers. Psychol.* 41: 731–43

Schneider B. 1987. The people make the place. *Pers. Psychol.* 40: 437–53

Schneider B, Wheeler JK, Cox JF. 1992. A passion for service: using content analysis to explicate service climate themes. *J. Appl. Psychol.* 77: 705–16

Schuler RS. 1992. Strategic human resource management: linking people with the needs of the business. *Organ. Dyn.* 21: 19–32

Schuler RS, Dowling PJ, DeCieri H. 1992. The formation of an international joint venture: Marley Automotive Components. *Eur. Manage. J.* 10: 304–9

Schuler RS, Jackson SE. 1987a. Linking competitive strategy and human resource management practices. *Acad. Manage. Exec.* 3: 207–19

Schuler RS, Jackson SE. 1987b. Organizational strategy and organization level as determinants of human resource management practices. *Hum. Res. Plan.* 10(3): 125–41

Schuler RS, Jackson SE, Dowling PJ, DeCieri H. 1991. Formation of an international joint venture: Davidson Instrument Panel. *Hum. Res. Plan.* 14: 51–9

Schuler RS, MacMillan IC. 1984. Gaining competitive advantage through HR management practices. *Hum. Res. Manage.* 23: 241–55

Schuler RS, van Sluijs E. 1992. Davidson-Marley BV: establishing and operating an international joint venture. *Eur. Manage. J.* 10: 428–37

Schwartz SH. 1992. Universals in the content and structure of values: theoretical advances and empirical tests in 20 countries. *Adv. Exp. Soc. Psychol.* 25: 1–66

Scott WR. 1987. The adolescence of institutional theory. *Admin. Sci. Q.* 32: 493–511

Sharf J. 1994. Legal and EEO issues impacting on personal history inquiries. In *Biodata Handbook: Theory, Research, & Application*, ed. GS Stokes, MD Mumford, WA Owens, pp. 351–90. Palo Alto, CA: *Consult. Psychol.*

Slocum JW, Lei D. 1993. Designing global strategic alliances: integrating cultural and economic factors. In *Organizational Change and Redesign: Ideas and Insights for Improving Performance*, ed. GP Huber, WH Glick, pp. 295–322. New York: Oxford Univ. Press

Slocum JW Jr, Cron WL, Hansen RW, Rawlings S. 1985. Business strategy and the management of plateaued employees. *Acad. Manage. J.* 28: 133–54

Smith KG, Mitchell TR, Summer CE. 1985. Top level management priorities in different stages of the organizational life cycle. *Acad. Manage. J.* 28: 799–820

Snell SA, Dean JW Jr. 1992. Integrated manufacturing and human resource management: a human capital perspective. *Acad. Manage. J.* 35: 467–504

Snow CC, Snell SA. 1993. Staffing as strategy. In *Personnel Selection in Organizations*, ed. N Schmitt, WC Borman, & Associates, pp. 448–78. San Francisco, CA: Jossey-Bass

Sonnenstuhl WJ, Trice HM. 1991. Linking organizational and occupational theory through the concept of culture. *Res. Sociol. Organ.* 9: 295–318

Strauss G. 1982. Workers participation in management: an international perspective. *Res. Organ. Behav.* 4: 173–265

Szilagyi AD Jr, Schweiger DM. 1984. Matching managers to strategies: a review and suggested framework. *Acad. Manage. Rev.* 9: 626–37

Terpstra DE, Rozell EJ. 1993. The relationship of staffing practices to organizational level measures of performance. *Pers. Psychol.* 46: 27–48

Thomas DA. 1993. Racial dynamics in cross-race developmental relationships. *Admin. Sci. Q.* 38: 169–94

Thompson JD. 1967. *Organizations in Action*. New York: McGraw-Hill

Thurow L. 1975. *Generating Inequality*. New York: Basic

Tolbert PS, Zucker LG. 1983. Institutional sources of change in the formal structure of organizations: the diffusion of Civil Service Reform, 1880–1935. *Admin. Sci. Q.* 28: 22–39

Tosi HL Jr, Gomez-Mejia LR. 1989. The decoupling of CEO pay and performance: an agency theory perspective. *Admin. Sci. Q.* 34: 169–89

Towers Perrin. 1992. *Priorities for Competitive Advantage*. New York: Towers Perrin

Triandis HC, Dunnette MD, Hough LM, eds. 1994a. *Handbook of Industrial and Organizational Psychology*, Vol. 4. Palo Alto, CA: Consult. Psychol. 2nd ed.

Triandis HC, Kurowski LL, Gelfand MJ. 1994b. Workplace diversity. See Triandis *et al.*, 1994a, pp. 769–827

Tsang MC, Rumberger RW, Levin HM. 1991. The impact of surplus schooling on worker productivity. *Ind. Relat.* 30: 209–28

Tung RL. 1993. Managing cross-national and intra-national diversity. *Hum. Res. Manage.* 32: 461–77

United States Department of Labor. 1993. *High Performance Work Practices and Firm Performance*. Washington, DC: US Dept. Labor

Van Maanen J, Barley SR. 1984. Occupational communities: culture and control in organizations. *Res. Organ. Behav.* 6: 287–365

van Sluijs E, van Assen A, den Hertog JF. 1991. Personnel management and organizational change: a sociotechnical perspective. *Eur. Work Org. Psychol.* 1: 27–51

Western B. 1993. Postwar unionization in eighteen advanced capitalist countries. *Am. Sociol. Rev.* 58: 266–82

Whyte WF, ed. 1991. *Social Theory for Action: How Individuals and Organizations Learn to Change*. Newbury Park, CA: Sage

Wickens P. 1987. *The Road to Nissan*. London: Macmillan

Wigdor AK, Sackett PR. 1993. Employment testing and public policy: the case of the general aptitude test battery. In *Personnel Selection and Assessment: Individual and Organizational Perspectives*, ed. H Schuler, JL Farr, M Smith, pp. 183–204. Hillsdale, NJ: Erlbaum

Williamson OE. 1979. Transaction-cost economics: the governance of contractual relations. *J. Law Econ.* 22(2): 233–61

Williamson OE. 1981. The modern corporation: origins, evolution, attributes. *J. Econ. Lit.* 19: 1537–68

Williamson OE. 1991. Comparative economic organization: the analysis of discrete structural alternatives. *Admin. Sci. Q.* 36: 269–96

Woodruff D. 1993. Saturn: labor's love lost? *Bus. Week* Feb. 8: 122–3

Woodward J. 1965. *Industrial Organization: Theory and Practice*. London: Oxford Univ. Press

Wright PM, McMahan GC. 1992. Theoretical perspectives for strategic human resource management. *J. Manage.* 18: 295–320

Wright PM, McMahan GC, McWilliams A. 1994. Human resources and sustained competitive advantage: a resource-based perspective. *Int. J. Hum. Res. Manage.* 5(2): 299–324

Youngblood SA, Tevino LK, Favia M. 1992. Reactions to unjust dismissal and third-party dispute resolution: a justice framework. *Empl. Responsib. Rights J.* 5(4): 283–307

Yu J, Murphy KR. 1993. Modesty bias in self-ratings of performance: a test of the cultural relativity hypothesis. *Pers. Psychol.* 46: 357–66

Zammuto RF, O'Connor EJ. 1992. Gaining advanced manufacturing technologies' benefits: the roles of organization design and culture. *Acad. Manage. Rev.* 17: 701–28

Zedeck S. 1992. *Work, Families, and Organizations*. San Francisco, CA: Jossey-Bass

Zucker LG. 1977. The role of institutionalization in cultural persistence. *Am. Sociol. Rev.* 42: 726–43

Zucker LG. 1987. Institutional theories of organization. *Annu. Rev. Sociol.* 13: 443–64

Chapter 3

Implications of the Converging Economy for Human Resource Management

Suzanne Zivnuska, David J. Ketchen, Jr., and Charles C. Snow

Introduction

In today's business world, there is continued fascination with New Economy firms and their methods of e-commerce, defined as the process by which business transactions are conducted via electronic networks (Boudreau, Loch, Robey & Straud, 1998). Organizations are building or extending various types of electronic networks that link them to customers, employees, suppliers, and partners. The versatility and speed of e-business are producing profound changes in the way both old and new firms compete, organize, and manage (Boudreau *et al.*, 1998; Christensen & Tedlow, 2000; Evans & Wurster, 1999; Sinha, 2000).

E-business, the most visible manifestation of the New Economy, is widely viewed as a revolutionary shift in business as we know it (Christensen & Tedlow, 2000; Evans & Wurster, 1999; Sinha, 2000), presenting managers and employees with sudden competitive threats as well as huge opportunities for growth in both new and existing markets (Boudreau *et al.*, 1998). The emergence and rapid growth of e-commerce are forcing practitioners and academics alike to rethink many traditional rules for running a business. For example, in the 1990s, equity markets handsomely rewarded firms such

S. Zivnuska, D. J. Ketchen, Jr., and C. C. Snow, "Implications of the Converging Economy for Human Resource Management," *Research in Personnel and Human Resource Management*, Vol. 20 (2001): 371–405.

as Amazon.com and Yahoo! that emphasized building large customer bases, brand identity, and market share to the detriment of profit. Although these organizations and other "dot.coms" have struggled recently, it is clear that the market is not ready to dismiss their business models. The implications of emerging business models are numerous and extensive, and managers and scholars alike are struggling to find the organizational responses appropriate for an uncertain future.

To date, much of the discussion about e-commerce has revolved around technical, economic, and marketing issues (Christensen & Tedlow, 2000; Christie & Levary, 1998; Evans & Wurster, 1999). One activity that is changing considerably in the evolving e-business environment, and yet has not been given much attention, is human resource management (HRM). The HRM function in both traditional as well as e-commerce firms is undergoing considerable change. In many firms, traditional HRM tasks such as recruiting, selecting, and training employees are being performed quite differently than in the past (Cascio, 1995). Internal organizational changes such as increased partnering, accelerating rates of innovation and learning, and new organizational structures are affecting the role that human resource specialists play in developing and fulfilling strategic objectives. Additionally, external market pressures, including labor market changes and increased emphasis on flexibility and responsiveness, are impacting the way that the HR role is performed (Snell & Wright, 1998).

The purpose of this paper is to focus on the effects of convergence between the "old" and "new" economies on human resource management. We begin with a discussion of the major driving forces of the Converging Economy. Second, we trace the influence of those forces on the HRM function and highlight some of the innovative practices companies have enacted in response. Finally, we discuss the concepts, methodologies, and theoretical perspectives that are needed in order to conduct future HRM research.

Drivers of the Converging Economy

The 21st century corporation is experiencing considerable turmoil as the Industrial Economy mixes with the New Economy to produce the Converging Economy. However, this turmoil is different from that of the 1980s and 1990s when many companies felt the pain of downsizing, de-layering, and disaggregating as they responded to the tightened economic environment. Since the mid-1990s, the typical large, established company has been in a growth mode, pursuing opportunities brought on by the technologies, mind-sets, and approaches associated with New Economy firms. If both traditional and newer companies are able to successfully navigate the Converging Economy, their future appears to be very promising.

Broadly speaking, three major forces are reshaping the global business terrain. The first is *information technology*. The Internet is perhaps the most influential of the new technologies, and it has spawned entirely new businesses as well as expanded the offerings of existing businesses (Ghosh, 1998). Also critical are the increasing array of ever more powerful computer software systems that help companies operate efficiently and effectively (Schmitz, 2000; Westland & Clark, 1999). The information environment in which companies operate is becoming increasingly rich, resulting in smarter, more effective partners and customers (Benjamin & Wigand, 1995). Managers in this type of environment may have to overcome fears about moving fast and cannibalizing, perhaps even eradicating, their current businesses. However, in all cases, managers will be held to high performance standards as evidenced by heavy use of "best practices" programs, and these standards can be achieved more easily by growing the business than by downsizing.

The second force is *globalization*. There is increasing convergence among economic and political systems around the world. In most countries, changes and reforms have led to more open markets for goods, capital, labor, technology, and ideas. Often, economic reform has led to political reform, as governments redefine their role to be more proactive, competent, and supportive of business firms. With the continued growth of multinational corporations, widespread use of benchmarking programs, and cross-border alliances in which knowledge is collaboratively created and shared, the ways in which resources are managed are beginning to look increasingly similar. Although human resources are less susceptible to a universal management style than capital, machinery, and software-based processes, they too can be accommodated by the sophisticated managerial approaches used by the leading multinational companies (Ohmae, 1999).

The third feature of the Converging Economy is the increasing importance of *intangible assets*, especially human assets. Compared to physical assets such as land, equipment, and money, intangible assets are now viewed by many companies as the primary source of value, growth, and sustained competitive advantage (Itami, 1987; Pfeffer, 1994). Intangible assets come in many forms, including the knowledge base that gives a company its capabilities; the relational capital amassed by forging links with customers, partners, and suppliers; and the brand equity that can be used to keep existing customers and attract new customers in a changing business environment. Progressive companies today are hard at work developing approaches to "knowledge management" – ways of leveraging organization members' knowledge and skills widely and quickly.

Together, these forces are having a profound impact on how companies obtain, manage, and develop their human resources. In the next few sections, we examine some of the specific ways that these forces are affecting the human resource function, as well as the innovative practices that have been devised in response.

Information Technology and Human Resource Management Practices

Changes in information technology are presenting HR professionals with important challenges (see Fig. 3.1). Information technology can be used to disseminate information, facilitate alternative work arrangements, and decentralize physical organizational structures. These potential advantages, however, also present organizations with difficult HR challenges. As organizations increasingly exist within a virtual context, the ability to be creative and build effective teams without the benefit of physical proximity

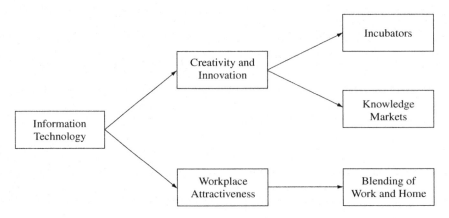

Figure 3.1   The influence of information technology on HRM.

may be taxed (Snell, Lepak & Youndt, 1999). For instance, the ability to generate creative sparks based on the synergy that occurs in group settings may be compromised by structures characterized by relatively isolated individuals working without face-to-face contact on a regular basis. Additionally, as more organizational information is made public, employees may be more aware of the HR packages offered by other employers. This knowledge may increase demand for competitive benefits and extra perks. In fact, employees may even be willing to switch employers multiple times to take advantage of attractive packages. To the extent that information technology influences employee willingness to be mobile, turnover costs may increase. To stem these costs, employers will need to make the workplace as attractive as possible to increase retention. These challenges are being met in a variety of ways.

Creativity and innovation

As the pace of technological innovation continues to increase, most organizations will have to bolster their capacity to be creative and innovative if they are to be successful in staying ahead of the change curve and harnessing a sustained competitive advantage. For instance, the Internet not only demands that existing organizations use new modalities of doing business, it also creates a climate wherein new companies are being built using the Internet as their business platform (Ghosh, 1998). Immense pressure exists for organizations to take advantage of new technology and paradigms for business as, or even before, they fully emerge in the marketplace. One HR response to this pressure to be creative and innovative is a broader focus on value creation (Boulton, Libert & Samek, 2000).

In the Converging Economy, organizations are increasingly relying on nontraditional value sources that may not be included on a firm's balance sheet such as customer loyalty, corporate reputation, and even ideas. For instance, in spring 2001, Microsoft's book value was $48.3 billion, but its market value exceeded $375 billion. This discrepancy in book and market value reflected the corporation's ability to create value in innovative ways and market it effectively to the public. Two HR responses designed to create value are the development of incubators, which create value out of the synergistic effects of amassing start-up energy with established HR policies and practices, and the creation of knowledge markets, which create value by encouraging and investing in creative processes and innovative thinking.

Incubators

idealab! is one company that is heavily leveraging its human assets to create value in the Converging Economy (Boulton *et al.*, 2000). idealab! was created as an incubator for Internet start-ups. As such, its purpose is to create, launch and operate Internet businesses by providing the structural and human resource support for promising newcomers to Internet businesses who do not have the financial reserves to make significant capital investments. Allowing several different new businesses to occupy the same physical space not only provides new businesses with structural and human resources support that they might otherwise lack, but also provides a single environment that allows increased communication, interaction, and teamwork among independent founders who would otherwise work in relative isolation. The combination of an innovative corporate culture supported by effective HR policies results in a dynamic organization where cross-fertilization of ideas and group problem-solving are encouraged, and individual learning can be gathered in a communal knowledge bank. Such benefits, taken in combination, are thought to increase each startup's capacity for creativity and innovation, as well as benefiting idealab!, a privately held company. By providing its organization members with physical and human resource support in a unique context, idealab! has responded to and created value out of the need that new Internet companies have to create strong teams and encourage creativity.

Knowledge markets

Knowledge "markets" are also developing to drive innovation forward in individual companies. Knowledge markets generally involve small entrepreneurial teams that operate within the structure of a larger organization, yet with a degree of independence that fosters a start-up mentality in the group (Stepanek & Weber, 1999). The approach is a logical extension of Wal-Mart's "store within a store" concept wherein employees operate store departments semiautonomously while sharing profits with the store (Walton, 1992). With the help of their HR departments, several companies are responding to the need for innovation through this strategy.

Nortel Networks Inc. is one such company. Nortel is a global communications company dedicated to building and strengthening the Internet. Despite its size, Nortel still must strive to maximize its creativity and ability to innovate. To achieve this goal, Nortel has implemented a program that encourages employees to be creative and actively take ownership in the company's direction. The HR department has facilitated the implementation of a program that allows employees to submit formal business proposals for new ideas. To reward these employees, Nortel then "buys" stock in them, encouraging employees to act independently on actualizing their plans. In this way, Nortel has created a system akin to an internal IPO for employees (Stepanek & Weber, 1999).

Similarly, Proctor & Gamble Co. operates an autonomous idea lab called "Corporate New Ventures" (Stepanek & Weber, 1999). This group encourages new product ideas and then funds the best ones to be put into quick production. Teams involved in these new ventures act independently, allowing them to be more responsive and flexible than would be expected from a company the size of Proctor & Gamble. These examples depart from the traditional "suggestion box" approach. In both Proctor & Gamble and Nortel Networks, the HR department has been instrumental in creating independent teams that manage their own resources, hire team members, create their own reward systems, and sometimes report directly to top management rather than working within the traditional hierarchy.

Workplace attractiveness

A second HR challenge that is driven by technology is the need to make the workplace more attractive to employees. As technological innovation has increased, the economy has become more mobile. The virtual workplace may decrease the intensity of personal ties and loyalty that employees feel towards their co-workers and employers, thereby increasing employee willingness to be mobile. The costs of resultant turnover and employee training are well known. In an effort to minimize these costs in an economy that encourages job mobility among workers, organizations must of necessity implement technology that allows their employees to more effectively blend their work and home life through nontraditional work designs. Interestingly, then, the very response to the challenge of a mobile work force can be found in its cause – using technology to benefit employees. When effective, the hope is that by using technology to improve work–life balance, employees will experience higher quality of life outcomes, feel more control over their ability to meet their work demands, and be less likely to pursue other employment opportunities.

Blending of work and home

Employees are increasingly demanding cutting-edge technology that makes their work easier, faster, and more portable. Additionally, people are demanding more personal time, and finding new uses for technology in their personal lives. If the technology that they want cannot be found in one organization, they may look to others. Therefore, in an attempt to simultaneously balance the needs of the corporation as well as the employees, some companies are providing their employees with personal and home access to technology that historically has been reserved for the office (Handy & Mokhtarian, 1996).

One clear example is the technology that enables employees to work from home, or telecommute. Employers are finding that telecommuting not only decreases overhead costs but is viewed as an important benefit that improves both recruitment and retention efforts, enabling organizations to attract the best possible employees (Handy & Mokhtarian, 1996). Additionally, despite common organizational fears of a loss of productivity, strong telecommuting policies can actually increase productivity as well as employee trust, employee morale, and organizational flexibility (Handy & Mokhtarian, 1996; Igbaria & Guimaraes, 1999).

This technology also benefits employees who are looking for more flexible ways of working in an attempt to balance complex, competing demands of work and home life. Socio-demographic trends such as dual-income couples raising children and taking care of aging parents, increased feelings of time pressure, and spiraling stress-related healthcare costs all contribute to individual decisions to telecommute (Handy & Mokhtarian, 1996). Employees may feel that telecommuting is one way of exercising greater control over the management of these competing demands. For instance, telecommuting allows greater flexibility in scheduling day care, allows employees to work from home when children are sick, and increases the time that employees can spend with their families by decreasing commute times (Handy & Mokhtarian, 1996). Viewed as a control-granting device, telecommuting may then result in lowered levels of experienced stress (Ganster & Schaubroeck, 1991; Schaubroeck & Merritt, 1997).

Employees who are not responsible for children or parents also may enjoy the extra time and freedom from commuting that telecommuting offers. As evidenced by the popularization of the term "road rage," commuting is widely acknowledged to add to stress, which costs American organizations $200–$300 billion annually (DeFrank & Ivancevich, 1998). In essence, innovative HR departments are implementing new ways of helping employees to more effectively blend their work and home lives. Beyond telecommuting benefits, some firms are offering employees access to the firm's resources to help with personal needs such as tax, home-buying, and legal advice.

One example of increased technology access and use can be found at Intel. The semiconductor manufacturer provides every employee with a new PC, ink-jet printer, Internet access, and technical support for their home use. Apple Computer gives their employees a new computer as part of their signing bonus. Even old-economy firms such as Ford Motor Company and Delta Airlines have similar programs.

In summary, the influence of information technology on HRM is large and increasing. As companies strive to obtain more creative thinking from their employees, they realize that they must provide access to the resources that support creativity and innovation. The progressive HR department can help by identifying linkages between technology and innovation, and then specifying where investments need to be made to retain key people and keep them productive.

Globalization and Human Resource Management Practices

Globalization is the second major force driving HR practices in the Converging Economy. As companies compete in the global workplace, the diversity of their clients and employees will increase. It may behoove progressive organizations to match the environmental diversity they face with similar levels of internal diversity. Additionally, globalization pressures may lead a firm to recognize that limiting its market by national boundaries may be outdated; rather, companies focusing on growth may experience the need to establish a physical presence overseas more than ever before (see Fig. 3.2).

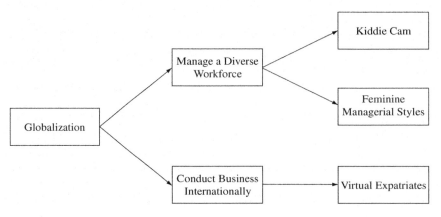

Figure 3.2   The influence of globalization on HRM.

Managing a diverse workforce

Workforce diversity, already a key concern in many organizations, is becoming even more salient as organizations expand into global markets and target increasingly diverse consumer groups. This environmental diversity requires that firms establish similar diversity within their organization, to better understand and respond to the demands of these new target markets. As the internal diversity in firms increases, employers will be met with a broad array of employee needs that may not have surfaced when the labor market was more homogeneous. Some HR departments are well equipped to help their organizations meet the challenges associated with diverse employees. Two HR practices that have been devised to cope with these challenges include the use of a "Kiddie Cam" to meet the specific needs of employees with small children, and attention to feminine managerial styles, aimed at the inclusion of many different groups and at a more holistic view of management.

Kiddie Cam

As the labor market continues to expand to include increasingly diverse groups, these groups must be appropriately supported. The increased presence of women with small children in the workforce is one such group. Additionally, societal changes have also resulted in fathers assuming more responsibility for child-rearing activities than may have been the case traditionally. Accordingly, some HR departments are helping their corporations implement policies that encourage employees to comfortably balance work and family demands. Cisco, a major Internet networking company, has created a $16 million childcare center equipped with Web-cams so parents can periodically check in on their children without leaving their desks. Ford Motor Company has adopted a similar approach. As noted in its 2000 Annual Report, "Recognizing that time and access to essential services are the two areas of greatest concern for working families, Ford is opening 30 Family Service and Learning Centers around the United States. Providing important services such as child care and educational resources in a single place locally, the Learning Centers will help simplify life for Ford people – and leave them free during the workday to concentrate on their jobs."

Feminine managerial styles

Another innovative HRM response to workforce diversity is the use of feminine managerial styles (or "WoManagement"). This management style not only accommodates more women in the workplace but is also thought to be more responsive to a variety of different workers. A key aspect of WoManagement is the acknowledgment that employees are whole people with lives outside of work and emotional responses that cannot be entirely separated from the work setting. This acknowledgment encourages the HR practice of offering employees unique, challenging, and interesting assignments congruent with personal interests and goals, rather than relying on financial incentives and perks to motivate production (Smith, 2000).

This approach extends far beyond the Management By Objectives type of goal setting popularized in the 1960s. Innovative companies like Apple Computer encourage managers to not only assign work based on employee interest but to actually shuffle and trade employees between departments based on employee needs and appropriate fit. Rather than employees being seen as a manager's individual property to hire, fire, or promote for the good of a single department, they are instead viewed in the context of the entire organization. A manager does not decrease his or her own power by moving an employee to an entirely different department but in fact is recognized for maximizing the employee's ability to contribute to the organization as a whole (Sharpe, 2000).

Additionally, feminine managerial styles encourage organizations to focus on the emotional side of corporate culture. Positive coworker relationships are being viewed as an essential component to organizational life that can stem the tide of high turnover rates (Smith, 2000). Therefore, today's most effective HR practices include a commitment to actively cultivate more "human moments" that exist outside of mediated communication channels and help employees to forge interpersonal bonds based on mutual trust and shared experiences (Hallowell, 1999). Specific HR initiatives that support these human moments may include internal activities like communal lunches that provide opportunities for employees at all levels to talk informally across hierarchical boundaries as well as intra-industry initiatives that transcend traditional competitive relationships. For instance, within the retail furniture industry, some managers are encouraged to attend periodic national or regional meetings that provide the opportunity for collaboration and shared learning that traditional models of competition would not support (Hallowell, 1999). Rubric, a provider of localization services to IT companies, is run with a philosophy to "overcommunicate" rather than to hoard information as a source of power (Sharpe, 2000).

A second example of the increased awareness of the importance of emotions at work can be found among private consulting groups like Traeger & Goleman, the Hay Group, and Gould, McCoy and Chadick Inc. These firms emphasize the importance of emotional expression, creative leadership, and consensus building (Gogoi, 2000), skills traditionally conceptualized as belonging within a more feminine domain and viewed skeptically within much of the business world. In reaction to this preconception of gender-based skills, many consultants offer men-only training and mentoring programs to help bring these new managerial skills to managers immersed in more traditional paradigms (Gogoi, 2000).

Conducting business internationally

Meeting the needs of diverse employees is not the only challenge that globalization presents to today's organizations. Increased globalization also motivates companies that once might have been focused on national markets to expand their products into international markets in an effort to achieve high growth rates. For many of these companies, creating an international market presence may require opening (and therefore staffing) international offices. To this end, companies rely on their HR departments to help open and staff international offices at unprecedented rates.

Virtual expatriates
International expansion challenges HR professionals to find employees who are willing and able to successfully relocate. Unfortunately, not only are US managers rather unique in their inability to successfully make international transitions (Black & Gregersen, 1999), but traditional relocations to remote offices often require long-term commitments (four or five years). Employees, who may perceive alternative employment opportunities within their local communities, are becoming less open to major relocations, and organizations may be less willing to invest the resources in long-term commitments given an estimated 80–90% expatriate failure rate (Black & Gregersen, 1999).

In response, some companies are trying to accommodate employees by offering alternative HR programs for international assignments. IBM Global Services offers their employees expatriate programs that allow managers to work two or three weeks in a remote location, alternated with one week at home. Other international options at IBM include allowing managers to supervise long-distance teams via computer- and phone-based communication, extreme commutes (e.g. Monday through Friday in Paris, weekends at home in New York), and year-long assignments rather than the traditional multi-year assignment (Armour, 2000).

In summary, globalization of the marketplace is changing the face of the labor market. These changes require that HRM policies and practices are flexible and support the needs of a broad array of people, all of whom have unique needs. Cutting-edge HR departments are able to recognize these labor market changes and react proactively to optimize their firms' ability to attract and retain high-quality employees while simultaneously reflecting environmental diversity internally.

Intangible Assets and Human Resource Management Practices

A strong interest in intangible assets is the third Converging Economy driver confronting the HR function. As organizations come to value "soft" resources like people and knowledge as assets, they will find themselves competing for the very best employees in the market. Increasingly, then, these firms will have to rely on HRM practices to strategically attract and manage their employees. The opportunity to act as a strategic partner also presents HR professionals with a major challenge. In today's environment,

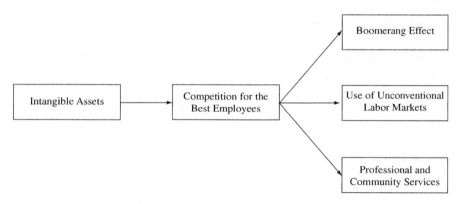

Figure 3.3   The influence of intangible assets on HRM.

HR managers must help their organizations design and manage the entire process of identifying, obtaining, developing, and retaining the best employees in an effort to increase the firm's competitive advantage (see Fig. 3.3).

Competition for the best employees

Companies are beginning to act upon their beliefs about the competitive value of intangible assets. Many firms are coming to believe that not only are physical assets like cash and property important components of success, but people and the knowledge that they possess are also critical. As many firms come to recognize employees as a key intangible asset, levels of competition for good people are rising. Therefore, HR professionals are challenged to devise new ways of attracting and retaining the very best. Below we discuss three creative techniques, including taking advantage of the boomerang effect to re-attract previous employees, capitalizing on unconventional labor markets in an effort to discover historically overlooked labor sources, and the implementation of professional services and community involvement policies to retain current employees.

Boomerang effect
Historically scorned as "traitors," ex-employees are viewed by some organizations as a potential source of human capital that can bring rich knowledge and experience back to the organization. These re-hired ex-employees are commonly referred to as "boomerangs" and are being pursued by a variety of organizations. Several large companies, including Microsoft, IBM, and Wells Fargo, have made formal decisions to hire boomerangs as part of their recruitment strategies (Yang, 2000). Some companies, such as Lockheed Martin (a systems integrator for government and commercial clients) and Sawtek (a high-tech producer for military and commercial customers), take this strategy a step further. These companies actively track their ex-employees with the intent of re-recruiting them after they have gained outside information and experience (Smith, 2000). To woo boomerangs, Sawtek invites former employees to an annual stock plan party. As a result, 5% of Sawtek's current employees have left the firm and later returned (Clarke, 2000).

Unconventional labor markets
Many organizations are developing creative responses to finding and recruiting from previously untapped labor markets. At the Bellagio Casino and Hotel in Las Vegas, employees with dubious pasts may be hired under a program that begins with work at a local fast-food restaurant. After eight months of successful employment, these fast-food employees are promoted to a more prestigious position at Bellagio at almost double their salary (Shapiro, 2000). Bellagio has found that a largely untapped labor market, ex-convicts, composes a particularly motivated and committed work force (Shapiro, 2000).

A second example is provided by the approach that Cisco Systems takes to layoffs (Olek & Prasso, 2001). When Cisco laid off 6,000 employees in April 2001, they implemented a new policy of allowing these employees to work for local nonprofit organizations for one year while still collecting 33% of their Cisco salary with benefits and continued stock options. The employees who take advantage of this program are also given first priority when the organization is prepared to re-hire. This program allows Cisco to retain strong ties to their ex-employees, may help to defray training costs when the firm is ready to re-expand its labor force, and also promotes a positive reputation as a socially responsible organization. These benefits may very well increase the company's competitive advantage in the long run, at least partially defraying the costs that many companies face in the wake of major layoffs.

Because using unconventional labor markets is a promising approach, new companies are emerging specifically to help with this task. Hire.com is one such organization. Hire.com offers employers a service that automates the recruiting process by providing them with pre-sorted, qualified resumes based on employer needs. Job seekers anonymously post profiles with potential employers, partially alleviating the pressure on HR professionals to recruit for specific positions (www.hire.com; Yang, 2000).

Organizations have also begun to modify time-tested recruiting tactics to better exploit labor pools. For example, beyond providing traditional signing bonuses, Honeywell offers extensive career development programs, paid degree programs, and formal mentoring to help employees advance. In areas where housing is difficult and expensive, like Silicon Valley near San Francisco, employees may be offered subsidized housing close to the office (Smith, 2000). Stalcorp has put a new twist on the practice of paying employees bonuses for their own recruitment efforts on behalf of the firm. Recognizing that retention, not merely recruitment, is critical, Stalcorp gives two bonuses to employees who successfully recruit for them: one based on the new employee's performance at a 90-day review, and then another after six months (Smith, 2000).

Providing professional services and community service
Finally, because employees are potentially the firm's most valuable asset, it is important to maximize employee productivity by eliciting the highest possible effort out of each individual. The primary means of doing so, of course, is the development and use of knowledge-management processes that are designed to create an entrepreneurial culture and to tap into what employees know and can do. Typically, such processes rely heavily on collaboration both within and outside the firm (Miles, Snow & Miles, 2000). In addition, firms can surround their knowledge-management processes with HR practices that enhance autonomy and flexibility as well as lower stress. For example,

firms can offer employees the opportunity to take care of personal business while at work. Organizations are also becoming quite creative in the services that they make available to employees. More than just offering a bank machine and a cafeteria, some organizations now provide employees with health spas and in-house massage programs. Oracle, an information management software company, lets workers accomplish "errands" while at work, providing access to services such as car detailing and film developing for their employees (Dillon, 2000).

Some companies go even further, satisfying not only employee needs for external services but allowing them to satisfy their desires for community involvement and service. Both LensCrafters and Ohio-based Corporate Research Consulting Group support charitable causes by allowing employees to volunteer their time during traditional work hours (Smith, 2000). The Gap and Levi Strauss, major clothing retailers, both have full corporate giving departments and separate foundations to support local activism and community events (www.gapinc.com; www.levistrauss.com).

In summary, as the competitive advantage afforded by the ability to attract and retain the highest quality employees becomes ever more apparent, enterprising HR managers are aligning their own strategic practices with those of the organization as a whole. In many cases, this process requires creative new methods for attracting and selecting applicants as well as for retaining those employees already with the firm. Success in this arena legitimizes the HR function and provides a tangible contribution to the overall well-being of the firm.

Implications for Future Research

The forces at work in the Converging Economy are producing dramatic challenges for the HR function in many firms. The ways in which companies are responding to those challenges, as evidenced by the innovative HRM practices described above, present a variety of opportunities for scholars in human resource management. We would like to explore two directions in particular that future research might take.

The first direction concerns the concept of employees as valuable resources. Scholarly inquiry focused on the fit between HR systems and competitive strategy has come to be labeled as "strategic human resource management" (SHRM). This growing body of research has recently come to rely heavily on the resource-based view of the firm for its theoretical inspiration. The resource-based view posits, in essence, that organizations should leverage their unique assets to develop sustained competitive advantages (Barney, 1991; Wernerfelt, 1984). SHRM researchers have adopted this perspective, asserting that employees can be unique assets (e.g. Snell et al., 1999; Wright & McMahan, 1992; Wright & Snell, 1991). However, most of this research focuses on human resources as assets to be *developed* while de-emphasizing or ignoring the notion of human resources as assets to be *assembled* and *organized*. Although the focus on developing resources has been valuable, increased insights could be generated by focusing attention on how organizations locate and configure these resources.

Viewing human assets from an entrepreneurial perspective, rather than from a developmental perspective, requires making a prediction about the future. In this view, the HR function is not reactive to the firm's competitive strategy; it is proactive in that it envisions the future business environment and then identifies the resources required to be effective in that environment. The concept of the Converging Economy would serve this endeavor well. Researchers need to identify key areas of convergence, derive their implications for organizations, and then determine what types of resource clusters need to be assembled and how they should be organized. The ultimate objective of this approach would be to add an entrepreneurial dimension to the current developmental emphasis of strategic human resource management.

A second important direction for future research concerns the management of the HR function. In those firms where the HR function becomes more proactive and entrepreneurial, who will perform this function? We envision three different candidates; in most cases they will probably join together in some combination to perform the HR role. The first candidate is composed of *employees organized by a market for human capital*. Increasingly, firms will employ sets of employees, either on staff or as contingent workers, whose value has been set by the market (Davis & Meyer, 2000). Some HR services for these employees, such as training and benefits, will be the responsibility of the individuals and groups involved.

Another group that will perform the HR function is the *existing HR department acting in partnership* with other firms' HR departments or with financial services firms. It is easy to imagine the various HR departments contained in a multi-firm network organization working together to build the human resource configurations necessary to operate their combined businesses. Similarly, one can imagine an HR department working closely with a financial services firm to develop the appropriate instruments for pricing and obtaining the services of scarce and/or unique human assets.

Finally, as has been the case with other functional areas, the HR function can be *outsourced*. Consultants, headhunters, and other firms that perform HR activities will be able to add value to their own businesses by increasing the value of the human resources that they locate for their clients. Such firms will also need to do research on the Converging Economy so that they can anticipate the types of requests made by their clients. Increasingly, this process may result in shifting the management of the HR function from firms to their human-resource suppliers.

In light of these possible areas of inquiry, a logical question arises: How should researchers investigate the effects of the Converging Economy on human resource management? We believe that research into the Converging Economy/human resource management nexus will require a mixture of qualitative and quantitative methods. The initial step of any investigation is defining the concepts of interest (Kerlinger, 1986). The drivers, challenges, and practices presented in this paper hopefully will serve in this capacity. We believe, however, that additional insights could, and should, be generated through tapping the meaning systems held by practitioners. For example, HR scholars should study the leading-edge firms that are experimenting with alternative arrangements for managing the HR function. Such case studies, combined with the entrepreneurial theoretical orientation described above, would considerably enhance our understanding of human resource management. More specifically, HR researchers should consider using techniques such as Q-sort interviews and Delphi approaches to discover the concepts and relationships perceived by managers. After a meaningful set of proposed concepts and relationships has been identified, HR researchers can then rely on the quantitative techniques with which they excel.

Throughout this process, careful attention should be paid to developing sound underlying theoretical frameworks. Although the resource-based view has been popular among SHRM scholars, debate has recently raged as to whether or not the resource-based view is in fact a theory or if it is simply a perspective (Barney, 2001; Priem & Butler, 2001). HR researchers interested in the Converging Economy should view this controversy as an impetus to consider the value of alternative theoretical perspectives.

At the most general level, we argue for exploring those theories that use an open systems perspective (Scott, 1998). The open systems perspective stresses the interdependence and reciprocal ties that exist between organizations and their environments. The premise that the Converging Economy will pose challenges to organizations therefore demands a theoretical perspective that accounts for key environmental effects on organizations. Although the global economy is not evolving in a totally predictable manner – the driving forces are too numerous and complex to determine causality – certain patterns are identifiable. The patterns described earlier, especially political and economic reform, are the province of developmental economics and international business theories. In addition, SHRM theory could benefit from incorporating ideas from other, narrower theoretical perspectives. Accordingly, we discuss aspects of several theoretical perspectives that have largely been untapped by strategic human resource management scholars. These theories are organized into four categories: evolutionary, economic, sociological, and critical.

Evolutionary approaches

Population ecology

With a focus on the birth and death of firms and its basis in evolutionary models, population ecology (Hannan & Freeman, 1977) suggests that in a new environment (like the Converging Economy), the firms most likely to survive are those that are best structured to fit the new conditions. As the Converging Economy unfolds, those organizations that do survive will provide a prototype for future organizations to model themselves on, thereby resulting in a new "species" of organization that has evolved to specifically meet the challenges of this new environment.

Furthermore, population ecology is focused on organizational survival in light of the organizational processes and routines that the organization as a whole develops in response to environmental pressures (Nelson & Winter, 1982). Specifically, firms' actions are thought to be based on their objectives (e.g. profit), their firm-based capabilities (e.g. organizational knowledge), and on their ability to maximize their choices (e.g. make the best choice possible given constraints and the inclination towards patterned, routinized behavior). This tripod that serves as the base of organizational action, therefore, is not rooted in individual or even departmental variables but in macro, organizational-level variables. The implication of this perspective is that individual managerial decisions will not have a great impact on the ultimate survival or demise of the firm.

Taken one step further, this logic suggests that strategic human resource management would be seen as a waste of energy to the extent that it is conceptualized as residing within individual managerial capacities. On the other hand, to the extent that strategic HR is seen as diffused throughout the organization, population ecology would lend a unique perspective to the understanding of the importance of SHRM. If strategic responses to managerial issues are viewed as entrenched in the organization and subsequently measured at the organizational level, rather than the individual managerial level, applying a population ecology lens to the relationship between SHRM and organizational survival might lead to some potentially interesting empirical inquiry.

The population ecology perspective encourages more research in the areas of both formal and informal organizational decision-making structures (e.g. Burgleman, 1994), absorptive capacity (Cohen & Levinthal, 1990), and advantages to be gained by learning from competitors (Barnett & Hansen, 1996). Therefore, although both population ecology and the resource-based view of the firm may be used primarily to explore challenges associated with the Converging Economy driver of intangible assets, the perspective that is offered by these two theories is quite different. While the resource-based view might lead one to assume that simply matching employee needs with organizational strategic goals is the key to successful SHRM, population ecology suggests that there is an internal, developmental process of growth which must be maximized for success.

Organizational learning
The organizational learning perspective serves as another evolutionary approach that illuminates the relationship between SHRM and the Converging Economy. The concept of patterned responses posited in population ecology suggests the relevance of cognitive learning theory and routinized behavior (Cohen & Levinthal, 1990; Levitt & March; 1988; March, 1991; Nelson & Winter, 1982). Every organization will approach the Converging Economy based on its prior experiences with either the Old or New Economies. Those past experiences, in turn, will influence how organizations make sense of their current circumstances (Weick, 1995) and even discover error in the original premises that guided their learning, a process which is termed double-loop learning (Argyris & Schön, 1978).

For instance, in the past an organization may have experienced high turnover due to low employee morale. If that same company experiences high turnover again, but in the new context of the Converging Economy, the cause of that turnover is nonetheless likely to be attributed to low employee morale a second time. This attribution might lead the HR team to respond by implementing morale boosters and focusing on increasing employee commitment rather than focusing on meeting the challenges of increasing workplace attractiveness and diversity management that are inherent in the Converging Economy.

An organizational learning perspective suggests that relying on past experience is only one part of a far more complex learning process that includes trial and error, creative discovery, and knowledge diffusion (Levitt & March, 1988). Because the Converging Economy presents a unique situation, relying too heavily on past response patterns is unlikely to be successful. Instead, to gain and maintain a competitive advantage, organizations must "learn to learn" by developing their absorptive capacity (Cohen & Levinthal, 1990). This type of learning requires that organizations learn to see value in new information, assimilate that information, and then exploit it.

The ability to see the value of new information may be largely dependent on the organization's ability to engage in double-loop learning (Argyris & Schön, 1978). Double-loop learning allows the organization to make sense not only of its past experiences but the very premises upon which organizational processes are built. It suggests that learning is a continual re-evaluation process that may allow organizations to continuously "re-invent" themselves. Therefore, according to a learning perspective, human resource managers must hone their ability to actively interface with the Converging Economy, employing a willingness to challenge their own assumptions with a sense of discovery and exploration (March, 1991). This willingness must then be followed by the ability to discern key information and mobilize the resources most applicable to their own work. Furthermore, HR managers then must actively work to disseminate their own learning throughout the rest of the organization.

Organizational learning is a process that cannot be hurried (March, 1991), nor can it be abandoned (Cohen & Levinthal, 1990). Dedication and persistence are required. One recommendation to organizations who wish to increase their absorptive capacity is to continually invest in research and development activities (Cohen & Levinthal, 1990). Although many people associate research and development with product innovation, it is also critical to other organizational processes, including human resource management. Therefore, to gain a strategic advantage, human resource managers must be willing to rely not only on learning from the competition or relying on their own histories, but they must also be willing to take risks, explore, and experiment with new, innovative policies and practices. This approach will be particularly important when meeting the challenges of creativity and innovation as well as workplace attractiveness, which are driven in the Converging Economy by information technology. Without this willingness, organizational learning in the HR area may come to a standstill, or even lockout, where new knowledge is no longer gained and an organization is doomed to, at best, incremental improvements (Cohen & Levinthal, 1990).

Some organizations may be so far along in the lockout process that they perceive new environmental contexts like the Converging Economy as threats rather than growth and learning opportunities. Those organizations may respond to its demands with a rigidity of behavior and over-reliance on previously functional responses that are now inappropriate (Staw, Sandelands & Dutton, 1981). Indeed, the concept of threat-rigidity provides us with a second anthropomorphic, cognitive perspective that can be applied to enhance our understanding of the interaction that occurs between organizations and their environment.

Threat-rigidity

Threat-rigidity suggests that organizations will react to threatening or adverse environmental conditions in one of two ways (Staw et al., 1981). Organizations may either restrict their information processing, or they may increase structural control, concentrating power and influence at higher hierarchical levels. These two responses are then thought to result in less flexibility and variation in organizational response to the environmental context. In a threatening environment that challenges the structure or process of organizing, organizations exhibit an interesting approach to information processing and learning. The intensity of information searching may vary as the threat unfolds and at some points may actually be quite high. Interestingly, however, it has been demonstrated that the general tendency is to embark upon this information search from a dominant, familiar precept and then interpret any new information from this *status quo* position (Holsti, 1971; Staw *et al.*, 1981).

In other words, threat-rigidity subverts the double-loop learning process and only allows information to be processed according to a predetermined set of givens that are not generally re-visited or questioned. This subversion, combined with the tendency to increase control and centralization, results in an organization with severely compromised decision-making capability, little potential for learning, and lack of adaptability to new circumstances. In contrast, companies best poised for success are those able to match the complexity of their internal structures with the high level of uncertainty in their environment (Hannan & Freeman, 1977; Weick, 1969). Thus, the organizations most likely to succeed in a new environment are those that are less likely to respond rigidly to the "threat" of that environment.

This perspective suggests that perhaps one of the most essential strategic HR practices to implement regards the organization's ability to be flexible in meeting all of the Converging Economy challenges. A bona fide strategic HR policy is not one that incorporates a standard set of rigid "best practices" for making the workplace attractive, managing diversity effectively, or maximizing recruiting and retention efforts, but is one that is able to adapt according to environmental demands.

Economic approaches

Transaction cost economics

Transaction cost economics provides us with another quite different perspective for examining the role that human resource management plays in responding to the Converging Economy. Transaction cost economics suggests that any transfer of goods and services is a transaction that may have associated friction or costs (Williamson, 1981; Williamson, 1985). Contracts are necessary to minimize these costs (Coase, 1937). Contracts increase control by reducing transactional uncertainty and defining the roles of the transaction participants (Ouchi, 1980; Williamson, 1981; Williamson, 1985). One of the key "transactions" that every organization must negotiate is that between the organization and its employees. Hence, human resource policies are a critical component of the contract that guides the employee-employer relationship.

A central premise of transaction cost economics is that frictions associated with transactions arise from human factors as well as environmental factors. The human factors that lead to transaction costs include bounded rationality (March & Simon, 1958) and the human predilection for opportunism. Because humans cannot have all possible relevant information, every transaction is fraught with uncertainty (a cost). Furthermore, because people tend to act in ways that protect their own self-interests rather than always dedicating themselves to the greater good, people cannot be entirely trusted to behave in ways that are beneficial to the organization.

This perspective has very interesting implications for human resource management. The employee-employer relationship is characterized primarily as one lacking in trust. A breakdown in the relationship between employees and employers, coupled with a decrease in the loyalty binding the employment contract, is certainly consistent with the New Economy. Clearly, this issue must be addressed in the Converging

Economy if organizations hope to attract and retain the very best employees. Therefore, the antecedents and consequences of mutual trust between employees and employers emerge as a key area of inquiry for SHRM under the lens of transaction cost economics.

Agency theory

Closely related to transaction cost economics is agency theory. The lack of trust that exists between transaction participants (in this context, employee and employer) leads to an agency problem (Eisenhardt, 1989). Agency theory explains the process by which the principal (employer) delegates work to the agent (employee) as guided by a metaphorical contract. Eisenhardt (1989) suggests that the mere existence of the contract is not enough to reduce transaction costs. Rather, the contract may result in the dual problems of agency and risk sharing. The agency problem centers around the difficulty that the principal may experience when trying to verify what work the agent is actually doing. The problem of risk sharing involves the different levels of acceptable risk that the principal and agent experience when negotiating and acting out their contract. Therefore, agency theory suggests that control is the central issue of concern to organizations.

Because of the need to control employees, monitoring systems must be implemented (Eisenhardt, 1985). One particularly common monitoring system is that of supervision by managers. Depending on the level of uncertainty and the programmability of the task being monitored, managers may implement different strategies of formal control (behavioral or outcome-based) (Eisenhardt, 1985; Kirsch, 1996). As we know from the threat-rigidity perspective (Staw *et al.*, 1981), however, increases in control may reduce the amount of learning and adaptability that organizations possess, thereby making it more difficult to respond effectively to Converging Economy factors. Thus, it appears that the needs for control and adaptability are somewhat adversarial. The nature of this conflict, and how organizations can manage it, must be better understood to fully grasp the implications that agency theory may have for achieving success in the Converging Economy.

Integrating the insights of transaction cost economics and agency theory further indicates that managers in the Converging Economy may have a difficult challenge to meet. Although managers are hired by the organization to protect its interest in the employer-employee contract, conditions in the Converging Economy suggest that employees hold substantial power that managers cannot ignore. To a great extent, in fact, employees may actually view management's role as a conduit between themselves and the organization. This view of the managerial role, coupled with the power that employees hold, suggests that managers who are unable to meet the demands of controlling employee behavior while still performing adequately as employee advocates may suffer the consequences of low morale, low productivity, and high employee turnover.

Furthermore, given the opportunism that is thought to drive behavior under an economic perspective, it may be that rather than working for the good of the organization as a whole, managers may simply act politically in an attempt to increase their own power (Ferris & Kacmar, 1992). In effect, managers in the Converging Economy may actually be seen as having a dual reporting structure to some extent, as they seek to please both the organization as well as the employee. When the necessity of also fulfilling their own opportunistic needs is factored into this equation, it is clear that managers may be pulled in three opposing directions, all of which may act as distractors from the central challenges posed by the Converging Economy. For instance, a manager who is more concerned with opportunistic gain may not be able to devote sufficient attention to meeting the challenges of international business concerns that are posed by the globalization process. To be effective, managers will have to find a way to satisfy all of these competing needs while still managing environmental demands. To be successful, these managers will have to depend upon the strategic ability of the human resources department and policies that support them in their multiple roles. These issues are thus important areas for scholarly inquiry.

Sociological approaches

Institutional theory

Institutional theory, a sociological approach to the open system perspective, is primarily used in two distinct ways to understand organizations. The first way focuses internally on organizations, considering the degree to which an organization is routinized, inert, and isomorphic (Meyer & Rowan, 1977; Meyer & Zucker, 1989; Zucker, 1977). This perspective suggests that to the extent organizations rely on established ways of decision making and behaving as they manage their human resources, they may find it difficult to meet the challenges associated with the converging factors of information technology, globalization, and intangible assets. In other words, in the Converging Economy, an institutional perspective suggests that relying on pre-existing solutions to new challenges may be ineffective. In this regard, institutional theory shares similarities with the organizational learning perspective discussed earlier.

The second approach that is commonly assumed under institutional theory relates to the external pressures confronting organizations. From keeping up with industry "best practices" to meeting the demands of consumer watchdog groups, there is considerable pressure to conform to specified business practices. This use of institutional theory is closely related to Barnett and Hansen's (1996) work on the "Red Queen effect," which focuses on the reciprocal causality that is commonly found between close competitors when it comes to developing and implementing strategic practices. An institutional perspective suggests that this "industry knowledge" may be less adaptive than it might seem on the surface. Organizations may enact particular HR practices not to leverage unique assets, but because managers witness successful organizations using those same practices (Schultz, Bennett & Ketchen, 1997). As entire industries become more homogeneous in their practices through the tendency of organizations to imitate their competitors, strategic thinking may be narrowed rather than enhanced (DiMaggio & Powell, 1983). Organizations may therefore find themselves struggling to implement "industry practices" that are inconsistent with, or even contrary to, their own unique culture and circumstance. This process may thereby inhibit the organization's capacity to learn and adapt.

Combining these two facets of institutional theory (internal and external), and applying them to SHRM research and practice may encourage us to explore new ways of understanding SHRM responses to the Converging Economy. For instance, in its totality, institutional theory encourages researchers to study HR with an eye to unique problem solving and capacity for creativity, rather than trying to define and promote a standard set of "best practices." Institutional theory also encourages researchers to study outliers, those cases which are unique and different from the norm, and which provide us critical opportunities to challenge the status quo and advance theory and practice (Daft & Lewin, 1990; Davis, 1971).

Resource dependence

Resource dependence theory argues that organizations are, for the most part, externally controlled, and therefore their actions are environmentally constrained (Pfeffer & Salancik, 1978). One of the trends found in the Converging Economy is the increasing importance given to optimizing intangible assets. To be successful, organizations must meet the challenge of attracting and retaining the very best possible employees. Resource dependence is particularly interesting when applied to this challenge as it illuminates the shift in the balance of power that is taking place between employees and employers. With the decline of unionization, there has been a steady decrease in the power that employees have held in the employment contract over the past century, as evidenced by frequent downsizing and reengineering. Today, forces in the Converging Economy are directing more attention to the need to proactively compete for intangible assets. With that competition increasing, some of the power that employees have lost is being recovered. Successful organizations are willing to recognize and respond adaptively to that shift (Emerson, 1962; Pfeffer & Salancik, 1978).

From a resource dependence view, the ability of HR departments to meet the competing demands of both employees as well as management is quite critical. When employees have power in the employer-employee relationship, the organization will benefit by incorporating HR as part of its strategic core, as the central responsibility of HR is to manage employees (thereby keeping their power in check). Therefore, as employees gain power, HR departments seem more likely to fulfill a strategic role as a defensive necessity on the part of the organization. As the power between employees and employer becomes more balanced, those likely to be found in the middle of any negotiations are likely to be human resource professionals. To achieve a strategic position in this circumstance will require that HR professionals amass and use their own power. This power perspective on the potential for HR to be a strategic organizational partner needs to be investigated further.

Critical approaches

Postmodernism

A postmodern approach to organizing is one that challenges the *status quo* and supports those views that have traditionally been marginalized or silenced (Alvesson & Deetz, 1999). In response to a modernist approach to organizational science, postmodernists focus on the myths of rationalism and positivism, the arbitrary nature of authority, the subordination of social life in favor of rationality, and the protection of dominant, powerful groups (Horkheimer & Adorno, 1979). The goal of the postmodernist is to understand the construction of social, historical, and political "truths," broaden the definitions of rationality, include a broad array of social groupings, and overcome domination (Alvesson & Deetz, 1999).

A postmodern approach to organizations may include a focus on the relationship between organizations and society, with attention to the social effects that institutions have on the public sphere and the process of consent and domination. More specifically, postmodern organizational scholars are interested in how increasing expertise in management leads to passivity on the part of employees and narrowed thinking throughout the organization (Alvesson & Deetz, 1999; Alvesson & Willmott, 1996). This approach is in direct opposition to the idea that the role of SHRM research is to more precisely understand the practices recommended for maximizing performance. A postmodern view of the role of SHRM in the Converging Economy would de-emphasize the importance of discovering a rational approach to best predict and manage the challenges posed by converging factors. Instead, inquiry would be dedicated to discovering individual creativity and meaningfulness of work (Sievers, 1986) while simultaneously decreasing the hierarchy, bias, and domination traditionally associated with organizing (Alvesson & Willmott, 1996; Calás & Smircich, 1999).

Emotions

Current thinking on the role that emotions play in organizations suggests that rationality – even bounded rationality – may be a modern myth, as emotion and cognition are perceived as inextricably entwined (Fineman, 1999). Furthermore, research in this area suggests that under situations of newness and perceived threat, organizations as a whole may react with child-like emotional–behavioral responses, refusing to cooperate, becoming aggressive, or becoming excessively dependent (Diamond & Allcorn, 1987). Therefore, learning to deal with these emotional tendencies, more than explicitly reacting to the external pressures posed by the Converging Economy, would be the focus of SHRM researchers and practitioners adopting an emotional perspective.

A second area of SHRM research that is spurred by an emotional approach is that of the emotional underpinnings of ethical practices. Focusing on the role that shame and guilt play in driving ethical behavior (Callahan, 1988; Fineman, 1999) is central to the development of fair practices that emerge in response to Converging Economy challenges. For instance, the perceived challenges of making the workplace more attractive, as well as attracting and retaining the best workers, may be driven by feelings of shame and guilt over past injustices or exploitations. Exploring these organizational feelings in light of the Converging Economy may result in a deeper understanding not only of organizations themselves but of the social movements and market pressures that influence organizations.

Theoretical summation

As evidenced by this discussion of nine theoretical perspectives that are not often applied to the study of SHRM, there is a considerable amount of research that may be spurred by adopting views less common than the resource-based view of the firm.

Table 3.1 Key strategic human resource implications of major theoretical perspectives

Theoretical perspective	*Key SHRM implications*
Population Ecology	• Individual attempts at SHRM matter little • Organizational diffusion of SHRM may influence firm survival • SHRM involves more than matching employee and organizational needs
Organizational Learning	• Over-reliance on past HR strategies is unlikely to be successful in the Converging Economy • Strategic HR managers must actively interface with their environment • HR managers must be willing to experiment and take risks
Threat-Rigidity	• HR flexibility in meeting Converging Economy challenges is critical for firm success • Rigid "best practices" may not position HR as responsive to the constantly shifting demands of the Converging Economy
Transaction Cost Economics	• Addressing issues surrounding employee-employer trust is critical for progressive HR managers
Agency Theory	• The need for HR control may be contrary to the need for HR adaptability • Strategic HR managers must meet the competing demands of employees and employer • Meeting their own opportunistic needs may detract from the benefit that HR managers can offer the organization
Institutional Theory	• Unique problem solving and creativity are key areas of competence for strategic HR managers • "Best practices" may not be the best HR approach
Resource Dependence	• HR must meet the competing demands of employees and upper management • A central HR function is to keep employee power in check • Investment in HR may be a defensive organizational strategy • To increase legitimacy, HR professionals must learn to amass and use their own power
Postmodernism	• HRM expertise leads to employee passivity • "Rational" approaches to management may be misguided • Discovery of meaning and exploration of creativity are two central goals of effective HR
Emotions	• SHRM researchers and practitioners must focus on emotional tendencies of employees rather than external pressures • The emotional underpinnings of ethical practices must be recognized by effective HR managers

Additionally, it is quite evident that several of the theories mentioned herein overlap; the approaches used to categorize the theories are meant to establish a general structure for understanding rather than a true typology. For instance, organizational learning and institutional theory both focus on breaking old response habits, and institutional theory in turn is somewhat closely related to population ecology, with a focus on the tendency of organizations to learn from their competitors. Each theory, however, has idiosyncrasies and thus provides a unique lens by which to study organizational responses to the Converging Economy. We believe that by importing established theory from other areas of the organizational sciences, researchers might not only help explain responses to Converging Economy trends and events but also provide a service to the broader field of human resource management. The key ideas that each theoretical perspective potentially contributes to SHRM are summarized in Table 3.1.

Conclusion

The concept of requisite variety suggests that, to be successful, organizations need to mirror the complexity of the environment with their internal capabilities (Ashby, 1956). The relationship between the Converging Economy and the human resource management function offers a good illustration of the need for requisite variety. Regardless of who is responsible for performing the HR function, the task is to anticipate environmental change, derive the implications for HRM, and develop appropriate responses. In this chapter, we have described several innovative practices firms have enacted to cope with the growing influence of information technology, globalization, and intangible assets. It is safe to predict that the extent to which each organization becomes equipped to meet these challenges, and those to follow, will influence if not determine its future success. Similarly, researchers interested in human resource management may find that their efforts to describe, explain, and predict organizational phenomena depend on the ability to incorporate the Converging Economy into their conceptual and empirical models.

REFERENCES

Alvesson, M., & Deetz, S. (1999). Critical theory and postmodernism: Approaches to organizational studies. In: S. R. Clegg & C. Hardy (eds.), *Studying organization: Theory and method* (pp. 185–211). London: Sage Publications.

Alvesson, M., & Willmott, H. (1996). *Making sense of management: A critical analysis.* London: Sage Publications.

Argyris, C., & Schön, D. (1978). *Organizational learning.* Reading, MA: Addison-Wesley.

Armour, S. (2000). Commute a chore? Try USA to London. *USA Today* (November 9), 3B.

Ashby, W. R. (1956). The effect of experience on a determinant system. *Behavioral Science, 1,* 35–42.

Barnett, W., & Hansen, M. (1996). The red queen in organizational evolution. *Strategic Management Journal, 17,* 139–58.

Barney, J. B. (1991). Firm resources and sustained competitive advantage. *Journal of Management, 17*, 99–120.

Barney, J. B. (2001). Is the resource-based "view" a useful perspective for strategic management research? Yes. *Academy of Management Review, 26*(1), 41–56.

Benjamin, R., & Wigand, R. (1995). Electronic markets and virtual value chains on the information superhighway. *Sloan Management Review, 36*(2), 62–72.

Black, J. S., & Gregersen, H. B. (1999). The right way to manage expats. *Harvard Business Review*, March–April, *53*, 52–60.

Boudreau, M. C., Loch, K. D., Robey, D., & Straud, D. (1998). Going global: Using information technology to advance the competitiveness of the virtual transnational organization. *Academy of Management Executive, 12*, 120–28.

Boulton, R. E. S., Libert, B. D., & Samek, S. M. (2000). A business model for the new economy. *Journal of Business Strategy*, July–August, 29–35.

Burgleman, R. (1994). Fading memories: A process theory of strategic business exit in dynamic environments. *Administrative Science Quarterly, 39*, 24–56.

Calás, M. B., & Smircich, L. (1999). From "the woman's" point of view: Feminist approaches to organization studies. In: S. R. Clegg & C. Hardy (eds.), *Studying organization: Theory and method* (pp. 212–51). London: Sage Publications.

Callahan, E. (1988). The role of emotion in ethical decision making. Hastings Center Report, June–July, 9–14.

Cascio, W. F. (1995). Whither industrial and organizational psychology in a changing world of work? *American Psychologist*, November, 928–39.

Christensen, C. M., & Tedlow, R. S. (2000). Patterns of disruption in retailing. *Harvard Business Review*, January–February, 42–5.

Christie, P. M. J., & Levary, R. R. (1998). Virtual corporations: Recipe for success. *Industrial Management*, July–August, 7–11.

Clarke, S. G. S. (2000). Boomerang hires bring experience. *Tallahassee Democrat*, December 27, E1–2.

Coase, R. H. (1937). The nature of the firm. *Econometrica, 4.* 386–405.

Cohen, W., & Levinthal, D. (1990). Absorptive capacity: A new perspective on learning and innovation. *Administrative Science Quarterly, 35*, 128–52.

Daft, R., & Lewin, A. (1990). Can organization studies begin to break out of the normal science straightjacket? An editorial essay. *Organization Science, 1*, 1–9.

Davis, M. (1971). That's interesting! Towards a phenomenology of sociology and a sociology of phenomenology. *Philosophy and Social Science, 1*, 309–44.

Davis, S., & Meyer, C. (2000). *Future wealth*. Boston, MA: Harvard Business School Press.

DeFrank, R. S., & Ivancevich, J. M. (1998). Stress on the job: An executive update. *Academy of Management Executive, 12*, 55–66.

Diamond, M. A., & Allcorn, S. (1987). The psychodynamics of regression in work groups. *Human Relations, 40*, 525–43.

Dillon, S. 2000. Preparing for a job interview. *U.S. News & World Report*, November 6, 62.

DiMaggio, D. J., & Powell, W. W. (1983). The iron cage revisited: Institutional isomorphism and collective rationality in organizational fields. *American Sociological Review, 48*, 147–60.

Eisenhardt, K. M. (1985). Control: Organizational and economic approaches. *Management Science, 31*, 134–49.

Eisenhardt, K. M. (1989). Agency theory: An assessment and review. *Academy of Management Review, 14*, 57–74.

Emerson, R. M. (1962). Power-dependence relations. *American Sociological Review, 27*, 31–40.

Evans, P., & Wurster, T. S. (1999). Getting real about virtual commerce. *Harvard Business Review*, November–December, 85–94.

Ferris, G. R., & Kacmar, K. M. (1992). Perceptions of organizational politics. *Journal of Management, 18*, 93–116.

Fineman, S. (1999). Emotion and organizing. In: S. R. Clegg & C. Hardy (Eds), *Studying organization: Theory and method* (pp. 289–310). London: Sage Publications.

Ganster, D., & Schaubroeck, J. (1991). Work stress and employee health. *Journal of Management, 17*, 235–71.

Ghosh, S. (1998). Making business sense of the Internet. *Harvard Business Review*, March–April, 127–35.

Gogoi, P. (2000). Teaching men the right stuff. *Business Week Online*, November 20. Available at http://www.businessweek.com/2000/00_47/b3708147.htm.

Hallowell, E. M. (1999). The human moment at work. *Harvard Business Review*, January–February, 58–66.

Handy, S. L., & Mokhtarian, P. L. (1996). The future of telecommuting. *Futures, 28*, 227–40.

Hannan, M. T., & Freeman, J. (1977). The population ecology of organizations. *The American Journal of Sociology, 82*, 929–64.

Holsti, O. R. (1971). Crisis, stress, and decision making. *International Social Science, 23*, 53–67.

Horkheimer, M., & Adorno, T. (1979). *The dialectics of enlightenment*. London: Verso.

Igbaria, M., & Guimaraes, T. (1999). Exploring differences in employee turnover intentions and its determinants among telecommuters and non-telecommuters. *Journal of Management Information Systems, 16*, 147–64.

Itami, H. (1987). *Managing invisible assets*. Cambridge, MA: Harvard University Press.

Kerlinger, F. (1986). *Foundations of behavioral research*. Fort Worth, TX: Harcourt Brace.

Kirsch, L. J. (1996). The management of complex tasks in organizations: Controlling the systems development process. *Organization Science, 7*, 1–21.

Levitt, B., & March, J. G. (1988). Organizational learning. *Annual Review of Sociology, 14*, 319–40.

March, J. G. (1991). Exploration and exploitation in organizational learning. *Organization Science, 2*, 71–87.

March, J. G., & Simon, H. A. (1958). *Organizations*. New York: John Wiley.

Meyer, J., & Rowan, B. (1977). Institutionalized organizations: Formal structure as myth and ceremony. *The American Journal of Sociology, 83*, 340–63.

Meyer, M. W., & Zucker, L. G. (1989). *Permanently failing organizations*. Newbury Park, CA: Sage Publications.

Miles, R. E., Snow, C. C., & Miles, G. (2000). TheFuture.org. *Long-Range Planning, 33*, 300–21.

Nelson, R. R., & Winter, S. G. (1982). *An evolutionary theory of economic change*. Cambridge, MA: Belknap Press of Harvard University Press.

Ohmae, K. (1999). *The invisible continent: Four strategic imperatives of the new economy*. New York: Harper Business.

Olek, J., & Prasso, S. (2001). Pink slips with a silver lining. *Business Week*, June 4, 14.

Ouchi, W. G. (1980). Markets, bureaucracies, and clans. *Administrative Science Quarterly, 25*, 129–41.

Pfeffer, J. (1994). *Competitive advantage through people: Unleashing the power of the workforce*. Boston: Harvard Business School Press.

Pfeffer, J., & Salancik, G. R. (1978). *The external control of organizations*. New York: Harper Row.

Priem, R. L., & Butler, J. E. (2001). Is the resource-based "view" a useful perspective for strategic management research? *Academy of Management Review, 26*, 22–40.

Schaubroeck, J., & Merritt, D. E. (1997). Divergent effects of job control on coping with work stressors: The key role of self-efficacy. *Academy of Management Journal, 40*, 738–54.

Schmitz, S. (2000). The effects of electronic commerce on the structure of inter-mediation. *The Journal of Computer-Mediated Communication*, 5(3). Available at http://www.ascusc.org/jcmc/vol5/issue3/schmitz.html.

Schultz, E., Bennett, N., & Ketchen, D. (1997). An examination of the relationship between strategic type and human resource practices among small businesses. *Journal of Small Business Strategy*, 8, 35–48.

Scott, W. R. (1998). *Organizations: Rational, natural, and open systems*. Upper Saddle River, NJ: Prentice Hall.

Shapiro, J. P. (2000). Prison to work: Employers look to the joint to fill jobs. *U.S. News & World Report*, November 6, 70.

Sharpe, R. (2000). As leaders, women rule. *Business Week Online*, November 20. Available at http://www.businessweek.com/2000/00_47/b3708145.htm.

Sievers, B. (1986). Beyond the surrogate of motivation. *Organization Studies*, 7, 335–52.

Sinha, I. (2000). Cost transparency: The net's real threat to prices and brands. *Harvard Business Review*, March–April, 43–50.

Smith, A. K. (2000). Charting your own course: The new workplace is risky, rugged, and rewarding. And guess what? You're in charge! *U.S. News and World Report*, November 6, 56–65.

Snell, S. A., Lepak, D. P., & Youndt, M. A. (1999). Managing the architecture of intellectual cap-ital: Implications for strategic human resource management. In: G. R. Ferris (ed.), *Research in personnel and human resources management* (pp. 197–93, Supplement 4). Greenwich, CT: JAI Press.

Snell, S. A., & Wright, P. M. (1998). Toward a unifying framework for exploring fit and flexibility in strategic human resource management. *Academy of Management Review*, 23, 756–72.

Staw, B. M., Sandelands, L. E., & Dutton, J. E. (1981). Threat rigidity effects in organizational behavior: A multilevel analysis. *Administrative Science Quarterly*, 26, 501–24.

Stepanek, M., & Weber, J. (1999). Using the net for brainstorming. *Business Week*, December 13, 55–7.

Walton, S. (1992). *Sam Walton: Made in America*. New York: Doubleday.

Weick, K. E. (1969). *The social psychology of organizing*. Reading, MA: Addison-Wesley.

Weick, K. E. (1995). *Sensemaking in organizations*. Thousand Oaks, CA: Sage Publications.

Wernerfelt, B. (1984). A resource-based view of the firm. *Strategic Management Journal*, 5, 171–80.

Westland, J. C., & Clark, T. H. K. (1999). *Global electronic commerce*. Cambridge, MA: The MIT Press.

Williamson, O. E. (1981). The economics of organization: The transaction cost approach. *The American Journal of Sociology*, 87, 548–77.

Williamson, O. E. (1985). *The economic institutions of capitalism*. New York: Free Press.

Wright, P. M., & McMahan, G. C. (1992). Theoretical perspectives for strategic human resource management. *Journal of Management*, 18, 295–320.

Wright, P. M., & Snell, S. A. (1991). Toward an integrative view of strategic human resource management. *Human Resource Management Review*, 1, 203–25.

www.gapinc.com

www.hire.com

www.levistrauss.com

Yang, D. J. (2000). Down (but not out) in Silicon Valley. *U.S. News and World Report*, November 6, 66–7.

Zucker, L. (1977). The role of institutionalization in cultural persistence. *Administrative Science Quarterly*, 42, 726–43.

Chapter 4

Human Resources and the Resource-Based View of the Firm

Patrick M. Wright, Benjamin B. Dunford, and Scott A. Snell

4.1 Introduction

The human resource function has consistently faced a battle in justifying its position in organizations (Drucker, 1954; Stewart, 1996). In times of plenty, firms easily justify expenditures on training, staffing, reward, and employee involvement systems, but when faced with financial difficulties, such HR systems fall prey to the earliest cutbacks.

The advent of the sub-field of strategic human resource management (SHRM), devoted to exploring HR's role in supporting business strategy, provided one avenue for demonstrating its value to the firm. Walker's (1978) call for a link between strategic planning and human resource planning signified the conception of the field of SHRM, but its birth came in the early 1980s with Devanna, Fombrun, and Tichy's (1984) article devoted to extensively exploring the link between business strategy and HR. Since then, SHRM's evolution has consistently followed (by a few years) developments within the field of strategic management. For example, Miles and Snow's (1978) organizational types were later expanded to include their associated HR systems (Miles & Snow, 1984). Porter's (1980) model of generic strategies was later used by SHRM researchers to delineate the specific HR strategies that one would expect to observe under each of them (Schuler & Jackson, 1987; Wright & Snell, 1991).

Though the field of SHRM was not directly born of the resource-based view (RBV), it has clearly been instrumental to its development. This was largely because of the

P. M. Wright, B. B. Dunford, and S. A. Snell, "Human Resources and the Resource-Based View of the Firm," *Journal of Management*, Vol. 27 (2001): 701–21.

RBV shifting emphasis in the strategy literature away from external factors (such as industry position) toward internal firm resources as sources of competitive advantage (Hoskisson, Hitt, Wan, & Yiu, 1999). Growing acceptance of internal resources as sources of competitive advantage brought legitimacy to HR's assertion that people are strategically important to firm success. Thus, given both the need to conceptually justify the value of HR and the propensity for the SHRM field to borrow concepts and theories from the broader strategy literature, the integration of the RBV of the firm into the SHRM literature should surprise no one.

However, two developments not as easily predicted have emerged over the past 10 years. First, the popularity of the RBV within the SHRM literature as a foundation for both theoretical and empirical examinations has probably far surpassed what anyone expected (McMahan, Virick, & Wright, 1999). Second, the applications and implications of the RBV within the strategy literature have led to an increasing convergence between the fields of strategic management and SHRM (Snell, Shadur, & Wright, 2001). Within the strategic literature, the RBV has helped to put "people" (or a firm's human resources) on the radar screen. Concepts such as knowledge (Argote & Ingram, 2000; Grant, 1996; Liebeskind, 1996), dynamic capability (Eisenhardt & Martin, 2000; Teece, Pisano, & Schuen, 1997), learning organizations (Fiol & Lyles, 1985; Fisher & White, 2000), and leadership (Finkelstein & Hambrick, 1996; Norburn & Birley, 1988; Thomas, 1988) as sources of competitive advantage turn attention toward the intersection of strategy and HR issues.

The purpose of this paper is to examine how the RBV has been applied to the theoretical and empirical research base of SHRM, and to explore how it has provided an accessible bridge between the fields of strategy and HR. To accomplish this, we will first review the specific benchmark articles that have applied the RBV to theoretical development of SHRM. We will then discuss some of the empirical SHRM studies that have used the RBV as the basis for exploring the relationship between HR and firm performance. Finally, we will identify some of the major topic areas that illustrate the convergence of the fields of strategy and HR, and propose some future directions for how such a convergence can provide mutual benefits.

4.2   Applying the RBV to SHRM

While based in the work of Penrose (1959) and others, Wernerfelt's (1984) articulation of the resource-based view of the firm certainly signified the first coherent statement of the theory. This initial statement of the theory served as the foundation that was extended by others such as Rumelt (1984), Barney (1996), and Dierickx and Cool (1989). However, Barney's (1991) specification of the characteristics necessary for a sustainable competitive advantage seemed to be a seminal article in popularizing the theory within the strategy and other literatures. In this article he noted that resources which are rare, valuable, inimitable, and nonsubstitutable can provide sources of sustainable competitive advantages.

Although debates about the RBV continue to wage (e.g., whether the RBV is a theory, whether it is tautological, etc.; Barney, 2001; Priem & Butler, 2001a,b) even its critics have acknowledged the "breadth of its diffusion" in numerous strategic research programs (Priem & Butler, 2001a, pp. 25–6). With its emphasis on internal firm resources as sources of competitive advantage, the popularity of the RBV in the SHRM literature has been no exception. Since Barney's (1991) article outlining the basic theoretical model and criteria for sources of sustainable competitive advantage, the RBV has become by far, the theory most often used within SHRM, both in the development of concept and the rationale for empirical research (McMahan, Virick, & Wright, 1999).

4.3   RBV and SHRM Theory

As part of *Journal of Management*'s Yearly Review of Management issue, Wright and McMahan (1992) reviewed the theoretical perspectives that had been applied to SHRM. They presented the RBV as one perspective that provided a rationale for how a firm's human resources could provide a potential source of sustainable competitive advantage. This was based largely on what was, at the time a working paper, but later became the Wright, McMahan and McWilliams (1994) paper described later.

Almost simultaneously, Cappelli and Singh (1992), within the industrial relations literature, provided an examination of the implications of the RBV on SHRM. Specifically, they noted that most models of SHRM based on fit assume that (1) a certain business strategy demands a unique set of behaviors and attitudes from employees and (2) certain human resource policies produce a unique set of responses from employees. They further argued that many within strategy have implicitly assumed that it is easier to rearrange complementary assets/resources given a choice of strategy than it is to rearrange strategy given a set of assets/resources, even though empirical research seems to imply the opposite. Thus, they proposed that the resource-based view might provide a theoretical rationale for why HR could have implications for strategy formulation as well as implementation.

Shortly thereafter, two articles came out arguing almost completely opposite implications of the potential for HR practices to constitute a source of sustainable competitive advantage. Wright *et al.* (1994), mentioned above, distinguished between the firm's human resources (i.e., the human capital pool) and HR practices (those HR tools used to manage the human capital pool). In applying the concepts of value, rareness, inimitability, and substitutability, they argued the HR practices could not form the basis for sustainable competitive advantage since any individual HR practice could be easily copied by competitors. Rather, they proposed that the human capital pool (a highly skilled and highly motivated workforce) had greater potential to constitute a source of sustainable competitive advantage. These authors noted that to constitute a source of competitive advantage, the human capital pool must have both high levels of skill and a willingness (i.e., motivation) to exhibit productive behavior. This skill/behavior distinction appears as a rather consistent theme within this literature.

In contrast, Lado and Wilson (1994) proposed that a firm's HR practices could provide a source of sustainable competitive advantage. Coming from the perspective of exploring the role of HR in influencing the competencies of the firm, they suggested that HR systems (as opposed to individual practices) can be unique, causally ambiguous and synergistic in how they enhance firm competencies, and thus could be inimitable. Thus, whereas Wright *et al.* (1994) argued for imitability of individual practices, Lado and Wilson noted that the system of HR practices, with all the complementarities and interdependencies among the set of practices, would be impossible to imitate. This point of view seems well accepted within the current SHRM paradigm (Snell, Youndt, & Wright, 1996).

Boxall (1996) further built upon the RBV/SHRM paradigm, suggesting that human resource advantage (i.e., the superiority of one firm's HRM over another) consists of two parts. First, human capital advantage refers to the potential to capture a stock of exceptional human talent "latent with productive possibilities" (p. 67). Human process advantage can be understood as a "function of causally ambiguous, socially complex, historically evolved processes such as learning, cooperation, and innovation" (p. 67). Boxall (1998) then expanded upon this basic model presenting a more comprehensive model of strategic HRM. He argued that one major task of organizations is the management of mutuality (i.e., alignment of interests) to create a talented and committed workforce. It is the successful accomplishment of this task that results in a human capital advantage. A second task is to develop employees and teams in such a way as to create an organization capable of learning within and across industry cycles. Successful accomplishment of this task results in the organizational process advantage.

Most recently, Lepak and Snell (1999) presented an architectural approach to SHRM based at least partly in the RBV. They proposed that within organizations, considerable variance exists with regard to both the uniqueness and value of skills. Juxtaposing these two dimensions, they built a 2 × 2 matrix describing different combinations with their corresponding employment relationships and HR systems. The major implication of that model was that some employee groups are more instrumental to competitive advantage than others. As a consequence, they are likely to be managed differently. While the premise of an architectural perspective is rooted in extant research in HR (cf., Baron *et al.*, 1986; Osterman, 1987; Tsui, Pearce, Porter, & Tripoli, 1997) and strategy (cf., Matusik & Hill, 1998), Lepak and Snell (1999) helped SHRM researchers recognize that real and valid variance exists in HR practices within the organization, and looking for one HR strategy may mask important differences in the types of human capital available to firms (cf., Truss & Gratton, 1994).

In essence, the conceptual development within the field of SHRM has leveraged the RBV to achieve some consensus on the areas within the human resource architecture in which sustainable competitive advantage might be achieved. Figure 4.1 depicts these components.

First, the human capital pool refers to the stock of employee skills that exist within a firm at any given point in time. Theorists focus on the need to develop a pool of human capital that has either higher levels of skills (general and/or firm specific), or achieves a better alignment between the skills represented in the firm and those required by its strategic intent. The actual stock of human capital can and does change overtime, and must constantly be monitored for its match with the strategic needs of the firm.

Second, an increasing consensus is emerging among researchers that employee behavior is an important independent component of SHRM. Distinct from skills of

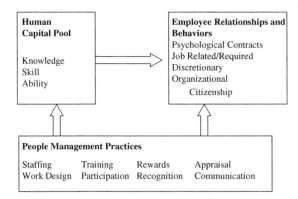

Figure 4.1   A model of the basic strategic HRM components.

the human capital pool, employee behavior recognizes individuals as cognitive and emotional beings who possess free will. This free will enables them to make decisions regarding the behaviors in which they will engage. This is an important, if subtle, distinction. A basic premise of human capital theory is that firms do not own it; individuals do. Firms may have access to valuable human capital, but either through the poor design of work or the mismanagement of people, may not adequately deploy it to achieve strategic impact. For example, MacDuffie (1995) focuses on the concept of discretionary behavior. Discretionary behavior recognizes that even within prescribed organizational roles, employees exhibit discretion that may have either positive or negative consequences to the firm. Thus, a machine operator who hears a "pinging" has discretion to simply run the machine until something breaks or to fix the problem immediately, and thus save significant downtime. Similar to March and Simon's (1958) concept of "the decision to contribute" SHRM's focus on discretionary behavior recognizes that competitive advantage can only be achieved if the members of the human capital pool individually and collectively choose to engage in behavior that benefits the firm.

Finally, while many authors describe HR practice or High Performance Work Systems, a broader conceptualization might simply be the people management system. By using the term *system*, we turn focus to the importance of understanding the multiple practices that impact employees (Wright & Boswell, 2002) rather than single practices. By using the term *people*, rather than HR, we expand the relevant practices to those beyond the control of the HR function, such as communication (both upward and downward), work design, culture, leadership, and a host of others that impact employees and shape their competencies, cognitions, and attitudes. Effective systems for managing people evolve through unique historical paths and maintain interdependence among the components that competitors cannot easily imitate (Becker & Huselid, 1998). The important aspect of these systems is that they are the means through which the firm continues to generate advantage over time as the actual employees flow in and out and the required behaviors change because of changing environmental and strategic contingencies. It is through the people management system that the firm influences the human capital pool and elicits the desired employee behavior. This dynamic process, while not depicted in the figure, will be taken up later in the paper.

The implications of our figure and this model are that while a firm might achieve a superior position in any one of the three, sustainable competitive advantage requires superior positions on all three.

This is because of three reasons. First, the value that skills and behaviors can generate requires that they be paired together (i.e., without skills, certain behaviors cannot be exhibited, and the value of skills can only be realized through exhibited behavior). Second, it is difficult to conceive of a firm's human capital pool containing both the highest levels of skills and exhibiting optimal behaviors in the absence of an aligned people management system. Finally, the effects of the people management systems are subject to time compression diseconomies (Dierickx & Cool, 1989). While these systems might be immediately imitated, a significant time lag will occur before their impact is realized, thus making it costly or difficult for competitors to imitate the value generated by the human capital pool. We will later build upon this model to explore how this fits within the larger organization.

4.3.1   Summary of RBV-based conceptual literature

In summary, the RBV has proven to be integral to the conceptual and theoretical development of the SHRM literature. Our brief review demonstrates how the RBV based SHRM research has evolved in the last decade. This evolution began when HR researchers recognized that the RBV provided a compelling explanation for why HR practices lead to competitive advantage. Ensuing scholarly debate about the specific mechanics of this relationship advanced the SHRM literature to its current state. The net effect has been a deeper understanding of the interplay between HRM and competitive advantage. The model depicted in Fig. 4.1 demonstrates that sustained competitive advantage is not just a function of single or isolated components, but rather a combination of human capital elements such as the development of stocks of skills, strategically relevant behaviors, and supporting people management systems. Although there is yet much room for progress it is fair to say that the theoretical application of the RBV has been successful in stimulating a substantial amount of activity in the SHRM arena. Having summarized the conceptual development, we now turn to the empirical research.

4.4   RBV and Empirical SHRM Research

In addition to the many applications of the RBV to theoretical developments within SHRM, this perspective also has emerged as one of the more popular foundations for exploring empirical relationships within SHRM. In fact, one is hard pressed to find any SHRM empirical studies conducted over the past few years that do not at least pay lip service to the RBV. In the interest of brevity, we will cover a sample of such studies that illustrate the application of RBV concepts to empirical SHRM research. We chose these studies either because they specifically attempt to build on resource-based theory or because they tend to be most frequently cited within the SHRM literature and at least tangentially rely on resource-based logic.

In an early application, Huselid (1995) argued at a general level that HR practices could help create a source of competitive advantage, particularly if they are aligned with the firm's competitive strategy. His study revealed a relationship between HR practices (or High Performance Work Systems) and employee turnover, gross rate of return on assets, and Tobin's Q. That study received considerable attention because it demonstrated that HR practices could have a profound impact on both accounting and market based measures of performance.

Koch and McGrath (1996) took a similar logic in their study of the relationship between HR planning, recruitment, and staffing practices and labor productivity. They argued that "... a highly productive workforce is likely to have attributes that make it a particularly valuable strategic asset" (p. 335). They suggested firms that develop effective routines for acquiring human assets develop a stock of talent that cannot be easily imitated. They found that these HR practices were related to labor productivity in a sample of business units, and that this relationship was stronger in capital intensive organizations.

Boxall and Steeneveld (1999) conducted a longitudinal case study of participants in the New Zealand engineering consultancy industry. They suggested that one of the firms in the industry had achieved a superior competitive position because of its human resource advantage in 1994, but that by 1997 two of the competitors had caught up in the competitive marketplace. They posited that this could mean that either the two competitors had been able to successfully imitate the former leader's human resource advantage, or that the former leader has developed an advantage about which there is presently uncertainty, but which will be exploited in the future.

Diverging from the focus on HR practices, Wright, Smart, and McMahan (1995) studied NCAA Men's basketball teams using an RBV framework. They focused on the skills of the team members and experience of the coach, and examined how a fit between skills and strategy impacted the team's performance. They found that the relationship between certain skills and team performance depended upon the strategy in which the team was engaged. In addition, their results indicated that teams whose coaches who were using a strategy different from their preferred strategy performed lower than teams where the coach was able to use his preferred strategy.

Recent empirical studies using the RBV build on Lepak and Snell's (1999) architectural framework discussed above. Lepak and Snell (2002) asked executives to describe the HR systems that existed for jobs that represented particular quadrants of their model. They found considerable support for the idea that the value and uniqueness of skills are associated with different types of HR systems within the same organization. These results were mostly consistent with the Lepak and Snell (1999) model, and supported the basic proposition that diverse HR strategies exist within firms. A follow up study (Lepak, Takeuchi, & Snell, 2001) indicated that a combination of knowledge work and contract labor was associated with higher firm performance. This finding not only raises some interesting ideas about the development of valuable human resources, but also highlights the importance of combinations of various types used in conjunction with one another.

In another example of examining the human capital pool, Richard (2001) used resource-based logic to examine the impact of racial diversity on firm performance. He argued that diversity provides value through ensuring a variety of perspectives, that it is rare in that very few firms have achieved significant levels of diversity, and that the socially complex dynamics inherent in diversity lead to its inimitability. He found in a sample of banks that diversity was positively related to productivity, return on equity, and market performance for firms engaged in a growth strategy, but negatively related for firms downsizing.

In an effort to look beyond human capital pool alone, Youndt and Snell (2001) studied the differential effects of HR practices on human capital, social capital, and organizational capital. They found that intensive/extensive staffing, competitive pay, intensive/extensive training and promotion from within policies were most important for distinguishing high levels of human capital in organizations. In contrast, broad banding, compressed wages, team structures, socialization, mentoring, and group incentives distinguished those with high social capital (i.e., relationships that engender knowledge exchange) but had very little effect on human capital itself. Finally, organizational capital (i.e., knowledge embedded in the organization's systems and processes) was established most through lessons learned databases and HR policies that reinforced knowledge capture and access.

4.4.1   Summary of RBV-based empirical research: limitations and future directions

Recent debate about the usefulness of the RBV provides an interesting commentary about the current state of SHRM research (Barney, 2001; Priem & Butler, 2001a). In response to claims that the RBV is tautological and does not generate testable hypotheses, Barney recognizes that most research applying the RBV has failed to test its fundamental concepts. Rather, he notes that much of the existing research has used the RBV to "establish the context of some empirical research – for example that the focus is on the performance implications of some internal attribute of a firm – and *are not really direct tests of the theory developed in the 1991 article*" (Barney, 2001, p. 46, emphasis added).

Much of the existing SHRM research falls into this category. Although the empirical application of the RBV has taken a variety of forms, ranging in focus from High Performance Work Systems and stocks of talent, to the fit between employee skills and strategy it has employed a common underlying logic: Human resource activities are thought to lead to the development of a skilled workforce and one that engages in functional behavior for the firm, thus forming a source of competitive advantage. This results in higher operating performance, which translates into increased profitability, and consequently results in higher stock prices (or market values) (Becker & Huselid, 1998). While this theoretical story is appealing, it is important to note that ultimately, most of the empirical studies assess only two variables: HR practices and performance.

While establishing such a relationship provides empirical evidence for the potential value of HR to firms, it fails to adequately test the RBV in two important ways. First, no attempt has yet been made to empirically assess the validity of the proposition that HR practices (or HPWS) are path dependent or causally ambiguous, nor whether they are actually difficult to imitate. While intuitively obvious and possibly supported by anecdotal data, the field lacks verifiable quantitative data to support these assertions. In fact, Boxall and Steeneveld's (1999) findings might suggest that HR systems are more easily imitated (or at least substitutable) than SHRM researchers previously believed. Certainly, efforts such as King and Zeithaml's (2001) study assessing causal ambiguity of competencies could be replicated with regard to SHRM issues. These authors asked managers to evaluate their firm's competencies and the generated measures of causal ambiguity based on these responses. While ambiguity was negatively related to firm performance in their study, they provide an example of how one might attempt to measure some of the variables within the RBV.

Second, few attempts have been made to demonstrate that the HR practices actually impact the skills or behaviors of the workforce, nor that these skills or behaviors are related to any performance measures. Arthur (1994) and Huselid (1995) did find a relationship between HR practices and turnover. Wright, McCormick, Sherman, and McMahan (1999) found that appraisal and training practices were related to executives' assessment of the skills and that compensation practices were related to their assessments of workforce motivation. However, as yet no study has demonstrated anything close to a full causal model through which HR practices are purported to impact firm performance.

In short, a major step forward for the SHRM literature will be to move beyond simply the application of RBV logic to HR issues toward research that directly tests the RBV's core concepts. In fairness, this state of affairs does not differ from attempts to study competitive advantage within the strategy literature. As noted by Godfrey and Hill (1995), it is impossible to assess the degree of unobservability of an unobservable, and inimitable resources are often purported to be unobservable. Thus, strategy researchers are often left to using proxy variables that may not be valid for measuring the underlying constructs (Hoskisson, Hitt, Wan, & Yiu, 1999).

However, given the single respondent, cross sectional, survey designs inherent in much of this research, one cannot rule out alternative explanations for the findings of empirical relationships. For example, Gerhart, Wright, McMahan, and Snell (2000) and Wright, Gardner, Moynihan, Park, Gerhart, and Delery (2001) both found that single respondent measures of HR practices may contain significant amounts of measurement error. Gardner, Wright, and Gerhart (2000) also found evidence of implicit performance theories suggesting that respondents to HR surveys might base their descriptions of the HR practices on their assessments of the organization's performance. This raises the possibility that research purporting to support the RBV through demonstrating a relationship between HR and performance may result from spurious relationships, or even reverse causation (Wright & Gardner, 2003). The point is not to discount the significant research that has been conducted to date, but rather to highlight the importance of more rigorous and longitudinal studies of HR from a RBV perspective.

Taking a deeper understanding of the resource-based view of the firm into empirical SHRM research entails focusing primarily on the competencies and capabilities of firms and the role that people management systems play in developing these. It requires recognizing that the inimitability of these competencies may stem from unobservability (e.g., causal ambiguity), complexity (e.g., social complexity), and/or time compression diseconomies (e.g., path dependence). This implies that rather than simply positing a relationship between HR practices and sustainable competitive advantage, one must realize that people management systems might impact this advantage in a variety of ways.

For instance, these systems might play a role in creating cultures or mindsets that enable the maintenance of unique competencies (e.g., the safety record of DuPont). Or, these systems may promote and maintain socially complex relationships characterized by trust, knowledge sharing, and teamwork (e.g., Southwest Airlines' unique culture). Finally, these systems might have resulted in the creation of a high quality human capital pool that cannot be easily imitated because of time compression diseconomies (e.g., Merck's R&D capability). Whichever the case, it certainly calls for a more complex view of the relationship between HR and performance than is usually demonstrated within the empirical literature.

In addition to a more complex view, such grounding would imply different strategies for studying HR and competitive advantage. For instance, recognizing time compression diseconomies implies more longitudinal or at least historical approaches to examining competitive advantage as opposed to the more popular cross-sectional studies. Focusing on causal ambiguity and social complexity might suggest more qualitative approaches than simply asking subjects to report via survey about the HR practices that exist. In sum, strategic HRM research more strongly anchored in the RBV of the firm would look significantly different than what currently exists. However, such research would shed light on both HR and strategy issues.

Extending this further, strategists who embrace the RBV point out that competitive advantage (*vis-á-vis* core competence) comes from aligning skills, motives, and so forth with *organizational systems, structures, and processes* that achieve capabilities at the organizational level (Hamel & Prahalad, 1994; Peteraf, 1993; Teece, Pisano, & Shuen, 1997). Too frequently, HR researchers have acted as if organizational performance derives solely from the (aggregated) actions of individuals. But the RVB suggests that strategic resources are more complex than that, and more interesting. Companies that are good at product development and innovation, for example, don't simply have the most creative people who continually generate new ideas. Product development capabilities are imbedded in the organizational systems and processes. People execute those systems, but they are not independent from them. So while core competencies are knowledge-based, they are not solely human. They are comprised of human capital, social capital (i.e., internal/external relationships and exchanges), and organizational capital (i.e., processes, technologies, databases) (Snell, Youndt, & Wright, 1996).

That doesn't negate the importance of HR; it amplifies it and extends it. The RVB provides a broader foundation for exploring the impact of HR on strategic resources. In this context, HR is not limited to its direct effects on employee skills and behavior. Its effects are more encompassing in that they help weave those skills and behaviors within the broader fabric of organizational processes, systems and, ultimately, competencies.

Notwithstanding a great deal of room for development, it is clear from the preceding review that the conceptual and empirical application of the RBV has led to considerable advancement of the SHRM literature. In a broader sense, the RBV has impacted the field of HRM in two important ways. First, the RBV's influence has been instrumental in establishing a macro perspective in the field of HRM research (Snell *et al.*, 2001). This macro view has provided complimentary depth to a historically micro discipline rooted in psychology. Relatedly, a second major contribution of the RBV has been the theoretical and contextual grounding that it has provided to a field that has often been criticized for being atheoretical and excessively applied in nature (Snell *et al.*, 2001).

4.5 The Convergence of RBV and SHRM: Potential Mutual Contributions

Thus far, we have discussed how the RBV has contributed to the field of SHRM. As noted before, however, RBV has also effectively put "people" on the strategy radar screen (Snell *et al.*, 2001). In the search for competitive advantage, strategy researchers increasingly acknowledge human capital (Hitt, Bierman, Shimizu, & Kochhar, 2001), intellectual capital (Edvinsson & Malone, 1997) and knowledge (Grant, 1996; Liebeskind, 1996; Matusik & Hill, 1998) as critical components. In so doing, the RBV has provided an excellent platform for highlighting the importance of people to competitive advantage, and thus, the inescapable fact that RBV strategy researchers must bump up against people and/or HR issues.

In fact, recent developments within the field of strategy seem to evidence a converging of that field and SHRM (Snell *et al.*, 2001). It seems that these areas present unique opportunities for interdisciplinary research streams that provide significant leaps forward in the knowledge base. We will discuss the concept of core competencies, the focus on dynamic capabilities, and knowledge-based views of the firm as potential bridges between the HR and strategy literatures. We choose these concepts because of both their popularity within the strategy literature and their heavy reliance on HR related issues.

4.6 Core Competencies

Prahalad and Hamel (1990) certainly popularized the core competency concept within the strategy literature. They stated that core competencies are "... the collective learning in the organization, especially how to coordinate diverse production skills and integrate multiple streams of technologies" (p. 64), and that they involve "many levels of people and all functions" (p. 64). While the distinction between core competencies and capabilities (Stalk, Evans, & Schulman, 1992) seems blurred, one can hardly conceptualize a firm capability or competency absent the people who comprise them or the systems that maintain them.

For example, competencies or capabilities refer to organizational processes, engaged in by people, resulting in superior products, and generally these must endure over time as employees flow in, through and out of the firm. Numerous researchers within the strategy field focus on firm competencies (e.g., King & Zeithaml, 2001; Leonard-Barton, 1992, 1995). These researchers universally recognize the inseparability of the competence and the skills of the employees who comprise the competence. In addition, some (e.g., Leonard-Barton, 1992) specifically also recognize the behavioral aspect of these employees (i.e., their need to engage in behaviors that execute the competency) and the supportive nature of people management systems to the development/maintenance of the competency. However, often these treatments begin quite specifically when examining the competency and its competitive potential within the marketplace. However, they then sometimes become more generic and ambiguous as they delve into the more specific people-related concepts such as knowledges, skills, abilities, behaviors, and HR practices.

This illustrates the potential synergy that might result from deeper integration of the strategy and strategic HRM literatures. To deeply understand the competency one must examine (in addition to the systems and processes that underlie them) the people who engage in the process, the skills they individually and collectively must possess, and the behavior they must engage in (individually and interactively) to implement the process. In addition, to understand how such a competency can be developed or maintained requires at least in part examining the people management systems that ensure that the competency remains as specific employees leave and new employees must be brought in to replace them. This again exemplifies the interaction of people and processes as they comprise competencies.

Focusing on the people-related elements of a core competency provides a linking pin between the strategy and HR literatures. Traditional HR researchers refer to a "competence" as being a work related knowledge, skill, or ability (Nordhaug, 1993) held by an individual. This is not the same as the core competencies to which strategy researchers refer. Nordhaug and Gronhaug (1994) argue that firms possess individuals with different competences that they refer to as a portfolio of competences. They further propose that a core (or distinctive) competence exists when a firm is able to collaboratively blend the many competences in the portfolio, through a shared mindset, to better perform something than their competitors. For SHRM researchers, this implies a need to develop an understanding of firms, the activities in their value chains, and the relative superiority in value creation for each of these activities. For strategy researchers, it suggests a need to more deeply delve into the issues of the individuals and groups who comprise the competency, and the systems that develop and engage them to exhibit and maintain the competency. Lepak and Snell's (1999) model provides one tool for making this link between the firm's competency, the people that comprise it, and the systems that maintain it.

4.7 Dynamic Capabilities

The RBV has frequently focused on resources or competencies as a stable concept that can be identified at a point in time and will endure over time. The argument goes that when firms have bundles of resources that are valuable, rare, inimitable, and nonsubstitutable, they can implement value creating strategies not easily duplicated by competing firms (Barney, 1991; Conner & Prahalad, 1996; Peteraf, 1993; Wernerfelt, 1984, 1995).

However, recent attention has focused on the need for many organizations to constantly develop new capabilities or competencies in a dynamic environment (Teece, Pisano, & Schuen, 1997). Such capabilities have been referred to as "dynamic capabilities" which have been defined as:

> The firm's processes that use resources – specifically the processes to integrate, reconfigure, gain, and release resources – to match and even create market change. Dynamic capabilities thus are the organizational and strategic routines by which firms achieve new resource reconfigurations as markets emerge, collide, split, evolve, and die.   (Eisenhardt & Martin, 2000)

Such dynamic capabilities require that organizations establish processes that enable them to change their routines, services, products, and even markets over time. While in theory, one can easily posit how organizations must adapt to changing environmental contingencies, in reality changes of this magnitude are quite difficult to achieve, and the difficulty stems almost entirely from the human architecture of the firm. The firm may require different skill sets implying a release of some existing employees and acquisition of new employees. The change entails different organizational processes implying new networks and new behavioral repertoires of employees. The new skills and new behaviors theoretically must be driven by new administrative (i.e., HR) systems (Wright & Snell, 1998).

This implies the centrality of HR issues to the understanding and development of dynamic capabilities. This centrality is well articulated by Teece *et al.* (1997) who note:

> Indeed if control over scarce resources is the source of economic profits, then it follows that such issues as skill acquisition, the management of knowledge and know how and learning become fundamental strategic issues. It is in this second dimension, encompassing skill acquisition, learning and accumulation of organizational and intangible or invisible assets that we believe lies the greatest potential for contributions to strategy. (pp. 514–15)

4.8   Knowledge-Based Theories of the Firm

Unarguably, significant attention in the strategy literature within the RBV paradigm has focused on knowledge. Efforts to understand how firms generate, leverage, transfer, integrate and protect knowledge has moved to the forefront of the field (Hansen, 1999; Hedlund, 1994; Nonaka, 1991; Svieby, 1997; Szulanski, 1996). In fact, Grant (1996) argues for a knowledge-based theory of the firm, positing that firms exist because they better integrate and apply specialized knowledge than do markets. Liebeskind (1996) similarly believes in a knowledge-based theory of the firm, suggesting that firms exist because they can better protect knowledge from expropriation and imitation than can markets.

Interestingly, knowledge-centered strategy research inevitably confronts a number of HR issues. Knowledge management requires that firms define knowledge, identify existing knowledge bases, and provide mechanisms to promote the creation, protection, and transfer of knowledge (Argote & Ingram, 2000; Henderson & Cockburn, 1994; Liebeskind, 1996). While information systems provide a technological repository of knowledge, increasingly firms recognize that the key to successful knowledge management requires attending to the social and cultural systems of the organization (Conference Board, 2000).

Knowledge has long been a topic within the HR literature, whether the focus was on testing applicants for job-related knowledge (Hattrup & Schmitt, 1990), training employees to build their job-related knowledge (Gephart, Marsick, Van Buren, & Spiro, 1996), developing participation and communication systems to transfer knowledge (Cooke, 1994), or providing incentives for individuals to apply their knowledge (Gerhart, Milkovich, & Murray, 1992). The major distinctions between the strategy and HR literatures with regard to knowledge has to do with the focus of the knowledge and its level. While the HR literature has focused on job-related knowledge, the strategy literature has focused on more market-relevant knowledge, such as knowledge regarding customers, competitors, or knowledge relevant to the creation of new products (Grant, 1996; Liebeskind, 1996).

In addition, while HR literature tends to treat knowledge as an individual phenomenon, the strategy and organizational literatures view it more broadly as organizationally shared, accessible, and transferable (cf., Argyris & Schon, 1978; Brown & Duguid, 1991; Snell, Stueber, & Lepak, 2001). Knowledge can be viewed as something that characterizes individuals (i.e., human capital), but it can also be shared within groups or networks (i.e., social capital) or institutionalized within organization processes and databases (organizational capital).

These distinctions represent something of a departure for HR researchers. However, the processes of creation, transfer, and exploitation of knowledge provide common ground across the two fields, again highlighting their potential convergence within the RBV paradigm. Although theorists such as Argyris and Schon (1978) argue that all learning begins at the individual level, it is conditioned by the social context and routines within organizations (Nonaka & Takeuchi, 1995). Coleman (1988), for example, noted that social capital has an important influence on the creation of human capital. What seems clear is that these different "knowledge repositories" complement and influence one another in defining an organization's capabilities (Youndt & Snell, 2001).

But there are substantial differences between HR systems that support individual learning and those that support organizational learning. Leonard-Barton (1992), for example, noted that organizational learning and innovation were built on four inter-related processes and their related values: (1) owning/solving problems (egalitarianism), (2) integrating internal knowledge (shared knowledge), (3) continuous experimentation (positive risk), and (4) integrating external knowledge (openness to outside). Each of these processes and values works systemically with the others to inculcate organizational learning and innovation. Each process/value combination is in turn supported by different administrative (HR) systems that incorporate elements of staffing, job design, training, career management, rewards, and appraisal. Again, the concept of knowledge brings together the fields of strategy and HR. But a good deal more work needs to be done to integrate these research streams. Strategy theory and research provides the basis for understanding the value of knowledge to the firm and highlights the need to manage it. The HR field has lacked such a perspective, but has provided more theory and research regarding how knowledge is generated, retained, and transferred among individuals comprising the firm.

4.9 Integrating Strategy and SHRM within the RBV

We have discussed the concepts of core competencies, dynamic capabilities, and knowledge as bridge constructs connecting the fields of strategy and SHRM. We proposed that both fields could benefit greatly from sharing respective areas of expertise. In fact, at the risk of oversimplification, the strategy literature has generated significant amounts of knowledge regarding who (i.e., employees/executives or groups of employees/executives) provides sources of competitive advantage and why. However, absent from that literature are specific techniques for attracting, developing, motivating, maintaining, or retaining these people. SHRM, on the other hand has generated knowledge regarding the attraction, development, motivation, maintenance, and retention of people. However, it has not been particularly successful yet at identifying who the focus of these systems should be on and why.

The strategy literature has also highlighted the importance of the stock and flow of knowledge for competitive advantage. However, it has not explored in great detail the role that individuals as well as their interactions with others contribute to this. Conversely SHRM has missed much of the organizational view of knowledge, but can provide significant guidance regarding the role that individuals play.

This state of affairs calls for greater integration between these two fields. Figure 4.2 illustrates this potential integration. Overall, the figure depicts people management systems at the left, core competencies at the right, intellectual capital and knowledge management as the bridge concepts between the two, and dynamic capability as a renewal component that ties all four concepts over time.

Note that the basic constructs laid out in Fig. 4.1 still appear in this expanded model, yet with a much more detailed set of variables. At the right-hand side of the model we place the people management systems construct. This placement does not imply that all competitive advantage begins with people management systems, but rather, that this represents the focus of the HR field. We suggest that these people management systems create value to the extent that they impact the stock, flow, and change of intellectual capital/knowledge that form the basis of core competencies.

Rather than simply focusing on the concepts of "skills" and "behavior" we propose a more detailed analysis with regard to the stock and flow of knowledge. To this end we suggest that the "skill" concept might be expanded to consider the stock of intellectual capital in the firm, embedded in both people and systems. This stock of human capital consists of human (the knowledge skills, and abilities of people), social (the valuable relationships among people), and organizational capital (the processes and routines

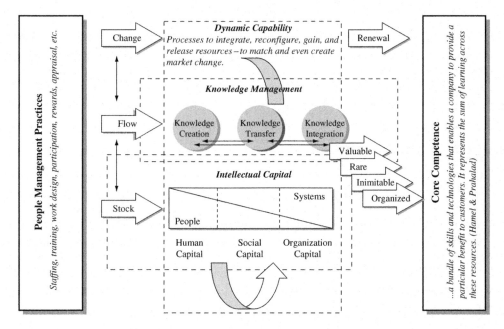

Figure 4.2 A model for integration strategy and strategic HRM.

within the firm). It broadens the traditional HR focus beyond simply the people to explore the larger processes and systems that exist within the firm.

The "behavior" concept within the SHRM literature can similarly be reconceptualized as the flow of knowledge within the firm through its creation, transfer, and integration. This "knowledge management" behavior becomes increasingly important as information and knowledge play a greater role in firm competitive advantage. It is through the flow of knowledge that firms increase or maintain the stock of intellectual capital.

At the right-hand side of the model we place the core competence, one of the major foci of the strategy literature. We propose that this core competence arises from the combination of the firm's stock of knowledge (human, social, and organizational capital embedded in both people and systems) and the flow of this knowledge though creation, transfer, and integration in a way that is valuable, rare, inimitable, and organized. This provides a framework for more specifically exploring the human component to core competencies, and provides a basis for exploring the linkage between people management systems and core competencies through the management of a firm's stock and flow of knowledge.

Finally, the dynamic capability construct illustrates the interdependent interplay between the workforce and the core competence as it changes overtime. It represents the renewal process that organizations must undergo to remain competitive. Dynamic capability requires changing competencies on the part of both the organization and the people who comprise it. It is facilitated by people management systems that promote the change of both the stock and flow of knowledge within the firm that enables the firm to constantly renew its core competencies.

This model by no means serves as a well-developed theoretical framework, but rather simply seeks to point to the areas for collaboration between strategy and SHRM researchers. These two fields share common interests in issues and yet bring complementary skills, knowledge, and perspectives to these issues. The RBV highlights these common interests and provides a framework for developing collaborative effort.

4.10   Conclusion

The RBV has significantly and independently influenced the fields of strategy and SHRM. More importantly, however, it has provided a theoretical bridge between these two fields. By turning attention toward the internal resources, capabilities and competencies of the firm such as knowledge, learning, and dynamic capabilities (Hoskisson *et al.*, 1999), it has brought strategy researchers to inescapably face a number of issues with regard to the management of people (Barney, 1996). We would guess that few strategy researchers are well versed in the existing research base regarding the effectiveness of various specific HR tools and techniques for managing people, and thus in addressing these issues with necessary specificity.

This internal focus also has provided the traditionally atheoretical field of SHRM with a theoretical foundation from which it can begin exploring the strategic role that people and HR functions can play in organizations (Wright & McMahan, 1992). In addition to the lack of theory, this literature has also displayed little, or at least an overly simplistic view of strategy, thus limiting its ability to contribute to the strategy literature (Chadwick & Cappelli, 1998). The RBV provides the framework from which HR researchers and practitioners can better understand the challenges of strategy, and thus be better able to play a positive role in the strategic management of firms.

We propose that both fields will benefit from greater levels of interaction in the future. This interaction should be deeper than simply reading each other's literature, but rather organizing conferences aimed at promoting face-to-face discussions of the common issues and challenges. In fact, we believe that future interdisciplinary research studies conducted jointly by strategy and SHRM researchers would exploit the unique knowledge and expertise of both fields, and synergistically contribute to the generation of new knowledge regarding the roles that people play in organizational competitive advantage.

REFERENCES

Argote, L., & Ingram, P. (2000). Knowledge transfer: A basis for competitive advantage in firms. *Organizational Behavior and Human Decision Processes*, 82 (1), 150–69.

Argyris, C., & Schon, D. A. (1978). *Organizational learning: A theory of action perspective*. Reading, MA: Addison-Wesley.

Arthur, J. B. (1994). Effects of human resource systems on manufacturing performance and turnover. *Academy of Management Journal*, 37 (3), 670–87.

Barney, J. (1991). Firm resources and sustained competitive advantage. *Journal of Management*, *17*(1), 99–120.

Barney, J. (1996). The resource-based theory of the firm. *Organizational Science*, *7*, 469.

Barney, J. (2001). Is the resource-based view a useful perspective for strategic management research? Yes. *Academy of Management Review*, *26*, 41–56.

Baron, J. N., Davis-Blake, A., & Bielby, W. T. (1986). The structure of opportunity: How promotion ladders vary within and among organizations. *Administrative Science Quarterly*, *31*, 248–73.

Becker, B. E., & Huselid, M. A. (1998). High performance work systems and firm performance: A synthesis of research and managerial applications. *Research in Personnel and Human Resources Management*, *16*, 53–101.

Boxall, P. F. (1996). The Strategic HRM debate and the resource-based view of the firm. *Human Resource Management Journal*, *6*(3), 59–75.

Boxall, P. F. (1998). Human resource strategy and industry-based competition: A conceptual framework and agenda for theoretical development. In P. M. Wright, L. D. Dyer, J. W. Boudreau, & G. T. Milkovich (eds.), *Research in personnel and human resources management* (Suppl. 4, pp. 1–29). Madison, WI: IRRA.

Boxall, P. F., & Steeneveld, M. (1999). Human resource strategy and competitive advantage: A longitudinal study of engineering consultancies. *Journal of Management Studies*, *36*(4), 443–63.

Brown, J. S., & Duguid, P. (1991). Organizational learning and communities-of-practice: Toward a unified view of working, learning, and innovation. *Organizational Science*, *2*, 40–57.

Cappelli, P., & Singh, H. (1992). Integrating strategic human resources and strategic management. In D. Lewin, O. S. Mitchell, & P. D. Sherer (eds.), *Research frontiers in industrial relations and human resources* (pp. 165–92). Madison, WI: IRRA.

Chadwick, C., & Cappelli, P. (1998). Alternatives to generic strategy typologies in strategic human resource management. In P. M. Wright, L. D. Dyer, J. W. Boudreau, & G. T. Milkovich (eds.), *Research in personnel and human resources management* (Suppl. 4, pp. 1–29). Greenwich, CT: JAI Press, Inc.

Coleman, J. S. (1988). Social capital in the creation of human capital. *American Journal of Sociology*, *94*, s95–120.

Conference Board. (2000). *Beyond knowledge management: New ways to work*. Research Report 1262-00RR.

Conner, K. R., & Prahalad, C. K. (1996). A resource-based theory of the firm: Knowledge versus opportunism. *Organization Science*, *7*, 477–501.

Cooke, W. (1994). Employee participation programs, group-based incentives, and company performance: A union–nonunion comparison. *Industrial and Labor Relations Review*, *47*, 594–609.

Devanna, M. A., Fombrun, C. J., & Tichy, N. M. (1984). A framework for strategic human resource management, *Strategic Human Resource Management* (Chapt. 3, pp. 33–51). New York: Wiley.

Dierickx, I., & Cool, K. (1989). Asset stock accumulation and sustainability of competitive advantage. *Management Science*, *35*, 1504–11.

Drucker, P. (1954). *The practice of management*. New York: Harper.

Edvinsson, L., & Malone, M. (1997). *Intellectual capital*. Cambridge, MA: Harvard Business School Press.

Eisenhardt, K. M., & Martin, J. A. (2000). Dynamic capabilities: What are they? *Strategic Management Journal*, *21*, 1105–21.

Finkelstein, S., & Hambrick, D. (1996). *Strategic leadership: Top executives and their effects on organizations*. Minneapolis/St. Paul: West Pub. Co.

Fiol, C. M., & Lyles, M. A. (1985). Organizational learning. *Academy of Management Review*, *10*, 803–13.

Fisher, S. R., & White, M. A. (2000). Downsizing in a learning organization: Are there hidden costs? *Academy of Management Review, 25* (1), 244–51.

Gardner, T. M., Wright, P. M., & Gerhart, B. (2000). The HR–firm performance relationship: Can it be in the mind of the beholder? Working Paper, Center for Advanced Human Resource Studies, Cornell University.

Gephart, M., Marsick, V., Van Buren, M., & Spiro, M. (1996). Learning organizations come alive. *Training and Development, 50*, 34–5.

Gerhart, B., Milkovich, G., & Murray, B. (1992). Pay, performance and participation. In D. Lewin, O. Mitchell, & P. Sherer (eds.), *Research frontiers in industrial relations and human resources.* Madison, WI: IRRA.

Gerhart, B., Wright, P. M., McMahan, G. C., & Snell, S. A. (2000). Measurement error in research on human resources and firm performance: How much error is there and how does it influence effect size estimates? *Personnel Psychology, 53*, 803–34.

Godfrey, P. C., & Hill, C. W. L. (1995). The problem of unobservables in strategic management research. *Strategic Management Journal, 16*, 519–33.

Grant, R. M. (1996). Toward a knowledge-based theory of the firm. *Strategic Management Journal, 17* (Winter Special Issue), 108–22.

Hamel, G., & Prahalad, C. K. (1994). Competing for the future. *Harvard Business Review, 72* (4), 122–29.

Hansen, M. T. (1999). The search-transfer problem: The role of weak ties in sharing knowledge across organization sub units. *Administrative Science Quarterly, 44* (March), 82–111.

Hedlund, G. (1994). A model of knowledge management and the N-form corporation. *Strategic Management Journal, 15*, 73–90.

Hattrup, K., & Schmitt, N. (1990). Prediction of trades apprentices' performance on job sample criteria. *Personnel Psychology, 43*, 453–67.

Henderson, R., & Cockburn, I. (1994). Measuring competence? Exploring firm effects in pharmaceutical research. *Strategic Management Research, 15*, 63–84.

Hitt, M. A., Bierman, L., Shimizu, K., & Kochhar, R. (2001). Direct and moderating effects of human capital on the strategy and performance in professional service firms: A resource-based perspective. *Academy of Management Journal, 44*, 13–28.

Hoskisson, R. E., Hitt, M. A., Wan, W. P., & Yiu, D. (1999). Theory and research in strategic management: Swings of a pendulum. *Strategic Management Journal, 25* (3), 417–56.

Huselid, M. A. (1995). The impact of human resource management practices on turnover, productivity, and corporate financial performance. *Academy of Management Journal, 38* (3), 635–72.

King, A. W., & Zeithaml, C. P. (2001). Competencies and firm performance: Examining the causal ambiguity paradox. *Strategic Management Journal, 22*, 75–99.

Koch, M. J., & McGrath, R. G. (1996). Improving labor productivity: Human resource management policies do matter. *Strategic Management Journal, 17*, 335–54.

Lado, A. A., & Wilson, M. C. (1994). Human resource systems and sustained competitive advantage: A competency-based perspective. *Academy of Management Review, 19* (4), 699–727.

Leonard-Barton, D. (1992). The factory as a learning laboratory. *Sloan Management Review, 34* (1), 23–38.

Leonard-Barton, D. (1995). *Wellsprings of Knowledge.* Boston: Harvard Business School Press.

Lepak, D. P., & Snell, S. A. (1999). The human resource architecture: Toward a theory of human capital allocation and development. *Academy of Management Review, 24*, 31–48.

Lepak, D. P., & Snell, S. A. (2002). Examining the human resource architecture: The relationships among human capital, employment, and human resource configurations. *Journal of Management, 28*, 517–43.

Lepak, D. P., Takeuchi, R., & Snell, S. A. (2001). An empirical examination of employment mode use and firm performance. Working paper, University of Maryland.

Liebeskind, J. P. (1996). Knowledge, strategy, and the theory of the firm. *Strategic Management Journal, 17* (Winter Special Issue), 93–107.

March, J., & Simon, H. (1958). *Organizations.* New York: Wiley.

MacDuffie, J. P. (1995). Human resource bundles and manufacturing performance: Organizational logic and flexible production systems in the world auto industry. *Industrial & Labor Relations Review, 48* (2), 197–221.

Matusik, S. F., & Hill, C. W. L. (1998). The utilization of contingent work, knowledge creation, and competitive advantage. *Academy of Management Review, 23*, 680–97.

McMahan, G. C., Virick, M., & Wright, P. M. (1999). Alternative theoretical perspective for strategic human resource management revisited: Progress, problems, and prospects. In P. M. Wright, L. D. Dyer, J. W. Boudreau, & G. T. Milkovich (eds.), *Research in personnel and human resources management* (Suppl. 4, pp. 99–122). Greenwich, CT: JAI Press, Inc.

Miles, R. E., & Snow, C. C. (1978). Organizational strategy, structure and process. New York: McGraw-Hill.

Miles, R. E., & Snow, C. C. (1984). Designing strategic human resources systems. *Organizational Dynamics*, Summer, 36–52.

Nonaka, I. (1991). The knowledge creating company. *Harvard Business Review, 69* (6), 96–104.

Nonaka, I., & Takeuchi, H. (1995). *The knowledge-creating company: How Japanese companies create the dynamics of innovation.* New York: Oxford Press.

Norburn, D., & Birley, S. (1988). The top management team and corporate performance. *Strategic Management Journal, 9*, 225–37.

Nordhaug, O. (1993). *Human capital in organizations: Competence, training and learning.* Oslo/London: Scandanavian University Press/Oxford University Press.

Nordhaug, O., & Gronhaug, K. (1994). Competences as resources in firms. *The International Journal of Human Resource Management, 5* (1), 89–106.

Osterman, P. (1987). Choice of employment systems in internal labor markets. *Industrial Relations, 26* (1), 48–63.

Penrose, E. T. (1959). *The theory of the growth of the firm.* New York: Wiley.

Peteraf, M. A. (1993). The cornerstones of competitive advantage: A resource based view. *Strategic Management Journal, 14*, 179–91.

Porter, M. E. (1980). *Competitive strategy.* New York: Free Press, pp. 34–46.

Prahalad, C. K., & Hamel, G. (1990). The core competence of the corporation. *Harvard Business Review*, May/June, 79–91.

Priem, R. L., & Butler, J. E. (2001a). Is the resource based "view" a useful perspective for strategic management research? *Academy of Management Review, 26* (1), 22–40.

Priem, R. L., & Butler, J. E. (2001b). Tautology in the resource based view and the implications of externally determined resource value: Further comments. *Academy of Management Review, 26* (1), 57–66.

Richard, O. C. (2001). Racial diversity, business strategy, and firm performance: A resource-based view. *Academy of Management Journal, 43* (2), 164–77.

Rumelt, R. (1984). Toward a strategic theory of the firm. In R. Lamb (ed.), *Competitive strategic management* (pp. 556–70). Englewood Cliffs, NJ: Prentice-Hall.

Schuler, R. S. & Jackson, S. E. (1987). Linking competitive strategies with human resource practices. Academy of Management Executive, 1 (3), 207–20.

Snell, S. A., Shadur, M. A., & Wright, P. M. (2001). The era of our ways. In M. A. Hitt, R. E. Freeman, & J. S. Harrison (eds.), Handbook of strategic management (pp. 627–9). Oxford: Blackwell Publishing.

Snell, S. A., Stueber, D., & Lepak, D. P. (2001). Virtual HR departments: Getting out of the middle. In Robert L. Heneman & David B. Greenberger, Human resource management in virtual organizations (Information Age Publishing).

Snell, S. A., Youndt, M. A., & Wright, P. M. (1996). Establishing a framework for research in strategic human resource management: Merging resource theory and organizational learning. In G. Ferris (ed.), Research in personnel and human resources management (Vol. 14, pp. 61–90).

Stalk, G., Evans, P., & Schulman, L. (1992). Competing on capabilities: The new rules of corporate strategy. Harvard Business Review, 70, 57–69.

Stewart, T. A. (1996). Human resources bites back. Fortune, May, 175.

Svieby, K. E. (1997). The new organizational wealth: Managing and measuring knowledge based assets. San Francisco: Berrett-Koehler.

Szulanski, G. (1996). Exploring internal stickiness: impediments to the transfer of best practice within the firm. Strategic Management Journal, 17 (Winter Special Issue), 27–43.

Teece, D. J., Pisano, G., & Shuen, A. (1997). Dynamic capabilities and strategic management. Strategic Management Journal, 18 (7), 509–33.

Thomas, A. B. (1988). Does leadership make a difference in organizational performance? Administrative Science Quarterly, 33, 388–400.

Truss, C., & Gratton, L. (1994). Strategic human resource management: A conceptual approach. International Journal of Human Resource Management, 5, 663–86.

Tsui, A. S., Pearce, J. L., Porter, L. W., & Tripoli, A. M. (1997). Alternative approaches to the employee–organization relationship: Does investment in employees pay off? Academy of Management Journal, 40, 1089–121.

Walker, J. (1978). Linking human resource planning and strategic planning. Human Resource Planning, 1, 1–18.

Wernerfelt, B. (1984). A resource-based view of the firm. Strategic Management Journal, 5, 171–80.

Wernerfelt, B. (1995). The resource based view of the firm: Ten years after. Strategic Management Journal, 16, 171–4.

Wright, P. M., & Boswell, W. (2002). Desegregating HRM: A review and synthesis of micro and macro human resource management research. Journal of Management, 28, 247–76.

Wright, P. M., & Gardner, T. M. (2003). Theoretical and empirical challenges in studying the HR practice–firm performance relationship. In D. Holman, T. Wall, C. Clegg, P. Sparrow, & A. Howard (eds.), The new workplace: People, technology, and organisation. New York: John Wiley and Sons, pp. 311–28.

Wright, P. M., Gardner, T. M., Moynihan, L. M., Park, H., Gerhart, B., & Delery, J. (2001). Measurement error in research on human resources and firm performance. Additional data and suggestions for future research. Personnel Psychology, 54, 875–902.

Wright, P. M., McCormick, B., Sherman, W. S., & McMahan, G. C. (1999). The role of human resources practices in petro-chemical refinery performance. The International Journal of Human Resource Management, 10, 551–71.

Wright, P. M., & McMahan, G. C. (1992). Theoretical perspectives for strategic human resource management. Journal of Management, 18 (2), 295–320.

Wright, P. M., McMahan, G. C., & McWilliams, A. (1994). Human resources and sustained competitive advantage: A resource-based perspective. *International Journal of Human Resource Management*, 5 (2), 301–26.

Wright, P. M., Smart, D. L., & McMahan, G. C. (1995). Matches between human resources and strategy among NCAA basketball teams. *Academy of Management Journal*, 38 (4), 1052–74.

Wright, P. M., & Snell, S. A. (1991). Toward an integrative view of strategic human resource management. *Human Resource Management Review*, 1 (3), 203–25.

Wright, P. M., & Snell, S. A. (1998). Toward a unifying framework for exploring fit and flexibility in strategic human resource management. *Academy of Management Review*, 23 (4), 756–72.

Youndt, M. A., & Snell, S. A. (2001). Human resource management, intellectual capital, and organizational performance. Working Paper, Skidmore College.

Chapter 5

The Complex Resource-Based View: Implications for Theory and Practice in Strategic Human Resource Management

Barry A. Colbert

Much of the writing in the field of SHRM has been concerned with either practical advice or presentation of empirical data. Without good theory, the field of SHRM could be characterized as a plethora of statements regarding empirical relationships and/or prescriptions for practice that fail to explain why these relationships exist or should exist. If, in fact, the criticism that the field of SHRM lacks a strong theoretical foundation is true, then this could undermine the ability of both practitioners and researchers to fully use human resources in support of firm strategy.   (Wright & McMahan, 1992: 297)

Made over a decade ago, this call for theory in strategic human resource management (SHRM) continues to ring through the literature in the field (Delery, 1998; Snell, Youndt, & Wright, 1996; Ulrich, 1997a). Rich, integrated theoretical frameworks will help focus and organize research efforts and will enable the practice of HR management to become a truly strategic discipline (Ulrich, 1997b). SHRM is predicated on two fundamental assertions. First is the idea that an organization's human resources are of critical strategic importance – that the skills, behaviors, and interactions of employees have the potential to provide both the foundation for strategy formulation and the means for strategy implementation. Second is the belief that a

B. A. Colbert, "The Complex Resource-Based View: Implications for Theory and Practice in Strategic Human Resource Management," *Academy of Management Review*, Vol. 29, No. 3 (2004): 341–58.

firm's HRM practices are instrumental in developing the strategic capability of its pool of human resources. A stronger theoretical foundation will help to affirm the first assertion, connect it to the second, and improve the focus and effectiveness of HRM research and practice, and it will help organizations to thrive more effectively in their particular operating contexts.

The basic precepts of SHRM have a natural affinity with the resource-based view (RBV) of competitive advantage in the strategy field (Barney, 1991; Grant, 1991; Wernerfelt, 1984). Proponents of the RBV argue that sustained competitive advantage can originate in a firm's resource base, and thereby draw attention to the internal workings of an organization. This view places more emphasis on the role of managers in the selection, development, combination, and deployment of a firm's resources, and not merely on selecting its competitive position in the operating environment.

The RBV has formed an integrating ground or "backdrop" for most of the work in SHRM over the past decade (Delery, 1998; Wright, Dunford & Snell, 2001). While the RBV has been helpful and relevant to the field of SHRM, there are aspects of the view that scholars have deemed critical but that are difficult to deal with in research and practice. This chapter extends the RBV by considering some of its difficult aspects through the lens of complexity (Kauffman, 1992; Kelly, 1994). Complexity as a research field includes the study of *complex adaptive systems*, in the many forms in which they appear: economies, ecosystems, thermodynamical systems, or computer-generated genetic algorithms, for example. The defining characteristics of such systems are that they are composed of large numbers of agents in linear and nonlinear relationships, and they exhibit emergent properties and order.

My purpose in this chapter is to consider the implications for research and practice in SHRM of a complex, living-systems extension of the RBV. I do so by demonstrating that concepts from complexity align well with many of the critical but difficult aspects of the RBV. Several of these difficult aspects, such as causal ambiguity, social complexity, and system-level resources, explicitly invite a more complex, less reductive view of organizations. This is useful for two reasons. First, it allows us to reframe the RBV in a way that admits some of its more important strategic aspects. Second, it sets the ground for the integration of a complexity view into the major modes of theorizing in SHRM. I present an integrated framework for SHRM that allows an application of complexity principles at the appropriate level of abstraction in the HR system.

Essential Contributions of the Paper

Wright *et al.* (2001) point out that the RBV has played a key role in legitimating the relevance of HRM to strategy research. By extending the RBV via a complexity lens, this chapter offers two conclusions that are relevant to SHRM. First, it suggests that some of the difficult aspects of RBV/SHRM research are made difficult by the way we approach them. Causal ambiguity, for example, is only problematic when we endeavor to disentangle the complex causal interactions in an organization's social system. If we accept that unpredictability and emergent properties are key features of complex systems, our focus shifts away from testing the effects of discrete HR practices (e.g. recruitment tactics, pay schemes) and toward consideration of processes by which the elements of the social system (e.g. the intentions, choices, and actions of people in the system) mingle and interact. Second, this chapter opens a potential avenue of research in SHRM through a focus on the HR system as a coherent whole, with managerial leverage points centered mainly at the HR *principles* level of the HR architecture.

The chapter proceeds as follows. First is an overview of the key questions in SHRM, including the role of the RBV as an integrating ground for HRM research. I then present a framework to describe the general shape of existing research in SHRM and the potential opportunities for extending the conceptual range of the field. Some critical but difficult aspects of the RBV are outlined to demonstrate consonance with a complexity view in order to make a case for applying complexity to SHRM. After this, I describe some key features of complexity and use living-systems principles from complexity to inform the principles level of the HR system architecture. The chapter closes with some ideas for future research.

Applied Domain: SHRM

In this section I outline some of the key questions in SHRM against the integrating ground of the RBV in strategy. I then draw together two concepts put forward independently in SHRM – specifically, the ideas of *modes of theorizing* in HRM research and the *levels of abstraction* in the HR system addressed by researchers. Integration of these two concepts will set the ground for extending both the RBV and SHRM research via complexity.

Key questions in SHRM

Research on the contribution of human resources (people) and HRM (practices) to organizational effectiveness has addressed a wide array of questions: What is the effect of HR practices on the development of a firm's human resources? Which HR practices lead to greater organizational performance? To what degree does that depend on firm strategy? How does a firm ensure that its HR practices "fit" with its strategy? How does it ensure that its individual HR practices fit with one another, or does fit even matter in HR practice? Must the attributes of a firm's base of human resources always align with an *a priori* strategy, or can its stock of skills, knowledge, and interactions *drive* strategic direction?

The key constructs and central debates in SHRM have grown out of the above questions: best practices versus fit (Becker & Gerhart, 1996), horizontal and vertical fit (Schuler & Jackson, 1987), fit versus flexibility (Wright & Snell, 1998), control-exerting versus creativity-enhancing aspects of HR systems (Snell *et al.*, 1996), univariate and multivariate effects (Doty, Glick & Huber, 1993), and appropriate theoretical frames (Delery, 1998; Delery & Doty, 1996; Lepak & Snell, 1999; Wright & McMahan, 1992). What is common to all of this work is a focus on the links among HR practices, the human resource pool, and organizational outcomes. At its heart, the key strategic questions for HRM research and HR practice are process questions, which tie practices to resource characteristics to organizational outcomes:

- How does a firm ensure resources are aligned to support current strategies, are adaptable to new strategies, and are able to influence new strategic directions?
- How does a firm actively build and continuously renew strategic human and organizational resources to fuel competitive advantage?

The RBV: an integrating ground for SHRM

These essential questions have been examined using a variety of perspectives drawn from organization theory, including institutional theory (Wright & McMahan, 1992), contingency theory (Lengnick-Hall & Lengnick-Hall, 1988), configurational approaches (Doty *et al.*, 1993), transaction cost analysis (Jones, 1984), behavioral perspectives (Schuler & Jackson, 1987), and organizational learning (Snell *et al.*, 1996). Some of these approaches are used centrally and frequently and others more tangentially and infrequently. The most prevalent perspective, often applied in conjunction with other frameworks, is the RBV of the firm (Barney, 1991, 1992; Barney & Wright, 1998; Lado & Wilson, 1994; Snell *et al.*, 1996; Wright, McMahan, & McWilliams, 1994). The RBV has helped to build a productive theoretical bridge between the fields of strategy and HRM (Wright *et al.*, 2001), and it serves as a backdrop (Delery, 1998) or integrating ground against which much of SHRM theory and research is presented.

The RBV states that a firm develops competitive advantage by not only acquiring but also developing, combining, and effectively deploying its *physical, human*, and *organizational* resources in ways that add unique value and are difficult for competitors to imitate (Barney, 1991). Most resource-based arguments are rooted in human resources – the skills, knowledge, and behavior of employees – or organizational resources – control systems, routines, and learning mechanisms – that are products of complex social structures built over time and, thus, are difficult to understand and imitate (Amit & Schoemaker, 1993; Barney, 1991, 1992; Conner, 1991; Mahoney & Pandian, 1992; Oliver, 1997; Peteraf, 1993). The strong and obvious connection to the RBV serves the SHRM field in two ways: (1) it foregrounds the role of human resources in questions of strategy, raising the importance of research and practice in SHRM, and (2) it encourages a more relevant focus for HRM, away from the HR practices themselves and toward their effect on firm resources (Delery, 1998; Wright *et al.*, 2001).

Following an examination of two theoretical frameworks in SHRM, I highlight particular aspects of the RBV that suggest complexity concepts could help in reframing some difficulties with the approach.

Dimensions for theory in SHRM

The framework constructed here draws together two useful concepts presented in the SHRM literature. The first is the idea of implicit *modes of theorizing* embedded in the SHRM field. Delery and Doty (1996) have identified three modes – *universalistic, contingency*, and *configurational* – discernible across a broad body of research, although not always explicitly acknowledged by the respective authors. The second concept is one of the *levels of abstraction* in the HR system, including *principles, policies*, and *practices*, over which theoretical constructs are often arrayed, also typically unacknowledged by the respective authors (Becker & Gerhart, 1996; Schuler, 1987; Wright, 1998). By bringing these two concepts together against the backdrop of the RBV, we can identify the room for contribution of ideas from complexity. It should be noted at the outset that this framework is most useful in delineating the general contours of the research in the field and identifying opportunities for advancement; I do not assert that every piece of research fits uniquely into one cell or another of framework.

Modes of theorizing in HR research

Delery and Doty (1996) have identified and contrasted universalistic, contingency, and configurational explanations of the effect of HR practices on organizational performance, with a slightly varying definition of "strategic HR practices" under each. The main differentiating characteristic across these categories is the level of system complexity assumed by the researcher and the capacity of various research approaches for modeling system complexity. Universalistic approaches pay little attention to interaction effects among organizational variables, a contingency perspective begins to allow for such effects, and the configurational school sees system interaction effects as critically important.

Universalistic perspective

Universalistic or "best-practice" approaches assert that certain independent-dependent variable relationships hold across whole populations of organizations – that is, some HR practices are always better than others, and all organizations should adopt them (Miles & Snow, 1984; Pfeffer, 1994). Under a universalistic approach, "strategic HR practices" are those that are found to consistently lead to higher organizational performance, independent of an organization's strategy. Examples are such practices as formal training systems, profit sharing, voice mechanisms, and job definition. One might argue that these are not strategic in the sense used elsewhere in the SHRM literature (i.e., contingent on strategy or explicitly aligned with specific strategy) and may simply be termed *prudent*, in the sense that they have been shown to consistently enable a given firm to perform better than it might otherwise.

Work in the universalistic perspective is largely unconcerned with interaction effects among organizational variables and implicitly assumes that the effects of HR variables are additive (e.g. Gerhart & Milkovich, 1990). Such a reductive, linear view of an organizational system ignores the notion of system-level resources – an important factor in the RBV. That is not to say that the insights provided by such approaches are not valuable; rather, they are only limited. Delery and Doty (1996) found strong empirical support for the universalistic perspective for some of their hypothesized variables.

Research under this perspective has been useful in identifying discrete HR practices that are universally sensible, but it has not contributed much to HRM in the strategic sense, if we take strategic to mean practices that differentiate the firm in its industry and that lead to sustainable competitive advantage. Practices that are universally adopted would have isomorphic rather than differentiating effects on competing firms. As such, the organization theory that best frames the best-practice approach is institutional theory (Baum, 1996; DiMaggio & Powell, 1983), which describes forces leading to a tendency to "sameness" across firms.

Contingency perspective

The contingency perspective goes beyond the simple, linear, causal relationships explored in universal theories and allows for interaction effects and varying relationships depending on the presence of a contingent variable – most often firm strategy. The task of the researcher is to select a theory of firm strategy and then specify how individual HR practices will interact with that strategy to result in higher organizational performance (e.g. see Fombrun, Tichy, & Devanna, 1984, and Schuler & Jackson, 1987). Effectiveness of HR practices is contingent on how well they mesh with other aspects of the organization (e.g. what discrete HR policies would be most appropriate if an organization were to pursue a low-cost strategy or wanted to encourage new product innovation). A contingency perspective draws a causal line from the HR policies and practices to the organizational performance metrics, and it allows for the moderating effects of strategy. The primary concern is with vertical fit (alignment with strategy) rather than horizontal fit (HR practices hanging together as a coherent, self-reinforcing system). While this mode directs attention toward effects among variables, internal system interaction effects are not a central concern.

Configurational perspective

The configurational school in organization studies follows a holistic principle of inquiry and is concerned with how patterns of multiple interdependent variables relate to a given dependent variable (Meyer, Tsui, & Hinings, 1993; Miller & Friesen, 1984). Researchers gather multiple dimensions of organizations, such as strategies, structures, cultures, and processes, into typologies of ideal types and treat the types as independent variables. This goes beyond the contingency approach, in which "researchers have been preoccupied with abstracting a limited set of structural concepts – centralization and formalization, for example – and measuring their relationships with a limited set of abstracted situational concepts, such as size, and technological uncertainty" (Meyer et al., 1993: 1175). A configurational view focuses on *patterns* of HR practices that together form an internally consistent whole (i.e., their effects are mutually reinforcing) and draws a correlation between those patterns and organizational performance (Doty & Glick, 1994).

The purported advantage of the configurational perspective is that it acknowledges system interaction effects – that the whole may be more or less than the sum of its parts. One significant shortcoming is that it is typically unmanageable to construct and test more than a few configurations, which understates the real-world complexity of organizational systems.

Levels of abstraction in the HR system

Becker and Gerhart (1996) have argued for clarity on the level of policy under examination – *HR principles, HR policies,* or *HR practices,* for instance–and proposed that an architectural approach be taken to understand the effects of HR system components on organization-level outcomes. Wright (1998) termed this distinction the *level of abstraction* at which HR is conceptualized and added the *product* level to capture the intended effects of the other three, usually in terms of the behavior of individuals, groups, or the organization. The notion of levels of abstraction differs from the notion of levels of analysis in organization studies, although both are grounds for caution and care by researchers. Where the latter normally denotes the structural level of a theoretical construct, such as individual, group, organization, or industry (Rousseau, 1985), the former is concerned with the level of thought abstraction under consideration and the associated construct definitions. Becker and Gerhart (1996) suggest that perhaps the mixed and conflicting results in HRM research are attributable to confusion in construct definition across the levels of abstraction.

An illustrative example makes this concept clear. A firm might adopt the guiding *HR principle* that "employee participation in all aspects of the business is critical to our success." In an architectural approach, this principle would serve as a guidepost to align lower, less abstract policies and practices. The next level holds the various *HR policy* alternatives capable of enacting the guiding principles, which in this example might be team-based work systems, problem-solving mechanisms, open book management, incentive pay, comprehensive communication processes, or suggestion systems. Once the appropriate policies are selected, the firm chooses from the available array of *HR practices,* or specific tools, to execute the policies. Quality circles or TQM teams; variable compensation schemes, profit sharing, or piecework (all types of incentive pay); newsletters, learning fairs, or town hall meetings to communicate – all are HR practices the firm can implement and align with the policy level and guiding principle in this example.

The *product* is the metric that describes behavior, or the effect of the behavior, induced by the practices. Behavior in this case might be assessed by the general level of cooperation, participation levels in problem-solving exercises, or demonstration of business knowledge by employees; the effects of the behavior could be measured by the number of problems solved, productivity, waste, or compensation payouts resulting from corporate performance. The menu of new practices available to a given firm depends on its unique context and history; the existing practices, management style, and the labor relations climate are factors that will likely expand or constrict the list of options. If, for example, an organization had an antagonistic relationship with its workforce, built over a long history of tough bargaining with the union, it is unlikely that the firm could successfully implement cooperative problem-solving teams, at least not without first taking steps to repair the organizational climate. Considerations of unique firm contexts and path dependence are critical features of the RBV.

Levels of abstraction and modes of theorizing: limitations and opportunities

The framework offered in this chapter draws together the concepts of levels of abstraction and modes of theorizing in order to consider the typical levels addressed by each mode and to identify opportunities for extending these ideas. The universalistic approach is primarily concerned with individual practices and, thus, is most often focused on the level of HR practices, with little consideration of system interaction effects.

Contingency research deals with multiple practices and their "vertical" interaction effects with contingent variables and, thus, is implicitly concerned with HR policies and the related practices. Interaction effects are deemed important, but only one or two variables are considered at once, and, typically, the contingent variable is limited to firm strategy.

Configurational approaches emphasize the importance of overall system interactions and effects and, thus, include the HR principles level as a critical cohesive force for the overall system. The limiting facet of the configurational approach is that complex organizational systems are reduced to a few possible configurations for the sake of manageability and are cast as typologies. For example, Miles and Snow's (1978) theory of strategy, structure, and process has been used to cast and test organizational types (prospector, analyzer, defender) and related sets of HR practices (Delery & Doty, 1996). Limiting the rich complexity of organizations to a few possible configurations constrains the range of possible combinations and interaction effects and understates both the creative and adaptive potential of a complex system. While configurational approaches come closest to modeling the complexity of organizations, they must stop short for analytical manageability.

These two concepts in SHRM – modes of theorizing and levels of abstraction – form a useful framework for considering future opportunities in SHRM research. In particular, they help to highlight the difficulty of acknowledging and dealing with (rather than artificially reducing) system complexity in SHRM, as well as highlight the idea of separating the principles level of the HR system from the focus on discrete practices as a means of accessing issues of dynamic complexity. To relate ideas from the field of complexity to SHRM, it is helpful to first consider some of the opportunities for extension of the RBV in strategy, especially since the RBV is central to and has been called a backdrop of SHRM research.

Opportunities for extending the RBV and SHRM

While the RBV has focused attention on organizational resources and has served as an integrating ground for research and theory, its main limitations are serious for the field: it offers little, in an explicit sense, in the way of prescriptions for managers, thus not answering the "how" questions central to SHRM. In assessing the issues of fit in SHRM, Delery notes that "while the resource based view provides a nice backdrop, explaining the importance of human resources to firm competitiveness, it does not specifically deal with how an organization can develop and support the human resources it needs for competitive advantage" (1998: 290). This is due, in large measure, to the somewhat paradoxical internal logic of the RBV, at least as it has been framed to date: the strategic value of firm resources lies in their inherent complexity, and attempts to causally unravel that complexity are counterproductive, if not futile. In a recent review of the contribution of the RBV to SHRM research, Wright *et al.* concluded that taking RBV deeper into SHRM research "requires recognizing that the inimitability of [organizational] competencies may stem from unobservability (e.g. causal ambiguity), complexity (e.g. social complexity), and/or time compression diseconomies (e.g. path dependence)" (2001: 709). The challenge to researchers and managers is to find a level of prescription that preserves the strategic value of the RBV without compromising its essence.

Throughout the large body of scholarly writing on the RBV – in strategy and with specific respect to SHRM – there have been a few key aspects widely acknowledged to be both critically important and exceedingly difficult to adequately represent. I identify four aspects here: (1) a focus on the *creative* as well as the *adaptive* aspects of the RBV; (2) the centrality of *complexity* and *causal ambiguity* to its logic; (3) the importance of *disequilibrium, dynamism,* and *path dependence;* and (4) the idea of *system-level characteristics.* It is with these four critical but difficult aspects of the RBV, generally and as applied to SHRM, that concepts from complexity best align. In the following sections I briefly elaborate on each of these aspects to set the ground for integrating ideas from the study of complex systems.

Focus on creativity and adaptivity
The strategic nature of HRM has often been characterized in the SHRM literature as an *adaptive* concept in terms of fit or flexibility (Wright, McMahan, McCormick, & Sherman, 1998; Wright & Snell, 1998): firms have an *a priori* strategy, or chosen market position, and the main challenges lie in strategy implementation. But limiting the discussion to adaptive concepts limits the range and power of the RBV as originally articulated by Penrose, who was interested in the *process* of firm growth and its relation to sustained advantage. She proposed that

> the availability of unused productive services within it create the productive opportunity of a given firm. Unused productive services are, for the enterprising firm, at the same time a challenge to innovate, an incentive to expand, and a source of competitive advantage. (1959: 85)

Thus, in its original conception, the RBV held that a firm's resource base contains not only adaptive potential but also *creative* potential. The "unused productive services," which in SHRM terms means the knowledge, skill, and behavioral dynamics of individuals and groups, are forces for creativity, innovation, growth, and relative industry advantage. To be of strategic value, HRM practices should be focused on building and leveraging both creative *and* adaptive sources of competitive advantage: the *latent creative potential* in the organization's human resource pool and the *idiosyncratic capabilities* that serve to realize that potential and that help the organization adapt to and thrive in its operating environment.

There have been relatively few attempts to explore the creative aspect of the RBV in SHRM. Snell *et al.* did explore the processes of knowledge creation through organizational learning processes and urged emphasis on creativity over control in SHRM research:

> In the context of achieving sustained competitive advantage, we need less research on the control attributes of SHRM and more research on how participative systems can increase the potential value of and impact of employees on firm performance. If human capital is valuable, we have to learn how to unleash that value. (1996: 65)

Holding the RBV as an explicit frame suggests that the HR system can help create advantage by recruiting, developing, and leveraging both creative and adaptive sources of competitive advantage.

Centrality of complexity and causal ambiguity

Under the RBV, inimitable competitive advantage is protected by the interrelated conditions of *causal ambiguity* and *complexity*. Causal ambiguity is the basic uncertainty surrounding the causal relationship between actions and results (Lippman & Rumelt, 1982; Reed & DeFillippi, 1990). Such uncertainty may be irreducible *ex ante* and *ex post* – fundamentally irreducible causal ambiguity – or may be understood only retrospectively – *ex ante* irreducible/*ex post* reducible causal ambiguity (Mosakowski, 1997). Although both of these types serve to protect against competitors' discerning and "reverse engineering" an organization's strategic resources, the former does so more than the latter. This feature of the RBV has been difficult to operationalize, however, because under fundamentally irreducible causal ambiguity, even the firm possessing the advantage must be uncertain of its source, or else diffusion to competitors will result (Lippman & Rumelt, 1982). This prime criticism of the RBV – that is, that it is tautological (Priem & Butler, 2001) – is related to its *ex ante* irreducibility.

Ambiguity arises from complexity as a byproduct of the complex nature of organizational interaction. It comes from *technical* complexity and, more significant, from *social* complexity in the way that a firm's inputs – physical, human, and organizational – are combined (Barney, 1991). Social complexity as a source of ambiguity, and therefore competitive advantage, is a common theme throughout the RBV literature (Barney, 1986; Grant, 1991; Nelson & Winter, 1982; Reed & DeFillippi, 1990; Schoemaker, 1990; Wright *et al.*, 1994). While the socially complex phenomena that give rise to ambiguity do change over time, deliberately orchestrating those changes is often beyond management control (Barney, 1992). Still, scholars in SHRM have pointed specifically to the advantages inherent in organizational complexity and to the distributed nature of the source of advantage:

> It is difficult to grasp the precise mechanisms by which the interplay of human resource practices and policies generates value. To imitate a complex system, it is necessary to understand how the elements interact. Are the effects additive or multiplicative, or do they involve complex nonlinearities? ... It is even difficult for a competing firm to imitate a valuable HR system by hiring away one or a few top executives because the understanding of the system is an organizational capability that is spread across many (not just a few) people in the firm. (Becker & Gerhart, 1996: 787)

Constructive, socially embedded resources are highly strategically important (in the sense that they are inscrutable to competitors) because of their inherent complexity, but they are difficult to deliberately build for precisely the same reason. The question for managers is how to act within that complexity so that the organization is encouraged to thrive, without having to unravel and codify the myriad causal effects at play in the social dynamic of the firm.

Importance of disequilibrium, dynamism, and path dependence
Rather than attempt to reduce and unbundle complex resources and capabilities in an effort to manage and control, management's task under the RBV is to *create uncertainty* – to "continually reinvest in the factors that create the ambiguity and barriers to imitation" for competitors (Reed & DeFillippi, 1990: 97). Strategy is a continuous competitive interaction, in which models should be built on ideas of disequilibria rather than static efficiency (Reed & DeFillippi, 1990). Similarly, Amit and Schoemaker have argued that, for strategy to be conceived more dynamically, "disequilibrium and process dynamics loom primary" (1993: 42).

Growth and rent creation are driven by creative disequilibrium at both the firm and industry levels. Early explications of the RBV included dynamic factors in their static descriptions of resource characteristics. "Historical dependence," "rate of decay," "embedded" in complexity over time – are all dynamic concepts referencing the processes by which strategic resources emerge, are created, or are destroyed (Barney, 1991; Grant, 1991). Dierickx and Cool (1989) focused particular attention on the process of accumulating strategic assets with their concept of the "time compression diseconomies" faced by imitators. Some strategic assets – reputation, for example – cannot be bought on the factor markets but must be accrued over time.

Recently, attempts have been made to identify and examine the effects of *dynamic capabilities*. Dynamic capabilities are the organizational and strategic processes through which managers convert resources into new productive assets in the context of changing markets (Galunic & Eisenhardt, 2001). Researchers have made several efforts to identify and prescribe dynamic capabilities in theoretical terms (Luo, 2000; Teece, Pisano, & Shuen, 1997), through empirical studies (Griffith & Harvey, 2001; Helfat, 1997, 2000; Rindova & Kotha, 2001), and through historical studies of response to technological change (Rosenbloom, 2000). Scholars have explored the factors contributing to the development of dynamic capabilities and have found that the effectiveness of capability-building mechanisms is contingent on features of the task to be learned, such as task frequency, homogeneity, and causal ambiguity (Zollo & Winter, 2002).

The dynamic capabilities view is useful in making the RBV operational by identifying specific organizational processes that build clearly identifiable valuable resources (Eisenhardt & Martin, 2000). While it has potential to contribute to SHRM research, the dynamic capabilities view has not, to date, been conceived to allow for complex system interaction effects, and is therefore more limited than the focus of this chapter. An overly reductive approach to examining system dynamics (i.e., attempting to reduce what is inherently not reducible) ignores the notion that irreducible system complexity and the resultant ambiguity are key to the RBV argument. Beyond this chapter, there is opportunity to apply a dynamic capabilities approach using the insights offered here – an issue I discuss in the conclusion.

Idea of system-level characteristics

Throughout the RBV strategy literature, there is reference to the importance of system-level, intangible resources. Such resources have been variously conceived as "organizational routines" (Grant, 1991; Nelson & Winter, 1982), "cultural resources" (Wernerfelt, 1989), "core competencies" (Prahalad & Hamel, 1990), "organizational capabilities" (Barney, 1992; Collis, 1994; Lado & Wilson, 1994; Ulrich & Lake, 1991). and "system-level resources" (Black & Boal, 1994). *System-level resources* are those organizational capabilities that exist only in relationships – in the interactions between things. In conceptual and empirical work, researchers have described the importance of the relationships between and among resources that display "cogency," "complementarity," or "cospecialization" or that generate rents at the system level or organization level (Amit & Schoemaker, 1993; Barnard, 1938; Black & Boal, 1994; Brumagim, 1994; Collis, 1994; Grant, 1991; Teece, 1986). Since such resources are system specific (and therefore firm specific, if the firm is the system under consideration), they are arguably the most "imperfectly mobile" type of resources within a given firm. Imperfect mobility is key to sustaining economic rent, and one of the "cornerstones of competitive advantage" identified by Peteraf (1993).

A few writers in SHRM have focused on the importance of system-level resources – those organizational qualities that only exist in relationship, rather than as self-contained, discrete entities. For instance, Brass (1995) took a social network perspective of HRM and focused not on the attributes of discrete human resources but on the benefit accruing from the relationships among them. Similarly, Snell (1999) reflected on the concept of *human capital*, regarding human resources from an investment and capital accumulation perspective, and allowed that there may be new insight found in the concept of *social capital*, which focuses on the value of relationships. However, less attention has been paid to this idea in SHRM than in the broader RBV strategy literature.

With a focus on these aspects of the RBV and SHRM that are ripe for extension – a focus on the creative as well as the adaptive; the centrality of complexity and causal ambiguity; the importance of disequilibrium, dynamism, and path dependence; and the idea of system-level characteristics – we can consider ideas offered from the field of complexity.

Complexity as an Extension of the RBV

These four critical but difficult aspects of the RBV are, in fact, central features of complex systems. This theoretical congruence between complexity and the RBV (and, by extension, SHRM) suggests that transferring ideas from one domain to the other via abstract analogical reasoning is not only legitimate but implicitly called for within the RBV literature. In this section I present key features of complexity as they align with those of the RBV. I close the chapter with principles from the field of complexity aimed at nurturing living systems and thoughts on how those principles might be integrated usefully into the HR system architecture.

Key features of complex systems

There is no one unified theory of complexity. *Complexity theory* generally denotes a wide-ranging body of work built on such fields as chaos theory (Gleick, 1987; Lorenz, 1963), cybernetics (Ashby, 1956; Weiner, 1948), and dynamic systems theory (Jantsch, 1980; Kauffman, 1992; Prigogene & Stengers, 1984). *Complexity science* includes, but is not limited to, the study of *complex adaptive systems* (CAS) – systems characterized by networks of relationships that are independent, interdependent, and layered (Holland, 1975; Langton, 1989; Zimmerman, Lindberg, & Plsek, 1998).

Each word in the phrase "complex adaptive system" is significant (Waldrop, 1992). *Complex* means more than just "complicated"; it describes a system in which the component agents operate with some measure of autonomy, as well as in relation to other system components – that is, independently and interdependently. That interaction gives rise to emergent properties that are irreducible – that exist only in relationship. (As Cilliers [1998] has noted, an airliner is merely *complicated*; a mayonnaise is *complex*. He describes these as "relational properties" to avoid the mystical qualities associated with "emergence.") *Adaptive* means that each agent, as well as the collective system, actively responds to whatever pushes it and works to turn events to its advantage and survival. *System* implies dynamism – an "alive" kind of dynamism that arises from the many linear and nonlinear (i.e., with amplifying and dampening interaction effects) interrelationships among system agents. Because of this adaptive, unpredictable dynamism, CAS have also been termed *living systems* by some writers in the field (Capra, 1996; Holland, 1995; Kelly, 1994).

In general terms, a CAS is composed of

> a large number of agents, each of which behaves according to its own principles of local interaction. No individual agent, or group of agents, determines the patterns of behavior that the system as a whole displays, or how those patterns evolve, and neither does anything outside the system.   (Stacey, Griffin, & Shaw, 2000: 106)

Difficult to concisely define, but easy to recognize (like organizations), complex systems are generally characterized by these two features: (1) a *large number of interacting agents* and (2) the presence of stable, observable *emergent properties* – the appearance of patterns due to the collective behavior of the components of the system (Morel & Ramanujam, 1999). Order emerges as the system under observation evolves and adapts with its contextual environment, although system boundaries are always somewhat arbitrarily drawn. Characteristics of CAS are recognizable across diverse domains, including ecologies, brains, ant colonies, political parties, economies, and corporations (Holland, 1995). Such living systems are integrated wholes whose properties cannot be reduced to those of smaller parts. Their essential, or "systemic," properties are properties of the whole, which none of the parts have. They arise from the "organizing relations" of the parts – that is, from a configuration of ordered relationships that is characteristic of that particular class of organisms, or systems. Systemic properties are destroyed when a system is dissected into isolated elements.   (Capra, 1996: 36)

The key features of complex systems resonate with the critical but difficult aspects of the RBV outlined earlier. They are *creatively adaptive* in that they seek novel means to evolve, by random mutation, self-organization, transformation of their internal models of the environment, and natural selection (Goldstein, 1999). Any attempt to reduce organizational complexity in order to exert control and adapt to the operating environment (i.e., to act as managers are taught to act) is counterproductive. In complex adaptive systems, it is the process of adaptation that builds complexity, and from that complexity emerges perpetual novelty (Holland, 1995). Such systems reach their creative state at *far-from-equilibrium* conditions, be they economies (Arthur, 1990), Boolean (binary) networks of light bulbs wired together that move to stable order based on localized blinking rules (Kauffman, 1995), or dissipative structures in thermodynamics that *build up* as energy moves through the system, in defiance of the second law of thermodynamics (Prigogene & Stengers, 1984). A CAS never reaches equilibrium; if it is not creating to adapt, it is dead (Holland, 1995). As complex adaptive systems evolve through time, they do so irreversibly. Their steps cannot be retraced, because the "arrow of time" only moves forward through the evolutionary creative process (Prigogene & Stengers, 1984); processes of emergence are *path dependent*.

By definition, emergent properties are *unpredictable* (i.e., fundamentally causally ambiguous), displaying what Goldstein (1999) terms *radical novelty*; they have features not previously evident in the complex system under observation and that are not able to be anticipated in their full richness before they actually show themselves. Emergence is

the arising of novel and coherent structures, patterns, and properties during the process of self-organization in complex systems. Emergent phenomena are conceptualized as occurring on the macro level, in contrast to the micro level components and processes out of which they arise.   (Goldstein, 1999: 49)

The notion of "coherent structures, patterns, and properties" sounds very much like the intangible, system-level resources deemed important by RBV writers.

Table 5.1 arrays the critical but difficult features of the RBV (call it "complex RBV") alongside some of the key features of complex systems. This similarity suggests that concepts from the study of complex living systems are well poised to inform and extend the RBV and, by extension, SHRM.

Table 5.1   Complex RBV: critical but difficult features of the RBV and key features of complex systems

Key features	RBV	Complexity
Creativity/ adaptivity	Competitive advantage grows from latent creative potential embedded in firm resources	Complex adaptive systems learn and create new responses to their contextual environment
Complexity and ambiguity	Inimitability arises from social complexity and causal ambiguity	Living systems are composed of complex interrelationships that are nonlinear, nondeterministic, and unpredictable
Disequilibrium, dynamism, path dependence	Complex relationships build over time and are historically dependent; disequilibrium is the creative state; dynamism and process issues are paramount	Systems thrive and create at far-from-equilibrium states; equilibrium leads to stagnation, decline, and death; history matters; paths unfold irreversibly through time
System-level resources	Some key strategic resources are intangible and exist only at the system level, in relationships	Some elements only exist at the system level, in the dynamic relationships *between* things

Complex RBV: heuristics for building system-level resources

Proponents of the RBV say that competitive advantage flows from *latent creative potential* and *idiosyncratic capabilities* (synchronous with the specific context) and that strategic resources must be valuable, rare, inimitable, and organizationally leveraged (Barney & Wright, 1998). Complex RBV focuses on the complex processes that build system-level resources over time. The value of such resources is grounded in their synchronicity with the firm's operating context; their inimitability is secured because they are inscrutably embedded in the complex interactions within the organization. Management heuristics drawn from complexity can influence the organizational system toward building and leveraging strategic resources. The notion of *self-organization* in the complexity frame asks us to think of an organization in a less control-oriented manner and acknowledges that an organization's social system is constructed out of the interplay among the intentions, choices, and actions of all organizational actors (Stacey *et al.*, 2000).

With an appropriate degree of humility (i.e., abandoning the objective of control, the most we intend is influence), we acknowledge the forces for creativity and adaptation inevitably embedded in a complex social system and offer guiding principles consonant with that view. This is consistent with the RBV literature, which asserts that management is, at its core, a "heuristic discipline," and calls for the development of useful heuristics to deal with organizational complexity (Amit & Schoemaker, 1993; Schoemaker, 1990). Heuristics are, according to *Chambers Concise Dictionary*, "principles used in making decisions when all possibilities cannot be fully explored."

Complexity Applied in SHRM

The purpose of illustrating these points of congruence is that they strongly suggest there is something to be learned from a complexity view in order to extend the RBV. The critical but difficult aspects of the RBV in strategy mark an opportunity to bring in ideas from complexity, and SHRM, with its natural affinity to the RBV, is a particularly useful means of operationalizing those insights. Because the framework constructed in this chapter is built along the dimensions of the levels of abstraction in the HR system and degrees of concern for system interaction effects in the modes of theorizing, there is a clear point of entry for complexity principles.

Figure 5.1 illustrates the integrated framework for SHRM described earlier. The modes of theorizing, with the addition of the complexity frame, are arrayed against the levels of abstraction. The RBV serves well as an integrating ground for the various modes of theorizing. Articulated within the RBV are the higher-order (more general, more abstract) objectives of unleashing latent creative potential and developing idiosyncratic capabilities that are common to all modes, and more are fully realized as we move from left to right on the spectrum. The ovals in the figure depict the typical prescriptive range of each mode along the levels of abstraction, and they are labeled with the most relevant theory of organization for each mode.

As we move from left to right across the figure, there is greater concern for the interaction effects among system variables and for system-level characteristics. The complexity perspective acknowledges that agent interactions are abundant and critical to system evolution and that there is a self-organizing aspect to them. In the context of the HR system architecture, this means that process principles reflecting a complexity perspective can be prescribed and that the policies, practices, and products will "self-organize," which can mean that they flow in concert with the particular idiosyncratic context of the firm, guided by the heuristics for growing CAS. The heuristics as HR principles can help to guide the dialogue processes in the organization: the interplay of the intent, choices, and actions of organizational actors (Stacey *et al.*, 2000). From a strategic perspective, organizational resources will be positioned to create maximum value when we expand the system boundaries to include the intent, choices, and actions of the firm's stakeholder base – customers, suppliers, shareholders, employees, operating communities, governments, and competitors, for example.

Dynamism and complex interaction among system components are issues of organizational *process*, which is consistent with the initial conception of the RBV. Penrose (1959) was concerned with the process of growth – in the ways that organizations grow – in contrast with economic theory of the time, which only addressed the pros and cons of *being* one size or another. Process issues have also been identified as important in SHRM, especially in the ways that HR system fit emerges over time:

> We would encourage researchers to examine the processes that lead to internal fit. Like other elements of the organization's infrastructure, creating internal fit among HR practices probably has an intentional as well as an emergent component. Researchers might try to sort out the extent to which HR systems are integrated rationally through a priori decision processes versus emerging over time as practices are adjusted incrementally.

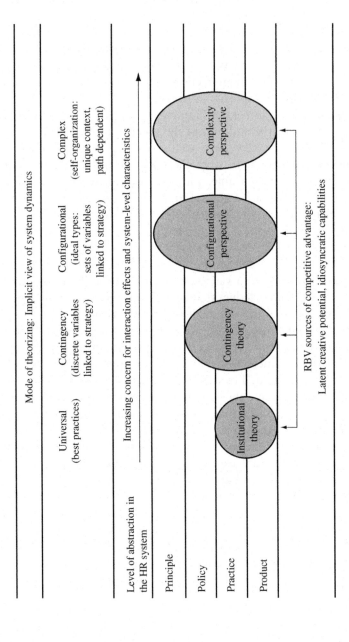

Figure 5.1   Dimensions of theory in SHRM with the addition of a complexity perspective.

> SHRM, in general, is an area that has focused far too exclusively on content issues to the exclusion of more process-oriented concerns.   (*Snell et al.*, 1996: 80)

The background shading in Fig. 5.1 indicates the primary range of prescription available under each mode of theorizing. Adding a complexity view to the framework extends consideration of the HR system out to a domain where system interaction effects are accepted as critical and allows that the properties and dynamics of the system are complex, unpredictable, and often irreducible to their component parts. Doing so via analogical *abstractions* will allow us to enter the framework at the appropriate level of abstraction – in this case, the principles level. Prescription here is focused on *process principles*: management heuristics for nurturing complex living systems.

Abstract analogical reasoning: transferring insights across knowledge domains

Rather than employ one concept or another from specific areas of study in complexity (e.g. fitness landscapes, cellular automata, nonequilibrium thermodynamics, dissipative structures, bifurcation points), we can consider living systems generally and abstractly – that is, take a set of abstract concepts generally observable across complex living systems and transfer them to the principles level of the HR architectural framework. Tsoukas suggests that such abstractions are particularly useful for theory building:

> From a theory-building point of view, abstractions are very important because they operate at a high level of generality, reveal the generic properties of a variety of phenomena, and can thus be used to explain phenomena across widely different domains.   (1993: 338)

Kelly (1994) put forward a set of abstract principles – a list of "laws" for growing living systems, synthesized from diverse streams of complexity research. The set of seven below is adapted from the nine offered in his wide-ranging work:

- Distribute being: Allow that systems are not contained in discrete bodies; living systems are distributed over a multitude of smaller units. All the mysteries we find most interesting – life, intelligence, evolution – are found in the soil of large distributed systems.
- Control from the bottom up: When everything is connected to everything in a distributed network, wide and fast-moving problems route around any central authority. Overall governance must arise from inter-dependent acts done locally in parallel and not from a central command.
- Cultivate increasing returns: Each time you use an idea, a language, or a skill, you strengthen it, reinforce it, and make it more likely to be used again. That is known as positive feedback or snowballing. Anything that alters its environment to increase production of itself is playing the game of increasing returns.
- Grow by chunking: Allow complex systems to emerge out of the links among simple systems that work well and are capable of operating independently. Attempts to *install* highly complex organization, without growing it, inevitably lead to failure.

Complexity is created by assembling it incrementally from simple modules that can operate independently.

- Maximize the fringes: A diverse, heterogeneous entity can adapt to the world in a thousand daily minirevolutions, staying in a state of permanent but never fatal churning. In economic, ecological, evolutionary, and institutional models, a healthy fringe speeds adaptation, increases resilience, and is almost always the source of innovations.
- Honor your errors: The process of going outside the usual method, game, or territory is indistinguishable from error. Even the most brilliant act of human genius is an act of trial and error. System evolution can be thought of as systematic error management.
- Pursue multiple goals: Survival is a many-pointed goal. A complicated structure has many masters, and none of them can be served exclusively. An adaptive system must trade off between exploiting a known path of success (optimizing a current strategy) and diverting energy to exploring new paths (thereby wasting energy and reducing efficiency).

These principles can be directed toward addressing the "how" questions central to HR research set out earlier: How does a firm encourage alignment of resources to strategy, and how does it continually build human and organizational (i.e., system-level) resources to fuel competitive advantage? As a prescription for managers, a complex RBV, living-systems view suggests that these principles be integrated into the HR architecture.

Table 5.2 offers an example of how such principles for nurturing living systems might translate to HR principles that are oriented toward process, focused on appropriately stirring the stew of creative forces embedded in the organization's social system – the intentions, choices, and actions at play. How these principles translate to HR policies and practices will depend on the historical experience of the organization and the nature and quality of the human relationships within the system. The third and fourth columns of Table 5.2 offer some possibilities of which HR practices might come into play, but they are only possibilities. Complex, system-level, path-dependent resources and capabilities only emerge out of the dynamic interplay within a given system and with its operating environment; it is beyond our prescriptive capacity to list what could, or should, be the particular actions of each organization. A complex systems view allows for the creation of valuable resources by encouraging an attitude of inclusiveness and humility on the part of managers: inclusiveness toward all system agents (stakeholders) and humility in that they are encouraged to relinquish the idea of tight control and focus on building "generative relationships" (Lane & Maxfield, 1996).

Coherence in the HR system

In reference to Fig. 5.1, there are single, discrete HR practices that researchers have identified as universally beneficial for organizations to adopt, there are HR practices that make sense in relation to particular firm strategies, and there are typological

Table 5.2 Living-systems coherence: translating complexity heuristics to the HR system

Heuristics for nurturing complex living systems	Possible translation to HR principles	Possible translation to HR policies	Possible effect on HR processes
Distribute being	• Eradicate arbitrary borders	• Encourage movement across departmental and organizational boundaries	• Work assignments (postings, projects) deliberately cross-functional
	• Build broad-based identity and capability	• Explicitly incorporate identity-building values into HR systems	• For example, recruitment, training, leadership development, performance management processes
Control from the bottom up	• Democratize the workplace	• Encourage formal and informal employee participation wherever possible	• Work structure design with a strong bias to full engagement
	• Feed information to all levels	• Take time to create an understanding of the business; coach at all levels	• Leadership development, internal communications
Cultivate increasing returns	• Seek opportunities to create positive reinforcement in the system	• Deliberately link reputation, external image, and internal identity in a virtuous cycle	• External and internal communication practices
	• Be deliberate with language and symbols	• Use and reuse consistent models and language in development programs	• Training – high customization of T&D programs (vs. outsourcing)
Grow by chunking	• Encourage local innovation	• Allow inconsistencies across departments	• Flexible interpretation of HR "rules"
	• Build learning capacity	• Foster knowledge exchange across organizational units	• Learning forums, communities of practice
Maximize the fringes	• Embrace debate	• Invite dialogue on alternate approaches	• Electronic discussion groups on pros/cons of HR systems
	• Experiment	• Create space for experimentation	• HR "skunkworks" – trials of new practices/processes
Honor your errors	• Encourage reflective practice	• Close learning loop on experimentation	• Reward systems – honor "greatest learning experiences"
Pursue multiple goals	• Incorporate stakeholder perspectives/aspirations	• Assess HR system impact on all stakeholders	• HR measures – build in stakeholder metrics
	• Tolerate multiple aims	• Create value on many fronts at once	• Solicit definition of "value" from diverse stakeholders

configurations of practices that work well together. Moving from configurational approaches to complexity approaches means loosening the coupling between conceptions of strategic types and full sets of related HR practices. It means introducing complexity principles at the appropriate level of the HR architecture and letting the system follow what Daneke (1997) calls its "unique geometries" – which is what complex systems will do, despite managerial efforts at total control.

The aim here is not to generate radical new ideas for HR practices in a discrete sense; each of the practices listed in Table 5.2 is at work in some organization today. Rather, the purpose of such a framework is to provide a measure of coherence and purpose to the HR system architecture, informed by complexity. What the overlapping aspects of the RBV and complexity suggest is that a set of principles drawn from the study of complex, living, thriving systems could serve well to nurture the creative and adaptive capabilities of the organization.

Implications for SHRM research

The framework offered in this chapter suggests a number of interesting research questions. What HR principles are most consistent with a complexity perspective? Some principles are offered here, but that list is by no means exhaustive. What range of HR policies and associated practices flows from complexity-based principles? How do the dialogic processes in organizations contribute to the development of HR policies and practices, and what role do HR principles play in moving to overall system coherence? Snell et al. (1996) observed that some HR practices emerge over time and are not thought out a priori. Investigation into those processes from a complex RBV perspective means focusing qualitatively on the human relationships in the system and on the processes of dialogue that lead to transformative change (Stacey et al., 2000).

Are the modes of theorizing compatible? That is, can we employ insights from a universalistic approach while at the same time injecting complexity principles to encourage emergent adaptive behavior of the whole system? What specific sources of advantage do organizational members attribute to the complex interactions encouraged by the HR principles? Is a complexity approach more appropriate for certain strategies, in certain industries? How does a complexity approach reframe the way we think of the concepts of "fit" and "flexibility" in SHRM research? Perhaps it asks us to accept that fit emerges out of ongoing, decentralized dialogic processes, and flexibility means adherence to a principles-driven view of the HR system. This might mean a continual, deliberate reinterpretation of HR policies and practices in the context of the organization, in the way that Holland (1995) describes complex systems as constantly revising and rearranging their building blocks as they gain experience. If the principles guiding the system are drawn from living-systems theory, versus a mechanistic organizational view, perhaps the prosperity odds are better.

One way to approach some of these questions would be to construct some high-level, exploratory hypotheses tying a complexity approach in the HR architecture to perceived strategic resources to organizational outcomes. One could construct a proposition regarding the significance of a complexity view, and another pertaining to the degree of institutionalization of the principles, covering the intention and execution of integration. For instance:

- Complex RBV advantage flows from complexity principles embedded in the HR architecture.
- Greater institutionalization of complexity principles in the HR system is associated with greater relative industry performance.

A possible method for exploring these propositions might be to select comparator companies, who occupy relatively equal strategic positions in the same industry, and collect qualitative data on their respective HR architectural schemes, along with supporting documentation. Principles may be explicit or implied, depending on the relative sophistication of the firm's HR system. The principles in action could be assessed for "complexity content" against the frameworks suggested in this paper to determine the relative presence of conditions for emergence and adaptive behavior. Qualitative data from actors inside the firm could be used to gather collective perceptions of strategic resources and their value to firm performance, their rarity, and conditions contributing to their inimitability, without trying to analytically break down causal ambiguity. Quantitative and qualitative comparisons of high- and low-performing firms in the same industry could be constructed to test the general propositions and to aid in the construction of others more specific.

Most significant and perhaps generalizable out of such a study would be not just the particular principles themselves but the process within the firm of drafting such principles (e.g. who is involved, over what time frames, through what dialogic processes, and based on which inputs) and the further process of consistently translating those principles to HR policies and practices. The *dynamic capabilities* view, highlighted earlier, could be usefully applied using the framework offered here. With a focus on HR principles, researchers could document the principles drafting and interpretation processes as strategic dynamic capabilities. Those processes that combine the intentions, choices, and actions of agents within and outside the organization will guide the development of the HR system over time, along paths that are unique and idiosyncratic to its operation environment – a complex RBV approach to addressing the "how" questions so important to SHRM.

Conclusion

My aim in this chapter has been to offer a general framework for extending the field of SHRM via a principles-based complexity approach. I have rationalized connecting these two fields of study based on congruence of key features of the RBV, a common strategic frame for SHRM, and key features from the study of complex living systems. While this chapter focuses on the particular relevance of these ideas to SHRM, extending the RBV via complexity may also have implications for strategy generally. Further work along this line could include a complex, principles-level view of strategy formulation and of the dynamics of strategy implementation. The framework constructed here allows for the introduction of complexity principles at the appropriate (principles) level of abstraction in the HR system. Pursuing a line of research in SHRM that focuses on coherence in the HR system, infused with a living-systems perspective, could help to inform the way organizations are studied and to improve the way they are managed.

REFERENCES

Amit, R., & Schoemaker, P. J. H. 1993. Strategic assets and organizational rent. *Strategic Management Journal*, 14: 33–46.

Arthur, W. B. 1990. Positive feedbacks in the economy. *Scientific American*, February: 92–9.

Ashby, W. R. 1956. *An introduction to cybernetics*. London: Chapman and Hall.

Barnard, C. 1938. *The functions of the executive*. Cambridge, MA. Harvard University Press.

Barney, J. B. 1986. Strategic factor markets: Expectations, luck, and business strategy. *Management Science*, 32: 1231–41.

Barney, J. B. 1991. Firm resources and sustained competitive advantage. *Journal of Management*, 17: 99–120.

Barney, J. B. 1992. Integrating organizational behavior and strategy formulation research: A resource-based analysis. In P. Shrivastava, A. Huff, & J. Dutton (eds.), *Advances in strategic management*, Vol. 8: 39–61. Greenwich, CT: JAI Press.

Barney, J. B., & Wright, P. M. 1998. On becoming a strategic partner: The role of human resources in gaining competitive advantage. *Human Resource Management*, 37: 31–46.

Baum, J. A. C. 1996. Organizational ecology. In S. R. Clegg, C. Hardy, & W. Nord (eds.), *Handbook of organizational studies* (1st ed.): 77–114. London: Sage.

Becker, B., & Gerhart, B. 1996. The impact of human resource management organizational performance. *Academy of Management Journal*, 39: 779–801.

Black, J. A., & Boal, K. B. 1994. Strategic resources: Traits, configurations and paths to sustainable competitive advantage. *Strategic Management Journal*, 15(Special Issue): 131–48.

Brass, D. J. 1995. A social network perspective on strategic human resource management. *Research in Personnel and Human Resource Management*, 13: 39–79.

Brumagim, A. L. 1994. A hierarchy of corporate resources. *Advances in Strategic Management*, 10A: 81–112.

Capra, F. 1996. *The web of life: A new scientific understanding of living systems*. New York: Anchor Books.

Cilliers, P. 1998. *Complexity and postmodernism: Understanding complex systems*. New York: Routledge.

Collis, D. J. 1994. Research note: How valuable are organizational capabilities? *Strategic Management Journal*, 15(Special Issue): 143–52.

Conner, K. R. 1991. A historical comparison of resource-based theory and five schools of thought within industrial organization economics: Do we have a new theory of the firm? *Journal of Management*, 17: 121–54.

Delery, J. E. 1998. Issues of fit in strategic human resource management: Implications for research. *Human Resource Management Review*, 8: 289–309.

Delery, J. E., & Doty, D. H. 1996. Modes of theorizing in strategic human resource management: Tests of universalistic, contingency, and configurational performance predictions. *Academy of Management Journal*, 39: 802–35.

Dierickx, I., & Cool, K. 1989. Asset stock accumulation and sustainability of competitive advantage. *Management Science*, 35: 1504–11.

DiMaggio, P. J., & Powell, W. W. 1983. The iron cage revisited: Institutional isomorphism and collective rationality in organizational fields. *American Sociological Review*, 48: 147–60.

Doty, D. H., & Glick, W. H. 1994. Typologies as a unique form of theory building: Toward improved understanding and modeling. *Academy of Management Review*, 19: 230–51.

Doty, D. H., Glick, W. H., & Huber, G. P. 1993. Fit, equifinality, and organizational effectiveness: A test of two configurational theories. *Academy of Management Journal*, 36: 1196–250.

Eisenhardt, K. M., & Martin, J. A. 2000. Dynamic capabilities: What are they? *Strategic Management Journal*, 21: 1105–21.

Fombrun, C. J., Tichy, N. M., & Devanna, M. A. 1984. *Strategic human resource management*, vol. 23. New York: Wiley.

Galunic, D. C., & Eisenhardt, K. M. 2001. Architectural innovation and modular corporate forms. *Academy of Management Journal*, 44: 1229–50.

Gerhart, B., & Milkovich, G. T. 1990. Organizational differences in managerial compensation and financial performance. *Academy of Management Journal*, 33: 663–91.

Gleick, J. 1987. *Chaos: Making a new science*. New York: Viking.

Goldstein, J. 1999. Emergence as a construct: History and issues. Emergence: *A Journal of Complexity Issues in Organizations and Management*, 1(1): 49–72.

Grant, R. M. 1991. The resource-based theory of competitive advantage. *California Management Review*, 33(3): 114–35.

Griffith, D. A., & Harvey, M. G. 2001. A resource perspective of global dynamic capabilities. *Journal of International Business Studies*, 32: 597–606.

Helfat, C. E. 1997. Know-how and asset complementarity and dynamic capability accumulation: The case of R&D. *Strategic Management Journal*, 18: 339–60.

Helfat, C. E. 2000. Introduction to the special issue: The evolution of firm capabilities. *Strategic Management Journal*, 21 (Special Issue): 955–59.

Holland, J. H. 1975. *Adaptation in natural and artificial systems*. Ann Arbor: University of Michigan Press.

Holland, J. H. 1995. *Hidden order: How adaptation builds complexity*. Reading, MA: Helix Books.

Jantsch, E. 1980. *The self-organizing universe: Scientific and human implications of the emerging paradigm of evolution*. Oxford: Pergamon.

Jones, G. 1984. Task visibility, free riding and shirking: Explaining the effect of structure and technology on employee behaviors. *Academy of Management Review*, 9: 684–95.

Kauffman, S. A. 1992. *Origins of order: Self-organization and selection in evolution*. Oxford: Oxford University Press.

Kauffman, S. A. 1995. *At home in the universe*. New York: Oxford University Press.

Kelly, K. 1994. *Out of control: The rise of neo-biological civilization*. Reading, MA: Addison-Wesley.

Lado, A. A., & Wilson, M. C. 1994. Human resource systems and sustained competitive advantage: A competency-based perspective. *Academy of Management Review*, 19: 699–724.

Langton, C. G. (ed.). 1989. *Artificial life*. Santa Fe Institute for Studies in the Sciences of Complexity. Redwood City, CA: Addison-Wesley.

Lengnick-Hall, C. A., & Lengnick-Hall, M. L. 1988. Strategic human resource management: A review of the literature and a proposed typology. *Academy of Management Review*, 13: 454–70.

Lepak, D., & Snell, S. A. 1999. The human resource architecture: Toward a theory of human capital allocation development. *Academy of Management Review*, 24: 31–48.

Lippman, S., & Rumelt, R. 1982. Uncertain imitability: An analysis of interfirm difference in efficiency under competition. *Bell Journal of Economics*, 13: 418–38.

Lorenz, E. 1963. Deterministic non-periodic flow. *Journal of the Atmospheric Sciences*, 20: 130–41.

Luo, Y. 2000. Dynamic capabilities in international expansion. *Journal of World Business*, 35: 355–78.

Mahoney, J. T., & Pandian, R. J. 1992. The resource-based view within the conversation of strategic management. *Strategic Management Journal*, 13: 363–80.

Meyer, A. D., Tsui, A. S., & Hinings, C. R. 1993. Configurational approaches to organizational analysis. *Academy of Management Journal*, 36: 1175–95.

Miles, R. E., & Snow, C. C. 1978. *Organizational strategy, structure and process.* New York: McGraw-Hill.

Miles, R. E., & Snow, C. C. 1984. Designing strategic human resource systems. *Organizational Dynamics*, 13(1): 36–52.

Miller, M., & Friesen, P. H. 1984. *Organizations: A quantum view.* Englewood Cliffs, NJ: Prentice-Hall.

Morel, B., & Ramanujam, R. 1999. Through the looking glass of complexity: The dynamics of organizations as adaptive and evolving systems. *Organization Science*, 10: 278–93.

Mosakowski, E. 1997. Strategy making under causal ambiguity: Conceptual issues and empirical evidence. *Organization Science*, 8: 414–42.

Nelson, R., & Winter, S. 1982. *An evolutional theory of economic change.* Cambridge, MA: Harvard University Press.

Oliver, C. 1997. Sustainable competitive advantage: Combining institutional and resource-based views. *Strategic Management Journal*, 18: 697–713.

Penrose, E. T. 1959. *The theory of the growth of the firm.* New York: Wiley.

Peteraf, M. A. 1993. The cornerstones of competitive advantage: A resource-based view. *Strategic Management Journal*, 14: 179–91.

Pfeffer, J. 1994. *Competitive advantage through people: Unleashing the power of the workforce.* Boston: Harvard Business School Press.

Prahalad, C. K., & Hamel, G. 1990. The core competence of the corporation. *Harvard Business Review*, 68(3): 79–91.

Priem, R. L., & Butler, J. E. 2001. Is the resource-based "view" a useful perspective for strategic management research? *Academy of Management Review*, 26: 22–40.

Prigogene, I., & Stengers, I. 1984. *Order out of chaos: Man's new dialogue with nature.* New York: Bantam Books.

Reed, R., & DeFillippi, R. J. 1990. Causal ambiguity, barriers to imitation, and sustainable competitive advantage. *Academy of Management Review*, 15: 88–102.

Rindova, V. P., & Kotha, S. 2001. Continuous "morphing": Competing through dynamic capabilities, form, and function. *Academy of Management Journal*, 44: 1263–80.

Rosenbloom, R. S. 2000. Leadership, capabilities, and technological change: The transformation of NCR in the electronic era. *Strategic Management Journal*, 21: 1083–103.

Rousseau, D. M. 1985. Issues of level in organizational research: Multi-level and cross-level perspectives. *Research in Organizational Behavior*, 7: 1–37.

Schoemaker, P. J. H. 1990. Strategy, complexity and economic rent. *Management Science*, 36: 1178–92.

Schuler, R. S. 1987. *Personnel and human resource management* (3rd ed.). St. Paul: West Educational Publishing.

Schuler, R. S., & Jackson, S. E. 1987. Organizational strategy and organizational level as determinants of human resource management practices. *Human Resource Planning*, 10(3): 125–41.

Snell, S. A. 1999. Social capital and strategic HRM: It's who you know. *Human Resource Planning*, 22(1): 62–5.

Snell, S. A., Youndt, M. A., & Wright, P. M. 1996. Establishing a framework for research in human resource management: Merging resource theory and organizational learning. *Research in Personnel and Human Resources Management*, 14: 61–90.

Stocey, R. D., Griffin, D., & Shaw, P. 2000. *Complexity and management: Fad or radical challenge to systems thinking?* New York: Routledge.

Teece, D. J. 1986. Profiting from technological innovation. *Research Policy*, 15: 285–305.

Teece, D. J., Pisano, G., & Shuen, A. 1997. Dynamic capabilities and strategic management. *Strategic Management Journal*, 18: 509–33.

Tsoukas, H. 1993. Analogical reasoning and knowledge generation in organization theory. *Organization Studies*, 14: 323–39.

Ulrich, D. 1997a. *Human resource champions.* Boston: Harvard Business School Press.

Ulrich, D. 1997b. Judge me more by my future than my past. *Human Resource Management*, 36: 5–8.

Ulrich, D., & Lake, D. 1991. Organizational capability: Creating competitive advantage. *Academy of Management Executive*, 5(1): 77–89.

Waldrop, M. M. 1992. *Complexity: The emerging science at the edge of order and chaos.* London: Viking.

Weiner, N. 1948. *Cybernetics.* New York: Wiley.

Wernerfelt, B. 1984. A resource-based view of the firm. *Strategic Management Journal*, 5: 171–80.

Wernerfelt, B. 1989. From critical resources to corporate strategy. *Journal of General Management*, 14(3): 4–12.

Wright, P. M. 1998. Strategy-HR fit: Does it really matter? *Human Resource Planning*, 21(4): 56–7.

Wright, P. M., Dunford, B. B., & Snell, S. A. 2001. Human resources and the resource based view of the firm. *Journal of Management*, 27: 701–21.

Wright, P. M., & McMahan, G. C. 1992. Theoretical perspectives for strategic human resource management. *Journal of Management*, 18: 295–320.

Wright, P. M., McMahan, G. C., McCormick, B., & Sherman, W. S. 1998. Strategy, core competence, and HR involvement as determinants of HR effectiveness and refinery performance. *Human Resource Management*, 37: 17–29.

Wright, P. M., McMahan, G. C., & McWilliams, A. 1994. Human resources and sustained competitive advantage: A resource-based perspective. *International Journal of Human Resource Management*, 5: 301–26.

Wright, P. M., & Snell, S. A. 1998. Toward a unifying framework for exploring fit and flexibility in strategic human resource management. *Academy of Management Review*, 23: 756–72.

Zimmerman, B. J., Lindberg, C., & Plsek, P. 1998. *Edgeware: Insights from complexity science for health care leaders.* Irving, TX: VHA Inc.

Zollo, M., & Winter, S. G. 2002. Deliberate learning and the evolution of dynamic capabilities. *Organization Science*, 13: 339–51.

Chapter 6

Alignment of HR Strategies and the Impact on Business Performance

Dave Ulrich

In Greek mythology, Sisyphus has the challenge of pushing a rock up a hill. He begins with great energy as he sees where he is headed, but as he is half-way up the hill, he finds that the rock obscures his view of the top of the hill, he loses his will, and the rock rolls over him and he and the rock end up at the bottom of the hill.

A similar rock-pushing, but not achieving, phenomenon often confronts HR professionals. At times, HR professionals push lots of rocks: action learning training, pay for performance programs, employee flexibility, high performing teams, and career banding systems. But, when these programs or initiatives fail to achieve an outcome, they become short term fads which lead to cynicism more than commitment.

The question this chapter addresses is straightforward: why and how does investment in HR practices impact business performance? The answer to this question is based on two premises. First, input must lead to output. Intuitively, people believe that HR inputs in staffing, training, development, communication, compensation, organization governance, etc. lead to positive business outputs. Empirically, theorists and researchers are beginning to show subtle, yet positive relationships between high performing work systems and market value (Becker, *et al.*, 1997; Huselid, 1995). As the intuitive relationship becomes empirical, more accurate statements may be made about the impact of HR on performance.

Second, the path between HR investment and business performance must be made clear for it to be replicated. Knowing that a path exists and understanding why the path exists and how it was created is like the difference between reading about the challenge of playing the piano and actually knowing how to play the piano. The

D. Ulrich, "Alignment of Human Resources and their Impact on Business Performance," *The Executive Handbook on Compensation* (Free Press, 2001): 17–31.

former can describe what to do, but without understanding the rigorous steps involved in successful piano playing, which includes both theory and practice, long term piano competence won't occur. In this essay, I will assume that the relationship between HR investment and business performance is nonrandom, can be described in some detail, and helps HR professionals show how investment in their practices impacts business performance. By validating these assumptions, HR professionals may be able to do more than push rocks up hills (initiate programs that start with enthusiasm, but end with entropy) and actually deliver business performance.

The chapter will answer the question of why and how investments in HR practices impact business performance by (1) defining the impact of investments in HR practices and business performance, (2) presenting a capability based view of organizations which shows the "why" and the "how" of the bridge connecting investment in HR and business performance, (3) reviewing ten critical capabilities which may link HR and performance, and (4) suggesting implications of these capabilities for HR functions and professionals.

Defining the Impact of Investments in HR and Business Performance

Sometimes relationships which we want to find and even assert between two variables are not as obvious as we would hope. The relationship between employee attitude and firm performance, for example, while intuitively appealing has not been consistently shown in the research. Likewise, in the 1980s, studies which examined the relationship between investments in HR activity and business performance came up somewhat empty (Delaney et al., 1988, 1989; Nkomo, 1987). Firms that invested more in HR were not more successful.

This research began to shift in the 1990s with more refined and subtle analyses which explored more elusive relationships between HR investments and business performance. First, efforts were made to identify contingent factors which affected investment in HR and business performance. Yeung and Ulrich (1990) found that under conditions of low environmental change, HR investments did not affect business performance, but under conditions of high environmental change, HR investments had a positive impact on business performance. So, for those companies where the external world was predictable and constant, investment in HR did not matter that much, while companies facing uncertainty and change would be well served to invest heavily in HR practices. Jackson and Schuler (1995) found that alignment of HR practices with strategy had a positive impact on business performance. While overall investment in HR did not affect performance, a unique strategic direction required a different set of HR practices prior to positive business performance. The alignment of a business's strategy and HR practices was pivotal to the relationship between investment in HR and performance.

Second, studies of overall investment in HR and business performance found nonlinear relationships. Becker, Huselid, and their colleagues (Becker and Gerhart, 1996; Becker et al., 1997; Delaney and Huselid, 1996; Huselid, 1995) found that

Figure 6.1   HR investments and firm results.

investments in HR practices impact business performance differently depending on the degree of integration or bundling of HR practices. HR investments most impact business performance when they are "bundled" or integrated. Firms investing in one or two "best practices" may not have high overall performance because at times the HR practices may contradict, or not complement, each other. For example, some firms do a competency model for staffing; a needs assessment for training; a 360° feedback for coaching; and a management by objective system for compensation. At times, the competencies for staffing, needs for training, behaviors for coaching, and MBO for compensation encourage different things. More successful firms have integrated HR systems; they might have, for example, one competence model that can be used for staffing, training, compensation, and coaching (Christensen, 1997). This research found that when investments in HR were made "one at a time" (e.g. fix the compensation system, then the training process, then the hiring system), the relationship between HR investment and performance was marginal.

Third, firms with extraordinary increases in market value seem to invest in high performing work practices (Pfeffer, 1994,1998). Pfeffer attributes extraordinary gains in market value to high performing HR practices in staffing, decision making, governance, and compensation. Ulrich, Zenger, and Smallwood (1999) found that firms in the same industry who have similar balance sheet and financial results may have different market values. Investors may value the financial results of one firm more than another. A portion of the differing market value for similar internal financial results may be explained by how investors perceive the quality of management within the firm. A higher perceived quality of management may be derived from HR practices which create better managers.

Collectively, these studies and perspectives suggest that investments in HR can and do impact business performance. However, these studies leave less clear answers to the questions "why" and "how" do investments in HR impact business performance. As the link between investments in HR and business performance becomes more precise by answering the "why" and "how" questions (Fig. 6.1), HR professionals may be able to make better investments in HR.

A "Capability" View of Organization as Bridge between HR Investments and Business Performance

An emerging view from the HR discipline itself and other disciplines has begun to show why and how HR investments affect firm performance. In the strategy field, work was traditionally divided into two parts: strategy formulation and strategy implementation. Formulation focused on positioning the firm in the market using competitive analysis, SWOT (strengths, weaknesses, opportunities, threats), five forces, or other analytic tools. Implementation often focused on management and organizational actions such as structure (e.g. structure follows strategy) or systems analysis (e.g. 7-s McKinsey model). More recently, strategists are finding a middle ground between formulation and implementation.

While the strategy work has tried to find the middle group between strategy and action, other disciplines have also attempted to define this "middle ground" between strategy and action. Those with a quality orientation focus on "processes" and work to reengineer those processes. Those with an organization development or change orientation have called this middle ground "culture." Those with an HR orientation have traditionally focused on "high performing organizations" or "work teams."

Currently, this "middle ground" between strategy and action remains somewhat murky. While most concur that there is a "middle ground" between strategy and results (or between HR investments and results as shown in Fig. 6.1), there are varying terms, concepts, and frameworks for defining this ground. The wide range of literatures and thinking on this "middle ground" indicates its pervasiveness and import.

Organizational capabilities offer a way of thinking about the missing link between strategy and action (Ulrich and Lake, 1990; Ulrich, 1998). Organizations possess capabilities which meet the following criteria:

- Offers integration: Capabilities are not individual competence or management systems, but organizationally based
- Adds value to customers: Capabilities are defined by those outside the firm as important
- Maintains continuity: Capabilities are stable over time
- Offers uniqueness: Capabilities are difficult to copy by competitors
- Engages employees: Capabilities create meaning for employees within the organization
- Establishes identity: Capabilities delineate an identity for the organization in the mind of customers, employees, and investors.

Capabilities represent the skills, abilities, and expertise of the organization. They describe what organizations are able to do and how they are able to do it. They are collections of individual competencies turned into organizational capabilities. They complement the technical, core competencies resident in an organization and may be characterized as the identity of the organization. Capabilities represent the ability of an organization to use resources, get things done, and behave to reach goals.

Capabilities become the results of HR; they fill in the middle ground between HR investments and firm performance (Fig. 6.1); they serve as the transition from mission, vision, strategies, and values to action as shown in Fig. 6.2. As leaders shift their organization's strategy (moving from cell 1 to cell 5 of Fig. 6.2), they create visions, strategies, and missions which depict how to win in the future. Often two mistakes are made once a future strategy (cell 5) is defined.

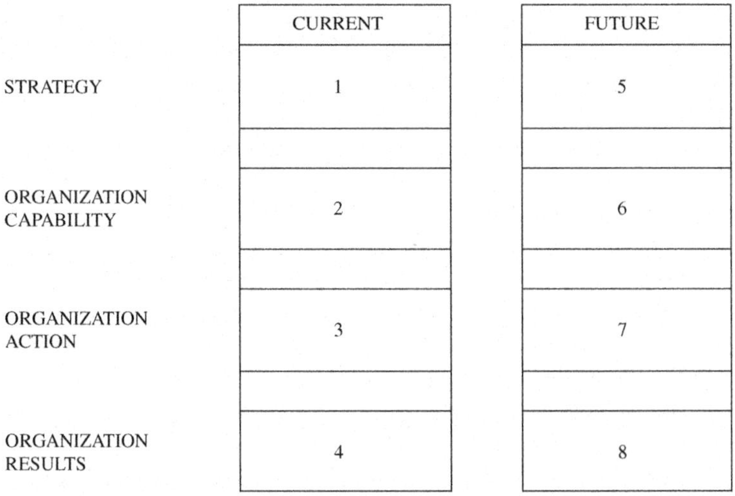

	CURRENT	FUTURE
STRATEGY	1	5
ORGANIZATION CAPABILITY	2	6
ORGANIZATION ACTION	3	7
ORGANIZATION RESULTS	4	8

Figure 6.2   Strategy/capability/organization assessment.

First, leaders try to implement a new strategy with the old capabilities (cell 2) and actions (cell 3). When Citibank purchased Traveler's Insurance, they were moving into a complete financial service provider. They had to realize, however, that the capabilities of providing financial advice were not the same capabilities required to sell insurance. The capabilities required to succeed in insurance were different from traditional banking services. As leaders at Citibank recognized the required capabilities, they invested in new management actions (cell 7) to assure that these capabilities were instilled within the company.

Second, leaders try to implement a new strategy (cell 5) by investing in the latest management fads and initiatives (cell 7). Managers who fall prey to quick fixes and latest fads often find that activities are disconnected and not long lasting. Unless different management actions (e.g. staffing, training, communication, organization design, compensation) create a set of capabilities, they are unlikely to have sustained impact.

General Managers and HR professionals have the challenge and obligation to work together to turn future strategies (cell 5) into future capabilities (cell 6) into future management actions (cell 7) to achieve organization results (cell 8). They do so by identifying the capabilities necessary to turn strategy into action. Capabilities represent the bridge between strategy and action; they become the theoretical basis for making sure that HR investments result in business performance and answer the "why" and "how" questions in Fig. 6.1:

Why do investments in HR lead to business performance?

> ...because investments in HR create capabilities which create an organization's unique ability to turn strategy into results.

How do investments in HR lead to business performance?

> ...by focusing or bundling HR investments on capabilities which in turn allow strategies to lead to results.

Critical Capabilities Which Link HR and Business Performance

If organizations can be defined by their capabilities and if an organization's capabilities may link investments in HR and business performance, it is important to identify potential capabilities an organization may possess. In this essay, 10 possible capabilities are identified which may bridge investments in HR and business performance. These capabilities are summarized in Table 6.1 and each is described below in terms of how it may help the organization achieve results and how investments in HR may create the capability.

HR operating efficiency

A basic tenet of HR capability is to make sure that HR practices occur more efficiently. Better, faster, and cheaper HR practices mean that the organization has the capacity to do better HR work at a lower cost. The efficiency of HR is being increased in many firms through appropriate deployment of technology (e.g. SAP, PeopleSoft), creating shared service departments, and increasing investments in training and development for HR professionals. Unless HR departments master the quality, speed, and costs of their delivery, they will not gain respect and credibility required to deliver more strategic value. In one firm, the CEO said that the HR department would have a hard time being credible in more strategic issues when they continually made mistakes on administrative tasks. In one case, a CEO said that an offer letter went out for a senior position with the decimal point wrong which caused the company to be embarrassed. He challenged the HR department to be 100% accurate in little things before they played aggressively in the larger strategic issues.

Human (intellectual) capital

Recent work on intellectual capital (Saint-Onge, 1996; Stewart, 1997) shows that the workforce within a firm becomes a critical predictor of overall firm success. At a broad level, intellectual capital represents the collective knowledge, skills, and abilities of all employees within a firm. Economists track intellectual capital by the calculation of market value divided by replacement value (Snell, Lepak, and Youndt, 1998). This equation offers a broad insight into the importance of knowledge and people within a firm, but it does not translate to specific managerial actions. More recent works on intellectual capital assess the competence and commitment of employees within a work unit (Ulrich, 1998). For example, McDonald's has found that when restaurants increase the competence and commitment of people who work within a restaurant (a measure of each establishment's intellectual capital), they find these restaurants reach higher performance goals. HR practices may clearly be used to increase both competence and commitment of employees. By hiring, training, incentivizing, and

Table 6.1   Potential capabilities

Capability	Definition	Measures	Company examples
1. HR operating efficiency	• Ability of organization to perform HR practices better, faster, and cheaper	• Cost of HR delivery • Quality of HR delivery • Speed of HR delivery	Hewlett Packard
2. Human (intellectual) capital	• Ability of an organization to attract and retain, throughout the company, employees who have competence and commitment	• Competence of employees • Commitment of employees	McDonald's
3. Leadership depth	• Ability of an organization to ensure high quality of leadership throughout the company	• Bench strength (backup in place for key jobs)	Johnson & Johnson
4. Learning	• Ability of an organization to generate and generalize ideas with impact	• Degree of innovation, training, experimentation, reengineering • Degree of sharing ideas across boundaries	Coca-Cola
5. Change	• Ability of an organization to move quickly (agility, flexibility, speed)	• Pace of change • Speed of decision making • Agility with which organization acts	3-Corn
6. Customer connection	• Ability of an organization to bond with targeted customers	• Share of target customer sales, profit, and mindset • Relationship or intimacy with target customers	Royal Bank
7. Shared mindset	• Ability of an organization to create a common culture among all employees	• Degree of common focus among employees • Degree of shared values	Continental
8. Strategic clarity	• Ability of an organization to have a focused and clear strategy	• Degree of common strategy focus • Degree to which strategy focuses on the future	Southwest Airlines
9. Accountability	• Ability of an organization to have clear standards and expectations	• Degree of clear processes • Degree of clarity around responsibility	Allied Signal
10. Boundaryless organization	• Ability of an organization to move people, authority and ideas, and to reward behaviors across boundaries	• Degree of boundaryless interaction	General Electric

governing employees with the right set of skills and in the right way, firms may increase their human capital (Ulrich, Zenger, and Smallwood, 1999).

Leadership depth

A recent study by McKinsey consulting firm has found that CEOs believe there is a "war for talent," particularly in finding successors for senior management positions. Companies with leadership bench have the ability to continue to adapt and change with new business conditions. Johnson and Johnson has invested heavily in building the next generation of leaders through formal training programs and stretch job assignments. These investments build leaders who have the capacity to make bold and difficult decisions and to shape an organization for the future. HR practices may be used to create leadership bench. When more talented leaders are hired, training, compensated, and when the organization is governed in such a way to give these leaders profit and loss accountability, they build depth and capacity. These organizations seem to have long term, not short term success; create new strategies for changing business conditions; and be built to last over time (Collins and Porras, 1995).

Learning

In recent years, learning organizations have become identified as central to a firm's success (Wick, 1993). Organizations that learn seem to have the capacity to reinvent themselves, to manage knowledge, and to adjust to changing competitive conditions (Senge, 1990). Yeung, Ulrich, Nason, and Von Glinow (1998) found that learning organizations had the capacity to both generate and generalize ideas with impact. Coca Cola, for example, has invested heavily in a learning consortia where innovative ideas from one country are codified and shared with other countries facing similar issues. By learning to share and implement ideas, Coke has become more of a learning organization. Investments in HR practices increase this capacity to learn by innovative training, compensation, and communication efforts which encourage sharing ideas. Organizations that learn tend to be more innovative, able to manage knowledge workers, and able to create new strategies.

Change

In a world where the pace of change is faster than ever, organizations that win will develop the capacity to adapt and adjust quicker than competitors. Organizations that change quicker have the capacity to anticipate rather than react, to enter new markets before competitors, and to transform new cultures for new work requirements. 3-Com continually works to reinvent itself, to identify new markets, and move quickly into those markets. Their move into the personal organizer (Palm) market was done before major competitors, which gave them a market advantage. HR practices may improve the capacity for change. Understanding how to bring new individuals into a company who have the ability to shape a culture; building incentive systems which encourage new, not old behaviors; and creating processes to share best practices help organizations create agility, or the ability to change.

Customer connection

Many firms have discovered that 20% of customers account for 80% of business performance. These target customers become absolutely critical for a firm to compete and win. In some firms, the focus on target customers has led to a definition of success as the "share of target customer." For example, Royal Bank has identified wealthy clients and has targeted these clients. With dedicated account managers and account teams, they have worked to gain a higher percentage of these clients' business. Success is measured by "share of client" rather than absolute revenue. This means that Royal Bank works to get a high share of targeted accounts: managing the stock, bond, loans, equity, insurance, pension, and other financial transactions of targeted customers. HR practices may increase this customer connection by forming account teams, building compensation programs based on account performance, and including key customers in HR practices. HR practices which increase customer connection, in turn, will lead to business results because of repeat business, customer loyalty, and lower costs to create revenue.

Shared mindset

Shared mindset, or common culture, represents the extent to which employees have a common focus or agenda (Ulrich and Lake, 1990). When a shared mindset exists, employees have a common focus and commitment to how to work to meet goals. A shared mindset helps a company set an agenda and make sure that it translates to employee behavior. When Continental executives worked to turn around Continental, they chose a shared mindset which started with key customers, business travelers who paid full fare. Business travelers wanted Continental to be known as the "on time" airline so that they could have a predictable schedule. With on time as the desired shared mindset, Continental executives worked to make sure that HR practices focused employee behaviors on this shared mindset. This meant building training programs so employees understood how to make on-time happen; creating compensation which incented employees to be on time; and enacting suggestion systems whereby employees could share their ideas on how to be on time. Shared mindset leads to business performance because employees are focused, attentive, and engaged in a common agenda.

Strategic clarity

If a test with a single question were given to a random set of employees to identify a firm's probability of success, a marvelous question would be: "what is the strategy of this business which sets us apart from competitors and helps us win with customers?" When employees have common answers to this question, strategic clarity exists. This clarity helps customers know how to differentiate a firm and helps employees know what is expected of them. Southwest Airlines has strategic clarity. Employees throughout Southwest know that the airline wants to be the low cost, high touch airline. Multiple management decisions support this strategy, for example, one aircraft to save money on gates and turnaround time at airports; no frills on the airline; cheaper tickets without using travel agents and the ticket technology; point to point departures; no assigned seating; etc. This strategic clarity helps Southwest create a distinct niche among customers. It also commits employees to a clear agenda and purpose. HR practices of who is hired, how they are hired, and how they are trained play a critical role in making strategic clarity real to employees.

Accountability

Many firms make promises … to investors, customers, and employees. Firms that meet those promises are more likely to be successful. Accountability increases the probability of meeting promises. When promises are met, firms are more successful because they have long term commitment from customers and investors. Allied Signal has created a culture where discipline and accountability matter. When Allied removed sectors and organized around business units, they were able to assign clear profit and loss accountability to business unit leaders. These leaders know they have to deliver business performance and they have resources necessary to make it happen. This accountability culture has helped Allied leaders make difficult decisions and accomplish what they promise. HR practices build accountability. When goals are set and made, good things happen; when goals are set and missed, bad things happen. At times this accountability resides within individuals and at other times with teams. Accountability also comes from clear and standard processes for doing work which may come from mastering quality and other processes.

Boundaryless

Over time, most firms create multiple boundaries (Ashkenas et al., 1995). Vertical boundaries separate lower from higher level employees. Horizontal boundaries separate functions or units from each other. Geographic boundaries separate countries. External boundaries separate a firm from suppliers and customers. These boundaries cost time and money to cross. Removing boundaries makes an organization both more efficient and quicker. General Electric has worked hard to remove many types of boundaries. They encourage information sharing, talent movement, teams, and rewards to be shared from top to bottom, side to side, inside-out, and around the world. The removal of boundaries comes in part from HR practices which provide forums to share information (e.g. workout), have team based compensation, and communicate clearly the removal of boundaries.

Table 6.1 summarizes these 10 capabilities. They are not the only capabilities a firm might seek, but they indicate why and how investments in HR may lead to sustained business performance. Once these capabilities are identified, accomplished, and measured, they will ensure that investments in individual HR practices integrate and eventually lead to business performance.

Implications of Capability Focus

The capability focus creates common measures of success for line managers and HR professionals. For example, one senior HR executive said he would never draft another "HR Plan" because his HR initiatives had to be the business initiatives, or he was focusing HR on the wrong things. He said that once the operating committee identified the capabilities required to succeed, his job was to make those capabilities happen. Line managers were responsible for delivering capabilities; so was he. When HR investments lead capabilities, then line and HR share responsibility.

Organizational diagnosis

A capability focus also leads to a new answer to the question, "what makes my organization effective?" Instead of focusing on the organization structure (e.g. how many levels of organization do we have), workforce (e.g. how many employees do we have), or systems (e.g. how well do we staff, structure, and use systems), an organizational diagnosis should focus on capability. This requires (1) identifying which of the 10 capabilities the organization requires to win (cell 6 in Fig. 6.2); (2) creating indicators of those capabilities that can be tracked over time (see Table 6.1 for examples of measures of each of the 10); and (3) making HR investments which result in these capabilities. When this is done, organizations are successful not because of the investment in HR, but because of the capability which derives from HR investments.

By knowing that the path between investments in HR and business performance must pass through capabilities, line managers and HR professionals may be able to better link investments in HR and business performance. They may be more explicit about what HR investments to make – those which establish critical capabilities. They may know how to sustain business performance over time, by monitoring and tracking capabilities, not just HR practices. They may have confidence that business performance is not coincidental, but lasting.

HR deliverables

HR departments and professionals should be measured by deliverables more than doables (Ulrich, 1997). Capabilities become the deliverables, or results for HR. Rather than measure number of people hired, it is better to assess the quality of those hires (e.g. to what extent do they help the organization innovate, change, and deliver other capabilities). Rather than measure training activity, the focus would be on outcomes of training such as speed to market, customer intimacy, knowledge of work force. Rather than track percentage of employees on variable pay programs, it might be better to measure the productivity which results from those investments.

The 10 capabilities in Table 6.1 might become the deliverables of an HR department. One company picked three capabilities (HR efficiency, intellectual capital, and change), and then committed to these deliverables by guaranteeing them and putting bonuses for the top HR leaders at risk against them. When capabilities become the deliverables of HR, it changes the discussion between HR professionals and business leaders. Rather than discuss how to run a training program, HR professionals and line managers may discuss the capabilities required to win and how HR can make investments to make them happen. A capability focus also bonds the HR professional and line manager by having both accountable for the capabilities. If the capabilities are critical to turning strategy into results (Fig. 6.2), then the line manager should be willing to not only pay attention, but put pay at risk against the critical capabilities. In successful companies, HR professionals and line managers share the accountability for defining and delivering on capabilities.

HR measures

Rather than measure investments in HR practices (e.g. how many individuals attended training, how many are on a pay at risk program), a capability focus shifts attention to outcomes of the HR practices. It is more important to measure the extent to which a firm has the ability to change, build leadership depth, create customer connect, or some of the other capabilities in Table 6.1. These measures may lead to accountability for both the HR professional and line managers. They may be used in a balanced scorecard as the indicators of building the right organization.

HR professionals

For HR to become more of a profession, it must define a body of knowledge which shapes how work is done. This body of knowledge should include both what investments need to be made in HR as well as the outcomes of those investments (capabilities). HR professionals have declared that they want to add value and deliver results. To do so requires focusing on capabilities and deliverables more than HR practices and doables.

Conclusion

This chapter accepts the current literature that shows that investments in HR impact business performance. But, it goes on to show why and how this happens. When a firm turns HR investments into capabilities which in turn lead to business performance, it may identify the reasons why HR investments affect business performance and thereby increase the probability that performance will be sustained. By making this path clear, HR professionals don't need to do endless rounds of pushing rocks up hills (proposing programs and/or practices), only to have the energy dissipate half-way up the hill. The alignment of HR strategies and business performance through capabilities will ensure lasting results.

REFERENCES

Ashkenas, Ronald N., Ulrich, Dave, Prahalad, C.K., and Jick, Todd. 1995. *The Boundaryless Organization: Breaking the Chains of Organizational Structure*. San Francisco: Jossey-Bass.

Becker, Brian and Barry Gerhart. 1996. The impact of human resource practices on organizational performance: Progress and prospects. *Academy of Management Journal*, 39, 779–801.

Becker, Brian E., Mark A. Huselid, Peter S. Pickus, and Michael F. Spratt. 1997. HR as a source of shareholder value: Research and recommendations. *Human Resource Management Journal*, 36(1), 39–48.

Christensen, Ralph. 1997. Where is HR? *Human Resource Management Journal*, 36(1), 81–4.

Collins, James and Jerry Porras. 1995. *Built to Last: Successful Habits of Visionary Companies*. New York: Harper.

Delaney, John Thomas, and Huselid, Mark A. 1996. The impact of human resource management practices on perceptions of performance in for-profit and non-profit organizations. *Academy of Management Journal*, 39, 949–69.

Delaney, John Thomas, David Lewin, and Casey Ichniowski. 1988. Human resource management policies and practices in American firms. Industrial Relations Research Center, Graduate School of Columbia University.

Delaney, John Thomas, David Lewin, and Casey Ichinowski. 1989. HR policies and practices in American firms. US Department of Labor, Bureau of Labor-Management Relations and Cooperative Programs, BLMR 173. US Government Printing Office, Washington D.C.

Huselid, Mark A. 1995. The impact of human resource management practices on turnover, productivity, and corporate financial performance. *Academy of Management Journal*, 38(3), 635–72.

Jackson, Susan and Randall Schuler. 1995. Understanding human resource management in the context of organizations and their environments. *Annual Review of Psychology*, 46, 237–64.

Nkomo, Susan M. 1987. Human resource planning and organizational performance: An exploratory analysis. *Strategic Management Journal*, 8(4), 387–92.

Pfeffer, Jeffrey. 1994. *Competitive Advantage through People: Unleashing the Power of the Work Force*. Boston: Harvard Business School.

Pfeffer, Jeffrey. 1998. *The Human Equation*. Boston: Harvard Business School Press.

Saint-Onge, Hubert. 1996. Tacit knowledge: The key to the strategic alignment of intellectual capital. *Strategy and Leadership*, March/April, 10–14.

Senge, P. M. 1990. *The Fifth Discipline: The Art and Practice of the Learning Organization*.

Snell, Scott, David Lepak, and Mark Youndt. 1998. Managing the architecture of intellectual capital: Implications for strategic human resource management. In Patrick Wright, Lee Dyer, John Boudreau, and George Milkovich (eds.), *Research in personnel and human resources management*, Greenwich, CT: JAI Press.

Stewart, Thomas. 1997. *Intellectual Capital*. New York: Doubleday.

Ulrich, Dave. 1997. *Human Resource Champions: The Next Agenda for Adding Value and Delivering Results.* Boston: Harvard Business School Press.

Ulrich, Dave. 1998. Integrating practice and theory: Towards a more unified view of HR. In Patrick Wright, Lee Dyer, John Boudreau, and George Milkovich (eds.), *Research in Personnel and Human Resources Management,* Greenwich, CT: JAI Press.

Ulrich, Dave and Dale Lake. 1990. *Organizational Capability: Competing from the Inside/Out.* New York: Wiley.

Ulrich, Dave, Jack Zenger, and Norm Smallwood. 1999. *Results Based Leadership.* Boston: Harvard Business School Press.

Wick, Cal. 1993. *The Learning Edge: How Smart Managers and Smart Companies Stay Ahead.* New York: McGraw-Hill.

Yeung, Arthur and Dave Ulrich. 1990. Effective human resource practices for competitive advantages: An empirical assessment of organizations in transition. In Richard J. Niehaus and Karl F. Price (eds.), *Human Resource Strategies for Organizations in Transition.* New York: Plenum Publishing Company, pp. 311–26.

Yeung, Arthur, Dave Ulrich, Steve Nason, and Mary Ann Von Glinow. 1998. *Learning Capability: Generate* Generalize Ideas with Impact.* New York: Oxford University Press.

Part II

Global Dimensions

The chapters in this part highlight unique issues in strategic human resource management that arise in firms that are operating in a global environment. Globalization has worked to increase competition worldwide and to make the effective management of people even more important. This force has resulted in the need for companies (multinational companies, MNCs) to be more knowledgeable in the dynamics of worldwide competition and country differences regarding human resource management practices. Newer organizational forms like international joint ventures and international mergers and acquisitions have resulted. New forms of competitive strategy for this global environment have also resulted. Together these are having a huge impact on the fields of HRM and SHRM. As a consequence of this, we have included several more chapters that discuss international aspects of HRM and SHRM; and several more chapters that discuss the use of HRM and SHRM for competitive advantage, particularly for global competitive advantage.

It is argued by some that the strategic human resource implications resulting from global firms are not only more complex and challenging than those of domestic firms, but more important as well. Similar complexity and challenges arise for global firms that need to operate in different countries and understand their external environment components, for example, national culture, laws and regulations, competition, and political conditions. So global firms have major implications for strategic human resource management, both from the viewpoint of requiring firms to align human resource management policies and practices with the unique internal requirements of MNCs, and from the viewpoint of requiring firms to align their human resource management policies and practices with the unique demands of the multiple country environments in which they operate.

The first chapter in this part by Gupta and Govindarajan discusses how MNEs can gain global competitive advantage. This extends the work of Barney described in his chapter in Part I. The authors identify five critical issues MNCs need to consider if they desire to exploit their global presence in order to gain global competitive advantage.

These five include: adapting to local market differences; exploiting economies of global scale; exploiting economies of global scope; tapping optimal locations for activities and resources; and maximizing knowledge transfer across locations. Each of these five, while an important issue for MNCs wishing to gain global competitive advantage, is also important for human resource management. Consequently, through understanding the human resource implications of each of these five, strategic human resource management can help MNCs gain global competitive advantage, and in ways that are different, yet consistent with, ways strategic human resource management can help domestic firms gain competitive advantage.

In the second chapter, Sparrow and Braun provide an excellent overview and update of the literature in human resource strategy in the international context, also referred to as strategic international human resource management. In their chapter, the authors review the main models and concepts in strategic international human resource management that have been proposed over the last twenty years. These models reflect the enhanced complexity of business strategy and strategic human resource management when done in an international or global context. For both areas, globalization adds more complexity to organizational issues such as differentiation (local) and integration (global), and both of these issues have significant implications for strategic human resource management as the authors describe. The authors also review and discuss the other major question in the field of strategic human resource management and that is, "to what extent do human resource strategies, policies and practices need to reflect the local country conditions, such as culture, politics, and labor markets, in which the MNC is operating?"

Whereas the Sparrow and Braun chapter addresses issues related to the human resource strategy of an MNC, the third chapter by Schuler, Jackson, and Fendt addresses issues related to managing human resources in cross-border alliances. In particular they discuss international joint ventures and international mergers and acquisitions. Drawing upon the extensive literature in these two forms of cross-border alliances, the authors review two models of these alliances that describe the business realities and necessities in stages, and then, in turn, describe the human resource implications of them. By doing this the authors illustrate the strategic linkage between cross-border alliances and international human resource management. These linkages are described in several testable propositions using a variety of theoretical perspectives, including the resource-based view.

In the fourth chapter, Pucik discusses a very central construct for MNCs, namely "global mindset." Based upon his extensive research in MNCs, whether describing themselves as pursuing a meganational (aka, transnational or global) strategy or multidomestic strategy, at the end of the day, both strategies require some attention to local (decentralized) and global (centralized) considerations and issues. To achieve this end of managing both (dualities) as effectively as possible, MNCs need to use the proper structure and processes. But they need to do more than this if they are to have the necessary flexibility to adapt to changing conditions. This can be done, Pucik proposes, through the development of the global mindset. He then goes on to describe in detail what it is, how it can be developed among managers, and how MNCs can develop policies and human resource practices to facilitate behaviors consistent with the global mindset.

As suggested by the first four chapters, there are three major levels of analysis in strategic human resource management when we go to the international or global arena. These include the local or country level, the regional or multi-country level, and the global or all-country level. Having these three levels is one of the many reasons why strategic human resource management at the international level is usually more complex than at the domestic level. This is equally true whether discussing strategic human resource management from the academic viewpoint or the practice viewpoint.

Whereas the first four chapters in this part applied mostly to the global or all-country level of analysis both academically and practically, the four concluding chapters in this part apply mostly to the regional and local levels. The first of these is the review chapter by Schuler and Jackson. In their chapter the authors review the last twenty-five years of work in human resource management in the United States. In it they describe the two main developments: strategic human resource management and strategic international human resource management, with the latter development being the more recent and perhaps less developed. The authors provide a review of the relevant theories and frameworks that can be used in both areas and suggest a growing interest in the application of these existing theories and frameworks in the area of strategic international human resource management.

Mayrhofer and Brewster, in the sixth chapter in this part, take a regional focus on international human resource management by looking at developments in Europe over time. The authors explore the question of the extent to which human resource practices amongst countries in Europe are converging, diverging, or remaining about the same (stasis) in their differences. Whilst detecting some convergence, the authors suggest that their fifteen years worth of data suggest that country differences within the European region still remain a key factor in human resource management throughout Europe. Their observations have important implications for practitioners and researchers in strategic international human resource management, in Europe and elsewhere.

Two significant examples of the importance of considering local differences in practice and research are China and India. With almost forty percent of the world's population, these two countries are important for MNCs everywhere, and subsequently for strategic international human resource management. Thus it behooves researchers and practitioners to know the human resource environment in each of these two countries, as well as the other countries of the world. In the first of these two chapters, Cooke describes the human resource environment in China. She describes such factors as forms of business, employment systems, the trade union movement, and government laws and regulations. She also describes some typical human resource practices for pay, recruitment, selection, and performance appraisal and concludes with a discussion of some key challenges facing human resource management in China.

Saini and Budhwar conclude the chapters in this part with a description of the human resource environment in India. They begin by describing the Indian economy and business environment and the evolution of human resource management in India, particularly focusing on the development of personnel management and the industrial relations regulations and practices in the 1920s. They describe the development of human resource development and the differences among personnel management, human resource development, and human resource management. These differences are important for an understanding of human resource management in India today. The authors also describe the impact of the country culture of India on human resource policies and practices and the extensive set of labor laws still relevant in India today. Their analysis and description of India, as Cooke's of China, represent important articles that can be useful to academics and practitioners working or researching in these countries. This applies equally to the rest of the nations of the world that are now to be studied more systematically for their relevance to strategic international human resource management.

Chapter 7

Converting Global Presence into Global Competitive Advantage

Anil K. Gupta and Vijay Govindarajan

In the early 1990s, PepsiCo, Inc. established an ambitious goal to more than triple its international soft drinks revenues – from $1.5 billion in 1990 to $5.0 billion by 1995. Charging boldly in the pursuit of these goals, Pepsi indeed built an extensive and wide-ranging global presence by the mid-1990s. Yet this global expansion did not translate into growth and profitability. In fact, by 1997, Pepsi withdrew from some major markets, such as South Africa, and had to take a nearly $1 billion loss from international beverage operations. While the global market for beverages continued to expand rapidly, Pepsi's international market share and revenues were actually shrinking, a situation that contrasted sharply with an aggressively growing Coca-Cola.[1]

As PepsiCo's experience demonstrates, securing global presence is anything but synonymous with possessing global competitive advantage. Building global presence gives you the right to play the game. However, it says little about whether and how you will actually win the game. Furthermore, winning one game does not ensure that you will win the next one. In short, transforming global presence into global competitive advantage requires systematic analysis, purposeful thinking, and careful orchestration, and is a never-ending process. Without a rigorously disciplined approach, global presence can easily degenerate into a liability that distracts management and wastes resources. The end result can even be a loss of competitive advantage in the domestic market.

A. K. Gupta and V. Govindarajan, "Converting Global Presence into Global Competitive Advantage," *Academy of Management Executive*, Vol. 15, No. 2 (2001): 45–58.

Sources of Global Competitive Advantage

To convert global presence into global competitive advantage, companies must exploit five value creation opportunities: adapting to local market differences, exploiting economies of global scale, exploiting economies of global scope, tapping the optimal locations for activities and resources, and maximizing knowledge transfer across locations.

We discuss the origins of each opportunity and the specific ways in which they can yield competitive advantage. We also outline the challenges and obstacles that often prevent firms from exploiting these opportunities to the fullest extent.[2]

Adapting to local market differences

A direct implication of being present in multiple countries is that companies must respond to the inevitable heterogeneity they will encounter in these markets. Differences in language, culture, income levels, customer preferences, and distribution systems are only some of the factors to be considered. Even in the case of apparently standard products, at least some degree of local adaptation is often necessary, or at least advisable. Cellular phone manufacturers, for example, must adapt their products to different languages and the magnitude of background noise on the street. By responding to country-level heterogeneity through local adaptation of products, services, and processes, a company can reap benefits in three fundamental areas: market share, price realization, and competitive position.[3]

Increased market share

By definition, offering standard products and services across countries reduces the boundaries of the served market to only those customers whose needs are uniform across countries. Local adaptation of products and services has the opposite effect, expanding the boundaries to also include those customers within a country who value different features and attributes. One of McGraw-Hill Companies' products, *Business-Week*, provides a good illustration of how local adaptation of products and services can enlarge the customer base. As the magazine's editor-in-chief explained: "Each week, we produce three editions. For example, this week's North American cover story is 'The New Hucksterism.' The Asian edition cover is 'Acer, Taiwan's Global Powerhouse.' And the European-edition cover is 'Central Europe.' In addition, our writers create an additional 10 to 12 pages of stories customized for readers in Europe, Asia, and Latin America. They also turn out four pages of international-finance coverage, international editorials, and economic analysis, and a regional feature column."[4]

Improved price realization

Tailoring products and services to the preferences of local customers (e.g. Baskin-Robbins's introduction of green-tea flavored ice cream in Japan) enhances the value delivered to them. As a corollary, a portion of this increased value should translate into higher price realization for the firm.

Neutralizing local competitors

One of the natural advantages enjoyed by most local competitors stems from their deep understanding of and single-minded responsiveness to the needs of the local market. For example, in the Japanese soft-drinks market, Suntory Ltd. and Asahi Soft Drinks Co. have been among the first movers in offering new concepts such as Asian teas and fermented-milk drinks. When a global player also customizes its products and services to local needs and preferences, it is mounting a frontal attack on the local competitors in their market niche. In its efforts to neutralize Suntory's and Asahi's moves and attack them on their home turf, Coca-Cola introduced several new products in Japan that are not offered by the company in other markets, including an Asian tea called Sokenbicha, an English tea called Kochakaden, and a coffee drink called Georgia.[5]

Challenges

While seeking the benefits of local adaptation, however, companies must be prepared to face a number of challenges and obstacles:

- In most cases, local adaptation of products and services will increase the company's cost structure. Given the inexorable intensity of competition in most industries, companies can ill afford any competitive disadvantage on the cost dimension. Managers have to find the right equilibrium in the trade-off between localization and cost structure. For example, cost considerations initially led Procter & Gamble to standardize diaper design across European markets, despite market research data indicating that Italian mothers, unlike those in other countries, preferred diapers covering the baby's navel. After some time, however, recognizing that this particular feature was critical to Italian mothers, the company consequently incorporated this design feature for the Italian market, despite its adverse cost implications.[6]
- In many instances, local adaptation, even when well-intentioned, may prove to be misguided. When the American restaurant chain TGI Fridays entered the South Korean market, it deliberately incorporated many local dishes, such as kimchi, in its menu. This responsiveness, however, backfired. Company analysis of the tepid market performance revealed that Korean customers anticipated a visit to TGIF as a visit to America, finding local dishes on the menu was inconsistent with their expectations. Companies must take the pulse of their market continually to detect if and when local adaptation becomes misguided adaptation.
- As with many other aspects of global marketing, the necessary degree of local adaptation usually will shift over time. In many industry segments, a variety of factors, such as the influence of global media, greater international travel, and declining income disparities across countries, may pave the way toward increasing global standardization. Consistent with the earlier example of *BusinessWeek*, we foresee a diminished need over time for geography-based customization. In other industry segments, particularly where the product or service can be delivered over the Internet (such as music), the need for even greater customization and local adaptation may increase over time. Companies must recalibrate the need for local adaptation on an ongoing basis; over-adaptation extracts a price just as surely as does underadaptation.

Exploiting economies of global scale

Building global presence automatically expands a company's scale of operations, giving it larger revenues and a larger asset base. However, larger scale will create competitive advantage only if the company systematically undertakes the tough actions needed to convert scale into economies of scale. The potential benefits of economies of scale can appear in various ways: spreading fixed costs, reducing capital and operating costs, pooling purchasing power, and creating critical mass.[7]

Spreading fixed costs over larger volume
This benefit is most salient in areas such as research and development, operations, and advertising. For instance, Merck, the pharmaceutical giant, can spread R&D costs over its global sales volume thereby reducing per-unit costs of development.

Reducing capital and operating costs per unit
This benefit is often a consequence of the fact that doubling the capacity of a production facility typically increases the cost of building and operating the facility by a factor of less than two.

Pooling global purchasing power over suppliers
Concentrating global purchasing power over any specific supplier generally leads to volume discounts and lower transaction costs. For example, as Marriott has raised its stakes in the global lodging business, its purchase of such goods as furnishings, linens, and beverages has stepped up dramatically. Exercising global purchasing power over a few vendors (e.g. PepsiCo for soft drinks) is part of Marriott's efforts to convert its global presence into global competitive advantage.

Creating requisite critical mass in selected activities
A larger scale gives the global player the opportunity to build centers of excellence for the development of specific technologies and/or products. To develop a center of excellence, a company generally needs to focus a critical mass of talent in one location. In view of the potential to leverage the output of such a center on a global scale, a global player will be more willing and able to make the necessary resource commitments required for such a center.

Challenges
Few, if any, of these potential strategic benefits of scale materialize automatically. The following challenges await firms in their efforts to secure these benefits:

• Scale economies can be realized only by concentrating scale-sensitive resources and activities in one or a few locations. Concentration is a two-edged sword, however. For example, with manufacturing activities, concentration means that firms must export centrally manufactured goods (e.g. components, subsystems, or finished products) to various markets. In making decisions about the location of any activity, firms must weigh the potential benefits from concentration against increased transportation and tariff costs.
• One unintended result of the geographic concentration of any activity is to isolate that activity from the targeted markets. Such isolation can be risky since it may

cause delayed, or inadequate, response to market needs. Another management challenge is to minimize the costs of isolation.

- Concentrating an activity in a designated location also makes the rest of the company dependent on that location. This sole-source dependence implies that, unless the location has world-class competencies, a firm may create a global mess instead of global competitive advantage. A European executive of Ford Motor Company, reflecting on the company's concentration of activities during a global integration program in the mid-1990s, said: "Now if you mis-judge the market, you are wrong in 15 countries rather than only one." The pursuit of global scale economies raises the added challenge of building world-class competencies at those locations in which the activities will be concentrated.

- In situations where global presence stems from cross-border acquisitions, as with British Petroleum's acquisition of Amoco, realizing economies of scale requires massive restructuring. Firms must scale up at those locations where activities are to be concentrated and scale down or even close shop at the other locations. This restructuring demands large financial investment, incurs huge one-time transition costs, and always results in organizational and psychological trauma. Furthermore, scaledowns or closures may damage the company's image and relations with local governments, local customers, and local communities. On top of all this, erroneous decisions in choosing locations are usually very difficult, expensive, and time consuming to reverse. Nonetheless, firms cannot realize the advantageous economies of scale without making tough decisions. Management must be willing to undertake a comprehensive and logical analysis and then have the courage of its convictions to carry out timely and decisive action.

Exploiting economies of global scope

Global scope refers to the multiplicity of regions and countries in which a company markets its products and services. Consider the case of two hypothetical advertising agencies, Alpha and Beta, whose sales revenues are roughly comparable. Assume that Alpha offers services in only five countries, whereas Beta is in 25 countries. In this instance, we would consider the global scope of Beta to be broader than that of Alpha. Global scope is rarely a strategic imperative when vendors are serving customers who operate in just one country or customers who are global but who engage in centralized sourcing. In contrast, the economic value of global scope can be enormous when vendors are serving customers who, despite being global, need the delivery of identical or similar products and services across many markets. In fulfilling the needs of such multilocation global customers, companies have two potential avenues through which to turn global scope into global competitive advantage: providing coordinated services and leveraging their market power.[8]

Providing coordinated services to global customers

Consider three scenarios: Microsoft, as it launches a new software product in more than 50 countries on the same day and needs to source advertising services in every one of the targeted markets; McDonald's, which must source virtually identical ketchup and mustard pouches for its operations in every market; and Shell Oil, which needs to source similar process-control equipment for its many refineries around the world. In all of these examples, a global customer needs to purchase a bundle of identical or similar products and services across a number of countries. The global customer could source these products and services either from a host of local suppliers or from a single global supplier that is present in all of its markets. Compared with a horde of local suppliers, a single global supplier can provide value for the global customer through greater consistency in the quality and features of products and services across countries, faster and smoother coordination across countries, and lower transaction costs.

Market power compared with competitors

A global supplier has the opportunity to understand the unique strategic requirements and culture of its global customer. Since it takes time to build this type of customer-specific proprietary knowledge, particularly in the case of multilocation global customers, potential competitors are initially handicapped and can more easily be kept at bay. Federal Express, a major supplier of logistics and distribution services to Laura Ashley, currently enjoys this advantage. As a global logistics provider, FedEx has had the chance to deepen its understanding of its role in Laura Ashley's value chain in all of its served markets. Such understanding is customer-specific and takes time to build. As long as FedEx continues to provide effective and efficient logistics services to Laura Ashley, this knowledge will serve as a major entry barrier for other local or global logistics suppliers.

Challenges

Despite these benefits, securing economies of global scope is not without its own challenges:

- A multilocation global vendor serving the needs of a multilocation global customer is conceptually analogous to one global network serving the needs of another global network. Every global network, however effectively managed, typically has a plethora of power centers, accompanied by competing perspectives on the optimal course of action. One of the management challenges for a global vendor is to understand the ongoing tug of war that shapes the needs and buying decisions of the customer network.
- Even for global customer accounts, the actual delivery of goods and services must be executed at the local level. Yet local country managers cannot be given total freedom in their operations with global customer accounts. They must orient their actions around their global customers' need for consistency both in product and service features and in marketing terms and conditions. Another challenge in capturing the economies of global scope lies in being responsive to the tension between two conflicting needs: the need for central coordination of most elements of the marketing mix, and the need for local autonomy in the actual delivery of products and services.

Tapping the optimal locations for activities and resources

Even though global economies have become increasingly integrated and influenced by the media so that cultures take on many of the same aspects, most countries will continue to be largely heterogeneous for years to come. Intercountry heterogeneity has an impact on the need for local adaptation in a company's products and services. But differences across countries also reveal themselves in the form of differences in cost structures and skill levels. A firm that can exploit these intercountry differences better than its competitors has the potential to create significant proprietary advantage.[9]

In performing the various activities along its value chain (e.g. R&D, procurement, component manufacturing, assembly, marketing, sales, distribution, and service), every firm has to make a number of crucial decisions, including where the activity will take place. Optimizing the location for every activity in the value chain can yield one or more of three strategic benefits: performance enhancement, cost reduction, and risk reduction.

Performance enhancement

Fiat's decision to choose Brazil, rather than its native Italy, to design and launch the Palio, its "world car," and Microsoft's decision to establish a corporate research laboratory in Cambridge, UK, are good examples of location decisions that were guided predominantly by the goal of building and sustaining world-class excellence in the selected activities. Location decisions can affect the quality with which any activity is performed in terms of availability of needed talent, speed of learning, and the quality of external and internal coordination.

Cost reduction

Two examples of location decisions founded predominantly on cost-reduction considerations are: Nike's decision to source the manufacture of athletic shoes from Asian countries such as China, Vietnam, and Indonesia; and the decision of Texas Instruments to set up a software development unit in India. Location decisions can affect the cost structure in terms of the cost of local manpower and other resources, the cost of transportation and logistics, as well as government incentives[10] and the local tax structure.[11]

Risk reduction

Given the wild swings in exchange ratios between the US dollar and the Japanese yen (in relation to each other as well as to other major currencies), a critical basis for cost competition between Ford and Toyota has been their relative ingenuity at managing currency risks. For these competitors, one of the ways to manage currency risks has been to spread the high-cost elements of their manufacturing operations across a few select and carefully chosen locations around the world. Location decisions can affect the risk profile of the firm with respect to currency, economic, and political risks.[12]

Challenges

There are challenges associated with using geographical differences to create global competitive advantage:

- The way in which activities are performed depends not only on the characteristics of the factor inputs but also on the management skills with which these inputs are converted into value-added outputs. The choice of a seemingly optimal location cannot guarantee that the quality and cost of factor inputs will be optimal. Managers must ensure that the comparative advantage of a location is captured and internalized rather than squandered because of weaknesses in productivity and the quality of internal operations. Ford Motor Company has amplified the proprietary advantage of locating some of its manufacturing operations in Mexico. People often assume that, in countries such as Mexico, lower wage rates come side-by-side with lower productivity. While this may be true statistically for the country as a whole, it does not have to be so for a specific firm. Because unemployment in Mexico is higher than in the US, Ford can be more selective about whom it hires in its Mexican operations. Given lower turnover of employees, the company can also invest more in training and development. Thus the net result can be not just lower wage rates but also higher productivity than in the US.

- The optimality of any location hinges on the cost and quality of factor inputs at this location relative to all other locations. This fact is important because countries not only evolve over time, but do so at different rates and in different directions. Thus for any particular activity, today's choice location may no longer be optimal three years down the road. A relentless pursuit of optimal locations requires the global company to remain somewhat footloose. Nike continuously assesses the relative attractiveness of various manufacturing locations and has demonstrated a willingness and ability to shift locations over time. Managers should not let today's location decisions diminish the firm's flexibility in shifting locations as needed.

- Optimal locations will generally be different for different resources and activities. Yet another challenge in fully capturing the strategic benefits of optimal locations is to excel at coordination across dispersed locations. Texas Instruments' high-speed telecommunications chip, TCM9055, was conceived in collaboration with engineers from Sweden, designed in France using software tools developed in Houston, produced in Japan and Dallas, and tested in Taiwan.[13]

Maximizing knowledge transfer across locations

Foreign subsidiaries can be viewed from several perspectives. One way to view Marriott's subsidiary in the UK is in terms of its market position within the UK's hotel industry. An alternate view of Marriott UK would be as a package of tangible assets, such as buildings, equipment, and capital. Yet another view would be to see Marriott UK as a reservoir of knowledge in areas such as real estate development, revenue management, hotel operations, and customer service. Building on this last perspective, we can view every global company not only as a portfolio of subsidiaries with tangible assets, but also as a portfolio of knowledge centers.

Given the heterogeneity of countries, every subsidiary has to create some degree of unique knowledge to exploit the resource and market opportunities of the local environment. Of course, not all locally created knowledge is relevant outside the local environment. For example, the ability to execute advertising in the Japanese language has little or no value outside Japan. However, other types of locally created knowledge may be relevant across multiple countries, and, if leveraged effectively, can yield strategic benefits to the global enterprise, ranging from faster product and process innovation to lower cost of innovation and reduced risk of competitive preemption.[14]

Faster product and process innovation
All innovation requires the incorporation of new ideas, whether they are developed internally or acquired and absorbed from others. A global company's skill at transferring knowledge across subsidiaries gives these subsidiaries the added benefit of innovations created by their peers. By minimizing, if not altogether eliminating, counterproductive reinvention of the wheel, product and process innovations get accelerated across the entire global network. Procter & Gamble's highly successful launch of Liquid Tide in the US market in the late 1980s occurred at least partly because the development of this product incorporated technologies pioneered in Cincinnati (a new ingredient to help suspend dirt in wash water), Japan (cleaning agents), and Brussels (ingredients that fight the mineral salts present in hard water).[15]

Lower cost of innovation
A second by-product of not reinventing the wheel is considerable savings in the costs of innovation. For example, the efficient stocklist-based distribution system developed by Richardson Vicks's Indian operations, now a part of Procter & Gamble India, found ready applicability in the company's Indonesian and Chinese operations.[16] Such cross-border replication of an innovation from one country to another eliminates or at least significantly reduces the costs associated with from-the-ground-up experimentation in that country.

Reduced risk of competitive preemption
A global company that demands constant innovations from its subsidiaries but does not leverage these innovations effectively across subsidiaries risks becoming a fount of new ideas for competitors. Procter & Gamble is keenly aware of these risks. Several of P&G's subsidiaries are dedicated to improving the fit, performance, and look of the disposable diaper. Over the last decade, P&G's ability to systematically identify the successful innovations and expedite a global rollout of these innovations has thwarted competitors from stealing its new ideas and replicating them in other markets. Effective and efficient transfer of knowledge across subsidiaries has helped P&G safeguard its innovations and enabled it to significantly reduce the risk of competitive preemption.

Challenges
Most companies tap only a fraction of the full potential in realizing the enormous economic value inherent in transferring and leveraging knowledge across borders. Some of the primary reasons are:

- Knowledge transfer from one subsidiary to another cannot occur unless the source and the target units and an intermediary, such as regional or corporate headquarters, recognize the existence of unique know-how in the source unit, and the potential value of this know-how in the target unit. Since significant geographic, linguistic, and cultural distances often separate subsidiaries, the potential for knowledge transfer can easily remain buried under a sea of ignorance. Companies face the management challenge of creating mechanisms to systematically and routinely uncover the opportunities for knowledge transfer.

- A subsidiary with uniquely valuable know-how is likely to enjoy a knowledge monopoly within the global enterprise. Power struggles are also both normal and ubiquitous in any organization. Thus at least some subsidiaries will view uniquely valuable know-how as the currency through which they acquire and retain power. The symptoms of this pathology are most obvious in the case of manufacturing facilities where relative superiority on an internal basis often serves as survival insurance in a footloose corporation. Management must ensure that subsidiaries are enthusiastic rather than reluctant to share what they know.

- Like the knowledge-is-power syndrome, the not-invented-here syndrome is also a chronic malady in many organizations. Two of the engines of this syndrome are ego-defense mechanisms that induce some managers to block information suggesting the greater competence of others, and power struggles that lead some managers to pretend that the knowhow of peer units is neither unique nor valuable. Global enterprises committed to knowledge transfer must also address the management challenge of making subsidiaries eager rather than reluctant to learn from peer units.

- Only a subset of an organization's knowledge exists in the form of codified knowledge, such as a chemical formula, an engineering blue-print, or an operations manual. Such codified knowledge readily lends itself to transfer and distribution across subsidiaries through electronic or other mechanisms for document exchange. However, much valuable know-how often exists in the form of tacit knowledge that is embedded in the minds, behavior patterns, and skills of individuals or teams – for example, a vision of a particular technology's future roadmap, and competencies at managing global customer accounts. With effort and investment, it might be possible to articulate and codify some of the tacit knowledge. Nonetheless, its embedded and elusive nature often makes tacit knowledge impossible to codify and thus difficult to transfer. The global enterprise must design and erect effective and efficient bridges for the transfer of knowledge (especially, noncodifiable tacit knowledge) across subsidiaries.

Creating Global Competitive Advantage: Action Implications

Focusing on the individual business as the unit of analysis, Table 7.1 summarizes the key issues that must be addressed to clarify the scope of each value-creation opportunity and to uncover the underlying challenges.

Exploiting any opportunity requires action. All action occurs at the level of activities in the firm's value chain. Therefore, capturing these five sources of value requires the firm to optimize on a global basis the organization and management of each value-chain activity – such as R&D, manufacturing, selling, and customer service.

As depicted in the star framework in Fig. 7.1, creating and managing an optimal network for each value-chain activity requires optimizing network architecture,

Table 7.1   Issues to consider in exploiting global presence

Adapting to local market differences

- Have we accurately drawn a distinction between those attributes where the customer truly values adaptation and those other attributes where the customer is either neutral or averse to adaptation?
- For those attributes where adaptation adds value, how much is the customer willing to pay for this value?
- Do we manage our product design and manufacturing activities in such a manner that we can offer the needed intercountry variety at the lowest possible cost?
- Do we have sensing mechanisms (such as market research and experimental marketing) that would give us early warning signals about increases or decreases in customers' preferences for local adaptation?

Exploiting economies of global scale

- In designing our products, have we exhausted all possibilities to utilize concepts such as modularization and/or standardization of subsystems and components?
- Have we accurately drawn a distinction between those activities that are scale-sensitive and those that are not?
- Have we fully assessed the benefits from economies of scale against any resulting increases in other costs, such as transportation and tariffs?
- Have we established effective and efficient coordination mechanisms so that we do not squander the benefits from scale economies?
- Have we built world-class competencies in the locations where we have chosen to concentrate the scale-sensitive activities?

Exploiting economies of global scope

- Is our internal coordination of marketing activities across locations at least on par with (and preferably ahead of) the extent to which our customers have integrated their own purchasing activities?
- How well do we understand the various pulls and pushes shaping the needs and buying decisions of our customer's global network?

Tapping the optimal locations for activities and resources

- Have we ensured that our location-based advantages are neither squandered nor neutralized by competitors because of any weaknesses in the quality and productivity of our internal operations at these locations?
- Do we have the organizational and resource flexibility to shift locations over time as some other locations begin to become more optimal than our current locations?
- How frictionless is the degree of our coordination across the various locations?

Maximizing knowledge transfer across locations

- How good are we at routinely and systematically uncovering the opportunities for knowledge transfer?
- How enthusiastic are our subsidiaries to share knowledge with other units?
- How eager are our subsidiaries to learn from any and all sources including peer subsidiaries?
- How good are we at codifying the product and process innovations generated by our subsidiaries? Have we built efficient communication mechanisms for the sharing of codified know-how across locations? How good are we at keeping codified knowledge proprietary to our company?
- Have we built effective mechanisms (e.g. people transfer, face-to-face interchange) for the transfer of tacit knowledge across locations?

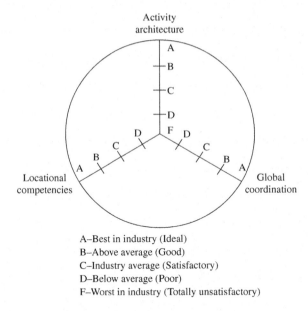

Figure 7.1   Drivers of global value: the star framework.

competencies at the nodes of the network, and coordination across the nodes. In other words, for any given business, exploiting global presence requires taking actions to create optimal R&D, purchasing, and manufacturing networks.[17]

Designing an optimal architecture

For any activity, network architecture refers to the number of locations in which that activity is performed, as well as the identity and specific charter of each location. Although an infinite number of choices exist, three of the most common architectural options are: concentration in one location (e.g. management of the reservation system at Marriott); differentiated centers of excellence (e.g. dedicated vehicle program centers at Ford); and dispersion to regional or local units (e.g. recruitment and training at McDonald's).

While activity architecture will shape organization structure decisions, it is not the same thing as organizational structure. For example, Honda's decision to build a design center in Italy is an activity-architecture decision. In contrast, organizational structure deals with such questions as who should report to whom (e.g. who should have direct control over the Italian design center – country manager for Honda Italy, president of Honda Europe, or the corporate design chief?). Because they require commitment of investment on the ground, architectural choices are less reversible than structural ones. Therefore, getting the activity architecture right is far more important than getting the organization structure right.

The issues that must be addressed in designing an optimal global architecture are: Does the number of locations where this activity will be performed ensure critical mass at each location and full exploitation of economies of scale? For each activity, does the choice of locations optimize both the quality with which this activity will be performed, and its cost competitiveness, while minimizing the political, economic, and currency risks associated with it? Is the charter of each location defined in a way that eliminates unneeded duplication across locations?

Reassessing the optimality of activity architecture on a periodic basis is essential. Some of the important factors that can render today's optimal architecture less than desirable tomorrow are: shifts in factor-cost differences across countries, changes in tariff regimes, trends in demand patterns across countries, variations in product design, and adoption of new manufacturing technologies. In 1997, Asea Brown Boveri's declaration that it would shift thousands of jobs from Western Europe to the emerging economies over the next five years illustrates the need for such ongoing reassessment. The company believed that this shift in manufacturing architecture would increase efficiency, take greater advantage of lower labor costs in the emerging economies, and heighten the company's responsiveness to customers in its largest growth markets.[18]

Building world-class competencies

Once a firm has chosen the locations at which a particular activity will be performed, the next step is to build the requisite competencies at those locations. Otherwise, the firm could easily lose all of the gains from creating a seemingly optimal architecture. As a hypothetical example, take an American heavy machinery company that has a significant European presence and two production centers, in Germany and in France, each supplying about 50 percent of its European market needs. With labor costs a significant portion, say 21 percent, of the total cost structure, the CEO weighs the option of consolidating all European production resources into one new facility in Spain. The CEO anticipates about a 12-percent net reduction in the total cost structure: a five-percent saving due to consolidating the two factories, and a seven-percent saving coming from the one-third reduction in labor costs that would result from lower manufacturing wages in Spain. Is this change in the architecture of the firm's European manufacturing operations the right move?

Despite the attraction of the projected reduction, the CEO should make this change only when confident that labor productivity in the Spanish plant will be greater than 67 percent of the average labor productivity in the existing German and French plants; the indirect effect of labor on other costs (e.g. raw material usage and machine utilization) will be either neutral or positive; and the quality and performance of products will remain world-class.

Many countries with relatively lower wage rates also suffer from lower levels of productivity. Nonetheless, companies should resist becoming prisoners of the aggregate statistics. It is often possible for a company to locate production in a low-labor-cost country and still achieve world-class productivity and quality levels. Both Motorola and Siemens have done this in China. This fortuitous combination of low labor costs and world-class operations is particularly feasible under the following conditions: the developing economy, despite its relative poverty, has a large pool of highly educated workers (as in India, China, and the Philippines); high unemployment levels furnish the multinational firm with a very talented and motivated pool of employees; and the company is setting up greenfield operations, where it is possible to establish world-class processes from day one, a task that often is far easier than shaking up the status quo in a well-entrenched organization.

As one would expect, the greater a business's dependence on a particular location, the greater is the need to have world-class competencies in the relevant activities there. The importance of any location is likely to be very high when it is the sole location, or one of only a few locations where the activity is concentrated, as is often true in the case of upstream activities such as R&D and manufacturing. But even in the case of downstream activities, such as sales, that are often dispersed across many locations, world-class market-sensing and selling competencies are critical, especially in the major markets. For example, any weakness in Ikea's market-sensing competencies in a moderately sized market such as Spain would be far less costly for the company than in such megamarkets as the US or China. Ikea's initial setbacks in the US market can be attributed in part to major blindspots in its market-sensing capabilities.[19]

Ensuring frictionless coordination

The final component in creating an optimal global network is to develop and maintain smooth, seamless coordination across locations. The worldwide business team needs to foster operational coordination between units performing similar activities (e.g. two R&D labs or two production centers), as well as those performing complementary activities (e.g. manufacturing and procurement and manufacturing and marketing), and the transfer of knowledge and skills across locations. The pursuit of seamless coordination along these dimensions requires creating eagerness among those managers whose cooperation is essential, and setting up mechanisms that will put the desired cooperation into practice.

Some of the high-leverage organizational mechanisms to create eagerness for cooperation among managers working in different subsidiaries are:

- Using an incentive system that links at least part of the subsidiary managers' rewards to the firm's regional or global performance. For instance, Procter & Gamble gives explicit weight to both country and regional performance in computing annual incentive payments to country managers.[20]
- Instituting a bench-marking system that routinely compares the performance of relevant subsidiaries along key indicators and makes these comparisons visible to the subsidiaries and their corporate superiors. A system of this kind puts the spotlight and pressure on the weak performers, encouraging them to learn from peers. For example, the typical business area headquarters within Asea Brown Boveri distributes internally detailed monthly information on critical parameters such as failure rates, throughput times, inventory turns, and days receivables for each factory belonging to the business area. ABB management believes that these reports put even more intense pressure on the managers than external marketplace competition.[21]
- Giving high visibility to individuals who achieve excellent business results through collaboration with peers in other subsidiaries. For instance, Procter & Gamble

regularly publicizes as success models those managers who demonstrate a zest for and ability to succeed at cross-border coordination.[22]

Some high-leverage mechanisms to make cooperation feasible are:

- Formal rules and procedures that enhance communication. Examples would be standard formats for reports, common terminology and language, and routine distribution of the reports to the relevant managers. Asea Brown Boveri's ABA-CUS system is an outstanding example of a formal communication system that works.[23]
- Global or regional business teams, functional councils, and similar standing committees that routinely bring key managers from various subsidiaries into face-to-face communication with each other. IBM's Global Software Team[24] and Ford's Capstone Project Team[25] are examples of effective coordination forums.
- Corporate investment in cultivating interpersonal familiarity and trust among the key managers of various subsidiaries. Managers from different subsidiaries can be brought together in executive development programs, managers can be rotated across locations, and language skills can be developed among these managers so that these get-acquainted encounters have high leverage. Motorola's Global Organizational Leadership Development (GOLD) program brings together 30 executives at a time from various subsidiaries within the Paging Group. Similarly, Unilever has long used rotation of managers across countries, as well as its Four Acres management-training center.[26]

Table 7.2 summarizes the typical criteria for assessing the optimality of any global network according to activity architecture, competencies at the nodes, and coordination across the nodes.

A Two-Step Approach to Building Global Advantage

General Motors, Ford, Toyota, and DaimlerChrysler were locked in a battle for global dominance in the automobile industry in 2001. Which firm will dominate five or 10 years in the future depends largely on the ability of each to convert its global presence into global competitive advantage.

Managers should never assume that global presence by itself is the same as global competitive advantage. Having global presence implies that a firm has available to it five distinct opportunities to create global competitive advantage: local adaptation, global scale, global scope, location, and knowledge advantage. Realizing these opportunities requires firms to adopt a two-step approach for analysis and action. They should first evaluate the optimality of the global network for each activity in the value chain along three dimensions: activity architecture, locational competencies, and global coordination. Based on this evaluation, firms should then design and execute actions to eliminate, or at least reduce, the suboptimalities.

Table 7.2 Assessment of global competitive advantage

Basis for global advantage	*Typical criteria for assessment*
Optimal architecture (for each value-chain activity)	• What is the size of the asset and employment base? • Have we captured economies of scale and scope in manufacturing, subcontracting, and raw material purchases? Are there any diseconomies of scale? • Do we have the needed sales and distribution strength in all key markets? Are our distribution systems too concentrated or too dispersed? • Do we have the needed critical mass in each key technology area? Is there unneeded duplication across technology centers? • Do locational choices automatically create push for excellence in the particular activity (e.g. miniaturization in Japan)? • Do we have critical talent available? • What will be the total impact on overall cost structure? • What will be the impact of government inducements and tax considerations? • What are the currency and political risks?
World-class competencies (by function; for each facility)	• Do we define quality from our customer's point of view? • Do we define quality narrowly (e.g. product durability only) or broadly (quality of products, services, and overall management)? • Do we use measurable indicators of quality or operate on gut feel? • Do we constantly compare ourselves with external benchmarks? • How do we compare with competitors on key attributes of quality- and time-based competition? • In delivering quality and speed, are we improving at a slower or faster rate than the competition?
Frictionless coordination (between similar activities; between complimentary activities)	• How direct and frictionless are the communication channels for customers' priorities and concerns to be heard, not just by marketing but also production and R&D personnel? • How direct and frictionless are the communication channels between units performing complementary activities? Between units performing similar activities? • Do reward systems encourage or discourage needed coordination? • Has the company created a frictionless internal market for ideas that rewards both the producers and the buyers of a great idea? Is the head office active or sleepy in carrying out its knowledge-broker responsibilities?

NOTES

1. Tomkins, R. Battered PepsiCo licks its wounds. *The Financial Times*, 30 May 1997, 26.

2. Our ideas in this section build on and extend the work of many scholars in the area of global strategy, including Caves, R.E. 1982. *Multinational enterprise and economic analysis*. Cambridge, UK: Cambridge University Press; Ghoshal, S. 1987. Global strategy: An organizing framework. *Strategic Management Journal*, 8: 425–40; and Porter, M.E. 1994. Global strategy: Winning in the world-wide marketplace. In L. Fahey & R.M. Randall (eds.), *The portable MBA in strategy:* 108–41. New York: John Wiley.

3. For an analysis of how local market differences affect entry strategies, see Root, F. 1994. *Entry strategies for international markets*. New York: Lexington Books.

4. As business goes global, so does *BusinessWeek*. *BusinessWeek*, 1 July 1996.

5. For Coca-Cola in Japan, things go better with milk. *Wall Street Journal*, 20 January 1997, B1.

6. Remarks by John Pepper, chairman and CEO, Procter & Gamble, to MBA class at Tuck School, Dartmouth College, Hanover, NH, May 1995.

7. See Chandler, A.D. 1990. *Scale and scope: The dynamics of industrial capitalism*. Cambridge, MA: Harvard University Press.

8. For an interesting case study on a company's efforts at capturing the economies of global scope, see Malnight, T.W. 1994. *Citibank: Global customer management*. Case No. 9-395-142. Boston: Harvard Business School.

9. For a recent review of the research literature dealing with choice of locations by multinational enterprises, see Dunning, J.H. 1998. Location and the multinational enterprise: A neglected factor? *Journal of International Business Studies*, 29,1: 45–66. See also Porter, M.E. 1994. The role of location in competition. *Journal of Economics and Business*, 1(1): 35–9.

10. See, for example, Globerman, S. & Shapiro, D.M. 1999. The impact of government policies on foreign direct investment: The Canadian experience. *Journal of International Business Studies*, 30(3): 513–32.

11. See Dunne, K.M. & Rollins, T.P. 1992. Accounting for goodwill: A case analysis of US, UK, and Japan. *Journal of International Accounting, Auditing, and Taxation*, 2: 191–207.

12. See, for example, Miller, K.D. & Reuer, J.J. 1998. Firm strategy and economic exposure to foreign exchange rate movements. *Journal of International Business Studies*, 29(3): 493–514.

13. Texas Instruments' global chip payoff. *BusinessWeek*, 7 August 1995.

14. See Gupta, A.K. & Govindarajan, V. 1991. Knowledge flows and the structure of control within multinational corporations. *Academy of Management Review*, 16(4): 768–92; Gupta, A.K. & Govindarajan, V. 2000. Knowledge flows within multinational corporations. *Strategic Management Journal*, 21: 473–96; Nobel, R. & Birkinshaw, J. 1998. Innovation in multinational corporations: Control and communication patterns in international R&D operations. *Strategic Management Journal*, 19(5): 479–96; and Kogut, B. & Zander, U. 1992. Knowledge of the firm, combinative capabilities, and the replication of technology. *Organization Science*, 3(2): 383–97.

15. Ingrassia, P. Industry is shopping abroad for good ideas to apply to products. *The Wall Street Journal*, 29 April 1985, 1.

16. Gurcharan Das. 1993. Local memoirs of a global manager. *Harvard Business Review*, March–April: 46.

17. Our ideas in this section build on the work of Kogut, B. 1985. Designing global strategies: Comparative and competitive value-added chains. *Sloan Management Review*, 15–28; and

Porter, M.E. 1986. *Competition in global industries*. Boston: Harvard Business School Press.

18.   Wagstyl, S. & Hall, W. ABB to cut jobs in Western Europe. *The Financial Times*, 9 June 1997, 1.

19.   Furnishing the world. *The Economist*, 19 November 1994, 79–80.

20.   Pepper remarks, op. cit.

21.   Taylor, W. 1991. The logic of global business: An interview with ABB's Percy Barnevik. *Harvard Business Review*, March–April.

22.   Pepper remarks, op. cit.

23.   Taylor, op. cit.

24.   Pepper remarks, op. cit.

25.   Wetlaufer, S. 1999. Driving change: An interview with Ford Motor Company's Jacques Nasser. *Harvard Business Review*, March–April: 76–88.

26.   Maljers, F.A. 1992. Inside Unilever: The evolving transnational company. *Harvard Business Review*, September–October.

Executive Commentary

Peter Roche

The London Perret Roche Group LLC

In a speech to the British-American Chamber of Commerce in March 1999, John Zeglis, then president of AT&T, said, "You are only going to have two kinds of companies in the future: those that go global and those that go bankrupt."[1] Zeglis's view appears to be widely shared, as there are now over 130 countries involved in global trade. Governments are lowering trade barriers with free trade agreements. Global bankers, like The World Bank and the IMF are eager to finance this internationalization of business. Further, a host of service providers and suppliers have declared themselves "global enterprises," as they step beyond their home shores to compete in the world market.

The management implications are significant for these entities. Competition is soaring. The complexity of the entity to be managed has increased exponentially because of sheer scale, business laws, business ethics, accounting procedures, and divergent cultures and habits, to name a few. The speed at which best practices are emulated is breathtaking – making that source of advantage less sustainable. Conducting business successfully in this environment requires a new business model.

The global enterprise described by Gupta and Govindarajan is a new species of organization. It is not the familiar multinational enterprise (MNE) simply expanded to a larger set of geographical locations. Rather, it is a new way of organizing designed for competitive advantage. What distinguishes a global enterprise with a competitive advantage from an MNE? According to Gupta and Govindarajan the differences are: how managers take advantage of economies of scale, rationalize production, develop a worldwide management talent pool, engage in R&D, and exchange knowledge and best practices across the globe. Many mergers designed to produce global entities have failed because they did not understand the distinctions between MNEs and global enterprises. They did not leverage the five "opportunities" outlined by Gupta and Govindarajan in their article: adapting to local market differences, exploiting economies of scale, exploiting economies of global scope, tapping the optimal locations for activities and/or resources, and maximizing knowledge transfer across locations. These opportunities are at the heart of Gupta and Govindarajan's framework. Their framework is not simplistic. Nor is it a clear-cut prescriptive set of dos and don'ts. Each of the five opportunities has multiple facets, challenges, and obstacles for each business and market. In other words, there is no single right answer, such as "always adapt the product to the local market." TGIF Fridays discovered this in South Korea, when it added local dishes to its menus. The restaurant found that local customers thought of a visit to TGIF as being a visit to America and they did not want to be served South Korean food. According to Gupta and Govindarajan, the right answer for any particular business could be adapting a little, adapting a lot, or not adapting at all. Moreover, the right answer could change over time.

Gupta and Govindarajan's framework suggests that, to be successful, businesses should institute an ongoing process of discovery, along with rigorous thinking and thoughtful application across the entire firm. Their framework is not a short-cut to *the* solution. At one point in my career I was an executive with an organization that manufactured products for the construction industry around the world. Applying Gupta and Govindarajan's framework to this business, it is clear that we did abide by one of their key recommendations – we adapted to local market differences for one customer but not for another. More specifically, for construction industry customers we adapted to the local language and how the products were packaged and shipped. For the home improvement industry, which sold many of the same products, but to a different set of customers, we needed many more adaptations from one market to the next. Many of these adaptations were a result of variable retail practices and different rules about product labeling. In both cases we competed very successfully. Yet in other circumstances, the organization's thinking was essentially MNE. That is, many of our adaptations to local markets were not optimal. Clearly, we were not always systematic in exploiting the five opportunities presented in Gupta and Govindarajan's framework.

Based on Gupta and Govindarajan's model, there are many powerful questions companies should ask themselves: Are you clear about the difference between an MNE and a global enterprise with a competitive advantage? If there were a scale with MNE at one end and global enterprise with a competitive advantage at the other, where would your company fall? Finally, what are the best leverage opportunities for your business? How these questions are answered just might inspire an organization to change the way it conducts its global business.

NOTE

1. http://www.att.com/speeches/item/0,1363,930,00.html.

Chapter 8

Human Resource Strategy in International Context

Paul R. Sparrow and Werner Braun

Introduction

In this chapter we address three questions central to the field of Strategic International Human Resource Management (SIHRM):

1. *What* are the main SIHRM strategy models and concepts?
2. *Should* a firm's strategy help decide its HR processes in other cultures?
3. *Do* HR strategies developed in western countries in reality apply to other cultures?

In this opening section we address the first question by concentrating on what is known so far in this area, including empirical research and the main conceptual models that have been proposed. HRM is a relatively new term even in Western society: it is said to have evolved in its best known form in the USA and arrived in the mid-1980s in the UK and much of Europe. HRM evolved as a concept in the 1980s clearly differentiating itself from the study and discipline of personnel administration and personnel management (Staehle, 1994; Storey, 1995). HRM introduces a view of people as resources that have strategic importance for the creation of competitive advantages for an organization. HRM, furthermore, seeks an 'internal fit' among the HRM functional areas (e.g. in the form of consistent 'bundles' of HRM policies and practices) (Tichy *et al.*, 1982; Schuler and Rogovsky, 1998) and an 'external fit' between such HRM policies and practices 'bundles' with the corporation's strategy (Tichy *et al.*, 1982;

P.R. Sparrow and W. Braun, "Human Resource Strategy in International Context," in *Handbook of Research in International Human Resource Management* (Erlbaum: 2005).

Schuler and Jackson, 1987; Schuler *et al.*, 2001) as well as its external environment (Beer *et al.*, 1985). HRM also introduces a change in perspective by involving top management in the HRM responsibility (Staehle, 1994) and proposes a shift of competences away from the central personnel departments back into line management in order to enhance the strategic integration (Wächter, 1987; Storey, 1995). In terms of outcomes, HRM does not merely seek the employees' compliance to rules and regulations of the organization or administrative efficiency, standard performance and cost minimization (Guest, 1991). The HRM outcome goals are rather a high employee commitment, high quality and highly flexible staff (Guest, 1997). Storey (1995: 5) defines HRM as: '... a distinctive approach to employment management which seeks to achieve competitive advantage through the strategic deployment of a highly committed and capable workforce, using an integrated array of cultural, structural and personnel techniques.'

In an international context we have seen the development of the field of strategic international human resource management (SIHRM). This has been defined as: 'human resource management issues, functions and policies and practices that result from the strategic activities of multinational enterprises and that impact on the international concerns and goals of those enterprises' (Schuler *et al.*, 1993). In contrast to comparative HRM, SIHRM essentially focuses on strategic HRM in MNCs and recognizes the importance of linking HRM policies and practices with organizational strategies of the MNC (e.g. Adler and Ghadar, 1990, 1993; Milliman *et al.*, 1991; Taylor *et al.*, 1996). The SIHRM literature reflects the growing importance of MNCs and the influence of complex global strategic business decisions on MNCs' HRM activities (Ferner, 1994; DeCieri and Dowling, 1997; DeCieri *et al.*, 2001; Schuler *et al.*, 2002; Schuler and Jackson, 2005). At a conceptual level, SIHRM frameworks have considered an increasing amount of independent variables as influencing factors on the IHRM activities of the MNC over the last few decades (Perlmutter, 1969; Perlmutter and Heenan, 1974; Adler and Ghadar, 1990, 1993; Adler, 1991; Milliman *et al.*, 1991; Schuler *et al.*, 1993; Taylor *et al.*, 1996; Schuler and Jackson, 2005). It is the recognition of this variety of influencing factors which leads to a heightened complexity in the perception of relationships between an MNC and its IHRM activities, and which makes the subject important and relevant for research (Schuler *et al.*, 2002; Schuler and Jackson, 2005).

Concepts Underpinning SIHRM

Before detailing the main strands of theoretical thought we draw attention to some fundamental principles that have shaped thinking in the area. Theoretical frameworks in SIHRM have been – and still are – influenced by three developments that emerged in broad historical sequence:

1. early attention to life-cycle models based on the concept of fit between HRM and progressive stages of HQ management attitude to international operations; product life cycles; or organizational life cycles;

2.   subsequent development of ideas about organizational design and the process through which strategy and structure can be matched, or ideal MNCs be created;
3.   development of integrative contingency frameworks premised on the need to both integrate and differentiate HRM policies.

Next we explain the influence that each of these developments has had. Having explained these influences we go on to outline four different theoretical underpinnings of the literature.

Life cycle models

The early attention to life cycle models reflected the need for strategic fit between HRM policies and practices and various ways of classifying the evolution of the firm, whilst the later development of broader contingency frameworks merely expanded the complexity of the 'fit' equation. One of the earliest set of studies to leave a strong mark on future SIHRM frameworks was by Perlmutter (1969) and Perlmutter and Heenan (1974). These studies suggested that staffing decisions within MNCs were a consequence of a progressive series of attitudes of the management at headquarters. With slight variations their differentiation between four distinct attitudes (ethnocentrism, polycentrism, regiocentrism and geocentrism) can be found throughout much of the theoretical SIHRM literature (see, e.g. Adler and Ghadar, 1993; Dowling *et al.*, 1994; Kamoche, 1996).

Proponents of life-cycle models argue that there is a link between the variation in MNC HRM policies and practices and either the product life cycles in companies or the organizational life cycle in these organizations. For Adler and Ghadar (1990, 1993) the different internationalization strategies of a MNC and the corresponding HRM strategies (expressed by different degrees of integration and differentiation of practice) are related to internationalization phases dependent on the organization's product life cycles with a 'fit' required between the HRM system and these cycles. Milliman *et al.* (1991) extended the model by Adler and Ghadar (1990) principally by looking at organizational life cycles rather than product life cycles. They argued that product life cycles are difficult to apply to MNCs because in many sectors (e.g. high technology industries) products have a short life cycle and in any event typically MNCs have multiple products each at different stages of their life cycle. Drawing upon work by Miller and Friesen (1980, 1984) that differentiates between four stages of organizational development (birth, growth, maturity and revival) they outlined phases of organization initiation, functional growth, controlled growth and strategic integration. In each of these organizational development stages different levels of external fit (between HRM activities and the MNC business context) and internal 'fit' (between the different HRM functional areas) are necessary. Consequently human resource flexibility becomes central to effective internationalization, and is dependent upon the capacity of HRM to facilitate the ability of the organization to adapt to changing demands both from within the MNC or from the MNC's context both effectively and in a timely manner (Milliman *et al.*, 1991).

Life cycle models can be criticized on three main grounds:

1. They focus on only one independent variable (i.e. the product life cycle or the organizational life cycle) and do not take further influencing variables into consideration. While large diversified MNCs are typically dealing with multiple product life-cycles simultaneously, in practice they are also confronted with a wide range of other endogenous and exogenous factors influencing their IHRM policies and practice design.
2. The exact description of a product or organizational life cycle can only be given *post hoc* which means that such models only have descriptive value rather than predictive qualities.
3. They fall short of discussing *how* an MNC can implement varying international policies and practices while also accounting for the contingencies of multiple host countries.

Organization design models

The second development to influence the literature has been the advent of organization design models. The challenge of considering *how* an MNC can best implement international policies and practices was taken up broadly when attention was given to organization design and the match between strategy and structure. Many of these assumptions about organization design in MNCs are in turn driven by information processing theory, a basic assumption of which is that organizations are open social systems that are exposed to both external and internal sources of uncertainty (defined as the difference between information possessed and information required to complete a task). MNCs need to develop information processing mechanisms capable of dealing with this uncertainty (Galbraith, 1973, 1977; Tushman and Nadler, 1978; Egelhoff, 1991). Information processing in organizations is generally defined as including the gathering of data, the processing and transformation of data into information, and the communication and storage of information in the organization (Tushman and Nadler, 1978; Egelhoff, 1991). According to this perspective, effective organizations are those that create a 'fit' between their information processing capacities and the information processing requirements determined by such factors as their strategy, task characteristics, inter-unit interdependence and their organizational environment.

Applying this perspective to MNCs, Egelhoff (1991) argues that such organizations are large and complex and have very high information processing requirements, especially if they are pursuing a transnational strategy which requires a reciprocal interdependence between affiliates and headquarters (Egelhoff, 1991). Information processing requirements are also high in MNCs because of their focus on flexible, people-based co-ordination and control mechanisms. Galbraith (1973:15) differentiates between different organizational design features all holding different levels of information processing capacity (in increasing order): rules and programmes; hierarchical referral; goal-setting; vertical information systems; and lateral relations. The higher the information processing requirement, the more organizations will steer towards the application of lateral relations (such as direct contact between individuals, liaison roles, task forces, teams, and matrix designs) (Egelhoff, 1991). MNCs therefore frequently reach the limits of their information-processing capacity.

Egelhoff (1999) went on to differentiate between two perspectives of the MNC that came to dominate thinking about strategy:

- *Traditional equilibrium models*, dominant in the 1970s and early 1980s, grounded in an industrial organization perspective and epitomized by the early strategy-structure models of Chandler (1962) and Stopford and Wells (1972) as well as the models of the process school of strategy (Prahalad, 1975) and a Porterian view of international strategy (Porter, 1986);
- '*New change models*', appearing towards the late 1980s, grounded in such theoretical perspectives as the resource-based or knowledge-based view of the firm and seen in the work of Bartlett and Ghoshal (1989) and Hedlund (1986, 1993).

We now discuss the more recent development of new change models. While the early strategy-structure models make a distinction between different structural and strategic MNC orientations depending on certain contingent factors, the new change models formulated an "ideal-type" MNC organizational structure and strategy (Egelhoff, 1999; Harzing, 1999). Some of the most noted examples of these 'new change models' include:

- The heterarchy (Hedlund, 1986)
- Paradigm S (Perlmutter and Trist, 1986)
- The transnational (Bartlett and Ghoshal, 1989)
- The horizontal organization (White and Poynter, 1990).

Among these models, Bartlett and Ghoshal's (1989) concept of the transnational as well as Hedlund's (1986) heterarchy can be regarded as the most influential in the area of strategic management as well as organizational behaviour (Harzing, 1999). The development of these ideal type MNC organizational structures can be linked to a general evolution of research into MNCs. Birkinshaw and Morrison (1995) noted that research into the MNC evolved in two critical directions during the mid-eighties:

- a shift away from seeing the MNC as a monolithic entity best viewed from a headquarters perspective towards an emphasis on the MNC affiliate as a unit of analysis (see also Gupta and Govindarajan, 1991; Wolf, 1997);
- a challenge of the old standing assumptions of equilibrium and 'fit' between a firm's strategy, structure and environment by introducing assumptions of permanently changing business environments which would require equally fast changing organizational responses.

Some important concepts continue to influence the field today as a result of discussion of ideal structures, notably the need to create a matrix in the mind of managers. The ideal type models suggest that adjustment is handled out of the same organizational design. They also began to change many assumptions about HR strategy. Organizational change cannot occur within conditions of equilibrium. Consequently Egelhoff (1999) asserts that in these models there is no attempt to make the organizational design dependent on variations in strategy and the environment. Moreover, under the assumption of an unpredictable, frequent and continuous change of strategic and environmental factors, they promoted the idea that the competitive advantage of a MNC cannot reside in any one operation or country and therefore the strategic importance of the affiliates worldwide and their employees is emphasized (see, e.g. Bartlett and Ghoshal, 1986). Consequently, organizational solutions to solve the simultaneous requirements of global integration and local responsiveness (the integration–differentiation dilemma) are less structure-based but rely instead on more informal, people based co-ordination and control mechanisms (Roth *et al.*, 1991). Hence, the solution is seen in creating a 'matrix in the minds' of MNC managers (Bartlett and Ghoshal, 1989, 1990).

Given the need to create a matrix in the mind, the emphasis shifted to creating shared values through: a corporate culture (Hedlund, 1986; Bartlett and Ghoshal, 1989; White and Poynter, 1990), a normative control system (Hedlund, 1986), the creation of an organizational context (Doz and Prahalad, 1981), and an input-control system (Hamilton and Kashlak, 1999). As Harzing (1999) points out, it is evident that this heightens the role of HRM within MNCs, as companies will increasingly depend on:

- the socialization of employees to ensure that employees share organizational values and goals and are socialized into a common organizational culture (see, e.g. Edström and Galbraith, 1977a,b, 1978; Ouchi, 1977, 1979, 1980; Mintzberg, 1979, 1983; Child, 1984; Baliga and Jaeger, 1984; Kenter, 1985; Pucik and Katz, 1986; Bartlett and Ghoshal, 1989; Martinez and Jarillo, 1989; Hennart, 1991; Evans *et al.*, 2002);
- informal, lateral or horizontal exchange of information which includes mutual adjustment, informal communication and co-ordination by feedback (see, e.g. March and Simon, 1958; Lawrence and Lorsch, 1967; Thompson, 1967; Mintzberg, 1979, 1983; Martinez and Jarillo, 1989; Evans *et al.*, 2002);
- formalized lateral or cross-departmental relations. These include (temporarily) formalized ways to exchange information such as task forces, cross-functional teams and integrative departments (see, e.g. Lawrence and Lorsch, 1967; Galbraith, 1973; Martinez and Jarillo, 1989; Evans *et al.*, 2002).

In addition to influencing the field through the idea of creating a matrix in the mind, organization design models have influenced our ideas on how MNCs build capability. It would be fair to say then that until very recently the international management literature adopted a fairly traditional stance to the building of such capabilities within MNCs. The vast majority of models of organizational design and internationalization, suggested a clear sequence of evolutionary stages through which the organization has to grow. A sequence of stages of organization design – variously called international, multinational, global and transnational/network/heterarchy – has been outlined (Bartlett and Ghoshal, 1989) which suggests a pattern can be found in the way in which the internationalization process has to be managed. In general, the organization structure has to respond to a series of strains that are faced, such as the challenges of growth, increased geographical spread, and the need for improved control and co-ordination across business units. Organizations have to build capability in each stage sequentially in order to maintain integrated standards for some business lines but remain locally responsive in others (Hamel and Prahalad, 1985; Yip, 1992; Ashkenas *et al.*, 1995). Some firms might develop through the various phases rapidly, and might be able to accelerate the process through acquisitions, but any attempt to leapfrog over intermediate steps is generally considered to result in dysfunctions.

Reflecting this view, there has been considerable research examining the role of HRM within MNCs pursuing a global/transnational SIHRM orientation (DeCieri and Dowling, 1997; Egelhoff, 1999; DeCieri *et al.*, 2001; Schuler *et al.*, 2002; Schuler and Jackson, 2005). Similarly, attention has been given to MNC structural attempts to facilitate global/transnational SIHRM orientations, such as an examination of the role of Regional Headquarters (Daniels 1986, 1987; Schütte, 1996, 1998).

However, there are two pressing research questions that need to be addressed today: can we accelerate the pace at which organizations progress through the constituent phases? Must organizations really work through each phase in a linear sequence to build organizational capability or can new organizational forms short circuit the process? In relation to the latter question, the assumption of linear and broadly sequential phases of organizational development no longer seems to fit the modern business environment in which there are many organizations (not necessarily MNCs of course) that begin life as global start-ups, without having to evolve through a series of levels of HRM flexibility and fit (Parker, 1998). Moreover, in relation to SIHRM practices, Braun and Warner (2002) note that many specifications are prescriptive and not based on any evidence that tests effectiveness. An example in the 'global' (Adler and Ghadar, 1990) or the 'strategic integration' (Milliman *et al.*, 1991) phases is the discussion of necessary SIHRM policies and practices such as recruiting globally irrespective of nationality, making international assignments and mobility a key for advancement into top management positions, appraising for and rewarding cross-cultural adjustment skills and mobility, and introducing global rewards structures. Research needs to ascertain whether this is a mere catalogue of prescriptive measures, and also provide contextual insight into the workability and effectiveness of such policies.

Contingency models

The third development to influence the literature has been the development of contingency models. In response to this need for greater sophistication, we have seen the specification of complex contingent relationships. In this last section on general influences we trace the roots of ideas about integration, differentiation, responsiveness and the transmission of strategic HR capabilities. The field has moved rapidly in recent years in the direction of uniting various theoretical perspectives and identifying a multitude of influencing independent variables, resulting in a number of contingency models (see, e.g. Schuler *et al.*, 1993, 2002; Taylor *et al.*, 1996; DeCieri and Dowling 1998). These contingency frameworks are now very elaborate and include an extensive array of independent variables. Common however to all these frameworks is the influence of the integration-differentiation concept by Lawrence and Lorsch (1967) as well as the Integration-Responsiveness (IR) model by Prahalad and Doz (1987). In other words, a MNC's perceived need for integration and control on the one hand and the perceived need for local responsiveness on the other provide a core influence for its choice of SIHRM policies and practices. Schuler and colleagues (Schuler *et al.*, 1993, 2002) refer to this dual need by emphasizing two strategic MNC components:

- an MNC's interunit linkages – representing the need for integration and control;
- an MNC's internal operations – representing the need for local sensitivity.

The dual need for integration and for local responsiveness reflects the fact that MNCs are geographically dispersed and goal-disparate organizations, which need to be co-ordinated or integrated in some form and to some degree. Ideally this integration is achieved with attention to being globally competitive, efficient, responsive, and flexible to local needs and conditions as well as being able to transfer learning across units (Bartlett and Ghoshal, 1989). Reflecting the increasing awareness of important explanatory variables, Schuler *et al.* (1993), Schuler *et al.* (2002) and Dowling *et al.* (1998) differentiate between two sets of factors: exogenous (growing by successive additions to the outside) and endogenous (increasing by internal growth and formed within). These influence the strategic HRM components and the IHRM policy and practice decisions. Exogenous factors include: industry characteristics; country/regional characteristics (Schuler *et al.*, 1993); country culture (Schuler *et al.*, 2002); and inter-organizational networks (DeCieri and Dowling, 1998; Dowling *et al.*, 1998). Endogenous factors include: the organizational structure of the MNC (international structure, intra-organizational networks, mechanisms of co-ordination); international entry mode (DeCieri and Dowling, 1998; Dowling *et al.*, 1998); headquarter's international orientation; competitive strategy (corporate-level, business-level strategy); experience in managing international operations (Schuler *et al.*, 1993); and organizational and industry life cycle.

The more recent contingency model by Taylor *et al.* (1996) develops the work of Schuler *et al.* (1993) by shifting the perspective towards factors at *three different organizational levels*: corporate level; affiliate level; and individual employee groups. At each level different independent variables are considered to influence the IHRM policies and practice design. In their contingency model they asked 'why should firms want to export their HRM system in the first place?'. Their work therefore has relevance to the second of our core questions – *should* a firm's strategy help decide its HR processes in other cultures? They explained the circumstances under which strategic HR capabilities are *considered to be generalizable* and capable of transmission or diffusion from the parent organization to affiliates. They argue that different levels of integration and responsiveness within a MNC's IHRM policies and practices are affected by an overall 'strategic international HRM (SIHRM) *system orientation*' and the degree of similarity of affiliates' HRM systems to the parent company's HRM system at the corporate level as well as at the affiliate level (see also Rosenzweig and Nohria, 1994; Hannon *et al.*, 1995; Lu and Björkman, 1997). Two factors shape an organization's SIHRM orientation. Whether:

1. the parent company actually has a global (as opposed to multi-domestic) strategy or not; and

2. top management believe that the HRM capability of the organization is a source of strategic advantage.

They further considered that there are three orientations (adapted forms of the categorization by Perlmutter, 1969) that result from the answers to these questions as the organization develops, the first of which results from a multi-domestic strategy and the second and third from a global strategy. The SIHRM orientations are:

1. *Exportive (ethnocentric)* (a wholesale transfer of HRM policies and practices successful in the parent organization to affiliates)
2. *Adaptive (polycentric)* (the creation of HRM systems with a maximum of adaptation to the local context and conditions)
3. *Integrative (geocentric)* (transfer best practice from wherever it might be found among affiliates in the organization).

These levels of similarity in systems at the subsidiary level are in turn influenced by four contingent factors, such as the strategic role of the subsidiary, whether the site is greenfield or an acquisition, and the cultural distance and legal distance between the parent and subsidiary.

Taylor *et al.*'s (1996) framework is however driven by the assumption that MNCs should develop an *integrative* approach to HRM, sharing best practices from all parts of the organization to create a worldwide system. The focus of the framework is on the need to create global integration – a geocentric orientation – yet they note that the mechanisms to identify and transfer best-HRM practice are *generally not in place in most MNCs.*

We make one final observation on the influence exerted by contingency models before analyzing the four main theoretical perspectives. The contingency frameworks by Schuler *et al.* (1993) and Taylor *et al.* (1996) have received praise as they have unified various theoretical perspectives and captured a wide array of independent variables influencing the design of IHRM policies and practices. There are also three criticisms of these models (Weber *et al.*, 1998):

1. The accumulation of independent variables makes these integrative frameworks increasingly untestable.
2. The 'independence' of a number of variables in the frameworks may be questioned. Just taking one example, Porter's (1986) work assumes that industry characteristics and competitive strategy influence one another.
3. Despite the large number of independent variables, existing contingency models still only explain a small part of the overall variance found in HRM policies and practices between MNCs operating in varying contexts. Context and institutional pressures are more complex than even these models assume.

There are then a series of research questions in relation to contingency models.

•   Given the limited variation explained by studies, are there situations in which an integrative approach to HRM globally is wholly '*undesirable*', and if so, what?

- Are there situations when *some elements* of the HRM system should converge (follow a geocentric path), whilst other elements may be allowed to remain different or even diverge?

Criticisms aside, the arrival of the integrative theoretical frameworks by Schuler *et al.* (1993) and Taylor *et al.* (1996), demonstrates that the field is drawing increasingly on theoretical perspectives from a variety of disciplines such as sociology, economics, management and psychology. Each theory has explained some organizational behaviour, but in so doing conveys different assumptions about the level and cause of influencing factors in the decision-making process of organizations (for an overview of these issues see Wright and MacMahan, 1992; Schuler and Jackson, 1995, 2005; Schuler, 2000a,b; Fenton-O'Creevy *et al.*, 2005).

Theoretical Underpinnings in the SIHRM Literature

Having explained how the three developments of life cycle organization design and contingency models have influenced thinking, in this second part of the chapter we consider the question *should* a firm's strategy help decide its HR processes in other cultures? We noted that Taylor *et al.*'s (1996) work touches on this question, but to answer this question we move into a discussion of some key theories. It is not possible to discuss exhaustively all the theoretical perspectives connected with the SIHRM field in this chapter, but we provide a brief outline of what we see as the four main perspectives:

- Resource dependence theory
- Resource-based view of the firm
- Knowledge-based view of the firm and organizational learning theory
- Relational and Social capital theory

We leave discussion on a fifth theory – institutional theory which asks '*do* HR strategies developed in western countries in reality apply to other cultures?' – to our treatment of this question in the final section of the chapter. However, let us return to the question of *should* the strategy help decide the HR processes across countries.

Resource dependence theory

The first of the four theoretical perspectives that answer the question of "should" is the resource dependence model (Pfeffer and Salancik, 1978; Pfeffer and Moore, 1980; Pfeffer and Cohen, 1984; Pfeffer and Davis-Blake, 1987). This focuses predominantly on power relationships and resource exchanges between an organization and its constituency. From this perspective, organizational decision-making is not seen as an outcome of strategic choice. Rather, the theory assumes that all organizations

depend on a flow of valuable resources (e.g. money, technology, management expertise) into the organization in order to continue functioning. A MNC affiliate may
have more or less dependence and power, as these resources are controlled by various
actors, internal to the MNC (e.g. parent company or regional operations) or external
to it (e.g. government institutions).

The ability to exercise control over any of these valued resources provides the actor
with an important source of power. The higher the scarcity of the valued resource,
the more the power of the entity that controls that resource increases (Wright and
McMahan, 1992). If external parties control vital resources, an organization is vulner-
able and will strive to acquire control in order to minimize its dependence (De Cieri
and Dowling, 1998). Pfeffer and Salancik (1978) and Scott (1987) argue that organizations can attempt to reduce this dependency through buffering (e.g. internalizing
control by coding of inputs for the production process, or stockpiling) as well as using
bridging strategies (e.g. bargaining for more independence, co-optation, joint ventures or the absorption of resource holders). The theory has been tested empirically
through the work of authors such as Pfeffer and Moore (1980), Pfeffer and Cohen
(1984) and Pfeffer and Davis-Blake (1987). This resource dependence perspective is
one of the main theoretical perspectives in the more recent integrative SIHRM frameworks (see Schuler et al., 1993; Taylor et al., 1996) discussed earlier and has also
helped to explain some of the empirical findings by Rosenzweig and Nohria (1994),
Hannon et al. (1995) and Lu and Björkman (1997).

Resource-based views of the firm

The second theoretical perspective that answers the "should" question is the resource-
based view (RBV) of the firm. Wright and Snell and various colleagues argue that this
view has emerged as perhaps the most predominant theoretical perspective (Wright
et al., 2001; Morris et al., 2005). They feel that it is particularly attractive to SIHRM
researchers because it focuses on the execution of various strategies and draws attention
to the potential value of a firm's internal asset stocks in this task. As seen earlier in
the chapter, SIHRM contingency frameworks have introduced the RBV perspective
in connection with top management attitudes regarding the transfer of HRM policies
and practices abroad (Taylor et al., 1996).

The idea of looking at a firm as a broader set of resources goes back to work of
Penrose (1959). The RBV sees the firm not through its activities in the product market but as a unique bundle of tangible and intangible resources (Wernerfelt, 1984).
While economic perspective views resources as immediately accessible on factor markets (which effectively eliminates firm resource heterogeneity and immobility as a
possible competitive advantage), in contrast, the RBV perspective stresses the inherent
immobility of valuable factors of production and the time and cost required to accumulate those resources (Peteraf, 1993). Firms are idiosyncratic. Throughout their history
they accumulate different physical assets and acquire different intangible organizational assets of tacit learning and dynamic routines (Collis, 1991). Imitation of these
assets is only possible if firms go through the same process of irreversible investment
or learning (Barney, 1989; Dierickx and Cool, 1989). Historical evolution of a firm in

practice constrains its strategic choice and so affects market outcomes. On the other hand, complex social phenomena can be a source of sustainable competitive advantage and will affect organization structure independently of strategic choice (Barney, 1991).

Barney (1991) and similarly Peteraf (1993) argue that in order for firm resources to hold the potential of sustained competitive advantage they must be:

- valuable, that is, the resource exploits opportunities and/or neutralizes threats in a firm's environment;
- rare among a firm's current and potential competitors;
- imperfectly imitable; that is other firms do not possess the same resources and cannot obtain them easily;
- non-substitutable with strategically equivalent resources (Ghemawat, 1986; Rumelt, 1987; Dierickx and Cool, 1989; Peteraf, 1993).

The RBV perspective has been discussed in connection with HRM for some time (see Schuler and MacMillan, 1984; Wright and McMahan, 1992; Wright et al., 1994) and considerable tacit knowledge is considered to reside within the whole HRM system (Lado and Wilson, 1994; Huselid, 1995).

However, RBV theories of the firm also present the clearest argument as to *why* firms must transfer capabilities globally. Morris, Snell and Wright (2005) argue that since MNCs operate in multiple environments they possess variations in both their people (reflecting the skillsets created by national business systems) and in their practices (which reflect local requirements, laws, and cultures). They benefit from a global workforce both by capitalizing on the superior skills that can be found by accessing global labour pools, and by exploiting the cultural synergies of a diverse workforce. SIHRM practices can contribute to the effective management of a firm's employees by enabling such outcomes. This variation is also a potential source of advantage at a local level. In discussing the transfer of HR best practice on a global basis, strategists argue that in a competitive marketplace the act of integrating disparate sources of knowledge within the bounds of the organization becomes a source of advantage (Grant, 1996). Indeed, one of the basic premises of internationalization research is that in order to succeed internationally a firm has to possess some highly advantageous, but intangible, knowledge-based asset.

Ghoshal, Bartlett and Nohria (Ghoshal and Bartlett, 1988; Bartlett and Ghoshal, 1997; Nohria and Ghoshal, 1997) argue that it is the utilization of organizational capabilities worldwide that provides MNCs with an important source of competitive advantage. The term organizational capability has been developed by both Ulrich (1987) in the HR field and Prahalad and Doz (1987) in the strategy field. As a concept it combines ideas from the fields of management of change, organizational design and leadership. Ulrich and Lake (1990) argued that organizational capability was about competing 'from the inside out'. Organizational capability therefore focuses on the ability of a firm's internal processes, systems and management practices to meet customer needs and to direct both the skills and efforts of employees towards achieving the goals of the organization.

This collection of capabilities reflects things such as a firm's 'key success factors', 'culture', 'brand', 'shared-mindset' or 'processes' (Ulrich and Lake, 1990; Lawler, 1997) and they reflect '… a firm's capacity to deploy resources, usually in combination, applying organizational processes to effect a desired end' (De Saá-Pérez and García-Falcón, 2002, p. 124). International expansion is only possible when firms can transfer their distinctive knowledge-assets abroad into new international markets (Dunning, 1993; Caves, 1996). If one chooses to follow this logic, then if there is any strategic advantage to be found in a firm's HRM capability (its philosophy, policies and practices) then this HR capability itself must also be transferred into different geographies around the world.

The capability to effect internal cross-border transfers of HRM practice (along with the knowledge needed to link this practice into local organizational effectiveness) becomes a core competence (Flood *et al.*, 2003). With regard to the question of should firms transfer their HRM systems, when organizations globalize they must (Stonehouse *et al.*, 2000):

- learn how best to co-ordinate and deploy their various capabilities and exploit them in a large number of countries and markets;
- identify new resources in untapped markets that will strengthen their existing core competences;
- enhance existing competences by reconfiguring value-adding activities across a wider geography or range of operations.

The RBV of the firm has been questioned more of late. Despite discussion of learning and knowledge transfer within the context of the RBV of the firm, until recently this perspective tended to emphasize the *role of the corporate centre in MNCs*, which is generally assumed to be one of shaping the strategic direction of the organization and designing the strategic change programmes pursued in the subsidiaries. The immobility in practice of many people and HRM practices also presents a challenge to the RBV of the firm. Ideas from this theory have to be combined with those from other perspectives to deal with the problem of stickiness in knowledge transfer. Though resources can provide a global advantage to the MNC as a whole, this is only *if* the knowledge, skills, and capabilities can be leveraged appropriately. We must draw upon organization learning perspectives, given that knowledge processes inside MNCs are central to the transfer of capability (Foss and Pedersen, 2004; Morris *et al.*, 2005). Attention also has to be given to the mechanisms that explain why such *mutual* transfer of capability is beneficial to the organization, and how it actually happens (Collis, 1991; Hedlund & Ridderstråe, 1997; Kogut, 1997). There are a series of research questions in relation to the RBV:

- Specifically, how do the following mechanisms develop the business and technological skills associated with mutual transfer of capabilities: International diversification into multiple markets, collaborating with organizations that have mutually complementary competences (e.g. through joint ventures), emphasizing strategic leadership roles for national subsidiaries, gaining access to foreign-based clusters of excellence, and building internal centres of excellence based on global best practice.

- Why must the organizational capabilities associated with strategic goals such as meeting customer needs be constituted in the same way in different international components of the firm?
- What does the pursuit of organizational capability mean for the design of IHRM functions and role of business partners. Do these issues make any difference to organizational effectiveness?

Organizational learning and knowledge-based views of the firm

The RBV of the firm is then still very influential, but a third theoretical perspective has also found much favour. Given the focus on knowledge transfer, organizational learning and knowledge-based views of the firm have come to influence progressively the field of SIHRM. Although certainly related to the RBV perspective, the knowledge-based view focuses more explicitly on tacit knowledge (as a resource). It is argued that the process of globalization that results from the transfer of such knowledge-based capabilities leads to some organizations building a superior 'knowledge transfer capacity'. There is as yet little confirmed empirical examination of this, but it is considered to involve two mutually reinforcing capabilities (Martin and Salomon, 2003):

1. the ability of a firm (or business unit) to articulate the uses of its own knowledge, assess the needs and capabilities of the main recipients for the knowledge, and transmit knowledge so it can be used in another location ('source transfer capacity');
2. the ability of the transferee to assimilate and retain information from a willing source, i.e. evaluate external knowledge, take in all its detail, and modify or create organizational procedures to accommodate the new knowledge ('recipient transfer capacity').

In practice, two positions have been taken on the transfer of knowledge and capabilities within MNCs (Tallman and Fladmoe-Lindquist, 2002):

1. The *capability-recognising* perspective notes that whilst MNCs do possess unique knowledge-based resources, these are typically treated as being home-country based or belonging to central corporate functions and top teams, there to be disseminated on a need-to-know basis.
2. The *capability-driven* perspective (also called the *dynamic capability* perspective) is concerned with a much wider process of building, protecting and exploiting mutual capabilities (Teece *et al.*, 1997). In this context across geographies: '... the world becomes an important source for new knowledge as well as new markets' (Tallman and Fladmoe-Lindquist, 2002, p. 116).

With regard to the question of should firms transfer HR systems, it is argued that by deploying these resources and progressively integrating them into the most value-adding activities, the organization can build a series of capabilities (such as industry-specific skills, relationships and organizational knowledge). The organizational learning literature which probably has had the biggest influence on SIHRM frameworks – such as the one by Schuler *et al.* (1993) – stresses the effect that time and experience have on organizational learning (e.g. Levitt and March, 1988; March and Olsen, 1988; Cohen and Levinthal, 1989, 1990; Barkema *et al.*, 1997; for a critique of such approaches see Prange, 1999). The focus on learning has brought two concepts into the international management field: absorptive capacity and progressing organizational simplicity. We explain the relevance of each.

According to these authors, prior learning facilitates the learning and application of new related knowledge. Prior related knowledge confers an ability to recognize the value of new information, assimilate it, and apply it to new ends (Cohen and Levinthal, 1989, 1990).

These abilities collectively constitute what Cohen and Levinthal (1990) call a firm's 'absorptive capacity'. This capacity increases incrementally as a function of the previous experiences of the firm and its learning processes (Barkema *et al.*, 1997). March and Olsen (1988) describe the learning cycle as a stimulus-response system in which individuals' actions result in organizational actions which evoke environmental responses. The latter are reported back to the organizations, where they affect individuals' cognition and preferences and influence their future actions. Levitt and March (1988) view organizational learning as routine-based, history-dependent and target-oriented. Organizations are seen as learning by encoding inferences from history into routines (e.g. forms, rules, procedures) that guide behaviour. In this way, learning can take place independently from individual actors through such processes as socialization, education and imitation. Knowledge transfer and integration are however only facilitated when respective parties have the absorptive capacity or prior experience necessary to understand related ideas (Szulanski, 1996; Tsai, 2002). Groups with large amounts of international experience are more likely to integrate knowledge from other parts of the organization than those that do not (Morris *et al.*, 2005).

Minbaeva, Pedersen, Björkman, Fey and Park (2003) asked recently whether absorptive capacity *can be enhanced* by MNCs? What managerial actions are the most important? They argued that the actions reside largely within employees in terms of their abilities and motivations. In International Joint Ventures (IJVs), for example, a series of managerial challenges, including differences in organizational culture and managerial style, the need to absorb new product lines, and varying dominant logics, all have to be managed (Vermuelen and Barkema, 2001). Success depends upon processes of organizational learning (and effective knowledge creation, acquisition and transfer between partners) (Barkema *et al.*, 1996; Glaister and Buckley, 1996; Inkpen, 1996; Pilkington, 1996; Schuler, 2001; Schuler and Jackson, 2001; Schuler *et al.*, 2003; Schuler and Tarique, 2005).

The second concept that organizational learning theory has brought to the field is that of progressing organizational simplicity. This concept has also been used to explain the (natural) negative forces that exist inside organizations, whereby repeated use of a knowledge base can lead to the tendency of organizations to become rigid, narrow and simple (Miller, 1993). It has been applied to cross border alliances by Vermuelen and Barkema (2001). Progressing organizational simplicity posits that firms are inclined to implement habitual ways of organizing and managing (Hedberg, 1981; Levinthal and March, 1993), concentrate on those aspects of their repertoire that appeared most successful in old situations, replicate them and transfer them into the new subsidiary, and install the same sets of technical systems, competitive actions and organization designs. This increasing routinization, dominance of previous expansion strategies and resulting narrowness of mental models pervading an internationalization strategy can lead to a failure to perceive and respond to important stimuli (Miller and Chen, 1996; Miller *et al.*, 1996, 1997).

There is a counter argument to this hypothesis. This considers that cross border alliances can in practice act as powerful catalysts of global knowledge management. Vermuelen and Barkema (2001) drew attention to some of the positive (from a knowledge management perspective) forces at play and examined the proposition that acquisitions might actually revitalize the organization, through exposure to manageable levels of shock, leading to superior long-term survival. They looked at the expansion patterns of 25 of the largest Dutch non-financial firms (excluding Royal Dutch Shell, Unilever, Philips and Akzo) over a period of three decades, and studied survival rates and increases in the viability of subsequent ventures. Firms that expanded through greenfield investments (setting up a subsidiary from scratch) did not exploit their knowledge base as effectively as those that expanded through acquisition (the takeover of an existing company).

Organizational learning gains might therefore outstrip short-term downsides to acquisitions, especially where differences between managerial teams create the opportunity for synergies and learning (Krishnan *et al.*, 1997), or when added value is created through processes of corporate renewal (Haspeslagh and Jemison, 1991). Barkema and Vermeulen (1998) believe that acquisitions bring powerful forces of cognitive change because they:

- engender conflicts that serve to unfreeze cognitive maps, structures and processes,
- preserve healthy levels of doubt, diversity and debate;
- increase the cognitive abilities of organization members;
- create new knowledge from the combination of existing forms of knowledge; and
- infuse unique knowledge and inculcate practices that lead to the creation of new knowledge.

There are a series of research questions that should be investigated in relation to progressing organizational simplicity. The above discussion of competing views on the organizational learning effects of cross border acquisitions presents a series of testable propositions that should in future be investigated. The key questions that must now be asked are:

- How might these forces of cognitive change (be it individual or collective) be engendered?
- What form must global knowledge management take in such situations?
- What can organizations do to help ensure some of the more positive learning outcomes?
- What learning can be influenced by global HR functions?

At a managerial level research should actually test whether the five cognitive changes that Barkema and Vermeulen (1998) specify do actually result from acquisitions. Moreover, a series of HRM practices are considered to be central to the management of these dominant logics, and the necessary migration of knowledge, knowledge appreciation and subsequent practice of 'knowledgeable action' (Iles and Yolles, 2002).

There have been some recent attempts to specify the contribution that HRM makes to global KM (Knowledge Management) processes. In the context of the debate around knowledge transfer, Jackson *et al.* (2003) have discussed some of the requirements for HR systems that enhance an organization's capability to gain and use its knowledge resources, identifying generic HR practices associated with four primary tasks of: encouraging knowledge-based competition behaviours (as applied to acquiring, creating, sharing, applying and updating knowledge), ensuring the associated competencies, providing motivation to engage in such behaviours, and providing opportunities through job and organizational design. They argued that we need to understand the combined effects of all elements of this system.

Finally, Sparrow (2005) has examined how each of five main forms of global knowledge management (centres of excellence, managing systems and technology-driven approaches to global knowledge management systems, capitalizing on expatriate advice networks, co-ordinating international management teams and developing communities of practice or global expertise networks) contributes to three knowledge-based capabilities of:

- Knowledge acquisition and creation (generation of new knowledge fundamental to the long-term viability of the enterprise);
- Knowledge capture and storage (creation of an inventory of knowledge so the organization knows what knowledge it possesses, and where it resides; the maintenance of current knowledge in usable form so that it remains valuable);
- Knowledge diffusion and transfer (subsequent mobilization and flow of knowledge within the organization that creates knowledge-based value).

The research questions that emerge are too numerous to relay here, but it is useful to note that he lists a series of outcomes that (in theory) should result for each capability from each knowledge management form and a series of propositions that need testing and validation and argues that we also need to test whether the prescribed HRM roles in fact take place, and if so, whether they are associated with producing the outcomes.

Relational and social capital theories

In this section on theoretical underpinnings of the field we now move to the fourth key perspective, which arises from relational and social capital theories. Organizational learning theories have then provided us with a much greater focus on the 'how' of internationalization processes. This focus on the how now also has been aided through reference to work on various forms of capital. We concentrate here on relational and social capital theory. Both the internal and external context for global firms within which knowledge has to be transferred have changed markedly in recent years.

As Buckley and Ghauri (2004, p. 83) note: '... The process of globalization is ... not only reorganizing power at world level but also at national and subnational levels. As domestic firms move part of their production to other countries, technology, knowledge and capital become more important'. Externally, we can look to the impact of e-commerce and more flexible networks of organizations. Decision makers in MNCs now face far more complex strategic options as a consequence of e-commerce and management through networks.

One response to the renewed complexity and opportunities has been the development of *business networks*. These networks might be built around groups of independent firms or neighbouring firms in regional industrial clusters or districts (Best, 1990; Rugman *et al.*, 1995). It is argued that internal changes, such as more transparent internal transfer pricing arrangements or service level agreements have brought internal prices more in line with external prices, and have allowed divisional managers to bypass weak or incompetent sections of the company and develop supply or production arrangements that service these broader cross-business networks. In relation to the question of should firms transfer HR systems globally, then the answer is yes, *if* HR system convergence is an antidote to incompetence.

Therefore the literature on inter-organizational trust has much relevance to the study of global organizations. Recently this literature has begun to give more attention to the role of what is termed *relational capital* (Chen *et al.*, 2004). Relational capital is primarily concerned with business networks and the inter-firm relationships that exist within these networks. It concerns the sets of interdependent business relationships upon which repeated business transactions are based and thereby includes the goodwill and trust that exists between a firm and its customers, suppliers, partners, government agencies, research institutions and so forth. Again, with regard to the question of should firms transfer HR systems globally, competitive advantage is assumed to result from this form of capital primarily for four reasons.

1. Knowledge sharing across these relational networks is considered to reduce the cost of transactions between network members, and thereby facilitate value creation and innovation (Tsai and Ghoshal, 1998).
2. Firms can access and deploy their existing capabilities in ways that help them seek new markets, resources, efficiencies and assets (Kale *et al.*, 2000; Dunning, 2002).
3. The social networks inherent in the relationships affect the rate of creation of inter-firm linkages within the MNC, improving its ability to align its organizational design with its global strategy (Tsai, 2000).
4. The ability of partners to absorb and learn from each other at more equal rates is facilitated, thereby extending the life cycle of arrangements such as joint ventures (Lane and Lubatkin, 1998; Yli-Renko *et al.*, 2001).

These assumed benefits all need testing. The underlying research question is as follows. In the context of international management, does knowledge about the relational capital inherent in local linkages determine the benefits (or otherwise) that a MNC might derive from its foreign investments? We might expect the trust that exists in business networks to be beneficial either because the other parties genuinely care about a 'trustor's' welfare, or it might exist from a more self-interested view (Saparito *et al.*,

2004). These different motivations should influence the ability to share and create knowledge within the network. Despite the growth of technology, face-to-face contacts with foreign partners are still crucial in cultivating trust, providing access to the flow of information within the network, and providing the opportunity to create new relationships (Dyer and Chu, 2000). Nonetheless, brokering knowledge *across* these organizational boundaries and relational networks, and processes of reciprocal inter-firm learning, has become a central feature of competitive strategy (Lubatkin *et al.*, 2001).

Social capital is related but different from relational capital. It concerns '... the goodwill that is engendered by the fabric of social relations and that can be mobilized to facilitate action' (Adler and Kwon, 2002, p. 17) and is defined as '... the sum of the resources, actual or virtual, that accrue to an individual or group by virtue of possessing a durable network of more or less institutionalized relationships of mutual acceptance or recognition' (Bourdieu and Wacquant, 1992, p. 119). Social capital theory has mainly been the preserve of economists and sociologists but the value of goodwill in broader terms means that organizational theorists now recognize the relevance of this social structure and the social ties it brings in relation to a wide range of work issues. It is considered to make the achievement of certain ends that would not be attainable in its absence possible. The management of social capital has become viewed as a critical business competence. Whilst human capital theory assumes that people, groups or organizations do better (i.e. receive higher returns for their efforts) because of their personal traits and characteristics, social capital theory assumes that they do better because they are better 'connected'. This 'connection' might be realized in the form of trust, obligation or dependency. Certain network structures, or certain locations in this set of exchange relationships, become an asset in their own right, and it is this asset that is the social capital.

Lengnick-Hall and Lengnick-Hall (2005) define social capital in the international context as '... the intangible resource of structural connections, interpersonal interactions, and cognitive understanding that enables a firm to (a) capitalize on diversity and (b) reconcile differences'. They argue that these two capabilities help international organizations manage the tension between pressures toward integration on a global scale versus local adaptation, and to cope with the challenges arising from diverse national values, economic systems, and workplace conditions, but point out that we now need more research in an international context to examine and understand social capital in an international context. Their work can be used to generate a series of research questions:

- Does dependence upon individuals in structural holes really result in a weakened competitive position and poorer strategic execution?
- How does top management social capital facilitate and constrain strategic choice and execution?
- With what other attributes must social capital be combined in order to lead to the creation of a global mindset?
- Which specific IHRM policies and practices shape the structural, relationship, and cognitive elements of social capital, and consequently how do these policies

influence a MNC's ability to learn and exploit what it knows despite cultural differences and geographic distance?

Again, these propositions now need to be tested empirically.

The management literature has long pointed to the role of international managers and expatriates as information brokers. Their brokerage opportunities exist in relation to participation in, and control of, information diffusion (Burt, 1992, 2000). Central to this process is the concept of 'structural holes' (holes in the social structure of a network that might not reflect a total unawareness of the other parties but do reflect a lack of attention to them). Structural holes are implicit in the boundaries between cohorts of employees, teams, divisions, and between firms. Individuals, units or organizations that have relationships that span these holes can create a competitive advantage depending on the nature of their brokerage. Holes act as buffers with people on either side of the hole circulating in different flows of information. They therefore offer an opportunity to broker the flow of information between people and to control the projects that bring people together from opposite sides of the hole. The research questions that emerge from recent discussion from a special capital perspective should be as follows:

- Which particular social capital structures are associated with greater role effectiveness for international managers, and in what ways?
- Is social capital separate to human capital or are there particular skills and competencies that help build social capital?
- What is the role of HR processes in building, protecting and capitalizing on social capital?

Summarizing the situation with regard to this fourth area of theory it would be fair to say that to date, in the international context what we have is theoretical frameworks only. Moreover, in any empirical testing it is difficult to divorce some aspects of social capital from the discussion of organizational learning above. Hansen (2002) argues that social networks provide a conduit for the sharing of knowledge because they: inform network members about the existence, location, and significance of new knowledge; create a more heterogeneous base of information and knowledge to draw from; and offer different reference points for members to make comparisons and explore new ideas. Consequently, social networks play an important role in knowledge creation (Morris *et al.*, 2005) and form a circulation system that carries information and ideas to those who need it, when they need it (Lengnick-Hall and Lengnick-Hall, 2005). Similarly, Kostova and Roth (2003) have combined ideas from organizational learning and social capital theories by proposing a contingency perspective that specifies the level of social capital needed in multinational corporations based upon different types of interdependencies between headquarters and foreign subunits. 'Simple interdependence' requires a few easily specified points of interaction supported by readily codifiable exchanges whereas 'Complex interdependence' requires many points of interaction and exchanges that are not easily codifiable. Therefore, as the degree and complexity of interdependence between headquarters and foreign subunits increase, higher levels of social capital are required. Relating back to the discussion of organizational designs, they predict that the level of social capital required will be highest for transnationals, followed by international MNCs, then global MNCs.

Do HR Strategy Theories Developed in Western Countries Apply to Other Cultures? (or, How Can HRM Strategies be Made to Apply in Different Cultures?)

We now move to the third and final section of the chapter which asks whether HRM strategies can be made to apply in different cultures. In the context of European HRM Sparrow and Hiltrop (1997) noted three areas of insight and knowledge that HR professionals need. These concern: the range of factors that engender distinctive national and local solutions to HRM issues; the strategic pressures that make these national models more receptive to change and development; and the firm-level processes through which such change and development in actual HRM practice will be delivered. Knowledge about the first area by proxy helps answer the question of whether HR strategy theories developed in western countries *do* actually apply to other cultures, and how HR strategies may be made to apply better in different cultures. This knowledge has largely been produced by the comparative HR researchers. This field has traditionally incorporated a country comparison perspective and asks questions such as: how is HRM structured in individual countries; what strategies are discussed; what is actually put into practice; what are the main differences and similarities; and to what extent are HR policies influenced by national factors such as culture, government policy, educational systems (Pieper, 1990; Brewster *et al.*, 1996)? A review of the field is well beyond the scope of this chapter, but readers should consider the work on:

- the culture-bound versus the culture-specific thesis (see, e.g. Harbison and Myers, 1959; Kerr *et al.*, 1960; Hickson *et al.*, 1974; Neghandi, 1974; Child and Kieser, 1979; Maurice *et al.*, 1980; Child, 1981; Birnbaum and Wong, 1985; Whitley, 1992, 1999; Redding, 1994; Staehle, 1994; Begin, 1997);
- literature that considers which HRM practices are more or less culture sensitive (see, e.g. Laurent, 1986; Kanungo and Jaeger, 1990; Poole, 1990; Van Dijk, 1990; Rosenzweig and Nohria, 1994; Lu and Björkman, 1997); and
- empirical examination of patterns of convergence or not in HRM (see, e.g. Brewster *et al.*, 2004).

The main conclusion of course is that the answer to the first part of the question – do HR strategies developed in western countries apply to other questions – is clearly no. Therefore attention is turned to the second part of the question, i.e. can HRM strategies be made to apply (better) in other cultures? We concentrate attention on institutional theory and what it has to say about the question. As the fields of international HRM and comparative HRM have begun to combine (under pressures for MNCs to work through partnerships, and to localize their management – and consequently to understand how HRM operates in different national contexts) we have seen an infusion of work to the international HRM field from studies that address these questions from the perspective of institutional theory. This work has been reviewed recently by Björkman (2005). He points out that until the early 1990s little reference to this approach could be found, excepting perhaps work on the following:

- Examination of the HRM practices found in foreign-owned subsidiaries of multinational corporations (MNCs) in terms of their degree of global 'integration' or MNC 'standardization' versus local 'responsiveness' or 'local adaptation'. Empirical studies usually ask subsidiary managers to estimate the extent to which the HRM practices resemble those of local firms and the MNC parent organization, respectively (e.g. Rosenzweig and Nohria, 1994; Hannon *et al.*, 1995; Björkman and Lu, 2001; Rosenzweig, 2005).
- Comparative studies of HRM practices across countries (e.g. Gooderham *et al.*, 1999).

Institutional theory developed from the work of Berger and Luckman (1967) who focused on the 'taken-for-granted' character of social reality in social institutions (e.g. religion, work, family, politics) and explained how such realities are created and institutionalized through processes such as typification and habitualization. Further theoretical developments (Meyer and Rowan, 1977; DiMaggio and Powell, 1983) focused on the nature and differentiation of a variety of institutional processes within organizations. An underlying assumption is that organizational structures increasingly arise as a reflection of rationalized institutional rules (Meyer and Rowan, 1977) and from 'myths' of their institutional environment (DiMaggio and Powell, 1983). Structures are not really determined by an organization's work activities, and the demands made by competition and the needs for efficiency, as much as we might believe (DiMaggio and Powell, 1983). In this sense, institutional theory again promotes a perspective where organizational decision making is not seen as an outcome of strategic choice. Similar to the buffering and bridging strategies developed by proponents of the resource dependence perspective, efforts have been made to highlight the strategic behaviours that organizations may employ in direct response to institutional processes (see, e.g. Oliver, 1991; Scott, 1995).

DiMaggio and Powell (1983) described isomorphic processes (the creation of similarity in unrelated forms) that are exerted by external 'institutional agencies' in an organizational field (defined as an aggregate set of organizations that constitute a recognized area of institutional life). They differentiated three isomorphic pulls:

- Coercive, that is, pulls resulting from pressures of external institutions such as the state, legal environment, cultural expectations of societies
- Mimetic, that is, organizations modelling themselves on other organizations in their 'field' as a standard response to uncertainty (e.g. triggered through employee transfers or explicitly through agencies such as consultancies)
- Normative, that is pulls resulting from the professionalization of functions and individuals (e.g. through educational institutions or practice dissemination by professional networks).

Therefore institutional theory soon began to also focus on the role of agencies from within an organization (Scott, 1987; Scott and Meyer, 1989): Scott (1983, p. 16) noted that 'The beliefs, norms, rules, and understandings are not just "out there" but additionally "in here"'. The environment is considered to enter the organization through processes of 'imposition', 'acquisition', 'authorization' (Scott, 1987). Pulls which emphasize the role of internal agents from within the organization (Scott and Meyer, 1989; Westney, 1993) include:

- 'Inducement' of organizational structure (where an organization that lacks power to impose patterns on other organizations instead offers inducements such as funding or certification)
- 'Incorporation' (where organizations come to replicate salient aspects of environmental differentiation in their own structure)
- 'Bypassing' (where institutionalized and shared values can substitute for formal structure)
- 'Imprinting' (where an organizational form retains some of the patterns, institutionalized at the time its industry was founded – though this may result from influences of both external and internal agencies).

The theory has left a strong mark on conceptual work in the area of SIHRM (see Wright and McMahan, 1992; Westney, 1993). From an empirical perspective Björkman (2005) also draws attention to the evidence that MNCs from different countries differ systematically in their overseas operations (e.g. Yuen and Hui, 1993; Rosenzweig and Nohria, 1994; Guest and Hoque, 1996; Bae *et al.*, 1998; Muller, 1998; Björkman and Lu, 2001; Faulkner *et al.*, 2002). Certainly, the current consensus is that firms are not as global or international as is often assumed and a clear country-of-origin effect is still evident. US MNCs, for example, tend to be more centralized and formalized than others in their management of HRM issues, ranging from pay systems through to collective bargaining and union recognition. They tend to innovate more and import leading edge practices from other nation-states. Japanese MNCs on the other hand have been at the forefront of work organization innovations through lean production, but expect their subsidiaries abroad to fit in with this approach. Even though standard world-wide policies and formal systems are not as apparent as in US MNCs, there is stronger centralized direction and ethnocentric attitudes. In short '… MNCs, far from being stateless organizations operating independent of national borders in some purified realm of global economic competition, continue to have their assets, sales, work-force ownership and control highly concentrated in the country where their corporate headquarters are located' (Ferner and Quintanilla, 1998, p. 710).

However, institutional theory does not just play a role in explaining the continuance of many comparative differences in HRM systems. It also has much to say about the key role of the global HR function in facilitating the transfer of *core processes and management practices*. Institutional theory asks whether this transfer is easy to engineer and automatic and indeed, can it actually be managed? It has gained much recent support in addressing these questions (Kostova, 1999; Martin and Beaumont, 2001; Fenton O'Creevy, 2003). We know that global strategies are characterized by particularly intense levels of uncertainty (Weick and Van Orden, 1990). Efforts at globalization within organizations are consequently hampered by problems of information overload (see the section on organization design), managerial complexity in the form of numerous conflicts or paradoxes ('domestic myopia' or only seeing things from within the mindset of the headquarters), and differences in national culture ('expanded socio-cognitive diversity') (Sanders and Carpenter, 1998). Managers in foreign subsidiaries become frustrated with requests to implement 'yet another programme' from headquarters and may – by intention or not – end up implementing one thing whilst reporting another.

Therefore we must consider models that outline *how* transnational transfer of organizational practices can happen successfully. How might an outsider make a judgement that an HRM practice has successfully transferred or not? By thinking about successful transfer of managerial practice as '... the degree of institutionalization of the practice at the recipient unit' Kostova (1999, p. 311). Convergence of practice ranges from simple implementation to evidence of *internalization*. Internalization should be measured by two things:

1. *Implementation* – following of rules implied by the practice and reflection of these rules in objective behaviours and actions. Diffusion of sets of rules to subsidiary employees seen in – and measured – by the actions of employees.
2. *Internalization of these rules by subsidiary employees* – ability to make sense of and attribute meaning to these rules in the same way as achieved by host country or headquarters employees, and the ability to infuse the practice with value. The ways in which recipient unit employees attach meaning to the practice is reflected in three psychological states: *practice commitment* (the relative strength of an employee's identification and involvement with the practice); *practice satisfaction* (a positive attitude towards the practice); and *psychological ownership* (the extent to which the employees claim that it is their practice).

Kostova (1999) argues that ideas will only transfer successfully internationally if they can be embedded into three contexts (social, organizational and relational). Kostova and Roth (2002) found support for this model when they examined the transfer of quality practices within an MNC to 104 locations in 10 countries through questionnaires given to 534 managerial informants and 3238 employees. They made a distinction between *ceremonial* or purely formal adoption and more *substantive* adoption of practices. Kostova and Roth's (2002) model of factors that determine the transfer of best practice is consistent with two important theoretical perspectives. First, it fits the strategic process perspective on the management of change (evidenced in the work of Pettigrew (1995)) in that it points out that international HR professionals have to make the socio-cultural, organizational and relational contexts more 'receptive to change'. International HR functions can influence the second and third of these contexts, if not the first. Second, it fits the business system and comparative literature in that it demonstrates the need for international HR professionals to understand how local practice is embedded in a complex set of relationships between national market structures, ways of organizing firms and authority systems.

However, Martin and Beaumont (2001, p. 1238) note that Kostova's model '... has usefully identified measures for evaluating the extent of institutionalization [but] ... is relatively silent on the process by which such states might be achieved'. Reflecting these criticisms, Björkman (2005) notes that institutional theorists remind us that organizations imitate each other in situations of uncertainty. He argues therefore that researchers should now study *macro and meso level processes of institutionalization* to examine, for example, the diffusion of 'high performance' work/HRM practices, the HR scorecard, outsourcing of HRM tasks, and the structure and roles of the HR department in the MNC.

Martin and Beaumont (2001), however, would argue that any model of HR change in MNCs must also incorporate an understanding of the ways in which managers create such 'strategic discourses' (Ford and Ford, 1995; Barry and Elmes, 1997). International HR practitioners have to 'habitualize' other parts of the organization to the new strategy, make the messages for change more objective as they are shared among employees, and ensure that the messages become 'sedimented' into the organization. Martin and Beaumont (2001) also note the importance of the process of 'design influence' exerted from the centre over local HR practice – exerted either as the direct source of innovation or by tacitly structuring the agenda in terms of what might be deemed acceptable in subsidiaries. This strategic influence role has also been examined by Napier *et al.* (1995). It includes being '…the change agent of corporate culture; the top management team's symbolic "communicator" to other levels of the organization; senior managers' mediator in development/career planning opportunities; and the corporate top management team's and particularly the CEO's reliable internal informal advisor' (Novicevic and Harvey, 2001, p. 1252).

Some researchers have considered specifically how MNCs develop organizational capability and consider that it is created out of the international networking at individual and functional levels that surrounds building research and development or production centres, logistic networks or indeed HR systems and processes on a global scale, and the conduct of these activities in global contexts (see, e.g. Collis, 1991; Fladmoe-Linquist and Tallman, 1994; Hedlund and Ridderstråe, 1997; Kogut, 1997; Tallman and Fladmoe-Lindquist, 2002). In order to understand how organizations develop, manage, and deploy such capabilities to support their business strategy (Montealegre, 2002) we generally have to conduct longitudinal studies. In doing so, Sparrow, Brewster and Harris (2004; Brewster *et al.*, 2005) apply a dynamic capability perspective to the field of SIHRM. They drew three key conclusions about the role of the HR function in international firms. First, the future of the global HR function will be both heavily dependent upon and will be shaped by the globalizing activity of two contiguous functions: information systems and marketing or corporate communications. Second, it is clear that the added value of the HR function in an international firm lies in its ability to manage the delicate balance between overall co-ordinated systems and sensitivity to local needs, including cultural differences, in a way that aligns with both business needs and senior management philosophy. Third, it is clear that there is a distinction to be made now between international HRM and global HRM. Traditionally, international HRM has been about managing an international workforce – the expatriates, frequent commuters, cross-cultural team members and specialists involved in international knowledge transfer. Global HRM is not simply about covering these staff around the world. It concerns managing SIHRM activities through the application of global rule-sets that carry meaning across cultures.

Conclusions

A large amount of the SIHRM literature focuses on the challenge for MNCs in coping with complex cultural, geographical, and institutional pressures. As the chapter
has made clear, the adoption of any one theoretical approach often appears somewhat dogmatic. In recent years then there has been a process of increasing transfusion
of theoretical ideas across the perspectives discussed in order to better understand
organizational behaviour. We are seeing some convergence and synthesis of ideas
between different combinations of the theories covered in this chapter. For example, the need to combine insights from institutional theory, knowledge-based theories
of the firm and social capital theory can be seen in recent models of MNCs centre-
subsidiary relationships based on the 'knowledge leveraging' perspective of Grant,
Almeida and Song (2000). This perspective appreciates that knowledge is created
in many sites and functions and is accessed in many locations. It argues that:
'… the movement of knowledge between different geographical locations is central
[to the process of adding value in knowledge development]' (Grant *et al.*, 2000,
pp. 115–16). Kostova and Roth's work (2002), though conducted mainly from
an institutional theory perspective, concluded that successful practice adoption is
largely dependent upon relationships based on trust and shared identity, requiring
insights from social capital theory. In relation to the study of MNCs, social capital has been defined as the knowledge that is embedded within social networks
(Nahapiet and Ghoshal, 1998). Others are drawing links between knowledge-based
theories and social capital theories. Knowledge flows are now understood to be mul-
tidirectional, unplanned and emergent (Iles and Yolles, 2002). Knowledge flows
can be understood through theories of tacit knowledge spread within top management teams through 'advice networks' (Athanassiou and Nigh, 2000); social capital
theory and the resources that accrue to international managers as a consequence
of their boundary spanning roles (Kostova and Roth, 2003); and the application
of knowledge transfer theory to the topic of expatriation (Bonache and Brewster,
2001).

Similarly, by integrating some organizational learning perspectives with resource-
based views of the firm, Morris, Wright and Snell (2005) argue that as MNCs
'… struggle to create and integrate practices across borders, they are faced with
unique challenges that either push for global efficiency or local responsiveness. These
challenges open the discussion for ways to actually manage both the creation and integration of knowledge on a global scale'. They have drawn attention to two competitive
capabilities: knowledge creation and knowledge integration at local level. They also
touch upon some institutional theory, by reference to Youndt, Subramaniam, and
Snell's (2004) discussion of organizational capital, which they consider to be knowledge and experiences that have become institutionalized and codified such that they
reside within an organization. They also note that trust provides the motive for actors
in the system of a MNC to interact with others, while shared identity provides an overlapping understanding of what is important to share. Perhaps the most striking of the
challenges that they argue remain to be addressed, however, is the need to understand
what the economic benefits (or rents) of the adoption of an integrated set of global

HR practices actually are, and to examine how such integration creates a source of sustainable competitive advantage.

In other chapters in this volume some attention is given to the geographical coverage and origin of much academic work. This question is less relevant to a chapter on theory, but we would make a general observation. Clearly, most of the theorizing is based on Anglo Saxon models of management and even where there has been empirical testing it tends to have been on UK or UK MNEs. It is also worth noting that US researchers have favoured the RBV whilst European researchers have been more attracted of late to both institutional theory and to some degree organizational learning perspectives. Certainly the comparative HR field, not featured in this chapter, is dominated by non-US researchers, perhaps not surprisingly. The field does now appear to be mature enough to combine these perspectives.

We make one final observation about the level of analysis that needs to be adopted in SIHRM research if it is to respond to this challenge. In addition to understanding what happens at the level of the firm in its totality – the traditional focus of many SIHRM researchers – we need to better understand how organizations enhance the ability of specific functions to perform globally. Many researchers argue that globalization within organizations is driven by what happens within business functions as they seek to co-ordinate (develop linkages between geographically dispersed units of a function) and control (regulate functional activities to align them with the expectations set in targets) their activities across borders (Kim *et al.*, 2003). As Malbright (1995, p. 119) pointed out: '… Globalization occurs at the level of the function, rather than the firm'. This observation has been reinforced by the longitudinal studies of Sparrow, Brewster and Harris (2004). However, the problem is that the HR function is not one that can be considered, currently, as being highly globalized. Indeed, a range of researchers have found that other departments are much more globalized (Yip, 1992; Hansen *et al.*, 1999; Kim *et al.*, 2003). If other functional activities are being better connected across geographical borders through flows of information that are intended to enhance levels of innovation and learning, then the HR functions that service them are themselves going to be forced to become more globalized but in a piecemeal and reactive manner. Clearly more attention needs now to be devoted to understanding the ways in which the HR function itself contributes effectively to the process of globalization.

REFERENCES

Adler, N.J. 1991. *International Dimensions of Organizational Behavior*. 2nd ed. Boston, MA: PWS-Kent.

Adler, N.J. & Ghadar, F. 1990. Strategic Human Resource Management: A Global Perspective. in Pieper, R. (ed.) *Human Resource Management: An International Comparison*. Berlin: de Gruyter: 235–60.

Adler, N.J. & Ghadar, F. 1993. A Strategic Approach to International Human Resources Management. In Wong-Rieger, D. & Rieger, F. (eds.) *International Management Research*. Berlin: de Gruyter: 136–61.

Adler, P.S. & Kwon, S.-W. 2002. Social capital: prospects for a new concept. *Academy of Management Review*, 27 (1): 17–40.

Ashkenas, R., Ulrich, D., Jick, T. & Kerr, S. 1995. *The Boundaryless Organization*. San Francisco, CA: Jossey-Bass.

Athanassiou, N. & Nigh, D. 2000. Internationalization, Tacit Knowledge and the Top Management Teams of MNCs, *Journal of International Business Studies* 31 (3): 471–88.

Bae, J., Chen, S.-J. & Lawler, J.L. 1998. Variations in human resource management in Asian countries: MNC home-country and host-country effects. *International Journal of Human Resource Management*, 9: 653–70.

Baliga, B.R. & Jaeger, A.M. 1984. Multinational Corporations: Control Systems and Delegation Issues. *Journal of International Business Studies*, 15: 25–40.

Barkema, H.G. & Vermeulen, F. 1998. International expansion through start-up or acquisition: a learning perspective. *Academy of Management Journal*, 41(1): 7–26.

Barkema, H.G., Bell, J.H.J. & Pennings, J.M. 1996. Foreign entry, cultural barriers, and learning. *Strategic Management Journal*, 17: 151–66.

Barkema, H.G., Shenkar, O., Vermeulen, F. & Bell, J.H.J. 1997. Working abroad, working with others. How firms learn to operate international joint ventures. *Academy of Management Journal*, 40 (2): 426–42.

Barney, J.B. 1989. Asset stocks and sustained competitive advantage: A comment. *Management Science*, 35 (12): 1511–13

Barney, J.B 1991. Firm resources and sustained competitive advantage. *Journal of Management*, 17: 99–120.

Barry, D. & Elmes, M. 1997. Strategy retold: toward a narrative view of strategic discourse, *Academy of Management Review* 22 (2): 429–52.

Bartlett, C.A. & Ghoshal, S. 1986. Tap your subsidiaries for global reach. *Harvard Business Review*, 64 (6): 87–94.

Bartlett, C.A. & Ghoshal, S. 1989. *Managing across Borders: The Transnational Solution*. Boston: Harvard Business School Press.

Bartlett, C.A. & Ghoshal, S. 1990. Matrix Management: Not a structure, a frame of mind, *Harvard Business Review*, 68 (4): 138–45.

Bartlett, C.A. & Ghoshal, S. 1997. *International Management: Text, Cases and Readings in Cross-Border Management*. 2nd edn. Boston, MA: Irwin.

Beer, M., Spector, B., Lawrence, P.R., Mills, D.Q. & Walton, R.E. 1985. *Human resource management*. New York: Free Press.

Begin, J. 1997. National HR systems: concepts and contexts. in j. Begin (ed.) *Dynamic human resource systems: cross-national comparisons*. Berlin: de Gruyter.

Best, M.H. 1990. *The New Competition: Institutions of Industrial Restructuring*. Polity Press: Oxford.

Birkinshaw, J.M. & Morrison, A.J. 1995. Configurations of Strategy and Structure in Subsidiaries of Multinational Corporations. *Journal of International Business Studies*, 26 (4): 729–53.

Birnbaum, P.H. & Wong, G.Y. 1985. Organizational structure of multinational banks in Hong Kong from a culture-free perspective. *Administrative Science Quarterly*, 30 (2): 262–77.

Björkman, I. 2005. International human resource management research and institutional theory, in I. Bjorkman & G. Stahl (eds.). *Handbook of Research into International HRM*. London: Edward Elgar.

Björkman, I. & Lu, Y. 2001. Institutionalization and Bargaining Power Explanations of HRM Practices in International Joint Ventures – The Case of Chinese-Western Joint Ventures. *Organization Studies*, 22 (3): 491–512.

Bonache, J. & Brewster, C. 2001. Knowledge transfer and the management of expatriation, *Thunderbird International Business Review* 43 (1): 145–68.

Bourdieu, P. & Wacquant, L.J.D. 1992. *An invitation to reflexive sociology*. Chicago, IL: University of Chicago Press.

Braun, W. & Warner, M. 2002. The 'culture-free' versus the 'culture-specific' management debate. In Warner, M. & Joynt, P. (eds.) *Managing across cultures*. 2nd ed. London: Thomson Learning: 13–25.

Brewster, C., Mayrhofer, W. & Morley, M. 2004. *Human Resource Management in Europe: evidence of convergence?* London, Elsevier.

Brewster, C., Sparrow, P.R. & Harris, H. 2005. Towards a new model of globalizing human resource management. *International Journal of Human Resource Management*, 16(2): 434–45.

Brewster, C., Tregaskis, O., Hegewisch, A. & Mayne, L. 1996. Comparative survey research in human resource management: a review and an example. *International Journal of Human Resource Management*, 7 (3): 585–604.

Buckley, P.J. & Ghauri, P.N. 2004. Globalisation, economic geography and the strategy of multinational enterprises. *Journal of International Business Studies*, 35 (2): 81–98.

Burt, R.S. 1992. *Structural holes*. Cambridge, MA: Harvard University Press.

Burt, R.S. 2000. The network structure of social capital. In B.M.Staw & R.I. Sutton (eds.) *Research in Organizational Behavior: An Annual Series of Analytical Essays and Critical Reviews. Volume 22.* New York: JAI Press.

Caves, R.E. 1996. *Multinational Enterprise and Economic Analysis*, Cambridge University Press: Cambridge.

Chandler, A.D. 1962. *Strategy and Structure: Chapters in the History of the Industrial Enterprise*. Cambridge, MA: MIT Press.

Chen, T.-J., Chen, H. & Ku, Y.-H. 2004. Foreign direct investment and local linkages. *Journal of International Business Studies*, 35 (4): 320–33.

Child, J. & Kieser, A. 1979. Organization and Managerial Roles in British and West German Companies: An Examination of the Culture-Free Thesis, In Lammers, C. J. & Hickson, D. J. (eds.) *Organizations Alike and Unlike*. London: Routledge.

Child, J. 1981. Culture, Contingency and Capitalism in the Cross-National Study of Organizations. In Cummings, L. L. & Staw, B. M. (eds.) *Research in Organizational Behavior Vol. 3.* Greenwich: JAI Press.

Child, J. 1984. Organization: a Guide to Problems and Practice. London: Harper and Row.

Cohen, W.M. & Levinthal, D.A. 1989. Innovation and learning: The two faces of R&D. *Economic Journal*, 99: 569–96.

Cohen, W.M. & Levinthal, D.A. 1990. Absorptive Capacity: A New Perspective on Learning and Innovations. *Administrative Science Quarterly*, 35: 128–52.

Collis, D.J. 1991. A resource-based analysis of global competition: the case of the bearings industry, *Strategic Management Journal* 12: 49–68.

Daniels, J.D. 1986. Approaches to European Regional Management by Large U.S. Multinational Firms, *Management International Review*, 26 (2): 27–42.

Daniels, J.D. 1987. Bridging national and global marketing strategies through regional operations, *International Marketing Review*, Autumn: 29–44.

DeCieri, H., Cox, J.W. & Fenwick, M. 2001. Think global, act local: from naïve comparison to critical participation in the teaching of strategic international human resource management. *TAMARA Journal of Critical Postmodern Organization Science*, 1(1): 68–78.

DeCieri, H. & Dowling, P.J. 1997. Strategic international human resource management: an Asia-Pacific perspective. *Management International Review*, 37 (1), Special Issue: 21–42.

DeCieri, H. & Dowling, P.J. 1998. *The Tortuous Evolution of Strategic Human Resource Management in Multinational Enterprises.* Department of Management, Working Paper in Human Resource Management and Industrial Relations No. 5, The University of Melbourne Australia.

De Saá-Pérez, P. & García-Falcón, J.M. 2002. A resource-based view of human resource management and organisational capabilities development, *International Journal of Human Resource Management* 13 (1): 123–40.

Dierickx, I. & Cool, K. 1989. Asset stock accumulation and sustainability of competitive advantage. *Management Science*, 25 (12): 1504–11.

DiMaggio, P.J. & Powell, W.W. 1983. The iron cage revisited: Institutional isomorphism and collective rationality in organizational fields. *American Sociological Review*, 48: 147–60.

Dowling, P.J., Schuler, R.S. & Welch, D.E. 1994. *International Dimensions of Human Resource Management.* 2nd edition. Belmont Cal: Wadsworth Publishing Company.

Dowling, P.J., Welch, D.E. & Schuler, R.S. 1998. *International Human Resource Management. Managing People in a Multinational Context.* Cincinnati etc: South-Western College Publishing.

Doz, Y.L. & Prahalad, C.K. 1981. Headquarters Influence and Strategic Control in MNCs. *Sloan Management Review*, 23 (1): 15–29.

Dunning, J.H. 1993. *Multinational Enterprises and the Global Economy.* Reading, MA: Addison-Wesley.

Dunning, J.H. 2002. Relational assets, networks and international business activity. In F.J. Contractor & P. Lorange (eds.) *Co-operative Strategies and Alliances.* Pergamon: New York. pp. 569–94.

Dyer, J. & Chu, W. 2000. The determinants of trust in supplier-automaker relationships in the US, Japan and Korea. *Journal of International Business Studies*, 31 (2): 259–85.

Edström, A. & Galbraith, J. 1977a. Transfer of Managers as a Coordination and Control Strategy in Multinational Organizations. *Administrative Science Quarterly*, 22: 248–63.

Edström, A. & Galbraith. J. 1977b. Alternative Policies for International Transfers of Managers. *Management International Review*, 17: 11–22.

Edström, A. & Galbraith. J.R. 1978. The Impact of Managerial Transfers on Headquarters-Subsidiary Relationships in a Multinational Company. In Ghertman, M.; Leontiades, J. (eds.) *European Research in International Business.* Amsterdam: North-Holland: 331–49.

Egelhoff, W.G. 1991. Information-Processing Theory and the Multinational Enterprise. *Journal International Business Studies*, 22 (3): 341–69.

Egelhoff, W.G. 1999. Organizational equilibrium and organizational change: two different perspectives of the multinational enterprise. *Journal of International Management*, 5: 15–33.

Evans, P.; Pucik, V.; Barsoux, J.-L. 2002. *The Global Challenge. Frameworks for International Human Resource Management.* Boston etc: McGraw Hill Higher Education.

Faulkner, D., Pikethly, R., & Child, J. 2002. International mergers and acquisitions in the UK 1985–94: A comparison of national HRM practices. *International Journal of Human Resource Management*, 13: 106–22.

Fenton-O'Creevy, M. 2003. The diffusion of HR practices within the multinational firm: towards a research agenda, *Beta: Scandinavian Journal of Business Research*, 17 (1): 36–47.

Fenton-O'Creevy, M., Gooderham, P. and Nordhaug, O. 2005. Diffusion of HRM to Europe and the Role of US MNCs. Management Revue, 16 (Special Issue 1).

Ferner, A. 1994. MNCs and Human Resource Management: An Overview of Research Issues. *Human Resource Management Journal*, 4: 79–102.

Ferner, A. & Quintanilla, J. 1998. Multinational, national business systems and HRM: the enduring influence of national identity or a process of 'Anglo Saxonization'?, *International Journal of Human Resource Management*, 9 (4): 710–31.

Fladmoe-Lindquist, K. & Tallman, S. 1994. Resource-based strategy and competitive advantage among multinationals, in P. Shrivastava, A. Huff and J. Dutton (eds.). *Advances in Strategic Management, Volume 10.* Greenwich, CT: JAI Press.

Flood, P.C., Ramamoorthy, N. & Liu, W. 2003. Knowledge and innovation: diffusion of HRM systems, *Beta: Scandinavian Journal of Business Research*, 17 (1): 59–68.

Ford, J.D. & Ford, L.W. 1995. The role of conversations in producing intentional organizational change, *Academy of Management Review*, 20 (3): 541–70.

Foss, N.J. & Pedersen, T. 2004. Organizing knowledge processes in the multinational corporation: an introduction, *Journal of International Business Studies*, 35 (5): 340–49.

Galbraith, J.R. 1973. *Designing complex organizations.* Reading, MA: Addison-Wesley.

Galbraith, J.R. 1977. *Organization design.* Reading, MA. Addison-Wesley.

Ghemawat, P. 1986. Sustainable advantage. *Harvard Business Review*, Sept–Oct: 53–8.

Ghoshal, S. & Bartlett, C.A. 1988. Creation, adoption, and diffusion of innovations by subsidiaries of multinational corporations, *Journal of International Business Studies*, 29: 365–88.

Glaister, K.W. & Buckley, P.J. 1996. Strategic motives for international alliance formation. *Journal of Management Studies*, 33: 301–32.

Gooderham, P. N., Nordhaug, O., & Ringdal, K. 1999. Institutional and rational determinants of organizational practices: Human resource management in European firms. *Administrative Science Quarterly*, 44: 507–31.

Grant, R. M. 1996. Toward a knowledge-based theory of the firm. *Strategic Management Journal*, 17(S2): 109–22.

Grant, R.M., Almeida, P. & Song, J. 2000. Knowledge and the Multi-national Enterprise, in Millar, C.J.M., Grant, R.M. and Choi, C.J. (eds.) *International Business: Emerging Issues and Emerging Markets.* Basingstoke: Macmillan, pp. 102–14.

Guest, D. & Hoque, K. 1996. The influence of national ownership in human resource management practices in UK greenfield sites. *Human Resource Management Journal*, 6(4): 50–74.

Guest, D.E. 1991. Personnel Management: The End of Orthodoxy? *British Journal of Industrial Relations*, 29: 149–75.

Guest, D.E. 1997. Human resource management and performance: a review and research agenda. *The International Journal of Human Resource Management*, 8: 263–76.

Gupta, A. & Govindarajan, V. 1991. Knowledge flows and the structure of control within multinational corporations. *Academy of Management Review*, 16: 768–92.

Hamel, G. & Prahalad, C.K. 1985. Do you really have a global strategy? *Harvard Business Review*, July/August, 139–48.

Hamilton, R.D. & Kashlak, R.J. 1999. National Influences on Multinational Corporation Control System Selection. *Management International Review*, 39 (2): 167–89.

Hannon, J. M., Huang, I.-C. & Jaw, B.-S. 1995. International human resource strategy and its determinants: The case of subsidiaries in Taiwan. *Journal of International Business Studies*, 26: 531–54.

Hansen, M. T. 2002. Knowledge networks: Explaining effective knowledge sharing in multiunit companies. *Organization Science*, 13: 290–302.

Hansen, M.T., Nohria, N. & Tierney, T. 1999. What is your strategy for managing knowledge?, *Harvard Business Review* 77 (2): 106–16.

Harbison F. & Myers C.A. 1959. *Management in the Industrial World*. New York: Mc Graw Hill.

Harzing, A.-W.K. 1999. Managing the Multinationals. An International Study of Control Mechanisms. Cheltenham, UK: Edward Elgar.

Haspeslagh, G. & Jemison, D.B. 1991. *Managing Acquisitions: Creating Value Through Corporate Renewal*. New York: Free Press.

Hedberg, B. 1981. How organizations learn and unlearn, in P.C. Nystrom & W.H. Starbuck (eds.), *Handbook of Organizational Design*. London: University Press.

Hedlund, G. 1986. The Hypermodern MNC – A Heterarchy? *Human Resource Management*, 25 (1): 9 ff.

Hedlund, G. 1993. Assumptions of hierarchy and heterarchy: an application to the multinational corporation. In Ghoshal, S. & Westney, E. (eds.). *Organization theory and the multinational corporation*. London: Macmillan: 211–36.

Hedlund, G. & Ridderstråe, J. 1997. Toward a theory of self-renewing MNCs, in B. Toyne & D.Nigh (eds.), *International Business: An Emerging Vision*. University of South Carolina Press.

Hennart, J.-F. 1991. Control in Multinational Firms: The Role of Price and Hierarchy. *Management International Review*, 31 Special Issue: 71–96.

Hickson, D.J., Hinings, C.R., McMillan, C.J. & Schwitter, J.P. 1974. The culturefree context of organization structure: a tri-national comparison. *Sociology*, 8: 59–80.

Huselid, M. 1995. The impact of human resource management practices on turnover, productivity and corporate financial performance, *Academy of Management Journal* 38 (3): 635–72.

Iles, P. & Yolles, M. 2002. International joint ventures, HRM and viable knowledge migration, *International Journal of Human Resource Management* 13 (4): 624–41.

Inkpen, A. 1996. Creating knowledge through collaboration. *California Management Review*, 39: 123–40.

Jackson, S.E., Hitt, M.A. & DeNisi, A.S. 2003. Managing human resources for knowledge-based competition: new research directions. In S.E. Jackson, M.A. Hitt & A.S. DeNisi (eds.) *Managing Knowledge for Sustained Competitive Advantage: Designing Strategies for Effective Human Resource Management*. San Francisco, CA: Jossey-Bass. pp. 399–428.

Kale, P., Singh, H. & Perlmutter, H. 2000. Learning and protection of proprietary assets in strategic alliances: building relational capital. *Strategic Management Journal*, 21: 217–37.

Kamoche K. 1996. The integration-differentiation puzzle: a resource-capability perspective in international human resource management. *The International Journal of Human Resource Management*, 7: 230–44.

Kanungo, R.N. & Jaeger, A.M. 1990. Introduction: the need for indigenous management in developing countries. In Jaeger, A. M. and Kanungo, R. N. (eds.) *Management in developing countries*. London: Routledge.

Kenter, M.E. 1985. Die Steuerung ausländischer Tochtergesellschaften. Instrumente und Effizienz. Frankfurt: P. Lang.

Kerr, C., Dunlop, J.T. Harbison, F.H. & Myers, C.A. 1960. *Industrialism and Industrial Man*. Cambridge MA: Harvard University Press.

Kim, K., Park, J-H. & Prescott, J.E. 2003. The global integration of business functions: a study of multinational businesses in integrated global industries, *Journal of International Business Studies* 34: 327–44.

Kogut, B. 1997. The evolutionary theory of the multinational corporation: within and across country options, in B. Toyne & D. Nigh (eds.). *International Business: An Emerging Vision*. Columbia, SC: University of South Carolina Press.

Kostova, T. 1999. Transnational transfer of strategic organizational practices: a contextual perspective, *Academy of Management Review* 24 (2): 308–24.

Kostova, T. & Roth, K. 2002. Adoption of an organizational practice by subsidiaries of multinational corporations: institutional and relational effects, *Academy of Management Journal* 45 (1): 215–33.

Kostova, T. & Roth, K. 2003. Social capital in multinational corporations and a micro-macro model of its formation. *Academy of Management Review*, 28 (2): 297–317.

Krishnan, H.A., Miller, A. & Judge, W.Q. 1997. Diversification and top management team complementarity: is performance improved by merging similar or dissimilar teams? *Strategic Management Journal*, 18: 361–74.

Lado, A. & Wilson, M. 1994. Human resource systems and sustained competitive advantage: a competency based perspective, *Academy of Management Review* 19: 699–727.

Lane, P. & Lubatkin, M. 1998. Relative absorptive capacity and interorganizational learning. *Strategic Management Journal*, 19: 461–78.

Laurent, A. 1986. The Cross-Cultural Puzzle of International HRM. *Human Resource Management*, 25: 91–102.

Lawler, E.E. 1997. *From The Ground Up*. San Francisco: Jossey-Bass.

Lawrence, J.W. & Lorsch, P.R. 1967. *Organization and Environment*. Boston: Harvard University Press.

Lengnick-Hall, M.L. & Lengnick-Hall, C. 2005. International human resource management research and social network/social capital theory, in I. Bjorkman & G. Stahl (eds.). *Handbook of Research into International HRM*. London: Edward Elgar.

Levinthal, D.A. & March, J.G. 1993. Exploration and exploitation in organizational learning. *Strategic Management Journal*, 14 (Winter): 95–112.

Levitt, B. & March, J.G. 1988. Organizational learning. *Annual Review of Sociology*, 14: 319–40.

Lu, Y. & Björkman, I. 1997. HRM practices in China-Western joint ventures: MNC standardization versus localization. *The International Journal of Human Resource Management*, 8: 614–27.

Lubatkin, M., Florin, J. & Lane, P. 2001. Learning together and apart: a model of reciprocal interfirm learning. *Human Relations*, 54 (10): 1353–82.

Malbright, T. 1995. Globalization of an ethnographic firm, *Strategic Management Journal* 16: 119–41.

March, J.G. & Olsen, J.P. 1988. The uncertainty of the past: organizational learning under ambiguity. in March, J.G. (ed.) *Decisions and Organizations*. Oxford: Basil Blackwell: 335–58.

March, J.G. & Simon, H.A. 1958. *Organizations*. New York: John Wiley.

Martin, G. & Beaumont, P. 2001. Transforming multinational enterprises: towards a process model of strategic human resource management change, *International Journal of Human Resource Management*, 12 (8): 1234–50.

Martin, X. & Salomon, R. 2003. Knowledge transfer capacity and its implications for the theory of the multinational corporation, *Journal of International Business Studies*, 34: 356–73.

Martinez, J.I. & Jarillo, J.C. 1989. The Evolution of Research on Coordination Mechanisms in Multinational Corporations. *Journal of International Business Studies*, 20 (3): 489–514.

Maurice, M., Sorge, A. & Warner, M. 1980. Societal Differences in Organizing Manufacturing Units: A comparison of France, West Germany, and Great Britain. *Organization Studies*, 1: 58–86.

Meyer, J. W. & Rowan, B. 1977. Institutionalized organizations: formal structure as myth and ceremony. *American Journal of Sociology*, 83 (2): 340–863.

Miller, D. & Friesen, P.H. 1980. Momentum and revolution in organizational adaptation. *Academy of Management Journal*, 23: 591–614.

Miller, D. & Friesen, P.H. 1984. A longitudinal study of the corporate life cycle. *Management Science*, 30: 1161–83.

Miller, D. 1993. The architecture of simplicity. *Academy of Management Review*, 18: 116–38.

Miller, D., Droge, C. & Vickery, S. 1997. Celebrating the "essential": the impact of performance on the functional favoritism of CEOs in two contexts. *Journal of Management*, 23: 147–68.

Miller, D. & Chen, M.-J. 1996. The simplicity of competitive repertoires: an empirical analysis. *Strategic Management Journal*, 17: 419–39.

Miller, D., Lant, T.K., Milliken, F.J. & Korn, H.J. 1996. The evolution of strategic simplicity: Exploring two models of organizational adaptation. *Journal of Management*, 22: 863–87.

Milliman, J., Von Glinow, M.A. & Nathan, M. 1991. Organizational Life Cycles and Strategic International Human Resource Management in Multinational Companies: Implications for Congruence Theory. *Academy of Management Review*, 16: 318–39.

Minbaeva, D., Pedersen, T., Björkman, I., Fey, C.F. & Park, H.J. 2003. MNC knowledge transfer, subsidiary absorptive capacity, and HRM. *Journal of International Business Studies*, 34: 586–99.

Mintzberg, H. 1979. *The structuring of organizations*. Englewood Cliffs, NJ: Prentice-Hall.

Mintzberg, H. 1983. *Structure in Fives. Designing Effective Organizations*. Englewood Cliffs, NJ: Prentice-Hall.

Montealegre, R. 2002. A process model of capability development: lessons from the electronic commerce strategy at Bolsa de Valores de Guayaquil, *Organization Science*, 13 (5): 514–31.

Morris, S.S., Snell, S.A. & Wright, P.M. 2005. A resource-based view of international human resources: towards a framework of integrative and creative capabilities, in I. Bjorkman & G. Stahl (eds.). *Handbook of Research into International HRM*. London: Edward Elgar.

Muller, M. 1998. Human resource and industrial relations practices of UK and US multinationals in Germany. *International Journal of Human Resource Management*, 9: 732–49.

Nahapiet, J. & Ghoshal, S. 1998. Social capital, intellectual capital, and the organizational advantage. *Academy of Management Review*, 23: 242–66.

Napier, N., Tibau, J., Jenssens, M. & Pilenzo, R. 1995. Juggling on a high-wire: the role of the international human resources manager, in Ferris, G., Rosen, S. and Barnum, D. (eds.) *Handbook of Human Resource Management*. Oxford: Blackwell, pp. 217–42.

Neghandi, A. R. 1974. Cross-cultural management studies: Too many conclusions, not enough conceptualizations. *Management International Review*, 14: 59–72.

Nohria, N. & Ghoshal, S. 1997. *The Differentiated Network: Organizing Multinational Corporations for Value Creation*. San Francisco, CA: Jossey-Bass Inc.

Novicevic, M.M. & Harvey, M. 2001. The changing role of the corporate HR function in global organizations of the twenty-first century, *International Journal of Human Resource Management*, 12 (8): 1251–68.

Oliver, C. 1991. Strategic Responses to Institutional Processes. *The Academy of Management Review*, 16 (1): 145–79.

Ouchi, W.G. 1977. The Relationship Between Organizational Structure and Organizational Control. *Administrative Science Quarterly*, 22: 95–112.

Ouchi, W.G. 1979. A Conceptual Framework for the Design of Organizational Control Mechanisms. *Management Science*, 25 (9): 833–48.

Ouchi, W.G. 1980. Markets, Bureaucracies and Clans. *Administrative Science Quarterly*, 25: 129–44.

Parker, B. 1998. *Globalization and Business Practice: Managing Across Boundaries*, London: Sage.

Penrose, E.T. 1959. *The Theory of Growth of the Firm*. New York: Wiley.

Perlmutter, H.V. 1969. The Tortuous Evolution of the Multinational Corporation. *Columbia Journal of World Business*, 4: 9–18.

Perlmutter, H.V. & Heenan, D.A. 1974. How multinational should your top managers be? *Harvard Business Review*, 52 (6): 121–32.

Perlmutter, H.V. & Trist, E. 1986. Paradigms for societal transition. *Human Relations*, 39 (1): 1–27.

Peteraf, M.A. 1993. The cornerstones of competitive advantage: a resource-based view. *Strategic Management Journal*, 14 (3): 179–91.

Pettigrew, A.M. 1995. Longitudinal field research on change: theory and practice, in Huber, G.P. and Van de ven, A. (eds.) *Longitudinal Field Research Methods: Studying the Processes of Organizational Change*. London: Sage.

Pfeffer, J. & Cohen, Y. 1984. Determinants of Internal Labor Markets in Organization. *Administrative Science Quarterly*. 29: 550–72.

Pfeffer, J. & Davis-Blake, A. 1987. Understanding organizational wage structure: A resource-dependence approach. *Academy of Management Journal*, 30: 437–55.

Pfeffer, J. & Moore, W. 1980. Power in university budgeting: A replication and extension. *Administrative Science Quarterly*, 25: 637–53.

Pfeffer, J. & Salancik, G. 1978. *The external control of organizations: A resource dependence perspective*. New York: Harper and Row.

Pieper, R. 1990. *Human Resource Management: an International Comparison*. Berlin: de Gruyter.

Pilkington, A. 1996. Learning from joint ventures: the Rover – Honda relationship. *Business History*, 38: 90–116.

Poole, M. 1990. Editorial: human resource management in an international perspective. *International Journal of Human Resource Management*, 1: 1–15.

Porter, M.E. 1986. Changing Patterns of International Competition. *California Management Review*, 28: 9–40.

Prahalad, C.K. 1975. *The strategic process in multinational corporation*. Unpublished doctoral dissertation. Harvard Graduate School of Business Administration.

Prahalad, C.K. & Doz, Y.L. 1987. *The Multinational Mission*. New York: The Free Press.

Prange, C. 1999. Desperately seeking theory? In Easterby-Smith, M., Burgoyne, J. & Araujo, L. (eds.). *Organizational Learning and the Learning Organization*. London: Sage.

Pucik, V. & Katz, J.H. 1986. Information, Control, and Human Resource Management in Multinational Firms. *Human Resource Management*, 25: 121–32.

Redding, S.G. 1994. Comparative Management Theory: Jungle, Zoo or Fossil Bed? *Organization Studies*, 15: 323–59.

Rosenzweig, P.M. 2005. The dual logics behind international human resource management: Pressures for global integration and local responsiveness. In G. Stahl & I. Björkman (eds.), *Handbook of research in international human resource management*. Cheltenham, UK: Edward Elgar.

Rosenzweig, P.M. & Nohria, N. 1994. Influences on human resource management practices in multinational corporations. *Journal of International Business Studies*, 25: 229–51.

Roth, K., Schweiger, D.W. & Morrison, A.J. 1991. Global Strategy Implementation at the Business Unit Level – Operational Capabilities and Administrative Mechanisms. *Journal of International Business Studies*, 22 (3): 369–402.

Rugman, A.M., D-Cruz, J.R. & Verbeke, A. 1995. Internationalisation and De-internationalisation: Will business networks replace multinationals? in G. Boyd (ed.) *Competitive and Co-operative Macromanagement*. Aldershot: Edward Elgar, pp. 107–29.

Rumelt, R.P. 1987. Theory, strategy, and entrepreneurship. in Teece, D. (ed.) *The Competitive Challenge*. Cambridge, MA: Ballinger: 137–58.

Saparito, P.A., Chen, C.C. & Sapienza, H.J. 2004. The role of relational trust in bank-small firm relationships. *Academy of Management Journal*, 47 (3): 400–10.

Schuler, R.S. 2000a. Human resource issues and activities in international joint ventures. *International Journal of Human Resource Management*, 12 (1): 1–52.

Schuler, R.S. 2000b. The internationalization of human resource management. *Journal of International Management*, 6: 239–60.

Schuler, R.S. 2001. Human resource issues and activities in international joint ventures, *International Journal of Human Resource Management*, 12 (1): 1–52.

Schuler, R.S., Budhwar, P.S. & Florkowski, G.W. 2002. International Human Resource Management: Review and Critique. *International Journal of Management Reviews*, 4 (1): 41–70.

Schuler, R.S., Dowling, P.J. & De Cieri, H. 1993. An integrative framework of strategic international human resource management. *International Journal of Human Resource Management*, 4: 717–64.

Schuler, R. & MacMillan, I. C. 1984. Gaining Competitive Advantage through Human Resource Management Practices. *Human Resource Management*, 23 (3): 241–55.

Schuler, R.S. & Jackson, S.E. 1987. Linking competitive strategy and human resource management practices. *Academy of Management Executive*, 1: 207–19.

Schuler, R.S. & Jackson, S.E. 1995. Understanding Human Resource Management in the context of organizations and their environments. *Annual Review of Psychology*, 46: 237–64.

Schuler, R.S. & Jackson, S.E. 2001. HR issues and activities in mergers and acquisitions, *European Management Journal*, June: 253–87.

Schuler, R.S. & Jackson, S.E. 2005. A quarter-century Review of Human Resource Management in the U.S.: The Growth in Importance of the International Perspective. *Management Revue*, 16 (1): 11–35.

Schuler, R.S. & Rogovsky, N. 1998. Understanding compensation practice variations across firms: The impact of national culture. *Journal of International Business Studies*, 29 (1): 159–77.

Schuler, R.S. & Tarique, I. 2005. International joint venture system complexity and human resource management, in I. Bjorkman & G. Stahl (eds.) *Handbook of Research into International HRM*. London: Edward Elgar.

Schuler, R.S., Jackson, S.E. & Luo, Y. 2003. *Managing Human Resources in Cross-Border Alliances*. London: Routledge.

Schuler, R.S., Jackson, S.E. & Storey, J. 2001. HRM and its Link with Strategic Management. in Storey, J. (ed.) *Human Resource Management A critical text*. London: Thomson Learning: 114–30.

Schütte, H. 1996. *Regional Headquarters of Multinational Corporations* (Unpublished doctoral thesis), Universität St. Gallen, Hochschule für Wirtschafts-, Rechts- und Sozialwissenschaften (HSG): St. Gallen.

Schütte, H. 1998. Between Headquarters and Subsidiaries: The RHQ solution, in Birken-shaw, J. and Hood, N. (ed.) *Multinational Corporate Evolution and Subsidiary Development*, St. Martin's Press: New York, 102–36.

Scott, W. R. 1995. *Institutions and Organizations*. London: Sage Publications.

Scott, W.R. & Meyer, J.W. 1989. *The Rise of Training Programs in Firms and Agencies: an Institutional Perspective*. Stanford University working paper.

Scott, W.R. 1983. Health Care Organizations in the 1980s: The Convergence of Public and Pro-fessional Control Systems. In Meyer, J.W. & Scott, W. R. (eds.) *Organizational Environments: Ritual and Rationality*. Beverly Hills, Ca.: Sage Publications: 99–113.

Scott, W.R. 1987. The adolescence of institutional theory. *Administrative Science Quarterly*, 32: 493–511.

Sparrow, P.R. 2005. Knowledge management in Global organizations, in I. Bjorkman & G. Stahl (eds.) *Handbook of Research into International HRM*. London: Edward Elgar.

Sparrow, P.R., Brewster, C. & Harris, H. 2004. *Globalizing Human Resource Management*. London: Routledge.

Sparrow, P.R. & Hiltrop, J.M. 1997. Redefining the field of European human resource manage-ment: a battle between national mindsets and forces of business transition, *Human Resource Management*, 36 (2): 1–19.

Staehle, W. 1994. *Management*, 7th ed, München: Verlag Franz Vahlen.

Stonehouse, G., Hamill, J., Campbell, D. & Purdie, T. 2000. *Global and Transnational Business: Strategy and Management*. Chichester: Wiley.

Stopford, J.M. & Wells, L.T. 1972. *Managing the Multinational Enterprise. Organization of the Firm and Ownership of Subsidiaries*. New York: Basic Books.

Storey, J. 1995. Human resource management: still marching on, or marching out? in Storey, J. (ed.) *Human Resource Management*. London: Routledge: : 3–32.

Szulanski, G. 1996. Exploring internal stickiness: Impediments to the transfer of best practice within the firm. *Strategic Management Journal*, 17: 27–44.

Tallman, S. & Fladmoe-Lindquist, K. 2002. Internationalization, globalization and capability-based strategy, *California Management Review*, 45 (1): 116–35.

Taylor, S., Beechler, S. & Napier, N. 1996. Toward an integrative model of strategic international human resource management, *Academy of Management Review*, 21 (4): 959–85.

Teece, D.J., Pisano, G. & Shuen, A. 1997. Dynamic capabilities and strategic management, *Strategic Management Journal*, 18 (7): 509–33.

Thompson, J.D. 1967. *Organizations in Action.Social Science Base of Administrative Theory*. New York: McGraw-Hill.

Tichy, N.M., Fombrun, C.J. & Devanna, M.A. 1982. Strategic Human Resource Management. *Sloan Management Review*, 23: 47–61.

Tsai, W. 2000. Social capital, strategic relatedness and the formation of intraorganizational linkages. *Strategic Management Journal*, 21: 925–39.

Tsai, W. 2002. Social structure of cooperation within a multiunit organization: Coordination, competition, and intraorganizational knowledge sharing. *Organization Science*, 13: 179–92.

Tsai, W. & Ghoshal, S. 1998. Social capital and value creation: the role of inter-firm networks. *Academy of Management Journal*, 41 (4): 464–76.

Tushman, M.L. & Nadler, D.A. 1978. Information processing as an integrating concept in organizational design. *Academy of Management Review*, 3: 613–24.

Ulrich, D. 1987. Organizational capability as competitive advantage: human resource profes-sionals as strategic partners, *Human Resource Planning*, 10: 169–84.

Ulrich, D. and Lake, D. 1990. *Organization Capability: Competing from the Inside Out*. New York: Wiley.

Van Dijk, J.J. 1990. Transnational management in an evolving European context. *European Management Journal*, 8: 474–9.

Vermuelen, F. & Barkema, H. 2001. Learning through acquisitions, *Academy of Management Journal* 44 (3): 457–76.

Wächter, H. 1987. Professionalisierung im Personalbereich. *Die Betriebswirtschaft*, 41: 141–50.

Weber, W., Festing, M., Dowling, P.J. & Schuler, R.S. 1998. *Internationales Personalmanagement*. Wiesbaden: Gabler.

Weick, K.E. & Van Orden, P. 1990. Organizing on a global scale. *Human Resource Management*, 29: 49–62.

Wernerfelt, B. 1984. A resource-based view of the firm. *Strategic Management Journal*, 5 (2): 171–80.

Westney, D.E. 1993. Institutional theory and the Multinational Corporation. In Ghoshal, S. & Westney, D.E. (eds.) *Organization Theory and the Multinational Corporation*. New York: St. Martin's Press: 53–76.

White, R. & Poynter, T. 1990. Organizing for world-wide advantage. In Bartlett, C.A., Doz, Y. & Hedlund, G. (eds.) *Managing the global firm*. London: Routledge: 95–113.

Whitley R.D. 1999. *Divergent Capitalisms: the social structuring and change of business systems*, Oxford University Press, Oxford.

Whitley, R.D. (ed.) 1992. *European Business Systems: Firms and Markets in Their National Contexts*, London: Sage.

Wolf, J. 1997. From "Starworks" to Networks and Heterarchies? Theoretical Rationale and Empirical Evidence of HRM Organization in Large Multinational Corporations. *Management International Review*, 37 (Special Issue): 145–69.

Wright, P. M., Dunford, B. B. & Snell, S. A. 2001. Human resources and the resource based view of the firm. *Journal of Management*, 27: 701–21.

Wright, P.M. & McMahan, G.C. 1992. Theoretical Perspectives for Strategic Human Resource Management. *Journal of Management*, 18 (2): 295–320.

Wright, P.M., McMahan, G.C. & McWilliams, A. 1994. Human resources and sustained competitive advantage: a resource-based perspective. *International Journal of Human Resource Management*, 5 (2): 301–26.

Yip, G.S. 1992. *Total Global Strategy*, Englewood Cliffs, NJ: Prentice-Hall.

Yli-Renko, H., Autio, E. & Sapienza, H. 2001. Social capital, knowledge acquisition, and knowledge exploitation in young technology-based firms. *Strategic Management Journal*, 22: 587–613.

Youndt, M. A., Subramaniam, M. & Snell, S. A. 2004. Intellectual capital profiles: An examination of investments and returns. *Journal of Management Studies*, 41: 335–61.

Yuen, E. & Hui, T. K. 1993. Headquarters, host-culture and organization influences on HRM policies and practices. *Management International Review*, 33: 361–83.

Chapter 9

Reframing Global Mindset: From Thinking to Acting

Vladimir Pucik

Several years ago, Nokia Networks, a leading provider of infrastructure equipment for mobile telecommunications, participated in a benchmark study at IMD to see how managers interpret their companies' global strategies. While Nokia's corporate documents carefully explained the need to achieve dual objectives – global efficiency and local responsiveness – managers did not understand the importance of this duality. The survey showed that managers in some parts of the company, such as product-focused business divisions, had a global orientation, while managers in other parts, such as sales and service divisions in rapidly growing markets, had a local orientation. Both groups were convinced that their interpretation of corporate strategy was correct – it is the others who "do not understand" and make it difficult to execute effectively.

The initial reaction of most top executives to this finding was positive – "This is exactly the type of differentiated focus we need – strongly integrated product lines worrying about global economies of scale and locally-oriented sales units worrying about local opportunities. We at the center then make the final decision." However, on reflection, their view changed. They realized that differences in understanding of corporate strategy caused the conflicts which were being pushed up to senior management for arbitration, overloading their own agendas, causing delays in decision-making and leaving them little time to focus on institutional leadership. While the product managers indeed needed to be global, they also had to understand the need to work through the conflicts with local sales units – and vice versa, the local units needed to

V. Pucik, "Reframing Global Mindset: From Thinking to Acting," in *Advances in Global Leadership*. Vol. VI (Elsevier/JAI: Oxford, 2005).

make sure that their sale initiatives were benefiting from and contributing to global synergies.

My experience with other global companies participating in our study shows that Nokia's experience is not unusual. Many firms competing globally are being pushed in contradictory strategic directions. In order to survive and prosper in the new global competition, companies must embrace closer regional and global integration to cut cost and improve efficiency, while at the same time, meet demands for local responsiveness to increase local acceptance, flexibility and speed. And, to further add to this complex task, demands for integration and responsiveness may vary from one subsidiary to another and from function to function.

These contradictory pressures represent a rather dramatic change from the early stages of internationalization when companies could align their organization around one simple strategic posture (Bartlett and Ghoshal, 1989). Some companies went international by following a *mega-national* strategy (Evans, Pucik and Barsoux, 2002). When adopting this approach, the whole company is run in a centralized fashion across national boundaries. Worldwide facilities are typically centralized in the mother country, products are standardized, and overseas operations are used as delivery pipelines to serve international markets. In such a firm, there is tight control of strategic decisions, resources, and information by the central hub. As a result, the competitive strength of the mega-national firm is its global integration, seen primarily in cost efficiencies of scale and cost. However, the firm's ability to respond to variations in local conditions is limited.

In contrast, firms following a *multi-domestic* strategy (Evans, Pucik and Barsoux, 2002) emphasize local differences by decentralizing responsibilities to their subsidiaries and local business units in order to be close to customers, to create a heightened sense of local accountability, and to encourage more local innovation and entrepreneurship. But, decentralization has also a shadow side. It often leads to reinventing of the wheel, the not-invented-here syndrome, duplication of back office functions, slowness in responding to technology change, difficulties in dealing with matrix pressures, lack of shared resources to respond to emerging needs. These costly byproducts of decentralization, often lead firms to try a more centralization approach . . . until bureaucracy, loss of responsiveness, and the inability to retain good people leads the pendulum to swing again to decentralization (Evans, Pucik and Barsoux, 2002).

To avoid the swinging pendulum, some global companies have adopted an alternative approach designed to simultaneously reap the benefits of centralization and decentralization. They recognize that decentralization (local autonomy) and centralization (global integration) are not contradictory, but form a duality. They attempt to maximize both dimensions, thus achieving high integration while remaining locally responsive.

To achieve this end, companies must create the proper structure and processes. But structure and process alone can not create this dual focus (Evans and Doz, 1989). Instead, the key to effective globalization is in the minds of people. Managers must frame problems in a way that recognizes the global nature of the firm. In short, managers must adopt a global mindset.

In the remainder of this paper, I consider the ways that global mindset contributes to the success of global firms. First, I review the evolution of the concept and answer the question "What is global mindset?" Then I consider how global mindset can be developed among managers in a global firm. Finally, I discuss the organizational processes required to make the global mindset actionable by facilitating behavior consistent with the mindset.

What is Global Mindset?

In his now classic typology of multinational firms, Perlmutter describes three types of companies (Perlmutter, 1969). In an ethnocentric firm, each subsidiary is required to confirm to the parent company way regardless of local conditions. In a polycentric firm, each subsidiary is allowed to develop with minimal interference, providing it remains profitable. In a geocentric firm, the subsidiaries are part of a whole whose focus is on worldwide as well as local objectives, each making its unique contribution with its unique competence (Perlmutter, 1969). Perlmutter then went on to argue that more "geocentric" managers would be needed in the future. Companies would need to find "the best men, regardless of nationality, to solve the company's problem anywhere in the world" (Perlmutter, 1969, p. 13). Since then many authors have argued that creating a global mindset among managers is a critical issue facing multinationals.

For example, early in its globalization efforts, Percy Barnevik, then the CEO of ABB made an explicit decision that, out of a workforce of over 200,000, the company would need about 500 global managers, handpicked and monitored by him, and made ready to move across countries, functions and businesses. This number proved to be far too few, creating severe coordination problems as the complexity facing the company increased beyond original expectations. It took the company some time and a major crisis (and several CEO's) to recognize the severity of its management capability gap, but even after this is fully recognized, it always requires time and substantial resources to fix it.

Dual Perspectives on Global Mindset

Following Perlmutter's now classic research, studies of the global mindset have developed within two different, but complementary perspectives: (1) a psychological approach, which describes the skills and psychological attributes of effective managers in multinational firms, and (2) a strategic approach which examines the ways that the strategic orientation of the firm affects attitudes and behavior of managers. Let us briefly review these two perspectives.

The psychology of global mindset

Three perspectives contribute to the psychological approach to global mindset. First, several authors define global mindset as a set of competencies and psychological attributes. For example, Rhinesmith (1993) observed that people with global mindsets tend to approach the world in six ways that differentiate them from domestic managers. They have broader perspectives, searching to understand the context for decisions and showing suspicion for "one best way" solutions. They accept life as a balance of contradictory forces, thereby facilitating their ability to handle the tensions of organizational life. They trust process rather than structure to provide the flexibility required to deal with ambiguity, unexpected events and other needs of the global firm. They value diversity and believe that diversity can be used to enhance teamwork. Change is viewed as an opportunity rather than a threat. And they have the curiosity that leads them to be open to surprise and to the constant need to redefine boundaries, meanings, and indeed themselves.

Others have suggested that the global mindset is *the ability to accept and work with cultural diversity*, leading to research that tries to map out the skill or competency sets associated with this ability. Gupta and Govindarajan (1968) say that a firm with a global mindset, in contrast to an ethnocentric mindset, "accepts diversity and heterogeneity as a source of opportunity." Kanter (1995) sees this as a difference between "cosmopolitan" and "local" mindsets, adopting the terms used by the sociologist Gouldner to describe the difference between people who identified with their profession as opposed to those who identified with the "local" interests of the firm. Adler and Bartholomew (1992) used the term "transnational manager" to indicate a global mindset. According to Adler and Bartholomew, the transnational manager is a cultural "citizen of the world," defined by his or her knowledge and appreciation of many cultures and by the ability to move smoothly and expertly within cultures and countries on a daily basis throughout their careers.

Others focus on the skills associated with global effectiveness. In one of the few empirical studies researchers at Ashridge (Barnham and Oates, 1991) studied sixty-one managers with track records of international success and found several competencies that distinguished successful international managers from those who did not have international experience. These competencies included the championing of international strategy (visioning the future), acting as a cross-border coach (giving and receiving feedback from international teams), cognitive complexity (the ability to step back and see new patterns), and emotional maturity (being able to handle emotional crises).

When this work is integrated, the psychological approach to global mindset presents a set of attributes and skills that contribute to effective leadership in a global corporation. However, this approach does not take into account the specific strategic focus of the firm. In contrast, the strategic perspective on global mindset is more concerned with mirroring the strategic dilemmas of the organization.

The strategic perspective on the global mindset

This perspective on global mindset focuses on a manager's appreciation for the strategic challenges facing the firm. Because the global firm must manage the contradictions of global integration, local responsiveness, and worldwide coordination,[1] this approach emphasizes the need for a "balanced perspective":

> Diverse roles and dispersed operations must be held together by a management mindset that understands the need for multiple strategic capabilities, views problems and opportunities from both local and global perspectives, and is willing to interact with others openly and flexibly. The task is not to build a sophisticated structure, but to create a matrix in the mind of managers.   (Bartlett and Ghoshal, 1989, p. 212)

Thus the strategic perspective on global mindset refers to *a set of attitudes that predispose individuals to balance competing business, country, and functional priorities which emerge in international management processes, rather than to advocate any of these dimensions at the expense of the others* (Murtha, Lenway and Bagozzi, 1998). It involves recognizing that organizational resources are deployed across all subunits and places high value on sharing information, knowledge and experience across boundaries.

The emphasis on the strategic dimension of global mindset helps to differentiate between global and expatriate managers. The former are defined as executives who are able to balance the simultaneous demands of global integration and local responsiveness and who have an ability to work effectively across organizational, functional, and cross-cultural boundaries. They are expected to have a hands-on understanding of global business and perceive global competition as an opportunity. In short, global managers are defined by their broad, open, global *state of mind*. In contrast, expatriate managers are identified *by location*, as executives in leadership positions outside their home country (Pucik and Saba, 1998). Some global managers may be expatriates, but not all expatriates are global managers. The international management literature is full of examples of expatriates with an ethnocentric orientation (Black, Gregersen and Mendenhall, 1992). At the same time, local managers in lead countries may not be expatriates, but they will need a global mindset.

Global mindset defined
Together, the psychological and the strategic perspectives provide a useful understanding of what a global mindset is. A manager with a global mindset understands the need for global integration and local responsiveness and works to optimize this duality. The global mindset includes an appreciation for diversity as well as homogeneity and an openness to learning from everywhere.

Developing the Global Mindset

Developing managers with a global mindset *starts at the top*. It is the responsibility of senior executives to articulate the global strategy of the firm and reinforce the importance of a global mindset in clear and consistent language, across all levels and units. During his tenure as ABB's first CEO, Percy Barnevik spent over 200 days per year visiting the operating companies around the world, personally presenting his vision of a global enterprise to thousands of managers and employees. For Barnevik, communicating the business vision, organizational values and management philosophy was not something that could be delegated. The same was true for GE's Jack Welch and other global leaders. Creating the proper context for the actions of the whole firm is the core of their leadership responsibilities.

Management development programs

Once the global vision is clearly understood, formal management development programs can be used to develop a global mindset among the participants. For example, in the late 1990s, Canon faced significant deterioration in profitability of its European operations, which for several decades were run successfully in a very decentralized fashion. Each country had essentially full blown sales and service organization with little or no pan-European integration. However, with deteriorating profitability, top managers felt that more coordination and integration was required.

Defining a new structure for a more effective regional organization was not difficult. They created a strong European headquarters and a product line organization, supported by pan-European management processes. But, the real challenge was developing a pan-European mindset among previously locally oriented managers. This reframing was the key requirement for successful change (Pucik and Govinder, 2004).

To create this mindset, Cannon made a massive investment in leadership development. Groups of key local managers spent three weeks at IMD over a six month period (three weekly modules with virtual project team work in between). At IMD they were exposed to the rationale for the new strategy. They were asked to identify and explore opportunities to be derived from the new way of operating and they developed specific integration plans for their business units and functions.

In addition, and perhaps most important, the program at IMD created a network of relationships among key executives from the head office and all major locations throughout Europe. Indeed, global firms are increasingly going to rely on flexible networks of relationships to foster global integration and coordination. Therefore, a significant component of a leadership developmental process should focus on the development of networks to support a sense of common purpose, trust and cooperation among employees across the whole global organization.

International mobility

International assignments can be used to reinforce and enhance the impact of formal global leadership programs on global mindset: international transfers, cross-border job swaps, or assignment to multi-cultural task forces and project teams are the most common. Indeed, cross-border mobility is one of the strongest mechanisms for developing global mindset. As shown already in the classic study by Galbraith and Edström (1977), international transfers help socialize people into the organization – a powerful tool for coping with the dilemmas and challenges facing the global firm, but they may also support many different aspects of global mindset. Such assignments develop a portfolio of integrative leadership skills, helping managers to learn how to deal effectively with the inevitable contradictions (championing global strategy, facing up to cross-border conflicts, handling complexity).

In addition, transfers enhance skills in handling cultural diversity. The person learns that there is more than one way of approaching a particular business or social issue, and that these different ways have some merits. This counteracts the tendency to think in terms of stereotypes. International transfers also create a network of cross-border personal relationships that can provide managers with rapid access to information and to other resources. These informal global networks supplement formal communication and may be seen as the core nervous system of the global firm.

However, it may be useful to differentiate between *demand-driven* and *learning-driven* international assignments (Pucik, 1992). The traditional expatriate jobs fit mainly in the former category; employees – in most cases managers or senior professionals – were dispatched abroad to control the foreign unit, to transfer knowledge or to solve a problem within the foreign unit. Learning was a secondary outcome. My experience tells me that most international assignments are still "demand-driven." Expatriates are used because sufficient know-how is not available locally, or because the authority of the center needs to be enforced. In other words, international managers are *teachers*, transferring new capabilities, or enforcers sent to maintain order.

Yet, as companies recognize that cross-border mobility is an indispensable tool for creating a global mindset, they are increasing the number of assignments where the primary driver is individual development. In fact, one may argue that in future the nature of cross-border mobility may change dramatically. With increasing sophistication of labor markets across the world there will be less need for knowledge transfer from the center, most international assignees will be *learners*, not teachers. They will learn through experience about market and cultural differences, while developing long-lasting networks of relationships – in the process enhancing the global mindset within the organization. And most importantly, they are likely to come from many parts of the organization, not just from the mother country.[2]

However, this new trend is not without barriers. International mobility can be very expensive, thus limiting the number of cross-border transfers to what the company can afford, not to what it needs. As a consequence, when global mindset and learning, rather then teaching, become the main reason behind the expatriation, it may be necessary to re-examine the rationale driving the traditional expatriate policies – changing the focus from financial incentives to learning opportunities.

At the same time, it is not just the expense that makes international mobility difficult. Social trends emerging across the world also increase the barriers to international transfer – dual career families, the constraints of children's education, parental care needs, fewer economic incentives to move, are all factors that may diminish the desire of employees to actively seek out international assignments. In response, global companies will have to become more and more creative in finding suitable alternatives to the traditional two or three year assignments – I believe that short-term cross-border transfers, international project work, and best practice exchanges and forums will greatly increase as tools to enhance global networks.

Whether long-term or short-term, international assignments are likely to remain the critical building blocks for developing global mindset. Therefore, they should commence relatively early in the professional career, when the learning impact is greatest, becoming an integrated part of the career and development process. They should involve rotations across the whole global network, eventually to replace the traditional exchanges between the corporate center and country affiliates.

Making Global Mindset Actionable

The development of global mindset through international assignments, action learning projects, formal education and other developmental experiences is the first step, but this learning is unlikely to stick unless it is reinforced by organizational processes that foster decisions and behaviors consistent with a global orientation. I saw this clearly when working with Nokia Networks.

Nokia Networks relies heavily on international transfers to implement mobile telecom projects around the world. Our research showed that expatriates managers were far more 'balanced' in their perspectives than their domestic counterparts, showing a high degree of understanding for the interplay between global and local forces and of the need for coordination. However, six months after they returned to their headquarters in Finland, there was no significant difference in mindset orientation between returned expatriates and those who never left home. Re-polarization of the mindset appears to quickly follow. Like other managers in Finland, returnees refocused on the global aspects of the business. To combat this problem, Nokia adjusted the performance management metrics to support a more balanced perspective. The company also changed the incentive schemes and profit and loss accountability, because it was clear to them that appraisal and reward systems that undermine a global mindset and global behavior can become a serious obstacle in making global mindset actionable.

Global performance management

Global performance management starts with global objectives (i.e., objectives for the firm as a whole) and global performance indicators. The scorecard for measurement should be global in order to make the different mechanisms of horizontal coordination work in a synchronized manner.

Of course, the specific goals will vary from one business to another and from one subsidiary to another, and different units will have different strategic priorities – thus different performance indicators will be given different weight. However, having all units work toward the global objectives and having performance measured at the global level facilitate the resolution of conflicts across boundaries. At the same time, it is important that the inevitable tensions regarding priorities are explicitly recognized and that there are clear guidelines and guiding principles on how these should be handled – such as customer must come first, the corporation second (including the business area and/or country), and the profit center third.

The second imperative is to recognize the conflict between individual job accountability and demands for lateral coordination and cross-boundary teamwork. This conflict is likely to be most acute when individuals are asked to work on horizontal cross-border projects and then penalized because of poor performance in their own jobs. Therefore, global teamwork usually requires top management sponsorship, explicitly recognizing the benefits and contributions of global behavior.

Beyond this, the specifics of appraisal and rewards need to be carefully considered, because the solution depends on the nature of the cross-boundary task. Rewards for full time delivery projects should be based on overall performance, not on the performance of the individual members. However, when the extent of cross-border linkage is moderate, then the best way of appraising and rewarding individuals for working on cross-boundary projects is to emphasize growth and development. Problem-solving projects provide intrinsic rewards in terms of learning challenges, increased visibility, and opportunities to build personal social capital (Evans, Pucik and Barsoux, 2002).

Appraisal and reward systems that take cross-boundary coordination activities into account are commonplace in organizations that are project-oriented, such as professional service firms, like McKinsey or Accenture. At these companies, senior partners spend up to a quarter of their time on this, collecting the views of clients, research and back office departments, managers and subordinates about the contribution of partners and managers (Ghoshal, 1991). In industrial firms, there has been a parallel spread of now well known 360° appraisal systems, where the appraisal and reward decisions are based not only on the view of the boss but also on that of project peers and subordinates.

Approaches to performance management that emphasize *both* responsibility for local financial results *and* cross-border collaboration to achieve global strategy are not clear-cut. Some argue that compensation should be only linked to outcomes that the employee can influence. This would limit linking pay to global results (directly or via stock options) to only a few executives in the organization. Others point to the evidence that firm performance improves when the individual rewards are at least partially tied to broader objectives even for people at low levels (Milkovich and Newman, 1996). And of course, in some country or industry environments it is accepted that employees may share some of the firm-level risk, whereas elsewhere such choices may be constrained by custom or regulation.

What guidance does existing research provide? The evidence suggests that the effectiveness of a performance management system – from pay-for-performance to team-based pay, from stock options to executive compensation – is highly dependent on cultural and institutional context.

But, within these limits, a firm may use rewards and personnel selection and socialization processes to create a unique, value-adding organizational culture by creating its own context (Bloom and Milkovich, 1999). For example, an American firm operating in China can pay attention to selecting and socializing people who fit with its approach to reward management (and the other elements of the performance process in which this is embedded) – just as Southwest Airlines with its distinctive culture pays great attention to selecting people who will thrive there rather than in a more "traditional" US airline.[3]

It is the internal consistency and coherence of practices and norms that create a powerful impact on global mindset. One cannot consider rewards separately from the other elements of performance management, as well as the wider context of recruitment and socialization – even though consistency creates its own constraints. In the same context, unless compensation is aligned to reward broader dimensions of performance beyond one's job or immediate business unit, it is unlikely that we will see strong collaborative behavior, or support for wider global corporate initiatives. In other words, if global synergy matters, then a global company should apply a consistent set of performance management practices irrespective of nominal cultural differences, but at the same time invest in selecting and socializing employees who will fit with such a system.

Of course, performance management is not a panacea that exists in isolation of other organizational processes. It is up to the senior managers (business unit, function and country leaders) to make global mindset actionable by creating conditions promoting cross-border coordination. Best practices forums, knowledge networks, international task forces, project teams, steering boards and other cross-border coordinating mechanisms are all useful tools supporting global mindset. However, it is important to remember that all these organizational mechanisms rest on a single foundation – person-to-person relationships built on trust and mutual respect. The fundamental requirement for global mindset to emerge in any organization is the recognition of diversity.

Supporting a culture of diversity

Making global mindset actionable depends on making global leadership development experiences open to all, not just those from the mother country or a few lead countries. When development opportunities are restricted (even if this is not intentional), local employees will inevitably tend to adopt local perspectives – that is the only direction for their own future. Thus a key task for current global leaders and those responsible for development of the next generation of global executives is to ensure equitable access to career opportunities for talented employees worldwide.

But, where will the future global leaders come from? Will global opportunities be available to employees all over the world, or only for those located in one or a few key countries or regions? In this context, the key challenge in developing managers with a global mindset is to secure equitable access for talented employees worldwide to take advantage of available opportunities. From a long-term perspective, a truly global enterprise must satisfy a simple but demanding test: Does it matter for one's future success, where an employee enters the organization? Today, there are probably only a few companies that can meet this benchmark, especially if global really means outside of the northern hemisphere. Among established multinational firms, how many have succeeded in developing a cadre of senior executives representing all continents in which the companies operate? It takes decades of effort to ensure that selection criteria are not biased toward one cultural group and that early identification of talent works equally well in Karachi as in New York.

Why do these barriers persist? Historically, most operational HR activities in multinational firms were decentralized into individual country organizations. Such an approach is, in principle, logical – after all, the vast majority of employees is and always will be "local," embedded in the local culture and impacted by the local legal and regulatory environment. However, when HR localization is taken too literally, and everyone is treated as local, who is then "global"? A natural outcome of this well-intentioned, but ultimately destructive localization bias, is that nationals of the country, where the corporate center is located, are considered implicitly "global," but all others are "local" with only a limited chance to advance on a corporate ladder. That's why the top leadership group, even among firms with extensive international experience, is generally not very representative of the employee population at large.

This deepening emphasis on global mindset requires a major shift in the HR orientation as the ethnocentric and parochial HR systems and policies, inherited from the past and focused on a single country or a select group of employees, are often the biggest barriers to the implementation of effective global human resources processes. The conventional focus of international HR is on selecting and supporting expatriates rather than serving the global employee population. In many corporations world-wide, the operational needs of the expatriate management system, much of it centered on compensation and benefit issues, still dominate the "international" agenda of the corporate Human Resource group.

Developing a global mindset inside the HR organization, including a deep understanding of the cultural and social context in which the firm operates, is the fundamental challenge facing many global firms. However, the role of HR should not be just to defend cultural traditions in the name of cultural diversity, but to implement the necessary organizational strategies with sensitivity to specific cultural influences. Unfortunately, where and how to "push," and where to "give in" to cultural differences, is the kind of specific "global" knowledge that not many HR leaders today have had the opportunity to develop.

Beyond cultural stereotypes

Managers with a global mindset recognize the benefits that can flow to the whole organization from encouraging and valuing cultural diversity in people, not just as members of distinct cultural groups, but as individuals. Success in building cross-border networks of relationships – the principal arteries of effective global organizations – depends on understanding and valuing cultural diversity. Yet valuing diversity must go well beyond the traditional emphasis on bridging the distance between clusters of national cultures by focusing on average – and stereotypical – national characteristics. We have stopped stereotyping about gender; perhaps we should tackle culture with the same determination.

The barrier that hinders effective cross-cultural communication is not just the "average" distance between national cultures. Variations in norms and values within cultures are just as important as variations across cultures (Pucik, 1997). Respect for cultural diversity in organizations requires understanding differences "within a culture" as well as "across cultures." In fact, it is due to outsiders' lack of comprehension of the diversity within a given culture, because they do not understand the historical, political and social context of "within-culture" differences, that they often rely on overused general assumptions and stereotypes. Thus, Western companies are told that because of the concept of "face" direct feedback is nearly impossible to implement in China. However, Haier, one of the leading Chinese multinationals, posts monthly appraisals of all managers in the company cafeteria. On average, it is probably true that most Chinese employees may resent direct negative feedback, but there are always those who accept this kind of "race-horse" environment as superior to the traditional emphasis on educational credentials and personal connections.

A genuine emphasis on global mindset implies recognizing not only cultural diversity but also human diversity. The acceptance of diversity should also include tolerance of people who are not "global," perhaps because of lack of opportunities, or perhaps because of personal choice or circumstances. Anything taken to an extreme risks becoming pathological – global mindset is no exception. This is true for companies as well as for individuals. International management textbooks are full of examples of "dumb" multinationals and their managers that are not sensitive enough to cultural differences – which the savvy "globals" navigate with ease. But years of successful navigation sometimes make one forget about the rocks below the water line.

Rethinking the Paradigm

During the last decade, a catchy slogan "Think globally, act locally" has often been used to capture the concept of a progressive global corporation which considers the whole world as its market, but which at the same time carefully nurtures and adapts to local priorities and requirements. Implementing this vision is, however, a longer and more difficult process than most companies envisioned.

Consider, for example, one multinational firm that used this popular slogan on the first page of its annual report. In response, one local subsidiary manager commented on its application in practice: "Our firm is organized on a simple premise. When operating under stress, and that is most of the time, *they* do the thinking, and *we* do the acting." In other words, the thinking and acting are two separate roles, performed by two separate groups. The headquarters takes the strategic initiatives, which the locals are left to implement. Although such a paradoxical outcome may not be what was intended, it may be unavoidable when tensions embedded in managing a business on a global basis are dealt with by separating decision-making responsibilities without an adequate support for developing shared ways of thinking.

In contrast, the key argument presented in this chapter is that global mindset is about a capability to appreciate and balance global and local perspectives. In their passion to promote global mindset, academics and others writing from a normative perspective sometimes tend to see global or cosmopolitan as superior to local, calling for a "universal way that transcends the particulars of places" (Kanter, 1995, p. 60). What is "local" is seen as parochial and narrowminded. However, in my view, global mindset requires an approach that may be seen as the opposite to such one-dimensional universalism – it calls for a dualistic perspective, an immersion in local particulars, while at the same time retaining a wider cross-border perspective, it requires an emphasis on local learning for the benefit of the whole organization.

In fact, global mindset is as much about learning as it is about doing. To be truly global implies openness to learn from the experience of others, and to understand and appreciate how others (local customers, employees, or competitors) may think. Because the very specific needs of local customers must be carefully assessed managers must learn and understand the local context through the *local* immersion. However, the ability to satisfy those needs with a superior value proposition is dependent on the *global* mobilization of corporate resources, be it leading edge technology, economies of scale, or global standards of performance and quality.

Perhaps the way to balance global/local dilemma is to return to the logic of the globalization process. Today, leveraging R&D investments, manufacturing assets, logistics, IT infrastructure, service platforms, and operational know-how for competitive advantage requires a world-scale approach. At the same time, customer needs are increasingly individualized, and customers worldwide exhibit a strong preference to be treated as individuals – the secret of the business model implemented by Dell, Ritz-Carlton and others. What, then, is the competitive advantage of a global firm? In simple terms, it is the ability to tap *global capabilities* and skills to satisfy *local customer needs*. It may be useful, therefore, to rephrase the original paradigm. Creating a global mindset inside an organization is really about developing leaders who *learn locally, and act globally*. Perhaps a contradiction, but that is the nature of globalization.

NOTES

A number of ideas presented in this chapter emerged through my long-term collaboration with Paul Evans, Professor of Organization, INSEAD, and Tom Murtha, Professor of Strategic Management and Organization, University of Minnesota.

1. *Responsiveness* refers to decisions on resource commitments taken autonomously by a subsidiary in response to primarily local competitive, political or customer demands. *Integration* refers to the centralized management of dispersed assets and activities to achieve scale economies. *Coordination* refers to the level of lateral interactions within and among the network of affiliates with respect to business, function and value chain activities.
2. Obviously, the distinctions in expatriate roles are often not so sharp. Most employees in learning assignments should create value (learning by doing is often the best way how to learn) thus responding to "demand." On the other hand, there is an expectation that employees in "agency" positions implicitly learn from the context of their jobs, enlarging personal skills as well as organizational competencies. Probably the smallest opportunity for fulfilling the multiple agenda is in traditional short-term "problem-solving" roles where time and resource constraints may limit learning opportunities. However, even here, appropriate mindset and sufficient support can make a difference.
3. Research on foreign companies in China shows significant differences in the degree of localization of practices such as recruitment, training, compensation, performance appraisal, and promotion criteria (Lu and Bjorkman, 1997).

BIBLIOGRAPHY

Adler, N. J. and S. Bartholomew (1992). "Managing globally competent people." *Academy of Management Executive* 6(3): 52–65.

Banham, K. and D. Oates (1991). The international manager. London: Economist Books.

Bartlett, C. A. and S. Ghoshal (1989). Managing across Borders: The transnational solution. Cambridge, Mass: Harvard Business School Press.

Black, J. S., H. B. Gregersen and M. E. Mendenhall (1992). Global Assignments: Successfully Expatriating and Repatriating International Managers. San Francisco: Jossey-Bass.

Bloom, M. and G. T. Milkovich (1999). "A SHRM perspective on international compensation and reward systems." Strategic Human Resources Management (Research in Personnel and Human Resources Management, Supplement 4). P. M. Wright, L. D. Dyer, J. W. Boudreau and G. T. Milkovich (eds.). Stamford, Conn.: JAI Press.

Edström, A. and J. R. Galbraith (1977). "Transfer of managers as a coordination and control strategy in multinational organizations." *Administrative Science Quarterly* (22): 248–63.

Evans, P. and Y. Doz (1989). The dualistic organization. In Human resource management in international firms: Change, globalization, innovation. P. Evans, Y. Doz, and A. Laurent (eds.). London: Macmillan.

Evans, P., V. Pucik and J. L. Barsoux (2002). The Global Challenge: Frameworks for International Human Resource Management. New York. N.Y. McGraw-Hill.

Ghoshal, S. (1991). "Andersen Consulting (Europe): Entering the business of business integration." Case series, INSEAD, Fontainebleau, France.

Gupta, A. K. and V. Govindarajan (2000). "Knowledge flows within multinational corporations." *Strategic Management Journal* 21: 473–96.

Kanter, R. M. (1995). World class: Thriving locally in the global economy. New York: Simon & Schuster.

Lu, Y. and I. Bjorkman (1997). "MNC standardization versus localization: HRM practices in China-Western joint ventures." *International Journal of Human Resource Management* 8(5): 614–28.

Milkovich, G. T. and J. M. Newman (1996). Compensation (Fifth Edition). Irwin: Homewood, Ill.

Murtha, T. P., S. A. Lenway, and R.P. Bagozzi (1998). "Global mind-sets and cognitive shift in a complex multinational corporation." *Strategic Management Journal* 19: 97–114.

Perlmutter, H. V. (1969). "The tortuous evolution of the multinational corporation." *Columbia Journal of World Business* 4: 9–18.

Pucik, V. (1992). Globalization and human resource management. Globalizing management: Creating and leading the competitive organization. V. Pucik, N. M. Tichy and C. K. Barnett (eds.). New York: Wiley.

Pucik, V. (1997). "Human resources in the future: An obstacle or a champion of globalization?" *Human Resource Management* 36(1): 163–68.

Pucik V. and Govinder N. (2004). Canon Europe (A)-(C), Lausanne, Switzerland: IMD.

Pucik, V. and T. Saba (1998). "Selecting and developing the global versus the expatriate manager: A review of the state-of-the-art." *Human Resource Planning* 21(4): 40–54.

Rhinesmith, S. H. (1993). A manager's guide to globalization: Six keys to success in a changing world. Homewood, Ill.: ASTD & Business One Irwin.

Chapter 10

A Quarter-Century Review of Human Resource Management in the US: The Growth in Importance of the International Perspective

Randall S. Schuler and Susan E. Jackson

The focus and context of human resource management in the US, both in its practice within organizations and its study within academia, have undergone major developments in the past quarter century (Schuler/Jackson 2004). These developments reflect the dramatic changes that began to occur during the 1980s. During that period, the focus of business shifted from domestic to multinational to global; the speed at which business was conducted increased; organizations recognized that labor costs and productivity must be addressed from a world-wide perspective; and many companies realized that competitive advantage could be seized and sustained through the wise utilization of human resources (Porter 1980; Kanter 1983, 1994; Drucker 1985; Prahalad 1995; Gupta/Govindarajan 2001).

Concurrently with these developments, businesses throughout the United States began to view human resource professionals as potential partners who should be involved in the strategic decision-making processes of the firm. Human resource departments had previously been given responsibility primarily for acquiring and motivating the firm's human resources, and doing so within specified legal and cost constraints. Now they are beginning to be viewed as human capital asset managers and as

R. S. Schuler and S. E. Jackson, "A Quarter-Century Review of Human Resource Management in the US: The Growth in Importance of the International Perspective," *Management Review*, Vol. 16, No. 1 (2005): 11–35.

potential sources of competitive advantage (Cappelli/Singh 1992; Pfeffer 1994, 1998; Bamey/Wright 1998; Chadwick/Cappelli 1999; Schuler/Jackson/Storey 2001). These changes have come at a rapid pace. This chapter provides an opportunity for us to pause and put the changes into perspective.

Our assessment is offered from the vantage point of the United States, where two major phenomena have developed during the past twenty-five years in the general area of human resource management – strategic human resource management and international human resource management. Our discussion reflects the substantial developments in scholarship and practice within these two areas of human resource management; it is grounded in scholarly research, the practitioner literature and discussions with numerous HR professionals and scholars.

Strategic human resource management and international human resource management both have roots in human resource management, which in turn grew out of personnel management. The term "personnel management" began to be replaced by "human resource management" in the mid-1970s (certainly its label continued in some companies well into the 1980s). This transformation coincided with: (1) a growing recognition of the importance of human resources to the success of companies and, therefore, the need to manage these resources systematically; (2) growing evidence by academics on how specific practices could be done more effectively; and (3) growing professionalism among human resource management practitioners.

Under the broad umbrella of human resource management we include the essential activities of resource planning, staffing, training and development, performance appraisal, compensation, safety and health, and labor relations – these comprise the traditional core of human resource management. We also include managing change and culture, work and organizational design and aligning HR activities – both externally and internally, as these activities follow naturally from HR's position as a strategic partner (Beer *et al.*, 1985; Ulrich 1998; Huselid/Becker/Beatty 2004).

The Practice of Strategic Human Resource Management

Among HR practitioners, the term "strategic human resource management" is used broadly to signal the view that human resource management activities should contribute to business effectiveness. This linkage between HRM activities, the needs of the business, and organizational effectiveness is the core of the area called strategic human resource management (Schuler/Jackson 1999). Two guiding assumptions of strategic human resource management are that (1) effective human resource management requires an understanding of and integration with an organization's strategic objectives, and (2) effective human resource management leads to improved organizational performance. When HR policies and practices are aligned with an organization's strategic objectives, the system can be described as "vertically integrated." The traditional activities of creating remuneration and benefits packages, tracking employee progress, bargaining collectively with unions and evaluating employee performance remain under the aegis of HR professionals (Lundy/Cowling 1996; Katz/Kochan 2000). The key defining aspect of strategic human resource management is not a change in the activities included under the HRM umbrella; rather, the essential shift is away from relying solely on professional and technical standards for evaluating the effectiveness of HR policies and practices, and toward the use of measures of organizational effectiveness as the primary criteria for judging effectiveness (Jackson/Hitt/DeNisi 2003; Huselid/Becker/Beatty 2004).

Understanding the strategic objectives of an organization requires developing a deeper understanding of the entire context in which organizations must function. Furthermore, it provides a basis for conceptualizing an organization's HR policies and practices as a system of many elements that are more or less well-aligned. The goal of developing HR policies and practices that are aligned to form a coherent system is often referred to as achieving "horizontal integration" among HRM activities. Achieving both vertical and horizontal integration requires that HR professionals work in partnerships with line managers and employees (and their representatives). In sum, strategic human resource management is about:

- vertical integration – understanding the organization and its context;
- horizontal integration – creating coherent HRM systems;
- demonstrating effectiveness – showing how HRM systems affect organizational performance;
- partnership – HR professionals working cooperatively with line managers as well as with nonmanagement employees.

Next, each of these points is discussed in more detail.

Understanding the context

In the US, the practice of human resource management has long been shaped by legal regulations, which provide to employees a variety of rights and protections against unfair and unsafe employment practices. Monitoring the legal and regulatory environment to ensure that a firm's HR practices comply with this aspect of the organization's environment has long been a primary responsibility of HR professionals. In addition, because an organization's pay practices must take into account the pay practices of other organizations competing for the same labor, HR's role has traditionally included monitoring the HR practices of competitors in the external environment. Likewise, because an organization's planning for future recruitment, staffing and development is affected by supply and demand in the external labor market, HR's traditional role generally included tracking labor market conditions. In recent years, however, the evolution of strategic HRM has meant that HR's responsibility for monitoring the external environment has grown.

Elsewhere (Jackson/Schuler 1995), we reviewed the empirical evidence which shows that a variety of environmental conditions can influence the approaches organizations use to manage their human resources. These conditions include aspects of the particular organization itself (e.g. its size, life cycle stage, competitive strategy, technology, job design and work characteristics, culture, structure, and characteristics of its workforce) as well as conditions of the external environment (e.g. industry dynamics, institutional pressures, economic and political conditions, and country cultures). Thus, it seems apparent that strategic human resource management needs to include continuous environmental scanning (see also Devanna/Fombrun/Tichy 1981; Fombrun/Tichy/Devanna 1984; Beer *et al.*, 1985; Kerr/Jackofsky 1989; Schuler 1992; Barney/Wright 1998; Dyer/Burdick 1998).

Although it is perhaps less apparent, strategic HRM also includes developing a comprehensive understanding of how the elements of the external environment affect the basic functioning of the organization. In his excellent discussion of strategic job modeling (which is a prime example of the shift from traditional job analysis to the strategic HRM approach), Jeffery Schippmann makes this point clearly when he states: "perhaps the most useful thing a strategic job modeler can do is develop his or her own understanding and framework for thinking about the customer's [organization's] problems. This means ... working to understand the underlying issues and developing working hypotheses about what is important and what is relevant in a given context" (Schippmann 1999: 37). More generally, HR professionals who demonstrate a deep understanding of business issues and their implications for HRM increase their own value and their ability to develop HR practices that recognize human resource management activities as sources of competitive advantage (Schuler/MacMillan 1984; Lado/Wilson 1994; Wright/McMahan/McWilliams 1994; Pfeffer 1994, 1998). Without an understanding of the broader organizational context, it is unlikely that the next task of strategic HRM – developing a coherent HRM system – will be successful.

It might be noted here that gaining competitive advantage through human resource management can be pursued in two ways. One approach is to adopt generic HR policies that have been shown to be effective across many types of organizations. An example of a generic HR policy that has been shown to be effective in a wide range of organizations is linking pay to performance. Organizations that effectively link pay to performance can be expected to outperform their competitors, all else being equal. Adopting HR policies that have been identified as among the "best" can be useful for moving the organization into a competitive position. However, because such practices are widely known and easily adopted by others, they are not likely to be a source of long-term, sustainable competitive advantage (Schuler/MacMillan 1984; Barney 1991). To achieve sustainable competitive advantage, a firm may need to develop HR practices that are appropriate for its specific context. For example, a US manufacturer competing on the basis of cost might adopt the policy of performance-based pay and then develop an individual piece-rate pay system that specifically supports that strategy and fits within the context of the American culture of individualism. Our interpretation of the academic and professional literature/practice is that both approaches to gaining competitive advantage exist, but that "lasting" competitive advantage from human resource management comes from developing HR practices that are appropriate for an organization's specific context (Boudreau/Ramstad 2002, 2003a).

HRM systems

Horizontal integration and coherence among the parts are hallmarks of an HRM system. An example of how adopting a systems perspective can influence the practice of HR is provided by Higgs, Papper, and Carr (2000). The authors begin by noting that the traditional HRM perspective treats selection primarily within the context of hiring decisions. Their discussion then elaborates on how systems thinking is transforming the way some HR professionals develop and manage selection processes.

As Higgs *et al.* explain, adopting a systems view of selection reveals that a large number of HR practices that were previously considered as distinct activities (e.g. hiring, training, performance evaluation, special assignments, career development) can all be considered selection processes. It follows that organizations should find a means for ensuring that these pieces fit together. It also follows that HR professionals who accept responsibility for the design and management of HRM systems must develop an understanding of HR that cuts across all HRM activities (policies and practices). That is, strategic HRM implies that HR professionals must nurture their capacity to operate as HR generalists rather than HR specialists. Higgs *et al.* identified competency modeling and managing against core values as two approaches being used by organizations to achieve the desired level of systemic, horizontal integration.

Competency modeling

Within the framework of traditional HRM, job analysis is firmly established as the appropriate basis for developing HR practices that meet legal requirements. These techniques were not developed originally to serve as the foundation of an HRM system that is aligned with the organization's strategic direction and provide guidance for creating an internally aligned HRM system. During the past decade, competency modeling has evolved to meet these strategic needs.

In comparison to traditional job analysis, which focuses on specific jobs, competency modeling places more emphasis on determining the knowledge, skills, abilities and other attributes needed *throughout* the organization; it also encourages more consideration of the organization's future needs rather than focusing on the details of specific jobs as they are carried out in the present (Schippmann 1999). Thus, at the level of the firm, competency modeling may provide the basis for developing an appropriate HR architecture (cf. Lepak/Snell 1999, 2003).

Vision and values

Declarations of the organization's vision and values may also provide guidance to the development of coherent HRM systems. Statements of organizational vision and values are sometimes derided as superficial, but when taken seriously these provide direction and a set of implicit decision rules for evaluating the firm-specific appropriateness of various HR practices. Regardless of whether vision and values statements are considered the foundations or reflections of the organization's culture, they provide a common understanding of what the organization is striving to be – its desired identity. Thus, vision and values statements serve as touchstones that employees and HR professionals alike can use to assess whether particular HR practices are internally consistent (Pfeffer 1998; see also Boswell/Boudreau 2001; Boudreau/Dunford/Ramstad 2001).

Demonstrating human resource management effectiveness

Traditionally, assessments of the "effectiveness" of an organization's HR practices relied heavily on technical criteria established by the profession (e.g. the validity of a selection tool, lack of bias in performance appraisals) and embodied in US legal regulations. More recently, HR professionals have been called on to demonstrate the effectiveness of HR practices – considered singly or as a total system – in monetary terms (Becker/Huselid/Ulrich 2001; Huselid *et al.*, 2004).

Monetary criteria

Twenty-five years ago, efforts to demonstrate effectiveness in monetary terms usually employed utility analysis (e.g. Schmidt *et al.*, 1979) or cost accounting (e.g. Cascio 2000). Regardless of the technical merits of such approaches, they have not been widely adopted by organizations. Instead, most firms continue to rely on subjective estimates and intuition when assessing the effectiveness of their HR practices (Becker *et al.*, 2001). Undoubtedly, there are many explanations for the slow adoption rate of utility analysis and cost accounting methods, including the fact that these measures may not reflect fundamental strategic objectives or the concerns of a broader set of important stakeholders (Donaldson/Preston 1995; Jayne/Rauschenberger 2000; Boudreau/Ramstad 2003a, b).

Nevertheless, recently in the US, interest in developing business-relevant HR metrics has mushroomed. HR consultants now offer a broad variety of sophisticated measures intended to assess the effectiveness of an organization's approach to managing human resources by estimating the economic value added or return-on-investment of HR activities (e.g. see Huselid *et al.*, 2004; Becker *et al.*, 2001; Fitz-Enz 2002). Thus, current practices for assessing HR effectiveness continue to place considerable emphasis on monetary metrics (Sturman *et al.*, 2003).

We believe that this narrow approach to assessing HR effectiveness primarily in economic terms is likely to continue to evolve in the future, as organizations improve their understanding of the underlying drivers of long-term organizational success. For example, using the logic of balanced scorecards and strategy maps (Kaplan/Norton 1996a,b, 2004), some firms have begun to develop sophisticated models of how HR practices directly influence internal operations as well as customer satisfaction. These models illustrate the specific means through which HR policies and practices can influence an organization's ability to achieve its strategic objectives (Rucci/Kim/Quinn 1998; Ulrich 1998; Becker *et al.*, 2001).

Looking ahead, we anticipate seeing further evolution in the approaches organizations use to assess the effectiveness of their HRM systems (Boudreau/Hopp/McClain/ Thomas 2003). Investors are among the most important stakeholders for a business because without their capital, the business could not continue. Thus, more sophisticated approaches to understanding how HRM systems influence investor satisfaction is one likely focus of future efforts. For example, the use of financial and stock market indicators to assess the effectiveness of HRM is often viewed as an approach designed to address the concerns of investors as stakeholders (Becker/Gerhart 1996; Becker/Huselid 1998; Gerhart 1999). But stock market indicators in particular tend to reflect the short-term orientation of some investors. For corporations that are partially owned by employees, via stock-based savings plans, these indicators may not be appropriate. For such investors, the long-term viability of the organization is more relevant (e.g. see Blasi/Kruse/Bernstein 2003).

Satisfying multiple stakeholders
A more complete assessment of HR's effectiveness would consider the impact of the HRM system on all of an organization's multiple stakeholders. The importance of developing HRM systems that address the concerns of all key stakeholders is not widely recognized in the US, however.

Certainly, the organization itself is a primary stakeholder, so it is appropriate to assess the impact of the HRM system against objectives such as improving productivity, improving profitability, sustainability, and ensuring the organization's long-term survival. Increasingly, employers also recognize that organizational strategies that depend on total quality, innovation and customer service cannot be met unless employees are willing to strive for the same goals on the organization's behalf. In other words, employees also are legitimate stakeholders, whose concerns must be addressed. Thus, "soft" indicators of employees' feelings about the organization (e.g. commitment, satisfaction) are being recognized as relevant indicators of effectiveness that are worthy of top management's attention (Schneider/Bowen 1995). In industries where innovation is essential, indicators of employee engagement and knowledge development are being recognized as important relevant measures of HR effectiveness (Boudreau/Ramstad 1999; Boudreau 2003).

The effectiveness of an HRM system can also be assessed by showing its effects on customers. HR practices can determine the quality and variety of products available to customers, the price at which those products can be purchased, the service received and so on. As the US economy evolved toward services, HR practices incorporated the voice of customers in numerous ways. Customer's expectations have been incorporated into job descriptions, their preferences have influenced criteria used to select new employees, their input is often sought to assess employee performance, and so on (Schneider/White 2004).

Other major stakeholders who can be affected by an organization's HR practices include suppliers and alliance partners. Through various forms of cooperative alliances, a company seeks to achieve goals that are common to all members of the alliance. Some alliances are formed to influence government actions. Research and development needs are another common reason for alliance formations. Joint ventures represent yet another type of alliance. Although organizations may understand that these stakeholders can all be affected by HRM, alliance partners are seldom included when organizations assess the effectiveness of their HRM systems.

Finally, within the US the effects of an organization's HR practices on the local community and the broader society have generally not been taken into account when assessing the effectiveness of HRM, except to the extent that these concerns are embodied in laws and regulations (Florkowski/Nath 1993). In recent years, numerous revelations of unethical and corrupt business practices serve as a reminder that a variety of HR practices (selection, training, performance measures, compensation) can contribute to such problems. Clearly, any organizational assessment of HR effectiveness that fails to consider its ability to reduce unethical or corrupt business practices is deficient.

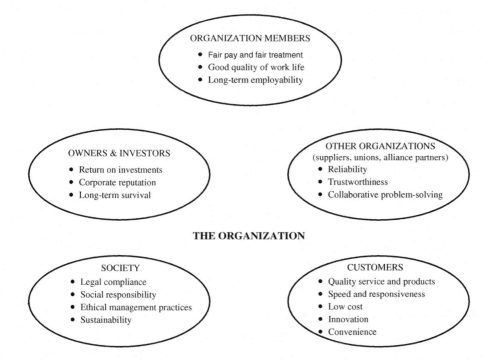

Figure 10.1   Stakeholders and their concerns. Adapted from S.E. Jackson and R.S. Schuler, *Managing Human Resources through Strategic Partnerships* 8th ed., Cincinnati, Ohio: South-Western 2003, p.17. Used with permission.

Figure 10.1 illustrates the variety of stakeholder concerns that effective organizations must consider and attempt to address. Choices about how to manage an organization's human resources often have unintended and unexamined consequences for stakeholders' perceptions of how well their concerns are satisfied. Thus, extending the domain of HRM to include a more nuanced consideration of stakeholders' concerns such as ethics and sustainability is an agenda item for the future practice of strategic HRM.

Partnership and the HR triad

As human resource management has evolved to become more strategic, it has become clear that effective HRM requires close cooperation between HR professionals and line managers. Unfortunately, HR practitioners in the US sometimes equate strategic HRM with "having a seat at the table" (i.e. being a member of the top executive decision making team), being a "business partner," and "showing bottom-line results." Such terminology does not adequately recognize HR's continuing and equally important responsibility for ensuring that employers meet the needs of all employees.

The fate of an organization, its investors, and its customers cannot be separated from the fate of all employees working for the organization (Pfeffer 1998;

Table 10.1   Examples of the roles and responsibilities of HR Triad members. Adapted from S.E. Jackson and R.S. Schuler, *Managing Human Resources through Strategic Partnerships*, 8th ed., Cincinnati, Ohio: South-Western 2003, p.14. Used with permission

Line managers	HR professionals	Employees/Unions
Include human resource professionals in the process of creating a business strategy and putting into place means of achieving the business strategy.	Assist line managers, employees and unions in developing and implementing elements of the human resource system.	Implement HR activities in conjunction with line managers and human resource professionals.
Work in tandem with human resource professionals, unions and employees to develop and implement elements of the human resource function.	Work in tandem with line managers to forge links between human resource activities and the business.	Become responsible for managing their own behavior and their careers in organizations.
Share responsibility for managing the human resources of the company.	Assist employees in voicing their concerns to management.	Recognize the value of and need for flexibility and adaptability.
Set policy that supports ethical behavior and sustainability.	Create policies and practices to support ethical conduct and an environment which supports them.	Represent the needs of all workers.

Schuler *et al.*, 2001; Beatty/Huselid/Schneier 2003). In our own work, we use the term "HR Triad" to describe the three key partners involved in effective HR partnerships – employees (and union representatives), line managers, and HR professionals. Some of the general roles and responsibilities of each member of the HR Triad are shown in Table 10.1. Much more specific roles and responsibilities can be found elsewhere (see Jackson/Schuler 2003).

Summary

To summarize, we have argued that the practice of strategic human resource management reflects the culmination and confluence of several trends that have unfolded during the past twenty-five years. These include developing a contextualized understanding of human resource management, thus facilitating vertical integration; developing systems of internally consistent and aligned HRM practices for horizontal integration; demonstrating the effectiveness of HR practices; and, forging an effective partnership among HR professionals, line managers, and employees and their representatives. It appears that a majority of large organizations in the US have embraced at least of some of these core elements of SHRM (Claus/Collison 2004; Huselid *et al.*, 2004).

Research in Strategic Human Resource Management

In the US, the science and practice of strategic HRM are related, but not tightly coupled, so we chose to summarize separately the key trends within each domain. Thus, we turn next to strategic HRM research.

US scholars have not yet adopted a common definition of "strategic HRM," but most would probably agree that it covers research intended to improve our understanding of the relationship between how organizations manage their human resources and their success in implementing business strategies (cf. Snell/Youndt/Wright 1996). As a focal topic for HRM research, strategic HRM began to emerge approximately twenty-five years ago (Galbraith/Nathanson 1978; Niniger 1980; Fombrun *et al.*, 1984; Schuler/MacMillan 1984; Dyer 1985). Since then it has evolved to include several streams of theory and empirical investigations. Due to space limitations, our tour of this work is necessarily too brief to adequately compare and contrast the numerous conceptual frameworks proposed, or to examine the ongoing methodological debates. Instead, we simply attempt to summarize a few key issues of interest to SHRM scholars in the United States. More detailed reviews can be found elsewhere (e.g. see Lengnick-Hall/Lengnick-Hall 1988; Wright/McMahan 1992; Snell/Youndt/Wright 1996; Becker/Huselid 1998; McMahan/Virick/Wright 1999; Martin-Alcazar/Romero-Fernandez/Sanchez-Gardey 2004).

High performance work systems, best practices, and HR bundles

As we have already noted, an element that differentiates the strategic HRM approach from earlier approaches is a focus on the entire HRM system. One stream of strategic HRM research has focused on demonstrating that more sophisticated HRM systems create more economic value. These more complex HRM systems are sometimes referred to as "best practices" or "high performance work systems" or "HR bundles" or "one best way" (e.g. Osterman 1984, 1987; Delaney/Lewin/Ichniowski 1989; MacDuffie/Drafcik 1992; Huselid 1995; MacDuffie 1995; Delery/Doty 1996; Becker/Huselid 1998; Cappelli/Neumark 2001).

In this stream of research, HR practices are assumed to operate in concert with each other. When properly aligned, several practices together may reinforce each other; when mismatched, they may work against each other and interfere with performance (Lawler 1992; Lawler/Mohrman/Ledford 1992; Delery 1998). Alternatively, some practices may serve as substitutes for each other (Ichniowski *et al.*, 1996). As noted in the discussion of competitive advantage, this stream of research tends to downplay the significance of context.

Several empirical studies have shown that firms that have an entire set of so-called high performance HR practices outperform firms with none or only a few of these practices (Becker/Huselid 1998). However, as critics have pointed out, there has been some inconsistency in the HR practices (or policies) that various authors consider to be among the preferred practices, making it difficult to draw general conclusions about which practices qualify as "best practices" (e.g. see Becker/Gerhart 1996). In order to continue moving forward with this line of research, more theory-driven research may be needed as well as a distinction between HR practices and HR policies. The result might be research that traces the causal chain that explains how particular HR practices or policies influence intermediate outcomes (e.g. motivation, productivity, turnover) and how those outcomes, in turn, are related to specific indicators of financial performance (Becker/Huselid 1998; Rogers/Wright 1998; Boswell/Boudreau 2001; Wright/Gardner 2002), or other indicators of organizational effectiveness (Boudreau/Hopp/McClain/Thomas 2003).

Research on high performance work systems, best practices, and HR bundles is considered by its advocates to fall within the realm of strategic HRM primarily because of its emphasis on predicting firm financial performance. That is, for some US researchers, strategic HRM research is defined primarily by the outcome of interest – firm performance. Next we consider strategic HRM research that puts more emphasis on creating alignment between the HRM system and a firm's context, for example, its particular strategy.

Strategic contingencies

The emergence of the strategic contingencies perspective in HRM research can be traced to early efforts to bridge the fields of strategic management (also referred to as business policy) and human resource management. The earliest works addressed the question of whether the effectiveness of a specific HR practice might depend on the strategic objectives of the firm that adopted the practice (e.g. Miles/Snow 1984; Schuler/Jackson 1987).

Prior to the emergence of strategic HRM, most empirical research sought to identify the most effective HR practices. The specific context in which a practice was used was considered to be of little consequence. The implicit assumption was that the most effective practices would be equally effective across firms. By asserting that the value of HR practices depends on the strategic context in which they are used, contingency advocates challenged the prevailing assumption of "one best way." [Although it is now less prevalent, this assumption has not been completely abandoned by some strategic HRM researchers; it remains implicit, for example, in research that seeks to establish the superiority of so-called "high performance work systems."]

Strategic contingency theory assumes that managers adopt strategies as means for competing in the specific environments they face (Lundy/Cowling 1996). Two of the most well-known typologies for describing the alternative strategies available to firms are the defender-reactor-analyser-prospector theory proposed by Miles and Snow (1984) and the competitive strategies identified by Porter (1980). Following the logic of strategic contingency theory, the choice of human resource practices can be understood as a process of matching HR practices to the strategies pursued by the organization (Lundy/Cowling 1996). For example, prospectors may look externally for people in order to bring in the cutting edge competencies needed for technological innovation. In contrast, an organization pursuing a reactor strategy may value knowledge about the organization's own internal processes over technological advances (Hambrick 2003).

Several studies provide some support for the contingency perspective. For example, drawing on Porter's work, Jackson, Schuler, and Rivero (1989) tested and found support for several hypotheses that specified the HR practices that should be found in firms pursuing strategies that emphasized cost reduction, quality improvement, or innovation (see also Cappelli/Crocker-Hefter 1993).

Configurational perspective

Closely associated with the development of this contingency perspective is the configurational perspective (Ketchen/Thomas/Snow 1993; Delery/Doty 1996; Martin-Alcazar *et al.*, 2004). In fact, in our view, the configurational perspective is conceptually indistinguishable from the earlier contingency perspective. Studies that have been cited in the literature as examples of the configurational perspective could just as easily be cited as examples of the contingency perspective (e.g. Schuler/Jackson 1987). By using the term configurational instead of contingency, those who view these two perspectives as different point out the importance of attending to each of two issues: one is the idea that HR practices need to be aligned with each other (horizontal integration), and the second is the idea that HR practices should be aligned with the broader context (vertical integration). That is, certain sets or "bundles" of HR practices may be more appropriate because they fit together to mutually support a defined set of employee behaviors, competencies and motivations, *and* these in turn are appropriate given the organization's specific context (Fombrun *et al.*, 1984; Miles/Snow 1984; Schuler/Jackson 1987; Baird/Meshoulam 1988; Gomez-Mejia/Balkin 1992; Ichniowski 1990; MacDuffie 1995; Delery/Doty 1996; Wright/Snell 1998; Delery/Shaw 2001; Boudreau 2003).

Theoretical frameworks

If one accepts the proposition that an HR practice that is effective in one context might be quite ineffective in another context, one challenge that follows is developing a logic for predicting which practices are most suitable for which contexts. Prominent explanations that have been offered to explain why and how a firm's strategy (and other contextual factors) influences its HRM system include the behavioral perspective, human capital theory, and the resource-based view of the firm.

Behavioral perspective
Grounded in role theory, the behavioral perspective focuses on the interdependent role of behaviors that serve as building blocks for an organizational system. Role

behaviors are 'the recurring actions of an individual, appropriately interrelated with the repetitive activities of others so as to yield a predictable outcome' (Katz/Kahn 1978). The primary means by which the organization sends role information through the organization, supports desired behaviors, and evaluates role performances is human resource management.

Schuler and Jackson (1987) used role theory to link HR practice with the competitive strategy of the organization (Porter 1980). They argued that different strategies require different role behaviors of the employees and thus require different human resource practices. Therefore, human resource management is effective when the expectations which it communicates internally and the ways in which it evaluates performance are congruent with the system's behavioral requirements (Fredericksen 1986). Since then, this approach for explaining why alternative strategies were likely to require different HRM systems has been referred to as "the behavioral perspective."

The behavioral perspective assumes that firms develop HR practices as a means for managing the behaviors of employees. It further assumes that different strategies impose differing behavioral imperatives. It defines an effective HRM system as one that (a) accurately identifies the behaviors needed to implement the firm's strategy, (b) provides opportunities for employees to engage in the behaviors needed, (c) ensures employees have the competencies required, and (d) motivates employees to behave as needed (Schuler/Jackson 1987; Treacy/Wiersema 1995; Jackson/Schuler 2002). Furthermore, the behavioral perspective argues that employees' decisions about how to behave reflect their interpretation and responses to an organization's entire HRM system – that is, employees imbue practices with meaning (see Daft/Weick 1984). Consequently, involving employees in the process of developing and implementing HR practices is essential.

Recently, the behavioral perspective was used to explain the effects of so-called "network building" HR practices on firm performance. Focusing on top management teams, Collins and Clark (2003) showed that several HR practices seemed to improve firm performance by encouraging executives to build their internal and external social networks, which they could then leverage to improve their firm's financial bottom line. Making somewhat similar arguments, Jackson, Hitt, and DeNisi (2003) recently extended the behavioral perspective to describe how HR practices might be used to encourage behaviors needed for knowledge-based competition.

Human capital theory

Grounded in economics, human capital theory provides an alternative logic for understanding the choices firms make in managing human resources. The crux of this theory is that people are of value to the organization to the extent they make it productive (Becker 1964; Becker/Huselid 1998; Lepak/Snell 1999). Thus, organizations make decisions about investments in people just as they make decisions about investing in machinery, viewing them as a form of capital. Costs related to training, retraining, motivating, and monitoring the organization are viewed as investments in the human capital of the firm, just as maintenance of machinery would constitute an investment in the capital of the firm (Flamholtz/Lacey 1981; Cascio 1991, 2000; Wright *et al.*, 1994; Wright/Dunford/Snell 2001). Efforts to develop HR metrics that establish the value of investments in HR practices are firmly grounded in the logic of human capital theory.

Human capital theory has also been used to gain insights into the decisions firms make about how to staff their operations. Human capital can be attained by either hiring from outside the organization or by training and developing human capital already within the organization (Wright *et al.*, 2001). The decision to "buy or make" depends on a comparison between the projected value to the organization, which will be realized when the capital is deployed and the costs to the organization of each option, given the current environmental context.

Resource-based view

The resource-based view of the firm emphasizes the need for resources as being primary in the determination of policies and procedures (Wernerfelt 1984). Organizations are viewed as being able to succeed by gaining and retaining control over scarce, valuable, and inimitable resources (Porter 1980; Barney 1991). The application of this theory to human resource management has led to an array of new insights for understanding how effective organizations manage their employees (Gupta/Govindarajan 2001).

Within the organization, the HR department can be viewed as controlling scarce resources to the extent that it controls access to the skills necessary for the achievement of strategic goals (Lepak/Snell 2003). On a broader level, a firm may gain a competitive advantage by using HR practices – for example, an appealing remuneration scheme – to lure and retain top talent (Gomez-Mejia/Balkin 1992). These competitive advantages are sustained through continued training, support of organizational culture, selection processes, and other traditional human resource practices.

The resource-based view has been invoked as the logic for explaining why coherent HRM systems lead to sustained competitive advantage: whereas it may be easy for competitors to copy or imitate any single HR practice, it should be more difficult to copy an entire system of aligned practices (Lado/Wilson 1994; Wright *et al.*, 1994). Furthermore, even if competitors are able to copy an entire HRM system, they may find that the system is not as effective because it is not aligned with the new organization's specific strategy or other elements of its broader context.

An integrative framework: contextualized and dynamic

By any standard, the field of strategic human resource management is still in its infancy. Nevertheless, there is an emerging consensus regarding the need to understand the interplay between human resource management systems and the broader context in which these systems are used – including characteristics of the immediate organization (technology, strategy, culture, and leadership) as well as characteristics of the external environment (laws, unions, country culture, and economic conditions) (Jackson/Schuler 1995; Delery/Doty 1996; Martin-Alcazar et el. 2004). Because the internal and external environments are dynamic, the process of managing human resources must also be dynamic. Success requires meeting the present demands of multiple stakeholders while also anticipating their future needs. Our interpretation of these essential elements of the emerging field of strategic HRM is illustrated in Fig. 10.2.

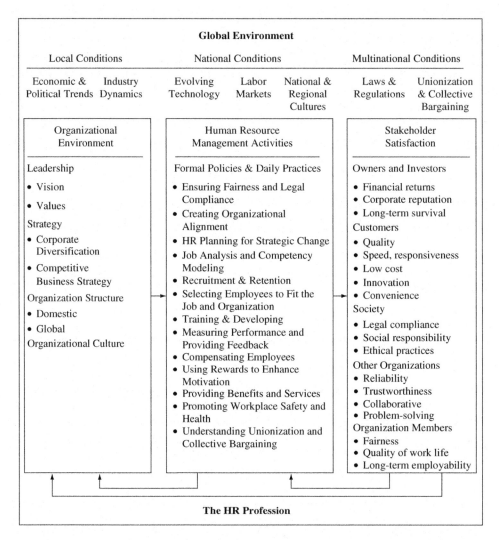

Figure 10.2 Contextual and dynamic framework for strategic HRM. Adapted from S.E. Jackson and R.S. Schuler, Managing Human Resources through Strategic Partnerships, 8th ed., Cincinnati, Ohio: South-Western 2003: 9. Used with permission.

The task of developing and implementing an effective HRM system presents numerous challenges. To date, research and theory have focused on the design question, that is, What comprises the best HRM system in a given context? Meanwhile, lacking clear answers to the design question, HR practitioners are faced with the challenges of interpreting the needs of multiple stakeholders, negotiating solutions that optimize their satisfaction, managing the process of change, monitoring effectiveness, and sustaining continuity while retaining the flexibility needed to adjust and improve. Looking ahead, it seems likely that the focus of academic work in the field of strategic HRM will evolve away from its current search for effective HRM system designs and toward understanding the processes through which HRM systems evolve and change in concert with their dynamic context. Gradually, the rather mechanistic view of HRM systems that prevails currently may be replaced by a perspective that recognizes the social aspects of human resource management and the processes through which organizational members create meaning from a complex array of signals.

Also needed in the future are studies that consider outcomes of concern to multiple stakeholders. To date, most strategic HRM research in the US has focused on financial performance and emphasized outcomes of interest to investors. Whether other stakeholders also benefit from these practices is not yet clear. A recent study of HR practices used in hospitals provides an example of how the concerns of multiple stakeholders can be taken into account. In that study (Brown/Sturman/Simmering 2003), the authors showed that compensation practices used in hospitals predicted both financial outcomes and patient care.

Research and Practice in International Human Resource Management

Within the US, the development of international HRM has been another significant trend during the past quarter century (Reynolds 2001, 2004; Schuler 1994). As a result of the globalization of industry, many firms now must compete on a worldwide basis rather than on the regional basis that was previously favored (Bartlett/Ghoshal 1991). Human resource management in this international context requires developing an understanding of the issues facing multinational enterprises (MNEs) (Evans/Pucik/Barsoux 2002; Briscoe/Schuler 2004).

Whereas there seems to be a significant gulf between research and practice in strategic HRM, research and practice in international HRM are more closely linked. Thus, in this section we discuss both together. Our brief review of developments in international HRM is organized around two topics – managing expatriates and managing MNEs – because these two topics have received the majority of research attention in the US during the past twenty-five years (Briscoe/Schuler 2004).

Managing expatriates

Managing a domestic workforce can differ drastically from managing a foreign workforce. Nevertheless, many US organizations that operated internationally for much of the past twenty-five years adopted the human resource practices of the parent country, the US. In addition, they used expatriates as a major means of staffing the senior management cadre of international locations. By staffing foreign operations with expatriates, the US parent could exercise control over the foreign operation (Tarique/Caligiuri 2004). Because this ethnocentric approach was widely adopted by US firms as they began to internationalize, most of the early practice and research in IHRM focused on expatriate selection and compensation (Tung 1988; Tarique/Caligiuri 2004; Adler 2002; Mendenhall et al., 2002).

Twenty-five years ago, international personnel professionals in US-based multinational firms devoted almost all of their time to managing expatriate assignments – in particular, expatriate compensation (Reynolds 1997). By the 1990s, expatriate compensation issues still consumed half of the time of corporate international HR staff (Reynolds 2001, 2004).

Today, considerably more of the time of US international HR staff is devoted to issues associated with managing local-nationals, and to issues such as global staffing, integration of worldwide HR practices, management development, and other topics considered to be of strategic value (Reynolds 2001, 2004). The number of HR professionals in the US who have responsibilities for international HR issues also has grown considerably. When the first professional association for international HR managers was established in the 1970s, it had only about 100 members. Today, some 8000 members of the major professional association for HR professionals (the Society for Human Resource Management) identify with this specialty. Recognizing that there is now an extensive body of knowledge that should be mastered by HR professionals with international responsibilities, the Society for Human Resource Management recently introduced a specialized testing and certification process.

Research in international HRM has followed a similar trajectory. Prior to the 1990s, the volume of US-based research in the field of international HRM was quite small, and it focused almost exclusively on managing expatriates. Much of the research sought to identify predictors of success in expatriate assignments. Numerous studies conducted during the past decade have shed light on individual characteristics that enable expatriates to adjust readily to new and unfamiliar circumstances. Research has also found that the cross-cultural training and developmental activities provided to expatriates can prepare them to work more effectively in other cultural contexts (e.g. see Black/Mendenhall/Oddou 1991; Caliguiri 2000; Ones/Viswesvaran 1997).

Managing expatriates continues to be a significant activity and an active area of research, but it no longer dominates IRHM in the United States. As the pace of globalization quickened, and as the costs associated with the growing numbers of expatriates came into question, US firms decreased their reliance on expatriates. Like other global firms, they turned to third country nationals and host country nationals as vital sources of staffing, for both nonmanagerial and managerial positions (Reynolds 2004; Pucik/Tichy/Barnett 1993). With the concurrent rise of multinational enterprises, practitioners and researchers alike are developing new ways of conceptualizing international HRM (Reynolds 2004).

Managing MNEs

As US MNEs have evolved, HR professionals have become more sensitive to cultural variations. Numerous studies have documented country differences in HR practices, and several have linked these to differences in the cultures and institutional environments of the US and other countries (e.g. Adler/Ghadar 1990; Rousseau/Schalk 2000; Sparrow/Schuler/Jackson 1994; Tung 1990). Such differences create special challenges for global firms.

One challenge that US MNEs continue to struggle against is adapting their HR practices to the new cultures in which they operate and doing so in a manner of operation that is both comfortable for the organization and appropriate for those cultures (Pucik *et al.*, 2002; Adler/Ghadar 1990). Of course, cultural differences are not the only challenge; as is true for domestic US firms, MNEs must align their HRM systems with other elements of the external environment – the laws, economic conditions, and political trends in each country of operation (Von Glinow/Drost/Tea-garden 2002).

A closely related challenge is developing a global approach to managing human resources that embraces a few universal principles that give the entire global system consistency and internal integrity, while also allowing local and regional autonomy. Achieving the right mix requires continual evaluation and discussion about which policies and practices can be global and which can or should be regional or even local (Gupta/Govindarjan 2001). As they have adopted local HR practices, many US MNEs have found it difficult to develop global HRM systems that are internally consistent and effective throughout the entire MNE (Schuler/Budhwar/Florkowski 2002; Boudreau/Ramstad/Dowling 2003).

Strategic international human resources

As is true for firms operating in a single country or region, MNEs strive to develop HRM systems that fit the contours of the present context – a context that is much more complex and multifaceted – yet anticipate the future concerns of its varied stakeholders. That is, effectively managing human resources in MNEs requires a framework for strategic international human resource management (Evans *et al.*, 2002; Briscoe/Schuler 2004). Strategic international human resource management has been defined as "human resource management issues, functions, policies and practices that result from the strategic activities of MNEs and that impact the international concerns and goals of those enterprises" (Schuler/Dowling/De Cieri 1993).

The practice of strategic international human resource management involves the management of inter-unit linkages and internal operations (Bartlett/Ghoshal 1991). Managing inter-unit linkages is needed to integrate, control and coordinate the units of a firm that are scattered throughout the globe (Ghoshal 1987; Galbraith 1992). Internal operations, on the other hand, encompass the remaining issues. For example, internal operations include the way a unit operates in concert with the laws, culture, society, politics, economy, and general environment of a particular location (Ballon 1992; Tung/Thomas 2003).

Managing cross-border alliances

Another important challenge for MNEs is managing cross-border alliances. Due in part to the high costs of developing new products and entering new markets, more and more US companies have elected to enter into cross-border alliances. Two types of cross-border alliances that present special HRM challenges are international mergers and acquisitions and international joint ventures (Schweiger/Very 2001). While international mergers and acquisitions have the tendency to reduce the number of companies in a market, international joint ventures typically increase the number of companies in a market. In both cases, costs can be reduced, profits enhanced, speed of market entry increased and risks managed.

Research suggests that many of the problems that arise in managing cross-border alliances are due to ineffective human resource management (Schuler/Jackson/Luo 2004). Research intended to improve our understanding of how to manage cross-border alliances is still in its infancy. Nevertheless, there is a growing volume of scholarship devoted to developing testable, theoretically-grounded frameworks that can serve as guides to new empirical research while also providing new insights to practicing HR professionals (Inkpen/Beamish 1997).

Some of the theoretical perspectives that have been used to guide studies of strategic HRM will undoubtedly prove useful for future research in strategic international HRM, including those theories we described above as well as institutional theory (Zucker 1987), agency theory (Jensen/Meckling 1976) and transactions-cost theory (Williamson 1985). In addition, the perspective of organizational learning theory (Kogut 1988; Cohen/Levinthal 1990) is proving useful. For many firms, the process of internationalizing involves expanding slowly from a domestic base into progressively distant areas. Establishing cross-border alliances may provide an efficient means for firms that seek to learn how to operate in new areas prior to investing heavily in them (Luo 2002; Shenkar/Zeira 1987). For this tactic to be effective, however, a variety of issues must be tackled; in the process, a firm's ability to manage human resources effectively within the cross-border alliance will be tested. Improving our understanding of this and other learning processes and developing guidelines for effectively managing cross-cultural organizational learning are challenges to be addressed by strategic international human resource management in the next quarter century.

Conclusion

The nature of US human resource management is changing rapidly as the 21st century gets under way. Increasingly, human resource management is being recognized as central to strategic planning and strategy implementation – for domestic firms as well as MNEs. With the objective of providing an overview of the past quarter-century of HRM in the US, we have briefly commented on a few major developments, including the importance of analyzing and interpreting the impact of context, the recognition of the importance of multiple stakeholders for HRM as well as organizations, the efficacy of a partnership involvement in the design, development and implementation of HRM activities, a growing professionalism in HRM both domestically and globally, and the use of data and theory for research advancements and contributions.

As we write this chapter we see the dynamics of the global economy and global labor markets rapidly evolving as dominant forces for human resource management in US companies, both domestic and multinational ones. These dynamics appear so powerful that the distinction between what constitutes domestic and multinational is fast disappearing. Consequently, we predict that the contextual and dynamic framework for studying and understanding HRM will apply to all organizations in the US and their HRM professionals in their efforts to manage human resources as effectively as possible.

REFERENCES

Adler, N. (2002): International dimensions of organizational behavior. Cincinnati, OH: South-Western.

Adler, N. J./Ghadar, F. (1990): Strategic human resource management. In: R. Pieper (ed.): Human resource management: An international resource comparison. New York: de Gruyter: 426–43.

Baird, L./Meshoulam, L. (1988): Managing the two fits of strategic human resource management. In: *Academy of Management Review*, 13: 116–228

Ballon, R. J. (1992): Foreign competition in Japan. New York: Routledge

Barney, J. B. (1991): Firm resources and sustained competitive advantage. In: *Journal of Management*, 17: 99–120.

Barney, J. B./Wright, P. M. (1998): On becoming a strategic partner: The role of human resources in competitive advantage. *Human Resource Management*, 37: 31–46.

Bartlett, C. A./Ghoshal, S. (1991): Managing across borders: The transnational solution. London: London Business School.

Beatty, R. W./Huselid, M./Schneier, C. (2003): New HR metrics. *Organizational Dynamics*, 2: 207–21

Becker, B. & Gerhart, B. (1996): The impact of human resource management on organizational performance: Progress and prospects. In: *Academy of Management Journal*, 39: 779–801.

Becker, B. E./Huselid, M. A. (1998): High performance work systems and firm performance: A synthesis of research and managerial implications. In: G. Ferris (ed.): Research in Personnel and Human Resources Management. Greenwich, CT: JAI Press.

Becker, B. E./Huselid, M. A./Ulrich, D. (2001): The HR scorecard: Linking people, strategy, and performance. Boston, MA: Harvard Business School Press.

Becker, G. S. (1964): Human capital. New York: National Bureau of Economic Research.

Beer, M./Spector, B./Lawrence, P. R./Mills, Q. D./Walton, R. E. (1985): Managing human assets. New York: The Free Press.

Black, J. S./Mendenhall, M./Oddou, G. (1991): Toward a comprehensive model of international adjustment: An integration of multiple theoretical perspectives. In: *Academy of Management Review*, 16, 291–317.

Blasi, J./Kruse, D./Bernstein, A. (2003): In the company of owners: The truth about stock options and why every employee should have them. New York: Basic Books.

Boswell, W. R./Boudreau, J. W. (2001): How leading companies create, measure and achieve strategic results through "line of sight." *Management Decision*, 39: 851–9.

Boudreau, J. W. (2003): Strategic knowledge measurement and management. In: S. E. Jackson/M. A. Hitt/A. S. DeNisi (eds.), Managing knowledge for sustained competitive advantage. San Francisco, Jossey-Bass: 360–98.

Boudreau, J. W./Dunford, B.B./Ramstad, P.M. (2001): The human capital impact on e-business: The case of the Encyclopedia Britannica. In: N. Pal and J.M. Ray (eds.) Pushing the digital frontier. New York, Amacom: 192–221.

Boudreau, J. W./Hopp, W./McClain, J.O./Thomas, L.J. (2003): On the interface between operations and human resource management. In: *Manufacturing and Service Operations Management*, 5 (3): 179–202.

Boudreau, J. W./Ramstad, P. M. (1999): Human resource metrics: Can measures be strategic? In: *Research in Personnel and Human Resources Management*, Supplement 4, 75–98.

Boudreau, J. W./Ramstad, P. M. (2002): From "professional business partner" to "strategic talent leader": What's next for human resource management? Working paper 02-10, Cornell University, New York.

Boudreau, J. W./Ramstad, P. M. (2003a): Strategic I./O psychology and the role of utility analysis models. In: W. Borman/D. Ilegen/R. Klimoski (eds.): Handbook of Psychology. New York: Wiley: 193–221.

Boudreau, J. W./Ramstad, P. M. (2003b): Strategic HRM measurement in the 21st century: From justifying HR to strategic talent leadership. In: M. Goldsmith/R.P. Gandossy/ M.S. Efron (eds.): HRM in the 21st Century. New York: Wiley: pp. 79–90.

Boudreau, J. W./Ramstad, P. M./Dowling, P. J. (2003): Global talentship: Towards a decision science connecting talent to global strategic success. In: W. Mobley/P. Dorfman (eds.): Advances in Global Leadership. New York, JAI Press./Elsevier Science: 63–99.

Briscoe, D. R./Schuler, R. S. (2004): International human resource management, 2e. London: Routledge. (www.routledge.com./textbooks./0415338344)

Brown, M. P./Sturman, M. C./Simmering, M. J. (2003): Compensation policy and organizational performance: The efficiency, operational, and financial implications of pay levels and pay structure. In: *Academy of Management Journal*, 46: 752–62.

Caliguiri, P. M. (2000): The big five personality characteristics as predictors of expatriates' desire to terminate the assignment and supervisor-rated performance. In: *Personnel Psychology*, 53: 67–88.

Cappelli, P./Crocker-Hefter, A. (1993): High Performance Work Practices and Firm Performance. Washington, D.C.: US Department of Labor.

Cappelli, P./Neumark, D. (2001): Do "high-performance" work practices improve establishment-level outcomes? In: *Industrial and Labor Relations Review*, 54: 737–75.

Cappelli, P./Singh, H. (1992): Integrating strategic human resources and strategic management. In: D. Lewin, O. S. Mitchell, and P. Sherer (eds.): Research Frontiers in Industrial Relations and Human Resources. pp. 165–92. Madison, Industrial Relations Research Association.

Cascio, W. F. (1991): Costing human resources, 3rd edn. Boston: Kent Publishing.

Cascio, W. F. (2000): Costing human resources:The financial impact of behavior in organizations, Mason, OH: South-Western Publishing.

Chadwick, C./Cappelli, P. (1999): Alternatives to strategic generaic strategy typologies in strategic human resource management. In: *Research in Personnel and Human Resource management*, Supplement 4: 1–29.

Claus, L./Collison, J. (2004): The maturing profession of human resources in the United States of America Survey Report. Alexandria, VA: SHRM./SHRM Global Forums.

Cohen, W. M./Levinthal, D. A. (1990): Absorptive capacity: A new perspective on learning and innovations. Administrative Science Quarterly, 35: 128–52.

Collins, C. J./Clark, K. D. (2003): Strategic human resource practices, top management team social networks, and firm performance: The role of human resource practices in creating organizational competitive advantage. In: *Academy of Management Journal*, 46: 740–51.

Daft, R. L./Weick, K. E. (1984): Toward a model of organizations as interpretation systems. In: *Academy of Management Review*, 9: 284–95.

Delaney, J./Lewin, D./Ichniowski, C. (1989): Human resource policies and practices in American firms. Washington D.C.: US Department of Labor, BLMR Report No. 137.

Delery, J. E. (1998): Issues of fit in strategic human resource management: Implications for research. *Human Resource Management Review*, 8: 289–309.

Delery, J. E./Doty, D. H. (1996): Modes of theorizing in strategic human resource management: Tests of universalistic, contingency, and configurational performance predictions. In: *Academy of Management Journal*, 39: 802–35.

Delery, J. E./Shaw, J. D. (2001): The strategic management of people in work organizations: Review, synthesis, and extension. In: Research in Personnel and Human Resource Management, 20: 165–97.

Devanna, M./Fombrun, C./Tichy, N. (1981): Human resources management: A strategic perspective. In: *Organizational Dynamics*, 51–67.

Donaldson, T./Preston, L. E. (1995): The stakeholder theory of the corporátion: Concepts, evidence, and implications. In: *Academy of Management Review*, 20: 65–91.

Drucker, P. (1985): The theory of the business. *Harvard Business Review*, 72 (5): 95–104.

Dyer, L. (1985): Strategic human resources management and planning. In: Rowland, K. M./ Ferris, G. R. (eds.): Research in Personnel and Human Resource Management. Greenwich, JAI Press: 1–30.

Dyer, L./Burdick, W. E. (1998): Personnel and Human Resource Management. In: M. F. Neufeld/J.T. Mckelvey (eds.): Industrial Relations at the Dawn of the New Millennium. Ithaca: New York State School of Industrial and Labor Relations: 63–85.

Evans, P./Pucik, V./Barsoux, J-L. (2002): The global challenge. London: McGraw-Hill.

Fitz-Enz, J. (2002): How to measure human resource management. New York: McGraw-Hill.

Flamholtz, E. G./Lacey, J. M. (1981): Personnel management, human capital theory and human resource accounting. Los Angeles: Institute of Industrial Relations, University of California.

Florkowski, G./Nath, R. (1993): MNC responses to the legal environment of international human resource management. In: *Journal of International Human Resource Management*, 4: 305–24.

Fombrun, C.J./Tichy, N.M./Devanna, M.A. (1984): Strategic Human Resource Management. New York: John Wiley & Sons, Inc.

Fredericksen, N. (1986): Toward a broader conception of human intelligence. In: *American Psychologist*, 41: 445–52.

Galbraith, J. R. (1992): The Value Adding Corporation. Center for Effective Organizations, University of Southern California.

Galbraith, J. R./Nathanson, D. (1978): Strategy Implementation: The Role of Structure and Process. St. Paul, MN. West Publishing.

Gerhart, B. (1999): Human resource management and firm performance. Research in Personnel and Human Resource Management. Supplement 4: 31–51.

Ghoshal, S. (1987): Global strategy: An organizing framework. In: Strategic Management Journal, 8: 425–40.

Gomez-Mejia, L./Balkin, D. B. (1990): Compensation, organizational strategy, and firm performance. Cincinnati, OH: South-Western.

Gupta, A. K./Govindarajan, V. (2001): Converting global presence into gobal competitive advantage. In: *Academy of Management Executive*, 15 (2): 45–56.

Hambrick, D.C. (2003): On the staying power of defenders, analyzers and prospectors. In: *Academy of Management Executive*, 17 (4): 115–18.

Higgs, A. C./Papper, E. M./Carr, L. S. (2000): Integrating selection with other organizational processes and systems. In: J. F. Kehoe (ed.): Managing selection in changing organizations. San Francisco: Jossey-Bass: 73–122.

Huselid, M.A. (1995): The impact of human resource management practices on turnover, productivity, and corporate financial performance. In: *Academy of Mangement Journal*, 38: 635–72.

Huselid, M.A./Becker, B./Beatty, R.W. (2004): The workforce scorecard. Boston: Harvard Business School Press.

Ichniowski, C. (1990): Human resource management systems and the performance of US manufacturing business. NBER Working Paper No. 3449, September.

Ichniowski, C. Kochan, T. A./Levine, D./Olson, C. & Strauss, G. (1996): What works at work: Overview and assessment. In: *Industrial Relations*, 35: 299–333.

Inkpen, A. C./Beamish, P. W. 1997. Knowledge management processes and international joint ventures. In: *Academy of Management Review*, 22: 177–202.

Jackson, S.E./Schuler, R.S. (1995): Understanding human rsource management in the context of organizations and their environments. In: M. Rosenweig/L. Porter (eds.): Annual Review of Psychology. Palo Alto, CA: Annual Reviews: 237–64.

Jackson, S. E./Schuler, R. S. (2003): Managing human resources through strategic partnerships, 8th ed. Cincinnati, OH: South-Western, 2003.

Jackson, S. E./Schuler, R. S. (2002): Managing individual performance: An individual perspective. In: S. Sonnentag (ed.): Psychological management of individual performance. New York: John Wiley and Sons: 371–90.

Jackson, S. E./Hitt, M. A./DeNisi, A. S. (eds.) (2003): Managing knowledge for sustained competitive advantage. San Francisco: Jossey-Bass.

Jackson, S. E./Schuler, R. S./Rivero, J. C. (1989): Organization characteristics as predictors of personnel practices. In: *Personnel Psychology*, 42: 727–86.

Jayne, M. E. A./Rauschenberger, J. M. (2000): Demonstrating the value of selection in organizations. In: J. F. Kehoe (ed.): Managing selection in changing organizations. San Francisco: Jossey-Bass: 73–122.

Jensen, M.C./Meckling, W.H. (1976): Theory of the firm: Managerial behavior, agency costs, and capital structure. In: *Journal of Financial Economics*, 3: 305–60.

Kanter, R. M. (1983): Frontiers for strategic human resource management. In: *Human Resource Management*, 22, 85–92.

Kanter, R.M. (1994): Change in the global economy: An interview with Rosabeth Moss Kanter. In: *European Management Journal*, 12: 1.

Kaplan, R. S./Norton, D. P. (1996a): Linking the balanced scorecard to strategy. In: *California Management Review*, 39 (fall): 53–79.

Kaplan, R. S./Norton, D. P. (1996b): Using the balanced scorecard as a strategic management system. In: *Harvard Business Review*, (January–February): 75–85.

Kaplan, R. S./Norton, D. P. (2004): Strategy maps. Boston: Harvard Business School Press.

Katz, H. C./Kochan, T.A. (2000): An introduction to collective bargaining and labor relations. New York: Irwin McGraw-Hill.

Katz, D./Kahn, R. L. (1978): The social psychology of organizations. New York: Wiley

Kerr, J. L./Jackofsky, E. F. (1989): Aligning managers with strategies: Management development versus selection. *Strategic Management Journal*, 10: 157–70

Ketchen, D. J./Thomas, J. B./Snow, C. C. (1993): Organizational configurations and performance: A comparison of theoretical approaches. In: *Academy of Management Journal*, 36: 1278–313.

Kogut, B. (1988): Joint ventures: Theoretical and empirical and perspectives. In: *Strategic Management Journal*, 9: 319–32.

Lado, A. A./Wilson, M. C. (1994): Human resource systems and sustained competitive advantage: A competency-based perspective. In: *Academy of Management Review*, 19: 699–727.

Lawler, E. E. III (1992): The ultimate advantage: Creating the high involvement organization. San Francisco: Jossey-Bass.

Lawler, E. E. III, Mohrman, S. A./Ledford, G. E. (1992): Employee involvement in America: An assessment of practices and results. San Francisco: Jossey-Bass.

Lengnick-Hall, C. A./Lengnick-Hall, C. A. (1988): Strategic human resource management: A review of the literature and proposed typology. In: *Academy of Management Review*, 13: 454–70.

Lepak, D./Snell, S. (1999): The human resource architecture: Toward a theory of human capital allocation and development. In: *Academy of Management Review*, 24: 31–48.

Lepak D. P./Snell, S. A. (2003): Managing the human resource architecture for knowledge-based competition. In: S. E. Jackson, M. A. Hitt, and A. S. DeNisi (eds.) Managing knowledge for sustained competitive advantage. San Francisco: Jossey-Bass: 127–54.

Lundy, O./Cowling, A. (1996): Strategic Human Resource Management. New York: Basic Books.

Luo, Y. (2002): Capability exploitation and building in a foreign market: Implications for multinational enterprise. In: *Organizational Science*, 13: 48–63.

Martin-Alcazar, F.M./Romero-Fernandez, P.M./Sanchez-Gardey, G.S. (2004): Strategic human resource management: Integrating the universalistic, contingent, configurational and contextual perspectives. In: *International Journal of Human Resource Management*, 16 (5): 633–59.

MacDuffie, J. P./Drafcik, J. (1992): Integrating technology and human resources for high-performance manufacturing. In: T. Kochan/M. Useem (eds.): Transforming organizations. New York: Oxford University Press: 210–26.

McMahan, G. C./Virick, M./Wright, P. M. (1999): Alternative theoretical perspectives for strategic human resource management revisited: Progress, problems and prospects. In: *Research in Personnel and Human Resources Management*, Supplement 4: 99–122.

MacDuffie, J. P. (1995): Human resource bundles and manufacturing performance: Organizational logic and flexible production systems in the world auto industry. In: *Industrial and Labor Relations Review*, 48: 197–221.

Mendenhall, M. E./Kuhlmann, M./Stahl, G. K./Osland, J. S. (2002): Employee development and expatriate assignments. In: M. J. Gannon/K. L. Newman (eds.): The Blackwell handbook of cross-cultural management. London: Blackwell Business.

Miles, R. E./Snow, C. C. (1984): Designing strategic human resource systems. In: *Organization Dynamics*, 16: 36–52.

Niniger, J. R. (1980): Human resources and strategic planning: A vital link. In: *Optimum*, 11 (4): 33–46.

Ones, D. S./Viswesvaran, C. (1997): Personality determinants in the predition of aspects of expatriate job success. In: Z. Aycan (ed.): Expatriate management: Theory and research, Volume 4. Greenwich, CT: JAI Press.

Osterman, P. (1984): How common is workplace transformation and who adopts it? In: *Industrial and Labor Relations Review*, 47: 173–88.

Osterman, P. (1987): Choice of employment systems in internal labor markets. In: Industrial Relations, 26: 46–67.

Pfeffer, J. (1994): Competitive advantage through people: Unleashing the power of the workforce. Boston: Harvard Business School Press.

Pfeffer, J. (1998): The human equation. Boston: Harvard Business School Press.

Porter, M. E. (1980): Competitive strategy: Techniques for analyzing industries and competitors. New York: Free Press.

Pucik, V./Tichy, N. M. & Barnett, C. K. (1993): Globalizing management. New York: John Wiley and Sons.

Prahalad, C.K. (1995): New view of strategy. In: *European Management Journal*, 13 (2): 47–56

Reynolds, C. (1997): Expatriate compensation in historical perspective. In: *Journal of World Business*, 32 (2): 118–32.

Reynolds, C. (2001): Compensation and benefits in a global context. In: C. Reynolds (ed.): Guide to global compensation and benefits. San Diego, CA: Harcourt: 3–12.

Reynolds, C. (2004): A short history of the evolution of IHRM in the US: A personal perspective. In: D.R. Briscoe/R.S. Schuler, International Human Resource Management, 2e, London: Routledge

Rogers, E. W./Wright, P. M. (1998): Measuring organizational performance in strategic human resource management research: Problems, prospects, and performance information markets. In: *Human Resource Management Review*, 8: 311–31.

Rousseau, D./Schalk, R. (eds.) (2000): Psychological contracts in employment: Cross-national perspectives. Thousand Oaks, CA: Sage.

Rucci, A. J./Kim, S. P./Quinn, R. T. (1998, January-February): The employee-customer-profit chain at Sears. In: *Harvard Business Review*: 83–97.

Schippmann, J. S. (1999): Strategic job modeling: Working at the core of integrated human resources. Mahwah, NJ: Lawrence Erlbaum.

Schmidt, F. L./Hunter, J. E./MacKenzie, R./Muldrow, T. (1979): The impact of valid selection procedures on workforce productivity. In: *Journal of Applied Psychology*, 64: 627–70.

Schneider, B./Bowen, D. E. (1995): Winning the service game. Boston, MA: Harvard Business School Press.

Schneider, B./White, S.S. (2004): Service Quality: Research Perspectives. Thousand Oaks, CA: Sage.

Schuler, R. S. (1992): Strategic human resource management: Linking the people with the strategic needs of the business. In: *Organizational Dynamics* (Summer): 18–32.

Schuler, R. S. (1994): Human resource management: Domestic to global. In: M. Warner (ed.): International encyclopedia of business and management. London: Routledge.

Schuler, R. S./Jackson, S. E. (1999): Strategic human resource management: A reader. London: Blackwell.

Schuler, R. S./Jackson, S.E. (1987): Linking competitive strategy with human resource management practices. In: *Academy of Management Executive*, 3: 207–19.

Schuler, R. S./Jackson, S. E. (2004): Human resource management in context. In: R. Blanpain/ C. Engels (eds.): Comparative labour law and industrial relations in industrialised market economies. The Hague: Kluwer Law International.

Schuler, R. S./MacMillan, I. C. (1984): Gaining competitive advantage through human resource management practices. In: *Human Resource Management*: 241–55.

Schuler, R. S./Budhwar, P./Florkowski, G. W. (2002, March): International human resource management: Review and critique. In: *International Journal of Management Reviews*: 41–70.

Schuler, R. S./Dowling, P./De Cieri, H. (1993, December): An integrative framework of strategic international human resource management. In: *International Journal of Human Resource Management*, 4(4): 717–64.

Schuler, R. S./Jackson, S. E./Luo, Y. (2004): Managing human resources in cross-border alliances. London: Routledge. (www.routledge.com)

Schuler, R. S./Jackson, S. E./Storey, J. (2001): HRM and its link with strategic management. In: J. Storey (ed.): Human Resource Management: A Critical Text. London: Thomson Learning: 114–30.

Schweiger, D. M./Very, P. (2001): International mergers and acquisitions: Special issue. In: *Journal of World Business*, 36: 1–3.

Shenkar, O./Zeira, Y. (1987): Human resource management in international joint ventures: Directions for research. In: *Academy of Management Review*, 12: 546–57.

Snell, S. A./Youndt, M. A./Wright, P. M. (1996): Establishing a framework for research in strategic human resource management: Merging resource theory and organizational learning. In: *Research in Personnel and Human Resource Management*, 14: 61–90.

Sparrow, P. R./Schuler, R. S./Jackson, S. E. (1994): Convergence or divergence: Human resource practices and policies for competitive advantage worldwide. In: *International Journal of Human Resource Management*, 5: 267–99.

Sturman, M.C./Trevor, C.O./Boudreau, J.W./Gerhart, B. (2003): Is it worth it to win the talent war? Evaluating the utility of performance-based pay. In: Personnel Psychology, 56 (4): 997–1035.

Tarique, I. & Caligiuri, P. (2004): Training and development of international staff. In: A. W. Harzing/J. Van Ruysseveldt (eds.): International human resource management Thousand Oaks, CA: Sage Publications.

Treacy, M./Wiersema, M. (1995): The discipline of market leaders. New York: Harper Collins.

Tung, R. L. (1990): International human resource management policies and practices: A comparative analysis. In: *Research in Personnel and Human Resources Management*, Supplement 2: 171–86.

Tung, R. L. (1998): The new expatriates: Managing human resources abroad. Cambridge, MA: Ballinger.

Tung, R. L./Thomas, D. C. (2003): Human resource management in a global world: The contingency framework extended. In: D. Tjosvold/K. Leung (eds.): Cross-cultural management: Foundations and future. UK: Ashgate.

Ulrich, D. (1998): Delivering results: A new mandate for human resource professionals. Boston: Harvard Business School Press.

Von Glinow, M. A./Drost, E. A./Teagarden, M. B. (2002): Converging on IHRM best practices: Lessons learned from a globally distributed consortium on theory and practice. In: *Asia Pacific Journal of Human Resources*, 40 (1): 146–66.

Wernerfelt, B. (1984): A resource-based view of the firm. In: *Strategic Management Journal*, 5: 171–80.

Williamson, O. E. (1985): The economic institutions of capitalism. New York: Free Press.

Wright, P. M./Gardner, T. M. (2002): Theoretical and empirical challenges in studying the HR practice-firm performance relationship. In: D. Holman/T. Wall/C. Cleff/P. Sparrow/A. Howard (eds.): The new workplace: A guide to the human impact of modern working practices. Chichester: John Wiley and Sons.

Wright, P. M./McMahan, G. C. (1992): Theoretical perspectives for strategic human resource management. In: *Journal of Management*, 18: 295–320.

Wright, P. M./Snell, S. A. (1998): Toward a unifying framework for exploring fit and flexibility in strategic human resource management. In: *Academy of Management Review*, 23: 756–72.

Wright, P. M./Dunford, B. B./Snell, S. A. (2001): Human resources and the resource-based view of the firm. In: *Journal of Management*, 27: 701–21.

Wright, P. M. McMahan, G. C./McWilliams, A. (1994): Human resources and sustained competitive advantage: A resource-based perspective. In: *International Journal of Human Resource Management*, 5: 301–26.

Wright, P. M. & Snell, S. A. (1991): Toward an integrative view of strategic human resource management. In: *Human Resource Management Review*, 1: 203–25.

Zucker, L.G. (1987): Institutional theories of organization. In: *Annual Review of Sociology*, 13: 443–64.

Chapter 11

European Human Resource Management: Researching Developments over Time

Wolfgang Mayrhofer and Chris Brewster

11.1 Introduction

Human Resource Management as a concept was formalised in the USA in the late 1970s and early 1980s, encapsulated in two famous textbooks (Fombrun *et al.*, 1984; Beer *et al.*, 1985). These approaches varied but both differentiated HRM from personnel management and argued that the former involved more integration of personnel policies across functions and with the corporate strategy (with HR being the downstream function); a greater role for line managers; a shift from collective to individual relationships; and an accent on enhancing company performance.

The notion of "European Human Resource Management" was developed largely as a counter to the hegemony of US conceptions of human resource management (HRM). This, in part, reflected developments in the arguments about how we should conceive of the notion of HRM (Kamoche 1996). It was argued (Brewster 1994; Sparrow/Hiltrop 1994) that US assumptions about the nature of HRM were inappropriate in this (and probably other) continents and that Europe needed models of its own. These notions were behind the establishment, towards the end of the 1980s, of a research network based on one university per country, dedicated to identifying trends in HRM in Europe. That network grew from the original five countries to

W. Mayrhofer and C. Brewster, "European Human Resource Management: Researching Developments over Time," *Management Review*, Vol. 16, No. 1 (2005): 36–62.

twenty-seven in Europe and some dozen others spread across the world. Some fifteen years after the start of the project, and at the point of the publication of the fourth edited book based on the network's outputs (Brewster *et al.*, 2004), this seems to be a good time to review what we have learned.

In particular, the long-term nature of the project allows us to identify trends in the management of human resources in Europe (see Gooderham/Brewster 2003 for a first attempt at doing so using this data). Are the European countries moving towards one another in the way that they manage HRM? If so, are they moving towards or away from a model similar to that operating in the USA? Or are they remaining separate and different?

In presenting these findings, this chapter is, therefore, ambitious in scope. First, it conceptualises the notion of "European HRM," setting it in the context of theories of international HRM and convergence and divergence in comparative HRM; it is argued that there are inevitably elements of universality and of national difference that have to be encompassed by such theories and that we need more nuanced approaches to the ideas of convergence and divergence. After briefly exploring the methodological and practical issues of researching large-scale developments in European HRM over an extended period, the chapter presents empirical evidence from the research of Cranet, the Cranfield Network of Human Resource Management, as a contribution to the European convergence/divergence debate which, finally, enables us to draw some conclusions about whether there is, indeed, evidence of convergence in European HRM.

11.2 Conceptual Background

11.2.1 Static views: specifics of European HRM?

Looking across national borders, how are we to conceive of the differences in HRM systems and approaches? What is the correct level of analysis? We have elsewhere (Brewster 1995b) used the analogy of a telescope. Changing the focus provides the viewer with ever more detail and the ability to distinguish ever-finer differences between aspects of the big picture that can be seen with the naked eye. None of the perspectives are "wrong" or inaccurate; some are more useful for some purposes than for others. So, we would argue, it is with HRM. There are some universals in the field (the need for organisations to attract, pay and deploy workers, for example). There are also some things which are shared within regions; some which are distinctive for certain countries; some which are unique to certain sectors; some ways in which each organisation or even sections of an organisation are different; and some factors which are unique to each individual manager. Each perspective sharpens the focus on some aspects but, inevitably, blurs others.

This chapter is concerned with identifying differences between the universalistic and contextual paradigms (Brewster 1999) and, within that, of establishing whether it makes sense to speak of a "European" version of HRM (Brewster 1994); with identifying the differences between countries in Europe in the way that they manage

HRM; and with establishing whether the trends in HRM are strong enough to lead us to speak of convergence. This section deals with the first of those issues.

Can we distinguish a version of HRM in Europe that is different from the versions existing in, for example, Japan or the USA? The latter case is of particular significance, given the power of the US version of human resource management. It has been argued that the US is an inappropriate model for Europe (see Cox/Cooper 1985; Pieper 1990; Thurley/Wirdenius 1991; Brewster 1994; Brewster 1995b). The vision of HRM that has come to us in Europe from the USA is culture bound (Adler/Jelinek 1986; Trompenaars 1994) and in particular, a view of HRM as based on the largely unconstrained exercise of managerial autonomy has been attacked as being peculiarly American (Guest 1990; Brewster 1993; Brewster 1995b). In Europe, organisations are not so autonomous. They exist within a system which constrains (or supports) them, first, at the national level, by culture and by extensive legal and institutional limitations on the nature of the contract of employment, and second, at the organisational level, by patterns of ownership (by the State, by the banking and finance system and by families) which are distinct from those in the USA. It has been argued elsewhere (Brewster 1993) that a new "European" model of HRM is required, one that takes account of State and trade union involvement – a concept of HRM which directs us to re-examine the industrial relations system approach outlined in 1958 by Dunlop (Brewster 1995a).

Of course, with a different turn of the focus screw, it is possible to distinguish distinct regional clusters even within Europe. Mostly these have been one-dimensional and limited to simple dichotomies. Thus, Hall and Soskice (2001) and Gooderham and colleagues (1999) contrast Anglo-Saxon style free-market capitalism with varieties where there is greater state intervention. Garten (1993) shares this view, though also noting the existence of government-induced market systems such as Japan. Hollingsworth and Boyer (1997a) focus on a different dimension, that of the presence or absence of communitarian infrastructures that manifest themselves in the form of strong social bonds, trust, reciprocity and co-operation among economic actors. Again, they find the Anglo cultures distinct from the rest of Europe, although they also distinguish France as an environment that, while not having a market mentality, is nevertheless deficient in communitarian infrastructures. Others distinguish between, on the one hand, countries such as the UK, Ireland and the Nordic countries, in which the state has a limited role in industrial relations, and the Roman-Germanic countries, such as France, Spain, Germany, Italy, Belgium, Greece and the Netherlands, in which the state functions as an actor with a central role in industrial relations (Due *et al.*, 1991: 90). Arguments have also been made for a "northern European" approach to HRM based around those countries where English is widely spoken and trade unions are stronger (Brewster/Larsen 2000).

One analysis of HRM practices found 'three clusters: a Latin cluster [which includes Spain, Italy, France]; a central European cluster ... and a Nordic cluster' (Filella 1991: 14). The Latin style of HRM is characterised, *inter alia*, by efforts to modernise HRM, a greater reliance on an oral culture and the presence of subtle 'political' structures which unconsciously nurture docile, dependent attitudes to authority. The Nordic approach to HRM would include the substantial, visible authority of the HR department, extensive written strategies, a widespread collective orientation to management, and extensive consultation. The continental central European model would involve lower authority for HR departments, extensive line management involvement in HR issues and legal support for collaboration with trade unions. Whether there is an 'offshore central European' model is open to question. Filella (1991) argues that the regional groupings may correspond to stages of socio-economic development.

Examining flexible (contingent) work practices, Brewster and Tregaskis (2001) found slightly different groupings in the manufacturing and service sectors. Spain tended to be a category on its own in both cases and, in manufacturing for example, Germany, the Netherlands, Norway and Switzerland were in the "high inclusive" group; France and Ireland in the moderately reactive group; in services the UK, Sweden, Denmark and Belgium were in the moderately reactive group. Gooderham and Brewster (2003) found four categories based on a matrix based around communitarianism and autonomy.

11.2.2   Dynamic views: convergence or divergence?

Whilst valuable in pointing us away from the universalistic prescriptions on HRM there are two major problems with these European or within-Europe approaches. First, whilst they emphasise the importance of culture and institutions, they underemphasise the level at which such differences are most cogent, the national level. Second, they are static: they leave little room for the change that we see all around us.

As far as the level of national differences is concerned, the evidence is widespread. A number of studies show the differences between various aspects of HRM in European countries (e.g. Pieper 1990; Vickerstaff 1992; Brunstein 1995; Brewster *et al.*, 2004).

However, the evidence concerning convergence or divergence is more equivocal: are the differences between nations being reduced or not?[1] There are at least two variations of the convergence thesis. The first is the market-driven approach, which tends towards arguing that the rest of the world will become increasingly similar to the United States of America, the most powerful market in the world and therefore the exemplar, in the way that organisations are managed, including how human resources are managed. The second explanator is institutional which, although there is a strand of this theory which argues for world-wide convergence, also includes a strand arguing that the institutional power of the European Union and its approaches to employment practices will lead to a convergence towards a specifically European model. The divergence thesis often uses institutional and/or cultural arguments.

Convergence: market-led
The first variation of the convergence thesis argues that policies of market deregulation and state decontrol are spreading from the US around the world. The power of markets will ensure that those firms that are more productive and whose costs are lower will be successful – others will be driven to copy them to survive. Since the USA is the technological leader, it followed that US management practices represented current "best practice," which other nations would eventually seek to emulate as they sought to adopt US technology. Thus "patterns in other countries were viewed as derivative of, or deviations from, the US model" (Locke *et al.*, 1995: xvi).

There is an institutional version of this theory (sometimes termed the "North-American phenomenological neo-institutionalism, Djelic/Bensedrine 2001) which argues that institutions reflect power relationships and that, therefore, the economic and technical pressures will be reflected institutionally. Thus there will be coercive pressure, to ensure that similar structures and practices are adopted throughout the world (such as the de-regulation "strings" typically tied to IMF loans to underdeveloped countries); normative pressures (from professional bodies, international associations and the growing internationalisation of executive education); and cognitive isomorphism (as international organisations attempt to spread their policies and cultures around the world; see DiMaggio/Powell 1983). It has been argued that one effect of this global institutional isomorphism is that the role of nation states becomes less significant (Meyer 2000).

The convergence thesis has also received support from transaction cost economics which also contends that at any one point of time there exists a best solution to organising labour (Williamson 1975; Williamson 1985). "Most transaction cost theorists argue that there is one best organisational form for firms that have similar or identical transaction costs" (Hollingsworth/Boyer 1997b: 34). Likewise, parts of the industrial organisation literature argue that firms tend to seek out and adopt the best solutions to organising labour within their product markets, long-term survival being dependent on their being able to implement them (Chandler Jr. 1962; Chandler Jr. 1977; Chandler Jr./Daems 1980). Thus there is a tendency for firms to converge towards similar structures of organisation.

This argument has been carried through into HRM. It is implicit in many of the universalist texts which simply ignore national differences and assume that findings from the USA are replicable elsewhere, and explicitly argued elsewhere (see, e.g. Locke *et al.*, 1995).

These various convergence perspectives are characterised by their functionalist mode of thought: practices are explained largely by reference to their contribution to technological and economic efficiency (Brewster/Tregaskis 2003). Management, including human resource management, is a dependent variable that evolves in response to technological and economic change, rather than with reference to the sociopolitical context. The effect is that regardless of auspices, effects on management and labour are similar (Kerr 1983).

Convergence: institutional driven
There is an alternative convergence argument, based on a different version of the institutional analysis.

This argues that since institutions are strong antecedents of difference the ongoing economic and political integration of European Union countries, for example, may create a convergence towards a distinctly European practice – different from the market convergence model. This concept would see regional convergence, but not global convergence, generating a specifically European model of convergence in HRM (Brewster 1995b). In Europe organisations are constrained at a national level, by culture and legislation and at the organisational level by trade union involvement and consultative arrangements. It is clear that, in general, European countries are more heavily unionised than the United States, and indeed most other countries.

Trade union membership and influence vary considerably by country, of course, but are always significant. Indeed in many European countries the law requires union recognition for collective bargaining. In most European countries many of the union functions in such areas as pay bargaining, for example, are exercised at industrial or national level, – outside the direct involvement of managers within individual organisations – as well as at establishment level (Hegewisch 1991; Morley et al., 1996; Traxler et al., 2001). Thus in Europe, unlike in the US, firms are likely to deal with well-founded trade union structures. It is worth noting that studies of HRM in the US have tended to take place in the non-union sector (Beaumont 1991b). In fact a constant assumption in research programmes in the US has been the link between HRM practices and non-unionism (see, e.g. Kochan et al., 1984; Kochan et al., 1986). "In the US a number of…academics have argued that HRM [the concept and the practice] is anti-union and anti-collective bargaining" (Beaumont 1991a: 300).

In HRM, state involvement in Europe is not restricted to the legislative role. Compared to the USA the state in Europe has a higher involvement in underlying social security provision. Equally it has a more directly interventionist role in the economy, provides far more personnel and industrial relations services and is a more substantial employer in its own right by virtue of a more extensive government-owned sector (for an overview about labour markets in Europe see Siebert 1997).

Finally, there are developments at the level of the European Union or the European Economic Area which impact upon all organisations in Europe. In a historically unique experiment, European Union countries have agreed to subordinate national legislative decision-making to European level legislation. These developments have indirect effects upon the way people are managed and direct effects through the EU's adoption of a distinct social sphere of activity. Thus, this strand of the debate would see convergence not on a world-wide basis, but rather towards different regional groupings based on the developing regional institutions. On such an analysis, the European Union, where these institutions are far stronger than they are in any other regional bloc, is a test case.

None of the "convergers" pretend that they do not see the variety of management approaches around the world. However, they argue that, in the long term, any variations in the adoption of management systems at the firm level are ascribable to the industrial sector in which the firm is located, its strategy, its available resources and its degree of exposure to international competition. Moreover, they claim, these factors are of diminishing salience. Indeed, once they have been taken account of, a clear trend toward the adoption of common management systems should be apparent.

Divergence: alternative models
Proponents of the divergence thesis argue, in direct contrast, that personnel management systems, far from being economically or technologically derived, epitomise national contexts that do not respond readily to the imperatives of technology or the market. This may be based upon an institutionalist perspective, in which organisational choice is limited by institutional pressures, including the state, regulatory structures,

interest groups, public opinion and norms (DiMaggio/Powell 1983; Meyer/Rowan 1983; Oliver 1991; Hollingsworth/Boyer 1997a). Or they may be based on the notion that cultural differences mean that the management of organisations – and particularly of people – is, and will remain, fundamentally different from country to country. National differences in ownership, structures, educational systems, and laws all have a significant effect on the architecture and the practices of employing in organisations. This literature has been synthesised in the work of such authors as Hall and Soskice (2001) who draw a sharp distinction between "co-ordinated market economics" of say Germany and Sweden and "liberal market" (Anglo-American) ones. A more subtle version is propounded by Whitley (1999) who sees six different possible varieties of capitalism (Fragmented, Co-ordinated industrial district, Compartmentalised, State organised, Collaborative, and Highly co-ordinated). He defines business systems as: " ... distinctive patterns of economic organization that vary in their degree and mode of authoritative co-ordination of economic activities, and in the organization of, and interconnections between, owners, managers, experts and other employees" (Whitley 1999: 33) – according human resource management a distinctive role in creating the difference between these systems.

These institutionalist writers tend to see cultural differences between nations as an aspects of this analysis. Others (e.g. Hofstede 1980; Trompenaars 1994; House et al., 2002) would see the cultural differences as underlying the institutional differences. Cultural values affect every aspect of work and organisation and are largely unseen by the actors involved.

Divergence theorists argue that national, and in some cases regional, cultures and institutional contexts are slow to change, partly because they derive from deep-seated beliefs and value systems and partly because major re-distributions of power are involved. More importantly, they argue that change is path dependent. In other words, even when change does occur this can only be understood in relation to the specific social context in which it occurs (Maurice et al., 1986; Poole 1986). Performance criteria or goals are thus, at any point in time, socially rather than economically or technologically selected so that they first and foremost reflect the national culture and the idiosyncratic principles of local rationality.

The general management discussion is beginning to be reflected in the specific field of comparative HRM (Brewster/Tyson 1991; Boxall 1995; Hollinshead/Leat 1995; Brewster et al., 2000). In this respect, HRM is catching up with another aspect of the study of employment relationships, the study of industrial relations, which has long recognised the importance of international differences (see, e.g. Poole 1986; Przeworski/Spague 1986; Stephans 1990; Due et al., 1991; Bean/Holden 1992; Visser 1992; Hyman 1994; Hollinshead/Leat 1995; Locke et al., 1995). Human resource management is increasingly acknowledged to be one of the areas where organisations are most likely to maintain a 'national flavour' (Schuler/Huber 1993; Rosenzweig/Nohria 1994; Adler 2002) and is the point at which business and national cultures have the sharpest interface, especially in areas such as forms of control (Harzing/Sorge 2003), work systems (Geppert et al., 2003), and team work (Woywode 2002). Even in companies that try to implement "world-wide" policies, practice is negotiated or varied at national level (Ferner 1997; Wächter et al., 2003).

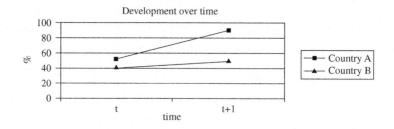

Figure 11.1   Directional convergence (type 1).

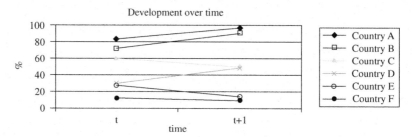

Figure 11.2   Final convergence (type 2).

11.2.3   Types of convergence

From a theoretical as well as an empirical point of view, the notions of convergence or divergence are complex. Although the general meaning, intuitively, is clear, it becomes more complex at a closer look. We propose to differentiate between two different forms of convergence: directional (type I) and final (type II) convergence (for a more in depth discussion of different forms of convergence[2] see Mayrhofer *et al.*, 2002).

Type I – directional convergence
Directional convergence occurs where the development tendency goes into the same direction. Regardless of a starting level in each country, if the variable analysed changes in the same direction in each country there is a convergence in direction at least. Figure 11.1 shows the basic idea. There, both in countries A and B the developments point in the same direction, for example the use of a certain management tool in each country increases. Nevertheless, the frequency of use in the two countries is at a different level.

Type II – final convergence
Final convergence exists when the developments of a variable in different countries point towards a common end point. In other words, the differences between countries decrease. This development is independent of directional convergence (type I) as different developments in terms of, for example, frequency of use of a certain management tool, can still result in final convergence. Figure 11.2 shows three country pairs as examples of final convergence. This is the meaning of convergence that is most commonly assumed in the literature, even if rarely stated explicitly and sometimes confused with the other forms. Each of the three examples shows a different case of final convergence for illustration.

Our results section discusses some of the empirical findings from the Cranet network on these issues, but first we address more general research issues raised by the process of comparative research.

11.3 Methodology

Researching large-scale developments in European HRM over an extended period of time raises not only conceptual, but also methodological and research practical problems (for basic views on international and/or cross-cultural research see, e.g. Adler 1983; Kochan *et al.*, 1992; Cavusgil/Das 1997). When doing the kind of longitudinal and comparative research that is addressed here, at least three major issues arise. First, basic decisions about methodology have to be made. Here, as in every other research effort, researchers have to position themselves within the available spectrum of epistemological and methodological options. Second, doing research across national and cultural boundaries adds specific elements to the "traditional" problems encountered in empirical research, for example, language barriers, different national traditions of doing research or varying practical circumstances of, say, data gathering. Third, such research efforts cannot be taken on alone. Working together in various forms of research networks seems to be a *conditio sine qua non*. Hence, the problems of working together in a culturally mixed, geographically dispersed group over a longer period of time and considerable network dynamics have to be taken into account.

Consequently, this chapter touches methodological issues at three levels. First, some basic problems of comparative research have to be addressed. Second, there is a need to discuss the consequences of doing research in a small team that is not anchored in a more or less homogeneous national background and, consequently, in a common understanding and, most often, sharing of joint standards of science. Third, the "usual" issues of the concrete research project have to be mentioned.

11.3.1 Basic problems of cross-cultural and comparative research

Choosing a methodological angle
Based on Cartesian dualism which distinguishes between the physical as external reality and thinking as internal world, two basic paradigms of scientific thought and methods have emerged: the objective, deductive and often called quantitative and the subjective, interpretative and frequently labelled qualitative paradigm (see, e.g. Lamnek 1988; Lueger 2000).

From a subjective, interpretative point of view the world is not simply given as an objective reality. Rather, it is subjectively constituted and socially pre-interpreted, formed by the observation schemes of the individual actors. In this process, objective and subjective meaning can be differentiated. Subjectively, the actors themselves attribute meaning to their own actions. On the other side, action can be linked with meaning without referring to the psyche of the actor through the observation of observers (Schütz 1981; Soeffner 1989). Given this background, the methods used within this paradigm usually have to meet specific criteria like openness, communicativity, contextuality or search for meaning (e.g. Lamnek 1988).

From an objective, deductive perspective the focus is on the world as "given" entity that can be looked at and analysed without referring to subjective interpretation.

Archetypically, this approach is reflected in the approach of natural science which strives for universal laws and testing of hypotheses via quantitative, experimental methods. Critical rationalism presupposes an objective reality, that is truth. Through a collective effort called science this truth can be approached more and more. Critique becomes crucial in this approach as it is essential for the core elements like intersubjectively checking results and methods (Popper 1972; Scholtz 1991). The methods used in this paradigm have to meet criteria like connection with theory, objective research process, operational definition and isolation of relevant measures, rational explanation, primacy of falsification (Friedrichs 1973).

Studies covering developments in European HRM are implicitly or explicitly rooted in the objective, deductive paradigm. Although using a variety of research methods including "typical" elements of "qualitative" research like single company cases studies or personal in-depth interviews, the basic assumption is quite clear: objective reality – in this case: developments in HRM in Europe – can be captured by using appropriate methods and operationalised through theory-based constructs.

Classic cross-cultural issues
In cross-cultural research a distinction between emic and etic approach has been made (see, e.g. Ronen 1986; Thomas 1993; Holzmüller 1995). "Whereas emics apply in only a particular culture, etics represent universality – they apply to all cultures in the world" (Ronen 1986: 47). If different cultures are compared on the basis of predefined categories (so called cultural dimensions), the researcher's position is outside the observed cultural system because cultures are compared on the basis of dimensions developed in the culture of the researcher. Hofstede's or Trompenaars' cross-cultural analyses are examples of etic research approaches. The main disadvantage and critique is the fact that an "ethnocentric bias" cannot be avoided, because one particular dimension (category) may have different meanings in different cultures or one cultural dimension may not exist in every culture. As far as the emic approach is concerned researchers are within the investigated cultural system, they try "to see how the natives conceptualise the world" (Ronen 1986). The emic approach can provide a culture specific level of understanding that gives the researcher an in-depth feel for the nation (Gannon 2001: 52). Though this can be characterised as a culture-adapted, non-ethnocentric approach, categorisation is under strong influence of the researcher's way of perception and the investigator's blind spot may cause distortions. In practical research, the emic/etic differentiation leads, among others, to the question of inclusion or exclusion of country representatives with local know-how and the effects of (not) doing so.

Specific problems in comparative research – noble and not so noble...
Different scientific traditions in methodological and epistemological terms exist across countries. Especially in continental Europe, there is a long tradition of interpretative research. Only in recent times, in spite of the domination of the "objective-deductive

perspective," has this angle become more acceptable, also in respected top journals (see, e.g. the increasing number of interpretative contributions in top management journals like the Academy of Management Journal). These different traditions, combined with a varying amount of methodological training researchers receive during their career and the problem of speaking a common language – even if English is the *lingua franca* in HR research, the command of English especially in its subtle nuances varies significantly – provide a background where it is not easy to agree on a common approach in international research networks consisting of members from a great number of countries.

Struggling with the issue of "likeness" and equivalence is one of the big topics in international comparative research (Cavusgil/Das 1997). Although it is not unique to that type of research but a 'universal' issue in research, it becomes especially salient at the international level. The same empirical phenomena can be labelled differently in different countries and, vice versa, different things can carry the same labels. Likewise, the same data gathering procedures can yield quite different results. Therefore, comparative research "is concerned with attempting to compare like with like. In international settings this is not an easy task." (Tregaskis *et al.*, 2004: 440)

In addition, practical circumstances of doing research in each country vary considerably. For example, different traditions of how to approach companies – via letter, personal interviews, the web etc. – or the financial resources available for an "average" researcher make a joint approach even more difficult.

11.3.2   Establishing and maintaining research networks

Ambitious international comparative research effort cannot be undertaken "alone" or with only a small group of people. Its scope in terms of content and methods, the geographical spread, the financial involvement and the time investment requires a larger research group with dedicated actors – in other words: an international research network. Establishing and sustaining such research networks has pitfalls of its own beyond the typical problems of multicultural work teams (see, e.g. Davison 1996; Erez/Somech 1996; Ely/Thomas 2001).

First, the question of who is starting the network comes up. This has an individual as well as an institutional component. At the individual level, a well-known figure in the field may use his or her reputation and contacts to bring together individuals often not (very well) known to each other. This can lead to a problematic communication structure at the beginning as much of the communication and integration is focused on the central actor. In addition, such a "father/mother figure" has, for a long time, a special place in the social structure of the network. This can have positive as well as negative consequences for the development of such networks. At the institutional level, the initiator's institutional affiliation is crucial. Its reputation as well as the country location plays a role that should not be underestimated in terms of the prestige and credibility ascribed to the network.

Second, the question of leadership, internal power distribution and decision mechanisms constitutes critical areas. The scientific communities are – at least at a superficial level – characterised by formal equality and a great amount of individualistic free-dom, the latter being for some members of the scientific communities one of the main motivational drivers. Nevertheless, in international research networks a num-ber of subtle (and less subtle) differences resulting in different power bases exist, for example, qualifications, reputation, seniority, available social capital, country of origin, commandment of the *lingua franca* of the network etc. In addition, larger research networks require some kind of decision mechanisms beyond basic – democratic "every-body is involved in and decides everything" – style of decisions. Thus, hierarchical differences return through the "backdoor." Handling the tension between the equal-ity/individualistic principle of the larger context and the concrete requirements of the research network is a crucial point.

Third, managing international research networks has its peculiarities. Due to the loose institutional bonds, the cultural diversity and the geographic spread such net-works have to rely on a number of mechanisms for co-ordination and control (for different types of such mechanisms see, e.g. Mayrhofer 1998; Turati *et al.*, 1998).

Fourth, if networks exist over a longer period of time, inevitably some internal net-work dynamics occur. Fluctuations in the membership, changes in the formal and/or informal status of network members based on developments in individual careers and professional development and, consequently, modified social relations, conflicts about the future course of the network, struggles about the use of especially promising find-ings and, linked with that, the distribution of reputation are just a few of the examples of issues arising. Processes become even more complicated if the research network consists of members from different reference systems, for example, from the scientific area and from the area of consulting. In addition to the issues just mentioned, new problems arise. The ultimate, often implicit understanding of the goal of one's effort – roughly characterised by knowledge creation/insight vs. practical applicability – is usually different. Likewise, different time frames, that is more long term vs. more short term, exist.

As can be seen from these few examples, the use of large international research networks – though essential for specific types of international comparative research – is fraught with dangers. Some of those networks are successfully managed and yield excellent output (see, e.g. the Globe-project in the area of comparative leadership research, House *et al.*, 1999). However, other research consortia (it would be invidious to name them here) either never take off or clearly lag behind their own ambitions.

11.3.3   The concrete research project

International HRM has recently experienced a steady growth in research efforts and publications. European researchers in particular have made a number of significant contributions to theoretical, empirical and methodological advances in the field (e.g. Pieper 1990; Poole 1990; Brewster 1995b; Brewster *et al.*, 1996; Gooderham *et al.*, 1999; Brewster *et al.*, 2000; Brewster *et al.*, 2004). Cranet has been part of these efforts, dedicated to analysing developments in the area of HRM in public and private organisations with more than 200 employees in a national, cross-national and quasilon-gitudinal way (see Brewster/Hegewisch 1994; Brewster *et al.*, 2000; Tregaskis *et al.*, 2004). At the outset, Cranet had two major goals: first, to research whether a pattern of "Europeanisation," that is convergence to a common pattern could be found over time and second, to identify whether changes in personnel policies towards a more strategic human resource management approach have occurred (Brewster *et al.*, 1996).

The Cranet survey is the largest and most representative independent survey of HRM policies and practices in the world. It includes 37 countries, 27 of them in Europe. Six major survey rounds have been conducted since 1990. Overall, data from roughly 30,000 respondents – public and private organisations – are now available and the number continues to increase. The survey concentrates on "hard data" like numbers, percentages, ratio etc. and avoids, as far as possible, attitudinal information. To reduce respondent and cross-country bias very few open-ended questions are included. In addition, the translation–retranslation technique (Brislin *et al.*, 1973; Brislin 1976) is used for every country in every survey round.

Inevitably, Cranet has to cope with the basic options and problems of comparative research in HRM highlighted above. From a methodological point of view, it is rooted in the objective and etic paradigm. The assumption made is that across cultures and countries data can be obtained focusing on "hard" evidence which is not very likely to be biased by cultural assumptions. Nevertheless, a number of variables are inevitably subject to culturally propelled interpretations. For example, concepts like performance evaluation are likely to be interpreted in a different way depending on one's cultural perspective. Although translation–retranslation techniques can help, they cannot solve the basic problems linked with doing objective, etic research in this area.

Cranet handles – not solves – the issues linked to the establishment and maintenance of international research networks by relying on a number of guiding principles. A basic decision has been made to adhere to a set of (network) universal standards. For example, a standard operating procedure has been set up for data collection and input, integration of new questions, and so forth. However, some local adaptations – for example, in the area of how to approach companies in the data collection process – have been made and are accepted within the network. In addition, the methodological discussion is kept going within the research network. This propels mutual learning processes and improves the solutions every network partner chooses for the respective country. In doing this, one has to manage skilfully the trade-off balances between practical necessities and methodological rigorousness. Likewise, there always has been a local partner in each country where Cranet collects data. Thus, the "ethnocentric bias/temptation" is reduced. In terms of network dynamics, Cranet has gone through various phases. In the initial start-up phase with a lot of growth in member countries, the emphasis was on data collection. The key actors remained quite stable. In the scientific community, the network started to get international attention. In a second phase, the growth rate declined. The focus switched from data collection to data analysis. At the same time, the fluctuation in the network increased as established members were leaving the network or re-positioning themselves within the network. In terms of reputation, the activities of the network gained visibility and respectability. In a third phase, many activities and individual members of the network have become well known and an accepted part of international comparative research in HRM. Some high profile publications in top journals (e.g. Gooderham *et al.*, 1999) indicate this. Still, the size of the network and the differentiated career paths its members pursue means that it remains a fragile unit.

In the following section, we will try to pull together insight from different pieces of the empirical work of Cranet over the past 15 years. As these come from various sources using different sub-sets of our own data as well as other authors' work, the necessary information about the used part of our sample is presented at the respective place in the text. Of course, for our own as well as for other authors' work, further information and details can be obtained by following the given references.

11.4   Results

By identifying major trends in the development of European HRM, the focus is "zoomed out": we do not want to point at specific countries or industrial sectors. Rather than commenting on such details, we would like to identify major, constituting characteristics of the overall picture. To be sure, this overall picture is by no means complete. Despite the efforts of Cranet and many other most valuable contributions, empirically and theoretically, we are far from understanding completely what goes on in European HRM. Nevertheless, parts of a picture are there and – with all the caution required – we can see at least four major trends constituting important characteristics of the evolving picture of HRM in Europe. The first two of them – "European HRM is different" and "Great variety of HR practices in European countries" – refer to a more static view. The latter two – "Frequent stasis" and "Some evidence of convergence" – include a dynamic component.

11.4.1   European HRM is different

As we have seen, there have been claims to identify a unique European model of HRM. The conceptual arguments have been outlined in Section 11.2 of this paper (see Brewster 1995b). Empirically, however, it is not easy to demonstrate convincingly that HR practices in Europe and the US (or, indeed, elsewhere) are clearly different, the main reason being a lack of adequate comparable data. Nevertheless, considerable evidence points in the direction of a distinctive European approach.

First, the legal environment relevant for HRM differs considerably between the US and Europe. Undeniably, even within Europe large differences exist between countries with a lot of labour related regulations like the German speaking area and comparatively less regulated countries like, for example, Ireland or the UK. Yet, clearly, the density of labour regulations is higher in Europe than in the US (Grubb/Wells 1993).

Second, the main actors in industrial relations have a different role in Europe and the US. Trade unions and employers' associations have more members and more influence in the former. The role of collective bargaining and collective agreements, the influence of trade unions in the political system and their importance for management decisions are just three of the important factors.

Third, a number of studies examining specific aspects of HRM point towards important differences between Europe and the US. These would include aspects like skill-level and available types of qualifications in the work force (Mason/Finegold

1997), the role of human resource development professionals (Nijhof/de Rijk 1997) and managerial attitude towards employees' participation in decision making (McFarlin *et al.*, 1992),

Fourth, and maybe especially relevant, is a situation where US and European views of HRM encounter each other directly: in the case of subsidiaries of US multinationals in Europe. Multinationals and their subsidiaries seem to play a special role in the diffusion of practices and know-how in HRM (see, e.g. Ferner 1997; Gooderham *et al.*, 1998; Müller 1998). The subsidiaries of US multinationals are different from indigenous organisations or multinationals from other countries which, by and large, adapt more to the local environment. US multinationals not only seem to have a rather ethnocentric approach to international HRM, with little re-transfer of best practices from their overseas operations, but are also particularly proactive in searching to by-pass local conditions that they see as constraints (Ferner 1997; Gooderham *et al.*, 1999). These are indicators for differences between how HRM is understood and implemented in the US and in Europe.

11.4.2   *Great variety of HR practices in European countries*

When "zooming in" towards HR practices in specific European countries, it becomes clear that in all major functional areas there are significant differences between European countries. Practices from four core functional areas of HR – organisational role, recruitment and selection, staffing, compensation – can serve as examples:

- formal representation of the HR function at the highest board of the organisation and the stage at which HR is involved in the development of corporate strategy – as indicators of its role and importance;
- the use of internal mechanisms for filling managerial vacancies – as an indicator of recruitment approaches for crucial parts of the work force;
- the proportion of workforce on part-time contracts – as an indicator of the configuration of the work force;
- the proportion of the annual salaries and wage bill spent on training and development – as an indicator of the importance of well-qualified labour.

When looking at these issues, the following picture emerges (see Table 11.1):

Without going into the detail – and the problematic – of such comparisons, the table illustrates a remarkable degree of difference: what is widespread or standard practice in one country plays little or no role in others.

11.4.3   *Frequent stasis*

We live in a world of full of change. The accepted wisdom is that individuals and organisations have – ideally: as quickly and as smoothly as possible – to adapt to ever changing contextual conditions. Massive change drivers like globalisation and the diminishing importance of national barriers, growing competitive pressures and

Table 11.1   Differences in HR practices in Europe[3]

	EU average	Highest	Lowest
Formal representation of HR function at the highest board	54.5	88.2 (F)	29.9 (P)
Involved in development of corporate strategy			
• From the outset	58.1	72.0 (I)	43.5 (NL)
• Through consultation	24.1	40.7 (P)	14.5 (Fin)
• On implementation	10.2	28.6 (Gr)	3.8 (S)
• Not Consulted	7.6	19.8 (A)	0.7 (F)
Internal recruiting			
• Senior Management	52.0	65.9 (GR)	7 (DK)
• Middle Management	76.3	82.0 (A)	62.4 (P)
• Junior Management	61.7	81.3 (S)	31.2 (F)
Proportion of workforce on non-standard contracts (part-time)			
• No part-timers employed	7.4	68.7 (P)	0 (NL)
• >10% of part-timers	24.9	63.3 (NL)	2.3 (P)
Proportion of annual salaries and wage bill spent on T&D			
• <1%	12.9	26.3 (I)	0.3 (F)
• 1–1.9%	27.3	42.0 (E)	7.8 (F)
• 2–2.9%	20.1	31.2 (DK)	12.1 (P)
• 3–4.9%	19.4	37.5 (F)	9.6 (E)
• 5–9.9%	15.6	31.1 (F)	1.8 (I)
• >10%	4.9	9.3 (P)	1.5 (FIN)

A = Austria; DK = Denmark; E = Spain; F = France; Fin = Finland;
  Gr = Greece; I = Italy; NL = Netherlands; P = Portugal; S = Sweden

virtualisation trigger new forms of organisations, work and careers. Indeed, *prima facie* plausibility and singular, eclectic evidence both seem to confirm the dictum of ubiquitous change.

However, Cranet's empirical results seem to be in striking contrast to such a dictum. In the area of European HRM, stability and little change seem to be not the exception but rather the rule. To be sure, this does not mean that everything stays exactly the same. Yet, very often even in areas where one might expect change (even the academics are seemingly caught up in the "change-frenzy" often generated by consultants or idealised cases), the data remain unclear or even point in the opposite direction. Let us look at three examples.

The question of *evaluation of HR departments* has been widely discussed in recent years. Due to an increasing pressure on all units not directly adding value, HR departments and their work are under close scrutiny, the acid test for HR being: is it worth it? The need to prove a contribution to the overall organisational performance leads to a growth in the formal evaluation of HR activities. Given this background, one would expect a sharp increase in the number of HR departments that are regularly and formally evaluated.

Table 11.2 HR departments formally evaluated (per cent of organisations)

Year	1989	1991	1992/93	1995/96	1999/2000
%	46.0	41.0	44.0	47.8	42.0
N	3773	4172	3397	3996	4991

Table 11.3 Importance of training and development – average training days per year by employee category

Year	1991	1992/93	1995/96	1999/2000
Management	6.7	6.6	6.0	6.0
Professional	6.6	6.4	6.2	6.4
Clerical	4.1	4.3	3.9	4.2
Manual	4.5	4.7	4.2	4.5

The empirical reality challenges these expectations. Our analyses use 18 European countries (i.e. all EU before the latest enlargement in 2004 except Luxemburg, with Germany split into the old and the new federal provinces, and in addition Turkey, Switzerland and the Czech Republic). Overall, for 20,610 private sector organisations with more than 200 employees appropriate data were available for the decade between 1989 and 2000.[4] For the longitudinal analyses only variables were included where identical or nearly identical questions were available for all survey rounds.

Across the surveyed countries there is no clear trend when looking at core variables for which a longitudinal analysis is possible. Several examples can illustrate this.

A first example is the degree to which HR departments are formally evaluated. When looking at the developments in this respect, the picture shown in Table 11.2 emerges.

Obviously some change occurs, but these changes do not all reflect any clear trend or a significant development into one direction or the other. Of course, this does not say anything about changes at the level of the individual country or organisation. Analysing aggregate data at the overall European level averages out such changes. But it provides a "bird's-eye" view of the overall situation across Europe.

A second example is *the importance of training and development measures.* Given the widely claimed emergence of the knowledge society, the changing demands of work processes and the increasing significance of a well-educated work force for handling organisational transformation processes, one would expect an ever-increasing amount of training in organisations.

However, if one looks at a major indicator for training and development activities – the number of training days per year for various groups of employees – no such trend whatsoever is discernable (see Table 11.3).

Again, a certain amount of variation is visible. However, nothing points in the expected direction. Practices seem to be quite stable.

A final example refers to *the role of the HR function* and its relationship to line management. The notion of a general decentralisation of HRM might leads us to expect that parts of the responsibility as well as the operational tasks will be shared with line management. Hence, the percentage of European companies devolving HRM responsibility away from specialists towards line management should have been increasing through the decade.

However, again, the data does not support such a hypothesis. The mean value of a composite index indicating the relative distribution of responsibility between HR specialists and line management reveals little momentum over time. Indeed, there is a slight tendency towards centralisation – on average 0.15 points per year between 1989/90 and 1999/2000, on a scale ranging from 5 to 20. In only two countries are there statistically significant changes, in all the other countries the changes are not significant and are as likely to go towards greater centralisation as greater decentralisation (for a more in depth discussion of these findings see Mayrhofer *et al.*, 2002; Larsen/Brewster 2003; Mayrhofer *et al.*, 2004).

These three examples were deliberately chosen from areas where one would, relying on "received wisdom," expect obvious changes. But even in such areas stability seems more common than change. Hence, one would not be surprised to find little variation in other areas. In fact, many of the areas researched by Cranet are remarkably stable in their development. Overall, the absence of change is an important part of the European picture.

Of course, in exploring these three examples a number of difficulties like the operationalisation of the variables or the problem of multi-level phenomena have to be kept in mind. Nevertheless, we would argue that if organisational practices had changed dramatically, the data would – notwithstanding research imperfections – reflect these changes. Put simply, they do not.

However, there is some evidence of change and the issue of convergence or divergence of HR practices in Europe still is open for debate

11.4.4 Some evidence of convergence

There are, perhaps, at least some first hints about areas of convergence in some aspects of the Cranet data. Our analyses focus on practices in various functional areas of HR that do seem to show signs of such changes. We want to analyse the effects of major change drivers – whether cultural, institutional or the market: do they lead to converging or diverging developments? For the analyses, the sample briefly described above from the 18 European countries was used.[5]

Directional convergence
Developments towards directional convergence in Europe can be found in four areas (more details and tables in Mayrhofer *et al.*, 2004):

- decreases in the size of the HR department relative to the overall work force;
- slight rises in the percentage of the annual salaries and wage bill spent on training (which, of course, may reflect a growing disparity between wage growth and the growing costs of training rather than a 'real' growth in the amount of training);

- increases in the amount of information being given to employees about company strategy and financial performance; and
- a more frequent use of performance related compensation systems.

In all these cases, the change in the average developments over all countries is statistically significant, all statistically significant changes at the country level point in the same direction and are compatible with the average development, and the majority of the non-significant changes at the country level are in the same direction as the significant changes overall and at the country level.

In all other patterns of practices analysed – the use of flexible work arrangements, the level at which the HR policy is determined and the responsibility shift from HR departments to line managers – the evidence is mixed or rather weak. Although there are some indications of converging developments, the empirical evidence is by no means clear and, therefore, we choose to be cautious in our claims.

Final convergence

Overall, the evidence for all the HR practices analysed is clear: there is no unequivocal trend towards final convergence. On the contrary, developments across European countries diverged during the 1990s, having a maximum point of convergence mostly around the middle of the decade rather than at the end (see Table 11.4 and, for a more detailed picture of the results, see Mayrhofer *et al.*, 2004). "Pure" final convergence would include a "narrowing down" of differences between European countries indicating a more common practice in the various countries. For the first part of the '90s, this is the case in some areas such as the use of variable and performance related elements of compensation or the use of flexible working practices. However, between the mid-'90s and the end of the '90s, the heterogeneity of HR practices in Europe increased again. Instead of a decrease of variety (in other words, final convergence, i.e., a movement towards a common or more similar 'endpoint'), the data shows increased divergence.

11.5   Concluding Remarks and Open Questions

Overall, how are we to understand the evidence in the light of the conceptual and empirical considerations? Neither the emergence of a European model of HRM nor the great variety of HR practices in European organisations comes as a big surprise. Conceptual as well as other empirical work has indicated this before. The empirical work reported here corroborates previous insight and puts new nuances to it. The empirical data show that in very "traditional" areas of HR country differences do continue to exist. Given the current situation within Europe this is again not very surprising. Despite the increasing common elements in the legislative framework of the EU countries, the access countries and even countries such as Switzerland that for a number of reasons make efforts to harmonise their legal system with essential legislative rules of the EU, country differences in institutional terms still matter. The role of trade unions and works councils, the level of safety and health regulations or

Table 11.4   Directional convergence (yearly change)

	Level of policy determination	Distribution of responsibility between HR department and line management	Relative size of HR department
Range and explanation of scales	Scale range: 0–5	Scale range: 5–20	
	0 The policy in all five major HR areas is determined by (international) headquarter	5 HR department is primarily responsible for crucial decisions in all five major HR areas	Percentage
	5 The policy in all five major HR areas is determined at the subsidiary/site level	20 Line management is primarily responsible for crucial decisions in all five major HR areas	
Average value, all countries and points in time	Scale value: 2.6	Scale value: 12.6	1.5% (15 HR specialists for every 1000 employees)

Developments between 1990 and 1999 (values indicate average yearly change)

Hypotheses about developments	HR policy determined at the subsidiary/ site level	HR responsibility shifts from HR departments to line management	Relative size of HR department decreases
Austria (2)*	−0.139	+0.045	+0.017
Belgium (2)	−0.028	−0.096	+0.044
Czech Republic (2)	−0.077	−0.089	+0.039
Denmark (4)	−0.037	−0.015	−0.012
Finland (3)	−0.060	+0.003	+0.014
France (5)	−0.062	−0.151	−0.024
Germany - East (3)	−0.034	+0.038	+0.065*
Germany - West (5)	−0.147	−0.027	+0.004
Great Britain (5)	−0.045	−0.039	+0.010
Greece (2)	−0.142	−0.150	+0.095
Ireland (3)	0.000	+0.130*	+0.018
Netherlands (4)	−0.035	+0.029	+0.021
Norway (4)	−0.041	+0.199 *	+0.064*
Portugal (2)	−0.032	−0.077	+0.044 *
Spain (5)	+0.011	−0.175	+0.038 *
Sweden (5)	−0.087	+0.064 *	+0.004
Switzerland (3)	−0.019	+0.034	+0.015
Turkey (3)	+0.142 *	+0.005	+0.022
Average of developments, all countries	−0.046	−0.015	+0.026 *
Proportion of countries with developments/ statistically significant developments according to hypotheses	11%	50%	89%

(Continued)

Table 11.4   (Continued) Training and development, communication with employees, compensation system and flexible work

	Proportion of annual salaries and wages bill spent on training	Information to employees about company strategy and financial performance (Scale: 0–8)	Compensation system includes variable/ performance related elements (Scale: 0–16)	Use of flexible work arrangements (Scale: 0–4)
Range and explanation of scales	percentage	Scale range: 0–4 0 none of the four groups of employees is informed 8 all of the four groups of employees are informed	Scale range: 0–16 0 none of the four groups of employees has variable/performance related compensation elements 16 all of the four groups of employees have variable/performance related compensation elements	Scale range: 0–4 0 none of four flexible work arrangements is used 4 all of four flexible work arrangements are used
Average value, all countries and points in time	3.1% (3.1% of the annual salaries and wages bill is spent on training)	Scale value: 4.8	Scale value: 3.9	Scale value: 2.1

(Continued)

the amount of regulation of the labour markets are just a few prominent examples of these institutional differences. Clearly more exciting from our point of view are the findings that deal with the more dynamic element of developments over time. In some circumstances, the absence of change is remarkable. The development or, more precisely, the non-development of various areas of HR are such a remarkable instance. As shown above, the data imply a relative constant picture during the 1990s. This is a clear antidote to the "change frenzy" that has infiltrated much of scientific and practitioner oriented writing about the situation in Europe. Combined with the previous point about the heterogeneity of the stable picture, this is a further attack on the messages of "ultimate solutions," "best-practices" that lead to organisational success and related models (Marchington/Grugulis 2000).

Table 11.4　(Continued) Developments between 1990 and 1999 (values indicate average yearly change)

Hypotheses about developments	Increasing investment into training and development	More information to employees about company strategy and financial performance	More use of compensation systems including variable/ performance elements	More use of flexible working arrangements
Austria (2)*	+0.061	+0.142 *	+0.086	+0.010
Belgium (2)	+0.209 *	−0.111	+0.012	+0.054 *
Czech Republic (2)	+0.060	+0.026	−0.204	−0.045
Denmark (4)	−0.005	+0.027	+0.032	+0.127 *
Finland (3)	+0.067	+0.044	+0.218 *	+0.026 *
France (5)	+0.069 *	+0.062 *	+0.540 *	+0.044 *
Germany – East (3)	−0.044	+0.061 *	+0.167 *	+0.090 *
Germany – West (5)	+0.028	+0.091 *	+0.103 *	+0.059 *
Great Britain (5)	+0.005	+0.079 *	−0.026	−0.004
Greece (2)	+0.195	+0.053	+0.220 *	−0.061
Ireland (3)	+0.101	−0.050	+0.040	−0.016
Netherlands (4)	+0.192 *	+0.082 *	+0.214 *	+0.063 *
Norway (4)	+0.182 *	−0.062	+0.055	+0.045 *
Portugal (2)	+0.214 *	+0.046	−0.128	+0.054 *
Spain (5)	+0.043	+0.132 *	+0.063 *	−0.103
Sweden (5)	+0.023	+0.127 *	+0.010	+0.016
Switzerland (3)	+0.190 *	+0.146 *	+0.117 *	+0.070 *
Turkey (3)	+0.072	+0.052	+0.065 *	−0.082
Average of developments, all countries	+0.092 *	+0.053 *	+0.088 *	+0.019
Proportion of countries with developments/ statistically significant developments according to hypotheses	89%	83%	83%	67%

* The values in brackets indicate the number of measurement points in time
* Significant regression coefficient at the .05 level, one-tailed test of hypotheses

The frequent stasis does not rule out change and even convergent developments. As was shown, there are some areas where at least directional convergence occurs. A closer look shows that directional convergence, that is the movement of a variable into the same direction, for example: more frequent use of certain instruments, occurs in areas where there is a clear and "overwhelming" pressure coming from various sources. If economic necessities, institutional requirements and/or management folklore point in the same direction, then a more or less consistent trend can be seen. The reduction in the comparative size of the HR department or the increasing amount of money spent for training and development measures can be mentioned as examples of this. Here, at least the mentioned sources seem to be supporting factors for the observable developments. One might speculate that only the joint appearance of a variety of factors pointing in the same direction has a measurable impact on the European landscape of HR. In all other cases, not much changes besides the rhetoric.

To be sure, this is not to say that HR stays the same at the level of the single organisation. However, without the combined effects of various sources we seem to experience replacement effects. It is likely that as some companies move in one direction, others move in the opposite one. The combined effect would be an observation of little change at the aggregate level of HR practices across countries.

In general, it seems clear that we need a more nuanced view of convergence in HRM policies and practices than has been apparent hitherto. Clearly, there are differences between European countries and, in turn, overall they differ from the general picture of HRM presented in the US literature. However, things appear to change slowly in HRM and perhaps the decade-long data presented here examines too short a period. From a directional convergence point of view, there seems to be at least some positive indication of convergence in some areas. However, looking at final convergence, things become more blurred. None of the HR practices converge at the end of the decade. Rather, the maximum point of convergence is reached in the middle of the decade with signs of divergence after that.

These broad conclusions leave us with a number of open questions:

- How are we to handle unresolved methodological questions, such as whether to measure HRM at local, national or regional levels? Which aspects of HRM to measure? What techniques to employ? and so on.
- What determines whether stasis, convergence or divergence occurs?
- What is a sufficient and appropriate time segment over which to measure convergence or divergence?

To answer these questions or at least have more insight, more evidence and more analysis, as so often, is clearly needed. Cranet members are committed to continuing the work they have started and a new round of the survey is currently underway. In addition, the Cranet network continues to expand, taking in more and more new countries. Other networks, such as the GLOBE network (House *et al.*, 2004), taking different approaches to these and related topics, will also add to our understanding. Support or challenge to these findings will also continue to be forthcoming from the groups applying more case study based and qualitative methods. There is much scope for expanding our understanding of comparative differences in HRM and how they are developing. It is a difficult, but worthwhile, task.

NOTES

1.   Our discussion here, for various reasons, including lack of space, is limited to convergence at the national level. Whilst we believe our analysis would have value with reference to

convergence or divergence at sectoral, size, interdependence and other levels, we leave that for future articles.

2. A third type of convergence – majority convergence – occurs if a population of organisations in a country becomes more homogeneous or heterogeneous, respectively, in the use of a certain management concept or tool. For example, if 50% of the organisations in a country use a specific management tool and 50% do not, one can assume maximum divergence within a country since there is a clear 'split' in the concrete use of this tool. In more general terms: the closer a value in a country has moved to the 50% level, the greater the majority divergence has become. Vice versa, the more the value approaches the 100% or 0% level, the greater the majority convergence has become. However, since within country comparisons are not the focus of this contribution we ignore this form of convergence here.

3. This analysis was made for those countries in the EU in 2000 only.

4. For a fuller description of the sample and the methodology see Müller *et al.*, 2001.

5. For a more detailed discussion about the methodology applied and the detailed results see Müller *et al.*, 2001; Mayrhofer *et al.*, 2002; Mayrhofer *et al.*, 2004.

REFERENCES

Adler, N. J. (1983): A Typology of Management Studies Involving Culture. In: *Journal of International Business Studies*, 14(1): 29–47.

Adler, N. J. (2002): International dimensions of organizational behavior. 4. Cincinnati, Ohio.

Adler, N. J./Jelinek, M. (1986): Is "organizational culture" culture bound? In: *Human Resource Management*, 25(1): 73–90.

Bean, R./Holden, L. (1992): Cross national differences in trade union membership in OECD countries. In: *Industrial Relations Journal*, 23(1): 52–9.

Beaumont, P. B. (1991a): Trade unions and HRM. In: *Industrial Relations Journal*, 22(4): 300–8.

Beaumont, P. B. (1991b): The US Human Resource Management Literature: A Review. In: Salaman, G. (ed.): Human Resource Strategies. The Open University.

Beer, M./Spector, B./Lawrence, P. R./Mills, D. Q./Walton, R. E. (1985): Human Resource Management New York, London.

Boxall, P. (1995): Building the theory of comparative HRM. In: *Human Resource Management Journal*, 5(5): 5–17.

Brewster, C. (1993): Developing a "European" model of human resource management. In: *International Journal of Human Resource Management*, 4(4): 765–84.

Brewster, C. (1994): European HRM: Reflection of, or Challenge to, the American Concept? In: Kirdbride, P. S. (ed.): Human Resource Management in Europe. London, 56–89.

Brewster, C. (1995a): IR and HRM: a subversive European model. In: *Industrielle Beziehungen*, 2(4): 395–413.

Brewster, C. (1995b): Towards a "European" model of human resource management. In: *Journal of International Business Studies*, 26(1): 1–21.

Brewster, C. (1999): Different Paradigms in Strategic HRM: questions raised by comparative research. In: Wright, P./Dyer, L./Boudreau, J./Milkovich, G. (eds.): Research in Personnel and HRM. Greenwich, Connecticut: 213–38.

Brewster, C./Hegewisch, A. (eds.) (1994): Policy and Practice in European Human Resource Management. The Price Waterhouse Cranfield Survey. London, New York.

Brewster, C./Larsen, H. H. (2000): The Northern European dimension. a distinctive environment for HRM. In: Brewster, C./Larsen, H. H. (eds.): Human Resource Management in Northern Europe. Routledge, Oxford: 24–38.

Brewster, C./Mayrhofer, W./Morley, M. (eds.) (2000): New Challenges in European Human Resource Management. Macmillan, London.

Brewster, C./Mayrhofer, W./Morley, M. (eds.) (2004): Human Resource Management in Europe. Evidence of convergence? Butterworth Heinemann, London.

Brewster, C./Tregaskis, O. (2001): Adaptive, reactive and inclusive organisational approaches to workforce flexibility in Europe. In: *Comportamento Organizacional e Gestão*, X(2): 209–32.

Brewster, C./Tregaskis, O. (2003): Convergence or divergence of contingent employment practices? Evidence of The Role of MNCs in Europe. In: Cooke, W. (ed.): *Multinational Companies and Global Human Resource Strategies*. Quorum Books, Greenwood, Ill.

Brewster, C./Tregaskis, O./Hegewisch, A./Mayne, L. (1996): Comparative research in human resource management: a review and an example. In: *The International Journal of Human Resource Management*, 7(3): 585–604.

Brewster, C./Tyson, S. (eds.) (1991): International comparisons in human resource management. Blackwell, London.

Brislin, R. W. (ed.) (1976): Translation Applications and Research. Sage, New York.

Brislin, R. W./Lonner, W. J./Thorndike, R. M. (1973): Cross-cultural research methods. Blackwell, London.

Brunstein, I. (ed.) (1995): Human Resource Management in Western Europe. de Gruyter, Berlin.

Cavusgil, S. T./Das, A. (1997): Methodological Issues in Empirical Cross-cultural Research: A Survey of the management literature and a framework. In: *Management International Review*, 37(1): 71–96.

Chandler Jr., A. D. (1962): Strategy and Structure. Boston.

Chandler Jr., A. D. (1977): The Visible Hand. The Managerial Revolution in American Business: Harvard University Press, Cambridge.

Chandler Jr., A. D./Daems, H. (eds.) (1980): Managerial Hierarchies: Comparative Perspectives on the Rise of the Modern Industrial Enterprise. MIT Press, Cambridge

Cox, C./Cooper, G. (1985): The irrelevance of American organisational sciences to the UK and Europe. In: *Journal of General Management*, 11(2): 27–34.

Davison, S. C. (1996): Leading and facilitating international teams. In: Berger, M. (ed.): Cross-Cultural Team Building. London *et al.*: 158–79.

DiMaggio, P. J./Powell, W. W. (1983): The Iron Cage revisited: institutional isomorphism and collective rationality in organizational fields. In: *American Sociological Review*, 48: 147–60.

Djelic, M.-L./Bensedrine, J. (2001): Globalisation and its limits: the making of international regulation. In: Morgan, G./Kristensen, P. H./Whitley, R. (eds.): The Multinational Firm. Oxford: 258–80.

Due, J./Madsen, J. S./Jensen, C. S. (1991): The social dimension: convergence or diversification of IR in the single European market? In: *Industrial Relations Journal*, 22(2): 85–102.

Ely, R. J./Thomas, D. A. (2001): Cultural diversity at work: The effects of diversity perspectives on work group processes and outcomes. In: *Administrative Science Quarterly*, 46(2): 229–74.

Erez, M./Somech, A. (1996): Is group productivity loss the rule or the exception? Effects of culture and group-based motivation. In: *Academy of Management Journal*, 39(6): 1513–37.

Ferner, A. (1997): Country of origin effects and HRM in multinational companies. In: *Human Resource Management Journal*, 7(1): 19–38.

Filella, J. (1991): Is there a Latin model in the management of human resources? In: *Personnel Review*, 20(6): 14–23.

Fombrun, C. J./Tichy, N./Devanna, M. A. (1984): Strategic Human Resource Management. New York et al.

Friedrichs, J. (1973): Methoden empirischer Sozialforschung. Reinbek b. Hamburg.

Gannon, M. J. (2001): Cultural Metaphors – Readings, Research Translations, and Commentary. Thousand Oaks, London, New Delhi.

Garten, J. E. (1993): A Cold Peace: America, Japan and Germany and the Struggle for Supremacy. New York.

Geppert, M./Williams, K./Matten, D. (2003): The social construct of contextual rationalities in MNCs: and Anglo-German comparison of subsidiary choice. In: Journal of Management Studies, 40(3): 617–41.

Gooderham, P./Brewster, C. (2003): Convergence, stasis or divergence? The case of personnel management in Europe. In: Beta, 17(1): 6–18.

Gooderham, P./Nordhaug, O./Ringdal, K. (1998): When in Rome, do they do as the Romans? HRM practices of US subsidiaries in Europe. In: Management International Review, 38(2): 47–64.

Gooderham, P./Nordhaug, O./Ringdal, K. (1999): Institutional and rational determinants of organizational practices: human resource management in European firms. In: Administrative Science Quaterly, 44: 507–31.

Grubb, D./Wells, W. (1993): Employment regulation and patterns of work in EC countries. In: OECD Economic Studies, (21): 7–58.

Guest, D. E. (1990): Human resource management and the American dream. In: Journal of Management Studies, 27(4): 377–97.

Hall, P. A./Soskice, D. (2001): An introduction to the varieties of capitalism. In: Soskice, D. (ed.): Varieties of Capitalism: The Institutional Foundations of Comparative Advantage. New York.

Harzing, A.-W./Sorge, A. (2003): The relative impact of country of origin and universal contingencies on internationalization strategies and corporate control in multinational enterprises: worldwide and European perspectives. In: Organization Studies, 24(2): 187–214.

Hegewisch, A. (1991): The decentralisation of pay bargaining: European comparisons. In: Personnel Review, 20(6): 28–35.

Hofstede, G. (1980): Culture's Consequence. International Differences in Work-Related Values. Newbury Park.

Hollingsworth, J. R./Boyer, R. (eds.) (1997a): Contemporary Capitalism. Cambridge.

Hollingsworth, J. R./Boyer, R. (eds.) (1997b): Coordination of economic actors and social systems of production. In: Contemporary Capitalism. Cambridge.

Hollinshead, G./Leat, M. (1995): Human Resource Management – An International and Comparative Perspective on the Employment Relationship. London.

Holzmüller, H. H. (1995): Konzeptionelle und methodische Probleme in der interkulturellen Management- und Marketingforschung. Stuttgart.

House, R. J./Hanges, P. J./Ruiz-Quintanilla, S. A./Dorfman, P. W./Javidan, M./Dickson, M./Gupta, V. (1999): Cultural influences on leadership and organizations – project GLOBE. In: Advances in Global Leadership, 1: 171–233.

House, R. J./Javidan, M./Hanges, P. J./Dorfman, P. W. (2002): Understanding cultures and implicit leadership theories around the globe: an introduction to project GLOBE. In: Journal of World Business, 37: 3–10.

House, R. J./Hanges, P. J./Javidan, M. (2004): Culture, Leadership and Organizations: The GLOBE Study of 62 Societies. Thousand Oaks.

Hyman, R. (1994): Industrial relations in western Europe: an era of ambiguity? In: Industrial Relations, 33(1): 1–24.

Kamoche, K. (1996): Strategic Human Resource Management within a resource-capability view of the firm. In: *Journal of Management Studies*, 32(2): 212–33.

Kerr, C. (1983): The Future of Industrial Societies. Cambridge.

Kochan, T. A./Dyer, L./Batt, R. (1992): International human resource management studies: a framework for future research. In: Lewin, D./Mitchell, O. S./Sherer, P. D. (eds.): Research Frontiers in Industrial Relations and Human Resources, Wisconsin: 309–37.

Kochan, T. A./Katz, H. C./McKersie, R. B. (1986): The Transformation of American Industrial Relations. New York.

Kochan, T. A./McKersie, R. B./Capelli, P. (1984): Strategic choice and industrial relations. In: *Industrial Relations*, 23(1): 16–39.

Lamnek, S. (1988): Qualitative Sozialforschung. Band 1: Methodologie. München.

Larsen, H. H./Brewster, C. (2003): Line Management Responsibility for HRM: what's happening in Europe? In: *Employee Relations*, 25(3): 228–44.

Locke, R./Piore, M./Kochan, T. (eds.) (1995): Introduction. In: Employment Relations in a Changing World Economy. i–xviii.

Lueger, M. (2000): Grundlagen qualitativer Feldforschung. Wien.

Marchington, M./Grugulis, I. (2000): 'Best Practice' Human resource Management: perfect opportunity or dangerous illusion? In: *International Journal of Human Resource Management*, 11(6): 1104–24.

Mason, G./Finegold, D. (1997): Productivity, machinery and skills in the United States and western Europe. In: *National Institute Economic Review*, 162(10): 85–99.

Maurice, M./Sellier, F./Silvestre, J. (1986): The Social Foundations of Industrial Power. Cambridge, MA.

Mayrhofer, W. (1998): Between market, bureaucracy, and clan – coordination and control mechanisms in the Cranfield Network on European Human Resource Management (Cranet-E). In: *Journal of Managerial Psychology*, 13(3/4): 241–58.

Mayrhofer, W./Morley, M./Brewster, C. (2004): Convergence, stasis, or divergence? In: Brewster, C./Mayrhofer, W./Morley, M. (eds.): Human Resource Management in Europe. Evidence of Convergence? London et al.: 417–36.

Mayrhofer, W./Müller-Camen, M./Ledolter, J./Strunk, G./Erten, C. (2002): The diffusion of management concepts in Europe – conceptual considerations and longitudinal analysis. In: *Journal of Cross-Cultural Competence & Management*, 3: 315–49.

McFarlin, D. B./Sweeney, P. D./Cotton, J. L. (1992): Attitudes toward employee participation in decision-making: A comparison of European and American managers in a United States multinational company. In: *Human Resource Management*, 31(4): 363–83.

Meyer, J. W. (2000): Globalization – sources and effects on national states and societies. In: *International Sociology*, 15: 233–48.

Meyer, J. W./Rowan, B. (1983): The structure of educational organisations. In: Meyer, J. W./Scott, W. R. (eds.): Organisational Environments: Ritual and Rationality. Beverly Hills, CA: 179–97.

Morley, M./Brewster, C./Gunnigle, P./Mayrhofer, W. (1996): Evaluating change in European industrial relations: research evidence on trends at organisational level. In: *International Journal for Human Resource Management*, 7: 640–56.

Müller, M. (1998): Human resource and industrial relations practices of UK and US multinationals in Germany. In: *International Journal of Human Resource Management*, 9(4): 732–49.

Müller, M./Mayrhofer, W./Ledolter, J./Erten, C./Strunk, G. (2001): Neue Formen der Arbeitsorganisation in Europa – eine empirische Studie. In: *Journal für Betriebswirtschaft*, 51(5–6): 265–77.

Nijhof, W. J./de Rijk, R. N. (1997): Roles, competences and outputs of HRD practitioners – a comparative study in four European countries. In: *Journal of European Industrial Training*, 21(6/7): 247–58.

Oliver, C. (1991): Strategic responses to institutional processes. In: *Academy of Management Review*, 16(1): 145–79.

Pieper, R. (ed.) (1990): Human resource management: an international comparison. Berlin *et al.*

Poole, M. (1986): Industrial Relations – Origins and Patterns of National Diversity. London.

Poole, M. (1990): Human resource management in an international perspective. In: *International Journal of Human Resource Management*, 1(1): 1–15.

Popper, K. (1972): Objective Knowledge. An Evolutionary Approach. Oxford.

Przeworski, A./Spague, J. (1986): Paper Stones: A History of Editorial Socialism. Chicago.

Ronen, S. (1986): Comparative and Multinational Management. New York.

Rosenzweig, P. M./Nohria, N. (1994): Influences on human resource development practices in multinational corporations. In: *Journal of International Business Studies*, 25(1): 229–51.

Scholtz, G. (1991): Zwischen Wissenschaftsanspruch und Orientierungsbedürfnis: Zu Grundlage und Wandel der Geisteswissenschaften. Frankfurt a.M.

Schuler, R. S./Huber, C. H. (1993): Personnel and Human Resource Management. 5. St.Paul.

Schütz, A. (1981): Der sinnhafte Aufbau der sozialen Welt. Eine Einleitung in die verstehende Soziologie. 2. Frankfurt a.M.

Siebert, W. S. (1997): Overview of European labour markets. In: Addison, J. T./Siebert, W. S. (eds.): Labour Markets in Europe – Issues of Harmonization and Regulation. London: 229–40.

Soeffner, H.-G. (1989): Auslegung des Alltags – Der Alltag der Auslegung. Zur wissenssoziologischen Konzeption einer sozialwissenschaftlichen Hermeneutik. Frankfurt a.M.

Sparrow, P./Hiltrop, J. M. (1994): European Human Resource Management in transition. Hempel Hempstead.

Stephans, J. (1990): Explaining Cross – National Differences in Union Strength in Bargaining and Welfare. In: Paper presented at the XII World Congress of Sociology, Madrid, July 9–13.

Thomas, A. (1993): Kulturvergleichende Psychologie – eine Einführung. Göttingen.

Thurley, K./Wirdenius, H. (1991): Will management become "European"? Strategic choices for organisations. In: *European Management Journal*, 9(2): 127–34.

Traxler, F./Blaschke, S./Kittel, B. (2001): National Labour Relations in Internationalised Markets. A Comparative Study of Institutions, Change and Performance. Oxford.

Tregaskis, O./Mahoney, C./Atterbury, S. (2004): International Survey Methodology: Experiences from the Cranfield Network. In: Brewster, C./Mayrhofer, W./Morley, M. (eds.): European Human Resource Management – Evidence of Convergence. London.

Trompenaars, F. (1994): Riding the Waves of Culture. Understanding Diversity in Global Business. Chicago, Ill. *et al.*

Turati, C./Usai, A./Ravagnani, R. (1998): Antecedents of co-ordination in academic international project research. In: *Journal of Managerial Psychology*, 13(3/4): 188–98.

Vickerstaff, S. (ed.) (1992): Human Resource Management in Europe. London u.a.

Visser, J. (1992): Union Organisation: Why Countries Differ. In: Paper presented at the IX World Congress of the IIRA, Sydney.

Wächter, H./Peters, R./Tempel, A./Müller-Camen, M. (2003): The "Country-of-Origin-Effect" in Cross-National Management of Human Resources. München, Mering.

Whitley, R. (1999): Divergent Capitalisms: The Social Structuring and Change of Business Systems. Oxford.

Williamson, O. E. (1975): Markets and Hierarchies. New York.

Williamson, O. E. (1985): The Economic Institutions of Capitalism. New York.

Woywode, M. (2002): Global management concepts and local adaptations: working groups in the French and German manufacturing industry. In: *Organization Studies*, 23(4): 497–524.

Chapter 12

HRM in China

Fang Lee Cooke

Introduction

HRM in China is as new as its market economy, with its traditional personnel administrative system undergoing a period of profound change. This chapter first outlines the historical development in personnel management and the role of trade unions and the Workers' Congress in China. It then analyzes the legislative, social, cultural and business factors that shape the HRM practices in terms of recruitment, training, working-time arrangements and pay. This is followed by a discussion of the major changes in recent years in the HR functions such as recruitment and performance appraisal. The chapter then contemplates key challenges facing HRM in China, notably the thorny issue of motivation-performance-reward, skill shortage and its associated problems of recruitment, retention and training, and the absence of strategic HRM. The chapter finally explores the implications of all these for HRM functions in the near future.

Throughout the chapter, relatively heavy references are made to state-owned enterprises (SOEs) and public sector organizations, although the private sector will also be discussed as much as possible. This is because the state has been a major employer in the past and because SOEs and public sector organizations are the areas where HRM has experienced the most radical changes in recent years under the economic and social (welfare) reforms. This chapter will also use the term HRM in a broad sense, although the term "personnel management" is used to describe personnel administrative policies prior to the 1980s when radical economic reforms started, leading to the proliferation of business ownership in addition to the state sector. It must be noted here that, while the concept of HRM has grown in popularity in recent years, there is considerable

F. L. Cooke, "HRM in China," In *Managing Human Resources in Asia-Pacific* (Routledge: London, 2004) : 18–34.

divergence in the ways in which "human resource management" is interpreted and understood in China. However, the scope of this chapter does not warrant the space to debate the origin and various versions of the concept in detail, a task made more difficult due to the lack of such a debate among academics and practitioners in China, who tend to accept the concept uncritically as a progressive given.

Historical Development in Personnel Management in China

Personnel management in China has a 50-year history following the founding of the "New China" in 1949 under the Communist Party. For the first three decades until the end of the Cultural Revolution, the personnel management system was highly centralized by the state under the planned economy regime. Personnel management during this period exhibited two major features in terms of its governance structure and content of the personnel policy.

First, the personnel policies and practices of organizations were strictly under the control of the state through regional/local labor departments. Centralization, formalization and standardization of the personnel policies and practices were the primary tasks of the Ministry of Labor (for blue-collar workers) and the Ministry of Personnel (for white-collar and managerial staff). The state not only determined the number of people to be employed and sources of recruitment, but also unilaterally set the pay scales for different categories of workers. State intervention also extended to the structure and obligations of the personnel functions at organizational level and managers of all levels were only involved in the administrative function and policy implementation under rigid policy guidelines (Child, 1994; Cooke, 2003a).

Second, for most people, entering employment was a "once-in-a-lifetime" event with "lifelong" job security. Wages were typically low but compensated by a broad range of workplace welfare provisions, including housing, pension, health, children's schooling, transportation to and from work, employment for spouses and school-leaving children, as part of the responsibility of the "nanny" employer (Warner, 1996a; Cooke, 2000).

These characteristics were once dominant in the personnel management system of the country because, until the 1980s, the vast majority of the Chinese employing organizations were state-owned, with a minority being collectively-owned and even fewer, privately-owned (see Table 12.1).

Today, four broad types of business ownership coexist in China's economic regime with the latter three rapidly gaining larger proportions:

1. state-owned enterprises;
2. collectively-owned enterprises in cities, townships and rural areas;
3. privately-owned firms and self-employed businesses;
4. foreign businesses, Sino-foreign joint ventures, and Sino-foreign cooperative enterprises (including investment from Hong Kong, Macao and Taiwan).

Table 12.1   Employment statistics by ownership in urban and rural areas in China* (figures in 100,000)

Ownership	1978	1980	1985	1990	1995	1998	2001
Number of employed in urban areas	951.4	1052.5	1280.8	1661.6	1909.3	2067.8	2394.0
State-owned units	745.1	801.9	899.0	1034.6	1126.1	905.8	764.0
Collectively-owned units	204.8	242.5	332.4	354.9	314.7	196.3	129.1
Cooperative units	—	—	—	—	—	13.6	15.3
Joint ownership units	—	—	3.8	9.6	5.3	4.8	4.5
Limited liability corporations	—	—	—	—	—	48.4	84.1
Share-holding corporations	—	—	—	—	31.7	41.0	48.3
Private enterprises	—	—	—	5.7	48.5	97.3	152.7
Units with funds from Hong Kong, Macao and Taiwan	—	—	—	0.4	27.2	29.4	32.6
Foreign funded units	—	—	0.6	6.2	24.1	29.3	34.5
Self-employed individuals	1.5	8.1	45.0	61.4	156.0	225.9	213.1
Number of employed in rural areas	3063.8	3183.6	3706.5	4729.3	4885.4	4927.9	4908.5
Township and village enterprises	282.7	300.0	697.9	926.5	1286.2	1253.7	1308.6
Private enterprises	—	—	—	11.3	47.1	73.7	118.7
Self-employed individuals	—	—	—	149.1	305.4	385.5	262.9

Sources: Figures for 1978–1998 come from *China Statistical Abstract* (2000), Beijing: China Statistics Press, p. 37; figures for 2001 come from *China Statistical Yearbook* (2002), Beijing: China Statistics Press, p. 117.

*Since 1990, data on economically active population, the total employed persons and the sub-total of employed persons in urban and rural areas have been adjusted in accordance with the data obtained from the 5th National Population Census. As a result, the sum of the data by region, by ownership or by sector is not equal to the total (original note from *China Statistical Yearbook*, 2002, p. 117).

The changing composition structure of business ownership since the 1980s with the shrinking share of state ownership and the rapid growth of private and foreign-related firms undoubtedly has major implications for the patterns of personnel management and industrial relations at a macro level (see discussion below). In addition, the state sector has witnessed radical changes in its personnel policy and practice in the last two decades, as part of the Economic Reforms and the Enterprise Reforms beginning in the early 1980s. One of the major changes has been the rolling back of direct state control and the consequent increase of autonomy and responsibility at enterprise level in major aspects of personnel management practice. This change was accompanied by a series of state-driven personnel initiatives which sent shock waves to individual employees as well as to the country's economy as a whole.

The objective of these initiatives was to bring to an end the planned state economy characterized by "high employment rate," "high welfare," "low wage" and "low productivity" and to introduce the market economy "with Chinese characteristics" in which competition and incentive were two major ingredients. As a result, rapid and fundamental changes in the Chinese HRM policies have taken place during the 1980s and especially the 1990s (Easterby-Smith *et al.*, 1995).

In particular, the "three systems" reforms have been implemented in most (state-owned) organizations since the mid-1990s. These include: fixed duration individual and collective labor contracts instead of jobs-for-life; new remuneration systems to reflect performance, post and skill levels; and new welfare schemes in which all employers and employees are required by law to make a contribution to five separate funds: pension, industrial accident, maternity, unemployment and medical insurance (Warner, 1996a, 1999). The new welfare system is intended to shift the huge welfare burden from the (state) employers towards individual employees.

Employment contracts were introduced for both managerial workers and ordinary workers to replace the old system in which managers were appointed by their superiors and workers were employed for life. The rationale of this contract system was to allow greater freedom for both organizations and individuals in entering and/or terminating their employment relationship. It also reduced the job security of individuals so that they would be more motivated to work and to update their skill. It should be pointed out here that all employers are now required by the Labor Law of China (1995) to sign an employment contract with their workers, by adapting a standardized employment contract provided by the local labor authority to each specific post. While the initial intention of introducing the employment contract in SOEs was to increase motivation by removing job security, the purpose of signing employment contracts in the private firms is primarily to protect individual workers against irresponsible employers who may try to evade their responsibilities as employers. Many of these workers come from rural areas and have little knowledge of their employment rights. According to the Labor Law (1995), the employment contract should include: length of contract, work content, health and safety protection and working conditions, remuneration, discipline, conditions for termination of contract, and liability for violating the employment contract.

In SOEs and public sector organizations, a system called "competing for the post" was also introduced in the mid-1990s in which employees would be assessed (through tests) once a year on their competence to work (Cooke, 2000, 2004b). Those who came last would be laid off and further training would be given to increase their competence while they were waiting for a post. This system has effectively injected an element of job insecurity which serves as an incentive for the employees to become more competitive by "up-skilling" themselves.

The State Economy Commission issued a document in 2001 (No. [2001] 230) which required SOEs to deepen the above "three systems" reforms by placing them as their top priority. The document reasserts that SOEs are required to establish a system in which managerial workers should compete for their posts with both upward and downward mobility. SOEs are also required to establish an independent employment system without interference from other bodies. Employment contracts are signed and employees need to compete for their post through competency tests. Finally, SOEs are required to establish a reward system which provides greater links between (individual) performance and reward as a motivational mechanism.

Many of the above changes in the state-owned sectors were initiated by the state and carried out at organizational level from the top down, with little involvement from trade unions and employees. These changes also took place alongside the most radical change in the SOEs in the last decade: downsizing. Started in the early 1990s as part of the program of restructuring and revitalizing the outmoded SOEs, this initiative reached its peak in the late 1990s after Premier Zhu Rongji's announcement of his SOE reform plan in 1997. This reform program included plans to make 10 million workers redundant within three years through early retirement and performance review. Laid-off workers were expected to receive re-training for re-employment, a process in which the trade union was able to play a more visible role.

Partnership in HRM

Only one trade union – the All China Federation of Trade Unions (ACFTU) – is recognized in China, with its formal national union structure dating back to the early 1920s in support of the Communist Party revolution. The current structure of the Chinese trade union organization has not changed drastically since 1949 (Warner, 1990), although there has been an expansion of union membership as urbanization has drawn more workers into industry (Ng and Warner, 1998). Drawing their membership from all sorts of occupations and sectors including manual and non-manual workers in factories, hospitals, schools and universities, the trade unions do not have any distinctive "trade" characteristics, as they all belong to the same "father" – ACFTU. Two major pieces of legislation provide the legal framework for the role of the union: the Trade Union Law (1950), which was replaced by the recently amended Trade Union Law (2001) in response to the rapid growth of the private sector, and the Labor Law (1995).

Traditionally, SOEs in China, which employ the majority of the workforce, have been the patron of the workers' welfare, as mentioned above. In the communist system in which labor and capital are perceived to share the same interests, trade unions in the SOEs in China play only a welfare role under the leadership of the Communist Party. They carry out this function effectively by acting as a "conveyor belt" between the Communist Party and the workers (Hoffman, 1981). Although union membership level is generally high, people join trade unions by default (to be seen as supportive to the Party and to enjoy the welfare benefits) rather than by desire. In some ways, it is a form of social exclusion not to be a union member in the state sector. For example, temporary workers (many of them from rural areas) who carry out laborious and tedious work unwanted by urban workers are usually non-union members and do not share the same level of workplace benefits as permanent workers.

In theory, trade unions have been given a newly regulated monitoring role. According to the Labor Law (1995), they are to "represent and protect the legal rights and interests of workers independently and autonomously and develop their activities according to the law" and to "monitor that employing units abide by labor disciplines and regulations." In practice, this proposition rarely materialized. Past and contemporary empirical evidence hardly supports the notion of trade union autonomy in China, whether it is for trade unions in large SOEs or in private- or foreign-owned enterprises (Warner, 1995, 2001; Ng and Warner, 1998; Cooke, 2002; Ding et al., 2002). Although union organizations have a relatively strong presence in some traditional state-owned industries, such as the railway industry (Cooke, 2000), union officials in China have generally been considered unfamiliar with the western style of collective bargaining, "with their serious lack of the necessary back-up bargaining resources, skills and capacities" (Warner and Ng, 1999: 307). Moreover, trade union officials in China are often in their post not because they are the best candidates for the job, but because they have appeared to be, for various reasons, "unsuccessful" in their previous managerial posts (Cooke, 2002).

Under the new ownership forms as a result of the privatization of SOEs in the 1990s, the welfare role of the state has largely disappeared. The seemingly harmonious management–labor relationship has been replaced with one characterized by conflicting interests, rising disputes and increasing inequality in contractual arrangements between management and labor. However, the role of the trade unions, or more specifically, the union officials' perception of their duties, remains little changed. They still continue to carry out their traditional functions such as organizing social events, taking care of workers' welfare, helping management to implement operational decisions, and coordinating relations between management and workers (Verma and Yan, 1995).

In the private sectors, union membership levels are far lower than those in the state sector and union activities are less popular (see Ding and Warner, 1999). Many firms do not recognize trade unions, claiming that the union's (welfare) functions are still carried out by the firm despite the absence of union organization. While labor officials often confuse the role of trade unions with that of a welfare function, demand from workers to establish a trade union may be low in part because they are unfamiliar with the concept of workplace representation but more so because of the perceived ineffectiveness of such an organization (Cooke, 2002).

According to the Labor Law (1995), the formal "representative function" of the unions is supplemented by the trade union guided Workers' Congress which is a format of workers' representation in the workplace. Initially introduced in the late 1940s, the Workers' Congress has been given an enhanced role since the 1980s as a result of the marketization programs. It has the legal right to:

> Deliberate such major issues as the policy of operations, annual and long-term plans and programmes, contract and leasing responsibility systems of management; it may approve or reject plans on wage reforms and bonus distribution as well as on important rules and regulations; it may decide on major issues concerning workers' conditions and welfare; it may appraise and supervise the leading administrative cadres at various levels and put forward suggestions for awards and punishments and their appointment and approval; and it democratically elects the director.   (Liu, 1989: 5–6)

Again, in reality, the role of the Workers' Congress remains less than effective (Benson and Zhu, 2000). The Workers' Congress is required by law to hold an annual meeting in which workers can raise issues of concerns. This, however, often does not happen. Even when it is held, it is mostly a symbolic gesture and an opportunity for a banquet party for everybody involved.

In short, there is no real "partnership" between management and the trade union or "employee voice" in the management–labor relations in China. However, the dominance of state influence in the state-owned sectors and the weak presence of trade unions in employment relations in China as a whole do not mean unilateral determination of HRM practices by the (state) employers.

Key factors determining HRM practices

Like those in other countries, HRM practices in both the state and the private sectors in China are, to a greater or lesser extent, shaped by a range of political, legal, cultural and economic factors. Major labor laws include: The Labor Law (1995), the Trade Union Law (1950, 2001), and the Provisions Concerning the Administration of the Labor Market (2000), which set out China's basic philosophy for the governance of the Labor Market. In spite of the perceived ineffectiveness of the employment regulations in China (Warner, 1996b; Cooke, 2001; Cooke and Rubery, 2002), these regulations do, at least in principle, provide a legal framework under which HRM practices, such as recruitment, training, working time and pay, should be carried out.

Regulations in recruitment are often aimed at removing gender discrimination. In recent years, external labor markets have been playing an increasingly important role in the (re)distribution of the labor resource as a result of the emergence of a market economy, sectoral restructuring, the decreasing role of the state as an employer and the consequent downsizing of its workforce. Instead of being assigned to a designated employing organization by the state when they enter employment, individuals are more likely to seek their jobs in a labor market inundated with candidates. This new way of recruitment and employment has on the one hand introduced dynamics to the country's employment system, and on the other hand brought new problems and conflicts to the system in general but more specifically to women's employment.

Although women (mostly full-time workers) make up nearly 40 percent of China's total workforce, recruitment is perhaps the most difficult barrier that women face in employment because of the current downsizing of SOEs, the mass migration of rural labor and the high unemployment rate (Cooke, 2001). Traditionally, male workers are considered to be more capable than female workers with higher participation rates, stronger adaptability, better mobility and attendance records, and a longer working life. Many employers are unwilling to recruit women because they are "inferior" to men and because of the "fuss" and cost associated with women's physiological conditions (e.g. child-bearing and caring). In order to eliminate gender discrimination, the state has issued a number of laws. These include the more recent laws such as the PRC Law on Protecting Women's Rights and Interests (1992) and the Labor Law (1995). These laws assert that men and women share the same labor rights. However, discrimination in different forms widely exists, often overtly, in the recruitment process against women who are at the higher end of the labor market as well as those who are sought for their low-cost and low-skill (Cooke, 2003a). Many job advertisements (including those issued by the public sector organizations) specify gender requirements and age limits even though the posts are suitable for both men and women, while the age limit is an attempt to avoid women job seekers of child-bearing age.

In terms of working-time arrangements, the Labor Law (1995) also specifies the number of hours (no more than 44) workers should work in a normal working week and the number of hours of overtime they should be expected to undertake (no more than 36 per month). It needs to be pointed out here that the vast majority of workers work full time in China, as part-time working is still a relatively new concept with insufficient interest from both the employers and the workers. While these working-time regulations are followed by most state sector organizations and many large private enterprises (Zhang *et al.*, 2002), they are often not adhered to by small business employers or township and village enterprises (TVEs). In general, workers in the private service sector such as retail and catering businesses work much longer hours than the norm, a situation compounded by the low level of rest days and holidays that are given to the workers. For example, Cooke's study 2005 of small retail shops found that few shops gave their workers one day per week for their rest days. Instead, the majority of shops gave their workers 2 or 3 days of rest per calendar month. Most owners did not allow their workers to take their statutory holidays, such as the Chinese New Year, because they were the busiest periods for the businesses.

In terms of training, there has always been a high level of state involvement/intervention in the training policies and practices of SOEs and public sector organizations (Cooke, 2004b). Since the start of economic reforms in 1979, a national network of Cadre Management Training Institutes has been established providing compulsory training courses for all (potential) managers (Warner, 1992). In 1981, the State Council of China stipulated that enterprises should allocate a minimum of 1.5 percent of the total wage bill as funding for employee education and training (Lu, 1987). In 1990, The Ministry of Labor issued another statutory requirement: "The Regulations for Worker's Technical Grade Examination." The examination content includes work attitude, performance and level of skill/competence. The regulations establish a system that links training, testing, deployment and remuneration together. In 1995, the "Temporary Regulations on Continuous Education for Professional and Technical Personnel in China" was introduced by the state. This is seen as an important policy document for the national continuous training, which marks the beginning of the formalization of continuous training for professional and technical staff. It specifies that all senior and middle-ranking professionals and technical staff should receive at least 40 hours of off-the-job training per year, and junior ranking staff no less than 32 hours. While these regulations provide a major momentum for (state-owned) workplace training, training provisions remain generally low and are unevenly distributed across different industries (see further discussion below).

Another factor that drives training provisions is the competitive business environment. For example, the increasing globalization of business in China has brought organizations to the recognition of the need to converge with international norms/practice. We have seen, in the last few years, a heat wave of applications of ISO 9000 quality series accreditation by many business organizations in China. This has led to an increase in training in some enterprises in order to fulfil the accreditation requirements. The accession to WTO likewise brought a tidal wave of training. One of the main reasons for the increase in the training provision in the last two years has been to do with the WTO-related legal framework. However, this training is far from sufficient for the Chinese organizations to deal with the surge of demand for WTO-related knowledge.

The pay system in China demonstrates a number of unique characteristics which differ from that in other societies, characteristics such as the egalitarian culture, the relatively heavy proportion of bonus in the total package of pay, and the significant role of workers in controlling the bonus. In Mao's era, the distribution principle was based on *the equality norm* which was "expected to lead to the best group harmony and stability" (Yu, 1998: 304). The espoused policy for employee motivation was based on moral teaching and the doctrine of "serve the people." During the Deng and now post-Deng period, bonus and perks have become the driving force. However, the basic wage is still based largely on the seniority-based egalitarian wage structure which does not reflect competence, and egalitarianism in the bonus distribution remains a key characteristic in order to maintain stability and harmonization.

Pay is perhaps the only aspect of HRM in China in which grass-root workers exert extensive control in its (even) distribution. It has been noted that the most noteworthy characteristic of the Chinese perspective on distributive fairness is one of egalitarianism. Chinese workers are said to be very sensitive and to have low tolerance toward income gaps between individuals or between different groups in the same company (Shirk, 1981; Easterby-Smith *et al.*, 1995). They regard this as potentially disruptive in collective social systems that put group harmony and social adhesion as the top priority (Yu, 1998; Cooke, 2002; Taylor, 2002).

A main feature of the pay system in the state sectors is the tension between the lack of employee input in establishing the formal wage set by the state, on the one hand, and their role in maintaining the low-earning differentials among themselves, on the other (Cooke, 2004a). While employees have little room to oppose the formal wage structure, they play a fundamental role in preserving the egalitarian and seniority culture in the distribution of bonuses and other material incentives, regardless of the relative efficiency of individuals. Attempts from the top to increase wage differentials between individuals according to performance may be mediated during implementation at the operational level.

In the private sectors, seniority and egalitarianism still remain characteristic in employees' attitude towards pay, albeit being diluted by employers' constant attempts to introduce performance-based pay and pay confidentiality, especially in joint ventures (JVs) and foreign firms. For example, Chen's Sino-American study (1995) found that Confucian values were still evident in the continued emphasis on the social hierarchy, with a higher ranking for differential rewards according to rank and seniority in the Chinese sample. While management's attempt to keep workers' bonuses confidential has been met with workforce resistance in Cooke's study (2002), resentment to widening pay differentials was felt by workers in Taylor's study (2002). However, Braun and Warner's small-scale study (2002) of multinationals in China found that the wide implementation of bonus pay systems seemed to be more accepted in Sino-western JVs. It appears that the new emphasis of Chinese employees towards an economic logic and rejection of equality-based rules is more a product of recent environmental pressure and institutional practice than any shift in underlying cultural values (Sparrow, 2000).

In short, the HRM practices are shaped, to varying degrees, by political, legal, economic and cultural factors specific to China. While there is a trend of the legal protection being extended to cover the private and informal sectors, there are also signs that the rapid growth of private businesses and joint ventures are adding forces for change in the SOEs and public sector, especially in areas such as recruitment, reward and performance management (see further discussion below).

Present changes within the HR functions

Existing studies on HRM in China suggest that personnel practices are in transition (Warner, 1998) from a highly centralized allocation process to a more market-oriented and merit-based system. This transition has strong implications for SOEs because of previous heavy influence of the state and current pressure from market competition (Zhu and Dowling, 2002). Until quite recently, the personnel function in SOEs was confined to job allocation, personnel record filing, and the provision of welfare benefits. The primary task for personnel management was to keep the employees politically and ideologically sound (Ding and Warner, 1999). Many of the HR functions which are familiar to their western counterparts were beyond the experience of personnel staff in China. However, economic reform and decentralization of decision-making in SOEs from the state have brought considerable changes to the HR functions in the state sectors. For example, Ding and Warner's study (1999) of twenty-four SOEs and JVs in four major cities found that the role of personnel managers has changed dramatically in both the SOEs and JVs. They were involved in making decisions in a range of HRM issues such as recruitment and selection, training, promotion, dismissal, reward and discipline. However, personnel management in the JVs exhibited more of the HRM characteristics than in the SOEs. While personnel departments in both SOEs and JVs had extensive involvement in training, the former still had less power than the latter in the determination of reward and disciplinary actions.

Similarly, Zhu and Dowling's study (2002) found that many traditional HR policies in China have changed and that there was clear evidence that a more complex and hybrid management model was emerging as a result of increasing levels of marketization and enterprise autonomy (Warner, 1998). For example, over half of the enterprises surveyed in Zhu and Dowling's study (2002) had written job analyses which were used for other HR activities such as HR planning, recruitment and selection and performance management. In addition, enterprises with different types of ownership all placed an emphasis on job-specific information for selection criteria, which demonstrated positive correlation with perceived effectiveness of staffing practices. Different external sources, such as advertising and the labor market, were used for recruitment purposes and more employees were hired on contractual basis. These findings all indicate some resemblance to HR practices used in advanced economies.

Recruitment and performance appraisal are perhaps the two aspects of HRM that have affected the personnel functions the most in governmental organizations as a result of the state-driven initiatives to modernize the workforce (Cooke, 2003b). There is a renewed emphasis on examination as a recruitment assessment mechanism in an attempt to block the influx of nepotism that has been a longstanding recruitment practice in governmental organizations in the past. The recruitment procedures specified by the state in the Provisional Regulations for State Civil Servants (1993) require that the whole examination and recruitment process be made public, including the exam content, procedure and result, so that the public can monitor its fairness. This is a bid for a fair and efficient system of recruitment and promotion that is transparent and competitive. Job applicants have to go through a competitive recruitment process that is ensured by intensive entrance examinations, coupled with other selection mechanisms, such as interviews and assessment centers. The regulations further specify that civil servants are required to have a formal annual assessment which includes written exams and performance record inspection. The assessment results are graded and referred to for promotion and reward. These new procedures of recruitment and performance appraisal create a considerable amount of planning and administrative work with which the recruitment personnel may not yet be familiar.

Key challenges facing HRM in China

HRM in China faces several challenges. First, Chinese enterprises in general do not have a systematic approach to HRM that is consistent with their enterprise business strategy. Second, despite the oversupply of labor, many employers are experiencing recruitment and retention problems. Third, there is a lack of an effective system which links long-term motivation and performance with reward. Fourth, there is a lack of coherence and continuity in enterprise training. The growth of human capital is obviously lagging behind that of enterprise profit. However, these problems are not encountered by the public and private sectors to the same degree. While some problems are generic to both sectors, others are more specific to the public or private sectors.

In terms of approaches to HRM, domestic private firms (many of which are very young) in China share a considerable level of similarities in the development of their HR functions. They source their HRs primarily from the labor markets, especially at the startup of their businesses. They lack a comprehensive HR strategy that provides skill training and career structure. They have not developed an organizational culture to elicit their employees' commitment and loyalty. By comparison, the state-sector organizations have a more established HR system due to the fact that they have a much longer history and have been subject to much state influence. However, many elements in their HR system have become outmoded and incompatible with recent developments in the economic environment and the labor markets. The rigidity of the HR system is also a major source of disadvantage SOEs and public sector organizations which are faced with two major problems in their HRM: how to retain and attract talent and how to motivate existing employees.

Retention of key technical staff has been a tough perennial problem encountered by many SOEs and public sector organizations in recent years. SOE workers are now much more likely to seek high wages in non-state firms (Ding *et al.*, 2001). It is believed that foreign firms and JVs have been poaching key technical personnel from SOEs. For example, an investigation by Beijing City Economy Commission of 150 large and medium-sized enterprises in Beijing on their HR composition revealed that SOEs had lost 64 percent of their university graduates since 1982 while high-tech private firms had lost 18.5 percent (Chu, 2002). It is also reported that the four major state-owned banks have lost many of their talented people to foreign banks in China in the last few years since China relaxed its policy for foreign banks to operate there (Chu, 2002). Wang and Fang (2001) found in their study of multinational companies (MNCs) in China that the vast majority of employees in these MNCs were no more than 30 years of age and over 95 percent of them possessed at least advanced diploma educational qualifications. Over 64 percent of the Chinese employees surveyed said that the most important reason for them to join MNCs was that they felt that they could utilize their talent and realize their own value. High income was the second most important reason (62.5 percent).

In the past, many SOEs and public sector organizations tried to retain their (key) staff by imposing a penalty clause in their employment contract. Those who wished to leave their employer before the prescribed number of years was fulfilled were often faced with a heavy financial penalty and their personnel file would not be released by their defiant employer. An increasingly popular method now used to retain staff is that of "negotiated wage" on an individual basis. This involves the abandoning of the conventional wage structure that does not differentiate performance in a real sense to a more tailored package for each individual worker based on his/her competence and market value. This often results in a general wage increase for the individuals concerned (Chen, 2002). It needs to be pointed out here that in recent years, there is a reverse trend of talent "returning" to the better managed SOEs which offer more attractive salaries and individualized reward packages.

There is a great scarcity of high-performing Chinese managerial and professional staff in China (Wong and Law, 1999). While foreign firms and JVs operating at the high end of the product markets are able to recruit good quality university and polytechnic graduates as technicians and skilled workers, many domestic companies are facing recruitment problems. Graduates are unwilling to go to or stay with enterprises that offer relatively low pay and have unhealthy prospects. While the increasing fluidity of the labor market may be beneficial for individuals who are in advantageous positions, organizations may find it difficult to establish a long-term employment relationship with key workers conducive to the organization's competitiveness. Keen competition for talent also tends to drive wages upward disproportionally (thus widening the wage gap and social inequality) and encourages opportunistic behaviors.

Foreign and domestic private firms also face the dilemma of whether to train up their employees for the key skills required at the risk of having them poached or to recruit from the market with attractive employment packages. Firms that provide training may have to readjust their training plan in order to reduce the cost associated with staff turnover. For example, Motorola (China) Ltd had to reduce its training period from 6–12 months to 3 months in order to stop trainee employees (who were sent to the USA for training) from abandoning the firm to stay in the United States (Editorial Team of *Development and Management of Human Resources*, 2001). Hence, firms that successfully recruit, develop and motivate their skilled employees may have significant competitive advantages (Björkman and Fan, 2002).

Another major challenge in HRM in China is the need to change the ideology of reward, distribution and performance, as discussed earlier in this chapter. Pay has not been an effective mechanism in China to reflect workers' performance or to motivate workers (Cooke, 2004a) and poor performance has always been a problem haunting the SOEs (Korzec, 1992; Chiu, 2002), if less so the private firms. However, Chinese workers have often been criticized by the managers of JVs, foreign and domestic private firms for a lack of motivation and pride in their work, and for showing little interest in advancing themselves. Therefore, a difficult task for HRM is to change the behavioral patterns of workers, to make them more motivated, to make them take greater ownership and responsibility for their own work and take greater pride in their organization. This will lead to a greater level of organizational congruence and ultimately productivity.

Perhaps the most severe challenge facing HRM in China at the national level is that of skills shortage and the insufficiency of training provision, an intertwined problem that has been touched upon several times so far in this chapter. One characteristic of the training system in China is the considerable variation in training provision between different forms of enterprise ownership and in different regions (Cooke, 2004b). In general, foreign firms, JVs and the state sector provide more training than other forms of business, with small private and self-employed business perhaps providing the least training. Firms located in the more developed east and southeast regions of the country provide more training in general than those in the north and west. Employees in manufacturing and public sector organizations also receive more training in general than those in the private-service sectors.

At the enterprise level, training practice displays a number of problems characterized by the lack of strategic planning and the low priority of training in organizational activities. Enterprises often carry out training without any strategic planning, costing or taking into account what the training needs of the enterprises are. Employee training is often seen as part of the non-core business for companies and the training department is often used to accommodate cadres who are deemed unsuitable for the front line of production. Training departments usually operate in a reactive mode. They are there to "fulfill' the task given by the higher authority," While training officers complain that senior management of the company neglect training, criticisms often leveled at the training provision are that it is irrelevant, out-of-touch, a formality to tick the training box and an opportunity for individuals to gold plate their qualifications (Xu, 2000). Borgonjon and Vanhonacker (1994) also pointed out that the Chinese SOEs were mostly concerned about technical training, and did not yet have the capability to run management training courses.

The Future of the HR Functions in China

The above key challenges facing HRM in China have profound implications for the HR functions at individual, organizational and national level. At the individual level, there is an urgent need to professionalize the HR functions. Human resource management as a discipline in higher education did not make its appearance until the mid-1990s, although it has been expanding rapidly since. In 1999, there were only thirty higher educational institutions that provided undergraduate degree courses on HRM. By July 2001, there were over ninety universities that recruited HRM undergraduates (Liao and Chen, 2002). The vast majority of HR officers in enterprises have therefore never received any formal training on HRM. Many of them came from a non-personnel background. Moreover, the nature of the personnel functions is experiencing significant changes from the reactive administrative role of the planned economy era to a more proactive and strategic role of the market economy. This is accompanied by an increasing level of labor mobility, more overt labor–management disputes, more complex reward systems, and the introduction of more labor regulations. HR personnel therefore need to equip themselves with the understanding of HR theories and labor regulations and their practical implications. They also need to understand the strategic role of HRM in relation to other functions of the organization.

At the organizational level, it is likely that in the next few years, the HR function in many Chinese organizations will continue to share its administrative and welfare roles with the trade unions. While the rapid expansion of the private sector and the recent amendment of the Trade Union Law are unlikely to change the power base (or the lack of it) of the union dramatically, the HR function has yet to develop to be part of the business strategy. The majority of entrepreneurs and CEOs in China have insufficient understanding of the strategic importance of HRM to organizational competitiveness and tend to underestimate the technicality of HRM. According to Xu (2001), their ideology of employment relationship is still largely of the transactional nature. A common mindset is that: "I have the money, I employ you, therefore you should do a good job for me." Much work needs to be done to convince them of the added value of human resources and the importance of winning employees' commitment for the success of the organization.

At the industry and national level, there is a need to establish industrial and national networks to share information of HR, to coordinate the HR functions such as skill training and recruitment, and to monitor the labor market trends and the conformity of labor regulations. Equally importantly, national professional bodies for HR professionals should be set up to link HR professionals and to facilitate the sharing of "best practices" in HRM. To date, no professional HR body exists at the national level. However, there are signs that some best practice sharing is taking place beyond the workplace level, albeit often in an unorganized manner. For example, blue-chip foreign firms and JVs are considered to have a sophisticated HR system, many elements of which are western practices transferred and adapted to suit the Chinese environment. Their HR policy and practice are often hailed by the media as good models to be followed by domestic firms in China. Delegate teams are sometimes organized by local governments or firms to visit these model companies in order to disseminate good practices.

Conclusion

This chapter has provided an overview of HRM in China, covering most aspects of HRM and its characteristics in different types of organizations such as SOEs, public sector organizations, foreign firms, JVs, TVEs and domestic private firms. It highlighted the most unique aspects of HRM practices in China. These include: gender inequality in recruitment and selection; the weak presence of trade unions and the absence of true workers' voices; the unofficial role of grass-root workers in maintaining the egalitarian distribution system; problems of skills shortage, training, recruitment and retention; and the need to professionalize the HR functions. While the current state of HRM in China is characterized by the withdrawal of state intervention at enterprise level and a trend towards greater diversity and marketization, these are taking place in parallel with the introduction of more statutory labor regulations and the radical reforms of workplace welfare and social security provisions. In short, the emerging HRM in China presents not only exciting opportunities but also severe challenges for the role of HR at all levels. Above all, HRM in China shares similar characteristics, to some extent, with that found in other economies, but at the same time displays its own strong national characteristics.

REFERENCES

Benson, J. and Zhu, Y. (2000) "A case study analysis of human resource management in China's manufacturing industry," *China Industrial Economy* 4: 62–5.

Björkman, I. and Fan, X.C. (2002) "Human resource management and the performance of Western firms in China," *International Journal of Human Resource Management* 13 (6): 853–64.

Borgonjon, J. and Vanhonacker, W. (1994) "Management training and education in the People's Republic of China," *International Journal of Human Resource Management* 5 (2): 327–56.

Braun, W. and Warner, M. (2002) "Strategic human resource management in western multinationals in China: The differentiation of practices across different ownership forms." *Personnel Review* 31 (5): 553–79.

Chen, B. (2002) " 'Negotiated wage': a method to stop staff turnover in SOEs," *Development and Management of Human Resources* 4: 11–12.

Chen, C.C. (1995) "New trends in rewards allocation preferences: a Sino-US comparison," *Academy of Management Journal* 38 (2): 408–28.

Child, J. (1994) *Management in China in the age of reform*, Cambridge: Cambridge University Press.

China Statistical Abstract (2000) Beijing: China Statistics Press.

China Statistical Yearbook (2002) Beijing: China Statistics Press.

Chiu, W.C.K. (2002) "Do types of economic ownership matter in getting employees to commit? An exploratory study in the People's Republic of China," *International Journal of Human Resource Management* 13 (6): 865–82.

Chu, L.Q. (2002) "Can your enterprise retain talent after WTO?," *Development and Management of Human Resources* 5: 7–8.

Cooke, F.L. (2000) "Manpower restructuring in the state-owned railway industry of China: The role of the state in human resource strategy," *International Journal of Human Resource Management* 11 (5): 904–24.

Cooke, F.L. (2001) "Equal opportunities? The role of legislation and public policies in women's employment in China," *Journal of Women in Management Review* 16 (7): 334–48.

Cooke, F.L. (2002) "Ownership change and the reshaping of employment relations in China: A study of two manufacturing companies," *Journal of Industrial Relations* 44 (1): 19–39.

Cooke, F.L. (2003a) "Equal opportunity? Women's managerial careers in governmental organisations in China," *International Journal of Human Resource Management* 14 (2): 317–33.

Cooke, F.L. (2003b) "Seven reforms in five decades: Civil service reform and its human resource implications in China," *Journal of Asia Pacific Economy* 8 (3): 380–404.

Cooke, F.L. (2004a) "Public sector pay in China: 1949–2000," *International Journal of Human Resource Management* 15 (4/5): 895–916.

Cooke, F.L. (2004b) "Vocational and enterprise training in China: Policy, practice and prospect," *Journal of Asia Pacific Economy* 20 (1): 26–55.

Cooke, F.L. (2005) "Employment relations in small commercial businesses in China," *Industrial Relations Journal* 36 (1): 19–37.

Cooke, F.L. and Rubery J. (2002) "Minimum wage and social equality in China," project report on *Minimum wage and employment equality in developed and developing countries*, Geneva: International Labour Organization (ILO).

Ding, D., Goodall, K. and Warner. M. (2002) "The impact of economic reform on the role of trade unions in Chinese enterprises," *International Journal of Human Resource Management* 13 (3): 431–49.

Ding, D., Lan, G. and Warner, M. (2001) "A new form of Chinese human resource management? Personnel and labour–management relations in Chinese township and village enterprises: A case study approach," *Industrial Relations Journal* 32 (4): 328–43.

Ding, D. and Warner, M. (1999) "'Re-inventing' China's industrial relations at enterprise-level: An empirical field-study in four major cities," *Industrial Relations Journal* 30 (3): 243–6.

Easterby-Smith, M., Malina, D. and Lu, Y. (1995) "How culture-sensitive is HRM?," *International Journal of Human Resource Management* 6 (1): 31–59.

Editorial team of *Development and Management of Human Resources* (2001) "Report of the Second Conference of Human Resource Development and Management in China," *Development and Management of Human Resources* 4: 9–15.

Hoffman, C. (1981) "People's Republic of China," in A. Albert (ed.) *International Handbook of Industrial Relations*, Westport, CT: Greenwood Press.

Korzec, M. (1992) *Labour and the failure of reform in China*, London: Macmillan.

Liao, C.W. and Chen, W.S. (2002) "Human resource management employee training system," *Development and Management of Human Resources* 7: 22–6.

Liu, T. (1989) "Chinese workers and employees participate in democratic management of enterprises," *Chinese Trade Unions* 2: 5–10.

Lu, H.J. (ed.) (1987) *Enterprise labour management*, Beijing: China Labour Press.

Ng, S.H. and Warner, M. (1998) *China's trade unions and management*, London: Macmillan.

Shirk, S.L. (1981) "Recent Chinese labour policies and the transformation of industrial organisation in China," *China Quarterly* 88: 575–93.

Sparrow, P. (2000) "International reward management," in G. White and J. Druker (eds.) *Reward management: A critical text*, London: Routledge.

Taylor, B. (2002) "Privatisation, markets and industrial relations in China," *British Journal of Industrial Relations* 40 (2): 249–72.

Verma, A. and Yan, Z.M. (1995) "The changing face of human resource management in China: Opportunities, problems and strategies," in A. Verma, T. Kochan and R. Lansbury (eds.) *Employment relations in the growing Asian economies*, London: Routledge.

Wang, C.G. and Fang, W. (2001) "Cultural adaptation and co-operation: An important aspect that MNCs face in China," *Xinhua Wenjai* 12: 19–24.

Warner, M. (1990) "Chinese trade unions: Structure and function in a decade of economic reform, 1979–1989," *Management Studies Research Paper No. 8/90*, Cambridge University.

Warner, M. (1992) *How Chinese managers learn*, London: Macmillan.

Warner, M. (1995) *The management of human resources in Chinese enterprises*, London: Macmillan and New York: St Martins Press.

Warner, M. (1996a) "Human resources in the People's Republic of China: The 'three systems' reforms." *Human Resource Management Journal* 6 (2): 32–43.

Warner, M. (1996b) "Chinese enterprise reform, human resources and the 1994 Labour Law," *The International Journal of Human Resource Management* 7 (4): 779–96.

Warner, M. (1998) "China's HRM in transition: Towards relative convergence?," in C. Rowley (ed.) *Human resource management in the Asia Pacific region: Convergence questioned*, London: Frank Cass, pp. 19–33.

Warner, M. (1999) "Human resources and management in China's 'Hi-tech' revolution: A study of selected computer hardware, software and related firms in the PRC," *International Journal of Human Resource Management* 10 (1): 1–20.

Warner, M. (2001) "Human resource management in the People's Republic of China," in P. Budhwar and Y. Debrah (eds.) *Human resource management in developing countries*, London: Routledge, pp. 19–33.

Warner, M. and Ng, S.H. (1999) "Collective contracts in Chinese enterprises: A new brand of collective bargaining under 'market socialism'?," *British Journal of Industrial Relations* 37 (2): 295–314.

Wong, L.S. and Law, K.S. (1999) "Managing localisation in the PRC: A practical model," *Journal of World Business* 34: 26–40.

Xu, Y.L. (2001) "Current situation of HRM in China," *Development and Management of Human Resources* 2: 8–10.

Xu, Z. (2000) "On format, style and methods of employee training," *China Smelter Education* 6: 79–80.

Yu, K.C. (1998) "Chinese employees' perceptions of distributive fairness," in A.M. Francesco and B.A. Gold (eds.) *International organisational behavior*, New Jersey: Prentice-Hall.

Zhang, H.Y., Ming, L.Z. and Liang, C.Y. (2002) *The development of private enterprises in China: Report no. 3*, Beijing: Social Science Documentation Publishing House.

Zhu, C. and Dowling, P. (2002) "Staffing practices in transition: Some empirical evidence from China." *International Journal of Human Resource Management* 13 (4): 569–97.

Useful websites

Asia-Pacific Human Resources Research Association:	http://www.aphr.org
ChinaHR.com Corporation:	http://www.chinaHR.com
ChinaHRD.net:	http://www.ChinaHRD.net
51e-training.com:	http://www.51e-training.com
The Ministry of Foreign Trade and Economic Co-operation of P. R. China:	http://www1.moftec.gov.cn/moftec

Chapter 13

HRM in India

Debi S. Saini and Pawan S. Budhwar

Introduction

This chapter presents a broad overview of the scenario of human resource management (HRM) in India. To provide the required context, this section presents some relevant demographic details of the Indian economy and society. India is a republic in South Asia. It has the second highest population in the world after China, which reached the 1 billion mark in June 2000. As per the latest census of 2001, the total population of the country is 1,027 million, which includes 531.28 million males and 495.73 million females. India's share of the world population is 16.7 percent. The literacy rate among the population for seven years and above for the country stands at 65.38 percent. The corresponding figures for males and females are 75.85 and 54.16 percent respectively. The density of population (per km^2) is 324 and the male : female ratio is 1000 : 933.

Being the largest democracy in the world, India is governed by a constitution that came into force on 26 January 1950. It attained independence from the British on 15 August 1947. The country comprises of 29 states and 6 union territories. There are six main religious groups: Hindus (83.2 percent), Muslims (11 percent), Sikhs (2 percent), Christians (2 percent), Jains and Buddhists (less than 1 percent). There are over three thousand castes. India has 179 languages and 544 dialects. The constitution recognizes sixteen languages, "Hindi" and English being the two official languages.

D. S. Saini and P. S. Budhwar, "HRM in India," in *Managing Human Resorces in Asia-Pacific* (Routledge: London, 2004); 114–137.

India has one of the largest English-speaking populations in the Asia-Pacific region (Budhwar, 2003).

As per the latest round of National Sample Survey (NSS) of Employment and Unemployment, the total workforce in the country is 397 million. Out of this, nearly 92 percent or more is engaged in the activities of the unorganized sector (including the so-called informal sector) while about 8 percent of the workforce is employed in the organized sector. Of the total, 60 percent of the workforce is engaged in agriculture. Of the 40 percent in the non-agriculture sector, the unorganized workforce is 82 percent and the remaining 18 percent or so belongs to the organized segment. Only about 12 to 15 percent of the total workforce in the country is estimated to fall in the category of wage/salary employment. Such employees constitute 6 percent of the workforce in the rural areas and about 40 percent of the workforce in the urban areas. (Economic Survey, Government of India 2002–3). The second National Commission on Labour (NCL) has estimated that only 5 percent of the workforce in the age group 20–24 has acquired some kind of a formal vocational training (Government of India, 2002a). This is a far lower percentage than those of developed countries, which range between 60 and 80 percent.

India is rich in both natural and human resources, even as it faces tremendous challenges in its efforts to enhance economic growth and development. It is estimated that around 200 million people in the country comprise the middle class, which is becoming larger with the liberalization of the Indian economy. This class is also viewed by the developed countries as an important market for exporting their goods from a long-term point of view. The country has multiplied its foreign direct investment (FDI) several times since adopting the New Economic Policy (NEP) in July 1991, but is still far behind its neighbor China and countries in Southeast Asia in this regard. There are now over 15,000 multinational firms operating in India and this number is increasing rapidly (for details, see Budhwar, 2001).

As global firms seek success in their Indian operations, and as Indian firms reach a higher degree of professionalism in the global context, they have to make critical decisions related to people management as strategic choices. This will necessitate an appreciation of the factors which influence HRM policies and practices in the Indian context. These factors, among others, include availability of requisite skills and competencies, required mindsets, desired values and customs, facilitative legal framework and institutions, and conducive cultural environment. They are the products of a country's socioeconomic and political realities (see Budhwar and Sparrow, 1998; Hofstede, 1993). A comprehensive understanding of such realities and insights helps a fuller comprehension of the HRM model of a country (Budhwar and Sparrow, 2002a). The contemporary HRM scenario of a country should be understood in the context of its general economic and business environment as it evolves over the years.

The Indian Economy and Business Environment

After independence, India put primacy on adopting self-reliance in its economic development policies and thus preferred an import-substitution model of development for

45 years or so. It set up the Planning Commission in 1950 to formulate national plans. Since then, a "mixed economy" approach (emphasizing both private and public enterprise) had been adopted until quite recently. This had the effect of reducing the incidence of entrepreneurship as well as global competitiveness – both necessary for national growth. Economic planning is carried out mainly through the five-year plans and industrial policies. Presently, the tenth five-year plan (2002–7) and the industrial policy of 1991 are in progress.

Despite the formalities of planning, the Indian economy was perhaps in its worst state in 1991. It witnessed a double-digit rate of inflation, decelerated industrial production, fiscal indiscipline, a very high ratio of borrowing to the GNP (both internal and external) and a dismally low level of foreign exchange reserves. Those had gone down so low that they were barely sufficient to meet the bill for three weeks' imports. The World Bank and the IMF agreed to bail out India on the condition that it changed from a regulated regime to a "free market economy." To meet the challenges, the government announced a series of economic policies, beginning with the devaluation of the rupee, followed by a new industrial policy and fiscal and trade policies. A number of reforms guided by the liberalization philosophy were made in the public sector, trade and exchange policy, the banking sector and the foreign investment policy (for details, see Budhwar, 2003).

The economy has responded positively to these reforms and India is now considered as one of the largest emerging nations, having bypassed the Asian economic crisis. The World Bank forecasts that, by 2020, India could become the world's fourth largest economy. In the last few years state control and ownership in the economy have been reduced. Bold steps have been taken to correct the fiscal imbalance, to bring about structural adjustments and to attract foreign direct investment. Foreign operators can now acquire immovable property in India, employ foreign nationals in their operations in India and buy and sell shares in Indian companies. Substantial reforms have been made in the telecommunications, financial and shipping sectors, as well as in direct tax structure and industrial policy. Significant reforms have already been initiated in the insurance sector by the present government. However, India still has a long way to go before it can compete fully with some of the more economically advanced Asian nations.

Liberalization of the Indian economy has resulted in sudden and increased levels of competition for Indian firms from international firms. At the same time it has also created opportunities for resource mobilization from new sources. HRM issues have now become more important with the firms' adoption of strategies of expansion, diversification, turnaround and internationalization. These developments have direct implications for HRM in India and the Indian HR function is under severe pressure to bring about large-scale structural changes in order to cope with the challenges brought about by economic liberalization. It has to develop a domestic workforce capable of taking on the challenges thrown up by the new economic environment. In such conditions the performance of the HR function has become more important than ever (for details, see Budhwar and Sparrow, 1997).

Despite many initiatives in response to the demands of the globalization process, India is comparatively slow in implementing the reforms process. AT Kearney's, a management consultancy firm, developed a 2003 globalization index for various countries

(*Times of India*, 2003: 11). It was found that the low pace of integration with the global economy together with the decline in portfolio capital investment caused India to slip to fifty-sixth rank from forty-ninth in the year 2002. Several factors have contributed to Indian business remaining much below world class. These include: lack of aspiration to be world class, lack of vision, lack of professionalism, lack of process sensitivity, lack of cost consciousness, little respect for time, and lack of a professional system of skill development, among others (Prahlad, 1998; Rao, 1999; Saini, 2000). Most enlightened employers are aware of these limitations. They also realize a greater need to tackle the problem of outdated technology, excessive workforce, inadequacy of skills, and lack of concern for customer satisfaction, and unsatisfactory levels of productivity.

Tackling these problems necessitated reorienting management systems and processes, and undertaking programs of attitudinal change. These included mixed bags of harder measures as well as attempts towards greater professionalism for HR empowerment. Vigorous downsizing of the excessive workforce became the order of the day both within the public and the private sectors. Several organizations devised voluntary retirement schemes (VRS) to facilitate the reform process. The NEP (announced in 1991), among others, envisaged the establishment of a National Renewal Fund (NRF). It was aimed to promote upgradation of skills of those affected by downsizing, finance VRS in the public sector enterprises, and support programs of skill enhancement in general. Ironically, almost no effective program of skill upgradation has been initiated so far; almost all spendings from the NRF has been confined to financing the VRS (Mishra, 2001). Even after more than a decade of liberalization policies a "skill development fund" has not been set up to facilitate a professionally managed macro program of human resource development (HRD). The aim of such a program would have been to develop appropriate skills and competencies as per social and economic demands, including changing the mindsets of the workforce so as to be in consonance with the needs of the business realities. If started, it will necessitate HRD programs at the macro level and adoption of HRM strategies at the micro level.

Evolution of Human Resource Management

The personnel function in India originated in the 1920s with the concern for labor welfare in factories. The Trade Union Act of 1926 gave formal recognition to workers' unions. The Royal Commission of Labor, 1931, recommended the appointment of labor welfare officers and the Factories Act of 1948 laid down the duties and qualifications of labor welfare officers. Further, the Indian judiciary played an important role in expounding the correct scope of the protection envisaged to the working class by the legislation that was enacted in several spheres of industrial relations (IR) as per the spirit of the constitution. Consequent to the passage of a number of labor and industrial relations laws, personnel managers began performing IR as a very significant role; one that formed such an important part of their work that they came to be known as children of the Industrial Disputes Act 1947 (IDA). All these developments formed the foundation of the personnel function in India (Balasubramanian, 1994, 1995) and paralleled the initial developments of the British personnel function. For example, provisions similar to those provided by Cadbury in Britain were provided by the Tata group in India in the early 1920s (see Budhwar and Khatri, 2001).

After Independence, in the 1950s, two professional bodies emerged: the Indian Institute of Personnel Management (IIPM), a counterpart of the Institute of Personnel Management in the UK, was formed at Calcutta and the National Institute of Labor Management (NILM) at Bombay. In the 1960s, the personnel function began to expand beyond the welfare aspect with three areas, labor welfare, industrial relations and personnel administration, developing as the constituent roles for the emerging profession (Venkata Raman and Srivastava, 1991). In the 1970s, the thrust of personnel function shifted towards greater organizational "efficiency," and by the 1980s it began to use and focus on terms and issues such as HRM and HRD. The two professional bodies, i.e. IIPM and NILM, merged in 1980 to form the National Institute of Personnel Management (NIPM) in Bombay. Thus, the status of personnel function in India has changed over the years (Amba-Rao, 1994; Budhwar and Sparrow, 1997).

In recent years, HRD has been seen as the main tool for improving business performance. Business survival has become an important aspect of HRD efforts. The vigorous efforts by academics (such as T.V. Rao, Udai Pareek and Ishwar Dayal, among others) helped to popularize the concept of HRD among both academics and practitioners. Programs of HRD and organizational development (OD) at the individual enterprise level in public as well as private sectors are being adopted. The formation of "The HRD Network," which today has a large membership of academics and HRM and other managers, symbolizes the need to debate HR interventions and sharpen abilities of HR professionals. This network has aroused tremendous sensitivity of the need for HRD in particular and for HRM in general. Greater focus has been put on developing HRD systems to produce synergy and employee contentment. During this period, the HR profession developed by leaps and bounds in both positive and negative senses. Several organizations resorted to indiscriminate appointment of HRD managers. This period also saw an elevation in the status of personnel managers to the board level; though only in professionally managed organizations. There was also a massive upsurge in re-labeling the title of personnel manager to HRD manager and personnel department to HRD department. Interestingly, however, some employers also perceived disillusionment with their decision as they felt that the investment in HRD did not deliver any tangible results. Thus they started downsizing or even abolishing their HRD departments. Efforts are also made to outsource HR activities. This gave rise to the need for the measurement of HR performance. Thus the concept of "HR audit" came into practice. Progressive employers like Aditya Vikram Birla asked all their companies to have their HR systems audited by consultants (Rao, 1999). The concept of the HRD scorecard is being used as a device to measure effectiveness of people-development activities.

As is well known, the HRM philosophy developed in the western countries during the 1980s and the 1990s both in its hard (instrumentalist) and soft (empowerment) dimensions (Legge, 1995). Empowerment was viewed as "the elixir of the 1990s." Finally, HRM now seems to have found wide application in both western organizations and MNCs. Ironically, no such debate on HRM as a philosophy in the Indian context existed, despite the immense contribution of various trainer-academics towards the implementation of the HRD philosophy (Saini, 2000). At the organizational level, the word HRM is rarely being used; it is substituted by HRD. However, MNCs operating in India do not confine their interventions to HRD and have undertaken wider programs and strategies of HRM (see Budhwar and Björkman, 2003). Some of the leading Indian organizations have also taken the initiative in this regard and have brought out newer issues in the strategic management of their human resources. Still, one fails to understand why Indian firms continue to use different terminology to denote their HR departments or the possible logic behind this.

Personnel Management, HRD or HRM: Some Reflections in the Indian Context

If one examines HRM books or courses taught in management schools in India, by and large it appears to be a case of old wine in new bottles; for the term "personnel management" has been replaced by HRD without much debate. Only recently some glimpses of reforms are visible in this regard. However, they are far from adequate. The writings of key scholars in the field such as Udai Pareek and T.V. Rao of the Indian Institute of Management (IIM) Ahmedabad, have helped in popularizing the term HRD in India (see for example, Pareek and Rao, 1981; Rao, 1999). But almost no attempt has been made to critically expound the term HRM as it has come to be understood in the advanced world. Pareek and Rao provide a very wide definition of the term HRD and view it as a philosophy by itself. They do not attempt to knit it into the HRM concept nor give any reasons as to why they have ignored the term HRM despite the long debate on it in the West. Almost nowhere do they differentiate between HRD and HRM. And it is certain that there is no Indianness in their explanation of the term HRD. They use the contribution of Nadler (1970) as a model in their formulations, and continue to preach his philosophy in the different versions of their text (i.e. the latest 1992 edition of Pareek and Rao, 1981; Rao, 1999). Today, Nadler's ideas have merged into the HRM philosophy. HRD is largely viewed as a developmental intervention in HRM. Almost the entire HRM community in the West has viewed it so, with very few exceptions (see, e.g. Walton, 1999). Indian academics have remained silent on the fate of HRM for long, knowingly or unknowingly, which has led to an uncritical popularization of the term HRD.

As a result, when scholars look for material on the HRM discourse in India, they receive only confusing signals, especially if they wish to put HRM thinking and practice in the context of global developments. For some strange reason, even most books in the HRM area bear HRD labels or linkages (Saini and Khan, 2000). This situation is partly attributable to the dominance of training and development and the psychologist–academics in the contemporary thinking on HRD/HRM in the country. It may partly be attributable to the renaming of the central government Ministry of Education as the Ministry of HRD in the early 1980s. Looking towards the courses in HRM offered at most business schools in India, they are not sufficiently equipped to face the challenges of this emerging subject, especially its strategic connotation. We have yet to witness most business schools and university departments devising innovative courses in this area, knowledge of which is necessary for realizing the goal of professional excellence in people management; in reality the basic HRM course for general MBA students is still personnel management. Courses in strategic HRM are hardly taught even as HR managers of most professionally managed organizations in the country are using the most modern methods and interventions of HRM (see Budhwar and Sparrow, 1997; Varkky *et al.*, 2001).

Budhwar (1998) empirically investigated in 137 Indian firms the preference for the usage of specific terms to denote HR departments in the Indian context, the nature of personnel function and the differences between personnel management (PM), HRD and HRM. His results show that the majority of Indian managers see the recently changed economic environment as the most significant factor responsible for major changes in the nature of their personnel/HR function. The liberalization of the Indian economy has created a pressure on the Indian HRM function to become more cre-ative and innovative. The HRM profession promises to commit itself to improve the efficiency and commitment of its human resources, obtain better results and improve industrial relations. This highlights, among others, the role of training and develop-ment and team or group-HRM activities. Due to such changes, the use of HRD-related terms is becoming popular and that of personnel management-related ones is going out-of-fashion. Interestingly, in MNCs operating in India, HRM is the preferred term to denote both HR departments and managers (see Budhwar and Björkman, 2003).

Indian managers define HRM as a holistic concept, which is more focused and proactive than PM; it integrates and incorporates both PM and HRD, and deals with satisfying and developing employees. HRD implies a long-term perspective for devel-oping the potential and capabilities of HR for future organizational needs. Personnel is seen as more of a policing type of department as it is now a secondary function, also called transactional HRM. This aspect of HRM is concerned with the day-to-day activities of control, attendance, compliance with legislation, discipline aspects and IR. The majority of Indian managers believe that the future of the HRM function is good and its status is improving. Some managers, however, feel that the existing legislation can be obstructive in this regard. Perhaps they rightly lament the functioning of the "EXIT" policy (a policy for voluntary retirement) as problematic due to the rigidities created by the IR laws (for details, see Budhwar, 2000).

Factors Influencing HRM and Related Challenges

National culture

The prevailing beliefs, values, traditions and behavior patterns among Indians form part of the national culture and can be attributed to several factors. Prominent among these are social customs and practices and the perpetration by the British of elitist values during their rule over India for more than a century. Perhaps the Britishers' biggest influence in this regard was through the promotion of feudalism. Their land cultivation system involved appointing feudal lords who exacerbated the values of hierarchy and subjugation. Also, their focus was on the supremacy of bureaucracy through the institution of an administrative service called the Indian Civil Service (ICS). The working of these institutions has made a lasting impact on the psyche of common people. They have strengthened hierarchy and power distance between the rulers and the ruled. The civil servants and the feudal lords constituted elite classes in society, whose position in the social hierarchy was strengthened by the policies of the British Indian government.

After Independence, the ICS was replaced by the Indian Administrative Service (IAS) with the projected intention of humanizing it and bringing it closer to people's aspirations. However, it inherited and sustained the culture of the ICS and the state system suffered from all the vices which are attributed to bureaucracy (see Saini, 1999). It has resulted in a two-tier system of the elite and the general public. While the law is enforced in a particular way for the former, the same law works to the detriment of the latter. Such a culture of elitism is known to have pervaded most types of organization. Such biases have been reflected even in the people management policies in general.

Feudalism created by the British promoted inequality and hierarchy amongst the urban as well as non-urban population. The caste system in India has also played a contributory role in this regard. The family-owned business houses have made full use of the inculcation of these values in society in practicing a kind of neofeudalism in industry. This is reflected in the organizational structures and social relations which reflect hierarchy, status consciousness, power distance and low individualism. These values have helped to strengthen hierarchical superior–subordinate relationships which act as a kind of mechanism of social control on the managed. Studies have shown that Indian managers attribute high priority to the importance of cultural assumptions which guide their employees' perceptions and organizational thinking. It is also revealed that the common Indian values, norms of behavior and customs exercise considerable influence on their HRM policies and practices (Budhwar, 2001).

The Indian social and cultural environment puts primacy on strong family ties that dilute individualism, resulting in greater dependence on others. This highlights the importance of interpersonal relations in people management in India, more than the importance given to it in other societies. The core bases of the management system in social and family relationships may then be attributed to various factors, including a strong caste system, an agrarian-based society, a high incidence of illiteracy, poverty and an indifference of the state system to the needs of the individual (Budhwar, 1999).

Kanungo and Mendonca (1994) have shown significant cultural differences between India and western countries on the basis of Hofstede's (1991) four initial dimensions of power distance, uncertainty avoidance, individualism and masculinity. India stands relatively high on uncertainty avoidance and power distance and relatively low on individualism and masculinity dimensions. Relatively high uncertainty avoidance implies an unwillingness to take risks and to accept organizational change. The relative low individualism implies that family and group attainments take precedence over work outcomes (Sharma, 1984). The relative high power distance implies that managers and subordinates accept their relative positions in the organizational hierarchy and operate from these fixed positions. Obedience is facilitated by the supposedly superior authority of the position holder and not by any rational basis. This is simply by virtue of the authority inherent in that status. The relative low masculinity implies that employees' orientation is towards personalized relationships rather than towards performance (Kanungo and Mendonca, 1994: 450). On the fifth dimension of long-term versus short-term orientation, traditionally, India is known as a long-term oriented nation (see Tripathi, 1990). However, results of a recent research (see Budhwar and Sparrow, 2002b) suggest that, due to the severe pressure created by the recent liberalization of economic policies and the presence of foreign operators in Indian organizations, the question of immediate survival has become more important. This explains a recent shift of emphasis towards short-termism. However, one should be cautious in generalizing any such analysis.

Nevertheless, on the same lines as the above analysis, other researchers (see, e.g. Sharma, 1984; Tayeb, 1987; Sinha and Kanungo, 1997) report that, on average, Indians resist change, hesitate to delegate or even accept authority, are fearful of taking an independent decision, are possessive towards their inferiors and frequently surrender to their superiors. A possible explanation for such behavior can be traced to the long imperialist history of India. Similarly, the traditional hierarchical social structure of India has always emphasized respect for superiors, who can be elders, teachers or superiors at work, i.e. the nature of Hinduism evidenced by the caste and social system (Sahay and Walsham, 1997; Budhwar et al., 2000).

From the above discussion, it may be deduced that the Indian societal culture has made a lasting impact on most management functions such as staffing, communication, leadership, motivation and control. Staffing for top managerial positions among Indian organizations (especially in the private sector) is generally restricted by familial, communal and political considerations. Authority in Indian organizations is likely to remain one-sided, with subordinates leaning heavily on their superiors for advice and directions. Motivational tools in the Indian organizations are more likely to be social, interpersonal and even spiritual (see Sparrow and Budhwar, 1997).

National institutions supporting industrial relations

The hallmark of the Indian IR law is massive state presence through the Industrial Disputes Act 1947 (IDA). This Act empowers the "appropriate government," in its discretion, to refer an industrial dispute for adjudication either on failure of conciliation or even without any resort to conciliation. Apart from the IDA, two other laws form part of the IR law in the country: the Trade Unions Act 1926 (TUA) and the Industrial Employment (Standing Orders) Act 1946 (IESOA). While the former confers on workers and unions freedom of association and immunity against civil and criminal liability for taking industrial action, the latter seeks to ensure standardization of the terms of employment and their certification by a government officer, who is obliged to satisfy himself that they are just and fair. These sets of laws were intended to facilitate the realization of individual and collective rights of workers. Promoting industrial peace with social justice has projectedly guided the IR policy of the government. Towards this end, apart from the legal framework, the central government has effectively used an institution called consultative tripartite conference – otherwise known as the Indian Labor Conference – consisting of representatives of employers, labor and government, whose meetings have been held annually since 1940. One of the most notable non-legislative initiatives in IR came from the government in 1958 as a result of the deliberations at this forum in the form of the Code of Discipline and the Joint Management Councils. These instruments were to be used as a formal basis for recognition of unions and collective bargaining. However, the impact of these bodies was merely transitory (Johri, 1998: 49). Legal means and interventions continued to dominate the IR policy in the country.

By conferring the working-class rights and individual labor rights, these laws, along with others, created working-class consciousness in the country. They led to a situation of clash between workers' aspirations and employers' willingness to grant benefits. Being a labor-surplus economy, the country's labor market realities helped the employers to obtain cheap labor and violate minimum labor employment standards by colluding with the labor bureaucracy. But the IDA model – which could not be replaced or even diluted despite a 55-year debate on its fate – substantially diluted collective labor rights by ensuring massive state presence in IR to control labor power. It resulted in juridification of IR (Saini, 1997, 1999). Its influence has been so strong that arbitration as a method of industrial disputes resolution is almost dead. Employers manage IR, among others, by diluting the efficacy of labor laws through consultation as well as adoption of extra-legal means. Variegated unfair labor practices (ULPs) are committed by them in the process. Over the years the pressure of unions, opposition parties and other pressure groups, and union federations have succeeded in influencing the state agencies to enact a large number of labor laws. One finds the situation paradoxical and perplexing. On paper, even industries which have become sick beyond hope are required to comply with these laws, including payment of minimum wages and minimum bonuses. In reality the system works such that employers have learnt to get away with these legal requirements. However, MNCs and other conscientious employers want an IR framework with simpler laws that do not require them to indulge in maneuverings and shenanigans. The IR law framework in larger organizations adversely affects the cause of forging workplace cooperation so as to meet the challenges of HRM in responding to the changed needs of industry in the era of globalization.

Unions

Being a democracy, India has at least a seemingly union-friendly legal framework of IR. Despite that, unionization rate has rarely exceeded 10 percent of the total working population in all sectors. Today this rate is believed to have slipped to around 7 percent. The compulsory adjudication system of the IDA has kept the unions weak (Saini, 1995, 1999). The first two decades after the independence witnessed rapid unionization of the organized sector in the country (both private and public). But unionization in India started declining after the famous Bombay Textile Strike which lasted more than a year and has not been officially withdrawn until today (Venkata Ratnam, 2001). This has brought a sea change in the concept of collective bargaining, which is less and less on industry basis and more on unit basis (*Business India*, 1998).

Membership of unions that are submitting returns is still low; as per the latest estimates it is barely 2 percent of the total workforce. Over 47,000 unions have a membership of 6,329,000. As per the latest available statistics, the number of members covered by collective agreements in the country is barely 1 percent of the total workforce (Mishra, 2001: 20). This is in spite of the fact that in the 1970s and 1980s the judiciary delivered several judgments in the area of industrial relations and labor laws which reflected its attitude of extreme sympathy with the working people, less to the basic principles of industrial organization.

However, in the present economic environment the existing legal framework is required to change its strong pro-labor stance. Early indications are positive in this regard. Lately, some of the recent labor judgments reflect the belief that the judiciary is more sympathetic to the employers and realizes their susceptibilities in the new environment. As noted above, the incidence of unionism is also declining. The number of strikes resorted to is much less than the lockouts (*Business India*, 1998; Mishra, 2001). This has also reduced workers' resistance to change to the new initiatives of HRM, despite patches of working-class success in resisting the individualization of IR through HRM (Ramaswamy, 2000: 219). Interestingly, in contrast to national firms, the impact of unions on the HRM policies and practices of MNCs operating in India is negligible (see Budhwar and Björkman, 2003). On the other hand, unions still significantly influence HRM policies and practices in Indian organizations. However, their stance is slowly changing and becoming more cooperative towards their employers.

The liberalization of the Indian economy has then put tremendous pressure both on the employees and employers. As a nation, India is lagging far behind in productivity standards and production of quality goods. These realities have begun influencing the mindsets of unions and union leaders who now seem to be meekly giving in to the legitimacy of the globalization agenda, as they are aware of these burning problems. Employees both in public as well as private sectors suffer from attitudinal indifference towards professionalism in work. Overall, one notices a lack of vision of being world class in India; this is largely true of government agencies as well as employers (Prahlad, 1998; Ghoshal *et al.*, 2001). In such circumstances, the possible consequence of the adoption of appropriate HRM policies will be salutary. They will lead to minimum wastage of human and financial resources at the micro level. Their adoption will also give due importance to "innovation, bench-marking, and organizing business and professional activities as per market exigencies" (Saini, 1999: 166). But, values of "association," "industrial justice," "workers' dignity" will face crisis; "minimum standards of employment" are also becoming clouded due to the unofficial support of the state to cost-cutting preferences of employers that is hidden in the globalization agenda. But being a democracy the country cannot openly adopt policies that disapprove of these IR values.

Diluting "workplace pluralism" as a value by superimposing HRM on it may work successfully if we have a significant chunk of workforce as gold-collared. The merger of the HRM and IR agenda many possibly work effectively in such a situation. If that happens, one may also forecast greater possibility of the use of HRM as a broad model of workplace justice. Some of the best examples in this regard are the software companies in the country, which have used HRM as a model of workplace justice, which automatically keeps the law and adversarialism away. The viability of the use of soft HRM as the principal philosophy in managing human resources increases in the case of such companies which employ knowledge workers. However, without question this will be too much to ask of national firms which do not have knowledge workers. Nevertheless, to a great extent this is successfully practiced in MNCs operating in India, irrespective of having knowledge or non-knowledge-based employees (see Budhwar and Björkman, 2003). It needs a macro level of overhauling of the Indian HRM system, which seems to have been initiated due to the pressure created by new economic environment on local firms (Ghoshal *et al.*, 2001). Still, India has a long way to go in this direction.

Judging by the way the Indian government has reacted to the situation, the continuance of its sympathy to the cause of social justice in the organized sector appears only remote. This is despite the fact that there has been no labor law reform at all in the post-liberalization era. This may appear surprising to the champions of globalization. But principally, governments' unwillingness to effect labor reforms in the past decade or so is largely explained by their fragility at the central level; they have not shown the courage to antagonize the trade unions openly by undertaking these reforms. Interesting, as it may appear, most employers have been able to manage the show despite the archaic laws. However, there is always a limit to everything, including the regulatory laws for workplace functioning.

At the executive level, state governments' attitudes are changing. Many of them have announced far-reaching changes in their labor policies, which henceforth appear to be helpful and in favor of the workers. Now they tacitly support hire and fire policies, forbidding *bandhs* (stoppages), as happened in the case of Kerala, and easing off requirements for labor inspection, as for example, in Rajasthan. The West Bengal government (which is headed by a Marxist party) has cancelled registration of hundreds of unions for non-submission of returns to the Registrar of Trade Unions, which is contrary to its earlier position. The incidence of granting permission for closure and retrenchment (as required under the IDA) in Tamil Nadu has gone up (Venkata Ratnam, 2001).

Workers' participation in management

Another important area of contention in IR is workers' participation in management. Today we have virtually no meaningful participation structures through law, except the works committees under the IDA, which are not fully functional (Saini, 1997). However, the Workers Participation in Management Bill 1990 is pending before the *Rajya Sabha* (upper house of Parliament). The bill is still under consideration of the Parliamentary Select Committee on Labour and Welfare (Government of India, 2002b: 22). This bill seeks to give substantial voice to employees in management, but it is unlikely that, given the changed priorities of the state, it will finally be enacted, despite the fact that the bill has recently been approved by the Cabinet Committee of the Government of India; and the present Labor Minister has shown his commitment to the cause of ensuring employee participation in industry through law. A debate on the bill is current among the social partners. One problem with granting such rights at this phase of economic development is that these efforts will exacerbate building of participation rights on the edifice of adversarial values, which in any case are at a low ebb almost everywhere. Despite such fleeting glimpses of state-sponsored attempts to help rejuvenate working-class rights, one may observe an ambience of well-recognized concerns for improving efficiency and productivity through HRM. The social goals of "association," "social justice" and "participation" are likely to remain subjugated, for they are not in tune with employers' needs for flexibility and autonomy. Workers involvement as an HRM strategy, however, is at a much higher level in foreign firms operating in India (see Budhwar and Björkman, 2003). However, employee involvement interventions are not built on adversarial foundations or any legal sanctions. Rather, they are viewed as part of an organization's voluntary efforts towards promoting commitment and performance culture, and also its unitarist goals. Such unitarism is inherent in HRM philosophy. The rationale of the "involvement" interventions is rooted in Japanization, which is increasingly becoming attractive for western organizations and for those who want to follow western HRM practices in other locales.

Urgency of IR reforms

The above developments in Indian IR augur fairly well for developing HRM; for it is difficult to sustain it in situations of zero-sum IR; this is especially important when India's HR systems and processes have to be conducive to facilitating efficiency and productivity, and eventually the export-promotion model of development. But the government's support may be said to be forthcoming indirectly, i.e. by remaining oblivious to the legal intent. The question is whether this is enough for the country's needs to attract higher levels of FDI. MNCs and other professional establishments need more tangible ways of state support, including having the changed legal framework itself. Intriguingly, it should be appreciated that one way of tackling the problem of flexibility at the micro level is the effective adoption of HRM. It has been used even alongside unions in many organizations including Reliance and Tata Steel (see Ghoshal *et al.*, 2001). This latter has nearly 50,000 workers and has downsized by some 20,000 in the past few years. But most other organizations are unable to follow this. The need for reforms in IR law for it to be facilitative to the globalization policies then remains paramount.

The labor law framework

India has a widespread network of labor laws which are believed to be too rigid. Due to this, wages do not necessarily respond to unemployment and productivity. Globalization warrants that areas are identified that require attention for infusing greater flexibility in the formal labor market; labor law is one such area. A large percentage of Indian managers (61.5 percent) have been found to believe that Indian national labor laws influence their HRM practices the most, for their actions and prerogatives are constricted by these laws (Budhwar, 2001: 82).

Today there are over 60 major central labor laws and about 150 state labor laws in India. All these laws may be grouped into five major categories: laws relating to working conditions; laws relating to wages and monetary benefits; laws relating to industrial relations; laws relating to social security; and miscellaneous labor laws. Some of the major central labor laws are as follows:

- Apprentices Act 1961
- Beedi and Cigar Workers (Conditions of Employment) Act 1966
- Bonded Labor System (Abolition) Act 1976
- Building and Other Construction Workers (Regulation of Employment Service) Act 1996
- Child Labor (Prohibition and Regulation) Act 1986
- Cine-Workers and Cinema Theatre Workers (Regulation of Employment) Act 1981
- Contract Labor (Regulation and Abolition) Act 1970
- Dangerous Machines (Regulation) Act 1983
- Dock Workers (Regulation of Employment) Act 1948
- Dock Workers (Safety, Health and Welfare) Act 1986
- Emigration Act 1983
- Employees' Provident Fund and Miscellaneous Provisions Act 1952
- Employees' State Insurance Act 1948
- Employers' Liability Act 1938
- Employment Exchanges (Compulsory Notification of Vacancies) Act 1959
- Equal Remuneration Act 1976
- Factories Act 1948
- Industrial Disputes Act 1947
- Industrial Employment (Standing Orders) Act 1946
- Inter-State Migrant Workmen (Regulation of Employment and Conditions of Service) Act 1979
- Labor Laws (Exemption from Furnishing Returns and Maintaining Registers by Certain Establishments) Act 1988
- Maternity Benefit Act 1961
- Mines Act 1952
- Minimum Wages Act 1948
- Motor Transport Workers Act 1961
- National Commission for Safai Karamcharis Act 1993
- Payment of Bonus Act 1965
- Payment of Gratuity Act 1972
- Payment of Wages Act 1936
- Plantations Labor Act 1951
- Public Liability Insurance Act 1991
- Sales Promotion Employees (Conditions of Service) Act 1976
- Trade Union Act 1926
- Weekly Holidays Act 1948
- Workmen's Compensation Act 1923

While labor laws are a necessary area of the focus of public policy in any enlightened society, they have to change with time. Some of the major points about the structure and working of Indian labor laws are discussed below.

1. The most problematic part in this regard is that some aspects of IR law are quite antithetical to the needs of globalization. Among others, the Industrial Disputes Act 1947 (IDA) has become the biggest epitome of rigidity in IR in the country. Chapter V-B of this Act requires all employers employing 100 or more workers in factories, mines and plantations to seek permission from the government in matters of lay-off, retrenchment and closure. The chapter gives bureaucratic discretion, which has often been exercised not at all or on extraneous factors. There have been cases of perennially sick establishments which have not been allowed to close or retrench excess labor force on extraneous considerations. The present government has proclaimed its commitment to increase the limit of 100 workers to 1,000 for the purpose of this chapter (V-B), but had to retreat twice under the pressure of its trade union wing, i.e. the Bhartiya Mazdoor Sangh (BMS), which today is the largest trade union federation in the country. Likewise, there are problems with section 9-A of the IDA, which requires that a notice of 21 days should be given by the employer for effecting change in any service conditions of workers. This section has also resulted in workers' resistance to the flexibility needs of the employers in this regard. The IDA also gives tremendous powers to the state to intervene in labor–management relations which produces their "juridification" (Saini, 1999) and consequently adversarialism, thus diluting the goals of HRM (Saini, 2000).

2. The Industrial Employment (Standing Orders) Act 1946 (IESOA), an important IR law, is proving to be problematic. Among others, it provides for uniformity in service conditions of all workers who are similarly placed. This is not quite in consonance with the current needs of industry where employers want to implement performance management principles and introduce new measures which discriminate between employees as per their competencies and/or performance.

3. The Contract Labor (Regulation and Abolition) Act 1970 (CLA) is another law whose structural features are being debated in academic and management circles. This law makes it very difficult to employ contract labor in permanent operations as it provides for abolition of contract labor in certain areas of employment specified by the central government. To the extent that this Act provides for regulating the service conditions of contract workers to make them reasonable, it is a welcome piece of legislation. It is well known that contract labor is highly exploited by contractors who do not observe minimum labor standards in their employment. Often, they are even denied minimum wages, appointment letters, identity cards, etc. (Shrouti and Kumar, 1994: 22). They work longer hours, are virtually denied provision of any social security benefit like protection under Employees' State Insurance (ESI) and provident fund (PF) laws. The recommendations of the second NCL (2002) will be disappointing to employers in this regard; for it has recommended continuance of provisions related to prohibition of contract labor in core activities. The commission has further recommended that if contract labor has to be temporarily employed in core activities, it must

be remunerated at the rate of a regular worker engaged in the same organization doing work of a similar nature. This move is being vehemently resisted by the employers.

4. The existing labor laws have different applicability in terms of industries and employees covered. Also, different sets of administrative mechanisms and dispute-resolving quasi-judicial bodies have been envisaged under various acts. For example, the definition of a worker is different under the IDA and the Factories Act. The term "wages" has been differently defined under different acts. Some laws cover employees receiving monthly wages as low as rupees 1,600 per month (e.g. the Payment of Wages Act, 1936); others cover even clerical and administrative employees (e.g. the Employees' State Insurance Act 1948; the Provident Fund Act, 1952; the Gratuity Act 1972); for some there is no wage limit for coverage (e.g. highly paid pilots are workmen under the IDA). A plethora of case law has been delivered by the judiciary to clarify these complexities in variegated situations. This has made the grasping of labor laws a very complex affair (for a detailed discussion, see Debroy, 1996). In fact, labor law complexity has converted union leaders into full time pleaders, who have set up labor law practice as a vocation (Saini, 1995a).

5. Keeping in mind the ambiguities involved, harmonization and unification of labor laws is an important area of reform. However, almost no serious efforts are being made to tackle this precarious situation. The National Labor Law Association (NLLA, 1994) came out with a proposal to enact a National Labor Code 1994 (draft), which should be a laudable effort so far as its unification agenda is concerned. But if one looks at its contents it has tried to take labor relations back to the welfare state era, which was not acceptable to the government as well as the employers. Hence, this proposed code stands shelved.

These are some of the critical issues in labor law reform which have to be addressed by the state as well as other stakeholders to facilitate shifting of labor–management relations assumptions from confrontational to cooperative mode.

Vocational education and training

Vocational education and training in India are divided into two subsystems. At the central (federal) level, while the vocational education is under the control of the Ministry of HRD, vocational training is basically regulated by the Ministry of Labor. Partly, the former ministry also exercises some control even in matters of training. Further, some 35 ministries of the central government are involved in providing and supporting some kind of training in their respective areas of operations (Saini, 2003). Vocational education is provided at the senior secondary stage in schools. This is over and above engineering, management and other technical education that takes place under the overall supervision of the University Grants Commission (UGC) and the All India Council of Technical Education (AICTE), both of which are central statutory bodies. State governments also exercise control in matters of accreditation of education at the engineering diploma level. Among the specialized vocational training institutions, more than 4,000 industrial training institutes (ITIs) are being run today; of these, 1,654 are run by government and 2,620 are run privately. Altogether, they have a training capacity of 750,000 students (Saini, 2003). Apart from these, the Apprentices Act 1961 has been applied to some notified industries. The Act obliges the employers covered under the Act to engage apprentices in certain predetermined trades as well as those holding degrees and diplomas as per specified ratio. This scheme, however, is working much below the projected capacity, for want of proper enforcement. Various government ministries and NGOs are running vocational training schemes for the informal sector. Apart from these, companies in public and private sectors are also involved in providing skills training and their upgradation. In the "Best 25 Employers in India" survey of 2002 conducted by Hewitt Associates, the average annual training hours in these organizations range from 24 to 120 (these hours are 24 in Indian Oil Corporation, a public sector organization, 47 in Infosys Technologies, 60 in Reddy's Laboratories, 64 in SmithKline Beecham, 86 in Tata Steel, 95 in Reliance, 71 in Tata Engineering, and 120 in LG Electronics).

After the initiation of economic reforms, the issue of skill upgradation and development has assumed critical significance in enabling the Indian economy to enhance its competitive strength. The export promotion model puts a much higher level of primacy on these issues than did the model of import substitution adopted earlier. Productivity, exports and economic growth depend on the quality of technical education and training imparted apart from programs of promoting attitudinal change and process sensitivity among employees. The performance of the existing system of state-regulated vocational training in the country is far from satisfactory (Adams and Krishnan, 2003). India has lost a valuable opportunity of occupation-based knowledge and skills in a more systematic manner at a very crucial stage of its economic development; interestingly, countries such as Singapore have been far more successful in developing competitive performance through enforcing comprehensive needs-driven schemes of skill development (Debrah *et al.*, 2000).

It should be understood that for a country of India's size and economic profile it is utopian to expect miraculous poverty-alleviation results merely through the promotion of organized industrial development. The complexity of the problem requires concerted efforts for ensuring a more meaningful vocational training system for the unorganized (including the informal) sector which employs 92 percent or more of the Indian workforce. Of course, even industry is far from happy about the availability of requisite skills for the organized sector, and a better skill development system is needed for the organized sector as well.

It is noticeable that private training-provider institutions have been able to grow with a good degree of effectiveness and have some remarkable success stories (Adams and Krishnan, 2003). The government-run ITIs, on the other hand, are functioning under several constraints and this should be kept in mind while planning for effective training strategies. A recent workshop on problems of delivering effective training in the country identified the following factors as critical, most of which were found wanting in the present training implementation framework: autonomy (operational, financial), quality of skills delivery, dedication of staff, holistic approach, focus on specific target groups and skills, freedom of admission and staff policy, effective management, adequate fees, employability of skills, marketability of products, capacity building of providers, networking, needs assessment, local resource base, and scientific support in training and technology design. It emphasized focus on soft skills apart from technical and job skills. From the self-employment perspective, aspects such as latest technology, bookkeeping, and market practices were identified as focus areas (Adams and Krishnan, 2003).

As discussed above, the original idea of the setting up of the National Renewal Fund (NRF) in July 1991 was an important step in providing a social safety net to labor affected by the globalization policies. The fund was to be utilized, among other things, for imparting training as a key plank for facilitating the reforms process. But in its actual working, its focus remained confined to funding the Voluntary Retirement Scheme (VRS) as a means of retrenching public sector employees, consequent to the downsizing program of the government (Mishra, 2001). There is then a need to develop a skill-agenda at the macro level that involves professionally organized programs, duly funded by suitable agencies. The second NCL (Government of India, 2002a) has emphasized the need for a modular approach in designing and imparting vocational training so that the individual aspirants receive inter-related multiple skills eventually to contribute to enterprise flexibility. This will help keep pace with the fast-changing technologies based on computerization and the IT revolution. The commission also emphasized a competency-based training system to provide avenues for competence assessment and certification at all levels of learning. This approach underscores developing specified competencies rather than the length of training time.

To operationalize these ideas, the commission has recommended the setting up of an independent regulatory authority. This body is intended to set standards of competence to be achieved at different levels of each trade. The government is collaborating with GTZ (an agency of the German government) to design a suitable law that will facilitate training as per the peculiar social and economic needs in the country. A law is soon expected to be introduced in Parliament to this effect under the name of the All India Authority of Vocational Training Act (AIAVT). This legislation is being designed to overcome various existing arrangements. If enacted, it will help reorient the existing ITI system to changing technological requirements. It is also expected to be an experience in professional excellence in the governance structure of the vocational training system in the country (for salient features of this proposed law, see Saini, 2003). However, it has been rightly emphasized that these efforts can be successful if they are well-knit and dovetailed in an appropriate "macroeconomic policy to maintain adequate aggregate demand and pace of economic growth, specifically in the non-agricultural sector" (Mathur, 2002: 17). This is one of the main challenges for HRD at the macro level that the country faces today. It remains to be seen whether the government is able to deviate from the past and show the requisite political sagacity in developing a workable skill-development agenda to facilitate the globalization process as well as poverty alleviation. The need of the hour is the government's commitment to a demand-driven, flexible and need-based training program guided by a professional rather than rule-based approach.

Shifting Agenda in the Twenty-First Century: Possible Directions for HRM in India

In the present competitive business environment the Indian HR function faces a large number of challenges as already discussed. To survive and flourish in the new dispensation, drastic changes are required at the national, organizational and individual levels. Some of these seem to be taking place, though possibly not with the required rigor and not quite in the right direction. One serious problem while making such judgments and analyses is the unavailability of reliable empirical research evidence.

The national level

The previous section highlighted some of the main national factors which significantly influence HRM in India (see also Budhwar and Sparrow, 1998, 2002a). Early indications suggest that the nature and accordingly the impact of most of the national factors (especially different institutions such as trade unions, legal framework, different pressure groups and the dynamic business environment) on Indian HRM is going to change. The legislations have to be amended so as to suit the present economic environment and help both workers and employers in the "real" sense. The stance of the unions is expected to become more cooperative. The dynamic business environment is further going to dictate the nature and type of HRM systems suitable for the country. With the rapid developments in the software and IT-enabled services (ITeS) sector and an increased emphasis on business process outsourcing (BPO), one may expect the emergence of sector-specific HRM patterns. For example, this will be the case for knowledge-based industries such as software and contact centers (see Budhwar and Singh, 2003).

The organizational level

At the organizational level the following is expected.

A strategic approach to HRM
Research evidence (see Budhwar and Sparrow, 1997, 2002b; Budhwar and Khatri, 2001) regarding the strategic nature of HRM in Indian national firms suggests that there is a low representation of the personnel function at board level, and few organizations have devised formal corporate strategies. Of these, a handful seem to consult the personnel function at the outset (this compares to a norm of around 50 percent in European organizations), many involve personnel in early consultation while developing corporate strategy and many also involve personnel during the implementation of that strategy. It seems that the status of the personnel function in India has improved over a short span of 10 years or so. The number of personnel specialists moving to the position of CEO has increased over the last few years, such that one out of every six CEOs of the top fifty Indian companies has been reported as a personnel

specialist (Venkata Ratnam, 1996). On the other hand, it seems that Indian firms are witnessing a significant devolvement of responsibility of HRM to line managers. This is noticeable in the areas of pay determination, recruitment, training, industrial relations, health and safety and expansion/reduction decisions. Moreover, Indian firms have been showing an increased emphasis on training and development of HR (see Budhwar and Sparrow, 2002b). However, if a strategy of devolvement is not associated with a closer integration of HRM into the business planning processes, it may create a situation of chaos in organizations as they attempt to cope with HRM implications of liberalization. Hence, the way forward is the adoption of a more strategic approach to HRM. Perhaps this agenda is already on the move and is being put into practice (see Agarwala, 2003; Singh, 2003). Certainly, this is the case with the MNCs operating in the country (see Budhwar and Björkman, 2003).

Structured and rationalized internal labor markets (ILMs)
The existing literature suggests the existence of unique ILMs in Indian organizations, based on social relations, political affiliations, political contacts, caste, religion and economic power (see Budhwar and Khatri, 2001). However, considering the present dynamic business environment, Indian organizations need to pursue more rationalized HRM practices and build strong ILMs (which should solely emphasize performance and be less influenced by the aforementioned social, economic, religious and political factors). There are some indications regarding such developments (in the form of increased emphasis on training and development, preference for talent in the recruitment and performance-based compensation), however, these tend to be more in the MNCs or the private sector. Globalization dynamics require that there is a need to speed up merit and performance-based decision-making in all sectors.

Open to change, sharing and learning
In the present competitive business environment, radical changes are taking place and it is difficult to keep track of many such changes. The new economic environment, although presenting a number of threats to local firms, also offers many opportunities to learn, collaborate and adapt to the new context. To make the best use of existing conditions, Indian firms need to be flexible and demonstrate readiness to change. Regular interaction with competitors and relevant stakeholders is becoming a necessity in the modern networked organizations. In this regard, much may be learnt from HR managers working in MNCs operating in India who are very open and flexible in their approach to managing human resources. For example, a recent research investigation with sixty-five top HR managers in as many foreign firms operating in India (see Budhwar and Björkman, 2003) reported that local firms are more rigid to change, less transparent in their operations, provide less learning opportunities and operate on traditional ILMs. However, the HR managers also perceived that the scenario is rapidly changing and such a gap between the working of MNCs and local firms is going to decrease in future. This should be one of the main agenda for Indian firms. The liberalization of economic policies, globalization realities and the operating practices of foreign firms will all put pressure on Indian firms for a more professional performance. The increasing number of Indian students graduating from the developed countries

and going back to India will also contribute a great deal towards resorting to a greater degree of professionalism by visionary Indian firms.

Crossvergence of HRM

With the arrival of a very large number of MNCs to India one may expect an active mixing-up of different management systems (such as the Japanese or American way of doing things). In such conditions, there will be a greater possibility of standardization of managerial roles across different firms. This is an outcome of the globalization exigencies (see Debrah and Smith, 2002) or some kind of *crossvergence*, that is, blending of work cultures (due to the active interface of diverse groups), that is taking place in India (see Ralston *et al.*, 1993; Gopalan and Stahl, 1998). Hence, one may expect cultural convergence and overlap among different types of firms operating in the country. Already, Japanese and many American firms operating in India are able to adopt their respective HR practices in their operations with minor modifications (see Budhwar and Björkman, 2003).

The Individual level

Many Indian educational institutions (such as the Indian Institute of Management and Indian Institute of Technology) are known to be producing world-class graduates. Considering the rapidly changing business environment and the emergence of a large number of MNCs in the country, a paradigm shift in the mindsets of individuals is evident. For example, tendencies for a strong preference to work in a reputed public sector organization, lifelong employment, making available only limited jobs for females, and so on, are all changing fast. The Indian worker has either preferred for a secured employment in the sluggish public sector or has been hostile to the exploitative practices of the family-run private enterprises. The HRM policies of the foreign companies have exercised considerable power in influencing this scenario. For example, professional customer handling by Citibank has been positively influencing the public sector banks in the country that now have to operate in a competitive environment. The Indian managers view these practices as benchmarks. Further, most foreign firms and an ever-larger number of local firms emphasize the need to attract talent. They are increasingly adopting formal, structured and rational approaches to attract, acquire and retain talent. This has significantly influenced behavior both at the individual and organizational levels. The opportunities provided by the new sectors such as software, contact centers and ITeS on the one hand and the MNCs on the other have encouraged females to come and join the mainstream workforce. Such developments are expected to continue and will eventually help transform the adoption of HRM practices in the country.

Conclusion

This chapter highlighted the state of people-management policies and practices in India and their roots in the country's historical background, environmental framework, institutions, contexts and styles. The analysis shows that there is remarkable progress in the professionalization of HRM in the organized sector; this is happening despite the tendency towards a shrinking percentage of the organized sector employment in the country. Attempts towards greater professionalism may be attributed partly to the progressive policies brought about and pursued by the MNCs and the professionally managed Indian organizations, including some of the public sector enterprises (see, e.g. Prasad, 1996; Uppal and Singh, 2001). The attitude towards business practice in general is changing, and people are realizing how far they need to change so as to cope. Among others, the key problems that have adversely influenced the management of HR in India include lack of a vision for skill and competency development, the rigidity caused by the labor law framework, the hierarchy-driven mindsets of employers, the government's indecisiveness in matters of privatization and dis-investment, and fragility of political coalitions that adversely affect the need to take bold decisions.

Another important factor affecting the HRM policies is the deceleration in the employment growth in the organized sector and the massive underemployment in a labor surplus economy. This increases the power of employers, and enables them to shape their HR strategies towards cost reduction. Thus a greater reliance may be placed on employment of peripheral rather than core employees. With the weakening of employee power, the HRM practices *vis-à-vis* this section of employees are bound to reflect hard devices including the resort to lower minimum standards of employment and commission of unfair labor practices (ULPs).

It is noticeable that the role of HRM managers is transforming from being the child of the Industrial Disputes Act to being responsible for culture building, communication, change management, performance management and measuring effectiveness of HR systems and interventions. Within the organized sector, however, the HRM practices are quite varied depending upon diverse factors. The majority of management schools, however, have not yet responded to the challenges of the new environment in terms of evolving appropriate courses, even as the professionals have responded well to the challenges by using the most modern interventions. A shift is noticeable in the attitude of the government, from dispensing social justice to ensuring the success of the export-promotion model of development. Interestingly, this has been possible to quite an extent despite the rigid labor law framework, for it is the governmental power which activates that framework. A rapidly growing industry of HR professionals has emerged, which is increasingly becoming sensitive to the needs of aligning HRM with business needs and strategies. Apart from the strategic performance of the traditional HR functions, new transformational themes are being identified (Saini, 2000; Varkky *et al.*, 2001). These, among others, include concepts like "People Capability Maturity Model," work–life balance, diversity management, six sigma and strategic leadership.

Some of the key challenges before the Indian state include the success of the second generation economic reforms which involve changing the legal framework, including streamlining the working of the unorganized sector and providing a workable model of competency and skill development at the national level. It will be interesting to see how the new government responds to the demands of this task, which has been on the reform agenda for more than a decade. Once the reforms in this sector take place, the matured HR professionals industry in the country is growing fast enough to respond to the emergent organizational justice issues, especially in professionally managed organizations. With the passage of time the number of such organizations is bound to increase. An era of people management issues being guided by appropriately carved-out HRM policies and practices is foreseeable, and the hitherto adversarial model of employee justice dispensation promoted by the present legal framework is likely to become weakened over time.

As noted earlier, Hofstede (1991) has attributed moderate uncertainty avoidance and power distance to Indian business configurations. This tends to defy initiative and thus proves counter to creativity. If HRM function grows fast it can help alter these cultural realities as well. Many MNCs are practicing progressive HRM practices in their Indian locales, which will help foster transparency and creativity to be benchmarked by progressive Indian organizations. For example, delayering has taken place in Indian organizations such as ICICI. In many Indian organizations bosses are being addressed by first name. Undoubtedly, however, internalizing soft HR as a way of organizational life is a complex task and one must refrain from indulging in platitudinous exhortations in this regard. Creating world-class competitors is an uphill task. It necessitates building "transaction governance capacity" (TCG) and requires that the economy upgrades itself (Prahlad, 1998). MNCs have multiple options and the country needs tremendous investment in capacity-building to attract them. They will also contribute towards a faster dawn of the era of soft HRM as a way of organizational life that will help expedite the realization of the goals of efficiency, productivity, trickle-down-effect and economic prosperity.

REFERENCES

Adams, S. and Krishnan, P. (2003) "Documentation of the consultative workshop on the project SCEC" under the program: Restructuring and Strengthening the National Vocational Training System (NVTS). Proceeding of a two-day workshop organized by GTZ (Germany) and DGET, Ministry of Labour, Government of India, India International Centre, New Delhi, 16–17 January 2003.

Agarwala, T. (2003) "Innovative human resource practices and organizational commitment: An empirical investigation," *International Journal of Human Resource Management* 14: 175–98.

Amba-Rao, S. (1994) "US HRM principles: Cross-country comparisons and two case applications in India," *International Journal of Human Resource Management* 5 (3): 755–78.

Balasubramanian, A.G. (1994) "Evolution of personnel function in India – A re-examination, Part I," *Management and Labour Studies* 19 (4): 196–210.

Balasubramanian, A.G. (1995) "Evolution of personnel function in India – A re-examination, Part II," *Management and Labour Studies* 20 (1): 5–14.

Budhwar, P. (1998) "Comparative human resource management: A cross-national study of India and Britain," Ph.D. Dissertation, Manchester Business School, Manchester.

Budhwar, P. (1999) "Indian management style and HRM" in M. Tayaeb (ed.) *International business text*, London: Pitman, pp. 534–40.

Budhwar, P. (2000) "Factors influencing HRM policies and practices in India: An empirical study," *Global Business Review* 1 (2): 229–47.

Budhwar, P. (2001) "Human resource management in India" in P.S. Budhwar and Y.A. Debrah (eds.) *Human resource management in developing countries*, London: Routledge, pp. 75–90.

Budhwar, P. (2003) "Culture and management in India," in M. Warner (ed.) *Culture and management in Asia*, London: RoutledgeCurzon, pp. 66–81.

Budhwar, P. and Björkman, 1. (2003) "A corporate perspective on the management of human resources in foreign firms operating in India," *2003 International HRM Conference*, 4–6 June 2003, Limerick, Ireland.

Budhwar, P. and Khatri, N. (2001) "Comparative human resource management in Britain and India: An empirical study," *International Journal of Human Resource Management* 13 (5): 800–26.

Budhwar, P. and Singh, V. (2003) "HRM in call centres in India: An exploratory study," *2003 International HRM Conference*, 4–6 June 2003, Limerick, Ireland.

Budhwar, P. and Sparrow, P. (1997), "Evaluating levels of strategic integration and development of human resource management in India," *International Journal of Human Resource Management* 8: 476–94.

Budhwar, P. and Sparrow, P. (1998) "National factors determining Indian and British HRM practices: An empirical study," *Management International Review* 38 (Special issue 2): 105–21.

Budhwar, P. and Sparrow, P. (2002a) "An integrative framework for determining cross-national human resource management practices," *Human Resource Management Review* 12 (3): 377–403.

Budhwar, P. and Sparrow, P. (2002b) "Strategic HRM through the cultural looking glass: Mapping cognitions of British and Indian HRM managers," *Organization Studies* 23 (4): 599–638.

Budhwar, L., Reeves, D. and Farrell, P. (2000) "Life goals as a function of social class and child rearing practices: A study of India," *International Journal of Inter-Cultural Relations* 24: 227–45.

Business India (1998) "Clutching at Straws," *Business India*, March 9–22.

Debrah, Y. and Smith, I. (2002) "Globalization, employment and the workplace: Diverse impacts?" in Y. Debrah and I. Smith (eds.) *Globalization, employment and the workplace*, London: Routledge, pp. 1–23.

Debrah, Y., McGovern, I. and Budhwar, P. (2000) "Complementarity or competition: The development of human resources in a growth triangle," *International Journal of Human Resource Management* 11 (2): 314–35.

Debroy, B. (1996) "The agenda for labour market reform in India," paper presented at the International Conference on Law and Economics, Project LARGE (A project of the UNDP and National Labour Law School for the Ministry of Finance, Government of India), New Delhi, 11–13 January 1996.

Ghoshal, S., Piramal, G. and Budhiraja, S. (2001) *World class in India*, New Delhi: Penguin Books.

Gopalan, S. and Stahl, A. (1998) "Application of American management theories and practices to the Indian business environment: Understanding the impact of national culture," *American Business Review* 16 (2): 30–41.

Government of India (2002a) *Report of the National Commission on Labour* (second), New Delhi: Ministry of Labour.

Government of India (2002b) *Annual report 2001–02*, New Delhi: Ministry of Labour.

Hofstede, G. (1991) *Cultures' consequences: Software of the mind*, London: McGraw-Hill.

Hofstede, G. (1993) "Cultural constraints in management theories," *Academy of Management Executive* 7 (1): 81–93.

Johri, C.K. (1998) "INDIA" in *International encyclopedia of laws: Labour law and industrial relations* (general editor: R. Blanpain), Deventer, the Netherlands: Kluwer Law International.

Kanungo, R.N. and Mendonca, M. (1994) "Culture and performance improvement," *Productivity* 35 (3): 447–53.

Legge, K. (1995) *Human resource management: Rhetorics and realities*, London: Macmillan.

Mathur, A. (2002) Background paper on "Skill acquisition and the Indian labour force" presented at the consultative Workshop on Employment and Labour market Reforms in India, organized by Institute of Human Development, New Delhi, 12–13 December.

Mishra, L. (2001) *Economy and labour*, New Delhi: Manak Publications.

Nadler, L. (1970) *Developing human resources*, Reading, MA: Addison-Wesley.

Pareek, U. and Rao, T.V. (1981) *Designing and managing human resource systems*, New Delhi: Oxford and IBH.

Prahled, C.K. (1998) "Globalization: pitfall, pain and potential" in B. Debroy (ed.) *Challenges of globalization*, New Delhi: Rajiv Gandhi Institute for Contemporary Studies and Konark Publishers.

Prahlad, C.K. (1999) "The power of imagination: India's legacy and the path to the future," *Business Today*, 22 February: 115–19.

Prasad, K. (1996) *Organizational development for organizational excellence*, New Delhi: Macmillan.

Ralston, D.A., Gustafson, D.J., Cheung, F.M. and Terpstra, R.H. (1993) "Differences in managerial values: A study of United States', Hong Kong, and PRC Managers," *Journal of International Business Studies* 24 (2): 249–75.

Ramaswamy, E.A. (2000) *Managing human resources*, New Delhi: Oxford University Press.

Rao, T.V. (1999) *HRD audit: Evaluating the human resource function for business improvement*, New Delhi: Response Books (a division of Sage Publications).

Sahay, S. and Walsham, G. (1997) "Social structure and managerial agency in India," *Organisation Studies* 18: 415–44.

Saini, D.S. (1995) "Compulsory adjudication syndrome in India: Some implications for workplace relations" in D.S. Saini (ed.) *Labour law, work and development: Essays in honour of P.G. Krishnan*, New Delhi: Westville.

Saini, D.S. (1995a) "Leaders or pleaders: The dynamics of brief-case trade unionism under the existing legal framework," *Journal of the Indian Law Institute* 37 (1): 73–91.

Saini, D.S. (1997) "Labour court administration in India," in ILO (ed.), *Labour adjudication in India*, New Delhi: International Labour Organization – South Asian Advisory Team.

Saini, D.S. (1999) "Labour legislation and social justice," *Economic and Political Weekly* (special issue on review of Labour), xxxiv (39): L-32 to L-40, 25 September.

Saini, D.S. (2000) "Introduction" in D.S. Saini and S.A. Khan (eds.) *Human resource management: Perspectives for the new era*, New Delhi: Response Books (a division of Sage Publications).

Saini, D.S. (2003) "Alleviating poverty through skills development: Lessons for law-making in developing countries," paper presented at workshop on law and poverty V, organized by CROP programme of the International Social Science Council and the Social Science Academy of Nigeria at Abuja (Nigeria) 24–6 November 2003.

Saini, D.S. and Khan, S.A. (eds.) (2000) *Human resource management: Perspectives for the new era*, New Delhi: Response Books (a division of Sage Publications).

Sharma, I.J. (1984) "The culture context of Indian managers," *Management and Labour Studies* 9 (2): 72–80.

Shrouti, A. and Kumar, N. (1994) *New economic policy, changing management strategies – impact on workers and trade unions*, New Delhi: Friedrich Ebert Stiftung.

Singh, S. (2003) "Strategic orientation and firm performance in India," *The International Journal of Human Resource Management* 14: 530–43.

Sinha, J.B.P. and Kanungo, R. (1997) "Context sensitivity and balancing in Indian organization behavior," *International Journal of Psychology* 32: 93–105.

Sparrow, P. and Budhwar, P. (1997) "Competition and change: mapping the Indian HRM recipe against world-wide patterns." *Journal of World Business* 32(3): 224–42.

Tayeb, M. (1987) "Contingency theory and culture: a study of matched English and the Indian manufacturing firms," *Organisation Studies* 8: 241–61.

Times of India (2003) "Executive digest section," *Times of India*, 10 January: 17.

Tripathi, R.C. (1990) "Interplay of values in the functioning of Indian organizations," *International Journal of Psychology* 25: 715–34.

Uppal, B. and Singh, U. (2001) "Dealing with corporate uncertainties: Mergers, acquisitions and others – SAIL, a case study," in B. Varkky *et al.* (2001). *Human resource management: Changing roles, changing goals*, New Delhi: Excel Books.

Varkky, B., Parashar, P. and Brahma, G. (2001) *Human resource management: Changing roles, changing goals*, New Delhi: Excel Books.

Venkata Ratnam, C.S. (1996) *Industrial relations in Indian states*, New Delhi: Global Business Press.

Venkata Ratnam, C.S. (2001) *Globalization and labour–management relations: Dynamics of change*, New Delhi: Response (a division of Sage Publications).

Venkata Ratnam, C.S. and Srivastava, B.K. (1991) *Personnel management and human resources*, New Delhi: Tata-McGraw-Hill Publishing Company.

Walton, J. (1999) *Strategic human resource development*, London: Financial Times–Prentice Hall.

Useful websites

National Human Resource Development Network:	http://www.hrdnetworkdelhi.com
Academy of Human Resource Development:	http://www.academyofhrd.org
Monthly Magazine on Human Resource Management (India):	http://www.humancapitalonline.com
All India Management Association:	http://www.aima-ind.org
Indian portal on Human Resource Development:	http://www.humanlinks.com
Human Internet:	http://www.humanresources.about.com
HR World:	http://www.hrworld.com
Executive Search Engine/Career's Search:	http://www.edgeindia.com
Recruitment Platform for IT Professionals:	http://www.jobcurry.com

Part III

Strategy into Action

The chapters in this part describe the viewpoints of several authors on the topic of linking human resource management activities with the firm. More specifically, they seek to answer the question: "Is there a better or preferred way of linking human resource activities with the firm?" In addressing this general question, they provide numerous examples illustrating that the answer may be that there are several ways, perhaps equally good, to link people with the firm. Those ways might depend upon several factors, many of which are discussed by the authors in Part I of this reader. These factors include characteristics of the internal environment such as top management values, the vision and mission of the firm, its size, strategy, technology, knowledge intensity, structure, products, services, and customers; and such external characteristics as whether it is service or manufacturing, degree of competition, size of the market, barriers to entry, ease of substitution for the products and services, legal and regulatory conditions, educational systems, demographics, political conditions, degree of unionization, and nature of the investment community. The other major question that the authors address in this part is: "What is the main purpose or reason for managing human resources as effectively as possible?" In general, they suggest that the purpose is to gain competitive advantage, attain higher levels of performance, satisfy the needs of employees and customers, and adhere to the rules and regulations of society.

The first chapter in this part by Boxall, drawing upon the work done in high-performance work systems in manufacturing, discusses human resource strategy and competitive advantage in the service sector. The author addresses whether or not it is possible to attain competitive advantage only in firms that are knowledge intensive, such as professional service firms. His work suggests that this may not be the case, but that the possibilities to attain competitive advantage in the service sector might be greater, although there may be substantial barriers to maintaining that advantage. Thus the work of strategic human resource management needs to be ongoing, one of monitoring and maintaining one's position in the marketplace. This adds a dynamic dimension to the area of strategic human resource management.

In the second chapter by Wright and Snell, the authors develop a unifying framework for understanding fit and flexibility in strategic human resource management. The authors focus their concerns on two major issues in strategic human resource management: establishing a fit or linkage between existing business strategy and the human resource system; and retaining enough flexibility to adjust the human resource system as the strategies of the business change (adding to the dynamic dimension referred to by Boxall). The authors review the literature on business strategy–HRM strategy fit that incorporates dimensions that enable the firm to find a temporary fit, but then to adjust as circumstances warrant. Figure 15.1 illustrates their model. Underlying the success of the firm's ability to have the fit and to have the ability to make adjustments are resource flexibility and coordination flexibility. Key measures of these are detailed in Table 15.1. The authors conclude with several implications for further research for strategic human resource management.

Associated with increased globalization and increased competition is the reality of the need to manage knowledge more systematically than ever before. In the third chapter, Lepak and Snell develop a very nice description of the human resource architecture for firms engaged in knowledge-based competition. This builds on their earlier work of the architectural perspective that views a firm as a portfolio of human capital. They review this perspective and then apply it in their discussion of human resource management in firms that are engaged in knowledge-based competition, such as professional service firms described by Boxall. They go on to describe the issues in and challenges of managing a portfolio of human capital competencies and leveraging knowledge across the HR architecture. The authors conclude with several interesting research implications for strategic human resource management.

As firms manage their human resources more strategically, they appear to ask the questions, "How can we measure our success?" and "What are the criteria against which we should measure our success?" The fourth chapter by Beatty, Huselid, and Schneier addresses these questions in their presentation of the business scorecard shown in Fig. 16.1. Their discussion moves to the component of the business scorecard most relevant to human resource management. Then they elaborate on this in their depiction of the HR scorecard (Fig. 16.2). Linking HR with the business is done through the use of competitive strategy and four aspects of HR: competencies, practices, deliverables, and systems. These are all tightly linked so that HR professionals and their managers can take the next step which is to link the HR scorecard back to the business scorecard (Fig. 16.6). This figure also illustrates the several criteria that organizations, and their HR departments, can use to evaluate their success. These criteria reflect the concerns of the multiple stakeholders described by Jackson and Schuler in the second chapter in Part I.

In the course of surviving and being more profitable in this intensely competitive world, firms are finding that they have to change, to restructure themselves. Not only may this move people and their work groups around, it may also move them out of the organization. Because employees are an important stakeholder in organizations, they deserve to have this process managed as effectively and with as much sensitivity as possible. In the fifth chapter, Cascio provides excellent examples from companies around the world and guidelines so that organizations can attain both of these concerns.

His suggestions are based on the premise that people are the source of innovation and renewal, especially knowledge-based organizations, and that the development of new markets, customers, and revenue streams depends on the wise use of a firm's human assets. His examples and guidelines are consistent with this premise.

Chapter 14

HR Strategy and Competitive Advantage in the Service Sector

Peter Boxall

One of the most important developments in the literature linking HR strategy and business performance is the growth in studies of high-performance work systems (HPWSs). The publication of *The New American Workplace*, by Appelbaum and Batt (1994), helped to popularise this term. A subsequent book on HPWSs in US manufacturing, *Manufacturing Advantage* (Appelbaum *et al.*, 2000), has built on this foundation. This book examines three US industries – steelmaking, clothing manufacture and medical electronics manufacture – and provides consistent evidence of mutually beneficial ('win-win') outcomes for firms and workers:

> Plant performance in each of the three industries examined is higher on the measures that matter to managers in those industries.[1] The opportunity-to-participate scale derived from the worker survey has a positive effect on worker outcomes as well. ...We find no support for the view that more participatory workplaces increase worker stress. Importantly, we find a significant improvement in wages associated with the extent of the opportunity to participate.

According to these authors, the work systems and employment models seen as supportive of high performance imply a mix of key practices: more rigorous selection and better training systems to increase ability levels, more comprehensive incentives (such as employee bonuses and internal career ladders) to enhance motivation and participative structures (such as self-managing teams and quality circles) that improve

P. Boxall, "HR Strategy and Competitive Advantage in the Service Sector," *Human Resource Management Journal*, Vol. 13, No. 3 (2003): 5–20.

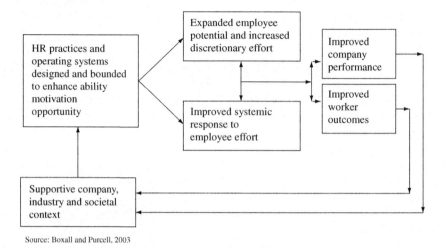

Source: Boxall and Purcell, 2003

Figure 14.1   High-performance work systems: commonly hypothesised linkages.

opportunity to contribute (Appelbaum *et al.*, 2000: 26–7, 39–46, 103–4). While there is significant debate about the particular mix of high-performance practices, one of the key arguments running through the literature is that the relevant practices work much better when 'bundled' together (Ichniowski *et al.*, 1996; MacDuffie, 1995). The idea is that productivity is best served by the systemic interactions among the practices. Adding only one of the practices is likely to 'have little or no effect on performance' (Ichniowski *et al.*, 1997: 311). Thus, HPWSs imply a high and consistent investment in human resources in order to reap greater benefits in the productivity and possibly in the agility of the firm. A map of the commonly hypothesised linkages in HPWSs is shown in Fig. 14.1 (Boxall and Purcell, 2003). As with the work of Appelbaum *et al.* (2000), the figure relies on the 'AMO' rubric: performance is seen as a function of employee ability (A), motivation (M) and opportunity to participate or contribute (O). If practices fostering these variables are enhanced, better use will be made of employee potential and discretionary judgment. In an organisational system that is truly receptive to this kind of work reform, the argument is that outcomes should be superior for both parties.

While there is ongoing debate over the extent to which HPWSs generate mutually beneficial outcomes (see, e.g. Godard 2001a, 2001b; Osterman, 2000; Ramsay *et al.*, 2000), the evidence on the employer side is that there are certain contexts in which such systems are likely to be cost-effective. While some would argue that the key contingency in manufacturing is competitive strategy, a close reading of the evidence suggests that employers more often find HPWSs cost-effective in high-technology or capital-intensive manufacturing (Arthur, 1994; MacDuffie, 1995; Osterman, 1994; Youndt *et al.*, 1996). This seems to be true irrespective of whether cost leadership or differentiation (or some mix of the two) is being pursued in competitive strategy (Boxall and Purcell, 2000, 2003). In other words, there are clearly parts of manufacturing where employers seek to complement high investment in physical capital with high investment in human capital in order to enhance total factor productivity. To understand this point, it helps to remember that a strategy of cost leadership in high technology or capital-intensive manufacturing rarely means that labour costs are in competition – a key point of contrast with the typical situation in services. On the other hand, in labour-intensive parts of manufacturing, competition is increasingly driven by plant location decisions in order to take advantage of lower labour costs, provided that quality and delivery standards are adequate. Tayloristic work systems and inexpensive HR practices are prevalent in these environments and are likely to remain so as long as they are cost-effective (Boxall and Purcell, 2003).

This chapter is concerned with the possibilities for HPWSs or, expressed more generally, HR advantage in services. HR advantage occurs where a firm builds and sustains competitive advantage substantially through the quality of its human capital and organisational processes (Boxall, 1996). The chapter examines the links between HR strategy and business performance in the service sector, asking two key questions:

- How do differences in market characteristics (including the knowledge content of services) lead to different competitive dynamics in services?
- In what circumstances can service firms build and sustain advantage through superior investments in human resources?

The chapter is structured as follows. It begins by reviewing the literature linking competitive positioning and HR strategy in services. The research discussed here is not an exhaustive review of the literature on work systems and employee relations in services. Rather, it selects those studies that show an awareness of market segmentation or strategic groups in services and which link these to HR strategy. The next section builds on this basis to create a new map or typology of the links from market characteristics to competitive dynamics and HR strategy in services. This analysis helps the chapter to explore the issue of whether competitive differentiation through human resources is possible only in high-skill areas such as professional services. The chapter concludes with a set of propositions on the conditions firms must meet to achieve and sustain HR advantage in services. These propositions are offered as a basis for further research, preferably of a longitudinal nature.

Market Segmentation

It is a commonplace to observe that the service sector covers a huge range of human services, varying significantly in the nature of the work and the level of skill required (Frenkel, 2000; Frenkel et al., 1999). After many years of domination by manufacturing studies in HRM and industrial relations (IR), more scholars are beginning to analyse the links between competitive strategy and HR strategy in services (e.g. Batt, 2000; Keltner et al., 1999; Lashley, 1998; Peccei and Rosenthal, 2001).

The only way we can make any serious progress on the nature of the links between competitive and HR strategies is through frameworks which help us handle the range of service markets and the reality of segmentation within service markets. Studies of markets that allow us to identify competitive segments (on the customer side) (Keltner et al., 1999) and/or strategic groups (on the firm side) are very important

(Bogner and Thomas, 1996; Fiegenbaum and Thomas, 1993; Gorman *et al.*, 1996; Peteraf and Shanley, 1997).

An industry may have several segments/strategic groups. In each group, firms are seeking to serve a particular set of customer needs in much the same way.[2] As a result, they become significant organisations for each other; benchmarking against other members of the group has obvious benefits. In other parts of the industry, firms are seeking to serve other client groups. It is not that easy to shift strategy from one of these groups to another; mobility barriers tend to be quite significant (Tallman and Atchison, 1996).

Major studies in the HR/IR literature which explore market segments or strategic groups include Batt (2000) on call centres in US telecommunications, Eaton (2000) and Hunter (2000) on US rest homes, Haynes and Fryer (1999, 2000) on New Zealand hotels, Rispoli (1996) on Italian hotels, Lashley (1998) on UK fast-food restaurants, and Doorewaard and Meihuizen's (2000) research on Dutch and German management consultancy firms. These studies show that there are discernible segments in each of these industries where competitive and HR strategies tend to co-vary.

Batt (2000), for example, analyses four segments in call-centre work in the US telecommunications industry. These segments vary in terms of the complexity and value of the employee-customer interaction. At the low end there are low-margin interactions of short duration, typically with predetermined scripts and with strong technological monitoring of employees. At the high end there are high-margin, low-volume interactions relying far more on employee skill and discretion and where technology is much more of an enabler than a monitor. One statistic alone is telling: at the low-margin end, operators deal with an average of 465 customers a day; in the two midrange segments they deal respectively with 100 and 64, and at the top end they deal with an average of 32 (Batt, 2000: 550). Batt finds significant differences in the contours of HR strategy across these market segments:

> Implementation of high involvement work practices varies systematically, according to the demand characteristics of the customer segment served, with the use of these systems more likely in higher value-added markets. Work practices that correlate with customer segment include the type of interaction with the customer; the extent to which technology is used as a control device versus a resource input; the skill requirements of jobs; discretion to influence work methods and procedures; and types and levels of compensation.   (*Batt, 2000: 555*)

Sectoral studies such as Batt's (2000) uniformly support the point that HR strategy is closely connected to competitive differentiation in services. Other compelling examples can be found in the US studies of rest homes cited earlier (Eaton, 2000; Hunter, 2000) where HR investments (in training, pay, career structures and staffing levels) are greater in firms that target higher value niches.

Lest these examples be criticised for focusing on less skilled service industries, it is worthwhile pointing out that customer differentiation can also be discerned in professional services. Doorewaard and Meihuizen's (2000) study of Dutch and German management consultancies is instructive. Here the authors discern two broad strategic types: firms oriented to efficiency and firms oriented to expertise. The former offer standard solution(s) to familiar problems in an efficient way, while the latter promote an individual professional's ability to offer new, client-specific solutions to new, unusual problems (Doorewaard and Meihuizen, 2000: 43). These are tendencies, not hard and fast categories, but they are associated with differentiation in HR strategy. Expertise-driven firms try to hire highly intelligent free spirits and retain them through challenging, high-discretion work, while those oriented to efficiency have a more bureaucratic model of HRM. Starbuck's (1992) discussion of knowledge-intensive firms can be used to add a dynamic element to this picture: management consultancies and similar firms may start up as expertise-oriented organisations. Some choose to stay small and stick with their expert culture, while others grow through routinisation and become efficiency-oriented in their production systems and HR strategy.

There ought to be more research based on longitudinal studies, but there is enough in these studies to suggest that we can do some productive theory-building at this point in time. This is the objective of this chapter.

Market Characteristics and Competitive Dynamics

Two building blocks help us to create a typology linking market characteristics, competitive dynamics and HR strategy in services. One is a typology of work systems developed by Herzenberg, Alic and Wial (1998) (cited approvingly by Batt (2000) and Frenkel *et al.* (1999)). This typology is shown in Fig. 14.2. While not recognising all complexity, it has the value of summarising four readily discernible categories of

Work systems	Tightly constrained	Unrationalised labour-intensive	Semi-autonomous	High-skill autonomous
Examples	Telephone operators, fast-food workers, cheque proofers	Some nurses' aides, hotel maids, domestics, long-distance truck drivers, childcare workers, clerical homeworkers	Clerical and administrative jobs with relatively broad responsibilities, low-level managers, some sales workers, UPS truck drivers	Physicians, high-level managers, laboratory technicians, electricians, engineers
Markets served	High volume, low cost; standardised quality	Low cost, low volume; often low or uneven quality	Volume and quality vary	Low volume (each job may differ); quality is often in the eye of the beholder
Task supervision	Tight	Loose	Moderate	Little
Formal education of workers	Low to moderate	Low to moderate (skill often unrecognised)	Moderate	High
On-the-job training	Limited	Some informal, unrecognised learning from other workers	Limited to moderate	Substantial
Source: Abridged from Herzenberg *et al.*, 1998:42-3				

Figure 14.2   Herzenberg et al.'s (1998) typology of work systems.

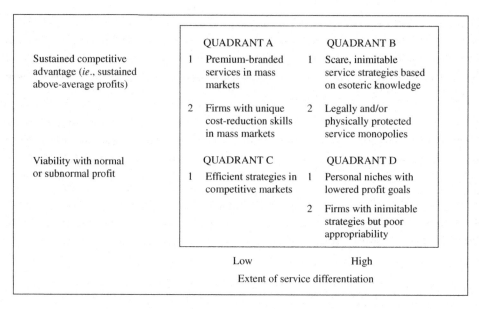

	QUADRANT A		QUADRANT B	
Sustained competitive advantage (*ie.*, sustained above-average profits)	1	Premium-branded services in mass markets	1	Scare, inimitable service strategies based on esoteric knowledge
	2	Firms with unique cost-reduction skills in mass markets	2	Legally and/or physically protected service monopolies
Viability with normal or subnormal profit		QUADRANT C		QUADRANT D
	1	Efficient strategies in competitive markets	1	Personal niches with lowered profit goals
			2	Firms with inimitable strategies but poor appropriability

Low   High

Extent of service differentiation

Figure 14.3   A typology of competitive strategies and business outcomes in services.

work, both in service and in manufacturing environments (Herzenberg *et al.*, 1998: 41). Work systems are a critical dimension of HRM and need to be incorporated in any model of the links between HR and competitive strategies (Boxall and Purcell, 2003).

The framework developed by Herzenberg *et al.* (1998) stretches from Taylorist work design to high-discretion systems, such as professional work, where Taylorism has rarely intruded. In-between are two other categories: one recognising the large amount of work which is labour-intensive, less skilled and unrationalised by management systems, and another recognising semi-autonomous work that requires midrange skills and is neither high in discretion nor highly constrained. This latter category, covering a lot of sales, clerical and associate-professional work, becomes important in the argument in this chapter.

The other building block is shown in Fig. 14.3. It provides important theory from strategic management, including (but not only) the resource-based view, which is needed to understand competitive dynamics in services. The figure plots service differentiation against business outcomes. Cost leadership is one of the two main competitive strategies analysed by Porter (1985). While ensuring 'cost parity or proximity' is an issue in any strategy (Porter, 1985: 14), firms can also differentiate in various ways. Miller's research (1992: 403) concurs with Porter's view that cost leadership is one strategic option and provides evidence of three broad types of differentiation: pioneering, salesmanship and quality leadership. His research also argues that possibilities for differentiation vary across industries. Thus, we can expect to find that some service sectors offer greater niche possibilities and have more strategic groups exploiting them than others.

Figure 14.3 recognises variation in the degree of service differentiability and argues that differentiation doesn't necessarily lead to sustained competitive advantage. It helps to define two broad business outcomes – viability and sustained competitive advantage

(Boxall and Steeneveld, 1999). Viability with normal profits is the primary goal of the firm, but the figure notes that in certain cases firms remain viable with sub-normal profits (e.g. because of family financing). Sustained competitive advantage only occurs where there is a sustained source of superior profitability, despite the best efforts of rivals to imitate or outflank it (Barney, 1991).

We should start at Quadrant C. This is the standard picture of perfect competition, as described in any basic economics textbook. In highly competitive markets (and many low-skill services fall into this category), firms need to be able to offer the relevant bundle of services at adequate quality, but costs are always in competition. Service firms in mass markets need to pay the market-clearing wage for the labour they employ, but are unlikely to pay much more than this because labour costs constitute such a significant proportion of total costs (Batt, 2000: 547). Over time, rents will be competed away and profits will tend to normalise. In this process, firms that are undercapitalised (which carry excessive financing costs) or which carry some other form of excess cost will fail (Tallman and Atchison, 1996).

In Quadrant A, first movers in mass-service markets can enjoy temporary windfalls. However, they fall back to Quadrant C, and normal profitability, as others execute good imitation strategies (Reed and DeFillippi, 1990; Tallman and Atchison, 1996). The only firms that sustain their presence in this desirable space are those that build outstanding brand recognition or which develop unique cost-reduction skills (Bogner and Thomas, 1996; Miller, 1992; Porter, 1985). Those that dominate market share may enjoy reputational advantages in the labour market which help them become more selective than other firms employing low-skilled, highly mobile labour. Lashley's (1998) analysis suggests we might place McDonald's fast food restaurants in this category.

Quadrant B contains two stable options. One is the terrain envisaged by Barney's (1991) description of resource-based advantage. The firm is doing something rare, valuable and hard to imitate or out-flank. The classic case here is the knowledge-intensive firm, which competes through valuable but esoteric expertise (Starbuck, 1992). Starbuck's case study of the elite New York law firm, Wachtell Lipton, is a celebrated example (Starbuck, 1993). As Coff (1997, 1999) and Kamoche (1996) have pointed out, it is also important to ensure that shareholders appropriate a healthy share of these rents, not an easy thing because key value generators are often well placed to exploit their special knowledge or negotiate for themselves. This is well demonstrated in the second category, where scarce resources stem from legal or physical protections. A famous historical example concerns the early chartered companies (such as the English East India Company and the Hudson's Bay Company) which were granted monopoly privileges in the 17th century (Jones and Ville, 1996). These companies experimented with various ways (such as bonds and oaths) to curb the opportunism of managers intent on amassing personal fortunes. Principal-agent problems were the constant travelling companion of the companies' rent-seeking behaviour.

Quadrant D notes that service differentiability does not necessarily lead to superior performance. There are two categories here. Small, specialist businesses at the edge of markets can survive as long as it remains sub-economic for the dominant firms that occupy the middle ground to move out to the edges, as argued by organisational ecologists who have developed the theory of resource partitioning

(Carroll and Hannan, 1995: 215–21). It is quite possible that some of these firms develop funding regimes (such as family financing) and adopt profit goals that are less demanding than would be the case in public companies. A second category involves firms in which there are sources of rent, but executives and/or other value generators capture them. This typically occurs through key executives using the special knowledge and power their positions confer to negotiate exceptional levels of remuneration and bonuses. Sometimes it is accompanied by fraud, as is graphically illustrated in several recent US cases of corporate collapse. Whether or not fraud is involved, these firms fail to deal effectively with what might be called the 'politics of appropriation'.

Predictions: Competitive Dynamics and HR Strategy

Figures 14.2 and 14.3 help to lay the basis for Fig. 14.4, which aims to relate market characteristics in services to competitive dynamics and HR strategy. The first two

Service market type	Knowledge content of service	Typical work design	Competitive dynamics in the sector	Predictions for HR strategy in firms
Type 1 Mass-service markets (e.g. petrol stations, fast food, supermarkets)	Low. Key managers or franchisees have critical knowledge, but general labour uses limited, mostly generic 'know-how'	Low discretion. May be highly 'Taylorised' in international franchises or major chains; otherwise unrationalised, low-skill work	Cost-based except to the extent limited by unions and state regulation; substitution of labour for technology and self-service; some branding strategies possible	Firms typically fit HR strategy to their cost-driven competitive strategies through paying only the market-clearing wage and complying minimally with labour laws; very limited prospects for HR advantage, except where premium brands can be created and sustained
Type 2 A mix of mass markets and higher value-added segments (e.g. elder care, hotels, call centres)	Low-to-moderate knowledge levels; mix of skill level needed in the workforce	Traditionally low-to-moderate discretion, but potential for job enrichment and HPWSs	Mix of cost and quality-based competition; greater profit opportunities for firms that identify higher value-added segments	In mass markets, HR strategies are Type 1, but possibilities exist for HR advantage in higher value-added segments; potential problems with imitability and appropriability
Type 3 Very significantly, if not totally, differentiated markets (e.g. high-level professional services)	High knowledge intensity	High discretion – the natural home of HPWSs	Expertise and quality-based competition, but with some anchors on relative pricing; some services may be routinised and migrate back to Type 2 competition	Extensive opportunities for HR advantage in expertise-driven niches; potential problems with imitability and appropriability; use of lower cost HR strategies where expertise is routinised

Figure 14.4   Market characteristics, competitive dynamics and HR strategy in services.

columns in Fig. 14.4 define the nature of the market: the type of knowledge used is an inherent feature of the service. Note that key variables referred to in the figure (such as differentiation and discretion) are really located on continua. To simplify things for theory-building, however, it helps to talk about three types.

The four types of work organisation referred to in Fig. 14.2 are spread across the three categories here, largely because the 'tightly constrained' and 'unrationalised labour-intensive' systems are typically found in low-cost, mass-service markets (Type 1 in Fig. 14.4) and, to some extent, in Type 2. Both these forms of work organisation are identifiable in service sectors, where labour costs are in stiff competition. One simply sees more attempts at Taylorism in some low-margin service sectors than in others. Employers find Taylorism useful for cost-effectiveness in some sectors, but they see no use for it in others.

Similarly, the four types of business outcome identified in Fig. 14.3 are all incorporated into the final column of Fig. 14.4, which outlines predictions for HR strategy. For example, both Quadrant C and A1 in Fig. 14.3 are noted in the Type 1 category in Fig. 14.4 and both Quadrant B1 and D2 are noted in Type 3.

Type 1: Mass-service markets

In mass-service markets, such as gas stations, fast food outlets and supermarkets, key managers or franchisees have critical knowledge, but general labour uses limited, mostly generic 'know-how'. Work design here typically involves one of two types in Herzenberg *et al.*'s (1998) framework. Some firms adopt Taylorism, while others use unrationalised practices. In both cases, costs, including labour costs, are in competition because customers are very price sensitive. Firms do not generally pay above market-clearing wages unless persuaded to do otherwise by unions and state regulation (see, e.g. Hunter, 2000). In their quest to survive in a cost-conscious environment, firms typically substitute labour for technology and self-service. While cost leadership and branding strategies are possible, the dynamics of cost-based competition in mass services have the effect of imposing major constraints on the HR strategies of firms. The key prediction here is that managers fit HR strategy to their cost-based competitive strategies through paying only the market-clearing wage and complying minimally with labour laws. There are very limited prospects for HR advantage, except where premium brands can be created and sustained. Apart from the latter case, firms find that investments in HPWSs are not cost-effective, as Batt (2000: 547, 555–6) argues. This is not an entirely deterministic argument (i.e. market structure determining HR strategy). It does not rule out firm-level creativity, and certainly not elements of managerial idiosyncrasy (good, bad and indifferent) (Purcell, 1999; West and DeCastro, 2001), but it does underline the severe economic constraints when firms operate in these kinds of service market.

Type 2: Mix of mass markets and higher value-added segments

The case studies cited above show that it is possible to break out of the Type 1 pattern in segments of certain service markets, such as elder care, hotels and call centres, where there is much greater variation in customer preferences and higher value-added customers can be targeted. A mix of skill levels is needed in the workforce (e.g. nurse aiding, nurses and other professionals in elder care). Jobs are traditionally low to moderate in discretion, but there is clearly potential for job enrichment (see, e.g. Eaton 2000). Competitive dynamics, then, are based around a mix of cost and quality-based competition. The key predictions for HR strategy are twofold. In mass-service segments, HR strategies will remain Type 1, but firms can discover possibilities for HR advantage in higher value-added segments. In these segments, investments in creating HPWSs are likely to be economically justified. The existence of high skills is not the necessary condition. Skill levels are variable. It is simply necessary that there are profitable higher value segments and that it is cost-effective to invest in developing greater employee skills and higher levels of motivation to serve them.

Type 3: Very significantly, if not totally, differentiated markets

In high-level, professional services and other knowledge-intensive services, work organisation has always involved high levels of employee discretion. This is the natural home of high-performance work systems in the service sector. Firms typically invest in building employee skills, enhancing motivation and providing opportunities to participate. However, following Doorewaard and Meihuizen (2000) and Starbuck (1992), there are two predictions in this model about competitive dynamics and HR strategy. Where high-level services are based on esoteric expertise (with some anchors on relative pricing), competitive strategy and HR strategy virtually merge. It seems silly to make much distinction between them. Committing to hiring certain experts (e.g. bringing them into partnership) will lead to emergent competitive strategies in their fields of expertise: they are the business. This is why it is helpful to think about competitive strategy in professional service firms in a federalist rather than top-down kind of way (Boxall and Steeneveld, 1999; Greenwood et al., 1990). There are extensive opportunities for HR advantage in these expertise-driven niches (admitting that firms may experience problems with appropriability). Where services become routinised (Doorewaard and Meihuizen, 2000), however, firms end up migrating back to Type 2 competition and one can expect to see greater use of lower cost HR strategies.

Barriers to imitation and the problem of appropriation

The discussion so far identifies opportunities for forms of HR advantage. However, it tends to suggest that seeing the opportunity will consistently lead to the result. This is obviously not the case. We need to push our dynamic analysis further. Management will need to foster barriers to imitation because sources of HR advantage will inevitably become subject to competition – from without and also from within. Imitative forces may set in more quickly in Type 2 competition because quality strategies are more easily imitated than those based on esoteric knowledge (Type 3) (Barney, 1991; Coff, 1999). As an aside, this has certainly been the case in automotive manufacturing, where quality is now a 'table stake' rather than a source of advantage (Leonard, 1998).

External competition for rents (sources of superior profitability) implies the firm needs to foster such barriers to imitation as path-dependence, social complexity and causal ambiguity (Barney, 1991; Wright *et al.*, 1994). Arguably, path dependence, or unique timing and learning, plays the primary role in creating barriers to imitation because it generates firm-specific assets and leads to social complexity and some degree of causal ambiguity (Boxall and Purcell, 2000,2003). This argument is supported by the Tallman and Atchison (1996) model of competence-based competition in which the timely and sustained investments of innovators and fast followers in a strategic group progressively exclude others from the game. Both innovators and fast followers have good targeting and timing: other firms don't. They then need to exploit this timing with a system of resources (physical human and organisational) that further differentiates the firm from others outside and, to some extent within, its strategic group (Tallman and Atchison, 1996: 355–7). Management skills in fostering ongoing, systemic learning must play a large role in any successful story of sustained competitive advantage (Boxall and Purcell, 2003; Leonard, 1998). Such skills need to be strongly embedded in the firm's routines and meta-routines (such as environmental sensing and strategic planning), and not solely dependent on heroic leaders, if they are to withstand imitation (Boxall, 1998; Mueller, 1996). There is thus an important role for an astutely formed HR strategy, for a blend of people-management practices and investments which helps the firm to develop innovative and agile behaviour, while not neglecting the stable harvesting of its existing operations.

Internal competition for rents (Coff, 1997,1999; Kamoche, 1996) implies that the firm will need to negotiate a suitable appropriation regime (Kamoche and Mueller, 1998: 1033). As with the problem of external competition for rents, HRM (broadly defined) plays an important role. Governance systems in the firm, including methods of managing managers, will need to ensure that rents are fairly split between investors, managers and other value creators. Clearly, executive management should not be the sole author of these systems: management is both an asset and a liability where appropriation is concerned. Executive managers have serious bargaining power because they have oversight of the production of tacit knowledge – the very tacit knowledge that generates sustained advantage gives key managers the power to dominate appropriation (Coff, 1999). As a result, investor representatives need to play a key role in the politics of governance, but contemporary debate about executive pay shows that this is far from easy.

Conclusions

The broad argument in this chapter is that the match, or fit, between competitive strategy and HR strategy is greater in services than it is in manufacturing. This is because competitive strategies of cost leadership and differentiation are both likely to imply high HR investment in capital-intensive or high-tech manufacturing. A strategy of cost leadership should not be equated with wage-based competition at this end of manufacturing. Management thinking about HR strategy in manufacturing is influenced by the employee-technology interface, not simply by the firm's desired competitive position. As in any sector, it is also, of course, influenced by employee responses, and by labour markets and labour law, among other factors (Boxall, 1996).

In services, however, one learns more about the likely shape of management strategy in HRM by looking closely at what is occurring at the employee-customer interface (Batt, 2000:542). Studies of market segments and strategic groups in services demonstrate the strong links between competitive and HR strategies. This chapter argues that cost-based, low-margin competition in mass services tends to drive out the possibilities for HR advantage, except where firms can fund greater HR investment out of premium branding. Where labour is plentiful, the only real constraints on this form of competition stem from effective forms of unionism and enforced regulation.

It is outside cost-based service competition that we can talk about possibilities for sustained advantage through the quality of human capital and organisational processes. The analysis here suggests that it is not simply high-level, knowledge-intensive services where the possibilities for HPWSs exist. Wherever there are important customer segments that extend beyond mass, low-cost services, there is potential for a pay-back from greater investment in human resources. Key studies on service markets such as call centres (Batt, 2000) and elder care (Eaton, 2000; Hunter, 1999) lead directly to this thesis. We ought, then, to avoid the impression that high-performance work systems are a category that is exclusive to certain elite industries. Rather, HPWSs are potentially available to a wide range of sectors. Putting the point more generally: there are work reform possibilities in many industries, where both parties might benefit or where one party might benefit while the other is not, overall, disadvantaged.

As a basis for further research, preferably of a longitudinal or history-sensitive nature, this chapter implies that five conditions must hold for HPWSs to be feasible in a firm operating in services.

1. *The customer proposition* A viable group of customers (an economic segment) must value some form of differentiation (e.g. higher quality of service of unique expertise). This can occur in midrange (Type 2) as well as knowledge-intensive services (Type 3). It can also occur in mass services (Type 1), where a firm creates and sustains premium branding, but the nature of Type 1 competition is such that this is much less likely.

2. *The HR proposition* Skills of workers do not have to be absolutely high, but the increments in know-how and in motivation that support the competitive differentiation must be a) achievable and b) economically worthwhile (cost-effective).

3. *The non-HR proposition* The business must have sufficient financial capital to support an HR premium (a higher level of investment in selectivity, training, pay, career structures *etc*).

4. *The cognitive and political proposition* Management needs the insight and political will to identify and meet the customer proposition through the right mix of HR and non-HR investment.

5. *The inimitability and appropriability proposition* In order to sustain and exploit a source of HR advantage, management will need to foster barriers to imitation, particularly those associated with path dependence: astute targeting and timing,

and ongoing, systemic learning. The firm will also need to effectively manage the politics of appropriation.

The argument, then, is that the potential for higher value market segmentation, not absolutely high skill levels, is decisive in creating a rationale for HPWSs – or space for HR advantage – in services. This is the point expressed in propositions one and two. Proposition three is needed because human and non-human resources are bundled in the firm (Penrose, 1959; Mueller, 1996): greater financial capital is needed to fund an HR premium. The fourth proposition is added because firms are managed entities, where cognitive limits and internal politics can always get in the way of a good idea (Child, 1972, 1997; Simon, 1947). Finally, not only must management be able to identify and act concertedly on the HR opportunity, but proposition five reminds us that management will also need to foster barriers to imitation and the firm will need to develop a suitable appropriation regime (Kamoche and Mueller, 1998). These are critical elements in any dynamic explanation. In other words, sources of HR advantage become subject to competition from without and, not least, from within (Coff, 1999). Management has a vital role to play, particularly in decisions about the targeting and timing of strategies and the related bundling of resources, and in the orchestration of ongoing, systemic learning. However, the centrality of management in this process also creates significant agency risks which, it goes without saying, should not be managed exclusively by executives.

All of this implies a critical role for astutely formed HR strategy. It helps to think about this role on two levels. On the first level, there is clearly a strategic question about which mix of HR practices and investments constitutes an HPWS in a particular firm and sector. The current literature in the area is obsessed with this question, but it is typically approached in a static manner. There is a second, more dynamic level on which HR strategy should also play a role. This level is concerned with shaping the managerial and broader context in which HPWSs are conceived, evolved and defended.

NOTES

1. For example, 'machine uptime' in the steel industry and 'sewing throughput time' in the apparel manufacturing industry.
2. For the sake of the theoretical argument and for ease of discussion, firms are assumed to be single business units. In reality, firms are often more complex. They may be competing in various industries and strategic groups.

REFERENCES

Appelbaum, E., Bailey, T. and Berg, P. (2000). *Manufacturing Advantage: Why High-Performance Systems Pay Off*, Ithaca: ILR Press.

Appelbaum, E. and Batt, R. (1994). *The New American Workplace*, Ithaca, New York: ILR Press.

Arthur, J. (1994). 'Effects of human resource systems on manufacturing performance and turnover'. *Academy of Management Journal*, 37:3, 670–87.

Barney, J. (1991). 'Firm resources and sustained competitive advantage'. *Journal of Management*, 17:1, 99–120.

Batt, R. (2000). 'Strategic segmentation in front-line services: matching customers, employees and human resource systems'. *International Journal of Human Resource Management*, 11:3, 540–61.

Bogner, W. and Thomas, H. (1996). 'From skills to competences: the "play-out" of resource bundles across bundles' in *Dynamics of Competence-Based Competition*. R. Sanchez, A. Heene and H. Thomas (eds.). Oxford: Elsevier.

Boxall, P. (1996). 'The strategic HRM debate and the resource-based view of the firm'. *Human Resource Management Journal*, 6:3, 59–75.

Boxall, P. (1998). 'Achieving competitive advantage through human resource strategy: towards a theory of industry dynamics'. *Human Resource Management Review*, 8:3, 265–88.

Boxall, P. and Purcell, J. (2000). 'Strategic human resource management: where have we come from and where should we be going?' *International Journal of Management Reviews*, 2:2, 183–203.

Boxall, P. and Purcell, J. (2003). *Strategy and Human Resource Management*, Basingstoke and New York: Palgrave Macmillan.

Boxall, P. and Steeneveld, M. (1999). 'Human resource strategy and competitive advantage: a longitudinal study of engineering consultancies'. *Journal of Management Studies*, 36: 4, 443–63.

Carroll, G.R. and Hannan, M.T. (eds) (1995). *Organizations in Industry: Strategy, Structure and Selection*, New York and Oxford: Oxford University Press.

Child, J. (1972). 'Organisational structure, environment and performance: the role of strategic choice'. *Sociology*, 6: 3, 1–22.

Child, J. (1997). 'Strategic choice in the analysis of action, structure, organizations and environment: retrospect and prospect'. *Organization Studies*, 18: 1, 43–76.

Coff, R. (1997). 'Human assets and management dilemmas: coping with hazards on the road to resource-based theory'. *Academy of Management Review*, 22: 2, 374–402.

Coff, R. (1999). 'When competitive advantage doesn't lead to performance: the resource-based view and stakeholder bargaining power'. *Organization Science*, 10: 2, 119–33.

Doorewaard, H. and Meihuizen, H. (2000). 'Strategic performance options in professional service organisations'. *Human Resource Management Journal*, 10: 2, 39–57.

Eaton, S. (2000). 'Beyond unloving care: linking human resource management and patient care quality in nursing homes'. *International Journal of Human Resource Management*, 11: 3, 591–616.

Fiegenbaum, A. and Thomas, H. (1993). 'Industry and strategic group dynamics: competitive strategy in the insurance industry'. *Journal of Management Studies*, 30: 1, 69–105.

Frenkel, S. (2000). 'Introduction: service work and its implications for HRM'. *International Journal of Human Resource Management*, 11: 3, 469–76.

Frenkel, S., Korczynski, M., Shire, K. and Tam, M. (1999). *On the Front Line: Organization of Work in the Information Economy*, Ithaca: ILR Press.

Godard, J. (2001a). 'Beyond the high-performance paradigm? An analysis of variation in Canadian managerial perceptions of reform programme effectiveness'. *British Journal of Industrial Relations*, 39: 1, 25–52.

Godard, J. (2001b). 'High-performance and the transformation of work? The implications of alternative work practices for the experience and outcomes of work'. *Industrial and Labor Relations Review*, 54: 4, 776–805.

Gorman, P., Thomas, H. and Sanchez, R. (1996). 'Industry dynamics in competence-based competition' in *Dynamics of Competence-Based Competition*. R. Sanchez, A. Heene and H. Thomas (eds.). Oxford: Elsevier.

Greenwood, R., Hinings, C. and Brown, J. (1990). '"P2-form" strategic management: corporate practices in professional partnerships'. *Academy of Management Journal*, 33: 4, 725–55.

Haynes, P. and Fryer, G. (1999). 'Changing patterns of HRM and employment relations in New Zealand: the large hotel industry'. *Asia Pacific Journal of Human Resources*, 37: 2, 33–43.

Haynes, P. and Fryer, G. (2000). 'Human resources, service quality and performance: a case study'. *International Journal of Contemporary Hospitality Management*, 12: 4, 240–48.

Herzenberg, S., Alic, J. and Wial, H. (1998). *New Rules for a New Economy: Employment and Opportunity in Postindustrial America*, Ithaca: ILR Press.

Hunter, L. (2000). 'What determines job quality in nursing homes?' *Industrial and Labor Relations Review*, 53: 3, 463–81.

Ichniowski C., Kochan, T., Levine, D., Olson, C. and Strauss, G. (1996). 'What works at work: overview and assessment'. *Industrial Relations*, 35: 3, 299–333.

Ichniowski, C., Shaw, K. and Prennushi, G. (1997). 'The effects of human resource management practices on productivity: a study of steel finishing lines'. *American Economic Review*, 87: 3, 291–313.

Jones, S. and Ville, S. (1996). 'Efficient transactors or rent-seeking monopolists? The rationale for early chartered trading companies'. *Journal of Economic History*, 56: 4, 898–915.

Kamoche, K. (1996). 'Strategic human resource management within a resource-capability view of the firm'. *Journal of Management Studies*, 33: 2, 213–33.

Kamoche, K. and Mueller, F. (1998). 'Human resource management and the appropriation-learning perspective'. *Human Relations*, 51: 8, 1033–60.

Keltner, B., Finegold, D., Mason, G. and Wagner, K. (1999). 'Market segmentation strategies and service sector productivity'. *California Management Review*, 41: 4, 84–102.

Lashley, C. (1998). 'Matching the management of human resources to service operations'. *International Journal of Contemporary Hospitality Management*, 10: 1, 24–33.

Leonard, D. (1998). *Wellsprings of Knowledge: Building and Sustaining the Sources of Innovation*, Boston: Harvard Business School Press.

MacDuffie, J.P. (1995). 'Human resource bundles and manufacturing performance: organizational logic and flexible production systems in the world auto industry'. *Industrial and Labor Relations Review*, 48: 2, 197–221.

Miller, D. (1992). 'Generic strategies; classification, combination and context'. *Advances in Strategic Management*, 8, 391–408.

Mueller, F. (1996). 'Human resources as strategic assets; an evolutionary resource-based theory'. *Journal of Management Studies*, 33: 6, 757–85.

Osterman, P. (1994). 'How common is workplace transformation and who adopts it?' *Industrial and Labor Relations Review*, 47: 2, 173–88.

Osterman, P. (2000). 'Work reorganization in an era of restructuring: trends in diffusion and effects on employee welfare'. *Industrial and Labor Relations Review*, 53: 2, 179–96.

Peccei, R. and Rosenthal, P. (2001). 'Delivering customer-oriented behaviour through empowerment: an empirical test of HRM assumptions'. *Journal of Management Studies*, 38: 6, 831–57.

Penrose, E. (1959). *The Theory of the Growth of the Firm*, Oxford: Blackwell.

Peteraf, M. and Shanley, M. (1997). 'Getting to know you: a theory of strategic group identity'. *Strategic Management Journal*, 18: S, 165–86.

Porter, M. (1985). *Competitive Advantage: Creating and Sustaining Superior Performance*, New York: Free Press.

Purcell, J. (1999). 'High commitment management and the link with contingent workers: implications for strategic human resource management' in *Research in Personnel and Human Resources Management (Supplement 4: Strategic Human Resources Management in the Twenty-First Century)*. P. Wright, L. Dyer, J. Boudreau and G. Milkovich (eds.). Stamford, CT and London: JAI Press.

Ramsay, H., Scholarios, D. and Harley, B. (2000). 'Employees and high-performance work systems: testing inside the black box'. *British Journal of Industrial Relations*, 38: 4, 501–31.

Reed, R. and DeFillippi, R. (1990). 'Causal ambiguity, barriers to imitation, and sustainable competitive advantage'. *Academy of Management Review*, 15: 1, 88–102.

Rispoli, M. (1996). 'Competitive analysis and competence-based strategies in the hotel industry' in *Dynamics of Competence-Based Competition*. R. Sanchez, A. Heene and H. Thomas (eds.). Oxford: Elsevier.

Simon, H.A. (1947). *Administrative Behavior*, New York: Free Press.

Starbuck, W. (1992). 'Learning by knowledge-intensive firms'. *Journal of Management Studies*, 29: 6, 713–40.

Starbuck, W. (1993). 'Keeping a butterfly and an elephant in a house of cards: the elements of exceptional success'. *Journal of Management Studies*, 30: 6, 885–921.

Tallman, S. and Atchison, D. (1996). 'Competence-based competition and the evolution of strategic configurations' in *Dynamics of Competence-Based Competition*. R. Sanchez, A. Heene and H. Thomas (eds.). Oxford: Elsevier.

West, G. and DeCastro, J. (2001). 'The Achilles heel of firm strategy: resource weaknesses and distinctive inadequacies'. *Journal of Management Studies*, 38: 3, 417–42.

Wright, P., McMahan, G. and McWilliams, A. (1994). 'Human resources and sustained competitive advantage: a resource-based perspective'. *International Journal of Human Resource Management*, 5: 2, 301–26.

Youndt, M., Snell, S., Dean, J. and Lepak, D. (1996). 'Human resource management, manufacturing strategy and firm performance'. *Academy of Management Journal*, 39: 4, 836–66.

Chapter 15

Managing the Human Resource Architecture for Knowledge-Based Competition

David P. Lepak and Scott A. Snell

The notion of knowledge-based competition has gained significant attention in recent years (Grant, 1996; Liebeskind, 1996), with scholars focusing on how firms create, transfer, and leverage knowledge for competitive advantage. And although there are many reasons for the success of firms competing on knowledge, human capital is at least in part a foundation for core competencies and an underlying source of competitive success (Hitt, Bierman, Shimizu, & Kochhar, 2001; Wright, Dunford, & Snell, 2001). Yet whereas all people contribute knowledge, innovation, creativity, and the like, not all employees are equal in their knowledge-based contributions.

Virtually all work performed in firms requires employees to use some knowledge and skill. Organizations must manage a wide assortment of employees; some contribute based on the knowledge they possess whereas others contribute based on the jobs they do (see, for example, Drucker, 1999). The challenge that organizations face is this: there are important distinctions between managing traditional work and managing knowledge work. Identifying these differences, and perhaps more importantly, understanding how to manage them, may be crucial for building competitive capability.

In some ways, the new focus on managing the knowledge of a firm's workforce represents a departure for human resource management. Traditionally, the field has viewed the job, rather than knowledge, as the fundamental unit of analysis. We believe that shifting our emphasis from job management to knowledge management – that

D.P. Lepak and S.A. Snell, "Managing the Human Resource Architecture for Knowledge-Based Competition," in *Managing Knowledge for Sustained Competitive Advantage* (Jossy-Bass, 2003): 127–54.

is, to what people know and how they use that knowledge – may have significant implications for HRM research and practice. One possible way to address these issues is to view a firm as a portfolio of multiple types of human capital that range in the kinds and levels of knowledge used to perform jobs. Once this distinction is made, we can address issues fundamental to the management of knowledge workers as well as to the management of other types of workers.

This chapter focuses on understanding how organizations make decisions to acquire, allocate, and manage the human capital they need to be successful, paying particular attention to the management of human capital in those organizations that compete based on knowledge. First, we review the notion of knowledge-based competition and discuss the implications that a shift toward knowledge management has on managing human capital. We then examine the human resource architecture presented by Lepak and Snell (1999), which provides a conceptual map for examining the decisions that firms make about the allocation of human capital to alternative modes of employment and the design of HRM systems to manage different groups of employees. To address issues related to managing human capital for knowledge-based competition, we use this architectural perspective to view three different levels of analysis: individual, cohort, and organizational. Throughout the chapter, we discuss implications for both research and practice.

An Architectural Perspective on Human Capital Management

To understand the importance that the traditional job-based approach has had for HRM, we need to look back at its history. In the past, and still in the present, jobs represent a microstructural artifact of a firm's operational imperatives. Put more simply, jobs are created as components of production and service processes. Once the jobs are created, individuals are sought to perform them efficiently. The logic of this approach is grounded in the principles of Weber's bureaucratic organization and Taylor's scientific management. By studying the tasks that workers performed, analyzing the necessary components of performing those tasks, and eliminating the unnecessary components, jobs could be designed so people could execute the needed tasks in the simplest way (Drucker, 1999). This is not to say that knowledge and experience were not important, but the knowledge of any one individual was deemphasized.

Adopting a job-based approach has proven to be effective for organizations, particularly when the environment is stable, change is slow, and jobs do not evolve quickly. As this became the fundamental job design strategy during the early part of the last century, HRM developed around these ideas. Indeed, most HRM textbooks acknowledge job analysis as the bedrock of the field (for example, Bohlander, Snell, & Sherman, 2001; Gomez-Mejia, Balkin, & Cardy, 2001). Without it, observers might ask, how would we know what task employees would perform? Without a clear understanding of the requisite tasks, how would we know what knowledge, skills, and abilities to emphasize in recruitment and selection? Similarly, how would we know the criteria for evaluating employee performance, rewarding pay, designing incentive systems, and so forth?

Perhaps the greatest difference between knowledge management and a traditional HRM approach is managing how employees contribute to a firm's core competencies rather than focusing solely on what jobs they do (Drucker, 1999; Snell, Lepak, & Youndt, 1999). As noted by Drucker (1999), "In manual work, the task is always given .... [I]n knowledge work the key question is: What is the task? One reason for this is that knowledge work unlike manual work, does not program the worker" (pp. 84–5). This is not to say that certain jobs do not correlate with certain types of knowledge. But the main emphasis is on leveraging the knowledge base of employees rather than making their job performance more efficient. In many cases, there may be no job to manage *per se*.

To extend traditional approaches to managing human capital so that they focus on contributions to core competencies in knowledge-based competition, we take an architectural perspective. As noted by Lepak and Snell (1999), *an architectural perspective* views a firm as a portfolio of human capital. This perspective is based on several assumptions. The first assumption is that a firm must often simultaneously rely on employees who contribute in different ways to its competitive advantage. Some contribute based on the knowledge they possess, some contribute primarily based on the jobs they perform, and many contribute based on a combination of the two. Therefore, it would be misleading to suggest that all employees are likely to be knowledge workers. Rather, knowledge workers are likely to make up a portion of the workforce, and the size of that portion depends on the firm.

An architectural perspective also assumes that organizations may draw on the knowledge of employees who are not necessarily a part of their permanent workforce but rather are part of the contingent labor pool (Lepak & Snell, 1999). Relying on external labor may enable firms to gain access to skills that would be too costly or difficult to develop internally (Matusik & Hill, 1998). Rather than constantly hiring and firing workers, firms use contingent workers to increase quickly both the number of workers at their disposal and the types of knowledge skills they possess (Pfeffer & Baron, 1988; Tsui, Pearce, Porter, & Hite, 1995).

Finally, an architectural perspective assumes that as the relative contributions of employees to a firm's core competencies differ, so too will the way they are managed. Whether the employees are internal or external or contribute based on their knowledge or on their job performance, a firm is likely to adapt its HRM system in an attempt to maximize their potential contribution. The challenge is to design an HRM system that facilitates the management of jobs and knowledge for both internal and external employees.

Applying the Architectural Perspective to Knowledge-Based Competition

For firms to apply the architectural perspective to human capital for knowledge-based competition, they must address two primary issues. First, they must ensure that their workforce possesses the needed competencies to contribute to their competitiveness, growth, and performance. Building the knowledge and skill base, however, is not

	Competencies	Contributions
Organizational level	• Managing the portfolio of human capital	• Knowledge sharing between internal and external employee cohorts • Appropriating knowledge across employee cohorts for competitive advangage
Employee group level	• Internalizing versus outsourcing employee competencies • Managing employment relationships of employee groups	• Enhancing employee group contribution
Individual level	• Understanding the profile of human capital • Mobility and retention	• Incentives to share knowledge

Figure 15.1   Multilevel perspective of the HR architecture in knowledge-based competition.

sufficient. In order for human capital to contribute to an organization's competitive ability on knowledge, a firm must also manage contribution and knowledge exchanges (Quinn, Anderson, & Finkelstein, 1996). In an HR architecture, these exchanges occur between organizational members as well as with knowledge contributors who reside outside a firm's boundaries.

For a firm to adopt an architectural perspective, it also needs to view its entire portfolio of human capital. We recognize here that knowledge management issues exist at the individual, employee group, and organizational levels. Knowledge, at its root, is an individual-level phenomenon (Argyris & Schon, 1978; Grant, 1996; Quinn *et al.*, 1996). As already noted, individual employees have differing types and degrees of knowledge, skills, and capabilities, and firms must understand their knowledge base and establish mechanisms for them to share it. And they rely on a variety of employee groups who contribute in different ways: some based on their knowledge, others on how they perform a job. Firms may also use different types of employees, such as contract workers, full-time employees, and consultants, to contribute to their competitiveness. Finally, a firm's portfolio of human capital and its respective knowledge base may be viewed also as an organizational asset that must be managed and leveraged. Figure 15.1 highlights the main issues that emerge when we consider how firms manage human capital competencies and knowledge contributions from multiple levels of analysis. We address these issues in the remainder of the chapter.

Individual Level of Analysis

At the individual level of analysis, it is first important to recognize that there are several fundamentally different forms of knowledge (Becker, 1964; Matusik & Hill, 1998; Schultz, 1961). Most individuals possess a degree of general or public knowledge, what economists refer to as *generic human capital*. As noted by Matusik and Hill

(1998), public knowledge "resides in the public domain" (p. 683). As a result, it is applicable in firms in a variety of industries.

Employees also may possess occupation-specific human capital – that is, a common body of knowledge that is relatively codified throughout a broader professional or institutionalized group. For example, although the talent of individuals may differ, doctors and lawyers draw primarily from a body of knowledge that is accessible to all in those communities.

Individuals are also likely to possess a certain degree of knowledge about a particular industry – that is, industry-specific human capital – such as biotechnology, retail, or utilities. Although still in the public domain, occupation and industry-specific knowledge should be viewed differently from purely generic human capital. These knowledge domains are often well established and consist of a body of knowledge that must be obtained in order for practitioners to be certified or gain legitimacy in the field. Unlike generic human capital, not all employees are likely to attain a significant level of these types of knowledge. Moreover, acquiring employees whose jobs involve primarily generic knowledge (that is, basic math, reading, writing, interpersonal skills, and so on) will likely be easier than acquiring employees whose contribution is based on industrial or occupational knowledge.

Finally, firm-specific knowledge is by definition limited in its application to a particular firm. As noted in transaction cost economics (Williamson, 1975), firm-specific knowledge and assets are only applicable or valuable in a particular firm. Matusik and Hill (1998) refer to this as private knowledge that is based on "such items as a firm's unique routines, processes, documentation, or trade secrets" (p. 583).

Although there are clearly different forms of knowledge, the reality is that employees do not possess only one but contribute to a company based on certain amounts of all four types. However, they differ substantially in their respective individual knowledge profiles. As Fig. 15.2 shows, we can map the knowledge profile of human capital by considering the relative degree of each form of knowledge that people use in their contribution. For instance, a recent college graduate (Employee A in Fig. 15.2) with an engineering degree might contribute to a firm based on a high amount of general knowledge and a modest amount of occupational knowledge but rely very little on industrial- or firm-specific knowledge. Another employee (Employee B) might use a great deal of occupational knowledge but rely to a lesser degree on general, industrial and firm-specific knowledge. A third employee (Employee C) might contribute based on her extensive firm-specific and indepth industry knowledge and rely very little on occupational or generic knowledge. The potential combinations of knowledge are unlimited, but the specific profile will likely have two main implications for the management of employees.

Mobility and retention of competencies

The first implication for the management of human capital for knowledge-based competition at the individual level is employee mobility (Teece, Pisano, & Shuen, 1997). The threat of mobility is a direct function of how transferable an employee's knowledge

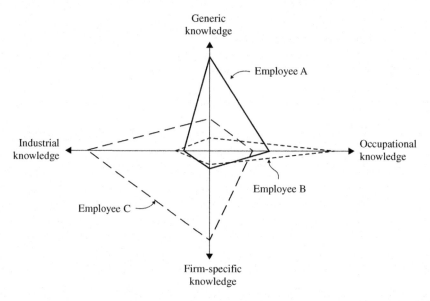

Figure 15.2 The knowledge profile of human capital.

and skills are in different contexts. In general, the threat of mobility increases as an individual's knowledge becomes less firm-specific and more generic (Galunic & Anderson, 2000; Williamson, 1975). Human capital theory (Becker, 1964) and transaction cost economics (Williamson, 1975) suggest that a firm invests in employees and provides employment security to the extent that these investments will translate into knowledge, skills, and abilities that are specific to that firm. In other words, firms provide security and rewards to employees in exchange for their diminished mobility.

Furthermore, employees are likely to have diminished mobility as their knowledge profile shifts from mostly generic knowledge to industry- or occupation-specific knowledge to firm-specific knowledge. Looking again at Fig. 15.2, increased mobility would likely be reflected in a greater proportion of an employee's knowledge profile in the top half of the profile. Similarly, decreased mobility would be reflected if a greater proportion of an employee's knowledge appeared in the bottom half of the profile. Thus, for the three hypothetical employees, Employees A and B likely have greater mobility than Employee C.

Contribution and knowledge exchange

Although mobility issues are not likely to be as critical for employees whose contributions are based on firm-specific knowledge, issues related to the sharing of their knowledge are. Horibe (1999) noted that "intellectual capital can only be invited" (p. 154). Compared with traditional assets such as property and machinery, competing on knowledge-based assets is somewhat paradoxical: firms base their success on something they do not technically own. Employees, not firms, own their knowledge

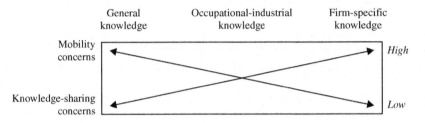

Figure 15.3 HR challenges associated with knowledge management.

(Becker, 1964; Drucker, 1999). This is a human capital dilemma: knowledge is a *corporate* asset that resides primarily in the minds of individuals who are free to do what they wish with it. Organizations may only secure and leverage knowledge if their employees cooperate (Coff, 1997).

As employees are able to command value in their own firm for what they uniquely know, there is an inherent dilemma in trying to encourage them to share their knowledge (Coff, 1997; Hansen, Nohria, & Tierney, 2000). From the employee's perspective, this may be the equivalent of a company sharing proprietary information with its industry. Doing so might diminish its proprietary value. Because information is power in a knowledge-based context, employees may not be willing to share. Unless there are adequate incentives to do so, employees, with firm-specific knowledge might hold the firm hostage in an effort to leverage their valued asset (Davenport & Prusak, 1998; Quinn *et al.*, 1996).

As shown in Fig. 15.3, these two fundamental problems associated with managing individual knowledge are inversely related. Problems of mobility increase when an individual's knowledge is proportionately more generic, and problems with knowledge sharing increase as an individual's knowledge becomes proportionately more firm-specific.

Looking at Fig. 15.3, the greatest challenge may be to manage employees who contribute based on occupational or industry-specific knowledge, those whose knowledge profile tends to fall to the left or right sides of the human capital profile. Compared with effort to recruit, retain, and replace workers who contribute based on general knowledge, efforts involving those who contribute based on these knowledge domains is often considerably more difficult. Employees with common knowledge may be more mobile, but the importance (or costs) of the mobility may be greater with employees who contribute based on occupational or industrial knowledge. Furthermore, the ability of these individuals to perform their roles effectively does not depend on specific firm context, even though it is limited to a specific task or industry domain.

These tensions may be particularly pronounced when the labor supply for these types of knowledge workers is tight. Interestingly, most professional service and consulting organizations are structured around industry (for example, utilities, biotechnology, and so on) or occupational knowledge domains (accounting, tax, strategic management, and so on). These firms are able to capitalize on their client organizations' concerns about mobility and retention while retaining an ability to apply their occupational or industrial knowledge to serve a variety of different companies.

Research implications

Perhaps the key research issue in managing knowledge at the individual level is to understand the implications of using different HRM practices for employees with different knowledge profiles. Researchers examining psychological contracts (Rousseau, 1995), social exchange theories (Tsui, Pearce, Porter, & Tripoli, 1997), and perceived organizational support (Eisenberger, Fasolo, & Davis-LaMastro, 1990) provide convincing evidence that employees display different attitudes and behaviors based on their perceptions of how they are managed by their firm. Do differences in employees' knowledge profiles influence how they view and respond to organizational investments?

Although employees may not use their full repertoire of knowledge in a particular organization, other forms of knowledge that they possess might be valued in other organizations. Thus the following dilemma: if employees are less mobile when they develop firm-specific knowledge what is their incentive to do so? Similarly, how do firms encourage employees with firm-specific knowledge to stay and share their knowledge with others when they possess a high degree of occupational or industrial knowledge that might be valued by competitors? Which combinations of HRM practices are most effective for encouraging knowledge sharing? Do these differ from practices that enhance employee retention? Are there trade-offs that must be made in focusing on retention rather than knowledge sharing? Although there is no clear answer to these questions, these research issues are likely to become more important when we focus on managing knowledge at an individual level of analysis rather than solely on managing jobs.

Employee Cohort Level of Analysis

Rather than focusing on understanding the knowledge profile of employees, at the cohort level we examine how firms deploy groups of employees who have similar forms of human capital in order to maximize their strategic contribution. It should be noted that we are not necessarily referring to individuals with the same knowledge content *per se*. Cohorts are individuals who have similar *profiles* or *combinations* of generic, industry, occupation, and firm-specific human capital. The particular content – that is, *what they know* – may differ substantially. This point will become clearer later on.

Managing the competencies of employee cohorts

Building on the resource-based view of the firm (for example, Barney, 1991), transaction cost economics (for example, Coase, 1937; Williamson, 1975), and human capital theory (for example, Becker, 1964), as well as the theoretical arguments of Snell, Youndt, and Wright (1996) and Ulrich and Lake (1991), an architectural perspective begins by focusing on the strategic value and uniqueness of human capital in order to understand its potential contribution (Lepak & Snell, 1999).

The *strategic value* of human capital can be ascertained by analyzing the benefits that employees provide to customers, shareholders, and other relevant stakeholders in comparison with the costs they incur in providing those benefits. What is valuable is likely to be distinct to each particular firm because each firm's goals and objectives differ. Theorists such as Barney (1991) and Quinn (1992) suggest that as the strategic value of human capital increases, so too does the likelihood that firms will employ it internally rather than outsource it or purchase it from outside. According to Bettis, Bradley, and Hamel (1992), outsourcing this kind of human capital is likely to jeopardize the competitive advantage of the firm by eroding its stock of core skills.

The contribution of human capital also depends on its *uniqueness* – the degree to which needed knowledge or skills are firm-specific or need to be applied in an idiosyncratic fashion (Lepak & Snell, 1999). We have previously discussed the idea that human capital ranges from completely generic to occupation-, industry-, and ultimately firm-specific. A fundamental tenet of the resource-based view of firms is that they are more likely to gain a competitive advantage when valued resources are firm-specific and not available to competitors (Barney, 1991). As noted in transaction cost economics (Williamson, 1975), firms have an economic incentive to sustain internal relationships with employees possessing firm-specific skills in order to overcome problems with information asymmetries and ensure a return on investment. Human capital theory (for example, Becker, 1964) posits that firms are more likely to invest in human capital when it is not transferable. Accordingly, individuals are expected to make their own investments in generic (transferable) skills, whereupon firms simply acquire these skills at a market rate (Schultz, 1961; Wallace & Fay, 1988).

Strategic value and uniqueness serve as contingency factors in determining how firms might balance both internal and external employment decisions. As employees are increasingly able to contribute directly to organizational outcomes such as efficiency, innovation, customer responsiveness, and the like, organizations have an incentive to internalize their employment relationship to capitalize on these productive capabilities. Uniqueness has its most direct effect on employment in its influence over a firm's commitment to development over time (ranging from task-focused to relationship-focused). And though this "make versus buy" decision is often made in the context of internal employment, Matusik and Hill (1998) suggest that firms might invest more in relationships with contingent workers when their partnership focuses on creating and transferring private knowledge.

Figure 15.4 provides a conceptual map for how a firm might allocate human capital to different employee groups to optimize their relative contributions to its core competencies (Lepak & Snell, 1999; Snell, Lepak, & Youndt, 1999).

Human capital that is unique and has high strategic value is most likely to contribute directly to a firm's core competencies on the basis of the employees' knowledge – that is, what they know and how they do something with it (Snell *et al.*, 1999; Purcell, 1999). Given uniqueness, managers are encouraged to focus on establishing a long-term relationship with these employees to enable them to develop firm-specific talents and contribution (Lepak & Snell, 1999). Given strategic value, firms have an incentive to internalize their employment and focus on developing and cultivating their knowledge, skills, and abilities to enhance their value-creating potential (Snell *et al.*, 1999). Because core knowledge workers are both valuable and unique, they have the

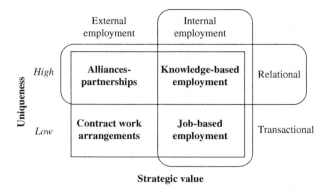

Figure 15.4 Human capital characteristics and employment modes. *Note:* Adapted from Lepak and Snell, 1999, and Snell, Lepak, and Youndt, 1999.

greatest potential to contribute to the competitive success of a firm that competes on knowledge.

Employee cohorts with knowledge that is valuable but not unique are likely to be managed for the job they do more than for their firm-specific use of knowledge. For example, sales clerks and production workers are often called upon to perform jobs that might require considerable knowledge, skill, and training. Yet when these employees are expected to contribute immediately to a firm by performing a specific set of tasks or activities based on a standardized knowledge domain, they are likely to be seen differently than core employees (Lepak & Snell, 1999). This is not to imply that these are simple jobs. In fact, they may be quite complex and require considerable knowledge and skills. However, although jobs that are valuable but of limited uniqueness are required for organizational effectiveness, often they do not differentiate any one firm from another, as is the case with a firm's core knowledge workers (Snell *et al.*, 1999).

Lepak and Snell (1999) suggested that firms are most likely to outsource work for tasks that are limited in scope, purpose, or duration. An organization's unskilled or semi-skilled positions often fall into this domain. Given their low uniqueness and high transferability, the capabilities of these workers are likely to be widely available. And given their limited value, organizations have little incentive to internalize their employment relationship. As the strategic value of these employees diminishes and the requisite skills approach that of a commodity, outsourcing may be more efficient and effective than internalization (Leonard-Barton, 1995; Stewart, 1997; Snell *et al.*, 1999).

In the top left quadrant of Fig. 15.4 we find employees with knowledge and skills that are of limited strategic value but unique to a firm. Some forms of unique human capital (for example, lawyers, consultants) may be employed so infrequently that they do not justify the cost of internal employment. Or a firm may desire these employees for their potential contribution but cannot hire them into the firm. In these scenarios, Lepak and Snell (1999) suggested that firms might establish ongoing alliances or partnerships with these external parties to perform some tasks or projects jointly. Consultants are perhaps the most direct example of this phenomenon, but the same can be true for legal aid, tax advising, enterprise resource planning solutions, and the like. Although both contract workers and alliance partners are external to a firm, alliance partners are expected to apply their skills in some unique capacity, usually over a longer time frame, whereas contract workers are expected to use their existing skills to perform a preset task or activity.

One of the key points of an architectural perspective is that although the employment options may be similar across firms, where employees or jobs actually fall in the matrix is likely to differ (Lepak & Snell, 2002). For instance, lawyers might be found in any of the four quadrants. In a law firm, staff attorneys may be viewed as an important element of the business operations. But although their knowledge would contribute to the core competence of the organization, it would not be an element that, on its own, substantially differentiates the firm from competitors. In those same firms, other (perhaps more senior) attorneys may develop specific knowledge that establishes a unique position with clients and customers. In other firms attorneys may serve as an external source of expertise and ongoing advice. Some organizations may establish continuing partnerships with a cadre of lawyers that facilitates the development of firm-specific knowledge that is necessary for them to function effectively. Lawyers who work with the same clients for a number of years may have idiosyncratic knowledge of the clients' history, operations, strategy, and so on that other lawyers do not possess. Yet other firms might view external relationships with lawyers in more transactional terms, using the lawyers' standardized occupational knowledge on a one-off basis to address more limited issues or only once or over a short period of time.

This example highlights an important component of this framework: decisions about employment are not fixed for a particular job but by the strategic value and uniqueness of how the human capital is used in firms. Though the title of the job may be the same, the role of the individual *vis-à-vis* the firm's competitive position may differ widely. As a result, some firms may internalize certain types of jobs whereas others may use external labor for them. And just as understanding the nature of employee contributions to a firm – their strategic value and uniqueness – is important for understanding how the firm employs its human capital, there are likely to be significant implications for HRM as well.

Managing employee cohort contributions

As we already suggested, an architectural perspective focuses on managing the contributions of multiple cohorts of workers. From an HR architectural perspective, a key issue is that HRM systems that are in place are likely to be different for each distinct employee group. Several researchers have examined variations in how firms manage different groups of employees. For instance, Jackson, Schuler, and Rivero (1989) found that "within organizations, different personnel practices are in effect for employees at different levels. Furthermore, the *relationships* between organizational characteristics and personnel policies are different for hourly and managerial employees" (p. 773).

Similarly, Tsui *et al.* (1997) found that the HRM practices used to manage permanent employees tend to fall into one of four coherent patterns that characterize the nature of the employee-organizational relationship: a long-term balanced approach, a short-term balanced approach, an underinvestment approach, or an overinvestment approach. Osterman (1987) suggested that firms might rely on salaried, wage, craft, or industrial employment subsystems in their management of different groups. Bamberger and Meshoulam (2000) suggested that firms might adopt a commitment, paternalistic, free agent, or secondary strategy for the management of their human capital. Though the focus of these authors varies, they converge on one point: there are different personnel practices for employees not only in different organizations but also *within* organizations. Although a discussion of the specific HRM practices that make up each system is beyond the scope of this chapter, we briefly review the nature of the HRM systems for different groups of employees in an architectural perspective.

Because of the value-creating potential of core knowledge workers, firms must have mechanisms in place to ensure their investment in and retention of these workers (Quinn *et al.*, 1996). Lepak and Snell (1999) suggest that a commitment-based HRM system (Arthur, 1992; Huselid, 1995) is likely to be most effective in encouraging knowledge workers to assume the risk of developing firm-specific knowledge and adopt a long-term perspective for organizational success. For instance, firms might structure knowledge work to allow for change and adaptation and provide empowerment and participation in decision-making to ensure these workers make their best contribution to company competitiveness.

In contrast, a productivity-based HRM system that emphasizes immediate contribution is consistent with the underlying expectations of job-based employees. This system most closely resembles traditional approaches to managing employees – that is, hiring employees to contribute immediately, paying them an equitable wage, and focusing on their job performance (Lepak & Snell, 1999). The job these people perform is the focus, not the idiosyncratic knowledge, skills, and abilities that they possess. Thus, the primary focus for these workers is likely to ensure that they immediately contribute to a firm's competitiveness. This represents the crux of the "make or buy" distinction for human capital.

Because contract workers are often solicited to apply a very standardized knowledge base to well-defined tasks, the main challenge for firms is to ensure that these workers comply with the necessary protocol and perform efficiently. And given the limited nature of the tasks these workers perform, a HRM system that focuses on ensuring compliance is likely to be most effective (Tsui *et al.*, 1995; Lepak & Snell, 1999). Finally, a collaborative-based HRM system might be particularly effective in managing strategic partners with limited value but great uniqueness. As noted by Snell *et al.* (1999), this type of idiosyncratic knowledge might be best leveraged if it is linked with other employee groups with more demonstrative value. This is likely to require a significant degree of knowledge sharing and information exchange.

Research implications

Researchers have long noted that differences exist based on exempt versus nonexempt status (Huselid, 1995), departmental differences (Snell & Dean, 1992, 1994), and the like. Although within-firm variations in the use of HRM systems are not new to HRM research, researchers have tended to focus primarily on full-time employees who contribute based on the jobs that they do. Research is needed on the potential trade-offs firms make in how they design their HRM systems to manage different employee groups.

Researchers including Rousseau (1995), Robinson (1996), Wayne, Shore, and Liden (1997), Tsui *et al.* (1997), and Shore and Berksdale (2000) have focused on understanding the employee outcomes from a firm's management of the social exchange. Though that research tends to focus on permanent employees, the logic of social exchange theories might extend to employees in other employment modes. For example, contract workers may expect limited investments in their development but organizations may "overinvest" in these employees or expect greater contributions. Similarly, core workers may expect extensive investments and support from organizations but be given investments that do not meet their expectations. The relative balance in this inducements-contribution exchange (March & Simon, 1958) is likely to influence the attitudes, behaviors, and productivity of employee groups significantly. As firms increasingly differentiate how they allocate their human capital, this is one research domain that would benefit from greater attention.

Although not all employees may have equal strategic importance (Stewart, 1997), all have the potential to affect a firm's bottom line. Although it clearly is important to understand how to manage core employees optimally, we would be remiss to assume that other workers in a firm, and the way they are managed, are not important as well. From an architectural perspective, several research questions need to be addressed. Which dimensions of employee contribution are most desirable for different employee groups? How should HRM practices be combined to enhance employee contributions across employee groups? It is imperative that HRM researchers clearly establish the relationships among different HRM practices and the logic for their inclusion or exclusion into HRM systems.

Organizational Level of Analysis

While managing the contributions of human capital in knowledge-based companies is gaining significant attention, it is important to remember that knowledge workers likely make up only a portion of any firm's workforce. They will likely be deployed alongside other employees, some contributing their manual skills, some the jobs they perform regardless of their knowledge or skills, some their industry or occupational knowledge, and some who are externalized. Figure 15.5 illustrates how a firm's HR architecture might look for a hypothetical company with regard to the strategic value and uniqueness of its employees. Each symbol represents the relative strategic value and uniqueness of the contributions of a particular employee across several job domains. We believe that viewing a firm's human capital in this fashion highlights several key issues for managing human capital in organizations.

Managing the portfolio of human capital competencies

At the organizational level of analysis, an architectural perspective suggests that firms must balance the use of multiple employment modes to optimize access to and use of knowledge. Decisions about which tasks and activities should be carried out internally and which should be outsourced are particularly important, and their complexity

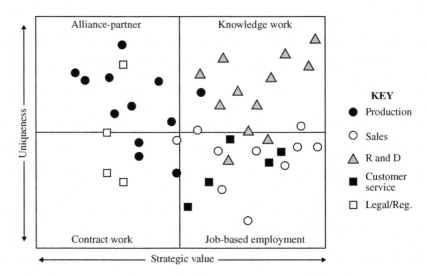

Figure 15.5   Example of human capital in an HR architecture.

should not be understated. For instance, a firm with a high reliance on knowledge workers may run a considerable risk because firm-specific investments take time to materialize, often involve extensive costs, and may be inefficient if the firm overinvests in employees who would not otherwise be deemed core. However, a firm that does not do so runs the risk of competing based on talent that competitors may already have or talent that they could lure away. At the same time, a firm that relies extensively on outsourcing runs the risk of failing to develop the core competencies it may need to compete in the future (Bettis *et al.*, 1992). However, for a firm that decides to deploy its human capital competencies, managing human capital moves beyond managing individual employees to focusing on coordinating and integrating the contributions of various employee groups.

It is also important to realize that the overall design of a firm's architecture, or its overarching framework for allocation and deployment of human capital and HRM systems, will likely be unique to its particular circumstances. Becker, Huselid, Pickus, and Spratt (1997, p. 41) note that at the firm level HRM systems "are highly idiosyncratic and must be tailored carefully to each firm's individual situation to achieve optimum results … . The appropriate design and alignment of the HRM systems with business priorities is highly firm-specific." Because firms differ in what they do and how they compete, the relative contributions of different groups of human capital will differ for them as well. The challenge for each firm is to identify the optimal mix of employment arrangements for its unique circumstances and to design HRM systems that maximize their relevant contribution to the firm's success.

A final issue needs to be addressed. A firm's portfolio of human capital should not be viewed as static but rather as dynamic, because the relative strategic value and uniqueness of human capital are likely to shift over time. For instance, when a firm alters its technology or strategic objectives, there are likely to be implications for the contributions of its human capital. As the core competencies of a firm change, the requisite human capital knowledge and skills will change as well. This point is underscored by Barney (1995) when he notes, "Although a firm's resources and capabilities have added value in the past, changes in customer tastes, industry structure, or technology can render them less valuable in the future" (p. 51).

Leveraging knowledge across the HR architecture

The notion of knowledge-based competition presupposes that organizations can leverage their employees' knowledge. At first glance, the logic of the HR architecture implies that only employees with high value and uniqueness contribute to a firm's core competencies. But that perspective may be simplistic. Although core competencies are certainly a function of people, they are also a function of processes and systems (Prahalad & Hamel, 1990; Wright *et al.*, 2001). Competencies are capabilities made up of aggregated knowledge, processes, technologies, and the like – not just human capital. And although not all workers are necessarily in the knowledge-worker category, some employees who themselves are not knowledge workers may perform activities or be involved in key processes that are instrumental to a firm's core competencies; they may have a link to a firm's competitiveness. For example, although the skills of aircraft maintenance employees at Southwest Airlines are not likely to be viewed as core competencies in themselves, they are instrumental in contributing to an operations system that allows Southwest to maintain one of the top rankings for on-time delivery. The challenge for organizations is to understand how employees in different employment cohorts – not just knowledge workers – contribute to core competencies and then enhance their potential contribution.

Although firms may want and need employees to possess a certain type or degree of knowledge, they may be unable to hire such employees full-time. Relying on external sources for human capital may enable greater flexibility and access to the types of knowledge a firm needs. As noted by Matusik and Hill (1998), "The use of contingent work also may stimulate the accumulation and creation of valuable knowledge within firms" (p. 686). Competing on knowledge likely requires organizations to establish mechanisms to exchange knowledge across employee groups to engender learning and innovation. This may be especially true in organizations that base their competitiveness on organizational learning and innovation.

In addition, firms must plan to manage how they can leverage their workers' contributions over time. They may be able to alter the strategic value and uniqueness of groups of human capital and change the nature of their contribution through firm-specific investments (uniqueness) and increased strategic value (Lepak & Snell, 1999). To increase firm specificity, firms may try to customize the uniqueness of an individual's contribution through on the job experiences that develop tacit knowledge that is not transferable to competing firms. Though employees may not currently be of particular value for a firm's competencies, they may be a source for future products or services (see, for example, Prahalad & Hamel, 1990; Leonard-Barton, 1995). The challenge is to design management systems that link the current knowledge of the employees with the firm's future growth. Though it certainly takes time to make the necessary human capital investments, firms that do so may enhance their ability to leverage the knowledge of their human capital.

Research implications

We believe that these issues point to several areas of research in how firms balance their portfolio of human capital. As firms increasingly rely on different types of human capital for the knowledge and skills they need, research is needed on how to manage the entire system – rather than just one group of employees – effectively. In addition, research is needed on different combinations in a firm's portfolio of human capital. For instance, do firms that rely more extensively on internal labor for knowledge generation outperform firms that rely more on external workers? Considering the potential costs related to investing in core knowledge workers, is there a point of diminishing returns in trying to shift noncore employees into this group? There are no clear answers to these questions, but their importance is likely to increase as firms continue to differentiate the nature of their employees' contributions.

When assessing effectiveness, it is also important to consider multiple performance outcomes. In the strategic HRM research, there is a tendency to focus primarily on accounting or market-based measures of firm performance (Rogers & Wright, 1998). Yet many possible outcomes are relevant. For example, Dyer and Reeves (1996) suggested several types of effectiveness measures: HRM outcomes (absenteeism, turnover), organizational outcomes (quality, service), financial-accounting outcomes (return on assets), and capital market outcomes (stock price). The key issue is to identify which outcome is most appropriate based on the context of the study (Becker & Gerhart, 1996). We would argue that performance measures should be more proximal to the actual outcomes required from employee groups. In some companies job-based employees may be held primarily to efficiency criteria whereas knowledge workers might be evaluated primarily on innovation and new ideas. Looking only at a firm-level performance measure such as return on assets or return on equity would not likely reflect how well (or poorly) a firm is managing these different groups of workers. Instead, it would capture an aggregated average across the groups.

In addition, there may be potential performance effects related to how firms manage the overall architecture that might exceed the management of any single group of employees. It may be the case that firms that effectively balance the concerns of multiple groups simultaneously are able to enhance the effectiveness of all their employees. It is possible that a firm that adequately manages all of its employees outperforms a firm that effectively manages its knowledge workers but is ineffective in managing other groups. As firms increasingly differentiate among their workforces, how well they can balance the demands of all of their employees will likely be a determinant of their performance.

Conclusion

The purpose of this chapter was to discuss how organizations that compete based on knowledge make decisions to acquire, allocate, and manage the human capital they need to be successful. To address this issue we took an architectural perspective and examined organizations as a portfolio of human capital from individual, cohort, and organizational levels of analysis. We believe that insights into the management of human capital for knowledge-based competition require consideration of both micro and macro perspectives.

To enhance employee contributions, we need to understand how individual employees and employee cohorts or groups contribute to a firm's success. This is most directly a function of a firm's core competencies and is reflected in their strategic value and uniqueness. At the same time, we also need to understand how different HRM practices and systems affect individuals and employee groups. Each employee group is likely to have a unique perception of obligations or a unique psychological contract with an organization. For example, job-based employees may have different expectations than knowledge workers, even though both groups are internal full-time employees (Tsui *et al.*, 1995). The extent to which firms can attend to these concerns while adhering to their own strategic demands and developing their core competencies should be positively related to their overall performance.

Clearly, many avenues for future research emerge when we view knowledge management from an architectural perspective. These two areas of the field are complementary; each ultimately depends on the other. The architectural perspective provides focus and clarity to the practice of knowledge management; knowledge management establishes a strategic context for activities designed in the architecture. We hope that this chapter has provided some interesting ideas to stimulate future work in this area.

REFERENCES

Argyris, C., & Schon, D. A. (1978). *Organizational learning: A theory of action perspective.* Reading, MA: Addison-Wesley.

Arthur, J. B. (1992). The link between business strategy and industrial relations systems in American steel minimills. *Industrial and Labor Relations Review, 45,* 488–506.

Bamberger, P., & Meshoulam, I. (2000). *Human resource strategy: Formulation, implementation, and impact.* Thousand Oaks, CA: Sage.

Barney, J. (1991). Firm resources and sustained competitive advantage. *Journal of Management, 17,* 99–129.

Barney, J. (1995). Firm resources and sustained competitive advantage. *Academy of Management Executive, 9*(4), 49–61.

Becker, B. E., & Gerhart, B. (1996). The impact of human resource management on organizational performance: Progress and prospects. *Academy of Management Journal, 39,* 779–801.

Becker, B. E., Huselid, M. A., Pickus, P. S., & Spratt, M. (1997). HR as a source of shareholder value: Research and recommendations. *Human Resource Management, 36,* 39–47.

Becker, G. S. (1964). *Human capital.* New York: Columbia University Press.

Bettis, R. A., Bradley, S. P., & Hamel, G. (1992). Outsourcing and industrial decline. *Academy of Management Executive, 6,* 7–22.

Bohlander, G., Snell, S., & Sherman, A. (2001). *Managing human resources.* Cincinnati, OH: South-Western.

Coase, R. H. (1937). The nature of the firm. *Economica, 4,* 386–405.

Coff, R. W. (1997). Human assets and management dilemmas: Coping with hazards on the road to resource-based theory. *Academy of Management Review, 22,* 374–402.

Davenport, T. H., & Prusak, L. (1998). *Working knowledge: How organizations manage what they know*. Boston: Harvard Business School Press.

Drucker, P. F. (1999). Knowledge-worker productivity: The biggest challenge. *California Management Review, 41*, 79–94.

Dyer, L., & Reeves, T. (1995). Human resource strategies and firm performance: What do we know and where do we need to go? *International Journal of Human Resource Management, 6*, 656–70.

Eisenberger, R., Fasolo, P., & Davis-LaMastro, V. (1990). Perceived organizational support and employee diligence, commitment, and innovation. *Journal of Applied Psychology, 75*, 51–9.

Galunic, D. C., & Anderson, E. (2000). From security to mobility: Generalized investments in human capital and agent commitment. *Organization Science, 11*, 1–20.

Gomez-Mejia, L. R., Balkin, D. B., & Cardy, R. L. (2001). *Managing human resources*. Englewood Cliffs, NJ: Prentice-Hall.

Grant, R. M. (1996). Toward a knowledge-based theory of the firm. *Strategic Management Journal, 17*, 109–22.

Hansen, M. T., Nohria, N., & Tierney, T. (2000, March-April). What's your strategy for managing knowledge? *Harvard Business Review*, pp. 106–16.

Hitt, M. A., Bierman, L., Shimizu, K., & Kochhar, R. (2001). Direct and moderating effects of human capital on strategy and performance in professional service firms: A resource-based perspective. *Academy of Management Journal, 44*, 13–26.

Horibe, F. (1999). *Managing knowledge workers: New skills and attitudes to unlock the intellectual capital in your organization*. New York: Wiley.

Huselid, M. A. (1995). The impact of human resource management practices on turnover, productivity, and corporate financial performance. *Academy of Management Journal, 38*, 635–72.

Jackson, S. E., Schuler, R. S., & Rivero, J. C. (1989). Organizational characteristics as predictors of personnel practices. *Personnel Psychology, 42*, 727–86.

Leonard-Barton, D. (1995). *Wellsprings of knowledge: Building and sustaining the sources of innovation*. Boston: Harvard Business School Press.

Lepak, D. P., & Snell, S. A. (1999). The human resource architecture: Toward a theory of human capital allocation and development. *Academy of Management Review, 24*, 31–48.

Lepak, D. P., & Snell, S. A. (2002). Examining the human resource architecture: The relationships among human capital, employment, and human resource configurations. *Journal of Management, 28*, 517–43.

Liebeskind, J. P. (1996). Knowledge, strategy, and the theory of the firm [Winter special issue]. *Strategic Management Journal, 17*, 93–107.

March, J. G. & Simon, H. A. (1958). *Organizations*. New York: Wiley.

Matusik, S. F., & Hill, C.W.L. (1998). The utilization of contingent work, knowledge creation, and competitive advantage. *Academy of Management Review, 23*, 680–97.

Osterman, P. (1987). Choice of employment systems in internal labor markets. *Industrial Relations, 26*, 46–67.

Pfeffer, J., & Baron, J. (1988). Taking the workers back out: Recent trends in the structuring of employment. In L. L. Cummings & B. M. Staw (eds.), *Research in organizational behavior* (pp. 257–303). Greenwich, CT: JAI Press.

Prahalad, C. K., & Hamel, G. (1990). The core competence of the corporation. *Harvard Business Review, 68*, 79–91.

Purcell, J. (1999). High commitment management and the link with contingent workers: Implications for strategic human resource management. In P. M. Wright, L. D. Dyer, J. W. Boudreau, & G. T Milkovich (eds.), *Research in personnel and human resource management* (pp. 239–57). Greenwich, CT: JAI Press.

Quinn, J. B. (1992). *Intelligent enterprise.* New York: Free Press.

Quinn, J.B., Anderson, P., & Finkelstein, S. (1996, March–April). Managing professional intellect: Making the most of the best. *Harvard Business Review*, pp. 71–80.

Robinson, S. L. (1996). Trust and breach of the psychological contract. *Administrative Science Quarterly, 41*, 574–99.

Rogers, E. W., & Wright, P. M. (1998). Measuring organizational performance in strategic human resource management: Problems, prospects, and performance information markets, *Human Resource Management Review, 8*, 311–31.

Rousseau, D. M. (1995). *Psychological contracts in organizations: Understanding written and unwritten agreements.* Thousand Oaks, CA: Sage.

Schultz, T. W. (1961, March). Investments in human capital. *American Economic Review, 52*, 1–17.

Shore, L. M., & Berksdale, K. (2000). Examining degree of balance and level of obligation in the employment relationship: A social exchange approach. *Journal of Organizational Behavior, 19*, 731–44.

Snell, S. A., & Dean, J. W. Jr. (1992). Integrated manufacturing and human resource management: A human capital perspective. *Academy of Management Journal, 35*, 467–504.

Snell, S. A., & Dean, J. W. Jr. (1994). Strategic compensation for integrated manufacturing: The moderating effects of job and organizational inertia. *Academy of Management Journal, 37*, 1109–40.

Snell, S. A., Lepak, D. P., & Youndt, M. A. (1999). Managing the architecture of intellectual capital: Implications for strategic human resource management. In. P. M. Wright, L. D. Dyer, J. W. Boudreau, & G. T. Milkovich (eds.), *Research in personnel and human resource management* (pp. 175–93). Greenwich, CT: JAI Press.

Snell, S. A., Youndt, M. A., & Wright, P. M. (1996). Establishing a framework for research in strategic human resource management: Merging resource theory and organizational learning. In G. R. Ferris (ed.), *Research in personnel and human resource management* (pp. 61–90). Greenwich, CT: JAI Press.

Stewart, T. (1997). *Intellectual capital.* New York: Doubleday-Currency.

Teece, D. J., Pisano, G., & Shuen, A. (1997). Dynamic capabilities and strategic management. *Strategic Management Journal, 18*, 509–33.

Tsui, A. S., Pearce, J. L., Porter, L. W., & Hite, J. P. (1995). Choice of employee-organization relationship: Influence of external and internal organizational factors. In G. R. Ferris (ed.), *Research in personnel and human resource management* (pp. 117–51). Greenwich, CT: JAI Press.

Tsui, A. S., Pearce, J. L., Porter, L. W., & Tripoli, A. M. (1997). Alternative approaches to the employee-organization relationship: Does investment in employees pay off? *Academy of Management Journal, 40*, 1089–121.

Ulrich, D., & Lake, D. (1991). Organizational capability. Creating competitive advantage. *Academy of Management Executive, 7*, 77–92.

Wallace, M. J., & Fay, C. H. (1988). *Compensation theory and practice.* Boston: PWS-Kent.

Wayne, S. J., Shore, L. M., & Liden, R. C. (1997). Perceived organizational support and leader-member exchange: A social exchange perspective. *Academy of Management Journal, 40*, 82–111.

Williamson, O. E. (1975). *Markets and hierarchies: Analysis and antitrust implications.* New York: Free Press.

Wright, P. M., Dunford, B. B., & Snell, S. A. (2001). Human resources and the resource-based view of the firm. *Journal of Management, 27*, 701–21.

Chapter 16

New HR Metrics: Scoring on the Business Scorecard

Richard W. Beatty, Mark A. Huselid, and Craig Eric Schneier

The role of the Human Resource function in firms has changed in parallel with the economic shift from agrarian to manufacturing to services – and now to information. Early on, HR was considered a staff function, not integral to the firm. Its role was administrative or transactional, its work-product often regarded as a commodity. One factor in changing HR's role is the increased reliance on knowledge workers. In our transitioning economy, observers, both inside and outside of organizations, have come to view a firm's workforce as far more valuable. Thus, if one views HR's primary role as influencing workforce mindset, competencies, and behavior, HR's role becomes central to the firm, for it is people who carry out its strategy. HR professionals need to recognize this change and adapt to it.

To enhance HR's organizational contribution, HR professionals not only will need to transform what they do but also how they are perceived. Early in its history, the "personnel" function was a refuge for line managers who were polite but ineffectual – employees "too nice to terminate." Three decades ago, empowered by federal and state legislation, HR became known as the "personnel police," often to the frustration of line managers. In the ongoing transformation to a services and information economy, HR wanted to be seen as a strategic partner, hopefully invited to the strategic planning party. But significant challenges await HR once invited to the party. It must have something to bring to the table.

We wish to address what and how HR can contribute to the strategic success of firms by transforming itself from a partner (that can be removed or outsourced) to a *player* – on the field, in the game, with the ability to score. The ability to score necessitates

R.W. Beatty, M.A. Huselid, and C.E. Schneier, "New HR Metrics: Scoring on the Business Scorecard," *Organizational Dynamics*, Vol. 32, No. 2 (2003): 107–21.

a new understanding of the rules of the game – a new perspective on what HR is to contribute, how its systems enable it to contribute, and how its ultimate deliverables can be measured. The rules of the game mean that HR should only attempt to score on an HR Scorecard integrated with the firm's Business Scorecard.

The shift to a services and knowledge economy has accelerated interest in the "intangibles" that have fueled market capitalization growth in the equity markets. Baruch Lev and others at New York University offer annual seminars on intangibles. *CFO* magazine has reported on how the value of knowledge workers in various industries can be captured in financial terms. Several studies have found that 30 to 40 percent of market appreciation is due to non-tangible factors. An Ernst & Young study has shown that intangible factors (e.g. strategy execution, managerial credibility, strategy quality, attracting and retaining talent, management experience, and compensation strategy) explain much of the variance in the market value of firms. These factors vary across industry; for example, in the computer industry, the quality of management explains as much as 13 percent of the total variance in market capitalization.

Thus, research has demonstrated that many targets of HR work can and do differentially impact a firm's financial outcomes. While this notion is often given lip service by firms, a growing body of evidence shows that what HR does can have a significant bottom-line effect. In a major research study, Huselid found that firms with sophisticated HR systems (also known as "high performance work systems") have a significant financial impact on profits per employee, sales per employee, and market value per employee. These findings have gained the attention of other academics and executives interested in better assessment of HR systems, as well as in redesigning executive appraisals to ensure that leaders are held accountable for enhancing their workforce's contribution to the bottom line.

One problem has been measurement effectiveness. A Conference Board survey of senior executives reported, as expected, that customer, financial, operational, and people measures were all seen as important but not equally effective. The test of measurement effectiveness was the executives' willingness "to bet their job" on the quality of the measures. The survey found significant discrepancies among domains, with the greatest discrepancy in people measures. Thus, substantial work is needed in the assessment of workforce measures in firms. Below we explore how to measure the workforce, the HR function, and firm leadership with respect to their impact on the workforce and ultimately upon a firm's strategic success.

From Business Scorecard to HR Scorecard

Our approach starts with Kaplan & Norton's Balanced Scorecard, a familiar concept in most firms. While maintaining the scorecard's core by retaining the financial, customer and business process success components, we have changed the component "Learning, Innovation, Etc." to "Workforce Success." We call this new scorecard the Business Scorecard (Fig. 16.1). Also notice that we prefer to use the word "success" as opposed to "satisfaction." Clearly firms can go out of business while satisfying customers and employees. Rather, the objective is to make both customers and employees

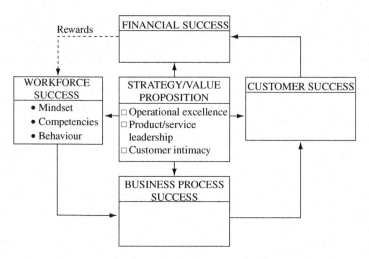

Figure 16.1　Business scorecard.

successful in order to make the enterprise successful. We have also replaced terms such as "mission" and "vision" from the center of the scorecard with "strategic choice." For a non-diversified firm or for a business unit within a diversified firm, we believe that a strategic choice (or value proposition) should be articulated, such that the workforce can understand and embrace how the unit intends to be successful in its chosen market. To simplify, we chose Tearcy & Wiersema's scheme in which firms pursue value propositions of low-cost provider (operational excellence), innovator (product or service leadership) or customization/unique solutions (customer intimacy). Strategic choice significantly impacts the definition of customer success, business process success, and plays an important role in assessing what the workforce must do to be successful.

To make the workforce successful in the context of the scorecard system, we must specify the major targets of an HR system, or HR's deliverables: workforce mindset, competencies, and behavior. To produce these deliverables, components of the HR system must be assessed on the competencies required of the *HR* workforce, the HR practices used to produce HR's deliverables (e.g. communication, work design, selection, development, measurement, rewards, etc.), and the HR system's integration and alignment with the strategy of the business.

This approach yields an HR Scorecard (Fig. 16.2) that enables the development of HR dashboards that capture HR's contribution. Several firms are pursuing such measurements systems and have made substantial progress. Boeing, General Electric, South-Corp Ltd., United Distillers & Vintners and Verizon are developing on-line, real-time metric systems to monitor HR processes and deliverables.

Assessing HR's Competencies

Assessing HR's competencies refers to the competencies of the HR workforce (i.e., the people who populate the HR function, their strengths and weaknesses in specific areas of expected HR performance). We look at HR competencies through the lens

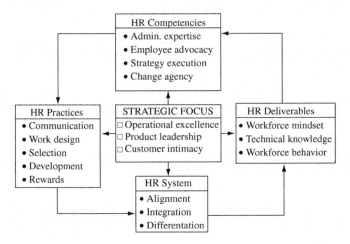

Figure 16.2   HR scorecard.

of Ulrich, whose book, *HR Champions*, analyzes HR's roles in terms of its focus on people or processes, as well as its strategic or operational focus. Thus, these roles can be depicted as a two-by-two matrix. First, the HR function can be conceived as having a process and tactical focus on administrative efficiency in the delivery of HR transactions. Second is HR's "employee advocacy" role (formerly "employee relations"), with an operational focus on serving the workforce (i.e. people) and the growth and retention of critical components of the workforce. HR's third role is strategic, whereby HR better enables the firm to execute its strategy by aligning HR practices with business strategy. The fourth role is concerned with changing the workforce – HR's "cultural change" role. Obviously, HR functions do not focus only on one role, nor should they. The point is to determine to what extent HR is currently focused on each role, and where it will need to be focused to enable the firm to be more successful.

The focus of the HR function should correlate with the firm's life cycle phase and strategic choice. As these shift, HR's focus must shift. For example, a firm pursuing an operational excellence strategy would want an HR function concerned with administrative efficiency. A firm moving from a product leadership to operational excellence strategy (a common occurrence with the commoditization of products and services) would likely require significant HR competencies in cultural change, as well as in strategy execution. Firms pursuing a product or service leadership strategy (i.e. innovation) would most likely want HR focused on providing "A players in A positions." In other words, the HR focus is to help populate the firm with the very best R&D or technical/innovative talent in order to distinguish itself from its competitors by building applied innovative and creative products (or services) that can create large-scale demand and command premium pricing.

How success in each role might be measured is easily understood. Measures of administrative efficiency are relatively simple (e.g. benefits cost per employee, processing cost per transaction, response time for benefit information requested, etc.). Employee advocacy measures are somewhat more complex. They involve issues such as retention rates of critical human capital, growth rate of core competency human capital, retention rate of critical human capital during organizational transitions or transformation, retention rate of "A" players in "A" positions, etc. Strategy execution measures might include: the extent to which the workforce understands the business's strategy (as measured by survey), line management feedback on the HR system's alignment with business strategy, or the HR workforce's level of understanding of the criticality of the HR function's integration. For firms active in mergers and acquisitions, another measure might be the depth of excess capacity of executives to export to recent acquisitions. The cultural change role measures might include: success rate of external hires brought in to "seed" firm change efforts, employee knowledge of the status of change efforts, depth of bench strength in change efforts, measures of employee mindset or mindset shift towards strategic goals and objectives, and certainly management's satisfaction with HR's contributions to organizational transformation efforts. Thus, there are some relatively straightforward measures of the HR function in terms of its competencies, all of which are driven by what the HR function needs to accomplish at any point in time.

Assessing HR's Practices

HR practices can be assessed against "best practices," or benchmarking. What can the HR function learn from other firms? How well is it doing relative to others? There are many best practice studies and many purveyors of best-practice information. Thus, one way HR can assess itself and its processes in delivering basic HR practices (e.g. selection, rewards, measurement, training and development, communications, work design, etc.) is to collect best practice data from available sources or actually conduct site visits. Once the data is gathered, the function can compare itself against a baseline and decide what improvement initiatives to undertake. Firms of substantial size can build internal scorecards, whereby critical HR practices can be compared across business units to determine how well one unit is doing relative to the firm's other business units on factors such as retention, labor costs, scarce-talent compensation, customer satisfaction, etc.

There is one caveat in using best practice assessment. Focusing on one practice or process in a system to the exclusion of others can drive the system out of tolerance, rather than enhancing the *system's* contribution to the firm. This very important point was often emphasized by W. Edwards Deming, who stimulated attention to operational measurement in the United States based on his work on quality in Japan. Thus, we must realize that enhancing a given HR procedure or practice can be useful, but in doing so we must avoid diminishing the efficacy of other components of the HR system. This leads us to HR *systems* as a third way of diagnosing the impact of the HR function on firms.

Assessing HR's Systems

We conceive of HR systems as the basic components of HR viewed as an interconnected whole with respect to a firm's strategy or value proposition. Our discussion explores three ways of assessing HR systems: alignment, integration, and differentiation.

Alignment relates to understanding that different business strategies require different cultures. Drawing on the seminal work of Schuler & Jackson, we use the three business strategies previously mentioned – operational excellence, product leadership, and customer intimacy – to demonstrate this point. In particular, there are significant cultural differences required of the primary workforce that must deliver the firm's value proposition.

Firms following an operational excellence strategy need a workforce that: identifies with business processes, is trainable, can learn rapidly, willingly follows the battle plan, is short-term focused, possesses a mindset that seeks to avoid waste and minimize costs, and is driven by incremental improvement. Because the objective of such firms is to build systems to drive the variance – and thus all the costs – out of the system, free spirits and ostentatious behavior are not welcome. The last thing that is needed in McDonald's is a creative hamburger-flipper! Firms that essentially follow this strategy include: Federal Express, Nucor, Wal-Mart, and, of course, McDonald's and most other fast-food franchisers. Such a value proposition offers it "our" way to the customer, at a price that is at or below all competitors. Ideally, the successful competitor can price the product or service at a level below a competitor's cost to produce, gain market share and thus leverage its operational excellence by serving a much broader customer base at an even lower price.

In product (or service) leadership, innovation is the value proposition. With an operational excellence strategy, the firm's uniqueness or competitive advantage is tied to cost. In product/service leadership, competitive advantage is tied to innovativeness of the offering. The workforce that produces innovations often identifies with, values, and is humbled by the discovery process. This is particularly true for the R&D workforce, which is largely responsible for the innovativeness, and the continued uniqueness, of firm offerings. Such a workforce tends to challenge the *status quo*, is anti-bureaucratic, has a longer-term focus, is driven by learning, has a greater tolerance for ambiguity, and is willing to take greater risks. It should not be structured or streamlined, because its members are expected to be innovative and creative, and think outside the box. Firms that generally follow this value proposition include Sony, GlaxoSmithKline, Merck, 3M, Intel, and Nike. These firms win in their markets by continuing to offer things "the new way" as opposed to "our way," as characteristic of an operational excellence strategy.

The customer intimacy value proposition offers unique solutions customized for the client. Such a strategy calls for a workforce constantly finding and improving solutions. Customer needs not only are satisfied but also anticipated. This requires a workforce that identifies with customers, shares "secrets" easily and readily with co-workers so that the entire system continuously leverages the firm's value proposition in order to grow by offering additional solutions to the client. Such a workforce should constantly seek customer intelligence, be adaptable and flexible, concerned with making results happen for the customer, be quick studies, and driven by customer success. It is not made up of clones, but employees who can think, capture and readily disseminate information, and better utilize that information in meeting a customer's unique requirements. Firms following a customer intimacy strategy include: the Four Seasons, Airborne, Roadway Express, Home Depot, Cott Corp., Cable & Wireless, PriceWaterhouseCoopers, and Dell Computer

Corp. The value proposition in customer intimacy is customization – you can have it "your way."

Alignment requires firms to understand that different value propositions require different cultures. There are many ways of looking at culture. One relatively straightforward approach is to use two very simple dimensions: firm structure (loose vs. tight) and firm focus (internal vs. external). Firms that are tight and internally focused are more typical of operational excellence. Because such firms are delivering a value proposition "our way," are trying to eliminate variance (and thus all avoidable costs) from the system, they must be tight and internally focused to achieve their strategy. On the other hand, product leadership firms, especially the R&D workforce responsible for creating the value proposition, need to be relatively loose. Just how loose? *Fortune* magazine featured a covering showing a prospective employee saying: "Yo, I'm the new corporation, man! I want an outlandish salary, a cappuccino machine, and by the way I'm bringing my bird to work." While the cover is a caricature, nevertheless flexibility, looseness, and tailoring to creative employees are important to yield the innovation necessary to leverage the product leadership value proposition. The challenge for line management, and especially the HR function, is to develop a core workforce focused on an applied innovation (i.e. an external focus) that delivers value to a customer. Thus, the culture needed for the product leadership value proposition to be successful is loose *and* external, especially for the core workforce that creates this value proposition.

The customer intimacy core workforce – those employees who interface with the customer – must be externally focused in a relatively tight platform. This enables the capture of customer information (i.e. customer intelligence) to build and efficiently deploy knowledge capital throughout the system, such that unique solutions are developed to leverage the relationship with the customer. The customer solutions culture not only solves immediate customer problems but also anticipates future customer needs based on learning occurring throughout the firm. Learning from customers enables further customization and requires a *very* strong external focus that operates through a smart and efficient dissemination platform. Airborne Express and Dell are examples where a firm finds unique solutions to customers' delivery problems but within a system that is tightly structured to capture customer intelligence and remain price competitive.

Strategic alignment means focusing HR practices on the firm's value proposition, as illustrated in Fig. 16.3. For example, in operational excellence one of the best workforce measures might be total cost productivity. The best rewards might be based on team productivity, since it would leverage the value proposition by creating "more with less." This would create self-funded productivity gains that can be shared with the workforce that enhanced productivity.

Product/service leadership measures might use sales from new products generated within, say, the last three years, and team innovation or revenue growth rewards based on new product sales, because these metrics are better measures of strategic success in delivering the value proposition created by the core workforce. Thus, revenue sharing incentives might be appropriate. Competency-based pay might also be appropriate for growing the competencies in the innovative, technical, and research units required by firms pursuing such a strategy.

WORKFORCE ALIGNMENT					
Strategic choices and traditional HR alignment					
Work design	**Performance measures**	**Selection**	**Competency development**	**Rewards**	**Communication**
• Right work • Key process • Job design • Organizational design	• Culture • Expections • Feedback • Levels	• Hire • Move • Exit	• Orientation • Current job • Career level	• Behavior • Consequences • Reward levels	• Strategy • Mindset • Status

• Centralized/controlled
• Strict policies
  Procedures
	• Total cost productivity
	• Errors
	• Wastes
	• Abandoned calls
	• Lost Customers/
	  accounts
	• Net sales → head-
	  count
	• Time/deadlines met
		• Strong basic
		  education;
		  –Quantitive
		  –Verbal
		• Written
		• Oral
		• Process
		  competence
		• Passive learners
			• Strong orientation on
			  exceptional rules
			• Predictable career
			  leader
			• Learning structured
				• Team productivity
				  awards
				• Profit sharing tied to
				  performance criteria
				• Skill based pay
					• Strategic choices
					• Teamwork
					• Encourage process
					  improvement
					• Productivity
					• Improvement
					  feedback

• More economy
• Team (cross
  functional)
	• % Sales from new
	  products (e.g., last 3
	  years)
	• Margin
	• New sales growth
	• Customer growth
	• Industry
	  accolade/recognition
	• Copyrights
	• Patents
		• Technical/reseach
		  correspondence
		• Outside–the–box
		  thinkers
		• Active learners
			• Employees
			  responsible for
			  learning
			• Mandatory
			  competency growth
			• Feedback on
			  professional
			  competency growth
				• Team innovation
				  award
				• Competency based
				  pay
					• Strategic choice
					• Antibureaucracy
					• Candor
					• Humble
					• Encourage
					  ideas/problem solving
					• Let winner "looks like"
					• Feedback on new
					  product sales

• Coordinated
• Know the customers
  needs
	• Customer guarantees
	• Customer relations
	  rate
	• No. from
	  current customers
		• Active learners
		• Networking
		  competence
		• Pecurrefuinss
			• Oriented toward long
			  learn relationship with
			  customer
			• Not a lot of ladders
			• Acts as a consultant
			  to customer/partner
				• Individual awards
				  system awards
				• Non financial award
				• "Fee for services"
				  awards
					• Strategic choice
					• Customer advises
					• Know your customers
					  need.

Figure 16.3 Aligning HR practices around value propositions.

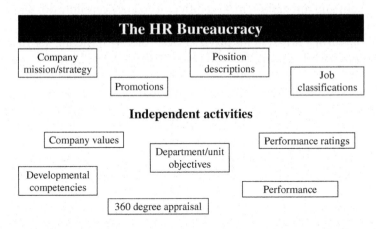

Figure 16.4 Common language.

In customer intimacy, customer guarantees, customer retention rates, and customer referrals might be important performance measures. Individual rewards for identifying new and better ways of serving customers, as well as system-wide team rewards, are appropriate for compensating the workforce for further leveraging the value proposition of customization.

Another *major* systems component is integration of the HR function. HR practices are seldom integrated (Fig. 16.4). In fact, one of the embarrassments of the HR profession is reliance on many different databases, all describing work or the workforce but using different languages. The compensation staff has its language for job evaluation, training and development uses the language of competencies, skills, knowledges, abilities, etc. The selection staff has a specific jargon having to do with job requirements and specifications found in job descriptions, different yet from the learning requirements of training and orientation efforts. Moreover, the performance measurement system often uses language entirely independent of workforce data from other areas of HR. In addition, top management can add to the language stew by using terms such as teamwork, integrity, leadership, etc. in a firm's mission and values statement. Such usage may not be conceptually different from HR's attempts to describe work or workforce but may not reinforce efforts to shape workforce mindset. Based on evidence, we believe that these systems need a common language and be supportive of one another.

Business strategy, communications about a firm's strategy and strategic direction, and the design of work all need to be aligned and integrated. Further, HR's basic system components – measurement, selection, development, and motivation – need to be aligned and integrated, with a common language as well. Since performance measurement is critical for gauging strategic progress, it must be consistent with the firm's value proposition. Because selection, development, and motivation efforts are all designed to enhance performance, it behooves firms to significantly improve their integration to leverage individual and firm performance. There is substantial evidence that this does not occur. Surveys report that neither managerial/professional nor hourly workers believe HR system components are well integrated.

Do alignment and integration make a difference? They certainly do. Substantial evidence from Huselid's survey of some one thousand firms indicates that alignment and integration of a firm's HR systems play a critical role, with the impact varying by the quality of a firm's work system. Huselid refers to these as "fit" and "complement," fit with respect to strategy and complement with respect to the components of the HR system. Huselid's findings demonstrate that substantial changes in market value occur based on the extent to which HR systems are aligned and integrated. For the least sophisticated one-fifth of firms in terms of HR, merely having an HR system is associated with >$40,000 increase in market capitalization per employee. However, for the next 40 percent of the sample, lack of alignment and integration does not seem to have much of an impact on market capitalization. (This may be one of the traps of best practices, for such firms may be engaging in various efforts to enhance one component of the HR system, without having a greater impact on the firm as a whole. In fact, best practices may create more variance within the HR function and therefore reduce its impact on the bottom line.) Finally, and most important, what the data shows is that for the top 40 percent, or most sophisticated HR systems, alignment and integration pay off substantially, adding *another* $40,000 to market capitalization per employee. Thus, alignment and integration of HR systems is not an academic issue. They impact a firm's financial returns.

Finally, a major emerging issue is workforce differentiation. Here we draw on the important recent work of Lepak and Snell. Figure 16.5 illustrates the competitive advantage of human capital in organizations and the availability of this human capital in the market. Readily available human capital with little strategic leverage is referred to here as contract services. In other words, this is work that is far from core in creating

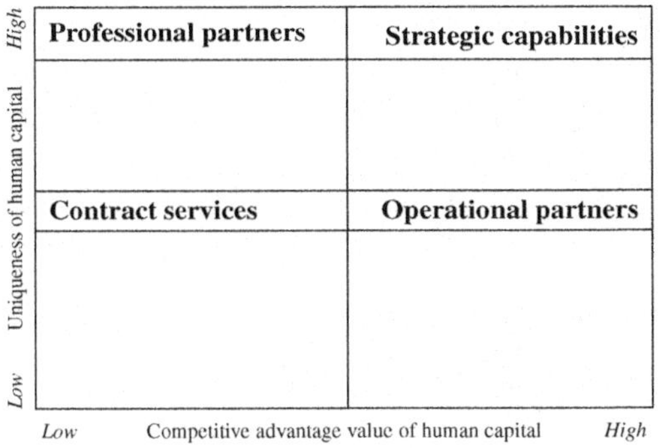

Figure 16.5   Differentiation: your organization's workforce(s).

or delivering the firm's value proposition and is a candidate for outsourcing. Strategic capabilities are those that are narrowly distributed in the labor market and have a significant impact on a firm's value proposition. Hence, the issue is how should a firm leverage its workforce. Another cell of the matrix we call professional partners – positions within firms not directly responsible for leveraging its value proposition. These positions differ depending on a firm's strategic pursuit. For a manufacturing firm, professional partners (i.e. not strategically core positions, yet professionals not abundant in the labor supply) include units such as law, finance, accounting, and even human resources. Although professional partners are narrowly distributed in the labor market, they do not directly contribute to the firm's competitive advantage in its chosen market. However, operational partners, although widely distributed in the labor market, have a significant impact on delivering the value proposition of the firm.

We concur with Lepak and Snell that each of these segments may call for a different focus in terms of HR systems. Contract services (work generally far removed from core) might require HR to assume a customer-supplier relationship with the firm, with HR's responsibility to make sure that the firm is getting the best, least expensive deal from a vendor. Obviously HR practices would be important here in terms of measurement, selection, and even development, and perhaps in terms of rewards to ensure that what is contracted for is delivered as specified. Professional partners would call for special treatment as professionals; at the same time, they are working outside their profession. They may be competent, but if they were *the* most competent, most likely they would be working in the professional firms within their discipline. Thus, from a compensation standpoint, they should probably be paid at or near midpoint and not much higher. Clearly if a firm finds itself in legal, financial or accounting trouble, it will likely go outside to find vendors with more qualified or specialized professionals.

Strategic capabilities, on the other hand, require the most care by HR because they leverage the firm's value proposition. How such individuals are selected, trained, measured, and compensated makes a difference.

These individuals may be compensated above or well above prevailing rates if a firm wishes to attract and retain the very best for positions that have strategic leverage. In fact it may be that one cannot pay too much for such individuals if they actually provide significant strategic leverage. Operational partners, on the other hand, probably should be paid at market value, but with significant group incentives, especially in systems such as operational excellence, where cost reduction is imperative. In other words, assessing HR performance involves not only HR alignment and integration (relatively new concepts to the HR function), but also differentiation – leveraging the HR system to maximize the contributions of the *core* workforce in delivering the firm's value proposition.

Linking to the Business Scorecard

As shown in Fig. 16.6, the HR Scorecard must be linked to the Business Scorecard, moving HR from focusing on doables to deliverables. What HR has been engaged in, as we have described it, is building competencies, aligning practices, and integrating and differentiating its systems to provide the workforce that can best leverage the firm's competitive advantage. But what it must *deliver* is a workforce. Workforce success is the ultimate objective of any HR system. How might this be assessed if we are truly to measure the HR system's effectiveness? One way is to measure the *mindset* of the workforce by eliciting answers to such questions as:

- Do employees know and understand the firm's strategy?
- Do employees know and understand the status of the firm's success with respect to the pursuit of that strategy?
- Do employees know and understand the firm's value proposition and how it is delivered?

Workforce mindset has been measured by various surveys. We believe such surveys should be much simpler and more frequent than in the past. For example, Sears' survey data, popularized in the *Harvard Business Review*, clearly support this. With

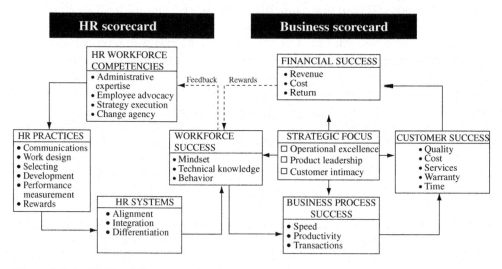

Figure 16.6 Linking HR scorecard to business scorecard.

ten questions Sears has been able to create a significant measure of workforce success (really a measure of workforce efficacy) and has demonstrated the impact of and improvements in workforce success on customer success and firm financial success.

Similar results have been reported else where using other scorecards (e.g. by many statewide Baldrige award winners). The Gallup Organization has used a 12-question survey that captures factors impacting productivity, retention, profitability, and customer satisfaction, as well as explaining a significant amount of variance in firm performance. Their questions are very similar to Sears' 10-question survey. Research is ongoing in this area, and survey data can help identify measurements of importance. Clearly a relationship exists between workforce behavior, operational success, customer success, and the financial success of firms.

HR's deliverables can also be measured by the *competency* of the workforce by eliciting answers to such questions as:

- Do employees know and understand what they are to do?
- Do employees believe they have the skills and knowledge necessary to do their job?
- Are employees provided the managerial support and support systems to do the job to the best of their ability?
- What level of competency is necessary in strategic resource positions now (and in the future)? Are individuals in these critical positions (e.g. sales representatives, customer service, etc.) delivering the behaviors expected of them?
- How many truly "A" players are there in "A" positions?
- How many "B" or "C" players are there in "A" positions?
- How many have passed behavior- or knowledge-based checkouts on specific competencies required for success in their jobs?
- Are our leaders behaving in ways that elicit "followership?"
- Do our leaders manage employee performance by detailing performance expectations, providing feedback, and conducting a meaningful review with an equitable reward conference?
- Are our leaders responsible for and assessed on their workforce's mindset, competency growth and behavior in strategic positions?

There have been many demonstrations of competency measure success, but the issue is which competencies to measure. Clearly competencies must be tied to business success. In fact, competencies should be tied to specific business deliverables (e.g. operational, customer and financial success). One problem in competency measurement is that competencies are often in "free-float" based on a firm's existing population, especially the firm's current executive officers, instead of the competencies necessary to win the firm's future. Competencies must be tied to business success and pass the "So what?" or "Because of?" test. Such competencies and their measurement are exemplified by mandated product knowledge and testing for sales associates (and executives) at Circuit City and Series 7 and 9 examinations in financial services to demonstrate General Electric's "Black Belt" proficiency.

The objective is to drive those behaviors with substantial impact on business process success that lead to customer success and ultimately result in financial success. Firms that are successful operationally and with their customers should experience firm financial success. From the perspective of HR, it is a continuous feedback loop. Financial success fuels the next generation of employee rewards. Customer success provides the feedback that enables the HR function to understand what needs to done to build better (or different) HR workforce competencies, enhance HR practices and determine the necessary steps to improve the alignment, integration, and differentiation of HR systems.

To achieve success HR must have a significant partnership with line management. While it is only reasonable to hold the HR function accountable for workforce success, line management should also be held accountable for the same workforce success metrics. If line managers wish to be successful in delivering on their business model (e.g. the Balanced Scorecard), they must be held accountable for workforce metrics such as workforce mindset, competency growth and behavior in delivering the unit's value proposition.

It is not unreasonable to ask what HR is willing to guarantee management in terms of workforce mindset, and behaviors. But the corollary is to ask what is line management willing to guarantee the firm, its workforce, customers, and its investors. Certainly line managers should be held accountable for financial success, customer success, business process success *and* workforce success. Workforce success for every manager can clearly be measured by metrics such as leader behavior (e.g. through 360° – or better yet 180° – assessments), workforce mindset, and workforce competencies. Indeed, if we are willing to accept the value of intangibles and their impact on market capitalization, it would be prudent to have a significant portion of all executive incentive compensation driven by leader behavior and workforce measures for any unit for which a manager is responsible.

Summary

Our objective has been to rethink the measurement of "soft-side" functions. While such measures may not always have the "hardness" of traditional business metrics, they are a step in the right direction – the right measures, on the business's scorecard, and with greater robustness. We believe it is essential that the HR function be assessed on its deliverables, using simple outcome measures such as the improvement of the workforce mindset, its competencies, and critical behaviors. It is equally essential to ensure that line managers be held accountable on the *same* workforce attributes or firms will not be able to deliver the workforce necessary to make the firm's business model a reality. Thus, a partnership between line managers and HR using the same attributes for the measurement of workforce success is mandatory to deliver the success of the firm's business model as intended.

Selected Bibliography

For those interested in the concept of human resources as a competitive advantage, see the work of D. Ulrich, especially *Human Resource Champions* (Harvard

Business School Press, 1997) and D. Ulrich and R. W. Beatty, "From Partners to Players: Extending the HR Playing Field," *Human Resource Management*, Winter 2001, 40(4), 293–307. For a discussion of the role of quality and measurement, see W. E. Deming, *Out of the Crisis* (MIT Press, 2000). On the growing importance of intangibles and the workforce in firm success, see B. Lev and P. Zarowin "Seeing is Believing," *CFO*, 1999. An illuminating discussion of non-financial measures can be found in Ernst & Young, *Measures That Matter: The Importance of Non-Financial Measures*, 1998. On the impact of HR systems on firms, see M. A. Huselid, "The Impact of Human Resource Management Practices on Turnover, Productivity, and Corporate Financial Performance," *Academy of Management Journal*, 1995, 38, 635–72.

Our approach to measurement starts with the concept of the Balanced Scorecard (R. S. Kaplan and D. P. Norton, *The Balanced Scorecard: Translating Strategy into Action* [Harvard Business School Press, 1996]). For a useful source on strategic choice, see M. Tearcy and F. Wiersema, *The Discipline of Market Leaders: Choose Your Customers, Narrow Your Focus, Dominate Your Market* (Perseus Books, 1997).

On improving various aspects of HR systems, see R. W. Beatty and C. E. Schneier, "New HR Roles to Impact Organizational Performance: From Partners to Players," *Human Resource Management*, 1996 and *The Performance Imperative: Strategies for Enhancing Workforce Effectiveness*, edited by H. Risher and C. Fay (Jossey-Bass, 1995), a collection of 20 essays offering an overview of the major issues affecting today's workforce.

On the issue of linkage, see B. E. Becker, M. A. Huselid, and D. Ulrich, *The HR Scorecard: Linking People, Strategy and Performance* (Harvard Business School Press, 2001). On the issue of designing an HR Architecture, see D. P. Lepak and S. A. Snell "The Human Resource Architecture: Toward a Theory of Human Capital Allocation and Development," *Academy of Management Review*, 1995, 24, 31–48. For a discussion of linking HR Strategies with role behaviors, see R. S. Schuler and S. E. Jackson "Linking Competitive Strategies with Human Resource Management Practices," *The Academy of Management Executive*, 1987, 1, 207–19.

Chapter 17

Strategies for Responsible Restructuring

Wayne F. Cascio

Employment Downsizing: The Juggernaut Continues

The job churning in the labor market that characterized the 1990s has not let up. If anything, its pace has accelerated. However, the free-agent mentality of the late 1990s that motivated some people to leave one employer so that they could make 5 percent more at another, a strategy that benefited men more than women,[1] is over. Layoffs are back – and with a vengeance. Thus, in 2001, companies in the United States announced layoffs of almost two million workers, with firms such as American Express, Lucent, Hewlett-Packard, and Dell conducting multiple rounds in the same year. Corporations announced 999,000 job cuts between September 11, 2001 and February 1, 2002 alone![2] Indeed, the 443,134 job cuts announced in the first quarter of 2002 exceeded those announced in the first quarter of 2001 by 9 percent.[3] Medium and large-sized companies announced most layoffs, and they involved *all* levels of employees, top to bottom. A study by Bain & Company's Worldwide Strategy Practice reported that in 2000, for example, 22 percent of the CEOs of the largest publicly traded companies either lost their jobs or retired, as opposed to just 13 percent in 1999.[4] Morgan Stanley estimates that about 80 percent of the US layoffs involved white-collar, well-educated employees. According to Morgan Stanley's chief economist, that's because 75 percent of the 12.3 million new jobs created between 1994 and 2000 were white-collar jobs. What the companies created, they are now taking away.

W. Coscio, "Strategies for Responsible Restructuring," *Academy of Management Executive*, Vol. 16, No. 3 (2002): 80–91.

Are there gender differences in the likelihood of layoffs and in their consequences? A longitudinal data set of more than 4,000 large Australian firms covering the period 1990–98 found that men were more likely than women to experience employment downsizing, but that women's re-employment rates after downsizing were lower than men's.[5] Evidence indicates that such career disruptions have particularly negative consequences on the future earnings of women.[6]

The Economic Logic That Drives Downsizing

What makes downsizing such a compelling strategy to firms worldwide? The economic rationale is straightforward. It begins with the premise that there really are only two ways to make money in business: either you cut costs or you increase revenues. Which is more predictable, future costs or future revenues? Anyone who makes monthly mortgage payments knows that future costs are far more predictable than future revenues. Payroll expenses represent fixed costs, so by cutting payroll, other things remaining equal, one should reduce overall expenses. Reduced expenses translate into increased earnings, and earnings drive stock prices. Higher stock prices make investors and analysts happy. The key phrase is "other things remaining equal." As we shall see, other things often do not remain equal, and therefore the anticipated benefits of employment downsizing do not always materialize.

What Does Research on the Economic Consequences of Employment Downsizing Tell Us?

In a series of studies that included data from 1982–94, 1995–2000, and 1982–2000; my colleagues and I examined financial and employment data from companies in the Standard & Poor's 500. The S&P 500 is one of the most widely used benchmarks of the performance of US equities. It represents leading companies in leading industries and consists of 500 stocks chosen for their market size, liquidity, and industry-group representation. Our purpose was to examine the relationships between changes in employment and financial performance. We assigned companies to one of seven mutually exclusive categories based upon their level of change in employment and their level of change in plant and equipment (assets). We then observed the firms' financial performance (profitability and total return on common stock) from one year before to two years after the employment-change events. We examined results for firms in each category on an independent as well as on an industry-adjusted basis.[7]

In our most recent study, we observed a total of 6,418 occurrences of changes in employment for S&P 500 companies over the 18-year period from 1982 through 2000. As in our earlier studies, we found no significant, consistent evidence that employment downsizing led to improved financial performance, as measured by return on assets or industry-adjusted return on assets. Downsizing strategies, either employment downsizing or asset downsizing, did not yield long-term payoffs that were significantly larger than those generated by Stable Employers – those companies in which the complement of employees did not fluctuate by more than ±5 percent.

This conclusion differs from that in our earlier analysis of the data from 1982 to 1994.[8] In that study we concluded that some types of downsizing, for example, Asset Downsizing, do yield higher ROAs than either Stable Employers or their industries. However, when the data from 1995–2000 are added to the original 1982–94 data, a different picture emerges. That picture suggests clearly that, at least during the time period of our study, it was not possible for firms to "save" or "shrink" their way to prosperity. Rather, it was only by growing their businesses (Asset Upsizing) that firms outperformed Stable Employers as well as their own industries in terms of profitability and total returns on common stock. With respect to such returns, Asset Upsizers generated returns that were 41 percent higher than those of Employment Downsizers and 43 percent higher than those of Stable Employers, by the end of Year 2.

This is not to say that firms should not downsize. In fact, many firms have downsized and restructured successfully to improve their productivity. They have done so by using layoffs as part of a broader business plan. As examples, consider Sears Roebuck & Company and Praxair, Inc. In January 2001 Sears cut 2,400 jobs as part of a restructuring that included closing 89 stores and several smaller businesses. Shares rose 30 percent in six months. Praxair, Inc., a $5 billion supplier of specialty gases and coatings, cut 900 jobs in September 2001 in response to the economic slowdown. At the same time, however, it also announced initiatives designed to pull it out of the slump, including two new plants for products where demand was on the rise. The result? The value of its shares rose 30 percent in three months.

In the aggregate, the productivity and competitiveness of many firms have increased in recent years. However, the lesson from our analysis is that firms cannot simply *assume* that layoffs are a quick fix that will necessarily lead to productivity improvements and increased financial performance. The fact is that layoffs alone will not fix a business strategy that is fundamentally flawed. Thus when Palm, Inc. trimmed 250 jobs in an effort to cut costs after a delayed product launch slowed demand, shares lost nearly half their value in one day and never recovered. In response, Palm's chief financial officer. Judy Bruner, noted, "There were a lot of questions about the viability of the business."[9]

In short, employment downsizing may not necessarily generate the benefits sought by management. Managers must be very cautious in implementing a strategy that can impose such traumatic costs on employees, both on those who leave as well as on those who stay.[10] Management needs to be sure about the sources of future savings and carefully weigh those against *all* of the costs, including the increased costs associated with subsequent employment expansions when economic conditions improve.

What's Different About Current Layoffs in the United States

In some important ways, the cuts that firms in the United States are making now differ from those they made in the 1990s.

Preemptive layoffs by large firms

Today's job cuts are not solely about large, sick companies trying to save themselves, as was often the case in the early 1990s (e.g., IBM, Sears). They are also about healthy companies hoping to reduce costs and boost earnings by reducing head count (e.g., Goldman Sachs and AOL). They are about trying to preempt tough times instead of simply reacting to them. These layoffs are radical, preventive first aid.[11] On the other hand, small companies, especially small manufacturers, tend to resist layoffs because they are trying to protect the substantial investment they made in finding and training workers.[12]

Tailoring the complement of skills

At the same time that firms are firing some people, they are hiring others, presumably people with the skills to execute new strategies. According to the American Management Association's annual survey of its member companies, which employ one-quarter of the American workforce, 36 percent of firms that eliminated jobs in the previous 12 months said they had also created new positions. That's up from 31 percent in 1996.[13] As companies lose workers in one department, they are adding people with different skills in another, continually tailoring their workforces to fit the available work and adjusting quickly to swings in demand for products and services. What makes this flexibility possible is the rise in temporary and contract workers.[14] On a typical day, they allow companies to meet 12 percent of their staffing needs. On peak days that figure may reach 20 percent.[15]

Sympathy toward an employer's reasons for layoffs, and a refusal to personalize the experience

From the perspective of employees, layoffs have a new character. More managers are briefing employees regularly about the economic status of their companies. This information raises awareness and actually prepares employees for what might happen to them. To many, the layoffs seem justified because of the slowdown in economic growth, the plunge in corporate profits, and the dive in stock prices. While being laid off even once used to be traumatic, some employees can now expect to go through that experience twice or even three times before they reach 50.[16]

Outplacement centers as hiring halls

Outplacement centers have become America's new hiring halls – gathering places for those between assignments. As the managing principal of the New York office of outplacement firm Right Associates put it. "These people are not ashamed, but they do feel dislocated, and there is anger. They were on track, and now they are trying to get back on track." Right has redesigned its offices to accommodate the new matter-of-factness about downsizing. Instead of enclosed offices and cubicles, where the downsized of the 1990s kept to themselves as they pursued jobs, there are many more glass walls and open gathering places where the downsized of the 21st century get to know each other. They socialize, and they even re-create office buzz. Said the managing principal, "It took us awhile to recognize that this had become important."

Layoffs in Other Countries

The phenomenon of layoffs is not limited to the United States. Asia and Europe have been hard hit as well. Japan's chip and electronics conglomerates have shed tens of thousands of jobs in the past year as the worldwide information-technology slump and fierce competition from foreign rivals have battered their bottom lines. High-profile firms such as Hitachi, Fujitsu, NEC, Toshiba, Matsushita Electric Industrial, and Sony have cut deeply, as has Mazda in automobile production.[17] In Hong Kong, fully 43 percent of firms in a recent survey expect to lay off workers in 2002, and in mainland China, more than 25.5 million people were laid off from state-owned firms between 1998 and 2001. Another 20 million are expected to be laid off from traditional state-owned firms by 2006.[18]

The incidence of layoffs varies among countries in Western Europe. Labor laws in countries such as Italy, France, Germany, and Spain make it difficult and expensive for companies to dismiss workers. In Germany, for example, all "redundancies" must by law be negotiated in detail by a workers' council, which is a compulsory part of any big German company and often has a say in which workers can be fired. Moreover, setting the terms of severance is tricky, because the law is vague and German courts often award compensation if workers claim that they received inadequate settlements. In France, layoffs are rare. As an example, consider that now-bankrupt appliance maker Moulinex, once considered an icon of French industry, repeatedly tried to restructure in 2001 but was blocked by the French Socialist government because its cost-cutting plans included layoffs. At present, even if companies offer generous severance settlements to French workers, as both Michelin and Marks & Spencer did in 2001, the very announcement of layoffs triggers a political firestorm.[19]

Multinational companies are dealing with this problem in several different ways. One strategy is to turn to other locations within the 15-nation European Union where labor laws are more flexible. Thus Britain has attracted car assembly plants from Nissan Motor Company and PSA Peugeot Citroen, while Ireland hosts EU-wide operations for such technology companies as Microsoft and Intel. A second strategy, practiced by multinationals such as General Motors and Ford, is to move production to Eastern Europe, Turkey, and other lower-cost areas.[20]

US-style layoffs are more common among some European multinationals. Thus London-based EMI Recorded Music, facing a declining global market and growing threat from Internet piracy, recently announced cuts affecting 18 percent of its work-force. Stockholm-based LM Ericsson, the world's largest manufacturer of equipment for cell-phone networks, with operations in 140 countries, had 107,000 employees in April 2001. By January 2002 it was down to 85,000, and in April 2002 it announced an additional 17,000 job cuts.[21] Such massive corporate and personal disruption once again raises important questions about the long-term benefits of strategies that emphasize reductions in the workforce. To put that issue into perspective, let us consider a key driver of business success in the new millennium: business concept innovation.

Business Concept Innovation

As Gary Hamel notes in his book *Leading the Revolution* (2000), the age of incremental progress is over. Its mantra – faster, better, cheaper – is true of fewer and fewer companies. Today change has changed. No longer is it additive. No longer does it move in a straight line. In many industries it is now discontinuous, abrupt, and distinctly non-linear, as radically different ideas and commercial developments render established products and services obsolete.[22] Perhaps the most far-reaching change of all is the Internet, which has rendered geography meaningless.

In the age of incremental progress, companies practiced rigorous planning, continuous improvement, statistical process control, six sigma quality-enhancement programs, reengineering, and enterprise resource planning.[23] If companies missed something that was changing in the environment – for example in TVs, stereos, and other consumer electronics, as in the 1970s and 1980s – there was plenty of time to catch up.

Today, if a company misses a critical new development – for example in digital phones, Internet auctions, or corporate extranets (networks that connect firms to their suppliers or customers, that is, the entire value chain) – it may never catch up. As an example of the latter, consider enterprise resource planning (ERP). Firms employed armies of consultants to help them use ERP to integrate internal operations like purchasing, manufacturing, and accounting. Such activities are important and useful, but now many companies use the Web to link up with suppliers and customers. Many ERP consultants (and their firms) are not players in this area, and the Web is the wave of the future.

Industrial-age management is a liability in a post-industrial world. Never before has there been such an incredible need for visionary leadership and the capacity to manage change effectively. Today the challenge is to think differently – to move beyond scientific management and kaizen (continuous improvement). As Hamel points out, the focus today is not on the slow accretion of scientific knowledge but on leaps of human imagination. In a non-linear world, only non-linear ideas will create new wealth and lead to radical improvements in human welfare.

The starting point today is not a product or a service. It's the entire business concept. Here are just a few examples:

- Internet telephony (the use of Internet facilities, where voice transmission is one form of communication) versus dedicated voice networks (e.g., telephones, allowing only voice transmission);
- buying insurance over the Internet versus going to a physical agency;
- searching for a job at Monster.com versus help-wanted ads in a local newspaper;

- downloading music via MP3 files versus purchasing CDs at a music store;
- instant buyer co-operatives (Mercata.com) versus shopping at a mall.

The list goes on and on. Now let's consider what business concept innovation is not.

What Business Concept Innovation Is Not

Some popular strategies today are spin-offs of non-core businesses, stock buy-backs, tracking stocks, and efficiency programs. All of these *release* wealth but they do not *create* wealth.[24] This is financial engineering, not business concept innovation. Strategies like these do not create new customers, markets, or revenue streams. Their only purpose is to wring a bit more wealth out of yesterday's strategies. Sure, money talks, but it doesn't think. Machines work efficiently, but they don't invent. Thinking and inventing are done by the only true, long-term source of innovation and renewal that organizations possess: smart, well-trained people.

How do you increase the probability that radical, new, wealth-creating ideas will emerge in your organization? Certainly not by indiscriminate downsizing of your workforce or by trying to imitate the best practices of other companies. Rather, a key task for leaders is to create an environment in which the creativity and imagination of employees at *all* levels can flourish. In many cases doing so requires a radical shift in the mindset of managers at all levels. That new mindset is called *responsible restructuring*.

Responsible Restructuring – What Is It?

In 1995 I wrote a publication for the US Department of Labor entitled *Guide to Responsible Restructuring*.[25] As I investigated the approaches that various companies, large and small, public and private, adopted in their efforts to restructure, what became obvious to me was that companies differed in terms of how they viewed their employees. Indeed, they almost seemed to separate themselves logically into two groups. One group of firms, by far the larger of the two, saw employees as *costs to be cut*. The other, much smaller group of firms, saw employees as *assets to be developed*. Therein lay a major difference in the approaches they took to restructure their organizations.

- *Employees as costs to be cut* – these are the downsizers. They constantly ask themselves: What is the minimum number of employees that we need to run this company? What is the irreducible core number of employees that the business requires?
- *Employees as assets to be developed* – these are the responsible restructurers. They constantly ask themselves: How can we change the way we do business, so that we can use the people we currently have more effectively?

The downsizers see employees as commodities – like paper clips or light bulbs, interchangeable and substitutable one for another. This is a "plugin" mentality: plug them in when you need them; pull the plug when you no longer need them. In contrast, responsible restructurers see employees as sources of innovation and renewal. They see in employees the potential to grow their businesses.

Downsizing's Hidden Risk to Learning Organizations

Learning organizations, from high-technology firms to the financial services industry, depend heavily on their employees – their stock of human capital – to innovate and grow. Learning organizations are collections of networks in which interrelationships among individuals, that is, social networks, generate learning and knowledge. This knowledge base constitutes a firm's "memory." Because a single individual has multiple relationships in such an organization, indiscriminate, non-selective downsizing has the potential to inflict considerable damage on the learning and memory capacity of organizations.[26] That damage is far greater than might be implied by a simple tally of individuals.

When one considers the multiple relationships generated by one individual, it is clear that restructuring which involves significant reductions in employees can inflict damage and create the loss of significant "chunks" of organizational memory. Such a loss damages ongoing processes and operations, forfeits current contacts, and may lead to foregone business opportunities. Which kinds of organizations are at greatest risk? Those that operate in rapidly evolving industries, such as biotechnology, pharmaceuticals, and software, where survival depends on a firm's ability to innovate constantly.

Ten Mistakes to Avoid When Restructuring

Downsizing a learning organization is not the only mistake that some companies make. Here are ten others to ponder and learn from.[27]

1. *Failure to be clear about long and short-term goals.* Always ask: What do our customers expect from us, and how will restructuring affect our ability to meet those expectations?[28]
2. *Use of downsizing as a first resort, rather than as a last resort.* In some cases, firms downsize because they see competitors doing it. This is a "cloning" response, in which executives in different firms follow one another's actions under conditions of uncertainty,[29] but it fails to consider alternative approaches to reducing costs. Such alternatives include delaying new-hire start dates, reducing perks, revoking job offers, freezing salaries and promotions, and asking employees to take unpaid vacations.[30]
3. *Use of non-selective downsizing.* Across-the-board job cuts miss the mark. So also do cuts based on criteria such as last-in-first-out (because then firms lose all their

bright young people), removing everyone below a certain level in the hierarchy (because top-heavy firms become even top heavier), or weeding out all middle managers (because firms lose a wealth of experience and connections).[31] Are all departments and all employees equally valuable to the firm? Probably not. With respect to employees, think about performance and replaceability.[32] Employees who are top performers and who are difficult to replace are most valuable. They are the "stars" that firms will depend on to innovate, to create new markets and new customers. Do everything you can to retain them.

4. *Failure to change the ways work is done.* Some firms mistakenly believe that they can keep making products or delivering services the same way as before downsizing. They fail even to consider changing from an old way to a new way of working. The same amount of work is simply loaded on the backs of fewer workers. Such a "pure-employment downsizing" approach does not lead to long-term improvements either in profitability or in total returns on common stock.[33]

5. *Failure to involve workers in the restructuring process.* It is a truism that employees are more likely to support what they helped to create. Yet many restructuring efforts fail to involve employees in any decisions either about the process or the desired outcome. As a result, employees feel powerless and helpless, and there is massive uncertainty in the organization. Conversely, when employees were asked to rate various factors that affect attracting, motivating, and retaining superior employees, one of the most important factors was "opportunities to participate in decisions."[34]

6. *Failure to communicate openly and honestly.* Failure to provide regular, ongoing updates not only contributes to the atmosphere of uncertainty; it also does nothing to dispel rumors. Open, honest communication is crucial if employees are to trust what management says, and trust is crucial to successful restructuring.[35] People trust leaders who make themselves known and make their positions clear.[36]

7. *Inept handling of those who lose their jobs.* Failure to treat departing employees with dignity and respect (e.g., having security guards escort them off company property), failure to provide training to supervisors in how to handle emotional factors, and failure to provide assistance to departing employees (financial, counseling, redeployment, training, outplacement) are other crucial mistakes.[37]

8. *Failure to manage survivors effectively.* Employee morale is often the first casualty of downsizing, as survivors become narrow-minded, self-absorbed, and risk averse.[38] Many firms underestimate the emotional damage that survivors suffer by watching others lose their jobs. In fact, a great deal of research shows that survivors often suffer from heightened levels of stress, burnout, uncertainty about their own roles in the new organization, and an overall sense of betrayal.[39] In unionized environments, downsizing may be related to increased grievances, higher absenteeism rates, workplace conflict, and poorer supervisor-union member relations.[40] In fact, survivors are looking for signals such as the following. Were departing employees treated fairly, and with dignity and respect? Why should I stay? What new opportunities will be available to me if I choose to do so? Is there a new business strategy to help us do a better job of competing in the marketplace?

9. *Ignoring the effects on other stakeholders.* In addition to survivors and victims, it is important to think through the potential consequences of restructuring on

customers, suppliers, shareholders, and the local community. A comprehensive program addresses and manages consequences for each of these groups.

10. *Failure to evaluate results and learn from mistakes.* Restructuring is not a one-time event for most firms. I have found in my research that unless firms are brutally honest about the processes and outcomes of their restructuring efforts, they are doomed to repeat the same mistakes over and over again. Don't be afraid to ask employees and managers at all levels, "What did you like most and like least about our restructuring effort?" Don't be afraid to ask customers if the firm is now meeting their needs more effectively, and for suggestions on how it might do so.

Three Downsizing Strategies for Responsible Restructuring

Now that we have seen what so many firms do wrong, let's examine three responsible restructuring strategies that some firms are doing right. These examples are by no means exhaustive, but they do represent the strategies of firms in several different industries (financial services, management consulting, high technology, telecommunications, manufacturing) and countries (the United States and Singapore).

Charles Schwab & Company: Use downsizing as a last resort; at the same time reinvent your business

At the end of the second quarter of 2001, Schwab's commission revenues were off 57 percent from their peak 15 months earlier. Overall revenue was down 38 percent, losses totaled $19 million, and the stock had dropped 75 percent from its high. Something had to give. How did the company respond? It took five steps *before* finally cutting staff.[41]

- When Schwab first saw business begin to deteriorate the year before, it put projects on hold and cut back on such expenses as catered staff lunches, travel, and entertainment. Management went out of its way to explain to employees the short-term nature of these cuts.[42]
- As it became clear that more savings were needed, top executives all took pay cuts: 50 percent each for the company's two CEOs, 20 percent for executive vice presidents, 10 percent for senior vice presidents, and 5 percent for vice presidents.
- It encouraged employees to take unused vacation and to take unpaid leaves of up to 20 days.
- Management designated certain Fridays as voluntary days off without pay for employees who didn't have clients to deal with.
- Only after the outlook darkened again, at the end of the first quarter of 2001, did the firm announce layoffs: 2,000 out of a workforce of 25,000. Even then the severance package included a $7,500 "hire-back" bonus for any employee

rehired within 18 months. It also included between 500 and 1,000 stock options, cash payments to offset the increased costs of healthcare insurance for laid-off employees, and a full range of outplacement services.[43] Further, everyone being laid off, nearly 5,000 people by the end of September 2001, was eligible for a $20,000 tuition voucher paid for by the founder himself. That could cost him as much as $10 million.

Over the past decade or so, Schwab & Company has had a lengthy record of product innovation. Perhaps its greatest innovation was one of the gutsiest moves of the 1990s: offering online trading in a bigger and better way than anyone else, even though it meant cutting commission rates by more than half. The result? In early 2000 Schwab could boast of having generated a better 10-year return for investors than Microsoft!

Today, however, the company is reinventing its business model. Sure, it is cutting costs by making its website easier to use, thus cutting down on expensive phone traffic, and it is raising fees for customers who don't trade very often and are unprofitable for the firm. But its biggest bet – where it thinks the bulk of its future revenue will come from – will be a radical new approach to winning and keeping business. The firm that was founded on the principle that it would never tell customers what stocks to buy is about to do just that – but with an ingenious twist.

The plan is to have computers analyze customers' portfolios, compare them with a computer-generated list of Schwab-recommended stocks for that investor's risk profile, and then convey that message to the client. When the objective analysis is supplemented with research reports from partner Goldman Sachs, plus occasional access to a salaried investment specialist, the company feels that these steps will fill in the final gap in what will be a complete set of services for virtually every investor.[44]

Schwab is practicing responsible restructuring. How? At the same time that it is demonstrating by its actions that it sees its employees as assets to be developed, it is developing business concept innovations that will allow it to generate new customers and new streams of revenue in order to grow its business.

Cisco Systems, Accenture, Motorola: "Park" the best; respect the rest

A second downsizing strategy is to retain top employees, while generating goodwill, even loyalty, among those departing. The United States has just sailed through five years of labor shortfalls on a scale not seen in more than three decades. What's more, the unemployment rate, while still rising, remains at historically low levels. Indeed, the unemployment rate for white-collar workers remains at just 2.2 percent.[45] Many employers are cautious about laying off too many workers, only to find themselves scrambling to refill the positions when demand picks up. To avoid that scenario, some are developing ingenious plans to "park" their most highly skilled employees until the economy recovers, and to promote goodwill, even loyalty, among those they have to let go.

Cisco Systems, which is shrinking its staff to 30,500 from 38,000 and paying six months' salary to those who sign severance agreements, is also trying a 21st-century version of the old industrial furlough. In a pilot program, it is paying 70 employees one-third of their salaries while lending them to non-profit organizations for a year. In effect Cisco is warehousing them until they might be needed.[46]

Accenture, a large management consulting firm, did cut 600 support staff last June. But to retain skilled employees, it developed the idea of partially paid sabbaticals. The firm pays 20 percent of each employee's salary for six to twelve months, plus benefits, and it lets the employee keep a work phone number, laptop, and email. About 1,000 employees took the offer. Said Accenture's managing partner for internal operations, "This is a way to cut costs that gives us the ability to hang onto people we spent so much time recruiting and training."[47]

Motorola has been hard hit by the global slowdown in telecommunications. As a result it is eliminating 30,000 jobs of the 147,000 that existed in January 2001, but at the same time it does not want to waste the results of its assiduous recruiting during the late 1990s. Every laid-off employee in the United States is getting a minimum of eight weeks' pay as severance, a benefit that until the late 1990s was not so broadly available to lower-ranking employees.

Motorola has also become more active in sponsoring job fairs and outplacement clinics where those leaving the company can receive help in writing resumes, honing interviewing skills, and making contacts.[48] Why is Motorola going to such lengths to generate goodwill among departing employees? It views these initiatives as subtle tools for future recruiting, once the economy revives and hiring resumes.

Philips Electronics Singapore: Offer training, counseling, and job-finding assistance to displaced workers

A third downsizing strategy for responsible restructuring is to help displaced workers find new jobs. Philips has operations in more than 60 countries in the areas of lighting, consumer electronics, domestic appliances, components, semiconductors, medical systems, business electronics, and information technology services. It began manufacturing operations in Singapore in 1969.[49]

Since the 1980s, manufacturing companies operating in Singapore have been following the global trend of relocating low-end production to lower-cost countries in the region. More recently, the trend has been to relocate to China and newly emerging economies with large supplies of low-cost labor and growing markets. In 1999 Philips Singapore took advantage of this opportunity to relocate part of its consumer electronics and domestic appliances business to China, Eastern Europe, and Mexico, thus lowering its operating costs while remaining based in Singapore. This restructuring exercise resulted in about 750 excess production operators, technicians, and related support staff.

In an effort to maintain a lean and flexible workforce in its low-end production in anticipation of an eventual relocation out of Singapore, Philips adopted the following human resource management strategies:

- Managers were required to assess long-term workforce projections carefully before recruiting new employees.

- Vacancies had to be filled from within the organization unless present staff could not meet the requirements.
- Philips recruited contract workers rather than full-time workers to meet increased demand and to provide flexibility when demand fluctuates.

When it became clear that the relocation would result in 750 excess employees, management informed the union, a branch of the Union of Workers in Electronics and Electrical Industries (UWEEI), of the situation. They worked together to ensure that the retrenched workers were given as much support and help as possible in finding alternative work.

Philips puts a high priority on employee self-development, with the belief that people are its most valuable resources. It has earned a reputation for being an enlightened and caring employer, having won several prestigious awards from the National Trade Union Congress (NTUC) and from the government. Its demonstrated commitment to its employees, as stated in its philosophy of management, is that employees should be respected, challenged, encouraged, and given equal opportunities.

Key initiatives at Philips

Skills upgrading and training for employability
Together with the UWEEI and the NTUC, Philips encouraged all of the affected workers to take advantage of a program that had been initiated by the NTUC: the Skills Redevelopment Program. That program provides attractive training grants to companies. Its objective is to help workers, especially those who are older and lower skilled, to become more employable through skills upgrading. Philips encouraged the 750 affected workers to enroll in the Certificate of Competence in Electronic Maintenance program under the Skills Redevelopment Program.

Counseling and employment assistance
On the day that the retrenchments were announced in December 1999, the company made sure that all affected workers were registered with the NTUC Employment Assistance Program, and company and union representatives were available to answer questions. Later, a job fair was organized by the Ministry of Manpower and union representatives to assist affected workers in their job search.

Job matching
The first priority was to help workers secure alternative employment, by trying to match them with vacancies in job data banks kept by the NTUC Employment Assistance Program and the government-sponsored Employment Services Department. In an initial effort in December 1999, more than 30 retrenched workers were identified as having the necessary qualifications to pursue further training for a higher skills job such as wafer fabrication. The union approached ST Micro-electronics, which had vacancies in this area, and got its agreement to interview interested workers. The union encouraged other workers who were qualified or interested to undergo training in order to qualify for higher-paying employment opportunities.

Financial assistance

To minimize financial hardship, retrenchment benefits were paid according to the collective bargaining agreement: one month's pay for every year of service for those with three or more years of service, and one week's pay for every year for those with fewer than three years' service. In addition, workers received one month's pay in lieu of notice of retrenchment, and those retrenched in December still received the one-month annual wage supplement normally paid at the end of the year.

Outcomes

Many of the laid-off workers had worked for Philips for more than 20 years, and this had been their first job. They understood the company's need to reduce operating costs and to remain competitive. At the same time, they appreciated the support provided both by the management and by the union in helping them to adjust to the sad reality. Such support also boosted the morale and confidence of those who continued to work in the plants.

Restructuring Responsibly: What To Do

At this point you are probably wondering how to proceed. We have highlighted some things not to do and have provided examples of how to use downsizing as part of a strategy for responsible restructuring. We believe it can all be put together by following these suggestions.

1. *Carefully consider the rationale behind restructuring.* Invest in analysis and consider the impact on those who stay, those who leave, and the ability of the organization to serve its customers.[50] Do you have a long-term strategic plan that identifies the future mission and vision of the organization, as well as its core competencies? Does the plan consider factors such as changes in the firm's external environment and industry, the business cycle, the stage of internationalization of the firm, market segments, and life cycles of products in the various segments? Does the plan consider how processes can be redesigned while retaining the high performers who will be crucial to the firm's future success? Is there a plan to sell off unprofitable assets? Is employment downsizing part of a plan or is it *the* plan? All of these factors could impact the need for and extent of restructuring.
2. *Consider the virtues of stability.* In many cases, companies can maintain their special efficiencies only if they can give their workers a unique set of skills and a feeling that they belong together. Teams work best if the team members get to know and trust each other and if each team member masters a broad enough range of skills to be able to fill in for absent colleagues. Moreover, profit sharing as a reward system makes sense only if the employees are around when profits are disbursed. Sometimes the virtues of stability outweigh the potential benefits of change.[51]
3. *Before making any final decisions about restructuring, managers should make their concerns known to employees and seek their input.* Sometimes workers have insightful

ideas that may make layoffs unnecessary. However, even if layoffs are necessary, seeking employee input will foster a sense of participation, belonging, and personal control. Make special efforts to secure the input of "star" employees or opinion leaders, for they can help communicate the rationale and strategy of restructuring to their fellow employees and can also help to promote trust in the restructuring effort.[52]

4. *Don't use downsizing as a "quick fix" to achieve short-term goals in the face of long-term problems.* Consider other alternatives first, and ensure that management at all levels shares the pain and participates in any sacrifices employees are asked to bear. Make downsizing truly a last resort, not a first resort.

5. *If layoffs are necessary, be sure that employees perceive the process of selecting excess positions as fair, and make decisions in a consistent manner.*[53] Make special efforts to retain the best and the brightest, and provide maximum advance notice to terminated employees.

6. *Communicate regularly and in a variety of ways in order to keep everyone abreast of new developments and information.* Use newsletters, emails, videos, and employee meetings for this purpose. Sharing confidential financial and competitive information with employees establishes a climate of trust and honesty. High-level managers should be visible, active participants in this process. Be sure that lower-level managers are trained to address the concerns of victims as well as survivors.[54]

7. *Give survivors a reason to stay, and prospective new hires a reason to join.* As one set of authors noted, "People need to believe in the organization to make it work, but they need to see that it works to believe in it."[55] Recognize that surviving employees ultimately are the people you will depend on to provide the innovation, superior service to customers, and healthy corporate culture that will attract and retain top talent. Do everything you can to ensure their commitment and their trust.

8. *Train employees and their managers in the new ways of operating.* Restructuring means change, and employees at all levels need help in coping with changes in areas such as reporting relationships, new organizational arrangements, and reengineered business processes. Evidence indicates clearly that firms whose training budgets increase following a restructuring are more likely to realize improved productivity, profits, and quality.[56]

9. *Examine all HR systems carefully in light of the change of strategy or environment facing the firm.*[57] Training employees in the new ways of operating is important, but so also are other HR systems. These include workforce planning based on changes in business strategy, markets, customers, and expected economic conditions; recruitment and selection, based on the need to change both the number and skills mix of new hires; performance appraisal, based on changes in the work to be done; compensation, based on changes in skill requirements or responsibilities; and labor relations, based on the need to involve employees and their unions in the restructuring process.

Above all, if you do choose to restructure, do it responsibly, and use it as an opportunity to focus ever more sharply on those areas of the business where your firm enjoys its greatest competitive strengths. By restructuring responsibly through the use of effective downsizing strategies, your organization will be better able to achieve the 3Cs of organizational success: Care of customers, Constant innovation, and Committed people.[58]

NOTES

1. Brett, J. M., & Stroh, L. K. 1997. Jumping ship: Who benefits from an external labor market career strategy? *Journal of Applied Psychology*, 82(3): 331–41.
2. Shadow of recession. 9 February 2002. *http://www. cbsmarketwatch.com.*
3. Planned job cuts continue fall. 3 April 2002. *http://www. cbsmarketwatch.com.*
4. Morris, B. White-collar blues. *Fortune*, 23 July 2001, 98–110.
5. Dawkins, P., & Littler, C. R. (eds.). July 2001. *Downsizing: Is it working for Australia? http://www.ceda.com.au.*
6. See, for example, Blau, F. D., & Ferber, M. A. 1987. *The economics of women, men, and work.* Englewood Cliffs. NJ: Prentice-Hall; Schneer, J. A., & Reitman, F. 1997. The interrupted managerial career path: A longitudinal study of MBAs. *Journal of Vocational Behavior*, 51(3): 411–34; and Schneer, J. A., & Reitman, F. 1995. The impact of gender as managerial careers unfold, *Journal of Vocational Behavior*, 47(3): 290–315.
7. Cascio, W. F., & Young, C. E. 2001. Financial consequences of employment-change decisions in major U.S. corporations: 1982–2000. In K. P. De Meuse & M. L. Marks (eds.). *Resizing the organization.* San Francisco: Jossey-Bass pp. 131–56. See also Cascio. W. F., Young, C. E., & Morris, J. R. 1997. Financial consequences of employment-change decisions in major U.S. corporations. *Academy of Management Journal*, 40(5): 1175–189; and Morris. J. R., Cascio, W. F., & Young, C. E. 1999. Have employment downsizings been successful? *Organizational Dynamics*, 27(3): 78–87.
8. Cascio et al., op. cit.
9. Bruner, J., quoted in Lavelle, L. Swing that ax with care. *Business Week*, 11 February 2002, 78.
10. Cascio, W. F. 1993. Downsizing: What do we know? What have we learned? *The Academy of Management Executive*, 7(1): 95–104. See also Cascio, W. F. Strategies for responsible restructuring. Keynote address presented at the National Manpower Summit, Singapore, 18 October 2001.
11. Morris, op. cit.
12. Ansberry, C. Private resources: By resisting layoffs, small manufacturers help protect economy. *Wall Street Journal*, 6 July 2001, A1, A2.
13. American Management Association. 2000. *2000 American Management Association survey: Staffing and structure.* New York: Author.
14. Eig, J. Shrinking week: Do part-time workers hold the key to when the recession breaks? *Wall Street Journal*, 3 January 2002. A1, A2.
15. Uchitelle, L. Pink slip? Now, it's all in a day's work. *New York Times*, 5 August 2001. *http://www.NYTimes.com.*
16. Ibid.
17. Hitachi decides another 4,000 workers in Japan must go. *South China Morning Post*, 31 January 2002. 1; Kunii, I. Under the knife. *Business Week*, 10 September 2001, 62: and Larimer, T. Worst-case scenario. *Time*, 26 March 2001, 54–56. See also Shirouzu, N. Leaner and meaner: Driven by necessity – and by Ford-Mazda downsizes, US-style. *Wall*

Street Journal, 5 January 2000, A1. A10. See also Sony's shake up. *Business Week*, 22 March 1999, 52, 53.

18. 43pc of firms plan to cut staff, says poll. *South China Morning Post*, 26 February 2002. China warns of 20 million urban jobless. *South China Morning Post*, 30 April 2002, 1.

19. Winestock, G. A reticent European right balks on labor. *Wall Street* Journal, 21 June 2002. A6, A7: and Matlack, C. The high cost of France's aversion to layoffs. *Business Week*, 5 November 2001, 56.

20. Winestock, op. cit.

21. Larsen, K. EMI plans job cuts, large cost savings. *Asian Wall Street Journal*, 21 March 2002, M6; Pritchard, S. Deregulation and debt serve to hasten inevitable. South *China Morning Post*, 26 March 2002, 2; and Gamel, K. Ericsson to cut 17,000 jobs. 22 April 2002. *http://www.cbsmarketwatch.com.*

22. Hamel, G. 2000. *Leading the revolution.* Boston: Harvard Business School Press.

23. Statistical process control (SPC) is a quality-control technique that is based on statistical theory. Its objective is to study the variation in the output of production processes. Six sigma is a standard in SPC where almost all variability in product or service output has been eliminated. In a six-sigma system, one expects only 3.4 defects per million units of output. Enterprise resource planning is a computer-based software system that integrates all departments and functions into a single information database.

24. Norris, F. Financial magic looked good, but left companies weak. *New York Times,* 28 September 2001. *http://www.NYTimes.com.*

25. U.S. Department of Labor. 1995. *Guide to responsible restructuring.* Washington. DC: U.S. Government Printing Office.

26. Fisher, S. R., & White, M. A. 2000. Downsizing in a learning organization: Are there hidden costs? *Academy of Management Review,* 25(1): 244–51.

27. The sources of these recommendations, unless otherwise noted, are my own research, as described in *Guide to responsible restructuring,* op. cit., as well as the following: Cravotta, R., & Kleiner, B. H. 2001. New developments concerning reductions in force. *Management Research News,* 24(3/4): 90–3. See also Moravec, M. The right way to rightsize. *Industry Week,* 5 September 1994, 46.

28. For more on this topic, see Seiders. K., & Berry, L. L. 1998. Service fairness: What it is and why it matters. *The Academy of Management Executive,* 12(2): 8–20.

29. McKinley, W., Zhao, J., & Rust, K. G. 2000. A sociocognitive interpretation of organizational downsizing. *Academy of Management Review,* 25(1): 227–43.

30. Lavelle, L. Thinking beyond the one-size-fits-all pay cut. *Business Week,* 3 December 2001. 45.

31. Ibid. See also The year downsizing grew up. *The Economist,* 21 December 1996. 97–9.

32. Martin, D. C., & Bartol, K. M. 1985. Managing turnover strategically. *Personnel Administrator.* 30(11): 63–73. See also Cascio. W. F. 2000. *Costing human resources: The financial impact of behavior in organizations.* 4th ed. Cincinnati, OH: South-Western College Publishing.

33. Cascio & Young, op. cit.

34. Mirvis, P. H. 1997. Human resource management: Leaders, laggards, and followers. *The Academy of Management Executive,* 11(2): 43–56.

35. Mishra, K. E., Spreitzer, G. M., & Mishra, A. K. 1998. Preserving employee morale during downsizing. *Sloan Management Review,* 39(2): 83–95. See also Gray, R. Internal communication: Its critical role during business reorganizations. Presentation to the Australian Human Resources Institute, Sydney, 1 November 2001.

36. Darling, J., & Nurmi, R. 1995. Downsizing the multinational firm: Key variables for excellence. *Leadership & Organization Development Journal*, 16(5): 22–8.
37. As one example of this, see Barrionuevo, A. Jobless in a flash, Enron's ex-employees are stunned, bitter, ashamed. *Wall Street Journal*, 11 December 2001, B1, B12.
38. Cascio, W. F. Downsizing: What do we know?, op. cit.
39. Appelbaum, S. H., Everard, A., & Hung, L. T. S. 1999. Strategic downsizing: Critical success factors. *Management Decision*, 37(7): 535–52.
40. Wagar, T. H. 2001. Consequences of work force reduction: Some employer and union evidence. *Journal of Labor Research*, 22(4): 851–62.
41. Vogelstein, F. Can Schwab get its mojo back? *Fortune*, 17 September 2001, 93–8. See also Bernstein, A. America's future: The human factor. *BusinessWeek*, 27 August 2001, 118–22.
42. Boyle, M. How to cut perks without killing morale. *Fortune*, 19 February 2001, 241, 242, 244.
43. Jossi, F. Laying off well. *HRMagazine*, July 2001, 48.
44. Schwab versus Wall Street. *BusinessWeek*, 3 June 2002, 64–70.
45. Bernstein, op. cit.
46. Uchitelle, op. cit.
47. Bernstein, op. cit.
48. Uchitelle, op. cit.
49. Source: Singapore Ministry of Manpower. February 2001. Managing excess manpower, case study series, Singapore: Author.
50. *Guide to responsible restructuring*, op. cit.
51. Cascio & Young, op. cit. See also Conlin. M. Where layoffs are a last resort. 8 October 2001. *http://www.businessweek.com*.
52. See Roth, D. How to cut pay, lay off 8,000 people, and still have workers who love you. *Fortune*, 4 February 2002. 62–8.
53. Colquitt, J. A., Conlon, D. E., Wesson, M. J., Porter, C. O. L. H., & Ng, K. Y. 2001. Justice at the millennium: A meta-analytic review of 25 years of organizational justice research. *Journal of Applied Psychology*, 86(3): 425–45.
54. Feldman, M., & Spratt, M. 1999. *Five frogs on a log: A CEO's field guide to accelerating the transition in mergers, acquisitions, and gut-wrenching change*. New York: Harper.
55. De Vries, M., & Balazs, K. 1997. The downside of downsizing. *Human Relations*, 50(1): 11–50.
56. Appelbaum, S. H., Lavigne-Schmidt, S., Peytchev. M., & Shapiro, B. 1999. Downsizing: Measuring the costs of failure. *Journal of Management Development*, 18(5): 436–63.
57. Becker, B. E., Huselid, M. A., & Ulrich, D. 2001. *The HR scorecard: Linking people, strategy, and performance*. Boston: Harvard Business School Press. See also Delery, J. E., & Doty, D. H. 1996. Modes of theorizing in strategic human resource management: Tests of universalistic, contingency, and configurational performance predictions. *Academy of Management Journal*, 39(4): 802–35.
58. Darling & Nurmi, op. cit.

Part IV

Role of the HR Department and HR Professionals

The chapters in this final part cover several issues related to the role of the HR department and HR professionals in strategic human resource management. Because the field of strategic human resource management depends upon detailed understanding of the activities of the firm as well as of its HR policies, it is often useful for the HR department and HR professionals to be closely involved, actually working in partnership, with line managers who are more directly involved in the firm's strategy formulation and implementation. In some firms, the senior HR professional may be quite knowledgeable about the strategy of the firm, making the resulting HR policies more aligned with the needs of the firm and the people more linked with the firm. Strategy formulation is only one part of the equation however. It is often in the details of implementation that business strategies get into difficulties. Here partnership among the HR professionals, line managers, and the employees themselves can help overcome the hurdles in implementation and ensure that the HR practices actually used are consistent with the HR policies and the needs of the firm. The chapters in this section talk about these issues in great detail. They also discuss the implications of strategic human resource management for competency development for the HR professionals, not only at the senior levels but throughout the HR department. They also discuss the implications for the structure of the HR department and what the HR department of the future may look like, particularly as it becomes a real strategic partner, practicing strategic human resource management in an expanding global environment.

The first chapter in this part by Gratton and Truss discusses three major components in the formulation of a people strategy for firms. Each part is important for HR departments and HR professionals to consider in their attempts to practice strategic human resource management. The first component is vertical alignment. Here the needs of the business, as determined in part by its strategy, structure, culture, and leadership, determine what the people strategy should be like. Because these are unique to each firm, the authors suggest that there is likely to be no one best way, at least at the very specific practice level. The second component is horizontal alignment. This implies that the human resource practices need to be consistent in sending the same messages to the employees about what behaviors and competencies are valued and needed. These first two components are the HR strategy formulation. While these two are important, it is the third that is most critical and that is the action dimension. Here the authors distinguish between HR policy and HR practice. It is the practice that is actually implemented that employees see and respond to and this must be consistent with the HR policy. So too, the behaviors and values of the managers must support the HR policies and be consistent with them. Without consistency in the action dimension, the HR strategy implementation part, the best formulated HR strategy will not have the impact for strategic human resource management to be effective. Needless to say, all three components provide a great deal of challenge for HR departments and HR professionals.

The second chapter in this part, by Mendenhall, Black, Jensen, and Gregersen, also provides HR departments and HR professionals with substantial challenges. These challenges result from the realities of globalization. The challenges that the authors identify and discuss in detail were uncovered in the years with senior HR professionals. The challenges include: enhancing global business strategy; aligning HR issues with business strategy; designing and leading change; building global corporate cultures; and developing global leaders. The authors provide excellent company examples to illustrate each of these and describe how HR professionals can respond effectively to them.

Furthering the theme of the challenges facing HR departments and HR professionals as a consequence of globalization, is the third chapter by Novicevic and Harvey. The authors argue that the HR department (*function* in their words) can play a more influential role in global organizations than it has in domestic organizations. This is consistent with the arguments of Gupta and Govindarajan (Part II) in their description of how MNCs can gain global competitive advantage. It is also consistent with the results reported in the article by Mendenhall and his colleagues. The authors suggest in their article that HR professionals can play a more important role because MNCs need strategic consistency and also flexibility (similar to what Pucik describes in his article on the Global Mindset in Part II). HR professionals can assist by: (a) linking human resource management to the needs of the firm; (b) forming and managing the top leadership teams; and (c) creating innovative global assignment options.

Tyson and Selbie conclude Part IV with their chapter on people processing systems and human resource strategy. The chapter is a valuable one for HR professionals seeking to add value to their organizations. In it they describe, through a case study of a telecom company as it evolved from a domestic to a global operation, how an HR department can evolve from transactional based to transformational based (aka, strategic human resource management). The authors do this through the explication of HRM systems, processes, and outsourcing. The use of outsourcing became critical to the HR department as it systematically decided how it could maximize its value and what was better left to others to do (hence, deciding what to outsource). The case study illustrates how transitioning the HR department from transactional to transformational may be more evolutionary than revolutionary, thus allowing individuals and departments to adapt to the changes over time. At the end, the case study also illustrates that HR departments and HR professionals can add value and be real players in organizations through strategic human resource management.

Chapter 18

The Three-Dimensional People Strategy: Putting Human Resources Policies into Action

Lynda Gratton and Catherine Truss

When we talk about people strategy, we mean a strategy, with its underpinning policies and processes, that an organization develops and implements for managing its people to optimal effect. Why is it that, despite their best efforts, organizations so often fail to develop and implement successful people strategies? We have just completed a ten-year study in seven large organizations: BT (a UK telecom company); Chelsea and Westminster NHS Trust (a public hospital); Citibank (a global bank); Glaxo (a global pharmaceutical company); HP (a computer company); Kraft Foods (a food company), and Lloyds-TSB (a UK national bank). The results from the sample of 4,500 employees we surveyed are not encouraging:

- 15% believed senior management was well-informed about what employees think and do.
- 34% did not have a great deal of trust in management.
- 20% agreed that their HR department had a clear strategy guiding its activities.
- 35% thought the appraisal system enabled an accurate assessment of people's strengths and weaknesses.
- 34% felt their HR department was competent at its job.

L. Gratton and C. Truss, "Three-Dimensional People Strategy: Putting Human Resources Policies into Action," *Academy of Management Executive*, Vol. 17, No. 3 (2003): 74–86.

- 48% thought people's work goals were clearly defined.
- 36% agreed that people received the training they needed to do their jobs well.

These discouragingly low percentages are the average responses for the total employee sample across three times studies (1994, 1997, and 2000). We did find that the people strategies of some companies were significantly stronger at some times than others. We shall later describe these results and how they were achieved. However, the average results do make depressing reading, and we have no reason to believe that better results would be obtained from other firms. If anything, these findings are likely to be more positive than most, since these organizations were keen participants in our study. Part of the problem is that most executives are unwilling to ask the difficult questions posed in our surveys, and so they never find out how successful their people strategy really is.

Our study of the development and implementation of people strategies has spanned seven different organizations and lasted the course of an entire decade.[1] During that time, we have witnessed line executives and their HR colleagues grappling with many of the complex situations that face all corporations at some time in their existence – mergers, takeovers, corporate crises, large-scale redundancy programs, and significant product and service market changes. We have seen how firms have gone about leveraging corporate success, despite the odds, through creative and innovative people-management strategies. We have also borne witness to the many mistakes, frustrations, and traumas inevitably experienced by these executives and their organizations over the same period. It is from this unique study that we draw our examples, cases, and lessons.

In this chapter we introduce a three-dimensional model of people strategy. It is based on a *vertical alignment* dimension between people strategy and business goals; a *horizontal alignment* dimension between individual HR policy areas; and, finally, an action or *implementation* dimension to represent the degree to which the people strategy is put into effect through the day-to-day experiences of employees and the behavior of line managers. Using detailed case studies, we illustrate the possible variety in people strategies, highlight the ways in which companies achieved strength along each dimension, and demonstrate the dramatic differences between the roles, competencies, and aspirations of the different HR functions. A key message is that the bridging from business goals to employee performance requires not only policies but also a determination to act, as seen through actual practices.

The Three Dimensions of a People Strategy

Should every company adopt a similar people strategy and simply aim to establish best practice in each of the HR policy areas? Over the last decade, there have been attempts to describe people strategy as an internally coherent set of HR policies and practices. This endeavor has proven to be both difficult and elusive. As one might expect, there appears to be no one single "ideal type" of people strategy with a set of HR policies and practices that can be adopted off the shelf by organizations seeking to manage their people more strategically.[2]

Vertical alignment

The reality is that an appropriate people strategy must vary according to organizational circumstances.[3] The key circumstances are business goals and strategies. Our argument is that, in order to play a strategic role in the organization, the HR policies and practices that make up an organization's people strategy should reflect, reinforce, and support the organization's business aims and objectives.[4] A strong linkage is needed between the overall vision of the organization that is held in the minds of the senior executives and the aims, objectives, and underlying philosophy of the organization's approach to managing people. This linkage will ensure that HR interventions can become a creator, and not an inhibitor, of sustained competitive advantage.[5] This link between people strategy and business-unit strategy we term *vertical alignment*.

We have chosen to refer to alignment and not fit; the distinction is fine, but significant. Fit implies a relationship between two discrete entities; alignment suggests a much more fluid dynamic that allows for variation and flexibility. We are not advocating a mechanistic "matching" exercise between business strategic objectives and people strategies; often, such matching is simply not feasible and, in any case, will act as a constraint.[6] Instead, the process is evolving, based on an understanding of what the business's goals are, their people implications, and the translation of these into an overarching people strategy that can be used as a basis for detailed HR policies.

Horizontal alignment

Vertical integration is a crucial dimension of a people strategy. But it is not sufficient. The second dimension is *horizontal alignment*.[7] The first dimension, vertical alignment, is concerned with the link between the corporate and business strategy as a whole and the firm's people-management strategy. The second dimension operates at the level of individual HR policy areas. The aim here is the achievement of a coherent and consistent approach to managing people that permeates the entire activities of the HR function and other organizational functional areas, and we are talking here at the *policy* level, not the *practice* level. This distinction is important, because we treat putting people strategies into action as a separate dimension. Achieving a high degree of horizontal alignment implies that an organization has embraced the value of developing and articulating clear HR policies that consistently relate to one another. At a more fundamental level, the firm is able to communicate consistent and reinforcing messages to employees.

Although at first sight vertical and horizontal alignment may appear to go hand in hand, our research has shown that this is not necessarily the case.[8] Firms that achieve high levels of vertical alignment may not exhibit strong horizontal alignment, and vice versa. This is because the two dimensions operate at different levels. Vertical alignment is concerned with whether or not the overarching people strategy pursued or implicit in an organization's actions supports the organization's strategic direction. Horizontal alignment, on the other hand, is concerned with the degree of internal coherence and consistency in the firm's stated HR policies.

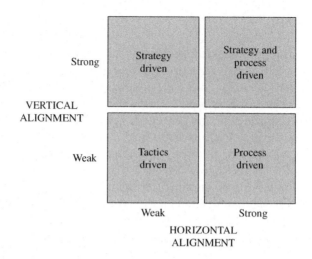

Figure 18.1　The two-dimensional model of people strategy.

These first two dimensions are depicted in Fig. 18.1. The upper-left quadrant represents an organization whose HR policies are, though inconsistent with each other, still aligned with the firm's business goals and strategies. In the lower-left quadrant, HR policies are neither coherent/consistent nor aligned with business goals/strategies. For the firm in the lower-right quadrant, HR policies are internally coherent/consistent but not aligned with the firm's business goals. The ideal situation – consistent and coherent HR policies aligned with business goals and strategies – is depicted in the upper-right quadrant. Now let us see what happens to these as yet theoretical or paper concepts when they are put, or not put, into action.

The action dimension

The third dimension is *action* or *implementation*. Much writing about HRM at the strategic level has tended to assume that the vertical and horizontal dimensions are sufficient. The mere existence of HR policies and a people strategy is believed to be sufficient to ensure action. The question of what actually happens once the strategy statement has been written or the policy document signed off has received scant attention.[9] Yet, as our research has shown, translating HR policies into action would appear to be absolutely fundamental to the question of whether an organization is delivering in the area of people management. For this reason, we separate out action as the third dimension of people strategy.[10]

This action dimension has two separate but closely interrelated aspects. The first concerns the *experiences by employees* of HR policies. For example, the policy on appraisal may state that employees have four performance feedback sessions with their manager every year and that they are appraised on five different competencies. If this is, indeed, the experience of employees, then policy has been turned into action. If, on the other hand, employees are rarely party to performance feedback and if, when they are, the manager concentrates on only one criterion, then the organization has failed to put policy into action. The second aspect of action is subtler and focuses on the *behaviors and values of the managers* as they are implementing policy. In their attitudes, conversations, and body language, managers send out very clear messages about their attitude toward and support of policy.[11]

The Three-Dimensional Model of People Strategy

Figure 18.2 adds the action/inaction dimension to Fig. 18.1. Our research has shown that there is much variety among companies in this three-dimensional model of people strategy. We found that at any point in time a company has its unique dimensional signature in terms of where it stands on the three dimensions:

- *Vertical Alignment:* the alignment between the business goals and the people strategy.
- *Horizontal Alignment:* the internal alignment between the set of HR policies making up the people strategy.
- *Action:* the degree to which HR policies are enacted or put into practice, as judged by employee experience and management behavior and values.

Our research also shows that organizations move about within the three-dimensional space. As our examples demonstrate, external events can occur and internal decisions can be taken that create new scenarios and shift the people strategy into a new dimension.

At the front of the three-dimensional cube shown in Fig. 18.2 are the four variations of the two-dimension model in which HR policies – in all their forms – are achieved.

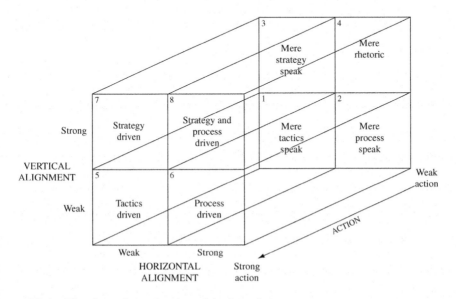

Figure 18.2 The three-dimensional model of people strategy

However, at the back of the cube are four corresponding variations of people strategy characterized by a total lack of action. We have termed these "mere tactics speak," "mere process speak," "mere strategy speak," and "mere rhetoric." We have found that executives benefit significantly from gaining a thorough understanding of these eight people-strategy variants and the continuums along which they vary. Often, executives are aware that their current people strategy has weaknesses as well as strengths, but they are unable to pinpoint the underlying reasons. Knowing their relative position in the cube enables them to identify precisely the source of the problem and take appropriate action.

We first turn to the non-action variations of people strategy. HR policies may (or may not) be internally consistent and may (or may not) be aligned with business strategies, but *nobody does anything about it*.

Mere tactics speak

Weak vertical alignment
Weak horizontal alignment
Weak action

At its worst, this variation occurs when the organization has no discernible people strategy and, therefore, there is no relationship (or only a very tenuous one) between people strategy and business unit objectives. Moreover, there is little discernible relationship between the various HR policies themselves, and in some cases, policies in one area may act to undermine those in another. This situation would hold, for instance, in an organization which evaluates employees on their deployment of a particular skill set in their work but then fails to provide them with the opportunity to acquire these skills. In such a situation, productive action is almost impossible. This type of people strategy is most often found in small organizations with no dedicated HR function or where HR is in an embryonic state, viewed as someone's part-time responsibility.

Chelsea and Westminster Hospital in 1994
In the 1993–94 study of the Chelsea and Westminster Hospital, the situation was "mere tactics speak." The incoming HR director was faced with a scenario where she had a workforce of over 2,000 staff but no statement or shared understanding of the people strategy. Only 27 per cent of employees thought the HR department had a clear overall strategy guiding its activities. There were few formalized HR policies, and no systematic attempts had been made to link them to each other or to the hospital's goals. For example, only 26 per cent agreed that people's work goals were clearly defined, and only 36 per cent agreed that people received the training they needed to do their jobs well. As a result, the hospital was failing to recruit and retain the individuals it needed at all levels, morale and attitudes towards the HR department were negative and, crucially, patient care needs were not being met in some areas. Only 23 per cent of staff surveyed agreed that the hospital inspired the very best in job performance from them. However, as we shall see, by the time of the 2000 study, this new HR director had significantly both strengthened the second dimension, the horizontal alignment of people policies, and, more significantly, put them into action.

Mere process speak

Weak vertical alignment
Strong horizontal alignment
Weak action

We saw this variation in firms where the HR function has a strong, integrated set of HR policy goals that are disconnected from the overall objectives of the business. Additionally, these well-described policies are inadequately put into effect. This situation can occur when there is a strong disconnect between the senior HR team and the business managers or where the senior HR team has weak strategic or business skills but high levels of process expertise. As a consequence, HR policies are developed in a sophisticated manner in isolation from the business imperatives. This expertise then fails to be translated into action, most often because of lack of line support for HR initiatives which are seen to be unrelated to business goals.

Citibank in 1997
In the 1997 study, Citibank was pursuing a strategy of organic growth through building strong relationships with key clients, a move away from its strategy in the early 1990s of a focus on products. The HR function in 1997 was undergoing a period of transformation: from administrative support to creating stronger horizontal alignment across its policy areas. A key plank in this change was the Talent Inventory, a new process with 10 key performance indicators to aid in employee selection, leadership, development, and succession planning. On the face of it, the Talent Inventory represented a significant step toward achieving horizontal alignment within HR.

However, we discovered that while the policy and instruments were well developed, the Talent Inventory was not being systematically *used* by line managers. Only 29 per cent of employees thought the appraisal system enabled the company to gain an accurate understanding of people's strengths and weaknesses. By the time of the 2000 study, the Talent Inventory had failed to gain traction in the company. It may have been the right tool, but those managers who had to make it work didn't think so. A sound and potentially beneficial process stayed at the level of "talk."

Mere strategy speak

Strong vertical alignment
Weak horizontal alignment
Weak action

We observed this combination when the people strategy is clearly articulated but is not translated into a coherent set of HR policies nor implemented by line managers. The senior HR team may be very close to the business and have high-level strategic skills, but for whatever reason they are not able to translate these business objectives into HR policies. For them, people strategy remains "mere strategy speak."

Glaxo, 1997–2000

We saw a number of companies migrate to this space in the early phases of a merger. Glaxo Pharmaceuticals was a case in point. During the 1997 study, the company experienced a major internal restructuring through the merger with Wellcome. The focus of the HR team was on partnering with the senior management team to manage the merger and on integrating one or two of the HR practices with the business goals. But this effort took time and, for a period of years, although the policies were aligned with the new business goals, the practices were far behind. As one member of the HR team put it, "We've come to a situation where none of our standard ways of doing things work any more, because they have rusted due to lack of use or because they don't reflect the new organization." The strategic intent was there, but without HR policies focused action was impossible. It would take focus and resilience for the company to realign itself over the coming years to become driven by people strategies and HR policies.

Mere rhetoric

Strong vertical alignment
Strong horizontal alignment
Weak action

Here, there is a strongly articulated people strategy that is linked into the business strategy and also demonstrates strong internal HR policy linkages, but the whole is not put into action in the day-to-day behavior of managers nor reflected in the experiences of employees. The HR team may be highly skilled in policy development but either may have weak implementation capability or may have senior line management who fail to support their activities. The people strategy looks good on paper but is nothing more than a paper reality.

BT in 1994

We observed this "mere rhetoric" clearly in the people-management strategies at BT Payphones in 1994. The strategies were geared toward achieving significant cultural change in order to enhance customer focus and individual performance in an organization previously characterized by a "jobs for life" mindset. Faced with severe competition and the threat of product substitution through the mass expansion of mobile telephone, the HR function aggressively pursued a number of interrelated initiatives. First, a change program reinforced the new set of values which was backed up by a Corporate Scorecard for measuring performance. Next, a series of extensive training and development programs was developed, including a Leadership Program, Total Quality Management, and "Involving Everyone." Finally, the Payphones People five-year plan was designed which included a staff attitude survey and a sophisticated performance management system. Each of these separate policies had been designed to achieve vertical alignment by linking into the business goals and horizontal alignment by linking to each other.

However, by the time of the 1997 study, the implementation problems were apparent. The sheer number and complexity of initiatives and policies had overwhelmed line managers and, as a consequence, the impact of each individual initiative had been lost. People were more confused than motivated. Perhaps more crucially, the cost-containment strategy pursued by the corporate center meant that annual redundancy targets were set, targeting between 17 and 20 per cent of managerial-level jobs. This redundancy program was supported by yet another program, termed Release. Clearly, the ethos of running a large redundancy program was at odds with the other, value-driven initiatives. We found that, as a consequence, the inability to put the values program into action had irreparably damaged the psychological contract between individual employees and the organization. As a consequence, cynicism about the gap between rhetoric and reality grew. By 1997, only 10 per cent of the employees we surveyed agreed that management cared about the needs and morale of employees. The gap between the strong rhetoric of the values program and the reality of weak action-taking had created suspicion and mistrust in the minds of employees.

Later in the chapter we explore the means by which these inert or "shadow" people strategies can move into the action dimension. We now turn to the four variations of the action dimension.

Tactics driven

Weak vertical alignment
Weak horizontal alignment
Strong action

This combination characterizes the traditional "administrative" HR function that focuses on the implementation of individual HR policies with limited relationship to the overall aims and objectives of the business or to each other. We found this variation associated with HR teams who were not regarded as a core business function but rather as "clerks of works" administering the support function, often for a set of business goals which is no longer appropriate.

Lloyds Bank in 1994
In the 1994 study, Lloyds Bank was the UK's most profitable clearing bank, pursuing an aggressive and very successful strategy of growth through acquisition. Massive changes in business goals during that era saw the automation of banking jobs combined with a renewed emphasis on selling. Like other HR functions in the banking sector at that time, many of the HR team had come from line management banking roles. As a consequence, the function historically had diligently followed the protocols and policies of the bank, focusing on day-to-day administration of personnel activities.

However, they were woefully ill-prepared to meet the significant structural changes that were occurring in their sector at that time. Employees, worn down by "change fatigue" and concerned about their jobs, failed to perceive any underpinning rationale to the changes. The traditional policies and practices of lifetime employment and stability which had so successfully supported the bank's relationship with its staff began to fall apart, and the incumbent HR team had neither the skill nor the experience to create policies and practices more fitting to the competitive environment of the bank. As one frustrated senior manager commented at that time, "Trust levels are devastated;

we have betrayed them." By the time of the 1997 study, much had changed. The HR team had been significantly professionalized and by 2000 was working as a key part of the strategic team of the business.

Process driven

Weak vertical alignment
Strong horizontal alignment
Strong action

This combination occurs in organizations where the HR team has weak business or strategic skills but excellent HR process skills, coupled with the capability to translate these skills into practice. We found this to be a natural evolution from the Tactics Driven combination.

Chelsea and Westminster Hospital 1997–2000

At the Chelsea and Westminster Hospital, as the 1990s progressed, the new HR director, working alongside the chief executive, began to effect some major changes. Her No. 1 priority was to establish the credibility of the department by improving the delivery of platform services, moving the hospital from *mere tactics speak* to *tactics driven*. The next phase was to examine in detail the HR policies and practices within the hospital and to ensure that they were mutually reinforcing. Key to this effort was developing an integrated people-strategy statement built around an "Employee Pledge." This Pledge was developed in consultation with the hospital employees and consisted of a set of "promises" that the hospital undertook to honor in the treatment of its staff. It included such matters as providing an Employee Assistance Program, providing staff with accessible information on all aspects of the hospital and its strategy, and helping to support staff in balancing home–work commitments. However, throughout this time, vertical alignment remained weak, hampered in part by the complexity of the hospital's business goals and the conflicting interests of the many stakeholders it served. Without a unifying goal, it was difficult for the team to establish strong vertical integration, and throughout the study they remained Process Driven.

Strategy driven

Strong vertical alignment
Weak horizontal alignment
Strong action

Here, we observed that the enactment of the business goals is primarily a line management responsibility. As a consequence, there is a strong vertical driver, often enacted through the performance-management processes. However, some of the subtleties of reinforcing HR practices are lost through weak horizontal alignment.

HP in 1994
In the 1994 study, HP in the UK operated with an extremely low-key HR department. At the corporate level, the strategy for managing people was strongly articulated in the visionary statement, the HP Way, whose ownership lay very much within the line management of the organization. In this way, the overarching people-strategy objectives were closely embedded within the strategic direction pursued by the corporation. In the UK, the actual HR department was perceived to be relatively peripheral in the management of people, focusing more on implementation issues than strategy. However, this failure to draw on HR professional expertise had implications. First, the focus on the HP Way occasionally meant that some elements of the people strategy peripheral to it failed to be developed. Second, the HR team did not always pick up on best practice in other companies. Finally, the HR team sometimes failed to configure the corporate initiatives to align with the specific nature of the changing UK context.

Strategy and process driven

Strong vertical alignment
Strong horizontal alignment
Strong action

In many senses, this represents the "ideal type" of people strategy: coherent HR policies aligned to business goals and strategies, the whole implemented effectively. Our study showed this ideal to be both difficult to achieve and hard to sustain.

Kraft Foods, 1994–2000
In Kraft Foods, we observed that over the period of study, the company achieved alignment and moved into action. In the early years of the decade, Kraft Foods went through a period of aggressive growth through acquisition. The HR team supported this initiative by developing an extremely efficient process for assimilating and integrating the HR systems of the acquired companies. As a consequence, the acquisition phase was dealt with rapidly, and new companies quickly became integrated into the parent firm. The firm's second strategic thrust of continuous improvement was supported by a coherent and highly embedded set of HR policies. These included recruiting and selecting people according to a clear set of criteria, providing targeted training and development, and offering line managers incentives to implement HR policy. At the same time, there was a strong performance-management process.

By the mid-1990s, the company experienced changed economic conditions, increased competition in its core brands, and a lack of potential takeover targets. In response to these developments, the business strategy changed to one of growth through innovation. This re-direction required a major cultural change, which was led by the HR team. A new vision and values statement was introduced and cascaded through the organization. Over a period of two years, the performance-management system was refined to align with the new values of creativity and risk taking. Programs were put in place to develop new leadership skills to support these values. Finally, recognizing that workforce diversity was becoming increasingly important to innovation, the HR team instituted location and time flexibility and work–life balance programs.[12]

Kraft's capacity to create a Strategy and Process Driven people strategy was reflected in extremely high levels of corporate performance in comparison with their peer group of companies in the food sector throughout the period of the study. We later return to examine the foundations of their success in more detail.

Our research has revealed many variations of people strategy which we have described along three dimensions. Knowing where your company is along each of these three dimensions enables you to understand the challenges you face. It also highlights those dimensions on which you should be focusing your attention.

The Appendix contains a short questionnaire listing the kinds of questions that executives can use to determine where the organization currently stands on each of the three dimensions. A scoring plan and guidance notes are also included. In the following section, we explore how certain companies strengthened their people strategy along each of the three dimensions.

Achieving Strong Vertical Alignment

Get quick wins

Faced with the need to strengthen vertical alignment, the most successful HR executives decided on a few key areas where they could quickly demonstrate a contribution and where the positive benefits of change would be readily visible to significant line managers. In establishing what interventions would be capable of delivering a short-term "quick win," they had a sophisticated understanding of which people processes would have a quick impact on the delivery of the business goal.[13] Lloyds TSB in 1997 had created a professional HR team keen to establish a couple of quick wins by responding to the strategic proposition of building an innovative product offering. Within a couple of months, they had recruited executives from FMCG (fast-moving consumer goods) companies to realign what was the marketing function of a traditional bank around the skills demonstrated within an FMCG context. They were also able to kick-start the "innovation" business goal fairly quickly by rapidly designing and implementing short-term training programs which communicated the new business goals, key concepts, and their new behaviors to a large number of employees.

Gain reputational effectiveness

The temptation for many of the HR functions in our study was that, when faced with organizational turbulence, they focused their resources on their own needs. As a consequence, they failed to gain real traction in these difficult times. We heard HR executives say, "We would do so much more if only we had more resources" or "We can't be strategic; we don't have time." However, the way that the most successful HR departments in our study secured the resources they needed was by meeting the business-goal expectations of their line-management colleagues (vertical alignment). By doing so they were creating "reputational effectiveness."[14] As a counter example, in another organization the HR function failed over a long period of time to achieve any reputational effectiveness. When we asked one line manager what he thought the HR department did, his comment was, "I think they do some administration and sometimes get things wrong." Needless to say, this particular HR department saw a steady dilution of its resource base over the 10-year period.

Build a business-focused HR team

In those organizations where vertical alignment was weak, inevitably the HR team was configured in a manner that precluded them from working closely with the line. In some cases, the whole HR team was physically distant from the business units and, as a consequence, rarely interacted with them. Where vertical alignment was strong, this strength was echoed in the team's configuration. In Kraft Foods, the HR staff were assigned to the business units to work alongside line managers as they made and implemented strategic decisions.

The same was true at the Chelsea and Westminster Hospital. While the decision to co-locate the HR and line executives had symbolic value, it was also often accompanied by cross-functional career development. As a director at the Chelsea and Westminster remarked, "We have benefited enormously as a directorate by having people seconded from the HR department to come and work with us and work with us only." Only by sitting alongside line executives can HR practitioners take part in day-to-day decision-making about the running of business units. As a consequence, HR managers are able to alter their mindset and view people strategies from a line perspective. An additional benefit of working alongside line managers is that HR policy implementation can also be enhanced.

Look up and out

The tendency in those organizations where we observed weak vertical alignment was for the HR executives and managers to focus inward on themselves: the HR department, their processes and policies. There was often a myopic, almost "fortress" view of the world. This was in stark contrast with those HR groups who were willing to extend their horizons, to look up – at what was happening at the top of the organization – and out – to see what was happening in their industry, their profession, their neighborhood, and the world.[15] We are thinking particularly here of the HR executives at Kraft Foods, who took the most active part in our Leading Edge workshops held over the course of the ten years. They attended more diligently than representatives from any of the other organizations, often with a large, international team. They contributed enthusiastically to the discussions and co-production of knowledge that was at the heart of our endeavor. They were willing to invest considerable time in engaging in an open and frank dialog with their peers from other organizations and with the research team, and to learning without a particular end-game in mind.

Achieving Strong Horizontal Alignment

Get the balance right

Getting the balance right is crucial to horizontal integration. In the 1994 study of Chelsea and Westminster Hospital, the ad hoc arrangements inherited by the incoming HR director meant that few clearly articulated HR policies were in place. Consequently, critical success factors such as the recruitment and retention of key staff fell down into the "black holes" within the overall people strategy. Only when she specifically focused on horizontal alignment did the source of these problems became apparent so they could be addressed.

Getting the balance right can also work in the opposite way. As we saw earlier, at BT Payphones the plethora of initiatives, programs, and activities they had developed under the banner of people strategy foundered because of their sheer complexity. This was compounded by the starkly conflicting messages being sent out by the enormous redundancy program, on the one hand, and the value change program on the other. The edifice of the people strategy crumbled because it was constructed on weak foundations. Attempting too many initiatives simultaneously also meant that it was impossible to track their relationships and implementation.

Foster creative dialog

The conversations that enable the continual, mutual adjustments that are crucial to horizontal alignment are an important feature of the most successful companies we studied. It was through these conversations that the HR teams and the business executives were able to design, plan, and make decisions. We found that these companies fostered a context for productive talk by creating time and space for conversations and by legitimizing big, broad questions.[16]

In some companies, we saw both space and time fragmentation within the HR function. The experts in each of the functional processes remained isolated; for example, the pay experts rarely talked with the career or the performance-management experts.[17] In those companies with strong horizontal alignment, the HR team worked closely together, even if they were geographically dispersed. When they did meet, it was not simply to reiterate known facts but rather to explore big, broad questions. The same was true of the relationships and conversations between the line and HR functions. A fine balance must be created between HR functioning as a cohesive team and yet operating as a business partner. In Kraft Foods, the balance was achieved by assigning HR staff to the business units. This enabled them to work alongside line managers as they made and implemented strategic decisions. At the same time, the HR team was kept together through regular meetings, sharing of best-practice initiatives, and e-communication. HR team members were appraised and rewarded for their achievements in support of the business and for their contributions to the HR team.

Think systemically

One of the challenges of horizontal integration is the sheer complexity of representing the various HR interventions, their potential relationships, and intended and unintended consequences. As a result, the people-strategy document, if it exists at all, does so as a simple, linear description of interventions. Not so at Kraft Foods, where the HR team worked with the line managers to create a more complete picture of what the organization would look like if it had the business goal of Innovation as a key business driver. Together, they created a systems map of the practices and processes and, more importantly, the relationships between the two. They were also able to model the intended and unintended consequences of the behaviors and values which these practices and processes would reinforce. This visual picture of the horizontal alignment of the policies and practices provided crucial insights for the management teams. For example, they began to understand that if they wanted teams to be innovative, then it would not simply be sufficient to reinforce innovative behavior with reward. They would have to do more to encourage innovation through the way in which they created and structured teams, in the way they encouraged personal autonomy and risk taking, and in the coaching and support they gave to managers.[18]

Achieving Strength in Taking Action

Build a complete picture of the organization's human resources

In those companies that excelled in putting coherent HR policies into action, we observed the HR teams working to collect and review data with executives at three levels of description:

- a review of all HR documentation and communication of the organization's strategic objectives to measure the degree of alignment between the stated HR objectives (of the people strategy) and the business goals and needs;
- measuring the enactment of the people practices;
- measuring and appraising the behavior and values of managers.

The methods involved collecting data from employee surveys, focus groups, and interviews, and data from appraisal and exit interviews. In our study, HP was particularly adept at data collection and review. Their complete picture of reality was built through consulting multiple stakeholders. For example, they made active use of peer assessment when teams from another business came to assess and comment upon the design and execution of HR policies and practices. This enabled the team to rapidly build a picture of where action was taking place – and where it was failing.

Take bold actions

We found that firms with action-oriented people strategies were willing to take bold, and sometimes unpopular, actions to demonstrate to the organization the behaviors they wanted to support. One example was Citibank in the 1994 study. Up until that time, the goals of the business had been firmly focused on maximizing the financial engine of the company. This focus on value creation and profitability had led to the rise of "lone star" executives who generated the most wealth and, consequently, won the biggest bonuses and the most rapid promotions. As the business goals changed in the direction of "serving a billion customers," the relationships between country teams and business lines became more important. The "lone stars" could not cross-sell in the way that the new business required. The HR team created a policy of cross-appraisal and 360-degree feedback, designed to measure the capability and motivation of managers to build relationships within their own teams and colleagues, across functions, and with other business lines. However, this goal of integration remained at the level of "rhetoric" for some time. Managers continued to behave as "lone stars," running roughshod across their team members and colleagues. Not until it became known that one of these "lone stars," who had indeed exceeded his financial target, had received only half of his anticipated bonus did people begin to take the creation of horizontal relationships more seriously. This "bold action" resulted in the "lone star" executive choosing to leave Citibank. But at the same time, it sent out a clear message that the business goal of building relationships would not simply remain at the level of rhetoric.

Keep the best

In the most successful firms we observed, there was a clear focus on the importance of continuity of *people* and *process* to ensure that action was sustained over time. At Kraft Foods, for example, the basic structure of the key performance-management practices remained intact throughout the time of our study. Within this time, the *focus* of the process changed (with a greater emphasis on the behaviors and values which reinforce innovation), but the *structure* of the process remained rock solid.

In the same way, continuity of people appeared to be a crucial factor. Throughout this ten-year study, we were able to track the membership of the HR teams. We saw clearly that changes in team membership could have an impact on both alignment and willingness to take action. On occasions, this change was positive. For example, at Chelsea and Westminster, the arrival of a strategic-thinking HR director to a team that had previously been administrative and tactical had a very positive impact on action orientation. Often, though, the impact of breaks in continuity, either through people changing or the new people coming in with a completely different perspective, had negative implications. At Kraft Foods, over the study period, there were only two HR directors. The first moved into a broader European role within Kraft Foods and was succeeded by his deputy, who had many years' experience in Kraft's HR function. This continuity ensured that the basic threads of the policies remained intact, while the shifting business goals could be reflected through subtle changes.

Focus on doing

In those firms most successful at achieving a strong degree of action-taking, we observed a clear ability to translate policies and strategies into definite action plans.

While many of the companies in our study were adept at managing business processes, few were equally adept at managing people processes. Our study revealed this lack of planning. We observed HR teams developing a plethora of unrelated people-process projects with limited integration. We observed projects begun and then not completed, unsophisticated tracking processes, and ambiguity around budgets and timescales. Of the companies we examined, Kraft Foods and HP had developed and implemented the most sophisticated project-management practices.

At HP, the people strategy was part of the whole business-strategy process, and from this came a number of priorities in the people-strategy area. These priorities were then treated to the same project-management practices as any major project. Project plans were created, outcomes agreed upon, and timelines discussed. Perhaps the most impressive aspect of their people strategy was the "HR War Room." This was a single room in which all the people-imperative projects were shown visually in detail with three illuminating colors. The color green signified a project which was on track; orange showed it was beginning to get off track; and red highlighted those projects which were in danger of not reaching their goals. Within a minute of entering the room, any manager was aware of the action-taking associated with the people strategy at HP.

Building and Delivering Excellent People Strategies

Delivering business strategy through people was key to the long-term performance of all seven companies we studied over the last decade. At the heart of this delivery is the competence and will to build vertical alignment, to craft horizontal alignment, and to move from rhetoric to the reality of action. This is never easy, particularly if organizational shocks such as downsizing and mergers rock the company's very foundation. And yet, we observed that it is possible to withstand these shocks and to create and embed people strategies that remain meaningful both to managers and to employees. The challenge for the HR department is to relentlessly learn how to achieve excellence in *all three dimensions* of people strategy.

APPENDIX

The three dimensions of people strategy

This short questionnaire is designed to help you to plot your people strategy in relation to the three dimensions.

For each question, please provide your own assessment of your organization on the scale:

1 = strongly disagree
2 = disagree
3 = neutral
4 = agree
5 = strongly agree

Score:

Section 1: Vertical Alignment

1. the senior HR director/manager is a full and equal member of the main board/strategic decision-making group. OR HR issues are actively represented on the main board/decision-making group. ...
2. The senior HR director/manager (or equivalent) actively helps to develop the strategic objectives of the business. ...
3. There is a clear statement of people strategy and how it supports the corporate strategy, either as a separate statement or contained within the general corporate strategy statement. ...
4. Senior line managers are actively involved in developing strategic people objectives. ...
5. Strategic people objectives are regularly reviewed to ensure their continuing relevance to strategic business objectives. ...

Total for Section 1:

Section 2: Horizontal Alignment

1. The people-strategy statement clearly demonstrates how policies in each individual HRM area support the overall people strategy ...
2. HR policies in each individual HRM area are always developed with reference to other HRM policies within the organization. ...
3. The HRM team works closely together in developing HRM policies. ...
4. HRM policies are regularly reviewed to ensure their continuing relevance to the overall people strategy. ...
5. When new HRM policies are developed, every effort is made to ensure that they are mutually supportive. ...

Total for Section 2:

Section 3: Action

1. If an outsider were to ask your senior line managers/directors how the people strategy supported the overall strategic objectives of the business, they would know the answer. ...
2. Think of the major current business strategic objective for your organization. Do your people strategy and policies actively work to support it? ...
3. Line managers in your organization are assessed or appraised against targets relating to the implementation of people strategy and policies. ...
4. Line managers are provided with the training they need to implement people strategy and policies. ...
5. Line mangers know what their individual role is in implementing people strategy and policies. ...
6. The effective implementation of people strategy and policies influences either the career progression or rewards of line managers. ...
7. If an outsider were to ask your employees whether the organization was recruiting people with the most appropriate skills and abilities to help the organization meet its objectives, they would agree. ...

8. If an outsider were to ask your employees whether they had the training and development they needed, they would agree. ...

9. If an outsider were to ask your employees whether their appraisals provided an accurate assessment of their strengths and weaknesses, they would agree. ...

10. If an outsider were to ask your employees whether their reward package was fair compared with that of others in the organization, they would agree. ...

11. If an outsider were to ask your employees whether the organization delivers on its promises in the area of people management, they would say 'yes.' ...

12. If an outsider were to ask your employees whether the way they are managed encourages them to help the organization deliver its strategic objectives, they would say 'yes.' ...

Total for Section 3:

Analysis

Your responses

Section 1
This section tests the strength of vertical alignment. If you achieved a score of 19 or over, then you have a strong level of alignment. Any scores below 19 indicate a weak level of alignment.

Section 2
This section tests the strength of horizontal alignment. If you achieved a score of 19 or over, then you have a strong level of alignment. Any scores below 19 indicate a weak level of alignment.

Section 3
This section tests whether or not your people strategy is put into action within your organization. A score of 40 or more indicates strong action. Any scores below 40 indicate weak action.

Scores:

Section 1	Section 2	Section 3	Result
Vertical	**Horizontal**	**Action**	
Below 19	Below 19	Below 40	Mere Tactics Speak
Below 19	Below 19	Above 40	Tactics Driven
Below 19	Above 19	Below 40	Mere Process Speak
Below 19	Above 19	Above 40	Process Driven
Above 19	Below 19	Below 40	Mere Strategy Speak
Above 19	Below 19	Above 40	Strategy Driven
Above 19	Above 19	Below 40	Mere Rhetoric
Above 19	Above 19	Above 40	Strategy and Process Driven

Acknowledgments

We would like to thank our colleagues on the Leading Edge Research Consortium project, in particular Professor Veronica Hope-Hailey, Dr. Philip Stiles, and Dr. Joanna Zaleska. We would also like to thank the corporate members of the consortium for their generous sponsorship of this research and the anonymous reviewers and the editors of this journal for their helpful comments on earlier drafts of this chapter.

NOTES

1. In each of the seven cases, we used a questionnaire, surveying the same business unit on three occasions: 1994 (1764 respondents); 1997 (1592 respondents); 2000 (1248 respondents). We also interviewed 20–35 employees in each firm and ran focus groups with the HR function.

2. Becker, B., & Gerhart, B. 1996. The impact of human resource management on organizational performance: Progress and prospects. *Academy of Management Journal*, 39(4): 779–801.

3. Baron, J. N., & Kreps, D. M. 1999. *Strategic human resources.* New York: Wiley.

4. See, for example, Ulrich, D. 1998. A new mandate for human resources. *Harvard Business Review*, 76(1): 124–34. Where we are extending this argument, however, is in the notion that people strategies have three separate, but interrelated, dimensions.

5. This perspective has been referred to as the "fit" approach, which has been contrasted with the "best practices" approach described above. These various theoretical frameworks on strategic HRM have been reviewed in Delery, J. E., & Doty, D. H. 1996. Modes of theorizing in strategic human resource management: Tests of universalistic, contingency and configurational perspectives. *Academy of Management Journal*, 39(4): 802–35.

6. See Wright, P., & Snell, S. 1998. Toward a unifying framework for exploring fit and flexibility in strategic human resource management. *Academy of Management Review*, 23(4): 756–72.

7. Baird & Meshoulam have provided a classic exposition of these two dimensions of alignment in strategic HRM. See Baird, L., & Meshoulam, I. 1988. Managing two fits of strategic human resources management. *Academy of Management Review*, 13(1): 116–28.

8. The findings from the 1994 and 1997 studies are described in Gratton, L. *et al.* 1999. *Strategic human resource management: Corporate rhetoric and human reality.* Oxford, UK: Oxford University Press.

9. For example, in Huselid's influential work exploring linkages between HRM and organizational performance, the focus is very much on stated HR policy. Data were collected from one single informant in each organization, most often an HR representative, and few items in his questionnaire tapped into the reality experienced by employees. See Huselid, M. A. 1995. The impact of human resource management practices on turnover, productivity and corporate financial performance. *Academy of Management Journal*, 38(3): 635–72.

10. This point is debated further in L. Gratton and C. Truss (2001). Complexities and controversies in linking HRM with organizational outcomes. *Journal of Management Studies*, 38(8): 1121–50.

11. The literature of process fairness has explored this in great detail. For a useful overview, see Greenberg, J., & Cropanzano, R. (Eds.). 2001. *Advances in organizational justice.* Stanford, CA: Stanford University Press.

12. The case of Kraft Foods is discussed in more depth in Gratton, L., *et al.*, *A decade of transformation*, op. cit.

13. We have described these timelines of enactment in more detail in Gratton, L. *et al.* 1999. Linking individual performance to business strategy: The People Process Model. *Human Resource Management*, 38(1): 17–31.

14. Tsui, A. 1984. A multiple constituency framework of managerial reputational effectiveness. In Hunt, J. *et al. Leadership*. New York: Pergamon.

15. Amabile, T. M. 1998. How to kill creativity. *Harvard Business Review*, 76(5): 76–87, highlights the importance of allowing people to have a large "network of wanderings," or intellectual space in which to explore possibilities and solve problems.

16. The role of conversation as a tool of mutual adaptation is described in Gratton, L., & Ghoshal, S. 2002. Improving the quality of conversations. *Organizational Dynamics*, 31(3): 209–23.

17. Abrahamson, E. 2000. Change without pain, *Harvard Business Review*, July–August: 75–9, describes similar examples of companies unwilling to share information across internal boundaries, with negative consequences for performance.

18. The visualization of horizontal alignment has been described by Lynda Gratton in Gratton, L. 2000. *Living strategy: Putting people at the heart of corporate purpose*. London: FT Prentice-Hall.

Chapter 19

Seeing the Elephant: Human Resource Management Challenges in the Age of Globalization

Mark E. Mendenhall, J. Stewart Black, Robert J. Jensen, and Hal B. Gregersen

In the early 1800s, an American farmer who had never seen an elephant decided to travel to a nearby town where a circus was scheduled to visit. Thinking to kill two birds with one stone, he loaded his wagon with vegetables, with the intent to sell them at the town's market after the performance of the circus. On the way to town he encountered the circus retinue, which was led by an elephant. The sight of the elephant terrified his team of horses, which promptly bolted – the result being an overturned wagon and spoiled vegetables littering the road. In response to this disaster, the farmer is said to have exclaimed: "I don't give a hang, for I have seen the elephant!"

In nineteenth century America, "seeing the elephant" denoted the encountering of an exotic phenomenon, an unequaled experience, an adventure of a lifetime, or a particularly dangerous situation. Gold prospectors planning to travel west in the 1850s announced they were "going to see the elephant." Those who returned home without making it to California claimed they had seen the "elephant's tracks" or the "elephant's tail." Gold Rush-era Californians sometimes described the phenomenon as simply, "the elephant."

What is the managerial "elephant" of the twenty-first century? Is there an unequaled, heretofore unknown, exotic sight, or some attractive, yet potentially overwhelming

M.E. Mendenhall, J.S. Black, R.J. Jensen, and H.B. Gregersen, "Seeing the Elephant: Human Resource Management Challenges in the Age of Globalization," *Organizational Dynamics*, Vol. 32, No. 3 (2003): 261–74.

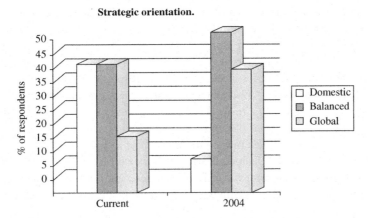

Figure 19.1 Strategic orientation.

condition that can make or break people and organizations? There is. The elephant, *globalization*, has upset the cart of traditional business rules: the new rules of globalization are often vague, unstable, counterintuitive, and full of exceptions.

The elephant and HR: When chief executive officers (CEOs) try to aggressively position their companies to be global players, they often find their efforts frustrated due to a lack of global competencies in their managerial corps. As the former CEO of Brunswick Corp., Jack Riechert, put it, "We have all the financial, technical, and product resources we need to be a dominant global player. What we lack are the human resources. We just don't have the people we need who understand global markets and players." When CEOs turn to their human resource specialists for help in developing globally competent managers and globally sophisticated HR systems, how ready are HR managers to confront the "elephant" of globalization?

To get richer insights about the challenges of globalization for HR managers, we interviewed HR executives from over 30 companies and collected surveys from executives attending several sessions at the University of Michigan Senior Human Resource Executive Program (please see Appendix A for a description of our study). We will first look at how globalization is influencing the strategic trends of the companies of these HR executives, and then we will report, and offer solutions to, what they characterized as the primary HR challenges they are facing due to globalization.

Going global: Four years ago, we asked these HR executives to describe the overall strategic orientation of their company, and what the overall strategic orientation would be in 2004 As Fig. 19.1 illustrates, their companies are migrating away from a domestic strategic focus and toward either a balanced or global focus. In the near term, most of this movement is from a domestic to a balanced focus (i.e., essentially equal focus on both domestic and international).

As one HR executive of a large discount retailer put it, "From our inception we have been a US company. However, this will not be the case going forward. Growth opportunities for us are in Europe, in Asia, and in Latin America. Also, our two biggest competitors are in Europe, and we need to beat them on their own turf."

Going from a domestic to balanced to global strategic focus is not an easy process and creates various HR challenges. A quick sketch of Black & Decker Corp.'s movement provides some initial insights. Prior to 1996, Black & Decker's eastern hemisphere regional headquarters was in Maryland. This regional office was responsible for virtually all the countries along the Pacific Rim. The US location of their Asia Pacific regional office largely reflected the US, or domestic orientation of the company. Subsequently, Black & Decker moved the eastern hemisphere regional office, first to Singapore. This put the office closer to the regional action and increased the focus on the region. Black & Decker put a similar increase in focus on other regions of the world. This move to a more balanced (equal weight on global and domestic concerns) strategic focus involved numerous HR challenges, such as: moving people around the world on international assignments, determining the extent to which important processes such as performance management should be harmonized with headquarters culture or with local business culture, determining cross-cultural issues associated with management development, and designing global compensation systems.

As senior executives within Black & Decker look forward to the future, they have determined that a balanced, but separate domestic and international strategic focus is not ideal for the firm. While the current balance provides greater focus on global market opportunities (and competitors) the separation aspect creates duplication and does not work to capture synergies or economies of scale and scope. In the future, Black & Decker wants to better integrate its operations worldwide so that information, ideas, innovations, products, and people can move more seamlessly across the entire global organization.

How prepared are you? Given that people, and in particular, leaders, are critical to the successful movement of organizations from domestic business outlooks towards global strategic orientations, one naturally wonders how well HR executives and HR groups are prepared to meet this challenge. When asked about HR's competence at managing global issues, the executives we surveyed painted a picture that raises some concern: only about one percent of the executives surveyed thought that their HR staff at headquarters or in their business units were "world class" in managing global issues.

Becoming world class at managing HR issues is a challenge for even the most highly regarded companies. Even the best companies and well-intentioned individuals can run aground on the unseen cultural reefs that lie in wait in the waters of global expansion. For example, when Jack Welch first took over as CEO of General Electric Co, only about 10 percent of its revenues were derived from international markets. It was a USA-centric organization. In addition to his mantra of be #1 or #2 (or get sold), he also pushed the major divisions to expand their strategic focus overseas. In response to this strategic shift, the Medical Systems division acquired companies in Japan and France. These acquisitions catapulted the division into the top position globally; however, things did not go well at first. Lack of international HR experience caused several missteps with GE's acquisition of *Cie Generale de Radiologie* in France. For example, during one of the initial integration meetings at a hotel in France, US managers put up English posters in the meeting room that declared, "GE is #1," and asked French managers to all wear T-shirts to the meeting with similar slogans on them. The French managers were insulted by these and other moves. As a result of these and other missteps, GE's new unit lost $25 million instead of making an anticipated $25 million in the first year after the acquisition. The second year also produced losses rather than anticipated profits. Today, the HR staff members at Medical Systems are considered to be some of the most capable anywhere.

However, the case illustrates two critical points. First, even a great company can have HR staff who are not world class when it comes to global competencies. Second, lack of those competencies in advance of global strategic expansion can (and often does) lead to mistakes that cost the company money, morale, and momentum.

Bringing an HR group up to speed in terms of global competency development in time for them to enhance global strategy implementation is a stiff challenge. While a firm can decide to shift its strategic direction from a domestic to a global focus in the space of a few years, developing the required HR competencies may not be done as rapidly. It takes time for an individual HR staff or for an entire HR group to increase their global management capabilities and competencies, and this development needs to start *in advance* of the actual implementation of the firm's strategic shift. An executive with TRW Inc. pointed out the importance of this when he stressed that:

> …just because you have taken an international assignment to China does not mean you can effectively manage across multiple countries. For most [leaders] an international assignment is a critical developmental experience, but that is not all it takes to turn you into a global leader. This means that we must have HR people who are global long before we need business people; otherwise how will we identify, train, and develop business leaders?

For this HR executive, this realization came after taking part in a global leadership development program for high-potential executives in the company that involved – among other things – action-learning projects in China. The executive admitted that the experience "opened his eyes" to the real demands of managing global HR, especially in terms of leadership development. It is interesting to note that in another study we undertook a few years ago, we found that only 11 percent of US HR executives had themselves lived or worked in a foreign country.

It is a troubling picture that these executives painted for us: Companies moving swiftly down the path to global strategy implementation, with HR systems and people who lack both system-wide and individual global expertise, and who have no time to adequately develop such expertise.

The "Big Five" global HR challenges: Regardless of how prepared companies are for global HR issues, they face them in real-time nevertheless. Consequently, we wanted to get a sense of what they felt were the biggest challenges they were currently wrestling with within the "context of ill preparation" discussed above. When we asked executives to identify the major challenges the HR function faced in terms of globalization concerns, the following five issues emerged:

- Enhancing global business strategy
- Aligning HR issues with business strategy
- Designing and leading change
- Building global corporate cultures
- Developing global leaders.

Just on the surface, these are incredible challenges, not easily met. For each one there is a long and steep learning curve; and to get to the top, you have to start early and climb hard. The question then becomes, "How do HR managers go about developing these competencies?"

Dealing with the "Big Five": Advice for Elephant Handlers

From both the interviews and surveys, it was clear that these challenges were of significant importance to all executives. We start with the issue of enhancing business strategy, then move to the challenge of aligning HR practices with the strategy. From there we move to facilitating change efforts and creating effective cultures. We end where global strategies are made – with global leaders and their development.

Enhancing the creation of global business strategies

In order for the HR group to play a role in the creation and implementation of global business strategy, HR managers must focus on three important issues: (a) integrating global HR issues into the company's mission, (b) encouraging senior managers to be catalysts for integrating HR with global strategy development and implementation, and (c) keeping global HR issues on managers' radar screens throughout the strategy-building and implementation process.

Mission integration
Organizations that possess world-class global HR competencies ensure that the HR dimension is central to a company's global mission. "People" issues are integrated into every aspect of business operations. For example, at ExxonMobil Aviation (EMA), the managing director, John Bell, insisted from the start of the new organization that people be at the core of the mission. EMA sells a true commodity – jet fuel. Jet fuel is the same the world over. It is made to very exacting standards – so exacting that it is co-mingled at the airports in storage tanks. Shell, BP, ExxonMobil, TotalFinaElf and everyone else's jet fuel is mixed together. Consequently, as John Bell puts it, "People are our only differentiator." If EMA cannot differentiate by the quality of employees it selects and develops, it has little hope of beating competitors such as Shell or BP, which also have large refineries, pipelines, and on-airport refueling capabilities.

Another indicator of pure integration between global HR and global mission is the diminished distinction between domestic and international HR. In all aspects of its operations, Molex Inc., for example, has worked hard to break the old paradigm of domestic vs. international. It was one of the first US firms to do away with distinctions between the two concepts in the HR realm. Molex HR staffs around the world have the same titles. Its corporate culture views Molex as a global family of firms, rather than a US-based conglomerate.

Top management as catalysts

Many companies often espouse concern for global HR issues – and sometimes even mention it in their mission statements – but few companies actually have integrated that concern into their strategic planning and policy crafting processes. This integration begins with the CEO. Until Kofi Annan became the seventh Secretary-General of the United Nations, there was little concern in that organization regarding such basic human resource concerns as HR planning, staff development, or performance management. This, though the United Nations is a worldwide organization with a staff of 8,500 who represent the interests of people in 188 nations!

Since taking the reins, Secretary-General Annan has launched numerous reforms throughout the United Nations Office of Human Resources Management. Initiatives around succession planning, HR planning, managerial competency training, and performance management are now in place and are taking hold in an organizational culture that was not historically focused on employee development. All because the CEO led the change, and believed in its importance.

Keeping global HR on managers' radar screens

To lead global HR change initiatives, top management must first understand the link between organizational performance and the social capital of the firm. The senior HR staff must constantly reinforce this truth – even if the CEO and other senior executives "get it." As the HR director at a large Canadian steel company put it,

> Much of my job is capturing and keeping the attention of senior management. These guys are steel guys. They pay attention to hard things not soft, so I have to demonstrate to them that people issues deliver both hard financial losses when they are not right and tangible gains when they are.

This mantra must be communicated constantly – along with the hard evidence to support its claims. Over time, a constant focus on the inextricable relationship between HR issues and productivity will pay dividends, as has been demonstrated in a number of recent domestic and international academic studies.

Aligning HR processes and programs with overall global business strategy

The natural challenge that flows from a foundation of valuing social capital in an organization is the need to align HR processes and programs with global business strategies – and vice versa! To do so, it is critical to focus on three things: maintaining a global vs. a headquarters-based perspective, paying attention to HR issues during strategy implementation, and balancing local vs. global issues in HR policies.

Maintain a global perspective, not a headquarters-based perspective

Rather than respond in a region-specific way to economic fluctuations by downsizing or expanding its human capital, Molex views both its business operations and social capital from a truly global perspective. For example, from mid-1997 to mid-1998, the American and European regions of Molex's operations performed very well, while its Asian operations struggled. In the past, however, Molex's Asian operations had been cash cows. In responding to the Asian financial crisis, Molex's CEO, Frederick A. Krehbiel, addressed all Molex employees at the company's annual worldwide telecommunications meeting with the following message:

> Let us celebrate the advantages of being global. Despite the fact that the Southeast Asia operations are down, the company has made enough money elsewhere to give salary increases to everyone. There have been no layoffs. In fact, we have spent money in all of our regions to make needed improvements to operations. In the past, the productivity of our Asian operations allowed us to improve our operations in Europe and America. Now it is time for Europe and America to carry the rest of the world, as Asia carried them in the past. (Solomon, "Brace for Change," in *Workforce* [January 1999], p. 10)

Pay attention to HR issues during implementation of global strategy
The acquisition of Parker Pen by Gillette Co in 1993 triggered a need to strategically restructure the organization of all units of Gillette (razors and toiletries, Duracell batteries, Oral-B dental care, and Braun appliances) into geographic units, each with a single sales force, to be more responsive to local needs. Gillette's senior executives wisely paid attention to human resource issues during the strategic planning and implementation of the restructuring, and because they did, the organizational transformation went more smoothly than it otherwise would have. For example, in Singapore, it was decided that all the Parker Pen and Gillette units were to be combined into one central "campus" rather than be spread out over the island. Parker employees who worked on the east side of the island threatened to quit if the campus was placed on the west side of the island, where the majority of the Gillette employees lived and worked. Conversely, the Gillette employees resented the idea that they might be asked to travel to the east side of the island to work. Rumors, fears, and poor morale began to fester, as everyone wondered what headquarters would do.

Rather than simply basing the location decision on the concentration of existing facilities, the preferences of senior managers, or the relative worth or power of dominant product units, Gillette senior management instead plotted on a map of Singapore the home of every single Gillette employee. The executives then chose a new site for the campus (rather than using existing facilities) based on the geographic location of all of Gillette's Singaporean employees. Valuable employees whose competencies (and customers!) could not easily be replaced were retained. Strategy and HR issues fused into the creation of a business decision that was more ideal than if it had been based on pragmatic organizational criteria alone.

Balance local vs. global issues in HR policymaking
A senior HR executive with DuPont Co, who has experience in Australia, USA, and several Asian countries, including Japan, explained that "even though DuPont has gone to global shared services in HR, it is impossible to have everything be the same the world over." Like many companies, DuPont has restructured human resources so that a vast majority of its activities are shared services done for all business units. While this works well in large countries with significant business operations, such as

the US or Germany, it works less well in smaller countries where DuPont's businesses are not equally invested, such as Thailand. With market conditions so different in Thailand from, say, Japan, it is hard to run a shared recruiting service effectively out of a single regional office in Singapore. Yet the challenge of not duplicating activities, and therefore costs, is significant. In this case, DuPont has worked hard to balance these tensions. It has discovered that despite the differences at upper managerial levels where they typically use search firms to help them with external recruiting, it is best to do this on a coordinated basis across countries. In this way they can leverage their size to get better prices and service from search firms. It also helps them avoid reinventing the wheel on a country-by-country basis. However, when it comes to less skilled line employees, the benefits of a local approach outweigh those of coordination.

Assisting in leading global change initiatives

A primary role of the HR function in any organization is to assist in crafting and implementing organizational change initiatives. The development of policies that actually help people adjust to and learn the new skills required for global organizational change is absolutely necessary if a company is to be successful in the global marketplace. To pull this off, HR managers must focus on enabling people not only to carry out the change initiative, but also to take the lead in creating and implementing global HR change initiatives.

Enable people to change – don't just tell them to
China Light and Power (CLP) in Hong Kong is expanding from a domestic-oriented, government-controlled monopoly to a market driven, global enterprise. It is a significant transformation, to say the least. The change in managers' focus from "what will the next set of government regulations be?" to "what are the market trends, who are our competitors, and what are they doing?" is a major challenge. It is, of course, not enough to say to these managers, "CHANGE!" Even if they all wanted to (and they don't), and even if they were all capable of changing on their own (and they're not), there is no guarantee they would move in the right direction.

Consequently, CLP implemented a set of new leadership competencies and communicated them to all managers. It then instituted a rather rigorous assessment program so that managers could get an idea of where they were relative to each of the competencies. Finally, those with the highest potential were put through a multi-phase, six-month program that included both traditional classroom education and study trips to deregulated electrical power markets, team projects, and an interactive (team-based) computer simulation of market competition. As a senior director of development explained, "If we don't show them the path and give them the tools, it's a bit unfair to let them go if they don't make the grade."

Taking the lead in creating and implementing global HR change initiatives
The corporate HR team of the Royal Dutch/Shell Group is an excellent example of an HR group that has created and led a global change initiative. In 1993, Shell, perceiving trouble among its expatriate staff, sent out a survey to 17,000 current and

former Shell expatriates and their spouses. Two major problems were identified: loss of spouses' careers and separation from children who had to return to their home countries for secondary education. These two problems were causing significant damage to international mobility, productivity, and global leadership development.

Six Shell task forces attacked the problem and implemented major policy changes in 1995. To assist in expatriate children's schooling. Shell now selects a local primary school and works with the school to develop and adopt curriculum that will prepare the expatriate children for secondary schooling in their home countries. Where this is not feasible and the number of expatriates in a specific location meet a threshold figure, Shell now builds and staffs a company elementary school. Traditionally, at the secondary school level, many expatriates had to send their children (from age 11) to boarding schools in their home countries. Shell has now contracted with International School Services to evaluate each locale and to strengthen existing schools by ensuring curriculum development, funding for lab equipment, etc. These curriculum-enhanced Shell programs are now in place at 800 secondary schools in 94 countries.

To meet the career needs of spouses and partners, Shell developed 'The Outpost" in 1995. Located in The Hague, it now has 40 local hubs around the world. The Outpost hubs, run by spouses of Shell employees, provide a rich information network about job openings, career advice, and support services on a within-country and between-country basis. The central Outpost has a database of roughly 11,000 families who have indicated that they are willing to share their insights and experiences with others. The Outpost matches new expatriates with existing expatriates, organizes welcome committees for new expatriates, publishes a magazine to help expatriates, and provides books and materials on topics of interest to expatriate families.

The teams' work has freed high-potential managers to pursue assignments overseas, which enhances their global business skills. And building global business competencies among Shell's managers aids directly in the achievement of Shell's global business strategies.

Strategically Assist in Building Global Corporate Cultures

The need to develop a global corporate culture that is strong enough to maintain a consistency of important company norms across nations, yet is also flexible enough to allow for local preferences in conducting business, is a difficult challenge. One way to achieve this balance is to focus on developing rituals that reinforce aspects of the corporate culture that top management wants to preserve. Another approach is to pay attention to local and cultural sensitivities and respect them despite the existence of a global, corporate culture.

Cement "global" rituals

People need symbolic reminders of the global scope and focus of the company because the vast majority of employees face local issues on a daily basis. Without the symbolic reminders, it is easy for day-to-day local demands to drive out global perspective. To tackle this dynamic, Molex has developed communications rituals to cement and reinforce the corporate norms they deem most important. Twice a month, each unit around the world has a communication meeting that lasts about an hour, but in some cases can go longer. Molex employees are informed of the status of the unit's performance and other issues that apply to that Molex unit.

Molex also conducts annual communication meetings. These meetings are attended in each unit by the chairman, the COO (chief operating officer), the executive vice president, the corporate vice president (VP) of HR, senior executives of the local entity, and senior executives from the region. Kathi Regas, corporate VP of HR for Molex, notes, Our annual communications meetings ensure that our employees know they're a part of something much bigger than their local entities. They know our history, our performance, and our plans for the future. This, combined with frequent contact among our employees from entities around the world, and common practices, helps maintain our culture and strengthens a global team of employees. (J. Laabs, "Molex Makes Global HR Look Easy," in *Workforce* [March 1999], p. 45)

Respect local cultural sensitivities
While great benefits can come from a unifying global corporate culture, local employees can and do resist the firm's culture if they view it as cultural imperialism vs. competitive unification. Although Black & Decker stumbled with its strategy for DeWalt power tools in Asia (which we describe just a bit later in this chapter), it was successful in folding Asia into one of the critical elements of its global corporate culture through sensitivity and respect for local values.

Black & Decker believed that one of the keys to its success had been a culture of direct and candid developmental feedback to managers. It used a 360-degree performance appraisal process for gathering feedback for managers on how they were doing relative to their bosses', their peers', and subordinates' perceptions. When it moved its eastern hemisphere headquarters from Maryland to Singapore, it also wanted to implement this developmental process.

As Black & Decker talked with local Asian employees, it became clear that it was a bit "counter-cultural" to give feedback (especially anything negative) to one's boss. When asked if employees felt bosses could benefit from the feedback, if employees wanted to give the feedback, and if they wanted to receive feedback, they almost universally said *yes*. The real cultural issue turned out to be face-to-face encounters and confidentiality. The HR director at the time, Robyn Mingle, created a system whereby comments from subordinates were submitted to HR, transcribed from hand to electronic format, and "scrubbed" to ensure that any hints in the comments as to who might have made them were removed. Then the original handwritten comments were shredded.

Black & Decker thus preserved a unifying element of its global corporate culture and values (i.e., 360-degree feedback and constant improvement) and at the same time respected the elements of the local culture that did not fit the exact way the practice was implemented in the US. As Robyn Mingle put it, "The critical thing is the end result – do you preserve the fundamental value? The fact that we had to implement it a bit differently in Asia than the US is fine and in fact necessary."

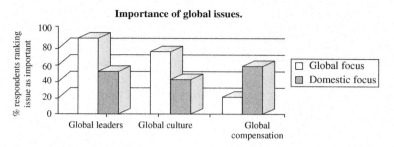

Figure 19.2   Importance of global issues.

Developing future leaders

It takes executives and managers with global mindsets, global competencies, and global experience to develop and implement global strategic initiatives. One major function of HR in the twenty-first century will be to transform domestic, ethnocentric managers into global managers.

Figure 19.2 provides an interesting perspective from our sample of HR executives regarding the influence of strategic focus on global leadership development. For example, executives whose companies currently have an international strategic focus view developing global leaders and managing an effective global corporate culture as being more important than those from companies with a domestic strategic focus. It is likely that global leaders were seen as the most important issue because – despite organizational structures, information systems, and the like – it is individual leaders and teams of executives that make decisions that either help or hurt the company's competitive position. In our talks with executives in these internationally focused companies, some general reasons surfaced that explained this state of affairs.

An HR executive from Black & Decker explained how the company suffered in Asia because the executives who were sent there had little previous international experience. As a consequence, in launching their leading power tool brand, DeWalt, in Asia they took the same approach that had worked miracles in the US.

The successful marketing strategy in the US called for taking the tools out to job sites and letting workers use the tools. This strategy "pulled" the tools into the market because after the first hand experience with the tools either the workers bought the tools themselves or influenced their bosses to buy them. When done in Asia, literally hundreds of workers would come down off the construction sites and try out the tools. Like their American counterparts, they were also impressed with the tools' functionality. However, unlike American counterparts, they did not own or buy their tools, and they had zero influence over their bosses or the company's tool purchasing decisions. Consequently, while the marketing events generated large crowds, they did not generate sales.

Developing global leaders is critical to global business success. To a great extent, executives interviewed were of the opinion that the success of a company's efforts in a new region or country could be no greater than the international savvy of the key leaders making strategic decisions for that market. One of the capabilities consistently mentioned was being sensitive to cultural and business differences and recognizing that what worked in one country may not work in another.

How, then, can global leaders be developed?

Expatriate assignments as vehicles for global leadership development
A plethora of social science research clearly indicates that to develop global leadership competencies in people, companies must make sure that managers have real global experiences. Thus, the strategic use of expatriates is critical in the development of global leaders. In fact, in a separate study, international assignments were found to be the single most powerful developmental experience. This may be part of the reason that we have seen a number of companies – such as 3M, Chevron Corp., Citicorp, GE, Nokia, Shell Oil Co, and Texas Instruments Inc – add an international assignment as one of the experiences managers need in order to be promoted to senior, corporate executive positions. John Pepper, recent chairman of Procter & Gamble Co put it this way, "My assignment to Italy when I was a young manager was one of the most important events in my entire career. It totally changed how I looked at the business. It also laid a solid foundation for when I later had responsibilities for our European operations. This in turn proved invaluable when I became CEO."

In particular, international assignments help leaders develop one of the most critical capabilities required in a global corporation – balancing global integration and local responsiveness. Mr. Pepper talked about his experience in Europe trying to introduce Visor laundry detergent into countries where there were different types of washing machines. Simplified, some countries had "top loaders" and others had "front loaders." While both cleaned clothes, the detergent tended to distribute unevenly in front loaders. Although they could have spent literally millions of dollars reformulating the detergent to work in front loading washing machines, they instead created a perforated plastic ball into which the detergent was placed and then tossed in with the clothes at the beginning of the wash cycle. As the ball tumbled with the clothes, the detergent flowed out. This invention allowed P&G to meet local differences and at the same time spread the development costs over a much larger revenue base and thus bring the per-unit development costs down.

Mr. Pepper explained that without these sorts of experiences as a leader outside your home market, you either take an imperial perspective as a CEO that your way can and should work everywhere in the world, or a fortress mentality that assumes that nothing from the outside can possibly be right for your market.

Create training programs that simulate expatriate assignments
Many companies are beginning to pay attention to developing leaders who have global competencies. Nokia, Shell, Unilever Bestfoods, TRW Inc., 3M, and the United Nations are examples of just a few organizations that are consciously trying to develop global leadership competencies in their managers. One of the more novel approaches is that of the Union Bank of Switzerland (UBS).

Managers of the Union Bank of Switzerland have participated in a project named *Seiten Wechsel* ("PerspectiveChange"), established by the "Schweizerische Gemeinnützige Gesellschaft," a nonprofit organization that brings together business executives with less privileged members of society, with the goal to further their mutual understanding. The purpose of this program is to expose managers to subcultures within their own country during short, compressed time periods. Managers of UBS were for a short period of time (usually about two weeks) assigned to social welfare projects that required them to look after homeless people, work with juvenile delinquents, care for HIV-patients who were terminally ill, or live together with immigrants seeking asylum. All involved benefited from the program – the people received much needed support and help, while the managers learned how to perceive the world through the eyes of people quite different from them.

According to the managers who participated in the program, "PerspectiveChange" helped them to reduce subjective barriers and prejudices, learn more about themselves, broaden their horizons, and increase their interpersonal skills – all competencies of global leadership. In addition, the program motivated managers to assume greater responsibility for those who need help; 60 percent of participants have supported the institution in which they volunteered after the program ended.

By exposing employees to subcultures within their own country, a foreign assignment can be simulated – they are immersed in a foreign culture at a relatively deep level, and they have to integrate into a different social system, function effectively in a strange environment, and deal with cultural diversity.

Conclusion

Clearly, some have seen the elephant of globalization and are hard at work changing themselves and their companies. However, there is increasing evidence that those who have not seen the elephant may not have a choice to avoid it for much longer. Given the steep and long learning curve for mastering international challenges such as enhancing strategy, aligning the organization with the strategy, facilitating global changes, creating an effective global culture, and developing global leaders, HR executives must lead – not lag – the global strategic focus of their firms.

To the extent that people are key to effective globalization and to the extent that international assignments are one of the most powerful developmental experiences, our research identified a shortage of HR executives with international assignment backgrounds. Some HR executives whom we interviewed suggested that this shortage existed in their companies because HR had been treated largely as a "local issue" (i.e., hiring and paying local employees). Others suggested that the perceived value of HR just did not offset the costs of sending an HR executive on an international assignment. Whatever the reasons for HR executives not having international assignment experience, it seems that this is a specific issue to change in the future.

Finally, to the extent that capable global leaders formulate strategy, implement structures, align the organization, champion needed changes, and determine and reinforce a unifying global culture, it is little wonder that those HR executives most experienced with globalization also ranked the challenge of global leader development as most important. The process of identifying and developing global leaders cannot be implemented overnight, nor will the results magically appear the next quarter. Consequently, building global leadership is perhaps the most important and hardest of the challenges, because working on it almost always precedes the obvious organizational need for it. It is quite easy to get people to jump off a burning oilrig platform, but much harder when they cannot yet smell smoke. This inherent resistance may in fact be why HR competency usually lags strategic focus.

Thus HR executives must lead globalization in part by example. If they have not identified and developed competent global HR talent, how much credibility – in advance of globalization – will they have for creating and implementing systems that identify and develop global leaders? Yet, if HR executives wait for the globalization demand to fully manifest itself as the company moves into new markets, acquires foreign companies, enters into joint ventures with partners abroad and then sees those efforts fail, HR executives will likely find their capabilities falling short of the demands. As "people problems" are identified as key causes for faltering globalization efforts, HR executives report to us that they increasingly see the finger of blame pointing at them.

Fundamentally, what we conclude from this study is that the largest globalization challenge HR executives confront is anticipatory change – changing before there is clear demand. While the challenges of anticipatory change are not unique to globalization, the need for it that globalization creates is nevertheless inescapable.

APPENDIX A: DESCRIPTION OF STUDY

The data presented here were gathered from both interviews and surveys. We interviewed HR executives in 30 firms headquartered in Europe (7 firms), North America (18), and Asia (5). These firms were selected based on ratings of a separate academic group and executive committee of a leading human resource professional association. We also conducted a survey commissioned by the Human Resource Planning Society. The survey was conducted at three sessions of the Senior HR Executive Program at the University of Michigan. HR executives from 84 out of 95 companies represented at the program participated in the study. The 84 companies had an average number of employees of 73,000 per company. The average firm size, in terms of annual revenue, was approximately $18 billion per year; all companies had operations outside of their home country, and most had substantial global operations. Of the respondents, 59.5 percent represented companies based in North America; 21.4 percent were based in Europe; and 16.7 percent were based in Asia, Australia, and South America.

Selected Bibliography

For a comprehensive discussion of the importance of human resource management functions in globalizing managerial cadres, see: J. S. Black, A. Morrison, and H. B. Gregersen, *Global Explorers: The Next Generation of Leaders* (New York: Routledge, 1999); P. Evans, V. Pucik, and J. Barsoux, *The Global Challenge: Frameworks for International Human Resource Management* (New York: McGraw-Hill, 2002); M. E. Mendenhall, T. M. Kühlmann, and G. K. Stahl, *Developing Global Business Leaders: Policies, Processes, and Innovations* (Westport, CT: Quorum Books, 2001).

For a detailed account of the relationship between HR issues and productivity, as has been demonstrated in a number of recent domestic and international academic studies, please see

B. E. Becker & B. Gerhart, "Human Resources and Organizational Performance: Progress and Prospects," *Academy of Management Journal*, 39(4) (special issue: *Human Resources and Organizational Performance*), 779–801. See also B. E. Becker and M. A. Huselid, "High Performance Work Systems and Firm Performance: A Synthesis of Research and Managerial Implications," *Research in Personnel and Human Resources Management*, 1998, 16, 53–101; B. E. Becker, M. A. Huselid, P. S. Pickus, and M. Spratt, "HR as a Source of Shareholder Value: Research and Recommendations," *Human Resource Management*, 1997, 36, 39–47; M. Carpenter, G. Sanders, and H. B. Gregersen, "Bundling Human Capital: The Impact of International Assignment Experience on CEO Pay and Multinational Firm Performance," *Academy of Management Journal*, 2001, 44(3), 493–512; and M. A. Huselid, S. E. Jackson, and R. S. Schuler, "Technical and Strategic Human Resource Management Effectiveness as Determinants of Firm Performance," *Academy of Management Journal*, 1997, 40, 171–88.

To read more about some of the case examples described in this chapter, see: J. S. Black, H. Gregersen, M. Mendenhall, and L. Stroh, *Globalizing People Through International Assignments* (New York: Addison-Wesley, 1999); C. M. Solomon, "Brace for Change," *Workforce*, January, 1999, 6–10; R. M. Kanter and T. D. Dretler, "Global Strategy and Its Impact on Local Operations: Lessons from Gillette Singapore," *Academy of Management Executive*, 1998, 12(4), 60–8; V. Frazee, "Tearing Down Roadblocks," *Workforce*, February, 1998, 50–5; J. Laabs, "Molex Makes Global HR Look Easy," *Workforce*, March, 1999, 42–6; C. Bingham, T. Felin, and J. S. Black, "An Interview with John Pepper: What it Takes to Be a Global Leader," *Human Resource Management*, 2000, 39(Summer/Fall), 287–92; and M. E. Mendenhall, and G. K. Stahl, "Expatriate Training and Development: Where Do We Go From Here?" *Human Resource Management*, 2000, 39(Summer/Fall), 251–65.

Finally, for more information regarding the historical phenomenon of "seeing the elephant," please see: J. Levy, *They Saw the Elephant: Women in the California Gold Rush* (Norman: University of Oklahoma Press, 1992).

Chapter 20

The Changing Role of the Corporate HR Function in Global Organizations of the Twenty-First Century

Milorad M. Novicevic and Michael Harvey

Introduction

The globalization of business activities in multinational corporations (MNCs) has cre-ated an increased pressure to link international human resource management (i.e. HRM) policies and practices with the firm-level outcomes (Chadwick and Cappelli, 1999). The increasing demands for modification of control and co-ordination mech-anisms in global organizations have distinctly imposed a commensurate need for structural changes within the headquarters human resource function of the MNCs (Roth and Ricks, 1994). Therefore, the focal point of the corporate human resource (i.e. HR) function in global organizations appears to be moving toward the need to design a supporting infrastructure for managers to manage competently the complex and competing demands for network co-ordination (i.e. consistency and efficiency) and differentiated responsiveness (i.e. flexibility and effectiveness) in global markets (Harvey *et al.*, 1999a). In addition, as these structural changes also entail heightened decentralization of global operations, the corporate HR function faces the com-plex issues associated with how to design flexible global assignments and leadership development systems (Ricks *et al.*, 1990).

M.M. Novicevic and M. Harvey, "The Changing Role of the Corporate HR Function in Global Orga-nizations of the Twenty-First Century," *International Journal of Human Resource Management*, Vol. 12, No. 8 (2001): 1251–68.

Recent research findings suggest that developing competent global managers is an issue of firm-level strategic relevance because global assignments and leadership are increasingly becoming the primary means of differentiating the global strategic thrust of the organization (Wieserma and Bantel, 1992). Thus, global assignments to develop global leaders represent one of the major areas of the corporate HR management involvement in corporate strategy formulation and implementation processes (Taylor and Beechler, 1993). If global leadership is to become one of the central facets of developing global strategies, the roles of the human resource function, department, and managers must be redefined in the context of this change. To address the growing strategic importance of leadership, companies like Gillette have implemented an international-trainee programme that exposes candidates for global assignments to corporate planning and strategy development prior to their being transferred overseas. As a result, 85 per cent of Gillette's global assignees come from the twenty-seven countries in which Gillette operates. Other MNCs, such as Coca-Cola, will not repatriate managers until there is solid evidence that they have had an impact on overseas performance and that they have developed a global mindset.

The primary focus of this paper is to examine how the increased demand for global corporate strategic consistency and flexibility redefines the roles of the corporate human resource function and its venues of influence. In particular, we analyse possible causal linkages among strategic international HR management, strategic leadership of corporate top management team (i.e. TMT), and alternative global assignment options. As globalization significantly changes not only the operating boundaries but also the symbolic context of the global organization, we argue that corporate HR function can play more influential roles in global organizations than it has in the past. This increased influence stems from a new set of the corporate HR's roles, characterized by blended political and strategic dimensions, which includes: the change agent of corporate culture; the TMT's symbolic 'communicator' to other levels of the organization; senior managers' mediator in development/career planning opportunities; and corporate TMT's and particularly the CEO's reliable internal informal adviser (Napier et al., 1995). Therefore, it would appear that supplementing the traditional strategic perspective with the political influence perspective on the IHRM function in global organizations provides unique insights into the emerging portfolio of roles that the corporate HR can play in global organizations when the demands for strategic flexibility and leadership development are salient.

In focusing on global leadership issues, we follow Napier's (1996) recommendation that the framework of a three-dimensional matrix (i.e. strategy, HR management, organizational outcomes) should include a fourth element, that being the type or level of employee affected by the other three factors (Napier, 1996: 239). Napier particularly hypothesized that organizations that grow internally within the existing structure will use 'transfers to promote managers to top management positions' based on subjective selection criteria, whereas the firms that diversify and acquire other firms will tend to draw upon the 'new' insiders using objective selection criteria. However, as corporate growth in the global context is increasingly becoming a mixed-mode growth, management-staffing processes have become political in nature, thus opening an opportunity for a new role for corporate HR influence and/or power. Therefore, we will analyse the corporate HR roles within the combined strategic and political influence perspective (Ferris *et al.*, 1995) by examining both the political and strategic forces driving global staffing and leadership development policies and practices. In particular, we will focus on the implicit influence of corporate HR on the design and implementation of global management staffing policies and practices to supply an adequate number of managers to implement the explicit corporate initiatives.

In the first section of the paper, we examine a strategic perspective on corporate HR roles in global organizations. We address the problems of control and co-ordination faced by corporate TMT as the firm globalizes its activities. Also, we examine the role of global management staffing in integration of control and co-ordination in a decentralized global organization. In the second part of the paper, we explore the relationship between TMT and corporate HR from the perspective of political influence theory. In the final part, we integrate the strategic and political perspective to devise specific alternative means of corporate HR political influence on global strategic leadership and management staffing choices. We conclude that this influence may result in a beneficial homogenization of 'best practices' in the global organization.

Strategic perspective on the corporate HR roles in global organizations

The international human resource literature appears to have not focused on the issue of how the transition from the multi-domestic MNC to a global integrated/co-ordinated network can affect the change in roles of the corporate HR function (Napier *et al.*, 1995). However, it is becoming clear that the increasing difficulty in staffing a global organization with competent leaders has put significant pressure on the corporate human resource function to elevate its corporate relevance for the TMT's strategic leadership and better relate its output to the firm performance (Wright and Snell, 1998). These new, latent in nature and global in scope, roles of the corporate HR function in a MNC are different from its traditional organizational roles in administering HRM programmes and processes involving identifying, selecting, training/developing, compensating, and appraising managers assigned overseas (Tung, 1994; Huselid *et al.*, 1997). Specifically, the increased emphasis on the globalization of corporate leadership through 'advice networks' (Athanassiou and Nigh, 2000) has given rise to the importance of corporate HR role in the global context and its influence on strategic staffing and leadership development policies and practices (Harvey, 1996). For example, the corporate HR function in 3M takes a competency approach to the selection of global assignees that focuses on the level of unique skills that each candidate has and then attempts to fit these competencies to the dimensions of the environment and task in the overseas assignment.

In a functionally organized MNC, as well as in multi-domestic MNCs, it might be possible to achieve a specific system 'fit' of HR management to the corporate strategy (Schuler, 1989: Wright and Snell, 1998). However, due to the multi-level globalization of organizational processes, the concept of this fit linkage has become elusive (Wright and Sherman, 1999). In a co-ordinated global network, rather than emphasizing the relevance of the behavioural 'fit', it would appear more appropriate that the emphasis be placed on the competence of HR management (Kamoche, 1997), as espoused by the resource-based view of the firm (Taylor *et al.*, 1996). The resource-based view of strategic international human resource management (i.e. SIHRM) opens the potential of emphasizing the organizational capability derived from the diversity of linkages in the various organizational configurations utilized in global organizations (Snell *et al.*, 1996). For example, Hewlett-Packard takes a global account management perspective in matching assignee competencies and maintaining consistency on a global strategy basis regardless of the number of countries where its key accounts are. Global account management attempts to balance the need for consistency (i.e. with key accounts) with the adaptation to local market demands. Therefore, the executives utilized on these global account management teams have a global mindset and at the same time recognize the need for unique strategies for individual countries.

Although the resource-based SIHRM models can frequently capture the form of these linkages, they lack the explanatory power relative to the content of the linkages (i.e. how, why and when they occur). Most empirical research supporting the resource-based view of SIHRM has tended to focus on associating the industrial relations strategy and its macro relationship of the high-performing flexible practices with the firm's performance indicators (Huselid, 1995; Becker and Gerhart, 1996). Though, clearly, the decisions related to employee relations and development have firm-level ramifications (i.e. training intensity, employment selectivity, union recognition, job grading, effective compensation/benefit system, labour force flexibility policies, and appropriate level of collective bargaining), it is difficult to assess the significance of these factors for the strategic management process in a global organization (MacDuffie, 1995).

In summary, the strategic perspective on the HR function leaves an array of questions unanswered relative to the corporate HR roles in a global organization, particularly those along the lines of the headquarters-subsidiary relationships. The questions, that would appear to have major implications, include:

1. How do the processes of global diversification and the trade-offs in global integration (i.e. efficiency) and local responsiveness (i.e. effectiveness) affect the headquarter-subsidiary HR management relations?
2. What are the forms of the fit and flexibility in the headquarters/subsidiary HR management relations that complement the strategic options in a global organization?
3. How can the corporate HR function exercise an effective influence over the subsidiary practices in the global context?
4. How do various institutional and cultural constraints affect the corporate HR design of the strategic global staffing policies and practices (Ferris *et al.*, 1999)?

We address the complexities of these specific strategic issues in the following section. In this analysis, we focus on the TMT headed by CEO as the primary 'customer' of the corporate HR function. The TMT-focus of the corporate HR function arises from the non-specific and non-competitive nature of the corporate HR's relationships with other stakeholders of a global organization

Strategic role of corporate TMT in controlling and co-ordinating activities in a global organization

The growing globalization of competition has enhanced a global leadership dilemma, which is how to design optimal governance mechanisms to resolve the tension between the needs for global integration among operating entities and those for local responsiveness (i.e. how to achieve 'contextualization' in the global strategies to compete effectively at the local market level) (Hamilton and Kashlak, 1999). The Gillette Co. has attacked this problem by ensuring that 80 per cent of its TMT members have extended international experiences. By doing so, Gillette feels that they will better understand the need for a global perspective in the HR function. In Gillette's case, this global mindset development is of particular importance because Gillette operates in 200 different markets, which challenge the TMT's leadership attempts to maintain consistency in the differentiated approach to each market. To maintain this consistency, the optimization of formal and informal control modes designed by the headquarters should resolve the problem of achieving the desired performance levels while supporting efficient co-ordinating efforts to induce cooperative behaviours among the globally networked subsidiaries (Gupta and Govindarajan, 1991). The balancing of control modes raises an increased demand for an agile strategic leadership supported by flexible co-ordination of differentiated activities in the global network (Harvey, 1996). To provide for the firm's strategic flexibility and global leadership, the TMT in a global organization should enhance its global mindset by diversifying the membership of its international assignees (Harvey *et al.*, 1999b). As the cultural diversity of global assignees may contribute to the development of performance-enhancing global capabilities, the appropriate strategic global staffing policies and practices should support a more multicultural network of assignees (Dulfer, 1998).

The increase in cultural diversity among the global assignees in MNCs could provide benefits for the control exercised over subsidiaries (Harvey and Buckley, 1997). In general, the control benefits of the assignees' cultural diversity depend on the internal and external conditions that create sources of uncertainty in the allocation of resources by the headquarters' TMT. The internal sources of uncertainty for the TMT include: the size of the global organization; the extent of its global diversification; and the extent of interdependence among its business units. Whereas, the external sources of uncertainty for TMT are: the perceived attractiveness of specific host country markets and the perceived country risk of host markets (Roth and Ricks, 1994; Gencturk and Aulakh, 1995).

MNCs typically design appropriate administrative mechanisms of formalization and centralization to mitigate uncertainty engendered by the internal and external sources, and thus increase the efficiency of the TMT's control (Roth *et al.*, 1991). Formalization provides explicit norms (i.e. such as rules and procedures) of desirable behaviour (Roth and Morrison, 1990), whereas centralization establishes legitimacy of the decision-making authority through a hierarchical design of governance. However, these 'hard' administrative mechanisms are generally not sufficient because, in addition to the explicit internal/external sources of uncertainty in a global organization, there are many latent sources of uncertainty in the decision-making environment (Pfeffer, 1989). These sources of uncertainty require 'soft' personnel control, which in turn requires prior development of global staffing policies and practices (Tung, 1987). When developing these policies and practices, MNCs have traditionally resisted decentralization of global assignments and have relied on the centralized practice of expatriation of home country personnel (i.e. expatriates) as the primary solution for appropriate control mechanism to mitigate uncertainties in foreign markets (Napier *et al.*, 1995).

Besides the support of the 'soft' control accentuated by globalization, an effective TMT's global strategic leadership needs the development of the co-ordination capability that is necessary for rationalization of reciprocal activities in a global network organization (Nohria and Ghoshal, 1994). The co-ordination capability helps integrate reciprocal interdependencies between the headquarters and subsidiaries as well as among the subsidiaries in the global network by securing consistency in the associated functional activities. The co-ordination in a global organization becomes more efficient if the TMT members and the subsidiary top managers share a common strategic philosophy and vision about the resources contributing to the firm's competitive advantage (Harvey *et al.*, 1999c). In addition, the efficiency of the global coordination increases if the geographic configuration and flow of the firm's resources match the organization's unique strategic positioning (Kogut, 1985). However, it is extremely difficult to efficiently map the globally distributed specific capabilities into the co-ordinated set of strategic activities. Moreover, it is highly challenging for expatriates to capture the context-specific efficiencies of this resource-activity mapping critical for global strategy implementation. Therefore, global assignments and leadership development activities, designed by the corporate HR function, should go beyond expatriation to support the TMT's strategic leadership in a global context and insure an efficient integration of control and co-ordination in the global organization.

The role of global staffing in integration of control and co-ordination in global organizations

The integrating personnel mechanisms, that may improve control and co-ordination under the conditions of uncertainty engendered by globalization, include strategic global staffing, global task forces and oversight committees (Taylor and Beechler, 1993). The positive externality of these mechanisms is an array of informal relationships among the members of these entities that are developed over time. These integrating mechanisms are intended to develop into the 'soft' structures within global organizations, which function both as informal control monitoring devices and as coordinating 'inducers' of subsidiary collaboration and competition for strategic projects (Birkinshaw and Hood, 1999). The process of lateral integration in a global organization is facilitated if the global assignees help the corporate and the subsidiary TMTs share the same strategic logic in their operating philosophies and orientations (Dowling *et al.*, 1999). Specifically, these integrating mechanisms can enhance the shared mindset in the global organization by increasing the level of trust in the network as the reference point of trust is shifted to subsidiaries. Therefore, the global staffing solutions for coordinating roles in lateral integration have increasingly been assigned to 'inpatriated' local and third country nationals usually carefully selected within the organization's network and intensively developed at the regional and/or corporate levels (Harvey and Buckley, 1997). Eventually, the inpatriates who are successful in globalizing corporate initiatives may become candidates for TMT openings in the future (Harvey *et al.*, 1999a). In this way, the level of cultural diversity in the MNC is raised to favourably influence the perceptions of procedural justice among the constituents of the global organization (Bartlett and Ghoshal, 1995).

The strategic global staffing issues, which influence the design of these complex integrating mechanisms, are supposed to be resolved through the global leadership development programmes that are necessary to help managers master the complex control and co-ordination tasks in global assignments (Harvey *et al.*, 1999c). In many ways, the staffing choices for individual assignments and global teams depend, most of all, on the nature of the assignment (i.e. the location and purpose of the assignment), as well as on the specific task of controlling and co-ordinating multiple interdependent activities associated with the TMT's strategic choices. Particularly, the task complexity of lateral integration among the subsidiaries is most affected by the firm's extent of related global diversity of goals and strategies (Gomez-Mejia, 1992). The global diversity in the organization's operations is a combined measure of the firm's product diversification and global market diversification (Hitt *et al.*, 1997). International diversity of operations is conceptualized as the firm's expansion across borders into new geographic markets (Prahalad and Doz, 1987), whereas product diversification is defined as expansion into new product markets (Yip *et al.*, 1997). Empirical findings have supported the hypothesis that the performance of a globally diversified firm is a quadratic function of the extent of its product diversification and is moderated by the extent of the number of country markets in which it is conducting business simultaneously (Vachany, 1999). However, this relationship is also moderated by risk that needs to be controlled and coordinated throughout the organization (Roth and Ricks, 1994).

Managing these complexities of a globally diversified firm under the conditions of growing global hypercompetition is a unique challenge for both TMT and human resource management (Murtha *et al.*, 1998). The top management must search for appropriate ways to effectively manage across the new emerging country markets in order to create a sustainable competitive advantage, while the corporate HR must support effectively these efforts. Past research findings suggest that product and market innovations and strategic flexibility are critical for creating sustainable competitive advantage as global organizations increasingly shift their organization design toward the integrated/co-ordinated network form of organization (Hedlund, 1986).

The integrated global networks, which require the development of a transnational capability through effective personnel-based horizontal co-ordination, attempt to maintain a positive linear relationship between international diversification and both innovation and firm performance (Hitt *et al.*, 1997). In this view, global diversity, supported by personnel-based control and co-ordination mechanisms, may produce superior firm performance because of increased economies of scale and scope, enhanced learning and innovation, and effective exploitation of core competencies

(Tsang, 1999). These processes enhance the firm's dynamic capability to appropriate returns from innovation in the global context. However, the problem of a globally diversified firm is that these value-adding processes are also accompanied by geometrically increasing costs of lateral co-ordinating because of institutional and cultural constraints imposed on the personnel-based control and co-ordination mechanisms (Ghoshal and Bartlett, 1995). Therefore, the solution to the problem of efficient control and horizontal coordination may require that the corporate TMT has to increase the firm stock of transcultural and transnational competencies to maintain a differentiated fit in managing the decentralized global firm (Bartlett and Ghoshal, 1989). In other words, an efficient lateral co-ordination requires the decentralization of the TMT's informal authority.

The primary problem in managing horizontal collaboration in a global organization is in co-locating the centralized decision rights with the decentralized specific/tacit knowledge (Jenssen and Meckling, 1999). Any co-location solution requires a trade off between costs and benefits of decentralization. Specifically, decentralization (i.e. delegation of autonomy to subsidiaries) sacrifices the efficiency of strategic control and co-ordination (Prahalad and Doz, 1987) whereas, centralization (i.e. retention of the headquarters directed hierarchy) sacrifices the effectiveness of responsiveness and innovativeness (Engelhoff, 1988). The strategic leadership of the TMT members and the effectiveness of the employed personnel integrating mechanisms determine how far the limits of the decentralization can be set in terms of the governance costs. The tradeoffs associated with the decentralization (i.e. delegation of TMT authority) in a global organization determine the level of uncertainties engendered by the extent of relatedness in global diversification.

A number of case studies reported by Ghoshal and Bartlett (1995) have shown that globally diversified firms' success depends on the corporate HR's capabilities to design and employ efficient differentiated and multicultural management systems across subsidiaries. In particular, horizontal integration among subsidiaries requires a distributed global leadership and project groups to develop the informal lines of horizontal co-ordination, relationships and shared values, while maintaining vertical control. Therefore, it would appear that an adaptive and transcultural management system requires that the vertical control mechanisms are mostly staffed by expatriates, whereas the horizontal co-ordination mechanisms are mostly staffed by inpatriates (Harvey et al., 1999c).

Political perspective on the relationship between TMT and corporate HR management in global organizations

The tendency for TMT to be conservative in decentralization, thereby emphasizing its formal corporate authority in the form of 'soft' control over subsidiaries, carries specific consequences for the subsidiaries' top managers (Hamilton and Kashlak, 1999).

Specifically, the consequences affect the subsidiary top managers' compensation and reputation, which are contingent to a degree to the subsidiaries' financial performance as well as other strategic goals established by corporate TMT for each subsidiary (Birkinshaw and Hood, 1999). Therefore, strategic staffing of subsidiary's executive positions strongly influences both the success/failure of TMT initiatives and the reputation and career progression of specific subsidiary executives. This 'strong' situation of competing values represents a heightened organizational problem for the corporate HR when selecting the appropriate base (i.e. parent organization or the subsidiaries) to design an adaptive global staffing system (Harvey, 1996).

The growing relevance of the global operating context for corporate actions mandates not only the new roles of the corporate HR function but also the corresponding globalization of the corporate HR manager's task domain (Harvey, 1996). First, the corporate HR manager needs more frequent face-to-face and indirect interactions with the HR managers in subsidiaries to properly assess the contextual relevance of staffing options. Second, the corporate HR manager has to become not only an efficient bureaucratic administrator in assessing the proper global staffing solutions but also an entrepreneurial promoter of corporate staffing policies. Third, the corporate HR manager's initiatives not only have to project this co-operative global dimension but also have to separate it from the administrative demands of impartiality when comparing managerial and labour performance and cost across countries. Finally, the corporate HR manager has to create specific direct and proactive political venues of influence on subsidiaries by bridging and/or buffering certain TMT-subsidiary conflict relationships.

This corporate HR political contribution to the TMT's global strategic leadership can be most effectively achieved through a proactive support of global management development programmes and experiences for the headquarters' and subsidiaries' senior managers who are candidates for or are already involved in global assignments. The smoothly programmed flexible transfer of senior managers across subsidiaries/cultures necessitates that the corporate HR's staffing policy criteria are tangible and explicit. Moreover, corporate HR support for global management development becomes particularly valuable if implemented through the subsidiaries' training and development departments (Tsang, 1999). In the following section, we develop a theoretical explanation for the new venues of political influence of the corporate HR function in global organizations.

Political influence theory to explain the increasing influence of corporate HR in global organizations

The political influence perspective, proposed by Ferris and Judge (1991), may be an appropriate frame to explain the new venues of corporate HR influence in global organizations. This perspective brings into question the inherent artificiality of the stand-alone rational strategic international HRM model, which assumes the possibility of maximizing both individual and organizational outcomes across borders through the elusive concept of 'organizational fit' (Judge and Ferris, 1992). Ferris and Judge (1991) argue that the supplementary 'issues of competing interests, power and politics' should be taken into account to explain the subjective evaluative reality of fit in the global organization. They define political influence as 'deliberate attempts to manage or control the meaning shared by others' in the organization (Ferris and Judge,

1991: 449). The shared meaning is a socially constructed aspect of the organizational reality in which the standard strategic factors such as competence, performance and fit are not assumed because of their subjective evaluative nature (Frost, 1989). In this perspective, the political influence in a global organization can be viewed as a value-neutral, specific form of social influence achieved by the use of symbolic means (Jennings, 1994).

In a co-ordinated global network, political influence is manifested as a rivalry, which takes place among the competing interests of the influential actors in the headquarters (i.e. HQ) and subsidiaries (Ferris *et al.*, 1992). The most critical areas of the interests relative to this latent competition include: strategic management staffing; managerial career mobility, and managerial compensation (Galang and Ferris, 1997). First, the HQ coalitions differentiated on the basis of, for example, functions, nationality and demographics often compete over the rules and decision criteria for global management staffing. The winning HQ coalition then needs the alliance of the corporate HR to have the management staffing system designed so that the coalition's interests are incorporated in the critical selection criteria. Second, competing interests at the firm level, manifested in the management of the shared meaning, exercise influence over information and decision criteria related to performance evaluation systems in the subsidiaries. The outcome of these processes forms the performance evaluation context within which corporate and subsidiary HR functions interact to manage the meaning attached to the appraised performance of each individual subsidiary. Third, internal labour market for international assignments and advancement opportunities toward the 'high potentials' circle are applicable for political influence (Ferris *et al.*, 1995). In this domain, the interests of the HQ coalitions can become influential and inclined to preserve the *status quo* through symbolic control of the corporate HR decision criteria which frequently favour social reproduction through perpetuation of expatriation practice (Dipboye, 1995).

The most sensitive aspect of managerial career mobility and advancement, where the political influence perspective becomes relevant at the firm level, is centred on the TMT succession planning process (Ferris *et al.*, 1992). The possible outcomes of the TMT succession are normally left silent but are informational concerning the dominant HQ and subsidiary coalitions' intents that wield the most influence over time (Galang and Ferris, 1997). The dominant interests in the headquarters attempt to ensure perpetuation of their control through succession/promotion of individuals supportive of those interests by raising the important political issue of 'cultural fit' in global management staffing decisions. Finally, political influence is particularly prominent in compensation system decisions both at the corporate and business levels (Pfeffer, 1989). Compensation systems involve allocation of scarce resources and thus are the subject of competing interests over the allocation decision criteria, particularly when long-term compensation elements like stock option and pension plans, that are dependent upon various national regulations, are addressed.

In summary, the political influence perspective of the corporate HR role in a global organization is supplementary to the rational strategic perspective (Ferris and Judge, 1991). Specifically, the rational strategic perspective focuses on the importance of the structure to control activities and secure the preservation of trust and co-operative interests against opportunism in global organizations. In contrast, the political influence perspective focuses on the importance of the process and the influence of competing interests on the collaboration and conflict in global organizations (Ferris *et al.*, 1999).

Alternative means of corporate HR political and symbolic influence in global organizations

Supplementing the strategic perspective with the political influence perspective implies a meta-theoretical view of corporate HR influence at the boundary between the functionalist and interpretative paradigms. From this view, which assumes the significance of social context (Ferris *et al.*, 1999), we need to offer answers to the following critical research and pragmatic questions: first, how does the political influence of corporate human resource moderate the relationship between the TMT strategic choices and the management staffing alternatives in globally diversified organizations? Second, what are the possible beneficial outcomes from this corporate human resource influence?

To articulate possible answers to these research and practical questions, we first need to provide a realistic preview of the traditional operating role of corporate HR in a MNC. First, the traditional area of technical and administrative responsibility for the human resource management function appears to be too narrow to influence the firm-level strategic decisions (Baron and Kreps, 1999). Second, the popular argument of HR effectiveness lacks both formal and practical legitimacy to enhance the corporate HR's marginal image of being commonly perceived as a mere derivative of the corporate strategy implementation (Galang *et al.*, 1999). Third, HR managers are usually isolated from major global strategic decisions unless some industrial relations-specific issue, such as union contract negotiation/administration, is involved (Schuler, 1989). Fourth, even in the cases of comprehensive corporate change, such as cross-border mergers and acquisitions, the IHRM-related strategic decisions are made *post hoc* (Jennings, 1994). Finally, IHRM issues, even when strategic, are not considered by TMT to belong to strategy formulation but strategy implementation phase; and even then, only within a narrow scope of country-specific employment implications, such as those related to corporate difficulties with bargaining situations (e.g. major lay-offs) (Russ *et al.*, 1998).

Therefore, it may be anticipated that the utilization of SIHRM structure in organizations globalizing their effort will not adequately address the unique requirements of a network organization. Rather, it is envisioned that a global human resource leadership system will be required to meet the challenge of global competition in the twenty-first century (Harvey *et al.*, 2001). The primary difference between these two HR systems is the ability of global HR leadership to address effectively the need to co-ordinate global processes with the flexibility to allow the adaptation of the processes for local subsidiaries. The development of a global HR leadership system will allow for the TMT and local subsidiary managers to effectively co-ordinate the distribution of political influence to develop/implement HR policies that are globally efficient (i.e. co-ordinated) and sometimes effective (i.e. adapted) to the unique needs of subsidiaries in various country markets (Harvey *et al.*, 1999a; Harvey *et al.*, 1999b; Harvey and Novicevic, 1999).

To be an effective and relevant actor in an leadership-driven globally diversified organization, the corporate HR has to redefine its traditional role of the bureaucratic

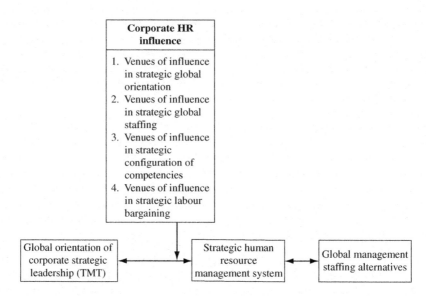

Figure 20.1   Model of corporate HR influence in global organizations.

administrator or the quasi-strategic partner of TMT and become an effective political 'influencer.' Specifically, corporate HR has to identify and establish new effective and relevant venues of its influence that are related to the firm global strategy. Establishing the new means of corporate HR influence requires taking part in certain discrete firm-level choices of political relevance to the strategic global leadership role of TMT in the following areas: venues of influence in strategic global orientation; venues of influence in strategic global staffing; venues of influence in strategic worldwide configuration of competencies; and venues of influence in strategic labour bargaining in the global context (see Figure 20.1).

These corporate-level choices can have a powerful political relevance to the corporate TMT and subsidiaries' TMTs because they influence the boundaries of responsibility and liability along the vertical levels and horizontal interfaces of the organization. In particular, when coupled with financial controls, these critical choices influence activities at the business level, which affect the competitive advantage creation. The first venue indicates that corporate HR must find a way to make a substantial contribution to the TMT strategic orientation in global strategic issues. Whereas, this contribution will be modest in the multi-domestic MNC, it is likely to be significant in the global organizational context. The second venue of the corporate HR influence falls in the domain of strategic global management staffing. Whereas, staffing is content-related (staffing with functional or generalist managers) in multi-domestic MNCs, it is process-related in global organizations (staffing with managers possessing cross-functional knowledge). The third venue of the corporate HR influence, strategic configuration of competencies, refers to the flexibility and responsiveness of the integrating mechanisms to enable and co-ordinate the development of specific capabilities within and among subsidiaries. This process of lateral co-ordination could be politically relevant to the corporate HR when identifying and selecting inpatriate candidates for corporate TMT succession planning. The fourth venue, strategic relevance of the level of labour bargaining, depends on the specific national labour-related regulations and may require a differentiated approach to country-specific policies on the global basis.

Of all these areas of potential corporate HR influence over subsidiary practices, the most politically sensitive area is that of creating the internal labour market for global managers, particularly its segment related to the career ladders toward TMT positions in the parent organization. In this domain, the subsidiary (i.e. business unit) executives and senior managers, with career orientation toward upper firm echelons, may be rationally prone to emphasize subsidiary cost minimization strategy at the cost of innovation in order to meet the tight financial control requirements set up by the TMT. To prevent such short-term focus, the corporate HR must design the appropriate appraisal and compensation criteria with bonuses for supporting lateral integration efforts. If successful, this practice of induced horizontal co-ordination could make the subsidiary executives' position central to the parent organization and the TMT would potentially heavily invest in their development initiating for them specific opportunities for future promotion and possible successful inclusion in the corporate TMT membership. As a result, the corporate HR has an opportunity to increase its political influence and become a 'voice' venue in the subsidiary managers' career progression process. Therefore, the corporate HR may become politically very influential across the management layers of the global organization.

Proposition 1.   The more salient the corporate HR's political influence in strategic global orientation, staffing, configuration of competencies, and bargaining, the greater the effect of the TMT's strategic leadership on globalization of the MNC's HRM system.

As a boundary condition, however, we need to explain why the globalization of the firm strategy is a necessary condition for corporate HR to attain the position of political influence. Specifically, we need to answer two critical questions: why is the corporate HR role of low strategic relevance in a multi-domestic MNC, but it may be of high strategic relevance in global organizations? (Harvey and Buckley, 1997); and why does the corporate HR in a multi-domestic MNC have a form of downsized bureaucracy whose destiny depends on its administrative ability to survive (Stewart, 1995)? First, the corporate HR in a multi-domestic MNC does not have a defined corporate role in tangible, bottom-line terms. Second, the traditional corporate HR operating policy-laden influence on subsidiaries has little appeal as the centralized source of power because the global decentralization and diversification processes in the consumer-centred global economy push the operating power centre toward subsidiaries' HR departments. Finally, corporate HR is often viewed by subsidiaries of a multi-domestic MNC as an unnecessary 'burden cost' because it may often merely duplicate the operating function of the subsidiary HR departments. However, in the global model, the corporate HR role becomes of greater importance because of its often-indispensable political support to the process-focused informal control and co-ordination in achieving lateral integration among subsidiaries. In particular, when the corporate TMT of a global organization searches for informal forms of influencing co-operative inter-dependencies among subsidiaries, corporate HR can significantly contribute to the development and maintenance of these innovative types of co-ordination and control.

The very important political tool of the corporate HR's informal influence in a global organization is the back-up infrastructure utilized by the integrating mechanisms, which enables the worldwide dispersion of corporate culture (i.e. the transnational infrastructure for efficient functioning of task forces, interlocking boards and over-sight committees). Specifically, the communication channels and media are critical for effective corporate culture dispersion throughout the global network. For exam-ple, the corporate HR-implemented intranet may sometimes be the most influential medium. The intranet-placed HR messages may take the form of informal web-memo summaries of guiding principles, which implicitly communicate the TMT view of cor-porate values in the mission-related terms. These generalized symbolic policies may have a powerful signalling influence on subsidiaries indicating which practices are and which are not viewed as acceptable by the corporate TMT. This means that corpo-rate HR, capable of skilfully communicating and brokering the strategic ambiguity in these informal general policies, may acquire a powerful referent base of political power in the global network. The power of such signalling messages is derived from their projected meaning designed to emphasize the achievement of consensus among subsidiaries rather than to serve as centralized TMT's instructions (see Boyd and Beg-ley, 2000, for a comprehensive field research on the high-tech MNCs' practices of incorporating worldwide input into the corporate HR policy making processes).

As a mediator of the TMT signals, the corporate HR management may build spe-cific political capital by managing the means of influence and thus provide a 'weak tie' among the subsidiary career-oriented executives and HR managers. The corpo-rate HR manager may also choose to initiate reverse prototyping of these signals by informing the corporate TMT on the emerging hurdles in the achievement of poten-tial consensus across subsidiaries. This informal advising can be grounded upon the previous informal interactions with the corporate co-ordinators who have participated in the meetings of interlocking directorates and personnel committees. It would also be tactically wise for the corporate HR to advise the TMT when to include in its co-ordination meetings the career-oriented and promising subsidiary line managers who are eager to qualify for the TMT-approved quotas in the executive development programmes and corporate career tracking databases. This strong influential base of the corporate HR referent power in a global organization could be maintained if the corporate HR manager succeeds in building an informal constituency (i.e. social capi-tal) among subsidiary senior managers. The symbolic positioning of the corporate HR as their 'voice venue', influential to capture the attention of the upper firm echelons, can pool this constituency. The reverse direction of this venue of the corporate HR political power could be built by enhancing the corporate HR image in the eyes of the subsidiary managers to perceive it as the competent disseminator of accepted corporate professional standards. However, the success of this political tactic of corporate HR highly depends upon the initial build-up of the critical mass of constituents among international assignees who originate from foreign subsidiaries.

Proposition 2.   A positive interaction of strategic and political dimensions in the corporate HR's efforts to globalize the MNC's HRM system will increase the diversity in global assignment and leadership development alternatives.

The role of inpatriate managers in implementation of corporate HR influence

The increasing corporate HR power base of political influence rests primarily in the globally dispersed informal managerial networks (Athanassiou and Nigh, 2000). This influence must be sustained and integrated by frequent communication and symbolic interactions during formal regional and corporate training and development programmes for the high potential senior managers form headquarters and subsidiaries. Besides having a formal function, these programmes can also have an informal function of facilitating the prototypical socialization of promising managers into the corporate upper echelons. Within this informal function of the development programmes, on the one hand, the senior managers from around the world learn to exchange their local/regional experiences and initiatives, interpreting and labelling them in terms compatible with the TMT initiatives. The informal function of the programme is, on the other hand, to communicate the corporate TMT attitude and approach to the emerging issues deserving managerial initiative. A politically beneficial role of the corporate HR manager is to engage in this informal function as a moderator and motivate the subsidiary managers to propose how they would implement and/or innovate specific corporate initiatives in other subsidiaries.

The regional and corporate programmes are particularly important for the social capital development and networking of young promising international managers. This is an opportunity for the corporate HR manager to influence young managers' expectancies about the company's goals and introduce them to the influential corporate managers during the development programmes. By becoming an embedded information broker or 'bridge of influence' in these managerial informal networks, the corporate HR manager can assess the expectancies of the upward-progressing managers coming from multiple nodes in the global network. In effect, these expectancies will later become reinforced and socially controlled by the implicit norms embedded in the network through cultural forms of influence exerted by the corporate TMT through the corporate HR mediation. Such an *ex ante* political influence of the corporate HR on the young 'fast track' global managers from around the world may also beneficially contribute to the success of their future international assignments.

In this way, the dense venue network of corporate HR influence may ensure that the main carriers of the cultural norms in the TMT initiatives become the global assignees coming from foreign subsidiaries. Their emerging primary role is less that of traditional subsidiary monitoring and reporting to the headquarters, but more that of transferring knowledge, skills and expertise across the global network. These globally mobile 'transpatriates' are continuously 'expatriated' from their homelands and also 'inpatriated' through the parent organization-sponsored socialization process (Harvey *et al.*, 1999c). For example, a globally mobile manager who has successfully implemented a TMT initiative in one subsidiary may be transferred as a corporate entrepreneur of that initiative in another subsidiary. The careers of the 'transpatriates' are shaped by their continuing acquisition of new competencies as well as by their reputation built on their successful completion of strategic projects when championing the corporate TMT's global initiatives.

Using the metaphor of top professional golf players, these global 'lead' managers can be viewed as high-impact players competing in the multinational tournaments for global reputation. The corporate TMT-influenced and corporate HR-implemented 'tournaments' serve the function of building interpersonal and interorganizational trust in the global network based on the reputation of these champions. The inpatriate champions thus become knowledgeable agents of organizational isomorphism of the 'best practices' in the global network. Such global management staffing and development practices may create socially complex, rare, inimitable, and non-substitutable organizational and human resources capable of creating competitive advantage. In the last instance, but far from the least important, they embody the implicit TMT-communicated vision of the global cultural control and co-ordination (Harvey and Buckley, 1997).

Conclusion

In summary, corporate HR influence in the global organization of the twenty-first century is envisioned to take a form of specific political venues with strategic ramifications. These venues of the symbolic political power of corporate HR provide various opportunities for the corporate HR to socially construct its global strategic relevance as a subsidiary resource. In the use of the venues of its influence, the corporate HR strives to achieve its ultimate goal – to complement the corporate TMT efforts to elicit homogenization of best practices in the global organization while preserving the specific capabilities and responsiveness of individual subsidiaries.

The responsiveness of the subsidiaries to corporate HR influence is motivated by their competition to become the regional centres of excellence in the global organization. This competition necessitates corporate HR-brokered cues on the TMT views of best practices. The corporate HR influence is further reinforced by the corporate TMT-referent comparison of subsidiary compliance to hard and soft norms promoted by focused corporate strategy and culture. These venues of the corporate HR influence may thus contribute to the successful institutionalization of a corporate culture of shared values across subsidiaries. The corporate HR symbolic actions help the subtle reproduction of corporate culture by supporting the isomorphism of best practices transferred by the global teams led by international assignees. In effect, the global staffing policies and practices increasingly rest on inpatriates, who are championing TMT initiatives through lateral co-ordination as potential candidates for the corporate TMT succession planning.

Practices of many MNCs go beyond global management staffing toward global employee involvement. For example, Dow Chemical started developing its specific global HRM system, branded as 'People Success', in 1992. Dow installed 35,000 global workstations that gave all employees across the globe open access to the same databases. This system, which supports Dow's business strategy implemented through a global network structure, provides to all employees opportunities governed by the same principles and values. As of now Dow's world-wide-spread employees have greater freedom to plan and control their careers; the primary responsibility for personal development is shifted to employees by the global HRM system.

At Dow, people have opportunities to enhance and develop various acquiring, applying, leveraging, and visioning competencies over time. The identified eight global competencies (i.e. in addition to specific competencies for the function) include initiative, innovation, interpersonal effectiveness, leadership, learning, market focus, teamwork, and value creation. As a result, Dow's global HRM system has moved to a competency platform. The most important feature of Dow's global HRM competency platform is its open access nature to previously confidential information/knowledge. This increased global relationalism in knowledge sharing forces managers to focus on leadership within the multiple contingencies of the global HRM system.

In summary, to enhance the strategic flexibility of the corporate TMT global orientation, the committing yet flexible influence of corporate HR in a global network organization depends upon the development of a global HR leadership system. This HR system allows for integration and localization of new aspects of HR management process. It would be difficult, if not impossible, for the traditional SIHRM structure to permit the opportunity and effectiveness requirements for distributed global leadership in a global network organization. Therefore, the development of a new role portfolio for the corporate HR function is critical for the distributed global leadership to flourish in global organizations of the twenty-first century.

REFERENCES

Athanassiou, N. and Nigh, D. (2000) 'Internationalization, Tacit Knowledge and the Top Management Teams of MNCs', *Journal of International Business Studies*, 31(3): 471–88.

Baron, J. and Kreps, D. (1999) 'Consistent Human Resource Practices', *California Management Review*, 41(3): 29–532.

Bartlett, C.A. and Ghoshal, S. (1989/1995) *Managing Across Borders: The Transnational Solution*. Boston, MA: Harvard Business School Press.

Becker, B. and Gerhart, B. (1996) 'The Impact of Human Resources Management on Organizational Performance: Progress and Prospects', *Academy of Management Journal*, 39: 779–801.

Birkinshaw, J. and Hood, N. (1999) 'An Empirical Study of the Development Process in Foreign-owned Subsidiaries in Canada and Scotland', *Management International Review*, 4: 339–64.

Boyd, P. and Begley, T. (2000) 'Incorporating Worldwide Input into HR Decision Making in High-tech Companies', *Human Resource Planning*, April, 22–37.

Chadwick, C. and Cappelli, P. (1999) 'Alternatives to Generic Strategy Typologies in Strategic Human Resource Management'. In Wright, P., Dyer, L., Boudreau, J. and Milkovics, G. (eds.) *Research in Personnel and Human Resources Management, Supplement 4*. Greenwich, CT: JAI Press, pp. 11–29.

Dipboye, R. (1995) 'How Politics Can Destruct Human Resources Management in the Interest of Empowerment, Support, and Justice', In Corpanzano, R. and Kacmar, K. (eds.) *Organizational Politics, Justice, and Support: Managing the Social Climate of the Workplace*. Wesport, CT: Quorum Books, pp. 55–80.

Dowling, P., Schuler, R. and Welch, D. (1999) *International Dimensions of Human Resource Management*, 3rd edition. Boston. MA: PWS-Kent.

Dulfer, E. (1998) 'Individualization of HRM Facing Intercultural Corporate Structures', *Management International Review*, 2: 27–46.

Engelhoff, W. (1988) *Organizing the Multinational Enterprise*. Cambridge, MA: Ballinger.

Ferris, G. and Judge, T. (1991) 'Personnel Human Resources Management: A Political Influence Perspective', *Journal of Management*, 17: 447–88.

Ferris, G., Buckley, M.R. and Allen, G. (1992) 'Promotion Systems in Organizations', *Human Resource Planning*, 13: 47–68.

Ferris, G., Galang, M., Thorton, M. and Wayne, S. (1995) 'A Power and Politics Perspective in Human Resource Management'. In Ferris, G., Rosen, S. and Barnum, D. (eds.) *Handbook of Human Resource Management*. Oxford: Blackwell, pp. 100–14.

Ferris, G., Hochwarter, W., Buckley, M.R., Harrell-Cook, G. and Frink, D. (1999) 'Human Resources Management. Some New Directions', *Journal of Management*, 25(3): 385–415.

Frost, P. (1989) 'The Role of Organizational Power and Politics in Human Resources Management'. In Ferris, G., Rowland, K. and Buckley, M. (eds.) *Human Resources Management*, 4th edition. Englewood Cliffs, NJ: Prentice-Hall, pp. 35–43.

Galang, M. and Ferris, G. (1997) 'Human Resource Department's Power and Influence Through Symbolic Action', *Human Relations*, 50: 1403–26.

Galang, M., Elsik, W. and Russ, G. (1999) 'Legitimacy in Human Resource Management'. In Ferris, G. (ed.) *Research in Personnel and Human Resources Management*, Vol. 17. Greenwich, CT: JAI Press, pp. 41–79.

Gencturk, E. and Aulakh, P. (1995) 'The Use of Process and Output Controls in Foreign Markets', *Journal of International Business Studies*, 26(4): 755–86.

Ghoshal, S. and Bartlett, C. (1995) 'Building the Entrepreneurial Organization: The New Organizational Processes, New Managerial Tasks', *European Management Journal*, 13(2): 139–55.

Gomez-Mejia, L. (1992) 'Structure and Process of Diversification, Compensation Strategy, and Firm Performance', *Strategic Management Journal*, 13: 38–397.

Gupta, A. and Govindarajan, V. (1991) 'Resource Sharing Among SBUs: Strategic Antecedents and Administrative Implications', *Academy of Management Journal*, 29: 695–714.

Hamilton, R. and Kashlak, R. (1999) 'National Influences on Multinational Control System Selection', *Management International Review*, 39(2): 167–89.

Harvey, M. (1996) 'Developing Leaders Rather Than Managers for Global Marketplace', *Human Resource Management Review*, 6(4): 279–304.

Harvey, M. and Buckley, M.R. (1997) 'Managing Inpatriates: Building Global Core Competency', *Journal of World Business*, 32(1): 35–52.

Harvey, M. and Novicevic, M.M. (1999) 'Trials and Tribulations of Addressing Global Organizational Ignorance', *European Management Journal*, 15: 63–84.

Harvey, M., Speier, C. and Novicevic, M.M. (1999a) 'The Role of Inpatriation in Global Staffing', *International Journal of Human Resource Management*, 10(3): 54–5.

Harvey, M., Novicevic, M.M. and Speier, C. (1999b) 'Inpatriate Managers: How to Increase the Probability of their Success', *Human Resource Management Review*, 9(1): 51–81.

Harvey, M., Speier, C. and Novicevic, M.M. (1999c) 'The Role of Inpatriation in Global Staffing', *Journal of International Management*, 5(3): 167–86.

Harvey, M., Buckley, M.R. and Novicevic, M.M. (2001) 'Strategic Global Human Resource Management'. In Ferris, G. (ed.) *Research in Personnel and Human Resources Management*.

Hedlund, G. (1986) 'The Hypermodern MNC – a Hierarchy?' *Human Resource Management*, 25(1): 9–35.

Hitt, M., Hoskisson, R. and Kim, H. (1997) 'International Diversification: Effects on Innovation and Firm Performance on Product-diversified Firms', *Academy of Management Journal*, 40: 767–98.

Huselid, M. (1995) 'The Impact of Human Resource Management on Turnover, Productivity, and Corporate Financial Performance', *Academy of Management Journal*, 38: 635–72.

Huselid, M., Jackson, S. and Schuler, R. (1997) 'Technical and Strategic Human Resource Effectiveness as Determinants of Firm Performance', *Academy of Management Journal*, 40: 171–88.

Jennings, P. (1994) 'Viewing Macro HRM from Without: Political and Institutional Perspectives'. In Ferris, G. (ed.) *Research in Personnel and Human Resources Management*, Vol. 12. Greenwich, CT: JAI Press, pp. 1–40.

Jenssen, M. and Meckling, W. (1999) 'Specific Knowledge and Divisional Performance Measurement', *Journal of Applied Corporate Finance*, 12(2): 8–17.

Judge, T. and Ferris, G. (1992) 'The Elusive Criterion of Fit in Human Resources Staffing Decisions', *Human Resource Planning*, 15: 47–67.

Kamoche, K. (1997) 'Knowledge Creation and Learning in International HRM', *International Journal of Human Resource Management*, 8(2): 279–304.

Kogut, B. (1985) 'Designing Global Strategies: Profiting from Operational Flexibility', *Sloan Management Review*, Fall, 27–38.

MacDuffie, J. (1995) 'Human Resource Bundles and Manufacturing Performance: Organizational Logic and Flexible Production Systems in the World of Auto Industry', *Industrial and Labor Relations Review*, 48: 197–221.

Murtha, T., Lenway, S. and Bagozzi, R. (1998) 'Global Mind-sets and Cognitive Shift in a Complex Multinational Corporation', *Strategic Management Journal*, 19: 97–114.

Napier, N. (1996) ' "Strategy, Human Resources Management and Organizational Outcomes" Coming Out from Between the Cracks'. In Ferris, G., Rowland, K. and Buckley, M. (eds.) *Human Resources Management*, 4th edition. Englewood Cliffs, NJ: Prentice-Hall. pp. 35–43.

Napier, N., Tibau, J., Jenssens, M. and Pilenzo, R. (1995) 'Juggling on a High Wire: The Role of International Human Resources Manager'. In Ferris, G., Rosen, S. and Barnum, D. (eds.) *Handbook of Human Resource Management*. Oxford: Blackwell, pp. 217–42.

Nohria, N. and Ghoshal, S. (1994) *The Differentiated Network*. San Francisco, CA: Jossey-Bass.

Pfeffer, J. (1989) 'A Political Perspective on Career: Interests, Networks, and Environments'. In Arthur, M., Hall, D. and Lawrence, M. (eds.) *Handbook of Career Theory*. New York: Cambridge University Press, pp. 380–96.

Prahalad, C. and Doz, Y. (1987) *The Multinational Mission: Balancing Local Demands and Global Vision*. New York: The Free Press.

Ricks, D., Toyne, B. and Martinez, Z. (1990) 'Recent Developments in International Management Research', *Journal of Management*, 16: 219–53.

Roth, K. and Morrison, A. (1990) 'An Empirical Analysis of Integration-Responsiveness Framework in Global Industries', *Journal of International Business Studies*, 21: 541–64.

Roth, K. and Ricks, D. (1994) 'Goal Configuration in a Global Industry Context', *Strategic Management Journal*, 15: 103–20.

Roth, K., Sweiger, D. and Morrison, A. (1991) 'Global Strategy Implementation at the Business Unit Level: Operational Capabilities and Administrative Mechanisms', *Journal of International Business Studies*, 22: 369–402.

Russ, G., Galang, M. and Ferris, G. (1998) 'Power and Influence of Human Resources Function Through Boundary Spanning and Information Management', *Human Resource Management Review*, 8: 125–48.

Schuler, R. (1989) 'Strategic Human Resource Management and Industrial Relations', *Human Relations*, 42: 157–84.

Snell, S., Youndt, M. and Wright, P. (1996) 'Establishing a Framework for Research in Strategic Human Resource Management'. In Ferris, G. (ed.) *Research in Personnel and Human Resources Management*, Vol. 14. Greenwich, CT: JAI Press, pp. 61–90.

Stewart, T. (1995) 'Human Resources Bites Back', *Fortune*, 13 May, 175.

Taylor, S. and Beechler, S. (1993) 'Human Resources Management System Integration and Adaptation in Multinational Firms', *Advances in International Comparative Management*, 8: 115–74.

Taylor, S., Beechler, S. and Napier, N. (1996) 'Toward an Integrative Model of Strategic International Human Resource Management', *Academy of Management Review*, 21: 959–85.

Tsang, E. (1999) 'The Knowledge Transfer and Learning Aspects of International HRM: an Empirical Study of Singapore MNCs', *International Business Review*, 8: 591–611.

Tung, R. (1987) 'Expatriate Assignments: Enhancing Success and Minimizing Failure', *Academy of Management Executive*, 1: 117–25.

Tung, R. (1994) 'Human Resource Issue and Technology Transfer', *Human Resource Management*, 5: 807–26.

Vachany, S. (1999) 'Global Diversification's Effects on Multinational Subsidiary's Autonomy', *International Business Review*, 8: 535–60.

Wieserma, M. and Bantel, K. (1992) 'Top Management Team Demography and Corporate Change', *Academy of Management Journal*, 35: 91–121.

Wright, P. and Sherman, W. (1999) 'Failing to Find Fit in Strategic Human Resource Management; Theoretical and Empirical Problems'. In Wright, P., Dyer, L., Boudreau, J. and Milkovic, G. (eds.) *Research in Personnel and Human Resources Management, Supplement 4*. Greenwich, CT: JAI Press, pp. 53–74.

Wright, P. and Snell, S. (1998) 'Toward a Unifying Theory in Exploring Fit and Flexibility in Strategic Human Resource Management', *Academy of Management Review*, 23: 756–72.

Yip, G., Johansson, K. and Ross, J. (1997) 'Effects of Nationality on Global Strategy', *Management International Review*, 4: 365–85.

Chapter 21

People Processing Systems and Human Resource Strategy

Shaun Tyson and Doone Selbie

21.1   Introduction

Processing people has always been an activity within personnel management. Human resource management (HRM) is identified as a strategic activity which nevertheless has to engage in business processes. These include bringing people in and out of the organisation, rewarding them, developing, managing performance and discipline.

   In the early 1990s, the notion that we can divide HR work into 'transactional' and 'transformational' grew in popularity [1,2]. Transformational HRM was seen as the strategic version of HRM – managing change, creating cultures, in parallel with marketing and business strategies, whereas transactional HRM was a term used to cover the routine processes of recruitment, selection, training, appraisal, compensation and benefits and all the systems and policies used to manage people day by day. Whilst not often explicitly stated, transformational HRM was considered to be strategic, transactional HRM was, by contrast, operational and administrative. Transformational HRM is the world of organisation development, of new ways of working, development and change, but has the concentration on processes and transactions produced a revolution in HRM and fundamental change to the nature of HRM [3]? In this chapter, we examine the concept of HRM systems and the processes covered, to show, through a case study example, the way system development through iterations over time, moved HRM to focus on value added activity. We also examine the closely interdependent relationship between HR processes, HR systems and the trend towards outsourcing.

   S. Tyson and D. Selbie, "People Processing Systems and Human Resources Strategy," *International Journal of Human Resources Development and Management*, Vol. 4, No.2, 2004: 117–27.

21.2   Developing HR Systems and Processes

In 1987 Tyson [4] argued that HRM was breaking down into a series of different processes. The 'Balkanisation' of HRM, its subdivisions into a series of activities
increasingly seen as separate and available to other functional specialists (e.g. communication experts, consultancies in reward, search and advertising, IT specialists etc.)
was foreseen as a consequence of the changes taking place. The shift to a business-
manager model, with sub-specialisms emerging as line managers took a central role,
was apparent in the late 1980s.

McGovern *et al.* [5] described how line managers' HR practices influenced and were
limited by organisational constraints. The institutional reinforcement of HR practices,
managerial short-termism, and delayering observed in their case study companies,
limited the amount of time line managers had for people management. Similarly, line
managers have been described as the delivery mechanisms of HR policies [6].

This need to give line managers a role without expecting them to become tied down
to the minutiae of personnel administration, no doubt encouraged the move towards
systems changes and the introduction of more advanced information technology [7].
As a consequence, procedural rulebooks were created. When activities were classified and described as systems and processes, so also HR roles could more easily be
outsourced. The further argument for outsourcing routine personnel administration
processes was to give more time to HR specialists to devote to strategic matters. There
was evidence, however, that instead HR managers spent their time 'firefighting' –
dealing with HR crises and urgent problems [8].

It has been argued that e-HRM can be introduced to create such a change in mindset
to be virtually a 'greenfield site' [9]. Tansley *et al.* see such a break from the past to be
similar to the greenfield site notion, providing for a more strategic approach to HRM.
They undertook a major case study to explore this idea but:

> The case evidence, however, demonstrated that the IT stimulus did not enable the design
> and implementation of an integrated HR information system that could enable significant
> change in employee management practices.   [9, p. 364]
> Amongst the reasons they cite for this failure were the lack of awareness and understanding
> of the HR information systems, the silo mentality of process owners, and the way processes
> were mapped independently, without linkages.

Although Ball [10] showed from successive surveys of HR information systems
that these were still largely used for administrative purposes, and were less likely to
be used for analysis and support, he did concede that the more sophisticated use of
HR information systems was in recruitment and training. Given that many of these
studies were undertaken at the end of the 1990s, often in smaller organisations, we
should look for more recent evidence. However, it is the classification of HR systems
as business processes which has grown, and which, although apparently downgrading
HRM, paradoxically can result in a more strategic perspective.

Cost savings and potential benefits to the accuracy of data, improved capacities
to obtain data and hence to inform strategic decisions could also be positive outcomes from treating the various HR transactional activities (e.g. sickness absence,

timekeeping, skills audits, training needs analyses, e-learning schemes and competency profiles) as processes. It was, however, the advent of a vision of HR processes as business processes which helped to change the mindset away from HR administration as an information system, and towards HR as a process for managing people.

Organisations, such as the European Foundation for Quality Management, stress HRM as part of the business process, alongside processes by which customer satisfaction and profit margins are obtained. By linking HR processes to business, the model encourages organisation members to see performance as an outcome of interlinking processes. IT systems have long been viewed as drivers for business redesign [11]. The argument that good quality internal systems lead to good quality service and customer satisfaction which is systematically linked into organisational performance thus gained ground.

From systems thinking and discrete processes, there is an easy step to outsourcing. The difficulty in outsourcing is maintaining the linkages to other systems. The trend towards outsourcing HR activities increased in the 1990s although to different degrees in organizations [12], but with obvious benefits from reducing costs in such areas as routine administration. Klaas *et al.* [13,14] examined HR outsourcing in the USA by researching the organisational determinants of firm outsourcing. They described four categories of outsourcing drawing upon their 1997 study: HR generalist activities; HR transactional activities; human capital activities; and recruiting and selection. HR generalists and transactional activities are most closely related to demand uncertainty – i.e. the uncertainty about a firms demand for labour, itself a function of firm performance and product demand. The results suggested that uncertainty facilitates greater reliance on outsourcing for these HR functions. The explanation for this may be that firms do not want to commit themselves to long-term internal systems and staffing when facing an unpredictable future. We could also argue that greater uncertainty in the environment produces more reviews of systems and more opportunities for the outsourcing option to be recommended.

There is clearly not a simple relationship between outsourcing and the adoption of systematic organisational processes. Different HR functions and objectives affect outsourcing decisions and external economic pressures are also significant. Monks and McMackin [15] rightly point to the complexity of HR systems – which include variations in policies and practices, and differences according to organisation structure. They show that system design is critical at the business unit level, whilst other levels (group or divisional) largely supported the business units in undertaking systems work. To study these processes, case study evidence on context is invaluable [9] and too, longitudinal evidence is invaluable [10].

It can be argued that choices about policies and processes influence later decisions about system architecture, that HR processes and the e-HRM methodologies adopted create different options.

21.3   Case History – Telecoms Company

To consider this interaction between systems, processes and strategy we describe below a case history, collected over 15 years, about a North American company operating in the UK/Europe but with global reach, in the high technology field and the fast moving telecommunications industry. At various stages, significant decisions were taken which had a major influence on the outcome of HR strategy.

21.3.1   *Regional operations*

In the late 1980s, like many other large international companies with North American parentage, the Company was very decentralised and regional with fairly small populations in most of the countries it operated in, except the USA. The impact of this regionalisation was that activities were managed in-country in an *ad hoc* way, with little requirement to interact with other countries or even other sites in the same country. This was regarded as 'normal' since the terms 'internationalisation' and 'globalisation' were still evolving and the impact of standard cross-border processes had yet to be seriously considered. There was minimal drive to find a common way of doing things, other than perhaps trying to encourage the North American way into each country. However, after a few attempts to do this, the countries were left alone to manage their own businesses for a few years. There was enough understanding of the complexities of differing legislation by country and possible costs associated with imposing a 'common way', especially in the compensation and benefits area, to dissuade the leaders from pursuing this as a strategic path at that time.

21.3.2   *International operations*

By the early to mid 1990s, the Company was growing steadily throughout the world. It had over 60,000 employees and a presence in about 90 countries. The establishment of standard in-country processes was becoming more important with the increasing headcount. The widespread usage of computers, the acceptance of home-based working, remote management and the significant increase in virtual teams, were starting to raise the visibility of inconsistencies in the way things were done. Audio conferencing enabled project teams to be created with employees based all over the world. They were able to work together with common objectives and be part of the same management groups.

The North American teams started to build some very sophisticated HR systems, using the basic HR database to support their local (North American) processes. These included early usage of the intranet for job postings and applications and manager self-service tools for annual salary planning. There was a strong desire to implement the same systems across the world, especially in a limited number of 'strategic' countries and also to get the whole company recorded in the organisational hierarchy tool for management reporting uses. The new tools were state of the art, very exciting and seemed critical to reducing the workload of the HR function and administration. They were built in-house, rather than bought off the shelf. However, local country acceptance (i.e. those countries outside North America) was slow and process changes associated with the implementations were minimal. So the full benefits of the toolsets were not realised by the business and HR organisations.

21.3.3   Global operations

The late 1990s saw exponential growth, both organically and through acquisition, with a headcount reaching about 90,000 and employees in over 120 countries. There was an urgent need to speed up all the processes, particularly in HR, where the recruiting need and integration of new company acquisitions into the main business was non-stop. The heavy usage of the intranet, and the thousands of websites often containing similar information, were really highlighting the fact that more global simplification, rather than just standardisation across single countries, was a necessity.

In order for a company to be able to really work globally, quickly and efficiently, avoiding employee frustration, duplication and confusion, it needed as many simple ways of doing things as possible. Understandably there were legislative reasons why some activities or processes had to be handled differently, but as long as this was the only reason for deviations, those objectives could start to be achieved.

During this period, the UK HR department realigned itself and created an in-house, centralised HR administrative function. Certain documentation management, intranet and call management tools were developed to assist this stage in the HR evolution process. The remaining UK HR staff became either strategic business partners or remained part of the corporate HR functions.

However, a catalyst was needed to align the inconsistent cross-country processes and further streamline the UK processes. It needed to be one that could minimalise the emotions associated with the changes, but which could be understood clearly.

The opportunity came when a significant decision was made to reduce the global HR system costs by cutting down the number of HR systems in use across the world. At the time, there were over 120 HR tools globally and the support costs and portfolio enhancement costs were over $15 m a year. The first step towards reducing these came with the plan to implement one global HR database and data warehouse that would be accessible throughout the world. There would still be a requirement to have functional tools using the data, but these would be the way the company would have the opportunity to differentiate itself. It could no longer afford to be in the business of building all of its own inhouse systems, as this was much too expensive to support, even though the system development and support skills existed within the company.

At the time this decision was being taken (1999), the business and HR strategies of acquisitive growth and significant recruitment were all encompassing. However, a system change as dramatic as the one proposed, could not happen overnight.

21.3.4   Systems planning and evaluation phase

The existing systems, which acted as data repositories and supported various HR processes, such as salary planning and job opportunities, were highly interdependent. There were also a number of separate core HR databases across the world, feeding data to the storage areas. The work of understanding the impact of retiring these core systems and replacing them with one global system took a considerable amount of time to analyse, explain and cost. In fact, a constant challenge throughout the project was tracking the knock-on impact of changes to downstream systems. Nevertheless, major budgets were approved, an HR SAP system, a new data warehouse and a new reporting toolset were selected and global implementation partners engaged.

HR SAP is one part of an SAP system, which is a global enterprise resource planning tool (ERP). An ERP is an information system tool that combines the needs of key business functions, for example, finance, supply management, customer relationship management and human resources, within one major system. Common data elements and structures are part of a technical platform upon which other modules and tools can be built, enabling cross-functional reporting and more efficient business management.

This planning phase took about nine months to achieve. During that time the business strategy moved on and the Company launched a campaign to review the major cost areas and the core strategic businesses in which it wanted to operate. The result was a significant shift and change in the way that the Company operated, especially in the manufacturing and transactional process areas. A key decision was made to outsource non-core businesses. This was the start of significant reshaping of the organisation.

By the end of the key outsourcing initiatives, the employee receivables, accounts payable and purchasing functions, had been moved to the outsource partner together with data entry, HR and training administration, payroll and the in-house HR systems development and support teams.

21.3.5   Systems design phase

Initially the HR teams were handling the employee relations side of outsourcing for non-HR departments within the business. They were also working closely with the system design teams for the HR SAP project and providing design input to the requirements for each country. These were slowly being refined in order to find some standard processes.

However, it was about 14 months into the new HR SAP project when the outsourcing began to focus on the key HR processes of data administration, policies and procedures advice, contractual change administration and employee training.

There was recognition that the future quality of the HR processes being outsourced, and consequently the success of the outsourcing itself, would be reliant on the new SAP system. So another significant decision was made. This time it meant changing the system implementation partner so that the new outsource partner could be responsible for the systems implementation, as well as the transactional activities associated with the HR administration outsourcing.

However, due to the complex systems architecture that had been created by the historical integration of all the legacy 120 HR systems, it took a further 12 months to complete the core database deployment.

21.3.6   Realising business benefits

This achievement was really just the beginning, rather than the end. The next objective was to work on the key supporting projects, which could be built around the new

HR platform. These were critical to the overall cost reduction objectives and the system retirements, consolidations and replacements that were required. Many of these projects had already been planned and were being worked in parallel with the HR SAP implementation.

Apart from the obvious bottom-line impacts, there was an increasing business requirement to push more people-management activities out to the line managers from the HR function. In order to do this, the aim was to create as many manager and employee self-service tools as possible. A further benefit was to improve the image of HR to one of a high tech function with accurate information that could be viewed and changed easily.

A major project was the replacement of the existing suite of resourcing tools with one that could be integrated with SAP and manage online applications and CVs via the internet from both internal and external candidates. When this project was planned and approved, there was still massive recruitment going on and it was high priority. By the time the system was fully implemented and the business benefits could start to be taken, the telecoms industry was in decline and recruitment was virtually on hold.

Another project included an integrated training administration system for self-registration on courses and online manager approval. The key deliverable from this project was the ability to measure training costs more thoroughly and track training attendance. The intent was for this information to then be fed into the business training needs analysis activities and future training plans. However, by the time it was up and running the company was running very few training courses relative to the previous year.

E-HR (or employee self-service) was gradually rolled out across the world for the countries as they came on board the SAP system. It provided the opportunity for employees to have ownership of their personal data, and control of changing it, wherever they were located in the world. Of course, it was necessary to have access to a computer terminal, but this was possible via a kiosk in the case of manufacturing sites, for example.

E-HR can reduce frustration, increase employee satisfaction and result in a significant improvement in data accuracy. This leads to administrative time saved in answering questions, pursuing and trying to change inaccurate data and ensuring the data is only changed in one place. The reduction in duplicate activities is especially valuable in organisations with a number of outsourced relationships and where downstream systems support various functional processes, for example, flexible benefits, payroll, pensions etc. The accurate information can improve internal customer satisfaction that in turn affects external customer satisfaction and enables the analytical and administrative departments to be focused on more added value activities.

For HR to become a truly strategic partner and accepted at the corporate business table, it needs to be able to measure HR processes, understand them and know where to improve them. Ultimately, they need to impact the bottom line by redirecting the department's attention to those areas of activity where streamlining can occur. In many cases this can also mean outsourcing. By transferring certain transactional HR work to outsource companies, there is more flexibility available to increase/decrease work load depending on external environmental factors. A good example is where the down turn in the telecommunications industry lead to significant headcount reductions and therefore reduced requirements for transactional HR staff. With the outsourcing in place, this flexibility could be managed more easily.

The service level agreements of an outsourcing contract require clearly documented and measurable processes in order that the partnership can agree and work with the relative contractual conditions. It is not a one-way contract. The Outsourcer must of course deliver its services against certain metrics but, in many cases, for these to actually be achievable, the Company itself may have to deliver against certain objectives too. An example of this could be the Company ensuring that the appropriate instruction to raise an offer letter actually arrives at the Outsourcer within the agreed timeline. This is needed before the Outsourcer can start its part of the process. The time it takes to raise the offer letter (which is the measure stated in the contract) can only start when the content information arrives. However, to recruiting managers, their view of the time an offer letter can take to be delivered, would be from when a notification was sent from their desk. The corporate policies in place would dictate the steps between the notification being sent and the letter being generated. This could be where the time delay really occurs, not in the transaction processing at all.

With the transaction and process boundary clarification that an Outsource/Company relationship creates, certain ambiguity is unravelled and both organisations are able to start focusing on process improvements.

One of the key objectives of both the HR SAP project and the outsourcing project was simplification of processes. If there is agreement over the way something can be done, then there is often the opportunity to automate it. The greater the consistency in process across the globe, the more it is possible to reuse technology and design development and therefore the greater the opportunity there is to spread and share costs across the business. Even if there are some requirements for legislative differences to be taken into account around the world, with a clear understanding of what they are, systems and processes can be appropriately customised to accommodate the exceptions. This speeds up the rollout of any tool supporting a process and enables positive communication messages to be transmitted across the business about even and fair treatment of employees.

21.4   Discussion

We have observed the key stages in the evolution of an HR department, its processes and systems in the case described above. It is easier, in hindsight, to see the iterative processes that occurred which contributed to the evolution of HRM as a number of discrete business processes and systems and also to see the difficulty in predicting the external environment impact on the business.

When HR strategy is closely linked to business strategy, for instance in periods of high growth, there is obviously a key focus on recruitment and retention practices. This leads to a requirement for tools to support the revised processes and speed up activities. Funding can be obtained when the business priorities are aligned with the system needs and there is likely to be strong sponsorship driving these new process and systems changes across the business.

The outsourcing of HR activities has been made possible through clear definition and standardisation. We can argue, therefore, that the most strategic question of all – who manages the HR process? – is fundamentally influenced by the adoption of different HR information systems.

Integration of HR into the business – the creation of the so-called 'business partner' model is also a consequence of the integration of HR processes. Within the international context, comparisons and international policies are only feasible if there are common system designs, supporting the decision. A mistake from earlier studies which suggested that 'informatics' – sophisticated, intelligent systems – would ultimately decide on HR issues was the failure to recognise that organisations are human creations, and the senior managers within them desire to retain the power to make decisions. HR information systems do, nevertheless, frame those decisions by setting out the options and choices, and choices such as outsourcing processes, once made, constrain and enable other decisions on the HR strategies available.

21.5   Conclusion

In this conclusion Dave Lepak provides a contemporary overview of the field of strategic human resource management and suggestions for future research. His chapter describes just how much knowledge exists in the field about the importance and impact of strategic human resource management. He suggests where future research might go to build on the successes of past work and what theoretical perspectives might be useful in doing so. His conclusion is that while much has already been accomplished by researchers worldwide, many opportunities for significant contribution still remain.

REFERENCES

1. Devanna, M.A. and Tichy, N.M. (1986) 'The transformational leader', *Training and Development Journal*, Vol. 4, No. 7, pp. 27–32.
2. Bass, B.M. (1994) 'From transactional to transformational leadership: learning to share the vision', *Organisational Dynamics*, Winter, pp. 19–31.
3. Hannon, J., Jelf, G. and Brandes, D. (1996) 'Human resources information systems: operational issues and strategic considerations in a global environment', *International Journal of HRM*, Vol. 7, No. 1, pp. 245–69.
4. Tyson, S. (1987) 'The management of the personnel function', *Journal of Management Studies*, Vol. 24, No. 5, pp. 49–53.
5. McGovern, P., Gratton, L., Stiles, P., Hope Hailey, V. and Truss, C. (1997) 'Human resource management on the line?', *Human Resource Management Journal*, Vol. 7, No. 4, pp. 12–29.
6. Storey, J. (1992) *Developments in the Management of Human Resources*, Oxford: Basil. Blackwell.

7. Hall, L. and Torrington, D. (1998) 'Letting go or holding on – the devolution of operational personnel activities', *Human Resource Management Journal*, Vol. 8, No. 1, pp. 41–55.

8. Colling, T. and Ferner, A. (1992) 'The limits of autonomy devolution line managers and industrial relations in privatised companies', *Journal of Management Studies*, Vol. 29, No. 2, pp. 157–80.

9. Tansley, C., Newall, S. and Williams, H. (2001) 'Effecting HRM style practices through an integrated HR information system an e-greenfield site?', *Personnel Review*, Vol. 30, No. 3, pp. 351–70.

10. Ball, K.S. (2001) 'The use of information systems: a survey', *Personnel Review*, Vol. 30, No. 6, pp. 677–93.

11. Hammer, M. and Champy, J. (1993) *Reengineering the Corporation: A Manifesto for Business Revolution*, New York: Harper Collins.

12. Csoko, L.S. (1995) 'Rethinking human resources: a research report', The Conference Board, Report No. 1124-95-RR.

13. Klaas, B.S., McClendon, J.A. and Gainey, T. (1999) 'HR outsourcing and its impact. The role of transaction costs', *Personnel Psychology*, Vol. 52, pp. 113–36.

14. Klaas, B.S., McClendon, J.A. and Gainey, T.W. (2001) 'Outsourcing HR: the impact of organisational characteristics', *Human Resource Management*, Summer, Vol. 40, No. 2, pp. 125–38.

15. Monks, K. and McMackin, J. (2001) 'Designing and aligning an HR system', *Human Resource Management Journal*, Vol. 11, No. 2, pp. 57–72.

Conclusion

Conclusion

Chapter 22

Strategic Human Resource Management: A Look to the Future

David P. Lepak

A clear pattern is emerging in strategic human resource management (HRM) research suggesting that HR systems geared toward increased commitment and employee involvement can have a dramatic impact on organizational outcomes. Despite differences in the terms used to denote which practices comprise an HR system, a consistently positive relationship between high investment HR systems (e.g., high performance work systems, high involvement, human capital enhancing, commitment-based HR systems, innovative employment practices) and aggregate performance measures at the plant, business-unit, and corporate level of analysis has been found (e.g., Arthur, 1994; Delery & Doty, 1996; Guthrie, 2001; Huselid, 1995; Ichniowski et al., 1997; Koch & McGrath, 1996; Youndt et al., 1996). Given these consistent findings, it should not be surprising that many researchers have suggested that people, more than other organizational resources, may be a strong potential source for achieving a sustainable competitive advantage (Barney, 1991; Pfeffer, 1994).

While establishing a relationship between HR systems and performance is certainly important and encouraging, as a field of research there remains considerable work to be done. The primary objective of this chapter is explore the future of strategic HRM research and offer some research suggestions to help move the field forward. While speculative, and certainly not exhaustive, the following research topics are areas of research that might provide additional insights into how to leverage HR systems to maximize individual and organizational performance. Viewed broadly, the proposed areas for future research focus on renewed examination of the "black box" in strategic HRM research and paying more attention to what we are actually measuring when we measure HR systems.

Examining the "Black Box"

Looking across the published research in strategic HRM, a major conclusion is that how firms structure their HR systems to manage employees is related to organizational effectiveness. Yet, while we know that HR relates to performance, and certain types of HR systems are positively related to performance, we know much less about *how* this process unfolds. Delery (1998: 290) suggested that, "a firm does not gain a competitive advantage from HR practices, per se, but from the human resources that the firm attracts and retains." Building on this point, one potentially useful way to approach this "black box" is to consider what impact HR systems are expected to have on employees that, if successful, would translate into organizational performance.

Employee ability and effort

At the individual level of analysis, Austin, Villanova, Kane, and Bernardin (1991), noted that individual performance is a function of ability and effort. Employees' human capital – their knowledge, skills, and abilities – provide them with the potential to positively impact firm performance while their effort displayed on the job – their attitudes and behaviors – determines the extent to which their potential is realized. In the context of strategic HRM research, this logic has been, at least implicitly, evoked in discussions of HR systems. For example, Wright and Snell (1991) suggested that HR practices may be viewed as two dimensions – managing competencies and managing behaviors. Huselid (1995) also arrived at a two factor solution, building skills and enhancing motivation, after analyzing a host of HR practices. Yet, while a conceptual link between HR systems, employee skills and effort, and organizational outcomes is fairly straightforward, many questions remain.

With regard to the role of human capital in this relationship, Snell and Dean (1992) noted that human capital adds value because of enhanced potential for productivity provided by higher knowledge and skills. Similarly, Pennings, Lee, and Van Witteloos-tuijn (1998: 426) noted that "professionals endowed with a high level of human capital are more likely to deliver consistent and high-quality services." Extending this logic, at a general level one of the mechanisms by which HR impacts performance is through its influence on human capital. But the question remains as to how. What specific aspects of human capital are most necessary for organizational success? Is it the level of human capital that is most important? Is it the type of human capital that is most important? Or is it some interaction between level and type that ultimately dictates how employees may add value within organizations. Employees vary in both the levels and types of human capital they possess and research is needed that examines the relative value of different forms and levels of experience, organizational tenure, occupational tenure, education, and the like for competitive advantage as well as the conditions under which different types and levels of human capital are most valuable.

Beyond human capital, we have to also consider the actual effort employees display on the job. One of the most prominent theoretical perspectives in strategic HRM – the behavioral perspective (Schuler & Jackson, 1987) – directly addresses this point. According to the behavioral perspective, firms use different HR practices in an attempt to elicit needed role behaviors for given organizational contingencies such as strategy and technology (Jackson et al., 1989; Schuler & Jackson, 1987). As noted by Jackson and colleagues (1989: 728), "A behavioral perspective assumes that employers use personnel practices as a means for eliciting and controlling employee attitudes and behaviors." While conceptually compelling, empirical testing of these employee attitudes behaviors as mediators of the HR–performance relationship is lacking (McMahan, Virick & Wright, 1999). Moreover, the specific attitudes and/or behaviors required in different settings have not been empirically established. Future research is needed to more deeply explore what attitudes and behaviors are necessary in different organizational contexts and how choices among different HR practices and/or systems may help, or hinder, the attainment of those attitudes and behaviors.

Finally, it is also important to look at the interaction between human capital and employee attitudes and behaviors to more fully understand how HR systems impact organizational performance. Conceptually, it is logical that organizations with high levels of human capital and high levels of collective employee effort toward organizational goals would realize greater performance. But what exactly is the nature of this interaction. Could high levels of human capital offset low levels of employee effort or vice versa? Or, is either the level/type of human capital more or less important than the discretionary efforts employees display on the job? Empirical investigations into the nature of the interaction between human capital and employee attitudes and behavior would help provide insights into this particular issue.

Intellectual capital

Recently, several scholars have shifted their focus to consider the role of social capital, and the broader notion of intellectual capital, in strategic HRM research. As noted by Youndt, Subramaniam, and Snell (2004: 337), intellectual capital can be broadly conceptualized as "the sum of all knowledge an organization is able to leverage in the process of conducting business to gain competitive advantage," and is comprised of human, social, and organizational capital (Youndt et al., 2004). As noted above, human capital refers to individual employee capabilities – their knowledge, skills, and abilities. Social capital reflects knowledge in groups and networks of people and may be viewed as the aggregate of resources embedded within, available through, and derived from the network of relationships possessed by an individual or organization (Brass, Galaskiewicz, Greve, & Tsai, 2004; Nahapiet & Ghoshal, 1998). Finally, organizational capital refers to "institutionalized knowledge and codified experience stored in databases, routine, patents, manuals, structures, and the like" (Youndt et al., 2004: 338).

In an empirical investigation of the relationship between these three facets of intellectual capital and both radical and incremental innovation, Subramaniam and Youndt (2005) found that organizational capital was positively associated with incremental innovative capability, social capital was related to both incremental and radical capabilities, and that human and social capital interacted positively to influence radical innovative capability. These findings have a potentially important implication for future strategic HRM research suggesting that the value of human capital is dependent on the level of social capital within organizations. As noted by Subramaniam and Youndt (2005), "unless individual knowledge is networked, shared, and channeled through relationships, it provides little benefit to organizations in terms of innovative capabilities." Certainly more research is needed but these findings seem to suggest that HR practices that facilitate the development of human capital are necessary but not sufficient for leveraging the potential talent of a workforce. Rather, companies must pay equal attention to the creation and effective utilization of social capital. Future strategic HRM research that focuses on identifying the HR practices that bolster human capital and the formation of social capital would prove beneficial.

Considering employee perceptions

A third avenue for future research is to shift our focus to examine employee perceptions of the HR practices that they are exposed to. While HR systems are implemented in an attempt to influence employees abilities (human capital) and their attitudes and behaviors, the effectiveness of HR systems are dependent on the employees themselves. HR practices such as performance appraisals and incentive systems, among others, are certainly designed to encourage certain actions by employees. Yet, it is important to recognize that employees do not always respond according to the intentions of organizational decision makers and the HR practices in place. Even within the same firm, employees may respond dissimilarly to HR practices as anticipated or expected by organizations.

Bowen and Ostroff (2004) recently pointed out that the effect of HR practices depends on the way in which employees interpret and respond to them, and it is reasonable to expect that not all employees will respond identically to the same HR practice. There are two factors to consider here. First, to be effective, employees must understand the HR practices to which they are exposed and the expected attitudes or behaviors that they are to display in response to this exposure. Employees are likely to vary, at least to a minimum degree, in how they interpret and react to the HR practices under which they are exposed. Accordingly, the impact of an HR practice on employee attitudes and behaviors may depend on the clarity or level of understanding that employees have regarding the intended purpose of the HR practices.

Second, even with clarity of what is expected of them, employees make decisions regarding how to act in their jobs. While some employees may choose to display the desired attitudes and behaviors such as productivity, on-time attendance, and citizenship behaviors that are desired by their organization and encouraged by HR practices, this relationship is not automatic. Rather, some employees may not engage in organization focused actions at all – even in the presence of HR practices. As noted by Kidwell and Bennett (1993), there are many circumstances associated with employee propensity to withhold effort that are manifest in behaviors such as shirking, social loafing, and free riding. The challenge is to identify individual and organizational factors that shape employees decisions whether or not to engage in actions that benefit the organization.

Interestingly, much of the HR literature implies that when employees are exposed to HR practices, they are fully informed and understand the objective of the HR practice and act accordingly, which may not always be true. Yet, employees are not simple receptors of organizational initiatives; they are cognitive beings and make choices about how to act on the job. To better understand how to strategically manage employees we have to have a better understanding of how employees understand and respond to HR initiatives that are designed to maximize their potential contributions toward competitive advantage. Research that explicitly incorporates individual differences as potentially important factors influencing the relationship between HR practices and employee actions and, ultimately, organizational performance, is needed.

Finally, HR policies may not translate into expected employee behaviors because managers may deviate in how they implement HR practices with their employees. While a company may have a certain HR policy, it is important to distinguish between the policies that are designed to be implemented at the organizational level of analysis and the actual practices that are carried out throughout the organization. Quite simply, it is possible that managers do not always implement the practices that they are supposed to. Moreover, while the practices and the policies may be consistent, the manner by which the practices are carried out may vary across managers. Managers are likely to vary in terms of the clarity they provide to employees regarding what is expected of them, the rationale for using a practice, or even the importance of a practice and the expected employee contributions for company success. Research that goes beyond simply examining the policies in place to examine variations in how HR practices are carried out through an organization would be beneficial to better understand how the process of how HR impacts performance.

What are We Measuring in Strategic HRM?

Beyond considering the intervening mechanisms in strategic HRM research, there are also several issues related to how we study strategic HRM. In particular, research is needed that provides greater insights into what HR systems are and how they operate.

One of the fundamental principles of strategic HRM research is that the impact of HR practices is best understood by examining the system of HR practices in place. Considering that HR practices are rarely used in isolation, failure to consider all of the HR practices that are in use neglects potential important explanatory value of unmeasured HR practices. Yet, while researchers may agree that a systems perspective is appropriate, there is a noticeable lack of agreement as to what these HR systems are and which practices comprise them. For instance, researchers have used terms ranging from high performance work systems (Huselid, 1995), human capital enhancing HR systems (Youndt et al., 1996), high involvement HR (Lawler, 1992), sophisticated HR practices (Koch & McGrath, 1996), and commitment oriented HR systems (Arthur, 1994), to name a few.

Perhaps more problematic, however, is that there are considerable differences in the practices that are used to comprise the systems. For instance, studies vary in the degree to which they include different HR practices such as due process, participation, selective staffing, and the like. For example, Becker and Gerhart (1996) noted differences in the use of variable pay in Arthur (1994), Huselid (1995) and MacDuffie (1995). A low emphasis on variable pay was included as part of high performance employment or "commitment" system in Arthur (1994) whereas a high emphasis on variable pay was included in the High Performance Work Systems in Huselid (1995) and MacDuffie (1995). Why is variable pay a key component of certain HR system conceptualizations and not of others? A key issue to consider is whether or not there is a single higher order HR system that is universally related to organizational performance or if there are multiple distinct HR systems that relate to different outcomes. One potential explanation may be that there are different HR systems that should be reflected by the use of distinct HR practices. One could conceptualize HR systems as directional or targeted in nature – HR systems may be oriented to foster commitment, high performance, or some other valued outcome.

The challenge is to understand, from a theoretical perspective, which HR practices should be included and excluded from either some higher level overarching high investment HR system or, if there really are different HR systems with different objectives, which HR practices should be included in these lower level HR systems. At this point in time, however, the lack of consensus regarding what these systems are, as well as what they should be, substantially limits our ability to build a cumulative body of knowledge regarding how HR systems influence important organizational outcomes. While there is a general consensus that high investment HR systems are beneficial for organizations, the specific nature of this relationship remains unclear. As a field, we know that different HR systems have been associated with performance measures. We do not know, however, what is really driving this relationship because these systems measure different HR practices.

Related, adopting a systems perspective raises the issue of how different components of the system are related. Unfortunately, most discussions of these systems read like a laundry list of which practices are included without as much discussion regarding how these different HR practices are related. For instance, is there a multiplicative effect or an additive effect when we consider HR practices simultaneously? While this is certainly an empirical question, there are also conceptual issues associated with the theoretical rationale underlying the relationships among the HR practices. Are some practices redundant with others, complementary to others, or substitutes for others? Without conceptually addressing these issues, our understanding of the use and effectiveness of HR systems is unnecessarily constrained due to failure to understand the mechanisms by which these work and, ultimately, influence performance.

Conclusion

The primary objective of this essay was to take a step back and think about areas of future research that are needed to continue to build on the growing area of strategic HRM research. In 1992, Wright and McMahan noted that strategic human resource management is primarily focused on "the pattern of planned HR deployments and activities" that are intended to help organizations achieve their objectives. Consistent with this logic, researchers have focused considerable energy examining if HR systems are in fact related with organizational performance. Looking over this body of research, it if fair to say that HR systems do make a difference. The challenge for the field of strategic HRM now is to better understand how.

While there are certainly many important areas of future research that might be considered, the focus of this paper was on two broad areas of research that are likely to prove valuable for strategic HRM researchers. First, with a greater focus on the intermediate linkages between HR and performance, and with a particular emphasis on how employees and their perceptions influence these relationships, we should be in a better position to identify the process by which HR impacts performance. Second, with a renewed focus on how we conceptualize HR systems, we may hopefully develop a greater understanding of how these systems operate to build a cumulative body of research.

Of course, there are many additional issues that must be examined as well. For example, while researchers are increasingly expanding strategic HRM research on a global level, research is needed that more directly examines cross-cultural issues in current models of strategic HRM. And with the emerging presence of off-shoring, research is needed to examine the short-term and long-term consequences of sending work to other countries as well as what HR systems might be used to maximize the benefits of off-shoring arrangements. Finally, we need to continue to build our conceptual logic for how and when HR systems make a difference. While researchers have built strong arguments for the importance of the resource based view of the firm (Barney, 1991), human capital theory (Becker, 1964), and the behavioral perspective (Jackson et al., 1989), it would be useful to continue to incorporate additional theoretical perspectives such as institutional theory (DiMaggio & Powell, 1983), resource dependency theory (Pfeffer & Salancik, 1978), or population ecology (Hannan & Freeman, 1977), to name a few, that would help further refine what we know about the relationship between HR systems and organizational performance.

While addressing these issues may seem like a daunting task, my view is that it is an exciting time to study strategic HRM. There are many conceptual and methodological challenges that remain to be addressed – all of which are critical to better understand strategic HRM and to help organizations leverage the potential contributions of their workforce.

REFERENCES

Arthur, J. B. (1994). Effects of human resource systems on manufacturing performance and turnover. *Academy of Management Journal, 37*, 670–87.

Austin, J. T., Villanova, P., Kane, J. S., & Bernardin, H. J. (1991). Construct validation of performance measures: Definitional issues, development, and evaluation of indicators. In G. R. Ferris (ed.), *Research in Personnel and Human Resource Management, 9*, 159–233. Greenwich, CT: JAI Press.

Barney, J. (1991). Firm resources and sustainable competitive advantage. *Journal of Management, 17*, 99–129.

Becker, G. S. (1964). *Human Capital*. New York: Columbia University Press.

Becker, B. & Gerhart, B. (1996). The impact of human resource management on organizational performance: Progress and prospects. *Academy of Management Journal, 39,* 779–801.

Bowen, D. E. & Ostroff, C. (2004). Understanding HRM-firm performance linkages: The role of "strength" of the HRM system. *Academy of Management Review, 29,* 203–21.

Brass, D. J., Galaskiewicz, J., Greve, H. R., & Tsai, W. (2004). Taking stock of networks and organizations: A multilevel perspective. *Academy of Management Journal, 47,* 795–817.

Delery, J. E. (1998). Issues of fit in strategic human resource management: Implications for research. *Human Resource Management Review, 8,* 289–309.

Delery, J. E. & Doty, D. H. (1996). Modes of theorizing in strategic human resource management: Tests of universalistic, contingency, and configurational performance predictions. *Academy of Management Journal, 39,* 802–35.

DiMaggio, P. J. & Powell, W. W. (1983). The iron cage revisited: Institutional Isomorphism and Collective rationality in organizational fields. *American Sociological Review, 48,* 147–60.

Guthrie, J. P. (2001). High-involvement work practices, turnover, and productivity: Evidence from New Zealand. *Academy of Management Journal, 44,* 180–192.

Hannan, M. T. & Freeman, J. (1977). The population ecology of organizations. *American Journal of Sociology, 82,* 929–64.

Huselid, M. A. (1995). The impact of human resource management practices on turnover, productivity, and corporate financial performance. *Academy of Management Journal, 38,* 635–72.

Ichniowski, C., Shaw, K., & Prennushi, G. (1997). The effects of human resource management practices on productivity: A study of steel finishing lines. *The American Economic Review, 87,* 291–313.

Jackson, S. E., Schuler, R. S., & Rivero, J. C. (1989). Organizational characteristics as predictors of personnel practices. *Personnel Psychology, 42,* 727–86.

Kidwell, R. E., Jr. & Bennett, N. (1993). Employee propensity to withhold effort: A conceptual model to intersect three avenues of research. *Academy of Management Review, 18,* 429–66.

Koch, M. J. & McGrath, R. G. (1996). Improving labor productivity: Human resource management policies do matter. *Strategic Management Journal, 17,* 335–54.

Lawler, E. E. (1992). *The Ultimate Advantage: Creating the High-Involvement Organisation.* San Francisco, CA: Jossey-Bass.

MacDuffie, J. P. (1995). Human resource bundles and manufacturing performance: Organizational logic and flexible production systems in the world auto industry. *Industrial and Labor Relations Review, 48,* 197–221.

McMahan, G. C., Virick, M., & Wright, P. M. (1999). Alternative theoretical perspectives for strategic human resource management revisited: Progress, problems, and prospects. In P. M. Wright, L. Dyer, J. Boudreau, & G. Milkovich (Eds.), *Research in Personnel and Human Resources Management, Supplement, 4,* 99–122. Greenwich, CT: JAI Press.

Nahapiet, J. & Ghoshal, S. (1998). Social capital, intellectual capital, and the organizational advantage. *Academy of Management Review, 23,* 242–66.

Pennings, J. M., Lee, K., & Van Witteloostuijn, A. (1998). Human capital, social capital, and firm dissolution. *Academy of Management Journal, 41,* 425–40.

Pfeffer, J. (1994). *Competitive Advantage Through People: Unleashing the Power of the Work Force.* Boston: Harvard Business School Press.

Pfeffer, J. & Salancik, G. R. (1978). *The External Control of Organizations.* New York: Harper & Row.

Schuler, R. S. & Jackson, S. E. (1987). Linking competitive strategies with human resource management practices. *Academy of Management Executive, 1,* 207–19.

Snell, S. A. & Dean, J. W., Jr. (1992). Integrated manufacturing and human resource management: A human capital perspective. *Academy of Management Journal, 35,* 467–504.

Subramaniam, M. & Youndt, M. A. (2005). The influence of intellectual capital on the types of innovative capabilities. *Academy of Management Journal, 48*, 450–63.

Wright, P. M. & McMahan, G. C. (1992). Theoretical perspectives for strategic human resource management. *Journal of Management, 18*, 295–320.

Wright, P. M. & Snell, S. A. (1991). Toward an integrative view of strategic human resource management. *Human Resource Management Review, 1*, 203–25.

Youndt, M. A., Snell, S. A., Dean, J. W., Jr., & Lepak, D. P. (1996). Human resource management, manufacturing strategy, and firm performance. *Academy of Management Journal, 39*, 836–66.

Youndt, M. A., Subramaniam, O., & Snell, S. A. (2004). Intellectual capital profiles: An examination of investments and returns. *Journal of Management Studies, 41*, 335–61.

Index